The rhetoric Of revolution

The rhetoric Of revolution

CHRISTOPHER KATOPE and **PAUL ZOLBROD**

THE MACMILLAN COMPANY

321.0908
K 20 n

Acknowledgments

The editors wish to thank the authors and the magazine and book publishers who have given permission to reprint the following.

Sir James Frazer, "Putting the King to Death," Reprinted by permission of S. G. Phillips, Inc., from *The New Golden Bough*, ed. by Theodor H. Gaster. Copyright © 1959 by S. G. Phillips, Inc. Reprinted by permission of the executors of Sir James G. Frazer and The Macmillan Co. of Canada.

"The Rebellion of the Maccabees," from *The Bible*, ed. by Ernest Sutherland Bates. Copyright © 1936, by Simon & Schuster, Inc. Reprinted by permission of Simon & Schuster, Inc.

Thomas Paine, "Thoughts on the Present State of American Affairs." Reprinted from *The American Tradition in Literature*, Third Edition. Edited by Sculley Bradley, Richard Croom Beatty, and E. Hudson Long. By permission of W. W. Norton & Company, Inc. Copyright © 1967, 1962, 1961, 1957, 1956 by W. W. Norton & Company, Inc.

"When Shall We Have Bread?" from Philip Dawson, ed., *The French Revolution*, © 1967. Reprinted by permission of Prentice-Hall, Inc., Englewood Cliffs, New Jersey.

Gamel Abdel Nasser, "The Seeds of Revolt," from *The Philosophy of the Revolution*. Reprinted by permission of Smith, Keynes and Marshall, Book Publishers.

Ho Chi Minh, "Declaration of Independence of the Democratic Republic of Viet Nam," from *Ho Chi Minh in Revolution*, ed. by Bernard B. Fall. Frederick Praeger and the New American Library.

Che Guevara, "Ideology of the Cuban Revolution," from "Notes on the Cuban Revolution," *Studies on the Left*, Vol. I, #3, 1960. Reprinted by permission of the Agenda Publishing Co.

22204

Arthur Schlesinger, Jr., "The Politics of Violence," August, 1968. Reprinted from *Harper's Magazine* by permission of the author, Arthur Schlesinger, Jr.

George Bernard Shaw, "Maxims for Revolutionists," from *Man and Superman*. Reprinted by permission of The Society of Authors, London SW. 10, Agent for the Bernard Shaw Estate.

Kingsley Widmer, "Thrust of the Underculture," *The Nation*, December 30, 1968. Reprinted by permission of *The Nation* and the author.

Herbert Marcuse, "The New Forms of Control," from *One-Dimensional Man*, Beacon Press. Reprinted by permission of the Beacon Press, Copyright © 1964 by Herbert Marcuse.

Herbert Read, "My Anarchism," from *The Cult of Sincerity*. Reprinted by permission of the publisher, Horizon Press, from *The Cult of Sincerity* by Frank Lloyd Wright. Copyright, 1969. Reprinted by permission of Benedict Read, and by permission of *Encounter*. This article appeared in *Encounter* (January, 1966), under the title, "Pragmatic Anarchism." Reprinted by permission.

Irving Howe, "The New 'Confrontation Politics' is a Dangerous Game." *The New York Times Magazine*, October 20, 1968. © 1968/1969 by the New York Times Company. Reprinted by permission.

Robert L. Scott and Donald K. Smith, "The Rhetoric of Confrontation," from *The Quarterly Journal of Speech*, February, 1969. Reprinted by permission of the Speech Association of America and the authors.

Charles B. Ketcham, "Towards the New Morality," from *The Search for Meaningful Existence* by Charles B. Ketcham. © 1968 Charles B. Ketcham. Reprinted by permission of Weybright and Talley, Inc.

Ivan Turgenev, "Bazarov's Nihilism," from *Fathers and Sons*, by Ivan Turgenev, translated by Bernard Guilbert Guerney. © Copyright 1961 by Bernard Guilbert Guerney. Reprinted by permission of Random House, Inc.

J. L. Simmons and Barry Winograd, "The Hang-Loose Ethic," from *It's Happening*, Marc-laird Publications, Santa Barbara, California. Reprinted by permission.

"The Nanterre Manifesto," translated by Peter Brooks. Reprinted from *Partisan Review*, Fall, 1968, Vol. 25, no. 4, by permission.

Albert H. Hobbs, "The SDS Trip." Reprinted by permission, from the Spring, 1969, issue of *The Intercollegiate Review.* © 1969 by The Intercollegiate Studies Institute, Inc., 14 South Bryn Mawr Avenue, Bryn Mawr, Pa., 19010.

James Reston, "The Cliches of the Radical Students." *The New York Times*, April 18, 1969. © 1969 by The New York Times Company. Reprinted by permission.

Stephen Spender, "What the Rebellious Students Want." *The New York Times Magazine*, March 30, 1969. © 1968/1969 by The New York Times Company. Reprinted by permission.

Sidney Hook, "The War Against the Democratic Process," *The Atlantic Monthly*, February, 1969. Reprinted by permission of the author.

Tom Wolfe, "The Pump House Gang," from *The Pump House Gang.* Reprinted with the permission of Farrar, Straus & Giroux, Inc., from *The Pump House Gang* by Tom Wolfe, Copyright © 1966 by The New York Herald Tribune, Inc. Copyright © 1968 by Tom Wolfe.

"John Gets the Better of Old Marster," reprinted from *American Negro Folktales*, compiled by Richard M. Dorson, by permission of Premier Books, Fawcett Publications, Inc. Copyright © 1956, 1967, by Richard Mercer Dorson. Copyright © 1958 by Indiana University Press.

Langston Hughes, "Dear Dr. Butts," from *Simple Takes A Wife.* Reprinted by permission of Harold Ober Associates Incorporated. Copyright 1953 by Langston Hughes.

Robert F. Williams, the Prologue to "Negroes with Guns," from *Black Protest: History, Documents, and Analyses, 1619 to the Present*, ed. by Joanne Grant, Fawcett Publications, Inc.

Eldridge Cleaver, "Notes on a Native Son," from *Soul on Ice* by Eldridge Cleaver. Copyright © 1968 by Eldridge Cleaver. Used with permission of McGraw-Hill Book Company.

LeRoi Jones, "The Black Artist and the Revolution." "State/Meant" from *Home: Social Essays* by LeRoi Jones. Reprinted by permission of William Morrow and Company, Inc. Copyright © 1965 by LeRoi Jones. "The Revolutionary Theatre," by LeRoi Jones. *Liberator*, Vol. 5, no. 7 (July, 1965). Copyright © 1965 by *Liberator*.

Christopher Lasch, "The Trouble with Black Power." Reprinted with permission from *The New York Review of Books*. Copyright © 1968, The New York Review.

Martin Luther King, Jr., "I Have a Dream." Reprinted by permission of Joan Daves. Copyright © 1963 by Martin Luther King, Jr.

Alfred North Whitehead, "The Century of Genius," reprinted with permission of the Macmillan Company from *Science and the Modern World* by Alfred North Whitehead. Copyright 1925 by The Macmillan Company. Renewed in 1953 by Evelyn Whitehead.

Sigmund Freud, "The Forbidden Exploration," from *The Basic Writings of Sigmund Freud*, trans and ed. by Dr. A. A. Brill. Copyright 1938 by Random House, Inc. Copyright renewed 1965 by Gloria Bennheim and Edmund Brill. Reprinted by permission.

Sir Ernest Rutherford, "The Stability of Atoms," from W. C. Dampier: *Readings in the Literature of Science*. Reprinted with permission of the publisher, Cambridge University Press.

Donald Fleming, "On Living in a Biological Revolution." Copyright © 1969, by the Atlantic Monthly Company, Boston. Reprinted with permission.

Zbigniew Brzezinski, "America in the Technetronic Age." Originally published under the title "The Technetronic Revolution," in *Encounter* (January, 1966). Reprinted by permission of *Encounter* and the author.

Aldous Huxley, "The Fertilizing Room." Chapter 10 in *Brave New World* by Aldous Huxley. Copyright, 1932, 1960 by Aldous Huxley. Reprinted by permission of Harper & Row, Publishers.

Hannah Arendt, "Man's Conquest of Space," from *Between Past and Future: Eight Exercises in Political Thought* by Hannah Arendt. Copyright © 1963 by Hannah Arendt. All rights reserved. Reprinted by permission of The Viking Press, Inc.

Barrington Moore, Jr., "Revolution in America?" Reprinted with permission from *The New York Review of Books*. Copyright © 1969, The New York Review.

Contents

Contents   xi

I

Introduction

As in so many instances, we begin by invoking Aristotle, even in this era of swift and compelling change that sometimes appears to seek the defoliation of the past. Rhetoric, he tells us, is the faculty of observing the available means of persuasion. That persuasion grows out of the personal character of the rhetorician, who is capable of instilling a certain attitude in the audience and whose language provides a proof or an apparent proof for the point he wishes to argue. He is a man who sincerely believes that he knows the truth about something and who desires to secure that truth among members of his audience and throughout his entire community. To do so, he must be sharply aware of the intricacies of the human mind; he must also have a conception of what is right and what is good; in addition, he must have the will to reason painstakingly and the ability to think logically; and finally, he must be aware of the inclinations and desires of his audience without himself being desposed to pander to those among it.

In the broadest sense, then, rhetoric has to do with knowing about argumentation. It is only in the narrower and more restricted sense that it has anything to do with the ornamentation and polish that cling to the surface of a written or spoken text. There is an ethical foundation to rhetoric, and the configurations of language that ultimately give the statement its outward form owe their existence to the security of that foundation. The rhetorician's chief devices are the sharpness of his mind and his eye, the genuineness of his consideration for the audience, the sincerity of his character, and the authenticity of his convictions. If ornamental polish or elegantly asserted style do exist in an effective sample of rhetoric, it is there only because the speaker or writer has discovered the means of effective persuasion, whereupon he could then invent techniques of getting his argument across to his audience convincingly. The eloquence of his words, the structure and cadence of his sentences, and the pattern and unity of his organization—not necessarily important in themselves—depend fundamentally upon his awareness that he is a man striving to persuade other men, and to persuade them with justification. Students should make that initial assumption about the rhetorician and his art, regardless of how our understanding of the term rhetoric has shifted since Aristotle's time.

There is no question that the conception of rhetoric has shifted, and in recent years the shift has been so abrupt that it sometimes appears more like a dislocation. In many classrooms, the term is often used to denote the traditional principles of grammar or the standards of correct and elegant diction; it includes rules pertaining to spelling and governing the accuracy of punctuation; and it incorporates such vague generalizations as those that admonish students to write their class compositions with clarity and unity. In short, such rhetoric is what might be called "schoolboy rhetoric," frequently nothing more than an elaborate set of formulas designed to elicit something called correctness pursued for the sake of academic grades. In public life, on the other hand, rhetoric has come to be associated with bombast and invective, with the building of images that frequently represent a cynical evasion of truth rather than a faithful and honest model of it, and with crowd-pleasing abstractions and trite or flashy (or both) figures of speech. One can recall, for example, certain campaign promises made by President Nixon prior to his election in 1968. After his inauguration, these same promises were apt to undergo modification or to be ignored, acknowledged at last only by statements that, after all, they were made in the heat of political contention and were used only to attract votes. We do not single out Mr. Nixon accusingly. He did merely what candidates are expected to do; such is the rhetoric of contemporary politics, and our point simply is that such a conception of rhetoric stands apart from Aristotle's conception of it. Likewise with the application of rhetoric found in the marketplace of commerce and industry, which represents a highly perfected technology more than it resembles a skilled and purposeful use of language. Rhetoric in this commercial sense promises young girls sex appeal in exchange for the purchase of a certain brand of toothpaste, middle-aged men the semblance of virility and success if they smoke a particular brand of cigar, and elderly matrons youth if they buy sugarless cola or cross-your-heart brassieres. Such rhetoric depends upon thd deft shuffling of graphic images and the well-engineered manipulation of electronic devices rather than an accurately intentioned assembly of words, sentences, and paragraphs. If it is artistic, its art is that of a certain manner of coercion rather than the knowledgeable application of persuasion. It too departs from the Aristotelian norm, perhaps more radically than other varieties of rhetoric.

We do not wish to generalize so wildly as to assert that such non-Aristotelian rhetorics are worthless or intrinsically bad. The question of their utility is not ours to settle. We merely wish to clarify what we ourselves have taken rhetoric to mean as we set about assembling our anthology. Quite deliberately, the essays collected here are offered in the spirit of the classical conception of what rhetoric is. All of them are models of persuasion in its various forms. Some serve better as models than others; a few are quite unsatisfactory when measured by the classical norm, which requires of a rhetorician the ability to make his statement credible by revealing his true character, to arouse conviction in his audience, and to demonstrate his point by some effectively rational means. We leave it to readers to discover the imperfections and the flaws where they exist. In fact, we invite value judgments with each selection, and we have purposely chosen several examples of spurious rhetoric to make our readers more appreciative of the real thing when they recognize it. We remind them to remain in relentless pursuit of the attitude of the speaker in each piece, to estimate the impact of that speaker on his audience, and to evaluate the effectiveness of his reasoning.

We do not wish to imply, however, that we are unconcerned with language, or that we would either disregard a consideration of it or denigrate that aspect of it called style. To the contrary. We recognize the importance of language; we recognize especially the significance of the language in the literature of persuasion. Recognizing as much, we have scrutinized the linguistic surface of each selection carefully, requiring complete effectiveness in every case. But, in setting up our standards, we have not forgot what some of the advocates and practitioners of newer conceptions of rhetoric overlook. Although language has its own effective purity and creates its own delightful beauty irrespective of what its user in any given case purports to say, it also has a more obscure dimension; for it bears a relationship with the individual who is using it, and it is this dimension that accounts for its ultimate value. The language a man uses has roots deep in his mind and psyche alike. The source of his words lies in his perception of reality, in his inner response to his environment and his society, in his desire for himself and his designs for his fellow men. The language of an individual is grounded deeply in his basicmost attitudes, and it is forced outward by his convictions, his passions, and the pressure of his commitments.

This brings us to an explanation as to why we have chosen revolution as the subject of this text. Aristotle says that rhetoric need not be confined to any particular subject matter; on the contrary, it can be matched with any. And few other themes serve our purpose as well, since few others are as likely both to arouse so wide a range of human passions and convictions and to illustrate so thoroughly the depth of man's basic need to recognize the self he truly is, and to relate to other men in his society. Yet few if any topics are as likely to make possible so completely the illustration that what an articulate man says actually does represent what he sees, what he stands for, and what he believes. On the other hand, few other topics allow so quickly the realization that language ill used—that is, language grounded upon a bogus conviction and assembled irrationally and without sincerity—is little more than prattle and bombast, no matter how slick and elegant its surface. The topic of revolution, we have discovered, serves amazingly well to demonstrate how human attitudes actually can govern language when the mind sets to work to build a verbal bridge between the self and others, and how language can be betrayed when reason fails and self-seeking passion alone makes an assault upon an audience or a community.

Thucydides provides a telling example in the third book of his history of the Peloponnesian War. Describing what he calls the Corcyraean revolution, in which the advocates of democracy rose up against the ruling oligarchy, he reports that as the revolution ran its course across the land, it carried to excess the inventions of those who fought each other, which became especially obvious in their language. "Words," he writes, "had to change their ordinary meaning and to take that which was now given them. Reckless audacity came to be considered the courage of a loyal ally; prudent hesitation, specious cowardice; moderation was held to be a cloak for unmanliness; ability to see all sides of a question, inaptness to act on any. Frantic violence became the attribute of manliness; cautious plotting a justifiable means of self-defence. The advocate of extreme measures was always trustworthy; his opponent a man to be suspected. To succeed in a plot was to have a shrewd head, to divine a plot still shrewder; but to try to provide against having to do either was to break up your party and to be afraid of your adversaries." Thucydides is describing a revolution he does not approve of, and we might even say that he is in fact describing what could more properly be called a civil war. But he still illustrates the general point that the language men use is governed by and is an accurate index of their attitudes and contentions; he illustrates the specific point that the rhetoric of revolution demonstrates with special clarity how language projects the character and attitude of the speaker, and how at the same time the character and attitude of that speaker give his words their special value. The same thing can possibly be said about the rhetoric of war or of violence, except that these categories of human activity depend somewhat less on the power of reason than revolution does, even where they overlap with it as is sometimes the case. Revolutionaries must know not only what they are saying and doing; they must also know what they are thinking. Indeed, they must know first that they *are* thinking, and they must be persistently aware of their ability to do so.

For better or for worse, language is the tissue of human behavior; the phenomenon we identify as revolution involves a variety of human behavior that puts a special coloration into the language that gives it its complexion. Another illustration of that fact comes from the word revolution itself and from the way it has been used. In her book *On Revolution*, Hannah Arendt reminds us that the term did not at first have a political application. Originally it meant the return or recurrence of a point or period of time. It was frequently used in a more precise and scientific sense by astronomers to designate the regular, circular movement of heavenly bodies. In using it, men acknowledged an awareness of the past and the existence of a fixed pattern of cycles. The term was not employed in a political sense until 1660, with the restoration of the monarchy in England. It was used politically a second time in 1668, when James II of England was removed from the throne in favor of William and Mary, thus restoring to the monarchy its former glory in an event that historians now call the "Glorious Revolution," which incidentally was bloodless and nonviolent. In both cases the word appears to mean just the opposite of what we take it to mean today. Miss Arendt, however, demonstrates that this is not merely an accident of semantics. "The revolutions of the seventeenth and eighteenth centuries," she writes, "which to us appear to show all evidence of a new spirit, the spirit of the modern age, were intended to be restorations." The earliest instances of political revolution as it has come to be understood in the modern world bear that point out. The spokesmen for both the American and the French Revolutions insisted that they desired to restore old liberties and values that had been suppressed by tyrants, and "that they wanted to revolve back to old times when things had been as they ought to be." Significantly, they used the word as a metaphor, acknowledging thereby a notion of heavenly movement and insisting that such irrepressible motion applies to human events just as surely as it applies to God's stars. In selecting a word used scientifically by astronomers, and in altering somewhat the meaning of that word, they performed a rhetorical act in which the term they chose to designate their actions displayed an attitude of certainty and righteousness toward what they advocated; and in which their sense of purpose gave the word a renewed force. Their special use of the term suggests a dedication to what they considered a higher cause and a zeal for what we now recognize as a more earthbound one. Ever since those two modern prototypes of political revolution, the emphasis of the term has been shifting away from the metaphorical sense that likens it to the motion of the stars and more toward the abstract concept of irrestibility.

Spokesmen for revolution, one then discovers, have behaved as though inevitability were on their side. They have come to be identified not necessarily by their political views, but rather by a marked sense of purpose and a certain fixed conception of reality that defy convention and reverberate in the language they use; it is this spirit—this frequently and sometimes seemingly threatening and unsavory attitude—that is the salient trait of a revolutionary. So that although revolution has come since the times of Jefferson and Robespierre to denote novelty and a sense of the future rather than the restoration of an old order and the reassertion of lost ideals, and although we recognize the reality of that semantic shift, we would still assert that revolution in the broadest sense applies to movements outside the political realm as well as it applies to political action itself. It is a man's state of mind that makes him a revolutionary, just as it is the state of his language that makes him one of revolution's effective rhetoricians. Because of the forcefulness of his state of mind, his language becomes especially suitable for the study of rhetoric: that is, for the study of the peculiar relationship between a man's verbal structures and his innermost convictions.

Hence, speaking again in a broad sense, we say that revolution has more to do with attitude than with politics, even where that attitude may sometimes manifest itself in the political arena. Broadly, we define revolution as either a change of attitude within a unit of society, or as an attitude that has been suppressed to the breaking point by an external force or else repressed internally beyond endurance. John Milton's ultimate declaration that kings can justifiably be deposed serves as an example, and so does Huck Finn's decision to go to hell by setting Jim free rather than going to heaven by sending Jim back to slavery. Sometimes the discovery a man makes about the nature of things forces him to alter his basic attitude about reality, as is the case with Newton, Darwin, or Freud, who clearly led revolutions that were nonpolitical; sometimes men finally decide to respond sharply to an awareness that they have hitherto harbored vaguely, as occurs with the tribesmen that Sir James Frazer discusses in "Putting the King to Death." In any event, the revolutionary social unit can be an individual or a group of individuals of any size, as long as all share the attitude that breaks forth in revolution. And the attitude can emerge in the sphere of social behavior or in art or science or religion or within the family unit.

In this text we recognize five categories of revolution, but we do so rather arbitrarily, realizing that any such classification must ultimately be artificial and limited. We certainly do not contend that the full spectrum of its variety can be fully or accurately exhibited. We do, however, maintain that, since revolution is so completely grounded within the mind and spirit of its advocates, it becomes significantly appropriate to be used for the study of rhetoric. Its appropriateness is extended, moreover, inasmuch as it frequently prompts spirited and rational replies from those who oppose it. A dialectic results that contains its own relevance to these times of controversy, contention, and crisis, yet that at the same time demonstrates that the only reasonable conflict in the contemporary world is the conflict of true rhetoric: The only clash that our society can safety sustain is the clash of words; the only tolerable weapons are the mind and spirit of man, brandished carefully and in full conjunction with one-another; and the only position a man can maintain relative to other men is to be true to himself and to represent himself honestly and skillfully with the fullest regard for members of his community.

DOVER BEACH

Matthew Arnold

The sea is calm tonight,
The tide is full, the moon lies fair
Upon the straits;—on the French coast the light
Gleams and is gone; the cliffs of England stand,
Glimmering and vast, out in the tranquil bay.
Come to the window, sweet is the night-air!
Only, from the long line of spray
Where the sea meets the moon-blanched land,
Listen! you hear the grating roar
Of pebbles which the waves draw back, and fling,
At their return, up the high strand,
Begin, and cease, and then again begin,
With tremulous cadence slow, and bring
The eternal note of sadness in.

Sophocles long ago
Heard it on the Aegean, and it brought
Into his mind the turbid ebb and flow
Of human misery; we
Find also in the sound a thought,
Hearing it by this distant northern sea.

The Sea of Faith
Was once, too, at the full, and round earth's shore
Lay like the folds of a bright girdle furled.
But now I only hear
Its melancholy, long, withdrawing roar,
Retreating, to the breath
Of the night-wind, down the vast edges drear
And naked shingles of the world.

Ah, love, let us be true
To one another! for the world, which seems
To lie before us like a land of dreams,
So various, so beautiful, so new,
Hath really neither joy, nor love, nor light,
Nor certitude, nor peace, nor help for pain;
And we are here as on a darkling plain
Swept with confused alarms of struggle and flight,
Where ignorant armies clash by night.

II

Revolution and the Body Politic

"Better to reign in Hell than serve in Heaven."

John Milton, *Paradise Lost*

PUTTING THE KING TO DEATH

Sir James George Frazer

At an early stage of his intellectual development man deems himself naturally immortal, and imagines that were it not for the baleful arts of sorcerers, who cut the vital thread prematurely short, he would live for ever. But in time the sad truth of human mortality was borne in upon our primitive philosopher with a force of demonstration which no prejudice could resist and no sophistry dissemble. Nevertheless, even if he reluctantly acknowledged the existence of beings at once superhuman and supernatural, he was as yet far from suspecting the width and the depth of the gulf which divided him from them. The gods with whom his imagination now peopled the darkness of the unknown were indeed admitted by him to be his superiors in knowledge and in power, in the joyous splendour of their life and in the length of its duration. But, though he knew it not, these glorious and awful beings were merely, like the spectre of the Brocken, the reflections of his own diminutive personality exaggerated into gigantic proportions by distance and by the mists and clouds of ignorance upon which they were cast.

Man in fact created gods in his own likeness and being himself mortal he naturally supposed his creatures to be in the same sad predicament. Thus the Greenlanders believed that a wind could kill their most powerful god, and that he would certainly die if he touched a dog. In answer to the enquiries of Colonel Dodge, a North American Indian stated that the world was made by the Great Spirit. Being asked which Great Spirit he meant, the good one or the bad one, "Oh, neither of *them*," replied he, "the Great Spirit that made the world is dead long ago. He could not possibly have lived as long as this." A tribe in the Philippine Islands told the Spanish conquerors that the grave of the Creator was upon the top of Mount Cabunian. Heitsi-eibib, a god or divine hero of the Hottentots, died several times and came to life again. His graves are generally to be met with in narrow defiles between mountains. When the Hottentots pass one of them, they throw a stone on it for good luck, sometimes muttering "Give us plenty of cattle." The grave of Zeus, the great god of Greece, was shewn to visitors in Crete as late as about the beginning

of our era. The body of Dionysus was buried at Delphi beside the
golden statue of Apollo, and his tomb bore the inscription, "Here lies
Dionysus dead, the son of Semele." According to one account,
Apollo himself was buried at Delphi; for Pythagoras is said to have
carved an inscription on his tomb, setting forth how the god had
been killed by the python and buried under the tripod. The god
Kronos was buried in Sicily, and the graves of Hermes, Aphrodite,
and Ares were shown in Hermopolis, Cyprus, and Thrace.

The great gods of Egypt themselves were not exempt from the
common lot. They too grew old and died. For like men they were
composed of body and soul, and like men were subject to all the
passions and infirmities of the flesh. Their bodies, it is true, were
fashioned of more ethereal mould, and lasted longer than ours, but
they could not hold out for ever against the siege of time. Age
converted their bones into silver, their flesh into gold, and their azure
locks into lapis-lazuli. When their time came, they passed away from
the cheerful world of the living to reign as dead gods over dead men
in the melancholy world beyond the grave. Even their souls, like
those of mankind, could only endure after death so long as their
bodies held together; and hence it was as needful to preserve the
corpses of the gods as the corpses of common folk, lest with the
divine body the divine spirit should also come to an untimely end. At
first their remains were laid to rest under the desert sands of the
mountains, that the dryness of the soil and the purity of the air
might protect them from putrefaction and decay. Hence one of the
oldest titles of the Egyptian gods is "they who are under the sands."
But when at a later time the discovery of the art of embalming gave
a new lease of life to the souls of the dead by preserving their bodies
for an indefinite time from corruption, the deities were permitted to
share the benefit of an invention which held out to gods as well as to
men a reasonable hope of immortality. Every province then had the
tomb and mummy of its dead god. The mummy of Osiris was to be
seen at Mendes; Thinis boasted of the mummy of Onouris; and
Heliopolis of that of Tum.

*If the high gods, who dwell remote from the fret and fever of this
earthly life, are yet believed to die at last, it is not to be expected
that a god who lodges in a frail tabernacle of flesh should escape the
same fate. The danger is a formidable one; for if the course of nature
is dependent on the man-god's life, what catastrophes may not be
expected from the gradual enfeeblement of his powers and their final
extinction in death? There is only one way of averting these dangers.
The man-god must be killed as soon as he shews symptoms that his
powers are beginning to fail, and his soul must be transferred to a
vigorous successor before it has been seriously impaired by the
threatened decay.*

The mystic kings of fire and water in Cambodia are not allowed to
die a natural death. Hence when one of them falls seriously ill and

the elders think that he cannot recover, they stab him to death. The people of Congo believed, as we have seen, that if their pontiff the Chitomé were to die a natural death, the world would perish, and the earth, which he alone sustained by his power and merit, would immediately be annihilated. Accordingly when he fell ill and seemed likely to die, his prospective successor entered his house with a rope or club and strangled or bludgeoned him to death.

The Ethiopian kings of Meroe were worshipped as gods; but whenever the priests chose, they sent a messenger to the king, ordering him to die, and alleging an oracle of the gods as their authority for the command. Customs of the same sort appear, moreover, to have prevailed in he same region down to modern times. Thus we are told that in Fazoql, a district of the Blue Nile, it was customary, as late as the middle of the nineteenth century, to hang a king who was no longer beloved. His relatives and ministers gathered round him and announced that since he was no longer pleasing to man or beast, he had better die.

The Shilluk of the White Nile regard the king as a reincarnation of Nyakang, the semi-divine hero who founded the dynasty and settled the tribe in its present territory. Accordingly they cherish "the conviction that the king must not be allowed to become ill or senile, lest with his diminishing vigour the cattle should sicken and fail to bear their increase, the crops should rot in the fields, and man, stricken with disease, should die in ever increasing numbers." To prevent these calamities it used to be the regular custom to put the king to death whenever he shewed signs of ill-health or failing strength. One of the fatal symptoms of decay was taken to be an incapacity to satisfy the sexual passions of his wives. When this ominous weakness manifested itself, the wives reported it to the chiefs, who are popularly said to have intimated to the king his doom by spreading a white cloth over his face and knees as he lay slumbering in the heat of the sultry afternoon. Execution soon followed the sentence of death. A hut was specially built for the occasion: the king was led into it and lay down with his head resting on the lap of a nubile virgin: the door of the hut was then walled up; and the couple were left without food, water, or fire to die of hunger and suffocation. This was the old custom, but it was abolished some five generations ago, and since then the Shilluk have adopted a quicker and more merciful mode of executing their kings. It is said that nowadays the chiefs announce his fate to the king, and that afterwards he is strangled in a hut which has been specially built for the occasion.

The Dinka are a congeries of independent tribes in the valley of the White Nile, whose territory, lying mostly on the eastern bank of the river and stretching from the sixth to the twelfth degree of North Latitude, has been estimated to comprise between sixty and seventy thousand square miles. They worship a supreme being whose name of Dengdit means literally Great Rain, and the human rain-maker (*bain*)

is a very important personage among the Dinka to this day; indeed
the men in authority whom travellers dub chiefs or sheikhs are in
fact the actual or potential rain-makers of the tribe or community.
Each of them is believed to be animated by the spirit of a great
rain-maker, which has come down to him through a succession of
rain-makers; and in virtue of this inspiration a successful rain-maker
enjoys very great power and is consulted on all important matters.
Yet, in spite, or rather in virtue, of the high honour in which he is
held, no Dinka rain-maker is allowed to die a natural death of
sickness or old age; for the Dinka believe that if such an untoward
event were to happen, the tribe would suffer from disease and
famine, and the herds would not yield their increase. So when a
rain-maker feels that he is growing old and infirm, he tells his
children that he wishes to die. Among the Agar Dinka a large grave is
dug and the rain-maker lies down in it on his right side with his head
resting on a skin. He is surrounded by his friends and relatives,
including his younger children; but his elder children are not allowed
to approach the grave lest in their grief and despair they should do
themselves a bodily injury. For many hours, generally for more than
a day, the rain-maker lies without eating or drinking. From time to
time he speaks to the people, recalling the past history of the tribe,
reminding them how he has ruled and advised them, and instructing
them how they are to act in the future. Then, when he has concluded his admonition, he tells them that it is finished and bids them
cover him up. So the earth is thrown down on him as he lies in the
grave, and he soon dies of suffocation. Even if a rain-maker is quite
young he will be put to death should he seem likely to perish of
disease. Further, every precaution is taken to prevent a rain-maker
from dying an accidental death, for such an end, though not nearly
so serious a matter as death from illness or old age, would be sure to
entail sickness on the tribe. As soon as a rain-maker is killed, his
valuable spirit is supposed to pass to a suitable successor, whether a
son or other near blood relation.

   In the Central African kingdom of Unyoro down to recent years
custom required that as soon as the king fell seriously ill or began to
break up from age, he should die by his own hand; for, according to
an old prophecy, the throne would pass away from the dynasty if
ever the king were to die a natural death. He killed himself by
draining a poisoned cup. If he faltered or were too ill to ask for the
cup, it was his wife's duty to administer the poison. When the king
of Kibanga, on the Upper Congo, seems near his end, the sorcerers
put a rope round his neck, which they draw gradually tighter till he
dies. If the king of Gingiro happens to be wounded in war, he is put
to death by his comrades, or, if they fail to kill him, by his kinsfolk,
however hard he may beg for mercy. They say they do it that he
may not die by the hands of his enemies. The Jukos are a heathen
tribe of the Benue river, a great tributary of the Niger. In their
country "the town of Gatri is ruled by a king who is elected by the

big men of the town as follows. When in the opinion of the big men
the king has reigned long enough, they give out that 'the king is
sick'—a formula understood by all to mean that they are going to kill
him, though the intention is never put more plainly. They then
decide who is to be the next king. How long he is to reign is settled
by the influential men at a meeting; the question is put and answered
by each man throwing on the ground a little piece of stick for each
year he thinks the new king should rule. The king is then told, and a
great feast prepared, at which the king gets drunk on guinea-corn
beer. After that he is speared, and the man who was chosen becomes
king. "

It appears to have been a Zulu custom to put the king to death as
soon as he began to have wrinkles or grey hairs. At least this seems
implied in the following passage written by one who resided for some
time at the court of the notorious Zulu tyrant Chaka, in the early
part of the nineteenth century: "The extraordinary violence of the
king's rage with me was mainly occasioned by that absurd nostrum,
the hair oil, with the notion of which Mr. Farewell had impressed
him as being a specific for removing all indications of age. From the
first moment of his having heard that such a preparation was attainable, he evinced a solicitude to procure it, and on every occasion
never forgot to remind us of his anxiety respecting it; more especially
on our departure on the mission his injunctions were particularly
directed to this object. It will be seen that it is one of the barbarous
customs of the Zoolas in their choice or election of their kings that
he must neither have wrinkles nor grey hairs, as they are both
distinguishing marks of disqualification for becoming a monarch of a
warlike people. It is also equally indispensable that their king should
never exhibit those proofs of having become unfit and incompetent
to reign; it is therefore important that they should conceal these
indications so long as they possibly can. Chaka had become greatly
apprehensive of the approach of grey hairs; which would at once be
the signal for him to prepare to make his exit from this sublunary
world, it being always followed by the death of the monarch." The
writer to whom we are indebted for this instructive anecdote of the
hair-oil omits to specify the mode in which a grey-haired and wrinkled Zulu chief used "to make his exit from this sublunary world";
but on analogy we may conjecture that he did so by the simple and
perfectly sufficient process of being knocked on the head.

The custom of putting kings to death as soon as they suffered from
any personal defect prevailed two centuries ago in the Caffre kingdom of Sofala, to the north of the present Zululand. These kings of
Sofala were regarded as gods by their people, being entreated to give
rain or sunshine, according as each might be wanted. Nevertheless, as
we learn from an old Portuguese historian, a slight bodily blemish,
such as the loss of a tooth, was considered a sufficient cause for
putting one of these god-men to death.

The king of Sofala who dared to survive the loss of his front tooth was thus a bold reformer like Ergamenes, king of Ethiopia. We may conjecture that the ground for putting the Ethiopian kings to death was, as in the case of the Zulu and Sofala kings, the appearance on their person of any bodily defect or sign of decay; and that the oracle which the priests alleged as the authority for the royal execution was to the effect that great calamities would result from the reign of a king who had any blemish on his body; just as an oracle warned Sparta against a "lame reign," that is, the reign of a lame king. It is some confirmation of this conjecture that the kings of Ethiopia were chosen for their size, strength, and beauty long before the custom of killing them was abolished. To this day the Sultan of Wadai must have no obvious bodily defect, and the king of Angoy cannot be crowned if he has a single blemish, such as a broken or a filed tooth or the scar of an old wound. According to the Book of Acaill and many other authorities no king who was afflicted with a personal blemish might reign over Ireland at Tara. Hence, when the great King Cormac Mac Art lost one eye by an accident, he at once abdicated. It is only natural, therefore, to suppose, especially with the other African examples before us, that any bodily defect or symptom of old age appearing on the person of the Ethiopian monarch was the signal for his execution.

Many days' journey to the north-east of Abomey, the old capital of Dahomey, lies the kingdom of Eyeo. "The Eyeos are governed by a king, no less absolute than the king of Dahomey, yet subject to a regulation of state, at once humiliating and extraordinary. When the people have conceived an opinion of his ill-government, which is sometimes insidiously infused into them by the artifice of his discontented ministers, they send a deputation to him with a present of parrots' eggs, as a mark of its authenticity, to represent to him that the burden of government must have so far fatigued him that they consider it full time for him to repose from his cares and indulge himself with a little sleep. He thanks his subjects for their attention to his ease, retires to his own apartment as if to sleep, and there gives directions to his women to strangle him. This is immediately executed, and his son quietly ascends the throne upon the usual terms of holding the reins of government no longer than whilst he merits the approbation of the people."

The Bambara, a large tribe in the French territory of Upper Senegal and Niger, have an ancient tradition that formerly their kings were only allowed to reign so long as they retained their strength and vigour. When they noticed that the king's strength was failing, they said "The grass is withering! The grass is beginning to wither," which had a sinister significance for the ageing king whose hair was beginning to grow grey.

Among the Banyankole, a pastoral people of the Uganda Protectorate, the king is known by the title of Mugabe. "No Mugabe ever allowed himself to grow old . . . he had to put an end to his life before his powers, either mental or physical, began to deteriorate. It was even thought undesirable that the Mugabe should look old, and treatment was applied to prevent his hair from growing grey. As soon as he felt his strength diminishing he knew it was time to end his life, and he called his chiefs, and also his sons, who never came to see him except on this occasion . . . when all was ready, he summoned the royal medicine-man and asked for the king's poison. This was always kept in readiness in the shell of a crocodile's egg. The white of the egg was dried and powdered and mixed with the dried nerve from the pointed end of an elephant's tusk and some other ingredients, the exact mixture being kept strictly secret. This had only to be mixed with a little water or beer to be ready for use, and when the Mugabe drank it he fell dead in a few moments."

The old Prussians acknowledged as their supreme lord a ruler who governed them in the name of the gods, and was known as God's Mouth (*Kirwaido*). When he felt himself weak and ill, if he wished to leave a good name behind him, he had a great heap made of thorn-bushes and straw, on which he mounted and delivered a long sermon to the people, exhorting them to serve the gods and promising to go to the gods and speak for the people. Then he took some of the perpetual fire which burned in front of the holy oak-tree, and lighting the pile with it burned himself to death.

Some peoples appear to have thought it unsafe to wait for even the slightest symptom of decay and have preferred to kill the king while he was still in the full vigour of life. Accordingly, they have fixed a term beyond which he might not reign, and at the close of which he must die, the term fixed upon being short enough to exclude the probability of his degenerating physically in the interval. In some parts of southern India the period fixed was twelve years. Thus, according to an old traveller, in the province of Quilacare, about twenty leagues to the north-east of Cape Comorin, "there is a Gentile house of prayer, in which there is an idol which they hold in great account, and every twelve years they celebrate a great feast to it, whither all the Gentiles go as to a jubilee. This temple possesses many lands and much revenue: it is a very great affair. This province has a king over it, who has not more than twelve years to reign from jubilee to jubilee. His manner of living is in this wise, that is to say: when the twelve years are completed, on the day of this feast there assemble together innumerable people, and much money is spent in giving food to Bramans. The king has a wooden scaffolding made, spread over with silken hangings: and on that day he goes to bathe at a tank with great ceremonies and sound of music, after that he comes to the idol and prays to it, and mounts on to the scaffolding, and there before all the people he takes some very sharp knives, and begins to cut off his nose, and then his ears, and his lips, and all his members, and as much flesh off himself as he can; and he throws it away very hurriedly until so much of his blood is spilled that he begins to faint, and then he cuts his throat himself. And he performs this sacrifice to the idol, and whoever desires to reign other twelve years and undertake this martyrdom for love of the idol, has to be present looking on at this: and from that place they raise him up as king."

The king of Calicut, on the Malabar coast, bears the title of Samorin or Samory, which in the native language is said to mean "God on earth." He "pretends to be of a higher rank than the Brahmans, and to be inferior only to the invisible gods; a pretention that was acknowledged by his subjects, but which is held as absurd and abominable by the Brahmans, by whom he is only treated as a Sudra." Formerly the Samorin had to cut his throat in public at the end of a twelve years' reign. But towards the end of the seventeenth century the rule had been modified as follows: "Many strange customs were observed in this country in former times, and some very odd ones are still continued. It was an ancient custom for the Samorin to reign but twelve years, and no longer. If he died before his term was expired, it saved him a troublesome ceremony of cutting his own throat, on a publick scaffold erected for the purpose. He first made a feast for all his nobility and gentry, who are very numerous. After the feast he saluted his guests, and went on the scaffold, and very decently cut his own throat in the view of the assembly, and his body was, a little while after, burned with great pomp and ceremony, and the grandees elected a new Samorin. Whether that custom was a religious or a civil ceremony, I know not, but it is now laid aside. And a new custom is followed by the modern Samorins, that jubilee is proclaimed throughout his dominions, at the end of twelve years, and a tent is pitched for him in a spacious plain, and a great feast is celebrated for ten or twelve days, with mirth and jollity, guns firing night and day, so at the end of the feast any four of the guests that have a mind to gain a crown by a desperate action, in fighting their way through 30 or 40,000 of his guards, and kill the Samorin in his tent, he that kills him succeeds him in his empire. In anno 1695, one of those jubilees happened, and the tent pitched near Pennany, a seaport of his, about fifteen leagues to the southward of Calicut. There were but three men that would venture on that desperate action, who fell in, with sword and target, among the guard, and, after they had killed and wounded many, were themselves killed. One of the desperados had a nephew of fifteen or sixteen years of age, that kept close by his uncle in the attack on the guards, and, when he saw him fall, the youth got through the guards into the tent, and made a stroke at his Majesty's head, and had certainly despatched him if a large brass lamp which was burning over his head had not marred the blow; but, before he could make another, he was killed by the guards; and, I believe, the same Samorin reigns yet. I chanced to come that time along the coast and heard the guns for two or three days and nights successively."

Putting the King to Death

When kings were bound to suffer death, whether at their own hands or at the hands of others, on the expiration of a fixed term of years, it was natural that they should seek to delegate the painful duty, along with some of the privileges of sovereignty, to a substitute who should suffer vicariously in their stead. This expedient appears to have been resorted to by some of the princes of Malabar. Thus we are informed by a native authority on that country that "in some places all powers both executive and judicial were delegated for a fixed period to natives by the sovereign. This institution was styled *Thalavettiparothiam* or authority obtained by decapitation. . . . It was an office tenable for five years during which its bearer was invested with supreme despotic powers within his jurisdiction. On the expiry of the five years the man's head was cut off and thrown up in the air amongst a large concourse of villagers, each of whom vied with the other in trying to catch it in its course down. He who succeeded was nominated to the post for the next five years." A similar delegation of the duty of dying for his country was perhaps practised by the Sultans of Java. At least such a custom would explain a strange scene which was witnessed at the court of one of these sultans by the famous traveller Ibn Batuta, a native of Tangier, who visited the East Indies in the first half of the fourteenth century. He says: "During my audience with the Sultan I saw a man who held in his hand a knife like that used by a grape-gleaner. He placed it on his own neck and spoke for a long time in a language which I did not understand. After that he seized the knife with both hands at once and cut his throat. His head fell to the ground, so sharp was the blade and so great the force with which he used it. I remained dumbfounded at his behaviour, but the Sultan said to me, 'Does any one do like that in your country?' I answered, 'Never did I see such a thing.' He smiled and replied, 'These people are our slaves, and they kill themselves for love of us.' Then he commanded that they should take away him who had slain himself and should burn him. The Sultan's officers, the grandees, the troops, and the common people attended the cremation. The sovereign assigned a liberal pension to the children of the deceased, to his wife, and to his brothers; and they were highly honoured because of his conduct. A person, who was present at the audience when the event I have described took place, informed me that the speech made by the man who sacrificed himself set forth his devotion to the monarch. He said that he wished to immolate himself out of affection for the sovereign, as his father had done for love of the prince's father, and as his grandfather had done out of regard for the prince's grandfather."

When once kings, who had hitherto been bound to die a violent death at the end of a term of years, conceived the happy thought of dying by deputy in the persons of others, they would very naturally put it in practice; and accordingly we need not wonder at finding so popular an expedient, or traces of it, in many lands. Thus, for example, the Bhuiyas are an aboriginal race of north-eastern India, and one of their chief seats is Keonjhur. At the installation of a Rajah of Keonjhur a ceremony is observed which has been described as follows by an English officer who witnessed it: "Then the sword, a very rusty old weapon, is placed in the Raja's hands, and one of the Bhuiyas, named Anand Kopat, comes before him, and kneeling sideways, the Raja touches him on the neck as if about to strike off his head, and it is said that in former days there was no fiction in this part of the ceremony. The family of the Kopat hold their lands on the condition that the victim when required shall be produced. Anand, however, hurriedly arose after the accolade and disappeared. He must not be seen for three days; then he presents himself again to the Raja as miraculously restored to life." Here the custom of putting the king's proxy to death has dwindled, probably under English influence, to a mere pretence; but elsewhere it survives, or survived till recent times, in full force. Cassange, a native state in the interior of Angola, is ruled by a king, who bears the title of Jaga. When a king is about to be installed in office, some of the chiefs are despatched to find a human victim, who may not be related by blood or marriage to the new monarch. When he comes to the king's camp, the victim is provided with everything he requires, and all his orders are obeyed as promptly as those of the sovereign. On the day of the ceremony the king takes his seat on a perforated iron stool, his chiefs, councillors, and the rest of the people forming a great circle round about him. Behind the king sits his principal wife, together with all his concubines. An iron gong, with two small bells attached to it, is then struck by an official, who continues to ring the bells during the ceremony. The victim is then introduced and placed in front of the king, but with his back towards him. Armed with a scimitar the king then cuts open the man's back, extracts his heart, and having taken a bite out of it, spits it out and gives it to be burned. The councillors meantime hold the victim's body so that the blood from the wound spouts against the king's breast and belly, and, pouring through the hole in the iron stool, is collected by the chiefs in their hands, who rub their breasts and beards with it, while they shout, "Great is the king and the rites of the state!" After that the corpse is skinned, cut up, and cooked with the flesh of an ox, a dog, a hen, and some other animals. The meal thus prepared is served first to the king, then to the chiefs and councillors, and lastly to all the people assembled. Any man who refused to partake of it would be sold into slavery together with his family. The distinction with which the human victim is here treated before his execution suggests that he is a substitute for the king.

Scandinavian traditions contain some hints that of old the Swedish kings reigned only for periods of nine years, after which they were put to death or had to find a substitute to die in their stead. Thus Aun or On, king of Sweden is said to have sacrificed to Odin for length of days and to have been answered by the god that he should live so long as he sacrificed one of his sons every ninth year. He sacrificed nine of them in this manner, and would have sacrificed the tenth and last, but the Swedes would not allow him. So he died and was buried in a mound at Upsala. Another indication of a similar tenure of the crown occurs in a curious legend of the disposition and banishment of Odin. Offended at his misdeeds, the other gods outlawed and exiled him, but set up in his place a substitute, Oller by name, a cunning wizard, to whom they accorded the symbols both of royalty and of godhead. The deputy bore the name of Odin, and reigned for nearly ten years, when he was driven from the throne, while the real Odin came to his own again. His discomfited rival retired to Sweden and was afterwards slain in an attempt to repair his shattered fortunes. As gods are often merely men who loom large through the mists of tradition, we may conjecture that this Norse legend preserves a confused reminiscence of ancient Swedish kings who reigned for nine or ten years together, then abdicated, delegating to others the privilege of dying for their country. The great festival which was held at Upsala every nine years may have been the occasion on which the king or his deputy was put to death. We know that human sacrifices formed part of the rites.

THE REBELLION OF THE MACCABEES*

I. THE GREEK TYRANNY

And it happened, after that Alexander son of Philip, the Macedonian, who came out of the land of Chettiim, had smitten Darius king of the Persians and Medes, that he reigned in his stead, the first over Greece, and made many wars, and won many strong holds, and slew the kings of the earth, and went through to the ends of the earth, and took spoils of many nations, insomuch that the earth was quiet before him; whereupon he was exalted, and his heart was lifted up. And he gathered a mighty strong host, and ruled over countries, and nations, and kings, who became tributaries unto him. And after these things he fell sick, and perceived that he should die. Wherefore he called his servants, such as were honourable, and had been brought up with him from his youth, and parted his kingdom among them, while he was yet alive. So Alexander reigned twelve years, and then died. And his servants bore rule every one in his place.

And after his death they all put crowns upon themselves; so did their sons after them many years; and evils were multiplied in the

*From the *First Book of the Maccabees.*

earth. And there came out of them a wicked root, Antiochus sur-named Epiphanes, son of Antiochus the king, who had been a hostage at Rome, and he reigned in the hundred and thirty and seventh year of the kingdom of the Greeks. In those days went there out of Israel wicked men, who persuaded many, saying,

"Let us go and make a covenant with the heathen that are round about us: for since we departed from them we have had much sorrow."

So this device pleased them well. Then certain of the people were so forward herein, that they went to the king, who gave them licence to do after the ordinances of the heathen: whereupon they built a place of exercise at Jerusalem according to the customs of the heathen, and made themselves uncircumcised, and forsook the holy covenant, and joined themselves to the heathen, and were sold to do mischief.

Now when the kingdom was established before Antiochus, he thought to reign over Egypt, that he might have the dominion of two realms. Wherefore he entered into Egypt with a great multitude, with chariots, and elephants, and horsemen, and a great navy, and made war against Ptolemee king of Egypt: but Ptolemee was afraid of him, and fled; and many were wounded to death. Thus they got the strong cities in the land of Egypt, and he took the spoils thereof.

And after that Antiochus had smitten Egypt, he returned again in the hundred forty and third year, and went up against Israel and Jerusalem with a great multitude, and entered proudly into the sanctuary, and took away the golden altar, and the candlestick of light, and all the vessels thereof, and the table of the showbread, and the pouring vessels, and the vials, and the censers of gold, and the veil, and the crowns, and the golden ornaments that were before the temple, all which he pulled off. He took also the silver and the gold, and the precious vessels: also he took the hidden treasures which he found. And when he had taken all away, he went into his own land, having made a great massacre, and spoken very proudly. Therefore there was great mourning in Israel, in every place where they were, so that the princes and elders mourned, the virgins and young men were made feeble, and the beauty of women was changed. Every bride-groom took up lamentation, and she that sat in the marriage chamber was in heaviness. The land also was moved for the inhabitants thereof, and all the house of Jacob was covered with confusion. And after two years fully expired the king sent his chief collector of tribute unto the cities of Juda, who came unto Jerusalem with a great multitude, and spoke peaceable words unto them, but all was deceit: for when they had given him credence, he fell suddenly upon the city, and smote it very sore, and destroyed much people of Israel. And when he had taken the spoils of the city, he set it on fire, and pulled down the houses and walls thereof on every side. But the women and children took they captive, and possessed the cattle.

Then builded they the city of David with a great and strong wall, and with mighty towers, and made it a strong hold for them. And they put therein a sinful nation, wicked men, and fortified themselves therein. They stored it also with armour and victuals, and when they had gathered together the spoils of Jerusalem, they laid them up there, and so they became a sore snare: for it was a place to lie in wait against the sanctuary, and an evil adversary to Israel. Thus they shed innocent blood on every side of the sanctuary, and defiled it: insomuch that the inhabitants of Jerusalem fled because of them: whereupon the city was made a habitation of strangers, and became strange to those that were born in her, and her own children left her. Her sanctuary was laid waste like a wilderness, her feasts were turned into mourning, her sabbaths into reproach, her honour into contempt. As had been her glory, so was her dishonour increased, and her excellency was turned into mourning.

Moreover King Antiochus wrote to his whole kingdom that all should be one people, and every one should leave his laws: so all the heathen agreed according to the commandment of the king. Yea, many also of the Israelites consented to his religion, and sacrificed unto idols, and profaned the sabbath. For the king had sent letters by messengers unto Jerusalem and the cities of Juda, that they should follow the strange laws of the land, and forbid burnt offerings, and sacrifice, and drink offerings in the temple; and that they should profane the sabbaths and festival days, and pollute the sanctuary and holy people, set up altars, and groves, and chapels of idols, and sacrifice swine's flesh, and unclean beasts; that they should also leave their children uncircumcised, and make their souls abominable with all manner of uncleanness and profanation: to the end they might forget the law, and change all the ordinances. And whosoever would not do according to the commandment of the king, he said, he should die. In the selfsame manner wrote he to his whole kingdom, and appointed overseers over all the people, commanding the cities of Juda to sacrifice, city by city. Then many of the people were gathered unto them, to wit, every one that forsook the law; and so they committed evils in the land, and drove the Israelites into secret places, even wheresoever they could flee for succour.

Now the fifteenth day of the month Casleu, in the hundred forty and fifth year, they set up the abomination of desolation upon the altar, and builded idol altars throughout the cities of Juda on every side, and burnt incense at the doors of their houses, and in the streets. And when they had rent in pieces the books of the law which they found, they burnt them with fire. And wheresoever was found with any the book of the testament, or if any consented to the law, the king's commandment was that they should put him to death. Thus did they by their authority unto the Israelites every month, to as many as were found in the cities. Now the five and twentieth day of the month they did sacrifice upon the idol altar, which was upon the altar of God. At which time according to the commandment they put to death certain women that had caused their children to be circumcised. And they hanged the infants about their necks, and rifled their houses, and slew them that had circumcised them.

Howbeit many in Israel were fully resolved and confirmed in themselves not to eat any unclean thing. Wherefore they chose rather to die, that they might not be defiled with meats, and that they might not profane the holy covenant: so then they died. And there was very great wrath upon Israel.

II. THE REBELLION

In those days arose Mattathias the son of John, the son of Simeon, a priest of the sons of Joarib, from Jerusalem, and dwelt in Modin. And he had five sons, Joannan, called Caddis; Simon, called Thassi; Judas, who was called Maccabeus; Eleazar, called Avaran; and Jonathan, whose surname was Apphus. And when he saw the blasphemies that were committed in Juda and Jerusalem, he said,

"Woe is me! wherefore was I born to see this misery of my people, and of the holy city, and to dwell there, when it was delivered into the hand of the enemy, and the sanctuary into the hand of strangers? Her temple is become as a man without glory. Her glorious vessels are carried away into captivity, her infants are slain in the streets, her young men with the sword of the enemy. What nation hath not had a part in her kingdom, and gotten of her spoils? All her ornaments are taken away; of a free woman she is become a bondslave. And, behold, our sanctuary, even our beauty and our glory, is laid waste, and the Gentiles have profaned it. To what end therefore shall we live any longer?"

Then Mattathias and his sons rent their clothes, and put on sackcloth, and mourned very sore. In the mean while the king's officers, such as compelled the people to revolt, came into the city Modin, to make them sacrifice. And when many of Israel came unto them, Mattathias also and his sons came together. Then answered the king's officers, and said to Mattathias on this wise,

"Thou art a ruler, and an honourable and great man in this city, and strengthened with sons and brethren. Now therefore come thou first, and fulfil the king's commandment, like as all the heathen have done, yea, and the men of Juda also, and such as remain at Jerusalem: so shalt thou and thy house be in the number of the king's friends, and thou and thy children shall be honoured with silver and gold, and many rewards."

Then Mattathias answered and spoke with a loud voice,

"Though all the nations that are under the king's dominion obey him, and fall away every one from the religion of their fathers, and give consent to his commandments: yet will I and my sons and my brethren walk in the covenant of our fathers. God forbid that we should forsake the law and the ordinances. We will not hearken to the king's words, to go from our religion, either on the right hand, or the left."

Now when he had left speaking these words, there came one of the Jews in the sight of all to sacrifice on the altar which was at Modin, according to the king's commandment. Which thing when Mattathias saw, he was inflamed with zeal, and his reins trembled, neither could he forbear to show his anger according to judgment: wherefore he ran, and slew him upon the altar. Also the king's commissioner, who compelled men to sacrifice, he killed at that time, and the altar he pulled down. Thus dealt he zealously for the law of God, like as Phinees did unto Zambri the son of Salom. And Mattathias cried throughout the city with a loud voice, saying,

"Whosoever is zealous of the law, and maintaineth the covenant, let him follow me."

So he and his sons fled into the mountains, and left all that ever they had in the city. Then many that sought after justice and judgment went down into the wilderness, to dwell there: both they, and their children, and their wives, and their cattle; because afflictions increased sore upon them.

Now when it was told the king's servants, and the host that was at Jerusalem, in the city of David, that certain men, who had broken the king's commandment, were gone down into the secret places in the wilderness, they pursued after them a great number, and having overtaken them, they camped against them, and made war against them on the sabbath day. And they said unto them,

"Let that which ye have done hitherto suffice; come forth, and do according to the commandment of the king, and ye shall live."

But they said,

"We will not come forth, neither will we do the king's commandment, to profane the sabbath day."

So then they gave them the battle with all speed. Howbeit they answered them not, neither cast they a stone at them, nor stopped the places where they lay hid, but said,

"Let us die all in our innocency: heaven and earth shall testify for us, that ye put us to death wrongfully."

So they rose up against them in battle on the sabbath, and they slew them, with their wives and children, and their cattle, to the number of a thousand people. Now when Mattathias and his friends understood hereof, they mourned for them right sore. And one of them said to another,

"If we all do as our breren have done, and fight not for our lives and laws against the heathen, they will now quickly root us out of the earth."

At that time therefore they decreed, saying,

"Whosoever shall come to make battle with us on the sabbath day, we will fight against him; neither will we die all, as our brethren that were murdered in the secret places."

Then came there unto him a company of Assideans, who were mighty men of Israel, even all such as were voluntarily devoted unto the law. Also all they that fled for persecution joined themselves unto them, and were a stay unto them. So they joined their forces, and smote sinful men in their anger, and wicked men in their wrath: but the rest fled to the heathen for succour. Then Mattathias and his friends went round about, and pulled down the altars, and what children soever they found within the coast of Israel uncircumcised, those they circumcised valiantly. They pursued also after the proud men, and the work prospered in their hand. So they recovered the law out of the hand of the Gentiles, and out of the hand of kings, neither suffered they the sinner to triumph.

Now when the time drew near that Mattathias should die, he said unto his sons,

"Now hath pride and rebuke gotten strength, and the time of destruction, and the wrath of indignation. Now therefore my sons, be ye zealous for the law, and give your lives for the covenant of your fathers. Call to remembrance what acts our fathers did in their time; so shall ye receive great honour and an everlasting name. Wherefore, ye my sons, be valiant, and show yourselves men in the behalf of the law; for by it shall ye obtain glory. And, behold, I know that your brother Simon is a man of counsel, give ear unto him alway: he shall be a father unto you. As for Judas Maccabeus, he hath been mighty and strong, even from his youth up: let him be your captain, and fight the battle of the people. Take also unto you all those that observe the law, and avenge ye the wrong of your people. Recompense fully the heathen, and take heed to the commandments of the law."

So he blessed them, and was gathered to his fathers. And he died in the hundred forty and sixth year, and his sons buried him in the sepulchres of his fathers at Modin, and all Israel made great lamentation for him.

Then his son Judas, called Maccabeus, rose up in his stead. And all his brethren helped him, and so did all they that held with his father, and they fought with cheerfulness the battle of Israel. So he got his people great honour, and put on a breastplate as a giant, and girt his warlike harness about him, and he made battles, protecting the host with his sword. In his acts he was like a lion, and like a lion's whelp roaring for his prey. For he pursued the wicked, and sought them out, and burnt up those that vexed his people. Wherefore the wicked shrunk for fear of him, and all the workers of iniquity were troubled, because salvation prospered in his hand. He grieved also many kings, and made Jacob glad with his acts, and his memorial is blessed for ever. Moreover he went through the cities of Juda, destroying the ungodly out of them, and turning away wrath from Israel: so that he was renowned unto the utmost part of the earth, and he received unto him such as were ready to perish.

THE TENURE OF KINGS

John Milton

No man who knows ought, can be so stupid to deny that all men naturally were born free, being the image and resemblance of God himself, and were by privilege above all the creatures, born to command and not to obey: and that they lived so. 'Till from the root of *Adam's* transgression, falling among themselves to do wrong and violence, and foreseeing that such courses must needs tend to the destruction of them all, they agreed by common league to bind each other from mutual injury, and jointly to defend themselves against any that gave disturbance or opposition to such agreement. Hence came Cities, Towns and Commonwealths. And because no faith in all was found sufficiently binding, they saw it needful to ordain some authority, that might restrain by force and punishment what was violated against peace and common right. This authority and power of self-defense and preservation being originally and naturally in every one of them, and unitedly in them all, for ease, for order, and lest each man should be his own partial Judge, they communicated and derived either to one, whom for the eminence of his wisdom and integrity they chose above the rest, or to more than one whom they thought of equal deserving: the first was called a King; the other Magistrates. Not to be their Lords and Masters (though afterward those names in some places were given voluntarily to such as had been Authors of inestimable good to the people) but to be their Deputies and Commissioners, to execute, by virtue of their entrusted power, that justice which else every man by the bond of nature and of Covenant must have executed for himself, and for one another. And to him that shall consider well why among free Persons, one man by civil right should bear authority and jurisdiction over another, no other end or reason can be imaginable. These for a while governed well, and with much equity decided all things at their own arbitrement: till the temptation of such a power left absolute in their hands perverted them at length to injustice and partiality. Then did they who now by trial had found the danger and inconveniences of committing arbitrary power to any, invent Laws either framed, or consented to by all, that should confine and limit the authority of whom they chose to govern them: that so man, of whose failing they had proof, might no more rule over them, but law and reason abstracted as much as might be from personal errors and frailties. While as the Magistrate was set above the people, so the Law was set above the Magistrate. When this would not serve, but that the Law was either not executed, or misapplied, they were constrained from

that time, the only remedy left them, to put conditions and take
Oaths from all Kings and Magistrates at their first instalment to do
impartial justice by Law: who upon those terms, and no other,
received Allegiance from the people, that is to say, bond or Covenant
to obey them in execution of those Laws which they the people had
themselves made, or assented to. And this ofttimes with express
warning, that if the King or Magistrate proved unfaithful to his trust,
the people would be disengaged. They added also Counselors and
Parliaments, nor to be only at his beck, but with him or without
him, at set times, or at all times, when any danger threatened to have
care of the public safety. Therefore saith *Claudius Seysell* a French
Statesman, *The Parliament was set as a bridle to the King;* which I
instance rather, not because our English Lawyers have not said the
same long before, but because that French Monarchy is granted by all
to be a far more absolute than ours. That this and the rest of what
hath hitherto been spoken is most true, might be copiously made
appear throughout all Stories Heathen and Christian; even of those
Nations where Kings and Emperors have sought means to abolish all
ancient memory of the People's right by their encroachments and
usurpations. But I spare long insertions, appealing to the known
constitutions of both the latest Christian Empires in Europe, the
Greek and German, besides the French, Italian, Aragonian, English,
and not least the Scottish Histories: not forgetting this only by the
way, that *William* the Norman though a Conqueror, and not unsworn
at his Coronation, was compelled the second time to take oath at St.
Albans, ere the people would be brought to yield obedience.

It being thus manifest that the power of Kings and Magistrates is
nothing else, but what is only derivative, transferred and committed
to them in trust from the People, to the Common good of them all,
in whom the power yet remains fundamentally, and cannot be taken
from them, without a violation of their natural birthright, and seeing
that from hence *Aristotle* and the best of Political writers have
defined a King, him who governs to the good and profit of his
People, and not for his own ends, it follows from necessary causes,
that the Titles of Sovereign Lord, natural Lord, and the like, are
either arrogancies, or flatteries, not admitted by Emperors and Kings
of best note, and disliked by the Church both of Jews, *Isai.* 26. 13.
and ancient Christians, as appears by *Tertullian* and others. Although
generally the people of Asia, and with them the Jews also, especially
since the time they chose a King against the advice and counsel of
God, are noted by wise Authors much inclinable to slavery.

. . .

We may pass therefore hence to Christian times. And first our
Savior himself, how much he favored Tyrants, and how much intended they should be found or honored among Christians, declares
his mind not obscurely; accounting their absolute authority no better
than Gentilism, yea though they flourished it over with the splendid

name of Benefactors; charging those that would be his Disciples to usurp no such dominion; but that they who were to be of most authority among them, should esteem themselves Ministers and Servants to the public. *Matt.* 20. 25. *The Princes of the Gentiles exercise Lordship over them,* and *Mark* 10. 42. *They that seem to rule* saith he, either slighting or accounting them no lawful rulers, *but ye shall not be so, but the greatest among you shall be your Servant.* And although he himself were the meekest, and came on earth to be so, yet to a Tyrant we hear him not vouchsafe an humble word: but *Tell that Fox, Luke.* 13. So far we ought to be from thinking that Christ and his Gospel should be made a Sanctuary for Tyrants from justice, to whom his Law before never gave such protection. And wherefore did his Mother the Virgin *Mary* give such praise to God in her prophetic song, that he had now by the coming of Christ *Cut down Dynasties or proud Monarchs from the throne,* if the Church, when God manifests his power in them to do so, should rather choose all misery and vassalage to serve them, and let them still sit on their potent seats to be adored for doing mischief. Surely it is not for nothing that tyrants by a kind of natural instinct both hate and fear none more than the true Church and Saints of God, as the most dangerous enemies and subverters of Monarchy, though indeed of tyranny; hath not this been the perpetual cry of Courtiers, and Court Prelates? whereof no likelier cause can be alleged, but that they well discerned the mind and principles of most devout and zealous men, and indeed the very discipline of Church, tending to the dissolution of all tyranny. No marvel then if since the faith of Christ received, in purer or impurer times, to depose a King and put him to death for Tyranny, hath been accounted so just and requisite, that neighbor Kings have both upheld and taken part with subjects in the action. And *Ludovicus Pius,* himself an Emperor, and Son of *Charles* the great, being made Judge, *Du Haillan* is my author, between *Milegast* King of the *Vultzes* and his Subjects who had deposed him, gave his verdict for the Subjects, and for him whom they had chosen in his room. Note here that the right of electing whom they please is, by the impartial testimony of an Emperor, in the people. For, said he, *A just Prince ought to be preferred before an unjust, and the end of government before the prerogative.* And *Constantinus Leo,* another Emperor, in the *Byzantine* Laws saith, *that the end of a King is for the general good, which he not performing is but the counterfeit of a King.* And to prove that some of our own Monarchs have acknowledged that their high office exempted them not from punishment, they had the Sword of St. *Edward* borne before them by an officer who was called Earl of the Palace, even at the times of their highest pomp and solemnities, to mind them, saith *Matthew Paris,* the best of our Historians, that if they erred, the Sword had power to restrain them. And what restraint the Sword comes to at length, having both edge and point, if any *Skeptic* will doubt, let him feel. It is also

affirmed from diligent search made in our ancient books of Law, that
the Peers and Barons of England had a legal right to judge the King:
which was the cause most likely, for it could be no slight cause, that
they were called his Peers, or equals. This however may stand im-
movable, so long as man hath to deal with no better than man; that
if our Law judge all men to the lowest by their Peers, it should in all
equity ascend also, and judge the highest. And so much I find both
in our own and foreign Story, that Dukes, Earls, and Marqueses were
at first not hereditary, not empty and vain titles, but names of trust
and office, and with the office ceasing, as induces me to be of
opinion, that every worthy man in Parliament, for the word Baron
imports no more, might for the public good be thought a fit Peer and
judge of the King; without regard had to petty caveats, and circumstances, the chief impediment in high affairs, and ever stood upon
most by circumstantial men. Whence doubtless our Ancestors who
were not ignorant with what rights either Nature or ancient Constitution had endowed them, when Oaths both at Coronation, and renewed in Parliament would not serve, thought it no way illegal to
depose and put to death their tyrannous Kings. Insomuch that the
Parliament drew up a charge against *Richard the second*, and the
Commons requested to have judgment decreed against him, that the
realm might not be endangered. And *Peter Martyr* a Divine of
foremost rank, on the third of *Judges* approves their doings. Sir
Thomas Smith[1] also a Protestant and a Statesman, in his *Commonwealth of England*, putting the question whether it be lawful to rise
against a Tyrant, answers that the vulgar judge of it according to the
event, and the learned according to the purpose of them that do it.
But far before these days, *Gildas*[2] the most ancient of all our
Historians, speaking of those times wherein the Roman Empire de-
caying quitted and relinquished what right they had by Conquest to
this Island, and resigned it all into the peoples' hands, testifies that
the people thus re-invested with their own original right, about the
year 446, both elected them Kings, whom they thought best (the
first Christian British Kings that ever reigned here since the Romans)
and by the same right, when they apprehended cause, usually deposed and put them to death. This is the most fundamental and
ancient tenure that any King of *England* can produce or pretend to,
in comparison of which, all other titles and pleas are but of yesterday. If any object that *Gildas* condemns the Britons for so doing, the
answer is as ready; that he condemns them no more for so doing
than he did before for choosing such, for saith he, *They anointed
them Kings, not of God, but such as were more bloody than the rest.*

[1] Secretary of State under Elizabeth I. His *Commonwealth of England*
was the best and most influential treatise on English government in the
sixteenth century.
[2] Gildas' (516?–570?) *History* and *Letters* are among the most useful
literary sources for our knowledge of early Anglo-Saxon England.

Next he condemns them not at all for deposing or putting them to death, but for doing it over hastily, without trial or well examining the cause, and for electing others worse in their room. Thus we have here both domestic and most ancient examples that the people of Britain have deposed and put to death their Kings in those primitive Christian times. And to couple reason with example, if the Church in all ages, Primitive, Romish, or Protestant, held it ever no less their duty than the power of their Keys, though without express warrant of Scripture, to bring indifferently both King and Peasant under the utmost rigor of their Canons and Censures Ecclesiastical, even to the smiting him with a final excommunion, if he persist impenitent, what hinders but that the temporal Law both may and ought, though without a special Text or precedent, extend with like indifference the civil Sword, to the cutting off without exemption him that capitally offends. Seeing that justice and Religion are from the same God, and works of justice ofttimes more acceptable.

. . .

There is nothing that so actually makes a King of *England*, as rightful possession and Supremacy *in all causes both civil and Ecclesiastical:* and nothing that so actually makes a Subject of *England*, as those two Oaths of Allegiance and Supremacy observed *without equivocating, or any mental reservation.* Out of doubt then when the King shall command things already constituted in Church, or State, obedience is the true essence of a subject, either to do, if it be lawful, or if he hold the thing unlawful, to submit to that penalty which the Law imposes, so long as he intends to remain a Subject. Therefore when the people or any part of them shall rise against the King and his authority executing the Law in any thing established civil or Ecclesiastical, I do not say it is rebellion, if the thing commanded though established be unlawful, and that they sought first all due means of redress (and no man is further bound to Law) but I say it is an absolute renouncing both of Supremacy and Allegiance, which in one word is an actual and total deposing of the King, and the setting up of another supreme authority over them.

THE LIBERTIES OF OUR COUNTRY

Samuel Adams

"Ambition saw that stooping Rome could bear a master, nor had virtue to be free."

I believe that no people ever yet groaned under the heavy yoke of slavery but when they deserved it. This may be called a severe censure upon by far the greatest part of the nations in the world who are involved in the miseries of servitude. But however they may be thought by some to deserve commiseration, the censure is just. Zuinglius, one of the first reformers, in his friendly admonition to the republic of the Switzers, discourses much of his countrymen's throwing off the yoke. He says that they who lie under oppression deserve what they suffer and a great deal more, and he bids them perish with their oppressors. The truth is, all might be free, if they valued freedom and defended it as they ought. Is it possible that millions could be enslaved by a few, which is a notorious fact, if all possessed the independent spirit of Brutus, who, to his immortal honor, expelled the proud tyrant of Rome and his 'royal and rebellious race'? If, therefore, a people will not be free, if they have not virtue enough to maintain their liberty against a presumptuous invader, they deserve no pity, and are to be treated with contempt and ignominy. Had not Caesar seen that Rome was ready to stoop he would not have dared to make himself the master of that once brave people. He was, indeed, as a great writer observes, a smooth and subtle tyrant, who led them gently into slavery: "and on his brow o'er daring vice, deluding virtue smiled." By pretending to be the people's greatest friend, he gained the ascendency over them; by beguiling arts, hypocrisy, and flattery, which are often more fatal than the sword, he obtained that supreme power which his ambitious soul had long thirsted for. The people were finally prevailed upon to consent to their own ruin. By the force of persuasion, or rather by cajoling arts and tricks, always made use of by men who have ambitious views, they enacted their *Lex Regia,* whereby *quod placuit princip legis habuit vigorem,* that is, the will and pleasure of the prince had the force of law. His minions had taken infinite pains to paint to their imaginations the godlike virtues of Caesar. They first persuaded them to believe that he was a deity, and then to sacrifice to him those rights and liberties which their ancestors had so long maintained with unexampled bravery and with blood and treasure. By this act they fixed a precedent fatal to all posterity. The Roman people afterwards, influenced no doubt by this pernicious example, renewed it to his successors, not at the end of every ten years, but for life. They transferred all their right and power to Charles the Great. *In eum transtulit omne suum jus et potestatem.* Thus they voluntarily and ignominiously surrendered their own liberty, and exchanged a free constitution for a tyranny.

It is not my design to form a comparison between the state of this country now and that of the Roman Empire in those dregs of time, or between the disposition of Caesar and that of —. The comparison, I confess, would not, in all its parts, hold good. The tyrant of Rome, to do him justice, had learning, courage, and great abilities. It behooves us, however, to awake, and advert to the danger we are in. The tragedy of American freedom, it is to be feared, is nearly completed. A tyranny seems to be at the very door. It is to little purpose, then, to go about coolly to rehearse the gradual steps that have been taken, the means that have been used, and the instruments employed to encompass the ruin of the public liberty. We know them and we detest them. But what will this avail, if we have not courage and resolution to prevent the completion of their system?

Our enemies would fain have us lie down on the bed of sloth and security, and persuade ourselves that there is no danger. They are daily administering the opiate with multiplied arts and delusions, and I am sorry to observe that the gilded pill is so alluring to some who call themselves the friends of liberty. But is there no danger when the very foundations of our civil Constitution tremble? When an attempt was first made to disturb the corner-stone of the fabric, we were universally and justly alarmed. And can we be cool spectators when we see it already removed from its place? With what resentment and indignation did we first receive the intelligence of a design to make us tributary, not to natural enemies, but infinitely more humiliating, to fellow-subjects! And yet, with unparalleled insolence, we are told to be quiet when we see that very money which is torn from us by lawless force made use of still further to oppose us, to feed and pamper a set of infamous wretches who swarm like the locusts of Egypt, and some of them expect to revel in wealth and riot on the spoils of our country. Is it a time for us to sleep when our free government is essentially changed, and a new one is forming upon a quite different system? A government without the least dependence on the people,—a government under the absolute control of a minister of state, upon whose sovereign dictates is to depend not only the time when, and the place where, the Legislative Assembly shall sit, but whether it shall sit at all; and if it is allowed to meet, it shall be liable immediately to be thrown out of existence, if in any one point it fails in obedience to his arbitrary mandates.

Have we not already seen specimens of what we are to expect under such a government, in the instructions which Mr. Hutchinson has received, and which he has publicly avowed and declared he is bound to obey? By one he is to refuse his assent to a tax bill unless the Commissioners of the Customs and other favorites are exempted; and if these may be freed from taxes by the order of a minister, may not all his tools and drudges, or any others who are subservient to his designs, expect the same indulgence? By another, he is forbid to pass a grant of the Assembly to any agent but one to whose election he has given his consent; which is, in effect, to put it out of our power to take the necessary and legal steps for the redress of those grievances which we suffer by the arts and machinations of ministers and their minions here. What difference is there between the present state of this Province, which in course will be the deplorable state of America, and that of Rome under the law before mentioned? The difference is only this, that they gave their formal consent to the change, which we have not yet done. But let us be upon our guard against even a negative submission, for, agreeable to the sentiments of a celebrated writer, who thoroughly understood his subject, if we are voluntarily silent as the conspirators would have us to be, it will be considered as an approbation of the change. "By the fundamental laws of England the two Houses of Parliament, in concert with the King, exercise the legislative power; but if the two Houses should be so infatuated as to resolve to suppress their powers, and invest the King with the full and absolute government, certainly the nation would not suffer it!" And if a minister shall usurp the supreme and absolute government of America, and set up his instructions as laws in the Colonies, and their governors shall be so weak or so wicked as, for the sake of keeping their places, to be made the instruments in putting them in execution, who will presume to say that the people have not a right, or that it is not their indispensable duty to God and their country, by all rational means in their power to resist them!

> Be firm, my friends, nor let unmanly sloth
> Twine round your hearts indissoluble chains;
> Ne'er yet by force was freedom overcome,
> Unless corruption first dejects the pride
> And guardian vigor of the free born soul;
> All crude attempts of violence are vain.
>   Determined hold
> Your Independence; for, that once destroyed,
> Unfounded freedom is a morning dream.

The liberties of our country, the freedom of our civil Constitution are worth defending at all hazards; and it is our duty to defend them against all attacks. We have received them as a fair inheritance from our worthy ancestors. They purchased them for us with toil, and danger, and expense of treasure and blood, and transmitted them to us with care and diligence. It will bring an everlasting mark of infamy on the present generation, enlightened as it is, if we should suffer them to be wrested from us by violence without a struggle, or be cheated out of them by the artifices of false and designing men. Of the latter, we are in most danger at present. Let us therefore be aware of it. Let us contemplate our forefathers and posterity, and resolve to maintain the rights bequeathed to us from the former for the sake of the latter. Instead of sitting down satisfied with the efforts we have already made, which is the wish of our enemies, the necessity of the times more than ever calls for our utmost circumspection, deliberation, fortitude, and perseverance. Let us remember that "if we suffer tamely a lawless attack upon our liberty, we encourage it, and involve others in our doom!" It is a very serious consideration, which should deeply impress our minds, *that millions yet unborn may be the miserable sharers in the event!*

"Candidus."

THOUGHTS ON THE PRESENT STATE OF AMERICAN AFFAIRS[1]

Thomas Paine

In the following pages I offer nothing more than simple facts, plain arguments, and common sense; and have no other preliminaries to settle with the reader, than that he will divest himself of prejudice and prepossession, and suffer his reason and his feelings to determine for themselves; that he will put on, or rather that he will not put off, the true character of a man, and generously enlarge his views beyond the present day.

Volumes have been written on the subject of the struggle between England and America. Men of all ranks have embarked in the controversy, from different motives, and with various designs; but all have been ineffectual, and the period of debate is closed. Arms as the last resource decide the contest; the appeal was the choice of the king, and the continent has accepted the challenge.

It hath been reported of the late Mr. Pelham[2] (who though an able minister was not without his faults) that on his being attacked in the House of Commons on the score that his measures were only of a

---

[1] "Thoughts on the Present State of American Affairs" was Part III of *Common Sense.* Part I discussed the British constitution in relation to "the origin and design of government"; Part II analyzed the weaknesses of "monarchy and hereditary succession." The American Declaration of Independence was promulgated six months later, on July 4.

[2] Henry Pelham, British prime minister (1743-1754).

temporary kind, replied, *"They will last my time."* Should a thought so fatal and unmanly possess the colonies in the present contest, the name of Ancestors will be remembered by future generations with detestation.

The sun never shined on a cause of greater worth. 'Tis not the affair of a city, a county, a province, or a kingdom; but of a continent—of at least one-eighth part of the habitable globe. 'Tis not the concern of a day, a year, or an age; posterity are virtually involved in the contest, and will be more or less affected even to the end of time by the proceedings now. Now is the seedtime of continental union, faith, and honor. The least fracture now will be like a name engraved with the point of a pin on the tender rind of a young oak; the wound would enlarge with the tree, and posterity read it in full grown characters.

By referring the matter from argument to arms, a new era for politics is struck—a new method of thinking has arisen. All plans, proposals, &c. prior to the nineteenth of April,[3] i.e. to the commencement of hostilities, are like the almanacks of the last year; which though proper then, are superseded and useless now. Whatever was advanced by the advocates on either side of the question then, terminated in one and the same point, viz. a union with Great Britain; the only difference between the parties was the method of effecting it; the one proposing force, the other friendship; but it has so far happened that the first has failed, and the second has withdrawn her influence.

As much has been said of the advantages of reconciliation, which, like an agreeable dream, has passed away and left us as we were, it is but right that we should examine the contrary side of the argument, and inquire into some of the many material injuries which these colonies sustain, and always will sustain, by being connected with and dependent on Great Britain. To examine that connection and dependence on the principles of nature and common sense; to see what we have to trust to, if separated, and what we are to expect, if dependent.

I have heard it asserted by some, that as America has flourished under her former connection with Great Britain, the same connection is necessary towards her future happiness, and will always have the same effect. Nothing can be more fallacious than this kind of argument. We may as well assert that because a child has thrived upon milk, that it is never to have meat, or that the first twenty years of our lives is to become a precedent for the next twenty. But even this is admitting more than is true; for I answer roundly that America would have flourished as much, and probably much more, had no European power taken any notice of her. The commerce by which

[3] April 19, 1775, the date of the battles of Lexington and Concord, where American minutemen defended their ammunition stores against British troops—the first armed engagements of the Revolution.

she hath enriched herself are the necessaries of life, and will always have a market while eating is the custom of Europe.

But she has protected us, say some. That she hath engrossed us is true, and defended the continent at our expense as well as her own is admitted; and she would have defended Turkey from the same motive, viz. for the sake of trade and dominion.

Alas! we have been long led away by ancient prejudices and made large sacrifices to superstition. We have boasted the protection of Great Britain without considering that her motive was *interest*, not *attachment*; and that she did not protect us from *our enemies* on *our account*, but from her enemies on her own account, from those who had no quarrel with us on any *other account*, and who will always be our enemies on the *same account*. Let Britain waive her pretensions to the continent, or the continent throw off the dependence, and we should be at peace with France and Spain were they at war with Britain. The miseries of Hanover's[4] last war ought to warn us against connections.

It hath lately been asserted in parliament, that the colonies have no relation to each other but through the parent country, i.e. that Pennsylvania and the Jerseys, and so on for the rest, are sister colonies by the way of England; this is certainly a very roundabout way of proving relationship, but it is the nearest and only true way of proving enmity (or enemyship, if I may so call it). France and Spain never were, nor perhaps ever will be, our enemies as *Americans*, but as our being the *subjects of Great Britain*.

But Britain is the parent country, say some. Then the more shame upon her conduct. Even brutes do not devour their young, nor savages make war upon their families; wherefore, the assertion, if true, turns to her reproach; but it happens not to be true, or only partly so, and the phrase *parent* or *mother country* hath been jesuitically adopted by the King and his parasites, with a low papistical design of gaining an unfair bias on the credulous weakness of our minds. Europe, and not England, is the parent country of America. This new world hath been the asylum for the persecuted lovers of civil and religious liberty from *every part* of Europe. Hither have they fled, not from the tender embraces of the mother, but from the cruelty of the monster; and it is so far true of England, that the same tyranny which drove the first emigrants from home pursues their descendants still.

In this extensive quarter of the globe, we forget the narrow limits of three hundred and sixty miles (the extent of England) and carry our friendship on a larger scale; we claim brotherhood with every European Christian, and triumph in the generosity of the sentiment.

It is pleasant to observe by what regular gradations we surmount

[4]The Prussian house of Hanover occupied the British throne from 1714 to 1901. Paine thus connects the repeated French invasions of Hanover, during the Seven Years' War (1756-1763), with the Franco-British rivalries.

the force of local prejudices as we enlarge our acquaintance with the world. A man born in any town in England divided into parishes, will naturally associate most with his fellow parishioners (because their interests in many cases will be common) and distinguish him by the name of *neighbor*; if he meet him but a few miles from home, he drops the narrow idea of a street, and salutes him by the name of *townsman*; if he travel out of the county and meet him in any other, he forgets the minor divisions of street and town, and calls him *country-man, i.e. county-man*; but if in their foreign excursions they should associate in France, or any other part of *Europe*, their local remembrance would be enlarged into that of *Englishman*. And by a just parity of reasoning, all Europeans meeting in America, or any other quarter of the globe, are *countrymen*; for England, Holland, Germany, or Sweden, when compared with the whole, stand in the same places on the larger scale, which the divisions of street, town, and county do on the smaller ones; distinctions too limited for continental minds. Not one third of the inhabitants, even of this province,[5] are of English descent. Wherefore, I reprobate the phrase of parent or mother country applied to England only, as being false, selfish, narrow, and ungenerous.

But, admitting that we were all of English descent, what does it amount to? Nothing. Britain, being now an open enemy, extinguishes every other name and title; and to say that reconciliation is our duty, is truly farcical. The first king of England, of the present line (William the Conqueror) was a Frenchman, and half the peers of England are descendants from the same country; wherefore, by the same method of reasoning, England ought to be governed by France.

Much hath been said of the united strength of Britain and the colonies, that in conjunction they might bid defiance to the world. But this is mere presumption, the fate of war is uncertain; neither do the expressions mean anything, for this continent would never suffer itself to be drained of inhabitants to support the British arms in either Asia, Africa, or Europe.

Besides, what have we to do with setting the world at defiance? Our plan is commerce, and that, well attended to, will secure us the peace and friendship of all Europe; because it is the interest of all Europe to have America a *free port*. Her trade will always be a protection, and her barrenness of gold and silver secure her from invaders.

I challenge the warmest advocate for reconciliation to show a single advantage that this continent can reap, by being connected with Great Britain. I repeat the challenge, not a single advantage is derived. Our corn will fetch its price in any market in Europe, and our imported goods must be paid for, buy them where we will.

But the injuries and disadvantages which we sustain by that con-nection are without number; and our duty to mankind at large, as

[5] *I.e.,* Pennsylvania.

well as to ourselves, instruct us to renounce the alliance: because any submission to, or dependence on, Great Britain, tends directly to involve this continent in European wars and quarrels, and set us at variance with nations who would otherwise seek our friendship, and against whom we have neither anger nor complaint. As Europe is our market for trade, we ought to form no partial connection with any part of it. 'Tis the true interest of America to steer clear of European contentions, which she never can do while by her dependence on Britain she is made the makeweight in the scale of British politics.

Europe is too thickly planted with kingdoms to be long at peace, and whenever a war breaks out between England and any foreign power, the trade of America goes to ruin, *because of her connection with Britain.* The next war may not turn out like the last,[6] and should it not, the advocates for reconciliation now will be wishing for separation then, because neutrality in that case would be a safer convoy than a man of war. Everything that is right or reasonable pleads for separation. The blood of the slain, the weeping voice of nature cries, *'Tis time to part.* Even the distance at which the Almighty hath placed England and America is a strong and natural proof that the authority of the one over the other, was never the design of heaven. The time likewise at which the continent was discovered, adds weight to the argument, and the manner in which it was peopled, increases the force of it. The Reformation was preceded by the discovery of America, as if the Almighty graciously meant to open a sanctuary to the persecuted in future years, when home should afford neither friendship nor safety.

The authority of Great Britain over this continent is a form of government which sooner or later must have an end. And a serious mind can draw no true pleasure by looking forward, under the painful and positive conviction that what he calls "the present con-stitution" is merely temporary. As parents, we can have no joy, knowing that *this government* is not sufficiently lasting to insure anything which we may bequeath to posterity; and by a plain method of argument, as we are running the next generation into debt, we ought to do the work of it, otherwise we use them meanly and pitifully. In order to discover the line of our duty rightly, we should take our children in our hand, and fix our station a few years farther into life; that eminence will present a prospect which a few present fears and prejudices conceal from our sight.

Though I would carefully avoid giving unnecessary offense, yet I am inclined to believe that all those who espouse the doctrine of reconciliation may be included within the following descriptions: Interested men, who are not to be trusted, weak men who *cannot* see, prejudiced men who *will not* see, and a certain set of moderate men who think better of the European world than it deserves; and

---

[6]The British were victorious in the French and Indian War, the Ameri-can phase of the Seven Years' War.

this last class, by an ill-judged deliberation, will be the cause of more calamities to this continent than all the other three.

It is the good fortune of many to live distant from the scene of present sorrow; the evil is not sufficiently brought to *their* doors to make *them* feel the precariousness with which all American property is possessed. But let our imaginations transport us a few moments to Boston;[7] that seat of wretchedness will teach us wisdom, and instruct us forever to renounce a power in whom we can have no trust. The inhabitants of that unfortunate city, who but a few months ago were in ease and affluence, have now no other alternative than to stay and starve, or turn out to beg. Endangered by the fire of their friends if they continue within the city, and plundered by the soldiery if they leave it, in their present situation they are prisoners without the hope of redemption, and in a general attack for their relief they would be exposed to the fury of both armies.

Men of passive tempers look somewhat lightly over the offenses of Great Britain, and, still hoping for the best, are apt to call out, *Come, come, we shall be friends again for all this.* But examine the passions and feelings of mankind; bring the doctrine of reconciliation to the touchstone of nature, and then tell me whether you can hereafter love, honor, and faithfully serve the power that hath carried fire and sword into your land? If you cannot do all these, then are you only deceiving yourselves, and by your delay bringing ruin upon posterity. Your future connection with Britain, whom you can neither love nor honor, will be forced and unnatural, and being formed only on the plan of present convenience, will in a little time fall into a relapse more wretched than the first. But if you say you can still pass the violations over, then I ask, Hath your house been burnt? Hath your property been destroyed before your face? Are your wife and children destitute of a bed to lie on, or bread to live on? Have you lost a parent or child by their hands, and yourself the ruined and wretched survivor? If you have not, then are you not a judge of those who have. But if you have, and can still shake hands with the murderers, then are you unworthy the name of husband, father, friend, or lover; and whatever may be your rank or title in life, you have the heart of a coward, and the spirit of a sycophant.

This is not inflaming or exaggerating matters, but trying them by those feelings and affections which nature justifies, and without which we should be incapable of discharging the social duties of life, or enjoying the felicities of it. I mean not to exhibit horror for the purpose of provoking revenge, but to awaken us from fatal and unmanly slumbers, that we may pursue determinately some fixed object. 'Tis not in the power of Britain or of Europe to conquer America, if she doth not conquer herself by *delay* and *timidity*. The present winter is worth an age if rightly employed, but if lost or

---

[7]Boston was then under British military occupation, and subject, then and later, to American siege.

neglected the whole continent will partake of the misfortune; and there is no punishment which that man doth not deserve, be he who, or what, or where he will, that may be the means of sacrificing a season so precious and useful.

It is repugnant to reason, to the universal order of things, to all examples from former ages, to suppose that this continent can long remain subject to any external power. The most sanguine in Britain doth not think so. The utmost stretch of human wisdom cannot, at this time, compass a plan, short of separation, which can promise the continent even a year's security. Reconciliation is *now* a fallacious dream. Nature has deserted the connection, and art cannot supply her place. For, as Milton wisely expresses, "Never can true reconcilement grow where wounds of deadly hate have pierced so deep."[8]

Every quiet method for peace hath been ineffectual. Our prayers have been rejected with disdain; and have tended to convince us that nothing flatters vanity or confirms obstinacy in kings more than repeated petitioning—and nothing hath contributed more than that very measure to make the kings of Europe absolute. Witness Denmark and Sweden.[9] Wherefore, since nothing but blows will do, for God's sake let us come to a final separation, and not leave the next generation to be cutting throats under the violated unmeaning names of parent and child.

To say they will never attempt it again is idle and visionary; we thought so at the repeal of the stamp act, yet a year or two undeceived us; as well may we suppose that nations which have been once defeated will never renew the quarrel.

As to government matters, it is not in the power of Britain to do this continent justice: the business of it will soon be too weighty and intricate to be managed with any tolerable degree of convenience, by a power so distant from us, and so very ignorant of us; for if they cannot conquer us they cannot govern us. To be always running three or four thousand miles with a tale or a petition, waiting four or five months for an answer, which, when obtained, requires five or six more to explain it in, will in a few years be looked upon as folly and childishness. There was a time when it was proper, and there is a proper time for it to cease.

Small islands not capable of protecting themselves are the proper objects for government to take under their care; but there is something absurd in supposing a continent to be perpetually governed by an island. In no instance hath nature made the satellite larger than its primary planet; and as England and America, with respect to each other, reverse the common order of nature, it is evident that they belong to different systems. England to Europe: America to itself.

[8]*Paradise Lost,* Book IV, 11. 98-99.
[9]Both Denmark and Sweden had recently been threatened by monarchical absolutism; Gustavus III of Sweden had imprisoned the entire Council in 1772.

I am not induced by motives of pride, party, or resentment to espouse the doctrine of separation and independence; I am clearly, positively, and conscientiously persuaded that 'tis the true interest of this continent to be so; that everything short of *that* is mere patchwork, that it can afford no lasting felicity—that it is leaving the sword to our children, and shrinking back at a time when a little more, a little further, would have rendered this continent the glory of the earth.

As Britain hath not manifested the least inclination towards a compromise, we may be assured that no terms can be obtained worthy the acceptance of the continent, or any ways equal to the expense of blood and treasure we have been already put to.

The object contended for ought always to bear some just proportion to the expense. The removal of North[10] or the whole detestable junto, is a matter unworthy the millions we have expended. A temporary stoppage of trade was an inconvenience which would have sufficiently balanced the repeal of all the acts complained of, had such repeals been obtained; but if the whole continent must take up arms, if every man must be a soldier, 'tis scarcely worth our while to fight against a contemptible ministry only. Dearly, dearly do we pay for the repeal of the acts, if that is all we fight for; for, in a just estimation, 'tis as great a folly to pay a Bunker-hill price[11] for law as for land. As I have always considered the independency of this continent an event which sooner or later must arrive, so from the late rapid progress of the continent to maturity, the event cannot be far off. Wherefore, on the breaking out of hostilities, it was not worth the while to have disputed a matter which time would have finally redressed, unless we meant to be in earnest; otherwise it is like wasting an estate on a suit at law, to regulate the trespasses of a tenant whose lease is just expiring. No man was a warmer wisher for a reconciliation than myself, before the fatal nineteenth of April, 1775,[12] but the moment the event of that day was made known, I rejected the hardened, sullen-tempered Pharaoh of England[13] forever; and disdain the wretch, that with the pretended title of *Father of His People* can unfeelingly hear of their slaughter, and composedly sleep with their blood upon his soul.

But admitting that matters were now made up, what would be the event? I answer, the ruin of the continent. And that for several reasons.

First. The powers of governing still remaining in the hands of the

[10]Frederick North, Earl of Guilford, prime minister (1770-1782), was held responsible for the British policy of colonial exploitation by taxation.
[11]American casualties at Bunker Hill (June 17, 1775) were reported to be one third of those engaged.
[12]Date of the battles of Concord and Lexington.
[13]King George III; here likened to the "hardened Pharoah," despotic captor of the Israelites (Exodus vii: 13-14).

king, he will have a negative over the whole legislation of this continent. And as he hath shown himself such an inveterate enemy to liberty, and discovered such a thirst for arbitrary power, is he, or is he not, a proper person to say to these colonies, *You shall make no laws but what I please*! And is there any inhabitant of America so ignorant as not to know, that according to what is called the *present constitution*, this continent can make no laws but what the king gives leave to; and is there any man so unwise as not to see, that (considering what has happened) he will suffer no law to be made here but such as suits *his* purpose? We may be as effectually enslaved by the want of laws in America, as by submitting to laws made for us in England. After matters are made up (as it is called), can there be any doubt but the whole power of the crown will be exerted to keep this continent as low and humble as possible? Instead of going forward we shall go backward, or be perpetually quarrelling, or ridiculously petitioning. We are already greater than the king wishes us to be, and will he not hereafter endeavor to make us less? To bring the matter to one point, Is the power who is jealous of our prosperity, a proper power to govern us? Whoever says No to this question is an independent, for independency means no more than this, whether we shall make our own laws, or whether the king, the greatest enemy this continent hath, or can have, shall tell us, *There shall be no laws but such as I like*.

But the king, you'll say, has a negative in England; the people there can make no laws without his consent. In point of right and good order, it is something very ridiculous that a youth of twenty-one (which hath often happened) shall say to several millions of people older and wiser than himself, "I forbid this or that act of yours to be law." But in this place I decline this sort of reply, though I will never cease to expose the absurdity of it, and only answer that England being the king's residence, and America not so, makes quite another case. The king's negative here is ten times more dangerous and fatal than it can be in England; for *there* he will scarcely refuse his consent to a bill for putting England into as strong a state of defense as possible, and in America he would never suffer such a bill to be passed.

America is only a secondary object in the system of British politics, England consults the good of *this* country no further than it answers her *own* purpose. Wherefore, her own interest leads her to suppress the growth of *ours* in every case which doth not promote *her* advantage, or in the least interfere with it. A pretty state we should soon be in under such a secondhand government, considering what has happened! Men do not change from enemies to friends by the alteration of a name: and in order to show that reconciliation *now* is a dangerous doctrine, I affirm *that it would be policy in the king at this time to repeal the acts for the sake of reinstating himself in the government of the provinces*; in order that *He May Accomplish by*

Craft and Subtlety, In the Long Run, What He cannot do by Force and Violence in the Short One. Reconciliation and ruin are nearly related.

Secondly. That as even the best terms which we can expect to obtain can amount to no more than a temporary expedient, or a kind of government by guardianship, which can last no longer than till the colonies come of age, so the general face and state of things in the interim will be unsettled and unpromising. Emigrants of property will not choose to come to a country whose form of government hangs but by a thread, and who is every day tottering on the brink of commotion and disturbance; and numbers of the present inhabitants would lay hold of the interval to dispose of their effects, and quit the continent.

But the most powerful of all arguments is, that nothing but independence, i.e. a continental form of government, can keep the peace of the continent and preserve it inviolate from civil wars. I dread the event of a reconciliation with Britain *now*, as it is more than probable that it will be followed by a revolt somewhere or other, the consequences of which may be far more fatal than all the malice of Britain.

Thousands are already ruined by British barbarity; (thousands more will probably suffer the same fate). Those men have other feelings than us who have nothing suffered. All they *now* possess is liberty; what they before enjoyed is sacrificed to its service, and having nothing more to lose they disdain submission. Besides, the general temper of the colonies towards a British government will be like that of a youth who is nearly out of his time; they will care very little about her. And a government which cannot preserve the peace is no government at all, and in that case we pay our money for nothing; and pray what is it that Britain can do, whose power will be wholly on paper, should a civil tumult break out the very day after reconciliation? I have heard some men say, many of whom I believe spoke without thinking, that they dreaded an independence, fearing that it would produce civil wars. It is but seldom that our first thoughts are truly correct, and that is the case here; for there is ten times more to dread from a patched up connection than from independence. I make the sufferer's case my own, and I protest, that were I driven from house and home, my property destroyed, and my circumstances ruined, that as a man, sensible of injuries, I could never relish the doctrine of reconciliation, or consider myself bound thereby.

The colonies have manifested such a spirit of good order and obedience to continental government as is sufficient to make every reasonable person easy and happy on that head. No man can assign the least pretense for his fears on any other grounds than such as are truly childish and ridiculous, viz., that one colony will be striving for superiority over another.

Where there are no distinctions there can be no superiority; perfect equality affords no temptation. The republics of Europe are all (and we may say always) in peace. Holland and Switzerland are without wars, foreign or domestic. Monarchical governments, it is true, are never long at rest: the crown itself is a temptation to enterprising ruffians at *home*; and that degree of pride and insolence ever attendant on regal authority, swells into a rupture with foreign powers in instances where a republican government, by being formed on more natural principles, would negotiate the mistake.

If there is any true cause of fear respecting independence, it is because no plan is yet laid down. Men do not see their way out. Wherefore, as an opening into that business I offer the following hints; at the same time modestly affirming that I have no other opinion of them myself than that they may be the means of giving rise to something better. Could the straggling thoughts of individuals be collected, they would frequently form materials for wise and able men to improve into useful matter.

Let the assemblies be annual, with a president only. The representation more equal, their business wholly domestic, and subject to the authority of a continental congress.

Let each colony be divided into six, eight, or ten, convenient districts, each district to send a proper number of delegates to congress, so that each colony send at least thirty. The whole number in congress will be at least 390. Each congress to sit and to choose a president by the following method. When the delegates are met, let a colony be taken from the whole thirteen colonies by lot, after which let the congress choose (by ballot) a president from out of the delegates of that province. In the next congress, let a colony be taken by lot from twelve only, omitting that colony from which the president was taken in the former congress, and so proceeding on till the whole thirteen shall have had their proper rotation. And in order that nothing may pass into a law but what is satisfactorily just, not less than three fifths of the congress to be called a majority. He that will promote discord, under a government so equally formed as this, would have joined Lucifer[14] in his revolt.

But as there is a peculiar delicacy from whom, or in what manner, this business must first arise, and as it seems most agreeable and consistent that it should come from some intermediate body between the governed and the governors, that is, between the congress and the people, let a *Continental Conference* be held in the following manner, and for the following purpose:

A committee of twenty-six members of congress, viz., two for each colony. Two members from each house of assembly, or provincial convention; and five representatives of the people at large, to be chosen in the capital city or town of each province, for, and in behalf of the whole province, by as many qualified voters as shall

[14]This was the name of Satan before he revolted against God; *cf.* Isaiah xiv: 12-20.

think proper to attend from all parts of the province for that purpose; or, if more convenient, the representatives may be chosen in two or three of the mst populous parts thereof. In this *conference,* thus assembled, will be united the two grand principles of business, *knowledge* and *power.* The members of congress, assemblies, or conventions, by having had experience in national concerns, will be able and useful counsellors, and the whole, being empowered by the people, will have a truly legal authority.

The conferring members being met, let their business be to frame a *Continental Charter,* or Charter of the United Colonies (answering to what is called the Magna Charta of England); fixing the number and manner of choosing members of congress, members of assembly, with their date of sitting, and drawing the line of business and jurisdiction between them (always remembering, that our strength is continental, not provincial); securing freedom and property to all men, and above all things the free exercise of religion, according to the dictates of conscience; with such other matter as it is necessary for a charter to contain. Immediately after which, the said conference to dissolve, and the bodies which shall be chosen conformable to the said charter, to be the legislators and governors of this continent for the time being: Whose peace and happiness, may God preserve. *Amen.*

Should any body of men be hereafter delegated for this or some similar purpose, I offer them the following extracts from that wise observer on governments, Dragonetti. "The science," says he, "of the politician consists in fixing the true point of happiness and freedom. Those men would deserve the gratitude of ages, who should discover a mode of government that contained the greatest sum of individual happiness, with the least national expense."[15]

But where, say some, is the king of America? I'll tell you, friend, he reigns above, and doth not make havoc of mankind like the Royal Brute of Great Britain. Yet that we may not appear to be defective even in earthly honors, let a day be solemnly set apart for proclaiming the charter; let it be brought forth placed on the divine law, the Word of God; let a crown be placed thereon, by which the world may know, that so far as we approve of monarchy, that in America *The Law is King.* For as in absolute governments the king is law, so in free countries the law *ought* to *be* king, and there ought to be no other. But lest any ill use should afterwards arise, let the crown at the conclusion of the ceremony be demolished, and scattered among the people whose right it is.[16] * * *

O ye that love mankind! Ye that dare oppose not only the tyranny but the tyrant, stand forth! Every spot of the old world is overrun

[15]"Dragonetti on 'Virtues and Rewards' " [Paine's note]. He referred to Giacinto Dragonetti, author of *Le Virtu ed i Premi* (1767).

[16]Popular sovereignty and a government by social contract are recurrent themes in Paine's later writings; *cf.* also the Declaration of Independence.

with oppression. Freedom hath been hunted round the globe. Asia and Africa have long expelled her. Europe regards her like a stranger, and England hath given her warning to depart. O receive the fugitive, and prepare in time an asylum for mankind.

"WHEN SHALL WE HAVE BREAD?"

While the National Assembly began debate on a new constitution, and the peasants in parts of the country experienced the panic and disorder known as the Great Fear, the population in Paris continued to have difficulty obtaining food. The atmosphere in some sections of the capital emerges clearly from the pages of a pamphlet published at the end of September.

Excerpts follow, from *Quand aurons-nous du pain? Vous Dormez, Parisiens, et vous manquez de pain!*

Go, keen expression of my rightful anguish, go and carry desolation and despair into all hearts if the Parisians do not have the courage to throw off the yoke of the tyrants, of the monopolists, who are oppressing them and causing them to die of hunger.

All kinds of governments, says Livy, are scrupulous to see that the citizens never lack food; the tranquillity of the State depends on it. A starved people is easily moved to excesses. But everyone knows the gentleness of the Restorers of French Liberty.

Why, Citizens, do La Fayette, Bailly, and the chiefs of the Commune leave you in want of *bread*? It is in order to grow fat at the expense of your substance.

Why do those villains bring troops to encircle Paris, Versailles, and the surrounding area with pikes and soldiers, on the pretext of guarding the King and the National Assembly?

It is to have the means of starving you and weakening you within a couple of days, in order to be able to slaughter you with no risk. But open your eyes: when shall we have *bread*?

You know that the King has come alone into your midst. You know that the King and the National Assembly were safe when you made sacrifices to the Patrie of Berthier, Foulon, De Launey, etc., etc. Now you are silent, and you are dying of hunger. . . .

The chiefs of your Committees are doing everything. They scorn the regulations and observations of the general Assembly of each District,. . . and you are asleep, and you do not have *bread*.

As the other Committees will not perhaps be so easy to corrupt, La Fayette reserves for himself the right to name your Military Chiefs. Ask him, then, when shall we have *bread*? . . .

You want to provide Ministers for the King, you want to name the

Generals, you want them to account to the Nation; but you throw yourselves into the arms of La Fayette, you give him a despotic power over you, you make him master of everything. Your life is safer, then, in the hands of that betrayer, La Fayette, of that Vampire, than in those of your good King: admit that you are fools, for you do not have *bread*.

How much does bread cost? a foreigner lately asked a workman's wife. Three *livres* and twelve *sous* for four pounds, she replied. What, he said, that is eighteen *sous* a pound! Yes, she said, it is fixed at twelve *sous* for four pounds, but one cannot get any. My husband has to spend an entire day at a baker's door to get a poor loaf weighing four pounds. He earns three *livres* a day, but not being able to work for lack of bread he loses his wages of three *livres*, so the bread comes to three *livres* and twelve *sous* for four pounds. Alas! When shall we have *bread*?

It used to be permitted to go into the Market; it is to the Market that they are supposed to transport the flour. What does the Cannibal Committee do? It prohibits the Bourgeois from entering the Market to keep them from seeing the infamies that are committed there. It sends the bakers to look for flour outside Paris, that is to say, in places where there is none because it has been secretly exported. Thus the poor baker is obliged to cheat you of one pound on each four-pound loaf. But when shall we have *bread*?

The Committee gives out that indiscreet Bourgeois have gone into the storage rooms in the Market where there is spoiled flour unfit for human consumption which is not even sold to the paperhangers. What do they do with this if they do not sell it? Why not throw it in the river? They keep it, but for what use if not to mix it with other flour to be eaten by the silly Parisians? Poor simpletons, you admire your chiefs, you are asleep. But when shall we have *bread*?

The Subsistence Committee sends Commissioners at great expense to buy flour in the provincial towns. The Petits Augustins District was assigned Brie, and in four or five days it performed prodigies, was well received by all the Farm stewards, from whom it brought eighty wagons to the Market.

The other Commissioners, thinking themselves Farmers-General of the Ovens, have amused themselves by giving dinners, and after more than a month had only five or six wagons of flour brought to the Market. Yet the Parisians are seeing their capitation tax increased; enormous expenses are counted as theirs; and we lack food. When shall we have *bread*?

More than a third of the inhabitants of the Capital are away; Heaven has poured its benefits profusely on our soil; the harvest has been very abundant; we should be overflowing with flour, and we have no bread. The Subsistence Committee's posters promise us food; it says it is sweating blood to go far and wide in search of flour; but hunger is pressing us; we are beginning to see that these unfulfilled promises are made only with the intention of deceiving us. They give us bread only in writing; when shall we have some in substance?

Although the grumbling of our intestines makes us aware that we are experiencing the horrors of need, they want to persuade us that our stomachs are full when they are empty, when we lack the food most precious to life. This will continue, and when shall we have *bread?* . . .

THE COMMUNIST MANIFESTO

Marx and Engels

A specter is haunting Europe—the specter of communism. All the powers of old Europe have entered into a holy alliance to exorcise this specter: Pope and Czar, Metternich and Guizot, French radicals and German police spies.

Where is the party in opposition that has not been decried as communistic by its opponents in power? Where the opposition that has not hurled back the branding reproach of communism against the more advanced opposition parties, as well as against its reactionary adversaries?

Two things result from this fact:

I. Communism is already acknowledged by all European powers to be itself a power.

II. It is high time that communists should openly, in the face of the whole world, publish their views, their aims, their tendencies, and meet this nursery tale of the specter of communism with a Manifesto of the party itself.

To this end, communists of various nationalities have assembled in London and sketched the following Manifesto, to be published in the English, French, German, Italian, Flemish, and Danish languages.

I. BOURGEOIS AND PROLETARIANS

The history of all hitherto existing society is the history of class struggles.

Free man and slave, patrician and plebeian, lord and serf, guild master and journeyman, in a word, oppressor and oppressed, stood in constant opposition to one another, carried on an uninterrupted, now hidden, now open fight, a fight that each time ended either in a revolutionary reconstitution of society at large or in the common ruin of the contending classes.

In the earlier epochs of history we find almost everywhere a complicated arrangement of society into various orders, a manifold gradation of social rank. In ancient Rome we have patricians, knights, plebeians, slaves; in the Middle Ages, feudal lords, vassals, guild masters, journeymen, apprentices, serfs; in almost all of these classes, again, subordinate gradations.

The modern bourgeois society that has sprouted from the ruins of feudal society has not done away with class antagonisms. It has but established new classes, new conditions of oppression, new forms of struggle in place of the old ones.

Our epoch, the epoch of the bourgeoisie, possesses, however, this distinctive feature: it has simplified the class antagonisms. Society as a whole is more and more splitting up into two great hostile camps, into two great classes directly facing each other: bourgeoisie and proletariat.

From the serfs of the Middle Ages sprang the chartered burghers of the earliest towns. From these burgesses the first elements of the bourgeoisie were developed.

The discovery of America, the rounding of the Cape opened up fresh ground for the rising bourgeoisie. The East Indian and Chinese markets, the colonization of America, trade with the colonies, the increase in the means of exchange and in commidities generally, gave to commerce, to navigation, to industry an impulse never before known, and thereby, to the revolutionary element in the tottering feudal society, a rapid development.

The feudal system of industry, under which industrial production was monopolized by closed guilds, now no longer sufficed for the growing wants of the new markets. The manufacturing system took its place. The guild masters were pushed on one side by the manufacturing middle class; division of labor between the different corporate guilds vanished in the face of division of labor in each single workshop.

Meantime the markets kept ever growing, the demand ever rising. Even manufacture no longer sufficed. Thereupon steam and machinery revolutionized industrial production. The place of manufacture was taken by the giant, modern industry, the place of the industrial middle class by industrial millionaires, the leaders of whole industrial armies, the modern bourgeois.

Modern industry has established the world market, for which the discovery of America paved the way. This market has given an immense development to commerce, to navigation, to communication by land. This development has, in its turn, reacted on the extension of industry; and in proportion as industry, commerce, navigation, railways extended, in the same proportion the bourgeoisie developed, increased its capital, and pushed into the background every class handed down from the Middle Ages.

We see, therefore, how the modern bourgeoisie is itself the product of a long course of development, of a series of revolutions in the modes of production and of exchange.

Each step in the development of the bourgeoisie was accompanied by a corresponding political advance of that class. An oppressed class under the sway of the feudal nobility, an armed and self-governing association in the medieval commune; here independent urban republic (as in Italy and Germany), there taxable "third estate" of the monarchy (as in France), afterwards, in the period of manufacture proper, serving either the semi-feudal or the absolute monarchy as a counterpoise against the nobility, and, in fact, cornerstone of the great monarchies in general, the bourgeoisie has at last, since the establishment of modern industry and of the world market, conquered for itself, in the modern representative state, exclusive political sway. The executive of the modern state is but a committee for managing the common affairs of the whole bourgeoisie.

The bourgeoisie, historically, has played a most revolutionary part.

The bourgeoisie, wherever it has got the upper hand, has put an end to all feudal, patriarchal, idyllic relations. It has pitilessly torn asunder the motley feudal ties that bound man to his "natural superiors," and has left remaining no other nexus between man and man than naked self-interest, than callous "cash payment." It has drowned the most heavenly ecstasies of religious fervor, of chivalrous enthusiasm, of Philistine sentimentalism in the icy water of egotistical calculation. It has resolved personal worth into exchange value and, in place of the numberless indefeasible chartered freedoms, has set up that single, unconscionable freedom—free trade. In one word, for exploitation, veiled by religious and political illusions, it has substituted naked, shameless, direct, brutal exploitation.

The bourgeoisie has stripped of its halo every occupation hitherto honored and looked up to with reverent awe. It has converted the physician, the lawyer, the priest, the poet, the man of science into its paid wage laborers.

The bourgeoisie has torn away from the family its sentimental veil, and has reduced the family relation to a mere money relation.

The bourgeoisie has disclosed how it came to pass that the brutal display of vigor in the Middle Ages, which reactionists so much admire, found its fitting complement in the most slothful indolence. It has been the first to show what man's activity can bring about. It has accomplished wonders far surpassing Egyptian pyramids, Roman aqueducts, and Gothic cathedrals; it has conducted expeditions that put in the shade all former exoduses of nations and crusades.

The bourgeoisie cannot exist without constantly revolutionizing the instruments of production, and thereby the relations of production, and with them the whole relations of society. Conservation of the old modes of production in unaltered form was, on the contrary, the first condition of existence for all earlier industrial classes. Constant revolutionizing of production, uninterrupted disturbance of all social conditions, everlasting uncertainty and agitation distinguish the bourgeois epoch from all earlier ones. All fixed, fast-frozen relations, with their train of ancient and venerable prejudices and opinions, are swept away, all new-formed ones become antiquated before they can ossify. All that is solid melts into air, all that is holy is profaned, and man is at last compelled to face with sober senses his real conditions of life and his relations with his kind.

The need of a constantly expanding market for its products chases the bourgeoisie over the whole surface of the globe. It must nestle everywhere, settle everywhere, establish connections everywhere.

The bourgeoisie has through its exploitation of the world market given a cosmopolitan character to production and consumption in every country. To the great chagrin of reactionists, it has drawn from under the feet of industry the national ground on which it stood. All old-established national industries have been destroyed or are daily being destroyed. They are dislodged by new industries, whose introduction becomes a life and death question for all civilized nations, by industries that no longer work up indigenous raw material, but raw material drawn from the remotest zones; industries whose products are consumed not only at home, but in every quarter of the globe. In place of the old wants, satisfied by the productions of the country, we find new wants, requiring for their satisfaction the products of distant lands and climes. In place of the old local and national seclusion and self-sufficiency we have intercourse in every direction, universal interdependence of nations. And as in material, so also in intellectual production. The intellectual creations of individual nations become common property. National one-sidedness and narrow-mindedness become more and more impossible, and from the numerous national and local literatures there arises a world literature.

The bourgeoisie, by the rapid improvement of all instruments of production, by the immensely facilitated means of communication, draws all, even the most barbarian, nations into civilization. The cheap prices of its commodities are the heavy artillery with which it batters down all Chinese walls, with which it forces the barbarians' intensely obstinate hatred of foreigners to capitulate. It compels all nations, on pain of extinction, to adopt the bourgeois mode of production; it compels them to introduce what it calls civilization into their midst, i.e., to become bourgeois themselves. In one word, it creates a world after its own image.

The bourgeoisie has subjected the country to the rule of the towns. It has created enormous cities, has greatly increased the urban population as compared with the rural, and has thus rescued a considerable part of the population from the idiocy of rural life. Just as it has made the country dependent on the towns, so it has made barbarian and semi-barbarian countries dependent on the civilized ones, nations of peasants on nations of bourgeois, the East on the West.

The bourgeoisie keeps more and more doing away with the scattered state of the population, of the means of production, and of property. It has agglomerated population, centralized means of production, and has concentrated property in a few hands. The necessary consequence of this was political centralization. Independent, or but loosely connected provinces, with separate interests, laws, governments and systems of taxation, became lumped together into one nation, with one government, one code of laws, one national class interest, one frontier, and one customs tariff.

The bourgeoisie, during its rule of scarce one hundred years, has created more massive and more colossal productive forces than have all preceding generations together. Subjection of nature's forces to man, machinery, application of chemistry to industry and agriculture, steam navigation, railways, electric telegraphs, clearing of whole continents for cultivation, canalization of rivers, whole populations conjured out of the ground—what earlier century had even a presentiment that such productive forces slumbered in the lap of social labor?

We see then: the means of production and of exchange, on whose foundation the bourgeoisie built itself up, were generated in feudal society. At a certain stage in the development of these means of production and of exchange, the conditions under which feudal society produced and exchanged, the feudal organization of agriculture and manufacturing industry, in one word, the feudal relations of property, became no longer compatible with the already developed productive forces; they became so many fetters. They had to be burst asunder; they were burst asunder.

Into their place stepped free competition, accompanied by a social and political constitution adapted to it, and by the economic and political sway of the bourgeois class.

A similar movement is going on before our own eyes. Modern bourgeois society with its relations of production, of exchange, and of property, a society that has conjured up such gigantic means of production and of exchange, is like the sorcerer who is no longer able to control the powers of the nether world whom he has called up by his spells. For many a decade past, the history of industry and commerce is but the history of the revolt of modern productive forces against modern conditions of production, against the property relations that are the conditions for the existence of the bourgeoisie and of its rule. It is enough to mention the commercial crises that by their periodic return put on its trial, each time more threateningly, the existence of the entire bourgeois society. In these crises a great part not only of the existing products but also of the previously created productive forces are periodically destroyed. In these crises there breaks out an epidemic that in all earlier epochs would have seemed an absurdity—the epidemic of overproduction. Society suddenly finds itself put back into a state of momentary barbarism; it appears as if a famine, a universal war of devastation had cut off the supply of every means of subsistence; industry and commerce seem to be destroyed; and why? Because there is too much civilization, too much means of subsistence, too much industry, too much commerce. The productive forces at the disposal of society no longer tend to further the development of the conditions of bourgeois property; on the contrary, they have become too powerful for these conditions, by which they are fettered, and as soon as they overcome these fetters they bring disorder into the whole of bourgeois society, endanger the existence of bourgeois property. The conditions of bourgeois society are too narrow to comprise the wealth created by them. And how does the bourgeoisie get over these crises? On the one hand, by enforced destruction of a mass of productive forces; on the other, by the conquest of new markets, and by the more thorough exploitation of the old ones. That is to say, by paving the way for more extensive and more destructive crises, and by diminishing the means whereby crises are prevented.

The weapons with which the bourgeoisie felled feudalism to the ground are now turned against the bourgeoisie itself.

But not only has the bourgeoisie forged the weapons that bring death to itself; it has also called into existence the men who are to wield those weapons—the modern working class—the proletarians.

In proportion as the bourgeoisie, i.e., capital, is developed, in the same proportion is the proletariat, the modern working class, developed—a class of laborers, who live only so long as they find work, and who find work only so long as their labor increases capital. These laborers, who must sell themselves piecemeal, are a commodity, like every other article of commerce, and are consequently exposed to all the vicissitudes of competition, to all the fluctuations of the market.

Owing to the extensive use of machinery and to division of labor, the work of the proletarians has lost all individual character and, consequently, all charm for the workman. He becomes an appendage of the machine, and it is only the simplest, most monotonous, and most easily acquired knack that is required of him. Hence the cost of production of a workman is restricted, almost entirely, to the means of subsistence that he requires for his maintenance and for the propagation of his race. But the price of a commodity, and therefore also of labor, is equal to its cost of production. In proportion, therefore, as the repulsiveness of the work increases, the wage decreases. Nay, more, in proportion as the use of machinery and division of labor increases, in the same proportion the burden of toil also increases, whether by prolongation of the working hours, by increase of the work exacted in a given time, or by increased speed of the machinery, etc.

Modern industry has converted the little workshop of the patriarchal master into the great factory of the industrial capitalist. Masses of laborers, crowded into the factory, are organized like soldiers. As privates of the industrial army they are placed under the command of a perfect hierarchy of officers and sergeants. Not only are they slaves of the bourgeois class, and of the bourgeois state; they are daily and hourly enslaved by the machine, by the overlooker, and, above all, by the individual bourgeois manufacturer himself. The more openly this despotism proclaims gain to be its end and aim, the more petty, the more hateful, and the more embittering it is.

The less the skill and exertion of strength implied in manual labor, in other words, the more modern industry becomes developed, the more is the labor of men superseded by that of women. Differences of age and sex have no longer any distinctive social validity for the working class. All are instruments of labor, more or less expensive to use, according to their age and sex.

No sooner is the exploitation of the laborer by the manufacturer over, to the extent that he receives his wages in cash, than he is set upon by the other portions of the bourgeoisie, the landlord, the shopkeeper, the pawnbroker, etc.

The lower strata of the middle class—the small tradespeople, shopkeepers, and retired tradesmen generally, the handicraftsmen and peasants—all these sink gradually into the proletariat, partly because their diminutive capital does not suffice for the scale on which modern industry is carried on, and is swamped in the competition with the large capitalists, partly because their specialized skill is rendered worthless by new methods of production. Thus the proletariat is recruited from all classes of the population.

The proletariat goes through various stages of development. With its birth begins its struggle with the bourgeoisie. At first the contest is carried on by individual laborers, then by the workpeople of a factory, then by the operatives of one trade, in one locality, against the individual bourgeois who directly exploits them. They direct their attacks not against the bourgeois conditions of production, but against the instruments of production themselves; they destroy imported wares that compete with their labor, they smash to pieces machinery, they set factories ablaze, they seek to restore by force the vanished status of the workman of the Middle Ages.

At this stage the laborers still form an incoherent mass scattered over the whole country and broken up by their mutual competition. If anywhere they unite to form more compact bodies, this is not yet the consequence of their own active union, but of the union of the bourgeoisie, which class, in order to attain its own political ends, is compelled to set the whole proletariat in motion, and is moreover yet, for a time, able to do so. At this stage, therefore, the proletarians do not fight their enemies, but the enemies of their enemies, the remnants of absolute monarchy, the landowners, the non-industrial bourgeois, the petty bourgeoisie. Thus the whole historical movement is concentrated in the hands of the bourgeoisie; every victory so obtained is a victory for the bourgeoisie.

But with the development of industry the proletariat not only increases in number; it becomes concentrated in greater masses, its strength grows, and it feels that strength more. The various interests and conditions of life within the ranks of the proletariat are more and more equalized, in proportion as machinery obliterates all distinctions of labor and nearly everywhere reduces wages to the same low level. The growing competition among the bourgeois and the resulting commercial crises make the wages of the workers ever more fluctuating. The unceasing improvement of machinery, ever more rapidly developing, makes their livelihood more and more precarious; the collisions between individual workmen and individual bourgeois take more and more the character of collisions between two classes. Thereupon the workers begin to form combinations (trade unions) against the bourgeois; they club together in order to keep up the rate of wages; they found permanent associations in order to make provision beforehand for these occasional revolts. Here and there the contest breaks out into riots.

Now and then the workers are victorious, but only for a time. The real fruit of their battles lies not in the immediate result, but in the ever expanding union of the workers. This union is helped on by the improved means of communication that are created by modern industry and that place the workers of different localities in contact with one another. It was just this contact that was needed to centralize the numerous local struggles, all of the same character, into one national struggle between classes. But every class struggle is a political struggle. And that union, to attain which the burghers of the Middle Ages, with their miserable highways, required centuries, the modern proletarians, thanks to railways, achieve in a few years.

This organization of the proletarians into a class, and consequently into a political party, is continually being upset again by the competition between the workers themselves. But it ever rises up again, stronger, firmer, mightier. It compels legislative recognition of particular interests of the workers by taking advantage of the divisions among the bourgeoisie itself. Thus the ten-hour bill in England was carried.

Altogether collisions between the classes of the old society further, in many ways, the course of development of the proletariat. The bourgeoisie finds itself involved in a constant battle. At first with the aristocracy; later on, with those portions of the bourgeoisie itself whose interests have become antagonistic to the progress of industry; at all times, with the bourgeoisie of foreign countries. In all these battles it sees itself compelled to appeal to the proletariat, to ask for its help, and thus to drag it into the political arena. The bourgeoisie itself, therefore, supplies the proletariat with its own elements of political and general education: in other words, it furnishes the proletariat with weapons for fighting the bourgeoisie.

Further, as we have already seen, entire sections of the ruling classes are, by the advance of industry, precipitated into the proletariat, or are at least threatened in their conditions of existence. These also supply the proletariat with fresh elements of enlightenment and progress.

Finally, in times when the class struggle nears the decisive hour, the process of disolution going on within the ruling class, in fact within the whole range of old society, assumes such a violent, glaring character that a small section of the ruling class cuts itself adrift and joins the revolutionary class, the class that holds the future in its hands. Just as, therefore, at an earlier period, a section of the nobility went over to the bourgeoisie, so now a portion of the bourgeoisie goes over to the proletariat, and in particular a portion of the bourgeois ideologists, who have raised themselves to the level of comprehending theoretically the historical movement as a whole.

Of all the classes that stand face to face with the bourgeoisie today, the proletariat alone is a really revolutionary class. The other classes decay and finally disappear in the face of modern industry; the proletariat is its special and essential product.

The lower-middle class, the small manufacturer, the shopkeeper, the artisan, the peasant, all these fight against the bourgeoisie, to save from extinction their existence as fractions of the middle class. They are therefore not revolutionary, but conservative. Nay, more, they are reactionary, for they try to roll back the wheel of history. If by chance they are revolutionary they are so only in view of their impending transfer into the proletariat; they thus defend not their present but their future interests, they desert their own standpoint to place themselves at that of the proletariat.

The "dangerous class," the social scum, that passively rotting mass thrown off by the lowest layers of old society, may, here and there, be swept into the movement by a proletarian revolution; its conditions of life, however, prepare it far more for the part of a bribed tool of reactionary intrigue.

In the conditions of the proletariat those of old society at large are already virtually swamped. The proletarian is without property; his relation to his wife and children has no longer anything in common with the bourgeois family relations; modern industrial labor, modern subjection to capital, the same in England as in France, in America as in Germany, has stripped him of every trace of national character. Law, morality, religion are to him so many bourgeois prejudices, behind which lurk in ambush just as many bourgeois interests.

All the preceding classes that got the upper hand sought to fortify their already acquired status by subjecting society at large to their conditions of appropriation. The proletarians cannot become masters of the productive forces of society, except by abolishing their own previous mode of appropriation, and thereby also every other previous mode of appropriation. They have nothing of their own to secure and to fortify; their mission is to destroy all previous securities for, and insurances of, individual property.

All previous historical movements were movements of minorities, or in the interest of minorities. The proletarian movement is the self-conscious, independent movement of the immense majority, in the interests of the immense majority. The proletariat, the lowest stratum of our present society, cannot stir, cannot raise itself up, without the whole superincumbent strata of official society being sprung into the air.

Though not in substance, yet in form, the struggle of the proletariat with the bourgeoisie is at first a national struggle. The proletariat of each country must, of course, first of all settle matters with its own bourgeoisie.

In depicting the most general phases of the development of the proletariat, we traced the more or less veiled civil war, raging within existing society, up to the point where that war breaks out into open revolution, and where the violent overthrow of the bourgeoisie lays the foundation for the sway of the proletariat.

Hitherto every form of society has been based, as we have already seen, on the antagonism of oppressing and oppressed classes. But in order to oppress a class certain conditions must be assured to it under which it can, at least, continue its slavish existence. The serf, in the period of serfdom, raised himself to membership in the commune, just as the petty bourgeois, under the yoke of feudal absolutism, managed to develop into a bourgeois. The modern laborer, on the contrary, instead of rising with the progress of industry, sinks deeper and deeper below the conditions of existence of his own class. He becomes a pauper, and pauperism develops more rapidly than population and wealth. And here it becomes evident that the bourgeoisie is unfit any longer to be the ruling class in society, and to impose its conditions of existence upon society as an overriding law. It is unfit to rule because it is incompetent to assure an existence to its slave within his slavery, because it cannot help letting him sink into such a state that it has to feed him instead of being fed by him. Society can no longer live under this bourgeoisie: in other words, its existence is no longer compatible with society.

The essential condition for the existence, and for the sway of the bourgeois class, is the formation and augmentation of capital; the condition for capital is wage labor. Wage labor rests exclusively on competition between the laborers. The advance of industry, whose involuntary promoter is the bourgeoisie, replaces the isolation of the laborers, due to competition, by their revolutionary combination, due to association. The development of modern industry, therefore, cuts from under its feet the very foundation on which the bourgeoisie produces and appropriates products. What the bourgeoisie, therefore, produces, above all, is its own gravediggers. Its fall and the victory of the proletariat are equally inevitable.

II. PROLETARIANS AND COMMUNISTS

In what relation do the communists stand to the proletarians as a whole?

The communists do not form a separate party opposed to other working-class parties.

They have no interests separate and apart from those of the proletariat as a whole.

They do not set up any sectarian principles of their own, by which to shape and mold the proletarian movement.

The communists are distinguished from the other working-class parties by this only: 1. In the national struggles of the proletarians of the different countries they point out and bring to the front the common interests of the entire proletariat, independent of all nationality. 2. In the various stages of development which the struggle of the working class against the bourgeoisie has to pass through, they always and everywhere represent the interests of the movement as a whole.

The communists, therefore, are on the one hand, practically, the most advanced and resolute section of the working-class parties of every country, that section which pushes forward all others; on the other hand, theoretically, they have over the great mass of the proletariat the advantage of clearly understanding the line of march, the conditions, and the ultimate general results of the proletarian movement.

The immediate aim of the communists is the same as that of all the other proletarian parties: formation of the proletariat into a class, overthrow of the bourgeois supremacy, conquest of political power by the proletariat.

The theoretical conclusions of the communists are in no way based on ideas or principles that have been invented, or discovered, by this or that would-be universal reformer.

They merely express, in general terms, actual relations springing from an existing class struggle, from a historical movement going on under our very eyes. The abolition of existing property relations is not at all a distinctive feature of communism.

All property relations in the past have continually been subject to historical change consequent upon the change in historical conditions.

The French Revolution, for example, abolished feudal property in favor of bourgeois property.

The distinguishing feature of communism is not the abolition of property generally, but the abolition of bourgeois property. But modern bourgeois private property is the final and most complete expression of the system of producing and appropriating products that is based on class antagonisms, on the exploitation of the many by the few.

In this sense the theory of the communists may be summed up in the single sentence: Abolition of private property.

We communists have been reproached with the desire of abolishing the right of personally acquiring property as the fruit of a man's own labor, which property is alleged to be the groundwork of all personal freedom, activity, and independence.

Hard-won, self-acquired, self-earned property! Do you mean the property of the petty artisan and of the small peasant, a form of property that preceded the bourgeois form? There is no need to abolish that; the development of industry has to a great extent already destroyed it, and is still destroying it daily.

Or do you mean modern bourgeois private property?

But does wage labor create any property for the laborer? Not a bit. It creates capital, i.e., that kind of property which exploits wage labor, and which cannot increase except upon condition of begetting a new supply of wage labor for fresh exploitation. Property, in its present form, is based on the antagonism of capital and wage labor. Let us examine both sides of this antagonism.

To be a capitalist is to have not only a purely personal but a social *status* in production. Capital is a collective product, and only by the united action of many members, nay, in the last resort only by the united action of all members of society, can it be set in motion.

Capital is, therefore, not a personal, it is a social power.

When, therefore, capital is converted into common property, into the property of all members of society, personal property is not thereby transformed into social property. It is only the social character of the property that is changed. It loses its class character.

Let us now take wage labor.

The average price of wage labor is the minimum wage, i.e., that quantum of the means of subsistence which is absolutely requisite to keep the laborer in bare existence as a laborer. What, therefore, the wage laborer appropriates by means of his labor merely suffices to prolong and reproduce a bare existence. We by no means intend to abolish this personal appropriation of the products of labor, an appropriation that is made for the maintenance and reproduction of human life, and that leaves no surplus wherewith to command the labor of others. All that we want to do away with is the miserable character of this appropriation, under which the laborer lives merely to increase capital, and is allowed to live only in so far as the interest of the ruling class requires it.

In bourgeois society living labor is but a means to increase accumulated labor. In communist society accumulated labor is but a means to widen, to enrich, to promote the existence of the laborer.

In bourgeois society, therefore, the past dominates the present; in communist society the present dominates the past. In bourgeois society capital is independent and has individuality, while the living person is dependent and has no individuality.

And the abolition of this state of things is called by the bourgeois abolition of individuality and freedom! And rightly so. The abolition of bourgeois individuality, bourgeois independence, and bourgeois freedom is undoubtedly aimed at.

By freedom is meant, under the present bourgeois conditions of production, free trade, free selling and buying.

But if selling and buying disappear, free selling and buying disappear also. This talk about free selling and buying, and all the other "brave words" of our bourgeoisie about freedom in general, have a meaning, if any, only in contrast with restricted selling and buying, with the fettered traders of the Middle Ages, but have no meaning when opposed to the communistic abolition of buying and selling, of the bourgeois conditions of production, and of the bourgeoisie itself.

You are horrified at our intending to do away with private property. But in your existing society private property is already done away with for nine tenths of the population; its existence for the few is solely due to its nonexistence in the hands of those nine tenths. You reproach us, therefore, with intending to do away with a form of property the necessary condition for whose existence is the nonexistence of any property for the immense majority of society.

In one word, you reproach us with intending to do away with your property. Precisely so; that is just what we intend.

From the moment when labor can no longer be converted into capital, money, or rent, into a social power capable of being monopolized, i.e., from the moment when individual property can no longer be transformed into bourgeois property, into capital, from that moment, you say, individuality vanishes.

You must, therefore, confess that by "individual" you mean no other person than the bourgeois, than the middle-class owner of property. This person must, indeed, be swept out of the way and made impossible.

Communism deprives no man of the power to appropriate the products of society; all that it does is to deprive him of the power to subjugate the labor of others by means of such appropriation.

It has been objected that upon the abolition of private property all work will cease and universal laziness will overtake us.

According to this, bourgeois society ought long ago have gone to the dogs through sheer idleness, for those of its members who work acquire nothing and those who acquire anything do not work. The whole of this objection is but another expression of the tautology that there can no longer be any wage labor when there is no longer any capital.

All objections urged against the communistic mode of producing and appropriating material products have, in the same way, been urged against the communistic modes of producing and appropriating intellectual products. Just as, to the bourgeois, the disappearance of class property is the disappearance of production itself, so the disappearance of class culture is to him identical with the disappearance of all culture.

That culture, the loss of which he laments, is, for the enormous majority, a mere training to act as a machine.

But don't wrangle with us so long as you apply, to our intended abolition of bourgeois property, the standard of your bourgeois notions of freedom, culture, law, etc. Your very ideas are but the outgrowth of the conditions of your bourgeois production and bour- geois property, just as your jurisprudence is but the will of your class made into a law for all, a will whose essential character and direction are determined by the economic conditions of existence of your class.

The selfish misconception that induces you to transform into eter- nal laws of nature and of reason the social forms springing from your present mode of production and form of property—historical relations that rise and disappear in the progress of production—this misconcep- tion you share with every ruling class that has preceded you. What you see clearly in the case of ancient property, what you admit in the case of feudal property you are of course forbidden to admit in the case of your own bourgeois form of property.

Abolition of the family! Even the most radical flare up at this infamous proposal of the communists.

On what foundation is the present family, the bourgeois family, based? On capital, on private gain. In its completely developed form this family exists only among the bourgeoisie. But this state of things finds its complement in the practical absence of the family among the proletarians, and in public prostitution.

The bourgeois family will vanish as a matter of course when its complement vanishes, and both will vanish with the vanishing of capital.

Do you charge us with wanting to stop the exploitation of children by their parents? To this crime we plead guilty.

But, you will say, we destroy the most hallowed of relations when we replace home education by social.

And your education! Is not that also social, and determined by the social conditions under which you educate, by the intervention, direct or indirect, of society, by means of schools, etc.? The com- munists have not invented the intervention of society in education; they do but seek to alter the character of that intervention, and to rescue education from the influence of the ruling class.

The bourgeois claptrap about the family and education, about the hallowed co-relation of parent and child, becomes all the more disgusting, the more, by the action of modern industry, all family ties among the proletarians are torn asunder and their children trans- formed into simple articles of commerce and instruments of labor.

"But you communists would introduce community of women," screams the whole bourgeoisie in chorus.

The bourgeois sees in his wife a mere instrument of production. He hears that the instruments of production are to be exploited in common and, naturally, can come to no other conclusion than that the lot of being common to all will likewise fall to the women.

He has not even a suspicion that the real point aimed at is to do away with the status of women as mere instruments of production.

For the rest, nothing is more ridiculous than the virtuous indignation of our bourgeois at the community of women which, they pretend, is to be openly and officially established by the communists. The communists have no need to introduce community of women; it has existed almost from time immemorial.

Our bourgeois, not content with having the wives and daughters of their proletarians at their disposal, not to speak of common prostitutes, take the greatest pleasure in seducing each other's wives.

Bourgeois marriage is in reality a system of wives in common and thus, at the most, what the communists might possibly be reproached with is that they desire to introduce, in substitution for a hypocritically concealed, an openly legalized community of women. For the rest, it is self-evident that the abolition of the present system of production must bring with it the abolition of the community of women springing from that system, i.e., of prostitution, both public and private.

The communists are further reproached with desiring to abolish countries and nationality.

The workingmen have no country. We cannot take from them what they have not got. Since the proletariat must first of all acquire political supremacy, must rise to be the leading class of the nation, must constitute itself *the* nation, it is, so far, itself national, though not in the bourgeois sense of the word.

National differences and antagonisms between peoples are daily more and more vanishing, owing to the development of the bourgeoisie, to freedom of commerce, to the world market, to uniformity in the mode of production and in the conditions of life corresponding thereto.

The supremacy of the proletariat will cause them to vanish still faster. United action, of the leading civilized countries at least, is one of the first conditions for the emancipation of the proletariat.

In proportion as the exploitation of one individual by another is put to an end, the exploitation of one nation by another will also be put to an end. In proportion as the antagonism between classes within the nation vanishes, the hostility of one nation to another will come to an end.

The charges against communism made from a religious, a philosophical, and, generally, from an ideological standpoint are not deserving of serious examination.

Does it require deep intuition to comprehend that man's ideas, views, and conceptions, in one word, man's consciousness, change with every change in the conditions of his material existence, in his social relations, and in his social life?

What else does the history of ideas prove than that intelleᶜtual production changes its character in proportion as material production is changed? The ruling ideas of each age have ever been the ideas of its ruling class.

When people speak of ideas that revolutionize society they do but express the fact that within the old society the elements of a new one have been created, and that the dissolution of the old ideas keeps even pace with the dissolution of the old conditions of existence.

When the ancient world was in its last throes, the ancient religions were overcome by Christianity. When Christian ideas succumbed in the eighteenth century to rationalist ideas, feudal society fought its death battle with the then revolutionary bourgeoisie. The ideas of religious liberty and freedom of conscience merely gave expression to the sway of free competition within the domain of knowledge.

"Undoubtedly," it will be said, "religious, moral, philosophical, and juridical ideas have been modified in the course of historical development. But religion, morality, philosophy, political science, and law constantly survived this change.

"There are, besides, eternal truths, such as freedom, justice, etc., that are common to all states of society. But communism abolishes eternal truths, it abolishes all religion, and all morality, instead of constituting them on a new basis; it therefore acts in contradiction to all past historical experience."

What does this accusation reduce itself to? The history of all past society has consisted in the development of class antagonisms, antagonisms that assumed different forms at different epochs.

But whatever form they may have taken, one fact is common to all past ages, viz., the exploitation of one part of society by the other. No wonder then that the social consciousness of past ages, despite all the multiplicity and variety it displays, moves within certain common forms, or general ideas, which cannot completely vanish except with the total disappearance of class antagonisms.

The communist revolution is the most radical rupture with traditional property relations; no wonder that its development involves the most radical rupture with traditional ideas.

But let us have done with the bourgeois objections to communism.

We have seen above that the first step in the revolution by the working class is to raise the proletariat to the position of ruling class, to win the battle of democracy.

The proletariat will use its political supremacy to wrest, by degrees, all capital from the bourgeoisie, to centralize all instruments of production in the hands of the state, i.e., of the proletariat organized as the ruling class, and to increase the total of productive forces as rapidly as possible.

Of course, in the beginning this cannot be effected except by means of despotic inroads on the rights of property and on the conditions of bourgeois production; by means of measures, therefore, which appear economically insufficient and untenable, but which, in the course of the movement, outstrip themselves, necessitate further inroads upon the old social order, and are unavoidable as a means of entirely revolutionizing the mode of production.

These measures will of course be different in different countries.

Nevertheless, in the most advanced countries the following will be pretty generally applicable:

1. Abolition of property in land and application of all rents of land to public purposes.

2. A heavy progressive or graduated income tax.

3. Abolition of all right of inheritance.

4. Confiscation of the property of all emigrants and rebels.

5. Centralization of credit in the hands of the state, by means of a national bank with state capital and an exclusive monopoly.

6. Centralization of the means of communication and transport in the hands of the state.

7. Extension of factories and instruments of production owned by the state; the bringing into cultivation of wastelands, and the improvement of the soil generally in accordance with a common plan.

8. Equal liability of all to labor. Establishment of industrial armies, especially for agriculture.

9. Combination of agriculture with manufacturing industries; gradual abolition of the distinction between town and country, by a more equable distribution of the population over the country.

10. Free education for all children in public schools. Abolition of children's factory labor in its present form. Combination of education with industrial production, etc.

When, in the course of development, class distinctions have disappeared and all production has been concentrated in the hands of a vast association of the whole nation, the public power will lose its political character. Political power, properly so called, is merely the organized power of one class for oppressing another. If the proletariat during its contest with the bourgeoisie is compelled, by the force of circumstances, to organize itself as a class, if, by means of a revolution, it makes itself the ruling class and, as such, sweeps away by force the old conditions of production, then it will, along with these conditions, have swept away the conditions for the existence of class antagonisms and of classes generally, and will thereby have abolished its own supremacy as a class.

In place of the old bourgeois society, with its classes and class antagonisms, we shall have an association in which the free development of each is the condition for the free development of all.

[The third part of the *Manifesto* is a somewhat technical comparison of "Socialist and Communist Literature," which ends with the ringing sentence: "Workingmen of All Countries, Unite!"]

THE SEEDS OF REVOLT

Gamal Abdel Nasser

Before proceeding with this discourse I would like to pause at the word "Philosophy." It looks big and sounds grand.

The truth is the Philosophy of the Revolution of July 23rd[1] should be treated by professors who should search deeply into it for the roots spreading at the very depth of our history. The stories of national struggles have no gaps that can be filled with nonsense. Neither have they the surprises that spring into existence without preludes.

I do not pretend to be a professor of history. This is the last thing my imagination may entertain. Nevertheless, if I were to attempt to study the story of our struggle like a schoolboy I would say, for instance, that the revolution of July 23rd is the realization of a hope that the people of Egypt, in modern times, have aspired to since they began to think of governing themselves and since they decided to be the masters of their fate.

One attempt failed to realize this hope when El Sayyed Omar Makram led the movement for appointing Mohamed Aly[2] viceroy of Egypt in the name of its people. Another attempt failed to fulfil this aspiration when Arabi[3] rose demanding a constitution. Other vain attempts followed during the intellectual fervour in the period between the revolt of Arabi and the Revolution of 1919. This latter was led by Saad Zaghloul[4] who again failed to reach his goal.

[1] On this date in 1952, Colonel Nasser, General Neguib, and their followers in a bloodless revolution, seized the Government of Egypt and on July 26 forced King Farouk off his throne.

[2] Led by the Azharite religious notable, Sheikh Omar Makram, and others, the people of Cairo saw in Mohamed Aly a champion against the tyranny of the Mameluke nobility and proclaimed him governor of Cairo. He became the founder of the dynasty which ended recently with Farouk.

[3] Colonel Arabi led a military revolt in 1881 on behalf of the Egyptian people, demanding a constitution and parliamentary government. At first successful and wildly popular, the revolution was put down by British troops in 1882—the beginning of the British occupation.

[4] Immediately after the First World War, the prominent Egyptian statesman and nationalist, Saad Zaghloul, sought to lead a deputation to England to treat for complete independence. He was refused; and after failing to gain for Egypt's claim the ear of the Peace Conference in Versailles, he returned home to organize the many postwar ideological and economic discontents at large in Egypt into a coherent demand for independence. The British exiled him to Malta, whereupon anti-British violence broke out all over Egypt. British troops only gradually restored order. He was released, and later formed the Wafdist Party.

68

It is not true that the revolution of July 23rd started on account of the results of the war in Palestine. Neither was it caused by defective arms, to which officers and men fell victims. It is still further from the truth to attribute it to the crisis of the elections of the Officers' Club.[5] In my opinion its causes are deeper and farther. Had the officers endeavoured to avenge themselves because they were cheated in Palestine or because the defective arms strained their nerves and because they suffered an indignity in the elections of the Officers' Club, the whole affair would not have deserved to be called a revolution. A mere mutiny was the likely description even if it were attributed to causes fair and just in themselves. All these were incidental. Perhaps their greatest influence was that they urged us to march forward along the road to revolution; but without them we were marching just the same.

Today I am trying to recall all the events that passed and, after years have elapsed since we first thought of the revolution, to go back to the first day I discovered the seeds of revolt within me. That day lies farther back in my life than November 1951, which marked the beginning of the crisis of the Officers' Club elections. The organization of the Liberal Officers[6] was then existing and active. I do not exaggerate when I say that the crisis of the Officers' Club elections was caused, more than anything else, by the activities of the Liberal Officers. We were determined to fight then in order to test the strength of our mass formation and real organization.

That day lies again farther back in my life than May 16, 1944, which marked the start of my life in the Palestine War. As I trace the details of our experience in Palestine I feel a strange sensation. We were fighting in Palestine but our dreams were in Egypt. Our bullets were aimed at the enemy lurking in the trenches in front of us, but our hearts were hovering round our distant Mother Country, which was then a prey to the wolves that ravaged it. In Palestine, Liberal Officers' cells were meeting in trenches and posts studying and searching. And it was in Palestine that Salah Salem and Zakaria Mohyy-el-Din came to me after having penetrated the siege of Falouga;[7] there we sat beseiged neither knowing what was to become of that siege nor when it would end. We spoke of nothing but our country and how to deliver it. It was in Palestine that Gamal-el-Din

---

[5] In the Club elections late in 1951, Farouk tried to force the election of Major-General Hussein Sirry Amer as President of the Administrative Council. Implicated in the arms scandal, Amer had nonetheless been put in command of the Frontier Forces, replacing General Neguib. The Club in defiance elected Neguib President.

[6] A secret movement organized in party cells.

[7] Elements of the Egyptian army were cut off and surrounded in the "Falouga Pocket" by Israeli forces during the Palestine War. A stubborn defense was put up by the encircled Egyptians who held out until liberated by the truce agreement.

Hussein sat beside me one day and spoke as his eyes wandered and his thoughts dispersed; "Do you know what Ahmad Abdel Aziz[8] had told me before he died?" he asked. "What did he say?" I asked in return. With a deep tone of voice and still deeper look he said, "Listen Gamal, Egypt is the field of our supreme war effort."

It was not only the friends I met in Palestine who spoke to me of the future of our country, but the enemy also played his part in reminding us of our homeland and its difficulties. A few months ago I read some articles written upon me by a Jewish officer named Yerdan Cohen. These were published in the Jewish Observer. In these articles he related how he met me during the contacts and discussions of the Armistice. "The subject that Gamal Abdel Nasser discussed with me," he stated, "was Israel's struggle against the English, how we organized our underground resistance in Palestine and how we succeeded in mobilizing world public opinion behind us against them."

The day I discovered the seeds of revolt within me was still further back than February 4, 1942 [when British tanks surrounded Abdin Palace seeking to force a change of government on King Farouk]. I wrote to a friend later saying, "What is to be done now that the catastrophe has befallen us, and after we have accepted it, surrendered to it and taken it submissively and meekly.

"I really believe," I continued, "that Imperialism is playing a one-card game in order to threaten only. If ever it knew that there were Egyptians ready to shed their blood and to meet force by force it would withdraw and recoil like a harlot. This, of course, is the state or habit of Imperialism everywhere."

Was it our duty, as an army, to do what we did on July 23, 1952?

I have just explained how the revolution of July 23rd was the realization of a hope that dangled before the eyes of the people of Egypt since they began, in modern times, to think of governing themselves and having the final word on their destiny. If this be so, and if what took place on July 23rd was only a military mutiny and not a popular revolt, why was the army then, apart from any other forces, destined to carry out this revolution?

Throughout my life I have had faith in militarism. The soldier's sole duty is to die on the frontiers of his country. Why then was our army compelled to act in the capital and not on the frontier?

Once more, let me reiterate that the defeat in Palestine, the defective arms, the crisis of the Officers' Club election were not the real springs from which the current flowed. They may have accelerated the flood but they could never be the original source. Why then did this duty fall upon the army? This question has often occurred to me. It came to me persistently during the stage of hoping, of thinking and of planning before July 23rd. It repeated itself several times during the experimental period after July 23rd. We had dif-

[8] Egyptian Commando Officer in the Palestine War.

ferent factors to justify action before July 23rd and to explain to us
why it was imperative that the army should act. "If the army does
not move," we said to ourselves, "who else will?"

I confess that after July 23rd I suffered fits in which I accused
myself, my colleagues and the rest of the army of rashness and folly
we committed on July 23rd.

Prior to that date I imagined that the whole nation was on tip-toes
and prepared for action, that it awaited the advance of the vanguard
and the storming of the outside walls for it to pour down in a solid
phalanx marching faithfully to the great goal. I thought we were only
the pioneers and the commandoes, that we would only be in the
front for a few hours, and that we would be soon followed by the
solid masses marching to the goal. My imagination often carried me
away. I felt I could hear the rattle of their solid, orderly rows as they
marched onwards to the main front. My faith was such as to render
everything I heard a concrete fact and not a mere vision.

After July 23rd I was shocked by the reality. The vanguard performed its task; it stormed the walls of the fort of tyranny; it forced
Farouk to abdicate and stood by expecting the mass formations to
arrive at their ultimate object. It waited and waited. Endless crowds
showed up, but how different is the reality from the vision! The
multitudes that arrived were dispersed followers and contrasted remnants. The holy march towards the great goal was interrupted. A
dismal picture, horrible and threatening, then presented itself. I felt
my heart charged with sorrow and dripping with bitterness. The
mission of the vanguard had not ended. In fact it was just beginning
at that very hour. We needed discipline but found chaos behind our
lines. We needed unity but found dissensions. We needed action but
found nothing but surrender and idleness. It was from this source and
no other that the revolution derived its motto.[9]

We did not expect this shock. We went to the men of ideas for
counsel and to the men of experience for guidance, but unfortunately
we did not find much of either.

Every leader we came to wanted to assassinate his rival. Every idea
we found aimed at the destruction of another. If we were to carry
out all that we heard, then there would not be one leader left alive.
Not one idea would remain intact. We would cease to have a mission

[9]Namely, "Unity, Discipline, Work." The great Egyptian thinker and
reformer, Sheikh Muhammad 'Abduh (1849-1905) put forward as the basis of
his political program the slogan, "Unity, Discipline, Justice." He anticipated the
Revolution in other ways, e.g., in his view that the regeneration of Egyptian
society could only be carried out by a just dictatorship. Popular representation
made no sense without popular conviction to support it. A just dictatorship, by
persuasion and force, could unite the community and instill healthy ideas.
Fifteen years would be enough to build the necessary foundations for free
representative government. But without such a sound authoritarian regime,
fifteen centuries would not suffice.

save to remain among the smashed bodies and the broken debris lamenting our misfortune and reproaching our ill-fate.

Complaints and petitions poured upon us in thousands. If these did refer to cases worthy of justice, or mentioned oppression that might be redressed, they would be understandable and logical. The majority of these were but persistent demands for revenge as if the revolution were meant to be a weapon for revenge and hatred.

If I were asked then what I required most my instant answer would be, "To hear but one Egyptian uttering one word of justice about another, to see but one Egyptian not devoting his time to criticize wilfully the ideas of another, to feel that there was but one Egyptian ready to open his heart for forgiveness, indulgence and loving his brother Egyptians." Personal and persistent selfishness was the rule of the day. The word "I" was on every tongue. It was the magic solution of every difficulty and the effective cure for every malady.

Often did I meet men, referred to in the press as "great men," of various tendencies and colours, from whom I sought the solution of a difficult problem. I could hear nothing from them save the word "I." He and only he was capable of understanding the problems of economics; the rest were but children creeping on all fours. He and only he was the expert statesman and the rest only learning their a & b and had not got to c. After interviewing any of these men I would go back to my colleagues bitterly exclaiming, "How utterly futile . . .! If we were to ask that man about a difficulty in fishing off the Islands of Hawaii his answer would only be 'I'."

I remember I once visited one of our universities and sat with professors endeavoring to profit by the experience of men of learning. Many spoke and spoke at length. Unfortunately not one of them presented a new idea. Every one introduced himself and listed his moral capacities which, in his view, could perform miracles. Every one eyed me as if I were to him more precious that the treasures of earth or the blessings of eternity. I could not help but remark to them all, "Everyone in his place can perform miracles. The primary duty is to put all energy into it and if you, as university professors, ever thought of students and rendered them, as you should, your principal care, you would provide us with a tremendous force wherewith to build up our country. Let every one remain at his post and strive hard at it. Do not look up to us. Circumstances have compelled us to leave our posts to perform a sacred task. We sincerely wish the country has no further use for us save as professional soldiers in the army. There we would have remained."

I did not wish then to set before them the example of the members of the Revolution Council[10] who, before the crisis summoned them for the supreme task, were performing their duties in the army most

[10]The cabinet of Neguib and Nasser, consisting mainly of Army officers who were Nasser's associates in the Free Officers movement and in the Revolution of July 23, 1952.

diligently. I did not wish to tell them that most of the members of the Revolution Council were professors in the Staff-College . . . a clear proof of their distinction as professional soldiers.

Every nation on earth undergoes two revolutions: One is political, in which it recovers its right for self-government from an imposed despot, or an aggressive army occupying its territory without its consent. The second revolution is social, in which the classes of society would struggle against each other until justice for all country-men has been gained and conditions have become stable.

Other nations have preceded us along the path of human progress and passed through the two revolutions but not simultaneously. Hundreds of years separated the one from the other. In the case of our nation, it is going through the two revolutions together and at the same time, a great experiment putting us to the test.

Political revolution demands, for its success, the unity of all national elements, their fusion and mutual support, as well as self-denial for the sake of the country as a whole.

One of the first signs of social revolution is that values are shaken and creeds are relaxed; fellow-countrymen struggle against each other, individuals and classes. Corruption, suspicion, hatred and selfishness dominate them. Between the anvil and the hammer we now live in two revolutions; one demanding that we should unite together, love one another and strain every nerve to reach our goal; the other forces us, in spite of ourselves, to disperse and give way to hatred, everyone thinking only of himself.

Between the anvil and the hammer the 1919 Revolution was lost and failed to achieve the results which it ought to have realized. The ranks that massed in 1919 to face tyranny were, after a while, occupied only by internal strife. Tyranny became more arbitrary whether it was in the form of the open forces of occupation or their veiled cat's paws, headed by Sultan Fouad and later by his son Farouk. The nation reaped nothing but a crop of self-suspicion, egoism and hatred, between individuals and classes alike. The hopes which the 1919 Revolution was expected to realize faded. The fact that they only faded and did not die out is due to the hopes that our nation always entertained. These hopes were still alive, and the natural resistance engendered by them was preparing for another trial. Such was the state of affairs that prevailed after the 1919 Revolution and which made the army the only force capable of action.

The situation demanded a homogeneous force. Its members should have faith in each other and should have in their hands such elements of material force as to ensure swift and decisive action. Such conditions did not prevail except in the army.

It was not the army, as I mentioned, that determined its role in the events. The opposite is nearer the truth. It was the events and their evolution that determined for the army its role in the mighty struggle for the liberation of the country.

I have realized from the very beginning that our success depended on our complete understanding of the nature of the conditions we live in as related to our national history.

It was imperative that we should proceed with the two revolutions together. The day we marched along the path of political revolution and dethroned Farouk we took a similar step along the path of social revolution by limiting the ownership of agricultural land.[11] I still believe until today that the revolution of July 23rd should retain its capacity for swift action and initiative in order that it may fulfill the miracle of proceeding with the two revolutions simultaneously, contradictory as our action may appear to be sometimes.

When a friend of mine came to me one day exclaiming, "You asked for unity to face the English and at the same time you permit the Graft Court to proceed with its work."[12] I listened to him with the image of our big crisis in my mind: the crisis of being between two millstones. One revolution demanded that we should stand in one row and forget the past, while another revolution forced us to restore the lost dignity of moral values and not forget the past.

This was not my will; nor was it the will of those who took part in the revolution of July 23rd. It was the will of fate, of the history of our nation and of the stage it is passing through today.

[11] On August 12, 1952, the new government announced its decision "in principle" to limit land ownership to 200 acres. The Agrarian Reform Law of 1952 was passed September 9, embodying the 200-acre rule.

[12] Referring, apparently, to the prosecutions going on against allegedly corrupt members of the *ancien regime* under the "Where Did You Get It?" law.

DECLARATION OF INDEPENDENCE OF THE DEMOCRATIC REPUBLIC OF VIET-NAM*
(September 2, 1945)

All men are created equal; they are endowed by their Creator with certain unalienable Rights; among these are Life, Liberty, and the pursuit of Happiness.

This immortal statement was made in the Declaration of Independence of the United States of America in 1776. In a broader

---

*The borrowing from the United States Declaration of Independence was open and intended. American members of the OSS mission parachuted to Ho in the summer of 1945 recall several of Ho's attempts to obtain a copy of the Declaration, or, failing this, a close approximation of its essential passages.

sense, this means: All the peoples on the earth are equal from birth, all the peoples have a right to live, to be happy and free.

The Declaration of the French Revolution made in 1791 on the Rights of Man and the Citizen also states: "All men are born free and with equal rights, and must always remain free and have equal rights."

Those are undeniable truths.

Nevertheless, for more than eighty years, the French imperialists, abusing the standard of Liberty, Equality, and Fraternity, have violated our Fatherland and oppressed our fellow citizens. They have acted contrary to the ideals of humanity and justice.

In the field of politics, they have deprived our people of every democratic liberty.

They have enforced inhuman laws; they have set up three distinct political regimes in the North, the Center, and the South of Viet-Nam in order to wreck our national unity and prevent our people from being united.

They have built more prisons than schools. They have mercilessly slain our patriots; they have drowned our uprisings in rivers of blood.

They have fettered public opinion; they have practiced obscurantism against our people.

To weaken our race they have forced us to use opium and alcohol.

In the field of economics, they have fleeced us to the backbone, impoverished our people and devastated our land.

They have robbed us of our rice fields, our mines, our forests, and our raw materials. They have monopolized the issuing of bank notes and the export trade.

They have invented numerous unjustifiable taxes and reduced our people, especially our peasantry, to a state of extreme poverty.

They have hampered the prospering of our national bourgeoisie; they have mercilessly exploited our workers.

In the autumn of 1940, when the Japanese fascists violated Indochina's territory to establish new bases in their fight against the Allies, the French imperialists went down on their bended knees and handed over our country to them.

Thus, from that date, our people were subjected to the double yoke of the French and the Japanese. Their sufferings and miseries increased. The result was that, from the end of last year to the beginning of this year, from Quang Tri Province to the North of Viet-Nam, more than two million of our fellow citizens died from starvation. On March 9 [1945], the French troops were disarmed by the Japanese. The French colonialists either fled or surrendered, showing that not only were they incapable of "protecting" us, but that, in the span of five years, they had twice sold our country to the Japanese.

On several occasions before March 9, the Viet Minh League urged the French to ally themselves with it against the Japanese. Instead of agreeing to this proposal, the French colonialists so intensified their terrorist activities against the Viet Minh members that before fleeing they massacred a great number of our political prisoners detained at Yen Bay and Cao Bang.

Notwithstanding all this, our fellow citizens have always manifested toward the French a tolerant and humane attitude. Even after the Japanese *Putsch* of March, 1945, the Viet Minh League helped many Frenchmen to cross the frontier, rescued some of them from Japanese jails, and protected French lives and property.

From the autumn of 1940, our country had in fact ceased to be a French colony and had become a Japanese possession.

After the Japanese had surrendered to the Allies, our whole people rose to regain our national sovereignty and to found the Democratic Republic of Viet-Nam.

The truth is that we have wrested our independence from the Japanese and not from the French.

The French have fled, the Japanese have capitulated, Emperor Bao Dai has abdicated. Our people have broken the chains which for nearly a century have fettered them and have won independence for the Fatherland. Our people at the same time have overthrown the monarchic regime that has reigned supreme for dozens of centuries. In its place has been established the present Democratic Republic.

For these reasons, we, members of the Provisional Government, representing the whole Vietnamese people, declare that from now on we break off all relations of a colonial character with France; we repeal all the international obligation that France has so far subscribed to on behalf of Viet-Nam, and we abolish all the special rights the French have unlawfully acquired in our Fatherland.

The whole Vietnamese people, animated by a common purpose, are determined to fight to the bitter end against any attempt by the French colonialists to reconquer their country.

We are convinced that the Allied nations, which at Teheran and San Francisco have acknowledged the principles of self-determination and equality of nations, will not refuse to acknowledge the independence of Viet-Nam.

A people who have courageously opposed French domination for more than eighty years, a people who have fought side by side with the Allies against the fascists during these last years, such a people must be free and independent.

For these reasons, we, members of the Provisional Government of the Democratic Republic of Viet-Nam, solemnly declare to the world that Viet-Nam has the right to be a free and independent country — and in fact it is so already. The entire Vietnamese people are determined to mobilize all their physical and mental strength, to sacrifice their lives and property in order to safeguard their independence and liberty.

IDEOLOGY OF THE CUBAN REVOLUTION*

Che Guevara

This is a unique revolution which some people maintain contradicts one of the most orthodox premises of the revolutionary movement, expressed by Lenin: "Without a revolutionary theory there is no revolutionary movement." It would be suitable to say that revolutionary theory, as the expression of a social truth, surpasses any declaration of it; that is to say, even if the theory is not known, the revolution can succeed if historical reality is interpreted correctly and if the forces involved are utilized correctly. Every revolution always incorporates elements of very different tendencies which, nevertheless, coincide in action and in the revolution's most immediate objectives.

It is clear that if the leaders have an adequate theoretical knowledge prior to the action, they can avoid trial and error whenever the adopted theory corresponds to the reality.

The principal actors of this revolution had no coherent theoretical criteria; but it cannot be said that they were ignorant of the various concepts of history, society, economics, and revolution which are being discussed in the world today.

Profound knowledge of reality, a close relationship with the people, the firmness of the liberator's objective, and the practical revolutionary experience gave to those leaders the chance to form a more complete theoretical concept.

The foregoing should be considered an introduction to the explanation of this curious phenomenon that has intrigued the entire world: the Cuban Revolution. It is a deed worthy of study in contemporary world history: the how and the why of a group of men who, shattered by an army enormously superior in technique and equipment, managed first to survive, soon became strong, later became stronger than the enemy in the battle zones, still later moved into new zones of combat, and finally defeated that enemy on the battlefield even though their troops were still very inferior in number.

Naturally we, who often do not show the requisite concern for theory, will not run the risk of expounding the truth of the Cuban Revolution as though we were its masters. We will simply try to give the bases from which one can interpret this truth. In fact, the Cuban Revolution must be separated into two absolutely distinct stages: that of the armed action up to January 1, 1959, and the political, economic and social transformations since then.

*Guevara wrote "Notes for the Study of the Ideology of the Cuban Revolution" for the October 8, 1960, issue of *Verde Olivo*, the magazine of Cuba's armed forces.

Even these two stages deserve further subdivisions; however, we will
not take them from the viewpoint of historical exposition, but from
the viewpoint of the evolution of the revolutionary thought of its
leaders through their contact with the people. Incidentally, here one
must introduce a general attitude toward one of the most controversial terms of the modern world: Marxism. When asked whether or
not we are Marxists, our position is the same as that of a physicist or
a biologist when asked if he is a "Newtonian," or if he is a "Pasteurian."

There are truths so evident, so much a part of people's knowledge,
that it is now useless to discuss them. One ought to be "Marxist"
with the same naturalness with which one is "Newtonian" in physics,
or "Pasteurian" in biology, considering that if facts determine new
concepts, these new concepts will never divest themselves of that
portion of truth possessed by the older concepts they have outdated.
Such is the case, for example, of Einsteinian relativity or of Planck's
"quantum" theory with respect to the discoveries of Newton; they
take nothing at all away from the greatness of the learned Englishman. Thanks to Newton, physics was able to advance until it had
achieved new concepts of space. The learned Englishman provided the
necessary stepping-stone for them.

The advances in social and political science, as in other fields,
belong to a long historical process whose links are connecting, adding
up, molding and constantly perfecting themselves. In the origin of
peoples, there exists a Chinese, Arab or Hindu mathematics; today,
mathematics has no frontiers. In the course of history there was a
Greek Pythagoras, an Italian Galileo, an English Newton, a German
Gauss, a Russian Lobachevsky, an Einstein, etc. Thus in the field of
social and political sciences, from Democritus to Marx, a long series
of thinkers added their original investigations and accumulated a
body of experience and of doctrines.

The merit of Marx is that he suddenly produces a qualitative
change in the history of social thought. He interprets history, understands its dynamic, predicts the future, but in addition to predicting
it (which would satisfy his scientific obligation), he expresses a
revolutionary concept: the world must not only be interpreted, it
must be transformed. Man ceases to be the slave and tool of his
environment and converts himself into the architect of his own
destiny. At that moment Marx puts himself in a position where he
becomes the necessary target of all who have a special interest in
maintaining the old—similar to Democritus before him, whose work
was burned by Plato and his disciples, the ideologues of Athenian
slave aristocracy. Beginning with the revolutionary Marx, a political
group with concrete ideas establishes itself. Basing itself on the giants,
Marx and Engels, and developing through successive steps with personalities like Lenin, Stalin, Mao Tse-tung and the new Soviet and
Chinese rulers, it establishes a body of doctrine and, let us say,
examples to follow.

The Cuban Revolution takes up Marx at the point where he himself left science to shoulder his revolutionary rifle. And it takes him up at that point, not in a revisionist spirit, of struggling against that which follows Marx, of reviving "pure" Marx, but simply because up to that point Marx, the scientist, placed himself outside of the history he studied and predicted. From then on Marx, the revolutionary, could fight within history.

We, practical revolutionaries, initiating our own struggle, simply fulfill laws foreseen by Marx, the scientist. We are simply adjusting ourselves to the predictions of the scientific Marx as we travel this road of rebellion, struggling against the old structure of power, supporting ourselves in the people for the destruction of this structure, and having the happiness of this people as the basis of our struggle. That is to say, and it is well to emphasize this once again: The laws of Marxism are present in the events of the Cuban Revolution, independently of what its leaders profess or fully know of those laws from a theoretical point of view. . . .

Each of those brief historical moments in the guerrilla warfare framed distinct social concepts and distinct appreciations of the Cuban reality; they outlined the thought of the military leaders of the revolution—those who in time would also take their position as political leaders.

Before the landing of the *Granma*, a mentality predominated that, to some degree, might be called "subjectivist": blind confidence in a rapid popular explosion, enthusiasm and faith in the power to liquidate the Batista regime by a swift, armed uprising combined with spontaneous revolutionary strikes, and the subsequent fall of the dictator. . . .

After the landing comes the defeat, the almost total destruction of the forces, and their regrouping and integration as guerrillas. Characteristic of those few survivors, imbued with the spirit of struggle, was the understanding that to count upon spontaneous outbursts throughout the island was a falsehood, an illusion. They understood also that the fight would have to be a long one and that it would need vast *campesino* participation. At this point, the *campesinos* entered the guerrilla war for the first time.

Two events—hardly important in terms of the number of combatants, but of great psychological value—were unleashed. First, antagonism that the city people, who comprised the central guerrilla group, felt towards the *campesinos* was erased. The *campesinos*, in turn, distrusted the group and, above all, feared barbarous reprisals of the government. Two things demonstrated themselves at this stage, both very important for the interrelated factors: To the *campesinos*, the bestialities of the army and all the persecution would not be sufficient to put an end to the guerrilla war, even though the army was certainly capable of liquidating the *campesinos'* homes, crops, and families. To take refuge with those in hiding was a good solution. In turn, the guerrilla fighters learned the necessity, each time more pointed, of winning the *campesino* masses. . . .

[Following the failure of Batista's major assault on the Rebel Army,] the war shows a new characteristic: The correlation of forces turns toward the revolution. Within a month and a half, two small columns, one of eighty and the other of a hundred forty men, constantly surrounded and harassed by an army that mobilized thousands of soldiers, crossed the plains of Camagüey, arrived at Las Villas, and began the job of cutting the island in two.

It may seem strange, incomprehensible, and even incredible that two columns of such small size—without communications, without mobility, without the most elementary arms of modern warfare—could fight against well-trained, and above all, well-armed troops.

Basic [to the victory] is the characteristic of each group: the fewer comforts the guerrilla fighter has, the more he is initiated into the rigors of nature, the more he feels himself at home; his morale is higher, his sense of security greater. At the same time, he has learned to risk his life in every circumstance that might arise, to trust it to luck, like a tossed coin; and in general, as a final result of this kind of combat, it matters little to the individual guerrilla whether or not he survives.

The enemy soldier in the Cuban example, which we are now considering, is the junior partner of the dictator; he is the man who gets the last crumbs left to him in a long line of profiteers that begins in Wall Street and ends with him. He is disposed to defend his privileges, but he is disposed to defend them only to the degree that they are important to him. His salary and pension are worth some suffering and some dangers, but they are never worth his life; if the price of maintaining them will cost it, he is better off giving them up, that is to say, withdrawing from the face of guerrilla danger. From these two concepts and these two morals springs the difference which would cause the crisis of December 31, 1958. . . .*

Here ends the insurrection. But the men who arrive in Havana after two years of arduous struggle in the mountains and plains of Oriente, in the plains of Camagüey, and in the mountains, plains, and cities of Las Villas, are not the same men, ideologically, who landed on the beaches of Las Coloradas, or who took part in the first phase of the struggle. Their distrust of the *campesino* has been converted into affection and respect for his virtues; their total ignorance of life in the country has been converted into a knowledge of the needs of our *guajiros* their flirtations with statistics and with theory have been fixed by the cement which is practice.

With the banner of Agrarian Reform, the execution of which begins in the Sierra Maestra, these men confront imperialism. They know that the Agrarian Reform is the basis upon which the new Cuba must build itself. They know also that the Agrarian Reform will give land to all the dispossessed, but that it will dispossess its unjust possessors;

*The day Batista was overthrown.

and they know that the greatest of the unjust possessors are also
influential men in the State Department or in the government of the
United States of America. But they have learned to conquer difficulties with bravery, with audacity and, above all, with the support of
the people; and they have now seen the future of liberation that
awaits us on the other side of our sufferings.

Counterrhetoric

OF TYRANNY

John Locke

As usurpation is the exercise of power which another has a right to,
so tyranny is the exercise of power beyond right, which nobody can
have a right to. And this is making use of the power any one has in
his hands, not for the good of those who are under it, but for his
own private separate advantage. When the governor, however entitled,
makes not the law, but his will the rule, and his commands and
actions are not directed to the preservation of the properties of his
people, but the satisfaction of his own ambition, revenge, covetous-
ness, or any other irregular passion.

  If one can doubt this to be truth or reason, because it comes from
the obscure hand of a subject, I hope the authority of a king will
make it pass with him. King James I. in his speech to the parliament,
1603, tells them thus: "I will ever prefer the weal of the public and
of the whole commonwealth, in making of good laws and constitutions, to any particular and private ends of mine—thinking ever the
wealth and weal of the commonwealth to be my greatest weal and
worldly felicity—a point wherein a lawful king doth directly differ
from a tyrant. For I do acknowledge that the special and greatest
point of difference that is between a rightful king and a usurping
tyrant is this: that whereas the proud and ambitious tyrant doth

think his kingdom and people are only ordained for satisfaction of his desires and unreasonable appetites, the righteous and just king doth, by the contrary, acknowledge himself to be ordained for the procuring of the wealth and property of his people." And again, in his speech to the parliament, 1609, he hath these words: "The king binds himself by a double oath to the observation of the fundamental laws of his kingdom. Tacitly, as by being a king, and so bound to protect as well the people as the laws of his kingdom, and expressly by his oath at his coronation; so as every just king, in a settled kingdom, is bound to observe that paction made to his people, by his laws in framing his government agreeable thereunto, according to that paction which God made with Noah after the Deluge. Hereafter, seedtime and harvest, and cold and heat, and summer and winter, and day and night, shall not cease while the earth remaineth. And therefore a king governing in a settled kingdom leaves to be a king and degenerates into a tyrant, as soon as he leaves off to rule according to his laws." And a little after, "Therefore all kings that are not tyrants, or perjured, will be glad to bound themselves within the limits of their laws. And they that persuade them the contrary are vipers and pests, both against them and the commonwealth." Thus that learned king, who well understood the notions of things, makes the difference betwixt a king and a tyrant to consist only in this, that one makes the laws the bounds of his power, and the good of the public the end of his government; the other makes all give way to his own will and appetite.

It is a mistake to think this fault is proper only to monarchies; other forms of government are liable to it as well as that. For wherever the power that is put in any hands for the government of the people and the preservation of their properties is applied to other ends, and made use of to impoverish, harass, or subdue them to the arbitrary irregular commands of those that have it, there it presently becomes tyranny, whether those that thus use it are one or many. Thus we read of the thirty tyrants at Athens, as well as one at Syracuse, and the intolerable dominion of the Decemviri at Rome was nothing better.

Wherever law ends tyranny begins, if the law be transgressed to another's harm. And whosoever in authority exceeds the power given him by the law, and makes use of the force he has under his command to compass that upon the subject which the law allows, not ceases in that to be a magistrate; and, acting without authority, may be opposed as any other man who by force invades the right of another. This is acknowledged in subordinate magistrates. He that hath authority to seize my person in the street may be opposed as a thief and a robber if he endeavor to break into my house to execute a writ, notwithstanding that I know he has such a warrant and such a legal authority as will empower him to arrest me abroad. And why this should not hold in the highest, as well as in the most inferior magistrate, I would gladly be informed. Is it reasonable that the eldest brother, because he has the greatest part of his father's estate, should thereby have a right to take away any of his younger brother's portions? Or that a rich man, who possessed a whole country, should from thence have a right to seize, when he pleased, the cottage and garden of his poor neighbor? The being rightfully possessed of great power and riches exceedingly beyond the greatest part of the sons of Adam is so far from being an excuse, much less a reason, for rapine and oppression, which the endamaging one another without authority is, that it is a great aggravation of it. For the exceeding the bounds of authority is no more a right in a great than a petty officer, no more justifiable in a king than a constable; but is so much the worse in him in that he has more trust put in him, has already a much greater share than the rest of his brethren, and is supposed, from the advantages of his education, employment, and counselors, to be more knowing in the measures of right and wrong.

May the commands then of a prince be opposed? May he be resisted as often as any one shall find himself aggrieved, and but imagine he has not a right done him? This will unhinge and overturn all polities, and, instead of government and order, leave nothing but anarchy and confusion.

To this I answer that force is to be opposed to nothing but to unjust and unlawful force; whoever makes any opposition in any other case draws on himself a just condemnation both from God and man, and so no such danger or confusion will follow, as is often suggested. For:

Firstly, as in some countries, the person of the prince by law is sacred, and so whatever he commands or does his person is still free from all question or violence, not liable to force, or any judicial censure or condemnation. But yet opposition may be made to the illegal acts of any inferior officer, or other commissioned by him, unless he will, by actually putting himself into a state of war with his people, dissolve the government, and leave them to that defense which belongs to every one in the state of nature. For of such things who can tell what the end will be? And a neighbor kingdom has shown the world an odd example. In all other cases the sacredness of the person exempts him from all inconveniences, whereby he is secure, whilst the government stands from all violence and harm whatsoever, than which there cannot be a wiser constitution. For the harm he can do in his own person not being likely to happen often, nor to extend itself far, nor being able by his single strength to subvert the laws, nor oppress the body of the people, should any prince have so much weakness and ill nature as to be willing to do it, the inconveniency of some particular mischiefs that may happen sometimes when a heady prince comes to the throne are well recompensed by the peace of the public and security of the government in the person of the chief magistrate thus set out of the reach of danger; it being safer for the body that some few private men should be sometimes in danger to suffer than that the head of the republic should be easily and upon slight occasions exposed.

Secondly, but this privilege belonging only to the king's person, hinders not, but they may be questioned, opposed, and resisted who use unjust force, though they pretend a commission from him which the law authorizes not. As is plain in the case of him that has the king's writ to arrest a man, which is a full commission from the king, and yet he that has it cannot break open a man's house to do it, nor execute this command of the king upon certain days, nor in certain places, though this commission have no such exception in it, but they are the limitations of the law, which, if any one transgress, the king's commission excuses him not. For the king's authority being given him only by the law, he cannot empower any one to act against the law, or justify him by his commission in so doing; the commission or command of any magistrate where he has no authority being as void and insignificant as that of any private man. The difference between the one and the other being that the magistrate has some authority so far and to such ends, and the private man has none at all. For it is not the commission, but the authority, that gives the right of acting, and against the laws there can be no authority; but, notwithstanding such resistance, the king's person and authority are still both secured, and so no danger to governor or government.

Thirdly, supposing a government wherein the person of the chief magistrate is not thus sacred, yet this doctrine of the lawfulness of resisting all unlawful exercises of his power will not, upon every slight occasion, endanger him or embroil the government. For where the injured party may be relieved, and his damages repaired by appeal to the law, there can be no pretense for force, which is only to be used where a man is intercepted for appealing to the law. For nothing is to be accounted hostile force but where it leaves not the remedy of such an appeal. And it is such force alone that puts him that uses it into a state of war, and makes it lawful to resist him. A man with a sword in his hand demands my purse in the highway, when perhaps I have not 12d. in my pocket; this man I may lawfully kill. To another I deliver £100 to hold only whilst I alight, which he refuses to restore me when I am got up again, but draws his sword to defend the possession of it by force if I endeavor to retake it. The mischief this man does me is a hundred, or possibly a thousand times more than the other perhaps intended me (whom I killed before he really did me any), and yet I might lawfully kill the one, and cannot so much as hurt the other lawfully. The reason whereof is plain, because the one using force, which threatened my life, I could not have time to appeal to the law to secure it, and when it was gone it was too late to appeal. The law could not restore life to my dead carcass. The loss was irreparable, which, to prevent the law of nature, gave me a right to destroy him who had put himself into a state of war with me, and threatened my destruction. But in the other case, my life not being in danger, I may have the benefit of appealing to the law, and have reparation for my £100 that way.

Fourthly, but if the unlawful acts done by the magistrate be maintained (by the power he has got), and the remedy which is due by law be, by the same power, obstructed, yet the right of resisting, even in such manifest acts of tyranny, will not suddenly or on slight occasions disturb the government. For if it reach no further than some private men's cases, though they have a right to defend themselves and recover by force what by unlawful force is taken from them, yet the right to do so will not easily engage them in a contest wherein they are sure to perish; it being as impossible for one or a few oppressed men to disturb the government, where the body of the people do not think themselves concerned in it, as for a raving madman or heady malcontent to overturn a well-settled state, the people being as little apt to follow the one as the other.

But if either these illegal acts have extended to the majority of the people, or if the mischief and oppression has light only on some few, but in such cases as the precedent, and consequences seem to threaten all, and they are persuaded in their consciences, and their laws, and with them their estates, liberties, and lives are in danger, and perhaps their religion too, how they will be hindered from resisting illegal force used against them I cannot tell. This is an inconvenience, I confess, that attends all governments whatsoever when the governors have brought it to this pass to be generally suspected of their people; the most dangerous state which they can possibly put themselves in, wherein they are the less to be pitied, because it is so easy to be avoided—it being impossible for a governor, if he really means the good of his people, and the preservation of them and their laws together, not to make them see and feel it, as it is for the father of a family not to let his children see he loves and takes care of them.

But if all the world shall observe pretenses of one kind and actions of another; arts used to elude the law, and trust of prerogative (which is an arbitrary power in some things left in the prince's hand to do good, not harm to the people) employed contrary to the end for which it was given. If the people shall find the ministers and subordinate magistrate chosen suitable to such ends, and favored or laid by proportionably as they promote or oppose them; if they see several experiments made of arbitary power, and that religion underhand favored (though publicly proclaimed against) which is readiest to introduce it, and the operators in it supported as much as may be; and when that cannot be done, yet approved still, and liked the better; if a long train of actings show the councils all tending that way, how can a man any more hinder himself from being persuaded in his own mind which way things are going, or from casting about how to save himself, than he could from believing the captain of the ship he was in was carrying him and the rest of the company to

Algiers when he found him always steering that course, though cross
winds, leaks in his ship, and want of men and provisions did often
force him to turn his course another way for some time, which he
steadily returned to again as soon as the wind, weather, and other
circumstances would let him?

AMERICA 1968:
THE POLITICS OF VIOLENCE*

Arthur M. Schlesinger, Jr.

The world today is asking a terrible question—a question which every
citizen of this Republic should be putting to himself: what sort of
people are we, we Americans?

And the answer which much of the world is bound to return is that
we are today the most frightening people on this planet.

We are a frightening people because for three years we have been
devastating a small country on the other side of the world in a war
which bears no rational relationship to our national security or our
national interest.

We are a frightening people because we have already in this decade
murdered the two of our citizens who stood preeminently before the
world as the embodiments of American idealism—and because last
night we tried to murder a third.

We are a frightening people because the atrocities we commit
hardly touch our official self-righteousness, our invincible conviction
of our moral infallibility.

The ghastly things we do to our own people, the ghastly things we
do to other people—these must at last compel us to look searchingly
at ourselves and our society before hatred and violence rush us on to
more evil and finally tear our nation apart.

We cannot take the easy course and blame everyone but ourselves
for the things we do. We cannot blame the epidemic of murder at
home on deranged and solitary individuals separate from the rest of
us. For these individuals are plainly weak and suggestible men,

*These words were spoken by Mr. Schlesinger while Senator Robert
Kennedy lay dying in a Los Angeles hospital. The occasion was the commencement ceremony at the City University of New York. The site was Bryant Park
behind the New York Public Library. Robed graduates and professors, loiterers,
bums, passing businessmen, parents, and mothers with small children made up
the audience; from everywhere came the violent sounds of the great city.

stamped by our society with a birthright of hatred and a compulsion toward violence.

We cannot blame our epidemic of murder abroad on the wickedness of those who will not conform to our views of how they should behave and how they should live. For the zeal with which we have pursued an irrational war suggests the internal impulses of hatred and violence demanding outlet and shaping our foreign policy to their ends.

We must recognize that the evil is in us, that it springs from some dark, intolerable tension in our history and our institutions. It is almost as if a primal curse had been fixed on our nation, perhaps when we first began the practice of killing and enslaving those whom we deemed our inferiors because their skin was another color. We are a violent people with a violent history, and the instinct for violence has seeped into the bloodstream of our national life.

We are also, at our best, a generous and idealistic people. Our great leaders—Lincoln most of all—have perceived both the destructive instinct and the moral necessity of transcending destruction if we are going to have any sort of rational and decent society. They have realized how fragile the membranes of our civilization are, stretched so thin over a nation so disparate in its composition, so tense in its interior relationships, so cunningly enmeshed in underground fears and antagonisms, so entrapped by history in the ethos of violence.

Now, as our nation grows more centralized, our energy more concentrated, our inner tensions more desperate, our frustrations in our own land and in the world more embittered, we can no longer regard hatred and violence as accidents and aberrations, as nightmares which will pass away when we awake. We must see them as organic in our national past; we must confront them; we must uncover the roots of hatred and violence and, through self-knowledge, move toward self-control. And we must exert every effort in the meantime to protect and strengthen the membranes of civility against the impulses of destruction.

In this effort, a special responsibility lies on our intellectual community. For one can expect primitive emotions on the part of those who occupy the right wing of our national politics But the intellectual community should be the particular custodian of the life of reason. It should be the particular champion of discipline and restraint. It should be the particular enemy of hatred and violence.

Little is more dismaying than the way in which some, a few, in the intellectual community have rejected the life of reason, have succumbed to the national susceptibility for hatred and violence, have, indeed, begun themselves to exalt hatred and violence as if primitivism in emotion constituted a higher morality. I do not suggest that such intellectuals are responsible for the atrocities committed at home and abroad. I do suggest that they have contributed to the atmosphere which has begun to legitimize hatred and violence. I do suggest that they are reinforcing the assault on civility and

hastening the decomposition of the American social process.
Some wonder, no doubt, whether that social process is worth
saving. But the alternative to process is anarchy, where those who use
the means of violence win out; and the intellectual community will
always lose in this competition. Our process, with all its defects, is a
process of change—peaceful change—on which all decency and rationality depend.

Let me make it clear that I am not talking about the student
uprisings of recent weeks. I have no question that on balance the
world stands to gain from student protest. No doubt such protest has
on occasion led to excess. But it is already a shameful state of affairs
when excess proves the only way of attracting the attention of
complacent university administrations and indifferent faculties to the
problems and perplexities of the coming generation.

The causes of student insurgency vary from college to college, and
from country to country. It would seem likely that the primary
incitement in our own nation has been the war in Vietnam—a war
which has tempted our government into its course of appalling and
insensate destruction, a war which, through the draft, has demanded
that young Americans kill and die where they can see no rational
relationship between personal sacrifice and national interest. But the
cause is also more than the Vietnam war. For that war has come for
many to prefigure a larger incomprehensibility, a larger absurdity,
even a larger wickedness, in our offical society. For some it has come
to seem, not an aberration, but the inevitable result of the irremedi-
able corruption of the American system.

I cannot share the belief that there was something foreordained and
ineluctable about the war in Vietnam—that the nature of American
society would have compelled any set of men in Washington to
pursue the same course of folly. This really seems determinist nonsense. One can still understand, though, why the contradictions of
our society weigh so heavily on the young—the contradictions between the righteousness of a Secretary of State and the ruthlessness
of a B-52; between the notion that violence is fine against simple folk
10,000 miles away and shocking against injustice in our own land;
between the equality demanded by our constitutional structure and
the equality denied by our social structure; even between the accepted habits of one generation and the emerging habits of the next,
as when a parent tipsy on his fourth martini begins a tirade against
marijuana.

The very weight of these contradictions has produced a rush of
despair about libertarian democracy itself. By libertarian democracy I
mean simply the system in which the rule of the majority at any
given time rests on the guarantee of the right of minorities to convert
themselves into new majorities. Such a system assumes political action to be in its essence a rational process—that is, a deliberate choice
of means to achieve desired ends. As a rational process, libertarian
democracy requires the widest possible freedom of discussion and

debate; and this implies, of course, a considerable indulgence of wrongheadedness and imbecility along the way.

This has been the American theory, as laid down, for example, in the Constitution and the Bill of Rights. And, in the course of our national history, libertarian democracy has led to many useful results. It has also led to many frustrations. It has left problems unsolved, wrongs unredressed, and sinners unpunished. It cannot be relied upon to produce rapid and conclusive change. The very insistence on reasonableness and due process has seemed at times a pretext for inaction and therefore a mask for injustice. This has been particularly the case in recent years. From the moment we started bombing North Vietnam in February 1965, our government appeared rigidly and sanctimoniously unresponsive to reasoned criticism of its course. Increasingly persuaded that change was impossible within the constitutional order, people started to turn to civil disobedience, emotional agitation, and even violent protest. A sense began to arise that libertarian democracy itself was impotent in the new world of economic, military, and intellectual corporatism. One saw a growing conviction, especially among the young, that party politics were a facade and a fake. One saw a growing cynicism about democratic institutions, a growing defection from the democratic process. In due course, the spreading sense of the impotence of libertarian democracy generated a creed systematically and candidly opposed to libertarian democracy.

The new creed has two parts. The first part is an attempt to clear away what its theorists regard as the noxious rubbish of the Bill of Rights. The new creed thus perceives the First Amendment as the keystone, not of liberty, but of a wicked apparatus of tolerance employed by an oppressive social order to thwart basic change. I do not wish to do this new doctrine an injustice, so I will state in the words of its leading advocate—that is, Herbert Marcuse—its belief that it is *necessary* and *right*, as a matter of principle, to suppress views with which one disagrees and to howl down those who utter such views.

Mr. Marcuse begins with the proposition that contemporary society has absorbed and abolished the historic means of social revolution. It has done this through an ingenious and despicable combination of welfarism, tolerance, and manipulation. Capitalism, in short, subverts potential opponents by offering a measure of apparent economic security and personal freedom.

Mr. Marcuse is determined to expose this state of affairs. As he sees it, any improvement in the condition of the powerless and the oppressed only plays into the hands of the rulers—and is therefore to be regretted. And the device of tolerance is particularly evil because it renders "the traditional ways and means of protest ineffective— perhaps even dangerous because they preserve the illusion of popular sovereignty."

The way to revive the hope of social change, Mr. Marcuse suggests, is therefore to do away with tolerance: "Certain things cannot be said, certain ideas cannot be expressed, certain policies cannot be proposed, certain behavior cannot be permitted without making tolerance an instrument for the continuation of servitude." He is commendably specific about what he would forbid. His program, as he states it,

...would include the withdrawal of toleration of speech and assembly from groups and movements which promote aggressive policies, armament, chauvinism, discrimination on the grounds of race and religions, or which oppose the extension of public services, medical care, etc. Moreover, the restoration of freedom of thought may necessitate new and rigid restrictions on teachings and practices in the educational institutions.

Mr. Marcuse's call for the forcible suppression of false ideas is, I have suggested, only the first part of the new creed. Nor is such an assault on the Bill of Rights new, even for radicals. The Stalinists of the 'thirties, for example, had no compunction in arguing in much the same way that civil freedom should be denied those who resist the Stalinist truth. What particularly distinguishes the New Left of the 'sixties from previous American radicalisms is the second part of its creed—and here not the summons to revolution, which again is familiar, but the refusal to state revolutionary goals except in the most abstract and empty language. To put it more precisely, what distinguishes the New Left is not only its unwillingness to define what it aims for after the revolution but its belief that such reticence is a virtue.

On its positive side, the new creed becomes, so to speak, a kind of existentialism in politics—a primitive kind, no doubt, but still rooted in some manner in the existential perception that man dwells in an absurd universe and defines himself through his choices. In extreme cases, this perception may lead to *voyages au bout de la nuit*: as Nietzsche said, "Nihilism represents the ultimate logical conclusion of our great values and ideals—because we must experience nihilism before we can find out what value these 'values' really had." In its serious form, existentialism can lead to an immense and intense sense of individual responsibility as every man realizes that only he can provide his own escape from the enveloping nothingness around him. In its vulgar form, however, with which we are dealing here, existential politics becomes the notion that we must feel and act before we think; it is the illusion that the experience of feeling and action will produce the insight and the policy.

Existential politics in this form springs much more from Sorel than from Kierkegaard. Georges Sorel, you will recall, drew a distinction between myths, which, he said, were "not descriptions of things, but expressions of a determination to act," and utopias, which were intellectual products, the work of theorists who "seek to establish a model to which they can compare existing society." Sorel regarded utopias—that is, rational programs—as contemptible. The myth must be the basis of action; the myth would produce the revolution, which would thereafter produce its own program; and "the myth," Sorel emphasized, "must be judged as a means of acting on the present; any attempt to discuss how far it can be taken literally as future history is devoid of sense." So, in the footsteps of Sorel, the New Leftists believe in the omnipotence of the deed and the irrelevance of the goal. The political process is no longer seen as the deliberate choice of means to move toward a desired end. Where libertarian democracy had ideally demanded means consistent with the end, and where the Stalinist left of the 'thirties contended that the end justified the means, the New Left propounds a different doctrine: that the means create the end.

Let us not ignore the attractions of the existential approach. After all, there are many absurdities in our world. Our country has never undertaken anything more absurd in its history than the Vietnam war. After all, a man does make himself by his decisions. After all, our conventional liberalism is to a discouraging degree a liberalism of promises and excuses. After all, social renewal can only come from personal commitment.

All these things help explain, I think, the appeal of the new creed. Yet this creed contains so much in the way of fakery and fallacy—to put it bluntly, it is so preposterous and so depraved—that I do not see how it can be long entertained by any serious democrat.

Let us look first at the negative part; the demand for the forcible suppression of false ideas. This immediately raises a self-evident question: how is one to tell which ideas are admissible and which are to be suppressed? "In the interplay of theory and practice," Mr. Marcuse replies, "true and false solutions become distinguishable. . . . Freedom is liberation, a specific historical process in theory and practice, and as such it has its right and wrong, its truth and falsehood." But who is to make this determination? What agency is the repository of final judgment on truth and falsehood? Here, alas, Mr. Marcuse lets us down. His standards are hopelessly vague, and in the end he places his confidence in what he mystically calls "the democratic educational dictatorship of free men."

This is not very satisfactory; so let us pursue the question a step further. I suppose that the new creed does not expect to make such judgments through a man. But, if not through a man, these judgments must be made through a mechanism, which means through men. Such a mechanism would plainly have to have an extraordinary degree of power. What assurance can there ever be that this power would be used disinterestedly—that is, for the good and the true, should there ever be a means of defining the good and the true— rather than in the interests of the men operating the mechanism? What will this mechanism become—what have such mechanisms ever become—but a means for the suppression of all criticism of the manipulators of the mechanism? So the mechanism, in the end, rests on an assumption of human infallibility.

But the assumption of human infallibility has never been justified in the long and varied history of mankind. It implies the rule of those whom Mr. Dooley long ago defined as men who do what they think "th' Lord wud do if He only knew the facts in th' case"—and Mr. Dooley was defining a fanatic.

Not only do men who claim infallibility in politics do far more evil than good; but the systematic suppression of supposedly false ideas would deeply constrict and impoverish human knowledge and understanding. "There is no error so crooked," Tupper said, "but it hath in it some lines of truth." Or, as Norman Mailer recently put it, "Sometimes a profound idea is buried in a particularly ugly notion." Human creativity takes a marvelous and sinister diversity of forms. How dare anyone assume the right to censor and deny the unlimited freedom of human expression? "I tolerate with the utmost latitude the right of others to differ from me in opinion without imputing to them criminality," wrote Jefferson. "I know too well the weakness and uncertainty of human reason to wonder at its different result."

The demand for the forcible suppression of "false" ideas would be an enormously effective way of calling a halt to human progress. Nor does the other half of the new creed make any more sense: that is, the conviction that one should feel and act first and think later, that the means create the end. The kind of action supremely required to strike through the mask of offical society, we are told, is violence. Without violence, official society, in its present sophisticated condition, will calmly co-opt and emasculate the opposition. Only violence will force official society to drop the smiling mask of tolerance and reveal its inner viciousness. More than this, violence becomes a means of social and individual redemption. As Frantz Fanon has written, "Violence is a cleaning force. It frees the native from his inferiority complex and from his despair and inaction; it makes him fearless and restores his self-respect. . . . Violence alone, violence committed by the people, violence organized and educated by its leaders, makes it possible for the masses to understand social truths."

This is hardly, of course, a new doctrine. Others in this century have propagated the cult of the deed. Mussolini and Hitler celebrated violence, because violence, by abolishing the procedures and civilities of society, opens the way for those who are most successful in the use of force. I do not know about the situation in developing countries; there violence in certain contexts may have the benign effects claimed by Fanon. But surely little is more pathetic than the view that violence in American society will benefit the left. A limited amount of violence may stimulate the process of democratic change; but, if the left, through the cult of the deed, helps create an atmosphere which destroys the process of democracy itself, the winners will be those who use violence best, and they will be on the right.

The new creed, with its dismissal of free discussion and its conviction that violence will mystically generate policy and program, represents an assault on rationality in politics—an assault based on the ultimate proposition that rights and wrongs in public affairs are so absolute and so easily ascertainable that opposition can be legitimately destroyed. This assault on the Bill of Rights and on libertarian democracy is in my judgment wrong, because no one is infallible. It is stupid, because the beneficiaries of this view will not be the idealists of the left but the brutalists of the right. It is dangerous because it represents a reversion to and rationalization of the strain of hatred and violence in our own national tradition: the politics of lynch law against the politics of Lincoln. It is a vote for the worst against the best in our political ethos.

The new creed above all overlooks the fact of human fraility. "Men are not flattered," wrote Lincoln, "by being shown that there has been a difference of purpose between the Almighty and them." Yet men are not gods. That is why absolutism always fails in human society. Democracy requires consent—it insists, that is, that a majority of the electorate be persuaded that one course is preferable to another. If men or mechanisms were infallible, there would be no need for persuasion. But, because they are not, the discipline of consent is indispensable to civilized society. The discipline of consent means the policies must triumph not through divine right or through a "democratic educational dictatorship" but through making sense to a majority of the people; and the condition of bringing a majority along is the best guarantee that policies relate, not to personal fantasy or personal power, but to the greatest good of the greatest number.

This discussion of the new creed may seem irrelevant to the pragmatic insurgencies of our society. And, indeed, so long as these insurgencies remain pragmatic—that is, related to specific issues and specific injustices—they represent a desperately needed pressure against the established complacencies of a self-righteous nation. Yet the new creed exists; it has received serious, if not convincing, formulation; it has won support because of the spreading sense in recent years of the impotence of libertarian democracy; and it has created among some of the young a mystical passion for revolutionary upheaval.

I have said that the new creed will only weaken democracy against its enemies. I would say further that it underestimates the power of rational democracy—that is, the power of the people, in one way or another, to modify the system and alter its course. We have had, I noted earlier, a season of despair about our democracy. But those whom despair led on to desperation underestimated the capacity of public opinion eventually to catch on to what is happening, even in fairly controlled and manipulated societies, and to demand a change in things. This has happened even in authoritarian states, like France. It has happened even in communist states, like Czechoslovakia. And it has happened in our own country.

Here the democratic process has turned out to be more effective than its critics had supposed. The rebellion against libertarian democracy gathered momentum, we have noted, because of the obstinate and righteous determination of our government to pursue a policy of military escalation in Vietnam. Yet in the last six months the democratic process, working in its own inscrutable way, has forced the President to abandon—for a moment, at least—the escalation policy; it has forced him to begin serious peace talks; it has forced him to withdraw from the Presidential contest. These are not inconsiderable accomplishments.

I do not contend that the process works swiftly. Obviously if President Johnson had given his March 31 speech a year earlier, many Americans and Vietnamese, now dead, might be alive; and the evidence against the escalation policy was just as strong on March 31, 1967, as it was on March 31, 1968. Nor do I contend that the process works surely. There is no guarantee against the reescalation of the war. Nor is there any guarantee, given the irresponsibility of the romantic left, against the election of a President committed to continue the persons and policies against which the rebellion began. Nor, alas, is there any guarantee against the resurgence of violence, bloodshed, and murder. Yet, with all its tardiness and inconclusiveness, democracy in America continues to show a certain vitality and efficacy. "The sober, second thought of the people," as Martin Van Buren said years ago, "is never wrong, and always efficient." At any rate, it is wiser in the long run than the certitudes of the absolutists.

Nietzsche once wrote, "Gaze not too deeply into the abyss, lest the abyss gaze into you." Those who claim to be bearers of absolute truth are men who have gazed too deeply into the abyss. They have committed what Hawthorne called the Unpardonable Sin—the sin of self-pride, which destroys discrimination, enslaves people, breeds fanaticism and violence, and concludes in madness and catastrophe. It is sad when the derelicts of our society surrender to the Unpardonable Sin; it is contemptible when our intellectuals exemplify it. Let us strike out against the concrete and particular evils of our time. But let us not yield to that awful despair which dissolves all distinctions in thought and action and hurtles us on to the politics of apocalypse. In the long run, any sane society must rest on freedom and reason. If we abandon this, we abandon everything.

If we are to survive as a nation, we must resist our inbred impulse to violence, not capitulate to it, not celebrate it. We must resist our inbred impulse to intolerance. We must resist our inbred impulse to absolutism. As we identify these impulses, as we strive against them wherever they appear—whether in the gutter press or in the abstractions of intellectuals—we create a chance of defying the winds of unreason. But we cannot suppose that this problem will solve itself. We must, indeed, define ourselves by our choices, but do so by making the choices which respect human reason and human dignity; the choices which acknowledge and nourish the human capacity for mutual respect and affection.

When Martin Luther King was murdered, Robert Kennedy broke the news of his death to a black audience on a street corner in Indianapolis. He said:

... we can make an effort, as Martin Luther King did, to understand and to comprehend, and to replace that violence, that stain of bloodshed that has spread across our land, with an effort to understand with compassion and love. ... I had a member of my family killed, but he was killed by a white man. But we have to make an effort in the United States, we have to make an effort to understand. ... What we need ... is not division; what we need ... is not hatred; what we need ... is not violence or lawlessness, but love and wisdom, and compassion toward one another, and a feeling of justice towards those who still suffer within our country, whether they be white or they be black.

Robert Kennedy concluded with a quotation from Aeschylus: "In our sleep, pain which cannot forget falls drop by drop upon the heart until, in our own despair, against our will, comes wisdom through the awful grace of God."

III

Revolution and the Social Order

"O God that madest this beautiful earth, when will it be ready to receive thy saints? How long, O Lord, how long?"

George Bernard Shaw, *Saint Joan*

THE APOLOGY OF SOCRATES

Plato

How you, O Athenians, have been affected by my accusers, I cannot tell; but I know that they almost made me forget who I was—so persuasively did they speak; and yet they have hardly uttered a word of truth. But of the many falsehoods told by them, there was one which quite amazed me;—I mean when they said that you should be upon your guard and not allow yourselves to be deceived by the force of my eloquence. To say this, when they were certain to be detected as soon as I opened my lips and proved myself to be anything but a great speaker, did indeed appear to me most shameless—unless by the force of eloquence they mean the force of truth; for if such is their meaning, I admit that I am eloquent. But in how different a way from theirs! Well, as I was saying, they have scarcely spoken the truth at all; but from me you shall hear the whole truth; not, however, delivered after their manner in a set oration duly ornamented with words and phrases. No, by heaven! but I shall use the words and argument which occur to me at the moment; for I am confident in the justice of my cause: at my time of life I ought not to be appearing before you, O men of Athens, in the character of a juvenile orator—let no one expect it of me. And I must beg of you to grant me a favour:—if I defend myself in my accustomed manner, and you hear me using the words which I have been in the habit of using in the agora, at the tables of the money-changers, or anywhere else, I would ask you not to be surprised, and not to interrupt me on this account. For I am more than seventy years of age, and appearing now for the first time in a court of law, I am quite a stranger to the language of the place; and therefore I would have you regard me as if I were really a stranger, whom you would excuse if he spoke in his native tongue, and after the fashion of his country:—Am I making an unfair request of you? Never mind the manner, which may or may not be good; but think only of the truth of my words, and give heed to that: let the speaker speak truly and the judge decide justly.

And first, I have to reply to the older charges and to my first accusers, and then I will go on to the later ones. For of old I have had many accusers, who have accused me falsely to you during many years; and I am more afraid of them than of Anytus and his associates, who are dangerous, too, in their own way. But far more dangerous are the others, who began when you were children, and took possession of your minds with their falsehoods, telling of one Socrates, a wise man, who speculated about the heaven above, and searched into the earth beneath, and made the worse appear the better cause. The disseminators of this tale are the accusers whom I dread; for their hearers are apt to fancy that such enquirers do not believe in the existence of the gods. And they are many, and their charges against me are of ancient date, and they were made by them in the days when you were more impressible than you are now—in childhood, or it may have been in youth—and the cause when heard went by default, for there was none to answer. And hardest of all, I do not know and cannot tell the names of my accusers; unless in the chance case of a comic poet. All who from envy and malice have persuaded you—some of them having first convinced themselves—all this class of men are most difficult to deal with; for I cannot have them up here, and cross-examine them, and therefore I must simply fight with shadows in my own defence, and argue when there is no one who answers. I will ask you then to assume with me, as I was saying, that my opponents are of two kinds; one recent, the other ancient: and I hope that you will see the propriety of my answering the latter first, for these accusations you heard long before the others, and much oftener.

Well, then, I must make my defence, and endeavour to clear away in a short time, a slander which has lasted a long time. May I succeed, if to succeed be for my good and yours, or likely to avail me in my cause! The task is not an easy one; I quite understand the nature of it. And so leaving the event with God, in obedience to the law I will now make my defence.

I will begin at the beginning, and ask what is the accusation which has given rise to the slander of me, and in fact has encouraged Meletus to prefer this charge against me. Well, what do the slanderers say? They shall be my prosecutors, and I will sum up their words in an affidavit: "Socrates is an evildoer, and a curious person, who searches into things under the earth and in heaven, and he makes the worse appear the better cause; and he teaches the aforesaid doctrines to others." Such is the nature of the accusation: it is just what you have yourselves seen in the comedy of Aristophanes, who has introduced a man whom he calls Socrates, going about and saying that he walks in air, and talking a deal of nonsense concerning matters of which I do not pretend to know either much or little—not that I mean to speak disparagingly of any one who is a student of natural philosophy. I should be very sorry if Meletus could bring so grave a charge against me. But the simple truth is, O Athenians, that I have nothing to do with physical speculations. Very many of those here present are witnesses to the truth of this, and to them I appeal. Speak then, you who have heard me, and tell your neighbours whether any of you have ever known me hold forth in few words or in many upon such matters. . . . You hear their answer. And from what they say of this part of the charge you will be able to judge of the truth of the rest.

As little foundation is there for the report that I am a teacher and take money; this accusation has no more truth in it than the other. Although, if a man were really able to instruct mankind, to receive money for giving instruction would, in my opinion, be an honour to him. There is Gorgias of Leontium, and Prodicus of Ceos, and Hippias of Elis, who go the round of the cities, and are able to persuade the young men to leave their own citizens by whom they might be taught for nothing, and come to them whom they not only pay, but are thankful if they may be allowed to pay them. There is at this time a Parian philosopher residing in Athens, of whom I have heard; and I came to hear of him in this way:—I came across a man who has spent a world of money on the Sophists, Callias, the son of Hipponicus, and knowing that he had sons, I asked him: "Callias," I said, "if your two sons were foals or calves, there would be no difficulty in finding some one to put over them; we should hire a trainer of horses, or a farmer, probably, who would improve and perfect them in their own proper virtue and excellence; but as they are human beings, whom are you thinking of placing over them? Is there any one who understands human and political virtue? You must have thought about the matter, for you have sons; is there any one?" "There is," he said. "Who is he?" said I; "and of what country? and what does he charge?" "Evenus the Parian," he replied; "he is the man, and his charge is five minae." Happy is Evenus, I said to myself, if he really has this wisdom, and teaches at such a moderate charge. Had I the same, I should have been very proud and conceited; but the truth is that I have no knowledge of the kind.

I dare say, Athenians, that some one among you will reply, "Yes, Socrates, but what is the origin of these accusations which are brought against you; there must have been something strange which you have been doing? All these rumours and this talk about you would never have arisen if you had been like other men: tell us, then, what is the cause of them, for we should be sorry to judge hastily of you." Now, I regard this as a fair challenge, and I will endeavor to explain to you the reason why I am called wise and have such an evil fame. Please to attend then. And although some of you may think that I am joking, I declare that I will tell you the entire truth. Men of Athens, this reputation of mine has come of a certain sort of wisdom which I possess. If you ask me what kind of wisdom, I reply, wisdom such as may perhaps be attained by man, for to that extent I am inclined to believe that I am wise; whereas the persons of whom I was speaking have a superhuman wisdom, which I may fail to describe, because I have it not myself; and he who says that I have, speaks falsely, and is taking away my character. And here, O men of Athens, I must beg you not to interrupt me, even if I seem to say something extravagant. For the word which I will speak is not mine. I will refer you to a witness who is worthy of credit; that witness shall be the God of Delphi—he will tell you about my wisdom, if I have any, and of what sort it is. You must have known Chaerephon; he was early a friend of mine and also a friend of yours, for he shared in the recent exile of the people, and returned with you. Well, Chaerephon, as you know, was very impetuous in all his doings, and he went to Delphi and boldly asked the oracle to tell him whether—as I was saying, I must beg you not to interrupt—he asked the oracle to tell him whether any one was wiser than I was, and the Pythian prophetess answered, that there was no man wiser. Chaerephon is dead himself; but his brother, who is in court, will confirm the truth of what I am saying.

Why do I mention this? Because I am going to explain to you why I have such an evil name. When I heard the answer, I said to myself What can the God mean? and what is the interpretation of his riddle? for I know that I have no wisdom, small or great. What then can he mean when he says that I am the wisest of men? And yet he is a god, and cannot lie; that would be against his nature. After long consideration, I though of a method of trying the question. I reflected that if I could only find a man wiser than myself, then I might go to the god with a refutation in my hand. I should say to him, "Here is a man who is wiser than I am; but you said that I was the wisest." Accordingly I went to one who had the reputation of wisdom, and observed him—his name I need not mention; he was a politician whom I selected for examination—and the result was as follows: When I began to talk with him, I could not help thinking that he was not really wise, although he was thought wise by many, and still wiser by himself; and thereupon I tried to explain to him that he thought himself wise, but was not really wise; and the consequence was that he hated me, and his enmity was shared by several who were present and heard me. So I left him, saying to myself, as I went away: Well, although I do not suppose that either of us knows anything really beautiful and good, I am better off than he is—for he knows nothing, and thinks that he knows; I neither know nor think that I know. In this latter particular, then, I seem to have slightly the advantage of him. Then I went to another who had still higher pretensions to wisdom, and my conclusion was exactly the same. Whereupon I made another enemy of him, and of many others besides him.

Then I went to one man after another, being not unconscious of the enmity which I provoked, and I lamented and feared this: but necessity was laid upon me,—the word of God, I thought, ought to be considered first. And I said to myself, Go I must to all who appear to know, and find out the meaning of the oracle. And I swear to you, Athenians, by the dog I swear!—for I must tell you the truth—the result of my mission was just this: I found that the men most in repute were all but the most foolish; and that others less esteemed were really wiser and better. I will tell you the tale of my wanderings and of the "Herculean" labours, as I may call them, which I endured only to find at last the oracle irrefutable. After the politicians, I went to the poets; tragic, dithyrambic, and all sorts. And there, I said to myself, you will be instantly detected; now you will find out that you are more ignorant than they are. Accordingly I took them some of the most elaborate passages in their own writings, and asked what was the meaning of them—thinking that they would teach me something. Will you believe me? I am almost ashamed to confess the truth, but I must say that there is hardly a person present who would not have talked better about their poetry than they did themselves. Then I knew that not by wisdom do poets write poetry, but by a sort of genius and inspiration; they are like diviners or soothsayers who also say many fine things, but do not understand the meaning of them. The poets appeared to me to be much in the same case; and I further observed that upon the strength of their poetry they believed themselves to be the wisest of men in other things in which they were not wise. So I departed, conceiving myself to be superior to them for the same reason that I was superior to the politicians.

At last I went to the artisans. I was conscious that I knew nothing at all, as I may say, and I was sure that they knew many fine things; and here I was not mistaken, for they did know many things of which I was ignorant, and in this they certainly were wiser than I was. But I observed that even the good artisans fell into the same error as the poets;—because they were good workmen they thought that they also knew all sorts of high matters, and this defect in them overshadowed their wisdom; and therefore I asked myself on behalf of the oracle, whether I would like to be as I was, neither having their knowledge nor their ignorance, or like them in both; and I made answer to myself and to the oracle that I was better off as I was.

This inquisition has led to my having many enemies of the worst and most dangerous kind, and has given occasion also to many calumnies. And I am called wise, for my hearers always imagine that I myself possess the wisdom which I find wanting in others; but the truth is, O men of Athens, that God only is wise; and by his answer he intends to show that the wisdom of men is worth little or nothing; he is not speaking of Socrates, he is only using my name by way of illustration, as if he said, He, O men, is the wisest, who, like Socrates, knows that his wisdom is in truth worth nothing. And so I go about the world obedient to the god, and search and make enquiry into the wisdom of any one, whether citizen or stranger, who appears to be wise; and if he is not wise, then in vindication of the oracle I show him that he is not wise; and my occupation quite absorbs me, and I have no time to give either to any public matter of interest or to any concern of my own, but I am in utter poverty by reason of my devotion to the god.

There is another thing:—young men of the richer classes, who have not much to do, come about me of their own accord; they like to hear the pretenders examined, and they often imitate me, and proceed to examine others; there are plenty of persons, as they quickly discover, who think that they know something, but really know little or nothing; and then those who are examined by them instead of being angry with themselves are angry with me: This confounded Socrates, they say; this villainous misleader of youth!—and then if somebody asks them, Why, what evil does he practise or teach? they do not know, and cannot tell; but in order that they may not appear to be at a loss, they repeat the ready-made charges which are used against all philosophers about teaching things up in the clouds and under the earth, and having no gods, and making the worst appear the better cause; for they do not like to confess that their pretence of knowledge has been detected—which is the truth; and as they are numerous and ambitious and energetic, and are drawn up in battle array and have persuasive tongues, they have filled your ears with their loud and inveterate calumnies. And this is the reason why my three accusers, Meletus and Anytus and Lycon, have set upon me; Meletus, who has a quarrel with me on behalf of the poets; Anytus, on behalf of the craftsmen and politicians; Lycon, on behalf of the rhetoricians: and, as I said at the beginning, I cannot expect to get rid of such a mass of calumny all in a moment. And this, O men of Athens, is the truth and the whole truth; I have concealed nothing, I have dissembled nothing. And yet, I know that my plainness of speech makes them hate me, and what is their hatred but a proof that I am speaking the truth? Hence has arisen the prejudice against me; and this is the reason of it, as you will find out either in this or in any future enquiry.

I have said enough in my defence against the first class of my accusers; I turn to the second class. They are headed by Meletus, that good man and true lover of his country, as he calls himself. Against these, too, I must try to make a defence:—Let their affidavit be read: it contains something of this kind: It says that Socrates is a doer of evil, who corrupts the youth; and who does not believe in the gods of the State, but has other new divinities of his own. Such is the charge; and now let us examine the particular counts. He says that I am a doer of evil, and corrupt the youth; but I say, O men of Athens, that Meletus is a doer of evil, in that he pretends to be in earnest when he is only in jest, and is so eager to bring men to trial from a pretended zeal and interest about matters in which he really never had the smallest interest.

And the truth of this I will endeavour to prove to you.

Come hither, Meletus, and let me ask a question of you. You think a great deal about the improvement of youth?

Yes, I do.

Tell the judges, then, who is their improver; for you must know, as you have taken the pains to discover their corrupter, and are citing and accusing me before them. Speak, then, and tell the judges who their improver is.—Observe, Meletus, that you are silent, and have nothing to say. But is not this rather disgraceful, and a very considerable proof of what I was saying, that you have no interest in the matter? Speak up, friend, and tell us who their improver is.

The laws.

But that, my good sir, is not my meaning. I want to know who the person is, who, in the first place, knows the laws.

The judges, Socrates, who are present in court.

What, do you mean to say, Meletus, that they are able to instruct and improve youth?

Certainly they are.

What, all of them, or some only and not others?

All of them.

By the goddess Here, that is good news! There are plenty of improvers, then. And what do you say of the audience,—do they improve them?

Yes, they do.

And the senators?

Yes, the senators improve them.

But perhaps the members of the assembly corrupt them?—or do they improve them?

They improve them.

Then every Athenian improves and elevates them; all with the exception of myself; and I alone am their corrupter? Is that what you affirm?

That is what I stoutly affirm.

I am very unfortunate if you are right. But suppose I ask you a question: How about horses? Does one man do them harm and all the world good? Is not the exact opposite the truth? One man is able to do them good, or at least not many;—the trainer of horses, that is to say, does them good, and others who have to do with them rather injure them? Is not that true, Meletus, of horses, or of any other animal? Most assuredly it is; whether you and Anytus say yes or no. Happy indeed would be the condition of youth if they had one corrupter only, and all the rest of the world were their improvers. But you, Meletus, have sufficiently shown that you never had a thought about the young: your carelessness is seen in your not caring about the very things which you bring against me.

And now, Meletus, I will ask you another question—by Zeus I will: Which is better, to live among bad citizens, or among good ones?

Answer, friend, I say; the question is one which may be easily
answered. Do not the good do their neighbours good, and the bad do
them evil?

Certainly.

And is there any one who would rather be injured than benefited
by those who live with him? Answer, my good friend, the law
requires you to answer—does any one like to be injured?

Certainly not.

And when you accuse me of corrupting and deteriorating the
youth, do you allege that I corrupt them intentionally or unintentionally?

Intentionally, I say.

But you have just admitted that the good do their neighbours good,
and the evil do them evil. Now, is that a truth which your superior
wisdom has recognized thus early in life, and am I, at my age, in
such darkness and ignorance as not to know that if a man with
whom I have to live is corrupted by me, I am very likely to be
harmed by him; and yet I corrupt him, and intentionally, too—so you
say, although neither I nor any other human being is ever likely to be
convinced by you. But either I do not corrupt them, or I corrupt
them unintentionally; and on either view of the case you lie. If my
offence is unintentional, the law has no cognizance of unintentional
offences: you ought to have taken me privately, and warned and
admonished me; for if I had been better advised, I should have left
off doing what I only did unintentionally—no doubt I should; but
you would have nothing to say to me and refused to teach me. And
now you bring me up in this court, which is a place not of instruction, but of punishment.

It will be very clear to you, Athenians, as I was saying, that
Meletus has no care at all, great or small, about the matter. But still I
should like to know, Meletus, in what I am affirmed to corrupt the
young. I suppose you mean, as I infer from your indictment, that I
teach them not to acknowledge the gods which the State acknowl-
edges, but some other new divinities or spiritual agencies in their
stead. These are the lessons by which I corrupt the youth, as you
say.

Yes, that I say emphatically.

Then, by the gods, Meletus, of whom we are speaking, tell me and
the court, in somewhat plainer terms, what you mean! For I do not
as yet understand whether you affirm that I teach other men to
acknowledge some gods, and therefore that I do believe in gods, and
am not an entire atheist—this you do not lay to my charge,—but only
you say that they are not the same gods which the city recognizes—
the charge is that they are different gods. Or, do you mean that I am
an atheist simply, and a teacher of atheism?

I mean the latter—that you are a complete atheist.

What an extraordinary statement! Why do you think so, Meletus?

Do you mean that I do not believe in the godhead of the sun or moon, like other men?

I assure you judges, that he does not: for he says that the sun is stone and the moon earth.

Friend Meletus, you think that you are accusing Anaxagoras: and you have but a bad opinion of the judges, if you fancy them illiterate to such a degree as not to know that these doctrines are found in the books of Anaxagoras the Clazomenian, which are full of them. And so, forsooth, the youth are said to be taught them by Socrates, when there are not infrequently exhibitions of them at the theatre (price of admission one drachma at the most); and they might pay their money, and laugh at Socrates if he pretends to father these extraordinary views. And so, Meletus, you really think that I do not believe in any god?

I swear by Zeus that you believe absolutely in none at all.

Nobody will believe you, Meletus, and I am pretty sure that you do not believe yourself. I cannot help thinking, men of Athens, that Meletus is reckless and impudent, and that he has written this indictment in a spirit of mere wantonness and youthful bravado. Has he not compounded a riddle, thinking to try me? He said to himself:—I shall see whether the wise Socrates will discover my facetious contradiction, or whether I shall be able to deceive him and the rest of them. For he certainly does appear to me to contradict himself in the indictment as much as if he said that Socrates is guilty of not believing in the gods, and yet of believing in them—but this is not like a person who is in earnest.

I should like you, O men of Athens, to join me in examining what I conceive to be his inconsistency; and do you, Meletus, answer. And I must remind the audience of my request that they would not make a disturbance if I speak in my accustomed manner:

Did ever man, Meletus, believe in the existence of human things, and not of human beings? ... I wish, men of Athens, that he would answer, and not be always trying to get up an interruption. Did ever any man believe in horsemanship, and not in horses? or in flute-playing, and not in flute-players? No, my friend; I will answer to you and to the court, as you refuse to answer for yourself. There is no man who ever did. But now please to answer the next question: Can a man believe in spiritual and divine agencies, and not in spirits or demigods?

He cannot.

How lucky I am to have extracted that answer, by the assistance of the court! But then you swear in the indictment that I teach and believe in divine or spiritual agencies (new or old, no matter for that); at any rate, I believe in spiritual agencies,—so you say and swear in the affidavit; and yet if I believe in divine beings, how can I help believing in spirits or demigods;—must I not? To be sure I must; and therefore I may assume that your silence gives consent. Now what are spirits or demigods? are they not either gods or the sons of gods?

Certainly they are.

But this is what I call the facetious riddle invented by you: the demigods or spirits are gods, and you say first that I do not believe in gods, and then again that I do believe in gods; that is, if I believe in demigods. For if the demigods are the illegitimate sons of gods, whether by the nymphs or by any other mothers, of whom they are said to be the sons—what human being will ever believe that there are no gods if they are the sons of Gods? You might as well affirm the existence of mules, and deny that of horses and asses. Such nonsense, Meletus, could only have been intended by you to make trial of me. You have put this into the indictment because you had nothing real of which to accuse me. But no one who has a particle of understanding will ever be convinced by you that the same men can believe in divine and superhuman things, and yet not believe that there are gods and demigods and heroes.

I have said enough in answer to the charge of Meletus: any elaborate defence is unnecessary; but I know only too well how many are the enmities which I have incurred, and this is what will by my destruction if I am destroyed;—not Meletus, nor yet Anytus, but the envy and detraction of the world, which has been the death of many good men, and will probably be the death of many more; there is no danger of my being the last of them.

Some one will say: And are you not ashamed, Socrates, of a course of life which is likely to bring you to an untimely end? To him I may fairly answer: There you are mistaken: a man who is good for anything ought not to calculate the chance of living or dying; he ought only to consider whether in doing anything he is doing right or wrong—acting the part of a good man or of a bad. Whereas, upon your view, the heroes who fell at Troy were not good for much, and the son of Thetis above all, who altogether despised danger in comparison with disgrace; and when he was so eager to slay Hector, his goddess mother said to him, that if he avenged his companion Patroclus, and slew Hector, he would die himself—"Fate," she said, in these or the like words, "waits for you next after Hector"; he, receiving this warning, utterly despised danger and death, and instead of fearing them, feared rather to live in dishonour, and not to avenge his friend. "Let me die forthwith," he replied, "and be avenged of my enemy, rather than abide here by the beaked ships, a laughing-stock and a burden of the earth." Had Achilles any thought of death and danger? For wherever a man's place is, whether the place which he has chosen or that in which he has been placed by a commander, there he ought to remain in the hour of danger; he should not think of death or of anything but of disgrace. And this, O men of Athens, is a true saying.

Strange, indeed, would be my conduct, O men of Athens, if I, who, when I was ordered by the generals whom you chose to command me at Potidaea and Amphipolis and Delium, remained where they placed me, like any other man, facing death—if now, when, as I conceive and imagine, God orders me to fulfill the philosopher's mission of searching into myself and other men, I were to desert my post through fear of death, or any other fear; that would indeed be strange, and I might justly be arraigned in court for denying the existence of the gods, if I disobeyed the oracle because I was afraid of death, fancying that I was wise when I was not wise. For the fear of death is indeed the pretence of wisdom, and not real wisdom, being a pretence of knowing the unknown; and no one knows whether death, which men in their fear apprehend to be the greatest evil, may not be the greatest good. Is not this ignorance of a disgraceful sort, the ignorance which is the conceit that a man knows what he does not know? And in this respect only I believe myself to differ from men in general, and may perhaps claim to be wiser than they are:—that whereas I know but little of the world below, I do not suppose that I know: but I do know that injustice and disobedience to a better, whether God or man, is evil and dishonourable, and I will never fear or avoid a possible good rather than a certain evil. And therefore if you let me go now, and are not convinced by Anytus, who said that since I had been prosecuted I must be put to death; (or if not that I ought never to have been prosecuted at all); and that if I escape now, your sons will all be utterly ruined by listening to my words if you say to me, Socrates, this time we will not mind Anytus, and you shall be let off, but upon one condition, that you are not to enquire and speculate in this way any more, and that if you are caught doing so again you shall die;—if this was the condition on which you let me go, I should reply: Men of Athens, I honour and love you; but I shall obey God rather than you, and while I have life and strength I shall never cease from the practice and teaching of philosophy, exhorting any one whom I meet and saying to him after my manner: You, my friend,—a citizen of the great and mighty and wise city of Athens,—are you not ashamed of heaping up the greatest amount of money and honour and reputation, and caring so little about wisdom and truth and the greatest improvement of the soul, which you never regard or heed at all? And if the person with whom I am arguing, says: Yes, but I do care; then I do not leave him or let him go at once; but I proceed to interrogate and examine and cross-examine him, and if I think that he has no virtue in him, but only says that he has, I reproach him with undervaluing the greater, and overvaluing the less. And I shall repeat the same words to every one whom I meet, young and old, citizen and alien, but especially to the citizens, inasmuch as they are my brethren. For know that this is the command of God; and I believe that no greater good has ever happened in the State than my service to the God. For I do nothing but go about persuading you all, old and young alike, not to take thought for your persons or your properties, but first and chiefly to care about the greatest improvement of the soul. I tell you that virtue is not given by money, but that from virtue comes money and every other good of man, public as well as private. This is my teaching, and if this is the doctrine which corrupts the youth, I am a mischievous person. But if any one says that this is not my teaching, he is speaking an untruth. Wherefore, O men of Athens, I say to you, do as Anytus bids or not as Anytus bids, and either acquit me or not; but whichever you do, understand that I shall never alter my ways, not even if I have to die many times.

Men of Athens, do not interrupt, but hear me; there was an understanding between us that you should hear me to the end: I have something more to say, at which you may be inclined to cry out; but I believe that to hear me will be good for you, and therefore I beg that you will not cry out. I would have you know, that if you kill such an one as I am, you will injure yourselves more than you will injure me. Nothing will injure me, not Meletus nor yet Anytus—they cannot, for a bad man is not permitted to injure a better than himself. I do not deny that Anytus may, perhaps, kill him, or drive him into exile, or deprive him of civil rights; and he may imagine, and others may imagine, that he is inflicting a great injury upon him: but there I do not agree. For the evil of doing as he is doing—the evil of unjustly taking away the life of another—is greater far.

And now, Athenians, I am not going to argue for my own sake, as you may think, but for yours, that you may not sin against the God by condemning me, who am his gift to you. For if you kill me you will not easily find a successor to me, who, if I may use such a ludicrous figure of speech, am a sort of gadfly, given to the State by God; and the State is a great and noble steed who is tardy in his motions owing to his very size, and requires to be stirred into life. I am that gadfly which God has attached to the State, and all day long and in all places am always fastening upon you, arousing and persuading and reproaching you. You will not easily find another like me, and therefore I would advise you to spare me. I dare say that you may feel out of temper (like a person who is suddenly awakened from sleep), and you think that you might easily strike me dead as Anytus advises, and then you would sleep on for the remainder of your lives, unless God in his care of you sent you another gadfly. When I say that I am given to you by God, the proof of my mission is this:—if I had been like other men, I should not have neglected all my own concerns or patiently seen the neglect of them during all these years, and have been doing yours, coming to you individually like a father or elder brother, exhorting you to regard virtue; such conduct, I say, would be unlike human nature. If I had gained anything, or if my exhortations had been paid, there would have been some sense in my doing so; but now, as you will perceive, not even the impudence of my accusers dares to say that I have ever exacted or sought pay of any one; of that they have no witness. And I have a sufficient witness to the truth of what I say—my poverty.

Some one may wonder why I go about in private giving advice and busy myself with the concerns of others, but do not venture to come forward in public and advise the State. I will tell you why. You have heard me speak at sundry times and in divers places of an oracle or sign which comes to me, and is the divinity which Meletus ridicules in the indictment. This sign, which is a kind of voice, first began to come to me when I was a child; it always forbids but never commands me to do anything which I am going to do. This is what deters me from being a politician. And rightly, as I think. For I am certain, O men of Athens, that if I had engaged in politics, I should have perished long ago, and done no good either to you or to myself. And do not be offended at my telling you the truth: for the truth is, that no man who goes to war with you or any other multitude, honestly striving against the many lawless and unrighteous deeds which are done in a state, will save his life; he who will fight for the right, if he would live even for a brief space, must have a private station and not a public one.

I can give you convincing evidence of what I say, not words only, but what you value far more—actions. Let me relate to you a passage of my own life which will prove to you that I should never have yielded to injustice from any fear of death and that "as I should have refused to yield" I must have died at once. I will tell you a tale of the courts, not very interesting perhaps, but nevertheless true. The only office of State which I ever held, O men of Athens, was that of senator: the tribe Antiochis, which is my tribe, had the presidency at the trial of the generals who had not taken up the bodies of the slain after the battle of Arginusae; and you proposed to try them in a body, contrary to law, as you all thought afterwards; but at the time I was the only one of the Prytanes who was opposed to the illegality, and I gave my vote against you; and when the orators threatened to impeach and arrest me, and you called and shouted, I made up my mind that I would run the risk, having law and justice with me, rather than take part in your injustice because I feared imprisonment and death. This happened in the days of the democracy. But when the oligarchy of the Thirty was in power, they sent for me and four others into the rotunda, and bade us bring Leon the Salaminian from Salamis, as they wanted to put him to death. This was a specimen of the sort of commands which they were always giving with the view of implicating as many as possible in their crimes; and then I showed, not in word only but in deed, that, if I may be allowed to use such an expression, I cared not a straw for death, and that my great and only care was lest I should do an unrighteous or unholy thing. For the strong arm of that oppressive power did not frighten me into doing wrong; and when we came out of the rotunda the other four went to Salamis and fetched Leon, but I went quietly home. For which I might have lost my life, had not the power of the Thirty shortly afterwards come to an end. And many will witness to my words.

Now, do you really imagine that I could have survived all these years, if I had led a public life, supposing that like a good man I had always maintained the right and had made justice, as I ought, the first thing? No, indeed, men of Athens, neither I nor any other man. But I have been always the same in all my actions, public as well as private, and never have I yielded any base compliance to those who are slanderously termed my disciples, or to any other. Not that I have any regular disciples. But if any one likes to come and hear me while I am pursuing my mission, whether he be young or old, he is not excluded. Nor do I converse only with those who pay; but any one, whether he be rich or poor, may ask and answer me and listen to my words; and whether he turns out to be a bad man or a good one, neither result can be justly imputed to me; for I never taught or professed to teach him anything. And if any one says that he has ever learned or heard anything from me in private which all the world has not heard, let me tell you that he is lying.

But I shall be asked, Why do people delight in continually conversing with you? I have told you already, Athenians, the whole truth about this matter: they like to hear the cross-examination of the pretenders to wisdom; there is amusement in it. Now, this duty of cross-examining other men has been imposed upon me by God; and has been signified to me by oracles, visions, and in every way in which the will of divine power was ever intimated to any one. This is true, O Athenians; or, if not true, would be soon refuted. If I am or have been corrupting the youth, those of them who are now grown up and have become sensible that I gave them bad advice in the days of their youth should come forward as accusers, and take their revenge; or if they do not like to come themselves, some of their relatives, fathers, brothers, or other kinsmen, should say what evil their families have suffered at my hands. Now is their time. Many of them I see in the court. There is Crito, who is of the same age and of the same deme with myself, and there is Critobulus his son, whom I also see. Then again there is Lysanias of Sphettus, who is the father of Aeschines—he is present; and also there is Antiphon of Cephisus, who is the father of Epigenes; and there are the brothers of several who have associated with me. There is Nicostratus the son of Theosdotides, and the brother of Theodotus (now Theodotus himself is dead, and therefore he, at any rate, will not seek to stop him); and there is Paralus the son of Demodocus, who had a brother Theages; and Adeimantus the son of Ariston, whose brother Plato is present; and Aeantodorus, who is the brother of Apollodorus, whom I also see. I might mention a great many others, some of whom Meletus should have produced as witnesses in the course of his speech; and let him still produce them, if he has forgotten—I will make way for him. And let him say, if he has any testimony of the sort which he can produce. Nay, Athenians, the very opposite is the truth. For all these are ready to witness on behalf of the corrupter, of the injurer of their kindred, as Meletus and Anytus call me; not the corrupted youth only—there might have been a motive for that—but their uncorrupted elder relatives. Why should they too support me with their testimony? Why, indeed, except for the sake of truth and justice, and because they know that I am speaking the truth, and that Meletus is a liar.

Well, Athenians, this and the like of this is all the defence which I have to offer. Yet a word more. Perhaps there may be some one who is offended at me, when he calls to mind how he himself on a similar, or even a less serious occasion, prayed and entreated the judges with many tears, and how he produced his children in court, which was a moving spectacle, together with a host of relations and friends; whereas I, who am probably in danger of my life, will do none of these things. The contrast may occur to his mind, and he may be set against me, and vote in anger because he is displeased at me on this account. Now, if there be such a person among you,—mind, I do not say that there is,—to him I may fairly reply: My friend, I am a man, and like other men, a creature of flesh and blood, and not "of wood or stone," as Homer says; and I have a family, yes, and sons, O Athenians, three in number, one almost a man, and two others who are still young; and yet I will not bring any of them hither in order to petition you for an acquittal. And why not? Not from any self-assertion or want of respect for you. Whether I am or am not afraid of death is another question, of which I will not now speak. But, having regard to public opinion, I feel that such conduct would be discreditable to myself, and to you, and to the whole State. One who has reached my years, and who has a name for wisdom, ought not to demean himself. Whether this opinion of me be deserved or not, at any rate the world has decided that Socrates is in some way superior to other men. And if those among you who are said to be superior in wisdom and courage, and any other virtue, demean themselves in this way, how shameful is their conduct! I have seen men of reputation, when they have been condemned, behaving in the strangest manner; they seem to fancy that they were going to suffer something dreadful if they died, and that they could be immortal if you only allowed them to live; and I think that such are a dishonour to the State, and that any stranger coming in would have said of them that the most eminent men of Athens, to whom the Athenians themselves give honour and command, are no better than women. And I say that these things ought not to be done by those of us who have a reputation; and if they are done, you ought not to permit them; you ought rather to show that you are far more disposed to condemn the man who gets up a doleful scene and makes the city ridiculous, than him who holds his peace.

But, setting aside the question of public opinion, there seems to be something wrong in asking a favour of a judge, and thus procuring an acquittal, instead of informing and convincing him. For his duty is, not to make a present of justice, but to give judgment; and he has sworn that he will judge according to the laws, and not according to his own good pleasure; and we ought not to encourage you, nor should you allow yourselves to be encouraged, in this habit of perjury—there can be no piety in that. Do not then require me to do what I consider dishonourable and impious and wrong, especially now, when I am being tried for impiety on the indictment of Meletus. For if, O men of Athens, by force of persuasion and entreaty I could overpower your oaths, then I should be teaching you to believe that there are no gods, and in defending should simply convict myself of the charge of not believing in them. But that it is not so—far otherwise. For I do believe that there are gods, and in a sense higher than that in which any of my accusers believe in them. And to you and to God I commit my cause, to be determined by you as is best for you and me.

[The vote is taken and Socrates is convicted.]

There are many reasons why I am not grieved, O men of Athens, at the vote of condemnation. I expected it, and am only surprised that the votes are so nearly equal; for I had thought that the majority against me would have been far larger; but now, had thirty votes gone over to the other side, I should have been acquitted. And I may say, I think, that I have escaped Meletus. I may say more; for without the assistance of Anytus and Lycon, any one may see that he would not have had a fifth part of the votes, as the law requires, in which case he would have incurred a fine of a thousand drachmae.

And so he proposes death as the penalty. And what shall I propose on my part, O men of Athens? Clearly that which is my due. And what is my due? What returns shall be made to the man who has never had the wit to be idle during his whole life; but has been careless of what the many care for—wealth, and family interests, and military offices, and speaking in the assembly, and magistracies, and plots, and parties. Reflecting that I was really too honest a man to be a politician and live, I did not go where I could do no good to you or to myself; but where I could do the greatest good privately to every one of you, thither I went, and sought to persuade every man among you that he must look to himself, and seek virtue and wisdom before he looks to his private interests, and look to the State before he looks to the interests of the State; and that this should be the order which he observes in all his actions. What shall be done to such an one? Doubtless some good thing, O men of Athens, if he has his reward; and the good should be of a kind suitable to him. What would be a reward suitable to a poor man who is your benefactor, and who desires leisure that he may instruct you? There can be no reward so fitting as maintenance in the Prytaneum, O men of Athens, a reward which he deserves far more than the citizen who has won the prize at Olympia in the horse or chariot race, whether the chariots were drawn by two horses or by many. For I am in want, and he has enough; and he only gives you the appearance of happiness, and I give you the reality. And if I am to estimate the penalty fairly, I should say that maintenance in the Prytaneum is the just return.

Perhaps you think that I am braving you in what I am saying now, as in what I said before about the tears and prayers. But this is not so. I speak rather because I am convinced that I never intentionally wronged any one, although I cannot convince you—the time has been too short; if there were a law at Athens, as there is in other cities, that a capital cause should not be decided in one day, then I believe that I should have convinced you. But I cannot in a moment refute great slanders; and, as I am convinced that I never wronged another, I will assuredly not wrong myself. I will not say of myself that I deserve any evil, or propose any penalty. Why should I? Because I am afraid of the penalty of death which Meletus proposes? When I do not know whether death is a good or an evil, why should I propose a penalty which would certainly be an evil? Shall I say imprisonment? And why should I live in prison, and be the slave of the magistrate of the year—of the Eleven? Or shall the penalty be a fine, imprisonment until the fine is paid? There is the same objection. I should have to lie in prison, for money I have none, and cannot pay. And if I say exile (and this may possibly be the penalty which you will affix), I must indeed be blinded by the love of life, if I am so irrational as to expect that when you, who are my own citizens, cannot endure my discourses and words, and have found them so grievous and odious that you will have no more of them, others are likely to endure me. No, indeed, men of Athens, that is not very likely. And what a life should I lead, at my age, wandering from city to city, ever changing my place of exile, and always being driven out! For I am quite sure that wherever I go, there, as here, the young men will flock to me; and if I drive them away, their elders will drive me out at their request; and if I let them come, their fathers and friends will drive me out for their sakes.

Some one will say: Yes, Socrates, but cannot you hold your tongue, and then you may go into a foreign city, and no one will interfere with you? Now, I have great difficulty in making you understand my answer to this. For if I tell you that to do as you say would be a disobedience to the God, and therefore that I cannot hold my tongue, you will not believe that I am serious; and if I say again that daily to discourse about virtue, and of those other things about which you hear me examining myself and others is the greatest good of man, and that the unexamined life is not worth living, you

are still less likely to believe me. Yet I say what is true, although a
thing of which it is hard for me to persuade you. Also, I have never
been accustomed to think that I deserve to suffer any harm. Had I
money I might have estimated the offence at what I was able to pay,
and not have been much the worse. But I have none, and therefore I
must ask you to proportion the fine to my means. Well, perhaps I
could afford a mina, and therefore I propose that penalty: Plato,
Crito, Critobulus, and Apollodorus, my friends here, bid me say
thirty minae, and they will be the sureties. Let thirty minae be the
penalty; for which sum they will be ample security to you.

[Socrates is condemned to death.]

   Not much time will be gained, O Athenians, in return for the evil
name which you will get from the detractors of the city, who will
say that you killed Socrates, a wise man; for they will call me wise,
even though I am not wise, when they want to reproach you. If you
had waited a little while, your desire would have been fulfilled in the
course of nature. For I am far advanced in years, as you may
perceive, and not far from death. I am speaking now not to all of
you, but only to those who have condemned me to death. And I
have another thing to say to them: You think that I was convicted
because I had no words of the sort which would have procured my
acquittal—I mean, if I had thought fit to leave nothing undone or
unsaid. Not so; the deficiency which led to my conviction was not of
words—certainly not. But I had not the boldness or impudence or
inclination to address you as you would have liked me to do,
weeping and wailing and lamenting, and saying and doing many
things which you have been accustomed to hear from others, and
which, as I maintain, are unworthy of me. I thought at the time that
I ought not to do anything common or mean when in danger: nor do
I now repent of the style of my defence; I would rather die having
spoken after my manner, than speak in your manner and live. For
neither in war nor yet at law ought I or any man to use every way of
escaping death. Often in battle there can be no doubt that if a man
will throw away his arms, and fall on his knees before his pursuers,
he may escape death; and in other dangers there are other ways of
escaping death; if a man is willing to say and do anything. The
difficulty, my friends, is not to avoid death, but to avoid unrighteousness; for that runs faster than death. I am old and move
slowly, and the slower runner has overtaken me, and my accusers are
keen and quick, and the faster runner, who is unrighteousness, has
overtaken them. And now I depart hence condemned by you to
suffer the penalty of death,—they too go their ways condemned by
the truth to suffer the penalty of villainy and wrong; and I must
abide by my award—let them abide by theirs. I suppose that these
things may be regarded as fated,—and I think that they are well.
   And now, O men who have condemned me, I would fain prophesy

to you; for I am about to die, and in the hour of death men are gifted with prophetic power. And I prophesy to you who are my murderers, that immediately after my departure punishment far heavier than you have inflicted on me will surely await you. Me you have killed because you wanted to escape the accuser, and not to give an account of your lives. But that will not be as you suppose: far otherwise. For I say that there will be more accusers of you than there are now; accusers whom hitherto I have restrained: and as they are younger they will be more inconsiderate with you, and you will be more offended at them. If you think that by killing men you can prevent some one from censuring your evil lives, you are mistaken; that is not a way of escape which is either possible or honourable; the easiest and the noblest way is not to be disabling others, but to be improving yourselves. This is the prophecy which I utter before my departure to the judges who have condemned me.

Friends, who would have acquitted me, I would like also to talk with you about the thing which has come to pass, while the magistrates are busy, and before I go to the place at which I must die. Stay then a little, for we may as well talk with one another while there is time. You are my friends, and I should like to show you the meaning of this event which has happened to me. O my judges—for you I may truly call judges—I should like to tell you of a wonderful circumstance. Hitherto the divine faculty of which the internal oracle is the source has constantly been in the habit of opposing me even about trifles, if I was going to make a slip or error in any matter; and now as you see there has come upon me that which may be thought, and is generally believed to be, the last and worst evil. But the oracle made no sign of opposition, either when I was leaving my house in the morning, or when I was on my way to the court, or while I was speaking, at anything which I was going to say; and yet I have often been stopped in the middle of a speech, but now in nothing I either said or did touching the matter in hand has the oracle opposed me. What do I take to be the explanation of this silence? I will tell you. It is an intimation that what has happened to me is a good, and that those of us who think that death is an evil are in error. For the customary sign would surely have opposed me had I been going to evil and not to good.

Let us reflect in another way, and we shall see that there is great reason to hope that death is a good; for one of two things—either death is a state of nothingness and utter unconsciousness, or, as men say, there is a change and migration of the soul from this world to another. Now, if you suppose that there is no consciousness, but a sleep like the sleep of him who is undisturbed even by dreams, death will be an unspeakable gain. For if a person were to select the night in which his sleep was undisturbed even by dreams, and were to compare with this the other days and nights of his life, and then were to tell us how many days and nights he had passed in the course of his life better and more pleasantly than this one, I think that any man, I will not say a private man, but even the great king will not find many such days or nights, when compared with the others. Now, if death be of such a nature, I say that to die is gain; for eternity is then only a single night. But if death is the journey to another place, and there, as men say, all the dead abide, what good, O my friends and judges, can be greater than this? If, indeed, when the pilgrim arrives in the world below, he is delivered from the professors of justice in this world, and finds the true judges who are said to give judgment there, Minos and Rhadamanthus and Aeacus and Triptolemus, and other sons of God who were righteous in their own life, that pilgrimage will be worth making. What would not a man give if he might converse with Orpheus and Musaeus and Hesiod and Homer? Nay, if this be true, let me die again and again. I myself, too, shall have a wonderful interest in there meeting and conversing with Palamedes, and Ajax the son of Telamon, and any other ancient hero who has suffered death through an unjust judgment; and there will be no small pleasure, as I think, in comparing my own sufferings with theirs. Above all, I shall then be able to continue my search into true and false knowledge; as in this world, so also in the next; and I shall find out who is wise, and who pretends to be wise, and is not. What would not a man give, O judges, to be able to examine the leader of the great Trojan expedition; or Odysseus or Sisyphus, or numberless others, men and women too! What infinite delight would there be in conversing with them and asking them questions! In another world they do not put a man to death for asking questions; assuredly not. For besides being happier than we are, they will be immortal, if what is said is true.

Wherefore, O judges, be of good cheer about death, and know of a certainty, that no evil can happen to a good man, either in life or after death. He and his are not neglected by the gods; nor has my own approaching end happened by mere chance. But I see clearly that the time had arrived when it was better for me to die and be released from trouble; wherefore the oracle gave no sign. For which reason, also, I am not angry with my condemners, or with my accusers; they have done me no harm, although they did not mean to do me any good; and for this I may gently blame them.

Still, I have a favour to ask of them. When my sons are grown up, I would ask you, O my friends, to punish them; and I would have you trouble them, as I have troubled you, if they seem to care about riches, or anything, more than about virtue; or if they pretend to be something when they are really nothing,—then reprove them, as I have reproved you, for not caring about that for which they ought to care, and thinking that they are something when they are really nothing. And if you do this, both I and my sons will have received justice at your hands.

The hour of departure has arrived, and we go our ways—I to die, and you to live. Which is better God only knows.

THE FREEDOM OF A CHRISTIAN

Martin Luther

Many people have considered Christian faith an easy thing, and not a few have given it a place among the virtues. They do this because they have not experienced it and have never tasted the great strength there is in faith. It is impossible to write well about it or to understand what has been written about it unless one has at one time or another experienced the courage which faith gives a man when trials oppress him. But he who has had even a faint taste of it can never write, speak, meditate, or hear enough concerning it. It is a living "spring of water welling up to eternal life," as Christ calls it in John 4 [:14].

As for me, although I have no wealth of faith to boast of and know how scant my supply is, I nevertheless hope that I have attained to a little faith, even though I have been assailed by great and various temptations; and I hope that I can discuss it, if not more elegantly, certainly more to the point, than those literalists and subtile disputants have previously done, who have not even understood what they have written.

To make the way smoother for the unlearned—for only them do I serve—I shall set down the following two propositions concerning the freedom and the bondage of the spirit:

A Christian is a perfectly free lord of all, subject to none.

A Christian is a perfectly dutiful servant of all, subject to all.

These two theses seem to contradict each other. If, however, they should be found to fit together they would serve our purpose beautifully. Both are Paul's own statements, who says in I Cor. 9 [:19], "For though I am free from all men, I have made myself a slave to all," and in Rom. 13 [:8], "Owe no one anything, except to love one another." Love by its very nature is ready to serve and be subject to him who is loved. So Christ, although he was Lord of all, was "born of woman, born under the law" [Gal. 4:4], and therefore was at the same time a free man and a servant, "in the form of God" and "of a servant" [Phil. 2:6-7].

Let us start, however, with something more remote from our subject, but more obvious. Man has a twofold nature, a spiritual and a bodily one. According to the spiritual nature, which men refer to as the soul, he is called a spiritual, inner, or new man. According to the bodily nature, which men refer to as flesh, he is called a carnal, outward, or old man, of whom the Apostle writes in II Cor. 4 [:16], "Though our outer nature is wasting away, our inner nature is being renewed every day." Because of this diversity of nature the Scriptures assert contradictory things concerning the same man, since these two men in the same man contradict each other, "for the desires of the flesh are against the Spirit, and the desires of the Spirit are against the flesh," according to Gal. 5 [:17].

First, let us consider the inner man to see how a righteous, free, and pious Christian, that is, a spiritual, new, and inner man, becomes what he is. It is evident that no external thing has any influence in producing Christian righteousness or freedom, or in producing unrighteousness or servitude. A simple argument will furnish the proof of this statement. What can it profit the soul if the body is well, free, and active, and eats, drinks, and does as it pleases? For in these respects even the most godless slaves of vice may prosper. On the other hand, how will poor health or imprisonment or hunger or thirst or any other external misfortune harm the soul? Even the most godly men, and those who are free because of clear consciences, are afflicted with these things. None of these things touch either the freedom or the servitude of the soul. It does not help the soul if the body is adorned with the sacred robes of priests or dwells in sacred places or is occupied with sacred duties or prays, fasts, abstains from certain kinds of food, or does any work that can be done by the body and in the body. The righteousness and the freedom of the soul require something far different since the things which have been mentioned could be done by any wicked person. Such works produce nothing but hypocrites. On the other hand, it will not harm the soul if the body is clothed in secular dress, dwells in unconsecrated places, eats and drinks as others do, does not pray aloud, and neglects to do all the above-mentioned things which hypocrites can do.

Furthermore, to put aside all kinds of works, even contemplation, meditation, and all that the soul can do, does not help. One thing, and only one thing, is necessary for Christian life, righteousness, and freedom. That one thing is the most holy Word of God, the gospel of Christ, as Christ says, John 11 [:25], "I am the resurrection and the life; he who believes in me, though he die, yet shall he lives"; and John 8 [:36], "So if the Son makes you free, you will be free indeed"; and Matt. 4 [:4], "Man shall not live by bread alone, but by every word that proceeds from the mouth of God." Let us then consider it certain and firmly established that the soul can do without anything except the Word of God and that where the Word of God is missing there is no help at all for the soul. If it has the Word of God it is rich and lacks nothing since it is the Word of life, truth, light, peace, righteousness, salvation, joy, liberty, wisdom, power, grace, glory, and of every incalculable blessing. This is why the prophet in the entire Psalm [119] and in many other places yearns and sighs for the Word of God and uses so many names to describe it.

On the other hand, there is no more terrible disaster with which the wrath of God can afflict men than a famine of the hearing of his Word, as he says in Amos [8:11]. Likewise there is no greater mercy than when he sends forth his Word, as we read in Psalm 107 [:20]:

"He sent forth his word, and healed them, and delivered them from destruction." Nor was Christ sent into the world for any other ministry except that of the Word. Moreover, the entire spiritual estate—all the apostles, bishops, and priests—has been called and instituted only for the ministry of the Word.

You may ask, "What then is the Word of God, and how shall it be used, since there are so many words of God?" I answer: The Apostle explains this in Romans 1. The Word is the gospel of God concerning his Son, who was made flesh, suffered, rose from the dead, and was glorified through the Spirit who sanctifies. To preach Christ means to feed the soul, make it righteous, set it free, and save it, provided it believes the preaching. Faith alone is the saving and efficacious use of the Word of God, according to Rom. 10 [:9]: "If you confess with your lips that Jesus is Lord and believe in your heart that God raised him from the dead, you will be saved." Furthermore, "Christ is the end of the law, that every one who has faith may be justified" [Rom. 10:4]. Again, in Rom. 1 [:17], "He who through faith is righteous shall live." The Word of God cannot be received and cherished by any works whatever but only by faith. Therefore it is clear that, as the soul needs only the Word of God for its life and righteousness, so it is justified by faith alone and not any works; for if it could be justified by anything else, it would not need the Word, and consequently it would not need faith.

This faith cannot exist in connection with works—that is to say, if you at the same time claim to be justified by works, whatever their character—for that would be the same as "limping with two different opinions" [I Kings 18:21], as worshiping Baal and kissing one's own hand [Job 31:27-28], which, as Job says, is a very great iniquity. Therefore the moment you begin to have faith you learn that all things in you are altogether blameworthy, sinful, and damnable, as the Apostle says in Rom. 3 [:23], "Since all have sinned and fall short of the glory of God," and, "None is righteous, no, not one;... all have turned aside, together they have gone wrong" (Rom. 3:10-12). When you have learned this you will know that you need Christ, who suffered and rose again for you so that, if you believe in him, you may through this faith become a new man in so far as your sins are forgiven and you are justified by the merits of another, namely, of Christ alone.

Since, therefore, this faith can rule only in the inner man, as Rom. 10 [:10] says, "For man believes with his heart and so is justified," and since faith alone justifies, it is clear that the inner man cannot be justified, freed, or saved by any outer work or action at all, and that these works, whatever their character, have nothing to do with this inner man. On the other hand, only ungodliness and unbelief of heart, and no outer work, make him guilty and a damnable servant of sin. Wherefore it ought to be the first concern of every Christian to lay aside all confidence in works and increasingly to strengthen faith alone and through faith to grow in the knowledge, not of works, but of Christ Jesus, who suffered and rose for him, as Peter teaches in the last chapter of his first Epistle (I Pet. 5:10). No other work makes a Christian. Thus when the Jews asked Christ, as related in John 6 [:28], what they must do "to be doing the work of God," he brushed aside the multitude of works which he saw they did in great profusion and suggested one work, saying, "This is the work of God, that you believe in him whom he has sent" [John 6:29]; "for on him has God the Father set his seal" [John 6:27].

Therefore true faith in Christ is a treasure beyond comparison which brings with it complete salvation and saves man from every evil, as Christ says in the last chapter of Mark [16:16]: "He who believes and is baptized will be saved; but he who does not believe will be condemned." Isaiah contemplated this treasure and foretold it in chapter 10: "The Lord will make a small and consuming word upon the land, and it will overflow with righteousness" [Cf. Isa. 10:22]. This is as though he said, "Faith, which is a small and perfect fulfilment of the law, will fill believers with so great a righteousness that they will need nothing more to become righteous." So Paul says, Rom. 10 [:10], "For man believes with his heart and so is justified."

Should you ask how it happens that faith alone justifies and offers us such a treasure of great benefits without works in view of the fact that so many works, ceremonies, and laws are prescribed in the Scriptures, I answer: First of all, remember what has been said, namely, that faith alone, without works, justifies, frees, and saves; we shall make this clearer later on. Here we must point out that the entire Scripture of God is divided into two parts: commandments and promises. Although the commandments teach things that are good, the things taught are not done as soon as they are taught, for the commandments show us what we ought to do but do not give us the power to do it. They are intended to teach man to know himself, that through them he may recognize his inability to do good and may despair of his own ability. That is why they are called the Old Testament and constitute the Old Testament. For example, the commandment, "You shall not covet" [Exod. 20:17], is a command which proves us all to be sinners, for no one can avoid coveting no matter how much he may struggle against it. Therefore, in order not to covet and to fulfil the commandment, a man is compelled to despair of himself, to seek the help which he does not find in himself elsewhere and from someone else, as stated in Hosea [13:9]: "Destruction is your own, O Israel: your help is only in me." As we fare with respect to one commandment, so we fare with all, for it is equally impossible for us to keep any one of them.

Now when a man has learned through the commandments to recognize his helplessness and is distressed about how he might satisfy the law—since the law must be fulfilled so that not a jot or tittle shall be lost, otherwise man will be condemned without hope—then, being truly humbled and reduced to nothing in his own eyes, he finds in himself nothing whereby he may be justified and saved. Here the second part of Scripture comes to our aid, namely, the promises of God which declare the glory of God, saying, "If you wish to fulfil the law and not covet, as the law demands, come, believe in Christ in whom grace, righteousness, peace, liberty, and all things are promised you. If you believe, you shall have all things; if you do not believe, you shall lack all things." That which is impossible for you to accomplish by trying to fulfil all the works of the law—many and useless as they all are—you will accomplish quickly and easily through faith. God our Father has made all things depend on faith so that whoever has faith will have everything, and whoever does not have faith will have nothing. "For God has consigned all men to disobedience, that he may have mercy upon all," as it is stated in Rom. 11 [:32]. Thus the promises of God give what the commandments of God demand and fulfil what the law prescribes so that all things may be God's alone, both the commandments and the fulfilling of the commandments. He alone commands, he alone fulfils. Therefore the promises of God belong to the New Testament. Indeed, they are the New Testament.

Since these promises of God are holy, true, righteous, free, and peaceful words, full of goodness, the soul which clings to them with a firm faith will be so closely united with them and altogether absorbed by them that it not only will share in all their power but will be saturated and intoxicated by them. If a touch of Christ healed, how much more will this most tender spiritual touch, this absorbing of the Word, communicate to the soul all things that belong to the Word. This, then, is how through faith alone without works the soul is justified by the Word of God, sanctified, made true, peaceful, and free, filled with every blessing and truly made a child of God, as John 1 [:12] says: "But to all who . . . believed in his name, he gave power to become children of God."

From what has been said it is easy to see from what source faith derives such great power and why a good work or all good works together cannot equal it. No good work can rely upon the Word of God or live in the soul, for faith alone and the Word of God rule in the soul. Just as the heated iron glows like fire because of the union of fire with it, so the Word imparts its qualities to the soul. It is clear, then, that a Christian has all that he needs in faith and needs no works to justify him; and if he has no need of works, he has no need of the law; and if he has no need of the law, surely he is free from the law. It is true that "the law is not laid down for the just" [I Tim. 1:9]. This is that Christian liberty, our faith, which does not induce us to live in idleness or wickedness but makes the law and works unnecessary for any man's righteousness and salvation.

This is the first power of faith. Let us now examine also the second. It is a further function of faith that it honors him whom it trusts with the most reverent and highest regard since it considers him truthful and trustworthy. There is no other honor equal to the estimate of truthfulness and righteousness with which we honor him whom we trust. Could we ascribe to a man anything greater than truthfulness and righteousness and perfect goodness? On the other hand, there is no way in which we can show greater contempt for a man than to regard him as false and wicked and to be suspicious of him, as we do when we do not trust him. So when the soul firmly trusts God's promises, it regards him as truthful and righteous. Nothing more excellent than this can be ascribed to God. The very highest worship of God is this that we ascribe to him truthfulness, righteousness, and whatever else should be ascribed to one who is trusted. When this is done, the soul consents to his will. Then it hallows his name and allows itself to be treated according to God's good pleasure for, clinging to God's promises, it does not doubt that he who is true, just, and wise will do, dispose, and provide all things well.

Is not such a soul most obedient to God in all things by this faith? What commandment is there that such obedience has not completely fulfilled? What more complete fulfilment is there than obedience in all things? This obedience, however, is not rendered by works, but by faith alone. On the other hand, what greater rebellion against God, what greater wickedness, what greater contempt of God is there than not believing his promise? For what is this but to make God a liar or to doubt that he is truthful?—that is, to ascribe truthfulness to one's self but lying and vanity to God? Does not a man who does this deny God and set himself up as an idol in his heart? Then of what good are works done in such wickedness, even if they were the works of angels and apostles? Therefore God has rightly included all things, not under anger or lust, but under unbelief, so that they who imagine that they are fulfilling the law by doing the works of chastity and mercy required by the law (the civil and human virtues) might not be saved. They are included under the sin of unbelief and must either seek mercy or be justly condemned.

When, however, God sees that we consider him truthful and by the faith of our heart pay him the great honor which is due him, he does us that great honor of considering us truthful and righteous for the sake of our faith. Faith works truth and righteousness by giving God what belongs to him. Therefore God in turn glorifies our righteousness. It is true and just that God is truthful and just, and to consider and confess him to be so is the same as being truthful and just. Accordingly he says in I Sam. 2 [:30], "Those who honor me I will honor, and those who despise me shall be lightly esteemed." So Paul says in Rom. 4 [:3] that Abraham's faith "was reckoned to him as righteousness" because by it he gave glory most perfectly to God, and that for the same reason our faith shall be reckoned to us as righteousness if we believe.

The third incomparable benefit of faith is that it unites the soul with Christ as a bride is united with her bridegroom. By this mystery, as the Apostle teaches, Christ and the soul become one flesh [Eph. 5:31-32]. And if they are one flesh and there is between them a true marriage—indeed the most perfect of all marriages, since human marriages are but poor examples of this one true marriage—it follows that everything they have they hold in common, the good as well as the evil. Accordingly the believing soul can boast of and glory in whatever Christ has as though it were its own, and whatever the soul has Christ claims as his own. Let us compare these and we shall see inestimable benefits. Christ is full of grace, life, and salvation. The soul is full of sins, death, and damnation. Now let faith come between them and sins, death, and damnation will be Christ's, while grace, life, and salvation will be the soul's; for if Christ is a bridegroom, he must take upon himself the things which are his bride's and bestow upon her the things that are his. If he gives her his body and very self, how shall he not give her all that is his? And if he takes the body of the bride, how shall he not take all that is hers?

Here we have a most pleasing vision not only of communion but of a blessed struggle and victory and salvation and redemption. Christ is God and man in one person. He has neither sinned nor died, and is not condemned, and he cannot sin, die, or be condemned; his righteousness, life, and salvation are unconquerable, eternal, omnipotent. By the wedding ring of faith he shares in the sins, death, and pains of hell which are his bride's. As a matter of fact, he makes them his own and acts as if they were his own and as if he himself had sinned; he suffered, died, and descended into hell that he might overcome them all. Now since it was such a one who did all this, and death and hell could not swallow him up, these were necessarily swallowed up by him in a mighty duel; for his righteousness is greater than the sins of all men, his life stronger than death, his salvation more invincible than hell. Thus the believing soul by means of the pledge of its faith is free in Christ, its bridegroom, free from all sins, secure against death and hell, and is endowed with the eternal righteousness, life, and salvation of Christ its bridegroom. So he takes to himself a glorious bride, "without spot or wrinkle, cleansing her by the washing of water with the word" [Cf. Eph. 5:26-27] of life, that is, by faith in the Word of life, righteousness, and salvation. In this way he marries her in faith, steadfast love, and in mercies, righteousness, and justice, as Hos. 2 [:19-20] says.

Who then can fully appreciate what this royal marriage means? Who can understand the riches of the glory of this grace? Here this rich and divine bridegroom Christ marries this poor, wicked harlot, redeems her from all her evil, and adorns her with all his goodness. Her sins cannot now destroy her, since they are laid upon Christ and swallowed up by him. And she has that righteousness in Christ, her husband, of which she may boast as of her own and which she can confidently display alongside her sins in the face of death and hell and say, "If I have sinned, yet my Christ, in whom I believe, has not sinned, and all his is mine and all mine is his," as the bride in the Song of Solomon [2:16] says, "My beloved is mine and I am his." This is what Paul means when he says in I Cor. 15 [:57], "Thanks be to God, who gives us the victory through our Lord Jesus Christ," that is, the victory over sin and death, as he also says there, "The sting of death is sin, and the power of sin is the law" [I Cor. 15:56].

From this you once more see that much is ascribed to faith, namely, that it alone can fulfil the law and justify without works. You see that the First Commandment, which says, "You shall worship one God," is fulfilled by faith alone. Though you were nothing but good works from the soles of your feet to the crown of your head, you would still not be righteous or worship God or fulfil the First Commandment, since God cannot be worshiped unless you ascribe to him the glory of truthfulness and all goodness which is due him. This cannot be done by works but only by the faith of the heart. Not by the doing of works but by believing do we glorify God and acknowledge that he is truthful. Therefore faith alone is the righteousness of a Christian and the fulfilling of all the commandments, for he who fulfils the First Commandment has no difficulty in fulfilling all the rest.

But works, being inanimate things, cannot glorify God, although they can, if faith is present, be done to the glory of God. Here, however, we are not inquiring what works and what kind of works are done, but who it is that does them, who glorifies God and brings forth the works. This is done by faith which dwells in the heart and is the source and substance of all our righteousness. Therefore it is a blind and dangerous doctrine which teaches that the commandments must be fulfilled by works. The commandments must be fulfilled before any works can be done, and the works proceed from the fulfilment of the commandments [Rom. 13:10], as we shall hear.

That we may examine more profoundly that grace which our inner man has in Christ, we must realize that in the Old Testament God consecrated to himself all the first-born males. The birthright was highly prized for it involved a twofold honor, that of priesthood and that of kingship. The first-born brother was priest and lord over all the others and a type of Christ, the true and only first-born of God the Father and the Virgin Mary and true king and priest, but not after the fashion of the flesh and the world, for his kingdom is not of this world [John 18:36]. He reigns in heavenly and spiritual things and consecrates them—things such as righteousness, truth, wisdom, peace, salvation, etc. This does not mean that all things on earth and in hell are not also subject to him—otherwise how could he protect and save us from them?—but that his kingdom consists neither in them nor of them. Nor does his priesthood consist in the outer splendor of robes and postures like those of the human priesthood of Aaron and our present-day church; but it consists of spiritual things through which he by an invisible service intercedes for us in heaven before God, there offers himself as a sacrifice, and does all things a priest should do, as Paul describes him under the type of Melchizedek in the Epistle to the Hebrews [Heb. 6-7]. Nor does he only pray and intercede for us but he teaches us inwardly through the living instruction of his Spirit, thus performing the two real functions of a priest, of which the prayers and the preaching of human priests are visible types.

Now just as Christ by his birthright obtained these two prerogatives, so he imparts them to and shares them with everyone who believes in him according to the law of the above-mentioned marriage, according to which the wife owns whatever belongs to the husband. Hence all of us who believe in Christ are priests and kings in Christ, as I Pet. 2 [:9] says: "You are a chosen race, God's own people, a royal priesthood, a priestly kingdom, that you may declare the wonderful deeds of him who called you out of darkness into his marvelous light."

The nature of this priesthood and kingship is something like this: First, with respect to the kingship, every Christian is by faith so exalted above all things that, by virtue of a spiritual power, he is lord of all things without exception, so that nothing can do him any harm. As a matter of fact, all things are made subject to him and are compelled to serve him in obtaining salvation. Accordingly Paul says in Rom. 8 [:28], "All things work together for good for the elect," and in I Cor. 3 [:21-23], "All things are yours whether ... life or death or the present or the future, all are yours; and you are Christ's. . . ." This is not to say that every Christian is placed over all things to have and control them by physical power—a madness with which some churchmen are afflicted—for such power belongs to kings, princes, and other men on earth. Our ordinary experience in life shows us that we are subjected to all, suffer many things, and even die. As a matter of fact, the more Christian a man is, the more evils, sufferings, and deaths he must endure, as we see in Christ the first-born prince himself, and in all his brethren, the saints. The power of which we speak is spiritual. It rules in the midst of enemies and is powerful in the midst of oppression. This means nothing else than that "power is made perfect in weakness" [II Cor. 12:9] and that in all things I can find profit toward salvation [Rom. 8:28], so that the cross and death itself are compelled to serve me and to work together with me for my salvation. This is a splended privilege and hard to attain, a truly omnipotent power, a spiritual dominion in which there is nothing so good and nothing so evil but that it shall work together for good to me, if only I believe. Yes, since faith alone suffices for salvation, I need nothing except faith exercising the power and dominion of its own liberty. Lo, this is the inestimable power and liberty of Christians.

Not only are we the freest of kings, we are also priests forever, which is far more excellent than being kings, for as priests we are worthy to appear before God to pray for others and to teach one another divine things. These are the functions of priests, and they cannot be granted to any unbeliever. Thus Christ has made it possible for us, provided we believe in him, to be not only his brethren, co-heirs, and fellow-kings, but also his fellow-priests. Therefore we may boldly come into the presence of God in the spirit of faith [Heb. 10:19, 22] and cry "Abba, Father!" pray for one another, and do all things which we see done and foreshadowed in the outer and visible works of priests.

He, however, who does not believe is not served by anything. On the contrary, nothing works for his good, but he himself is a servant of all, and all things turn out badly for him because he wickedly uses them to his own advantage and not to the glory of God. So he is no priest but a wicked man whose prayer becomes sin and who never comes into the presence of God because God does not hear sinners [John 9:31]. Who then can comprehend the lofty dignity of the Christian? By virtue of his royal power he rules over all things, death, life, and sin, and through his priestly glory is omnipotent with God because he does the things which God asks and desires, as it is written, "He will fulfil the desire of those who fear him; he also will hear their cry and save them" [Cf. Phil. 4:13]. To this glory a man attains, certainly not by any works of his, but by faith alone.

From this anyone can clearly see how a Christian is free from all things and over all things so that he needs no works to make him righteous and save him, since faith alone abundantly confers all these things. Should he grow so foolish, however, as to presume to become righteous, free, saved, and a Christian by means of some good work, he would instantly lose faith and all its benefits, a foolishness aptly illustrated in the fable of the dog who runs along a stream with a piece of meat in his mouth and, deceived by the reflection of the meat in the water, opens his mouth to snap at it and so loses both the meat and the reflection.

You will ask, "If all who are in the church are priests, how do these whom we now call priests differ from laymen?" I answer: Injustice is done those words "priest," "cleric," "spiritual," "ecclesiastic," when they are transferred from all Christians to those few who are now by a mischievous usage called "ecclesiastics." Holy Scripture makes no distinction between them, although it gives the name "ministers," "servants," "stewards" to those who are now proudly called popes, bishops, and lords and who should according to the ministry of the Word serve others and teach them the faith of Christ and the freedom of believers. Although we are all equally priests, we cannot all publicly minister and teach. We ought not do so even if we could. Paul writes accordingly in I Cor. 4 [1], "This is how one should regard us, as servants of Christ and stewards of the mysteries of God."

That stewardship, however, has now been developed into so great a display of power and so terrible a tyranny that no heathen empire or other earthly power can be compared with it, just as if laymen were not also Christians. Through this perversion the knowledge of Christian grace, faith, liberty, and of Christ himself has altogether perished, and its place has been taken by an unbearable bondage of human works and laws until we have become, as the Lamentations of Jeremiah [1] say, servants of the vilest men on earth who abuse our misfortune to serve only their base and shameless will.

THE BLOODY TENENT OF PERSECUTION

Roger Williams

To every courteous reader:

While I plead the cause of Truth and innocency against the bloody doctrine of persecution for cause of conscience,' I judge it not unfit to give alarm to myself and all men to prepare to be persecuted or hunted for cause of conscience.

Whether you stand charged with ten or but two talents, if you hunt any for cause of conscience, how can you say you followest the Lamb of God who so abhorred that practice?

If Paul, if Jesus Christ were present here at London, and the question were proposed what religion would they approve of: the Papists, Prelatists, Presbyterians, Independents, etc. would each say, "Of mine, of mine."

But put the second question: If one of the several sorts should by major vote attain the sword of steel, what weapons doth Christ Jesus authorize them to fight with in His cause? Do not all men hate the persecutor, and every conscience, true or false, complain of cruelty, tyranny, etc.?

Two mountains of crying guilt lie heavy upon the backs of all that name the name of Christ in the eyes of Jews, Turks, and pagans.

First, the blasphemies of their idolatrous inventions, superstitions, and most unchristian conversations.

Secondly, the bloody irreligious and inhumane oppressions and destructions under the mask or veil of the name of Christ, etc.

Oh how like is the jealous Jehovah, the consuming fire, to end these present slaughters in a greater slaughter of the holy witnesses? (Rev. 11.)

Six years preaching so much truth of Christ (as that time afforded in King Edward's days) kindles the flames of Queen Mary's bloody persecutions.

Who can now but expect that after so many scores of years preaching and professing of more truth, and amongst so many great contentions amongst the very best of Protestants, a fiery furnace should be heated; and who does not now see the fires kindling?

I confess I have little hopes till those flames are over, that this discourse against the doctrine of persecution for cause of conscience should pass current—I say not amongst the wolves and lions, but even amongst the sheep of Christ themselves. . . . I have not hid within my breast my soul's belief. And although sleeping on the bed either of the pleasures or profits of sin, you think your conscience bound to smite at him that dares to waken you? Yet in the midst of all these civil and spiritual wars, I hope we shall agree on these particulars:

First, however the proud (upon the advantage of a higher earth or ground) overlook the poor and cry out, "Schismatics! Heretics!, etc.," "Shall blasphemers and seducers escape unpunished? etc.," yet there is a sorer punishment in the Gospel for despising Christ than Moses, even when the despiser of Moses was put to death without mercy (Heb. 10:28,29). He that believeth not shall be damned (Mark 16:16).

Secondly, whatever worship, ministry, ministrations, [if] the best and purest are practised without faith and true persuasion that they are the true institutions of God, they are sinful worships, ministries, etc. And however in civil things we may be servants unto men, yet in divine and spiritual things the poorest peasant must disdain the service of the highest prince: Be ye not the servants of men. (I Cor. 14.)

Thirdly, without such search and trial, no man attains this faith and right persuasion. (I Thes. 5.) Try all things.

In vain have English parliaments permitted English Bibles in the poorest English houses and the simplest man or woman to search the scriptures, if yet against their souls' persuasions from the scripture they should be forced (as if they lived in Spain or Rome itself, without the sight of a Bible) to believe as the church believes.

Fourthly, having tried, we must hold fast, . . . we must not let go for all the flea bitings of the present afflictions. Having bought truth dear, we must not sell it cheap; not the least grain of it for the whole world, no not for the saving of souls, though our own most precious; least of all for the bitter sweetening of a little vanishing pleasure; for a little puff of credit and reputation from the changeable breath of uncertain sons of men; for the broken bags of riches on eagles' wings; for a dream of these, any or all of these which on our death-bed vanish and leave tormenting stings behind them.

Oh how much better is it from the love of truth, from the love of the Father of lights, from whence it comes, from the love of the Son of God, who is the way and the truth, to say as He (John 18:37), "For this end was I born, and for this end came I into the world, that I might bear witness to the truth."

CHAPTER I

Truth. In what dark corner of the world, sweet Peace, are we two met? How has this present evil world banished me from all the coasts and quarters of it, and how has the righteous God in judgment taken you from the earth? (Rev. 6:4.)

Peace. 'Tis lamentably true, blessed Truth, the foundations of the world have long been out of course; the gates of earth and Hell have conspired together to intercept our joyful meeting and our holy kisses. With what a wearied, tired wing have I flown over nations, kingdoms, cities, towns to find out precious truth!

Truth. The like inquiries in my flights and travels have I made for peace, and still am told she has left the earth and fled to Heaven.

Peace. Dear Truth, what is the earth but a dungeon of darkness where truth is not?

Truth. And what's the peace thereof but a fleeting dream, thine ape and counterfeit?

Peace. Oh where's the promise of the God of Heaven that righteousness and peace shall kiss each other?

Truth. Patience, sweet Peace; these heavens and earth are growing old and shall be changed like a garment (Psalm 102). They shall melt away and be burnt up with all the works that are therein; and the most high eternal Creator shall gloriously create new heavens and new earth wherein dwells righteousness (II Pet. 3). Our kisses then shall have their endless date of purest and sweetest joys. Till then both you and I must hope, and wait, and bear the fury of the Dragon's wrath, whose monstrous lies and furies shall with himself be cast into the lake of fire—the second death (Rev. 20).

Peace. Most precious Truth, you know we are both pursued and laid for. Mine heart is full of sighs, mine eyes with tears. Where can I better vent my full oppressed bosom than into thine, whose faithful lips may for these few hours revive my drooping, wandering spirits, and here begin to wipe tears from mine eyes and the eyes of my dearest children?

Truth. Sweet daughter of the God of peace begin. Pour out your sorrows, vent your complaints! How joyful am I to improve these precious minutes to revive our hearts, both yours and mine, and the hearts of all that love the truth and peace! (Zach. 8.)

Peace. Dear Truth, I know your birth, your nature, your delight. They that know you will prize you far above themselves and [their] lives and sell themselves to buy you. Well spoke that famous Elizabeth to her famous attorney, Sir Edward Coke: Mr. Attorney, go on as thou hast begun and still plead not *pro Domina Regina* but *pro Domina Veritate* [not for Mistress Queen but for Mistress Truth].

Truth. 'Tis true my crown is high, my scepter's strong to break down strongest holds, to throw down highest crowns of all that plead (though but in thought) against me. Some few there are—but oh how

few are valiant for the truth and dare to plead my cause as my
witnesses in sackcloth! (Rev. 11.) While all men's tongues are bent
like bows to shoot out lying words against me!

Peace. Oh how could I spend eternal days and endless dates at
your holy feet in listening to the precious oracles of your mouth! All
the words of your mouth are truth and there is no iniquity in them.
Your lips drop as the honeycomb. But oh! since we must part anon,
let us (as you said) improve our minutes and (according as you
promised) revive me with your words, which are sweeter than the
honey and the honeycomb.

CHAPTER II

Dear Truth, I have two sad complaints:

First, the most sober of your witnesses that dare to plead your
cause, how are they charged to be my enemies—contentious, tur-
bulent, seditious?

Secondly, your enemies, though they speak and rail against you,
though they outrageously pursue, imprison, banish, kill your faithful
witnesses, yet how is all vermillioned o'er for justice 'gainst the
heretics? Yea, if they kindle coals and blow the flames of devouring
wars that leave neither spiritual nor civil state, but burns up branch
and root, yet how do all pretend an holy war? He that kills, and he
that's killed, they both cry out it is for God and for their conscience.

'Tis true, nor one nor other seldom dare to plead the mighty Prince
Christ Jesus for their author, yet both (both Protestant and Papist)
pretend they have spoke with Moses and the prophets, who all, say
they (before Christ came), allowed such holy persecutions, holy wars
against the enemies of holy Church.

Truth. Dear Peace (to ease your first complaint), 'tis true your
dearest sons, most like their mother, peace-keeping, peace-making
sons of God, have borne and still must bear the blurs of troublers of
Israel and turners of the world upside down. And 'tis true again,
what Solomon once spoke: The beginning of strife is as when one
lets out water; therefore (says he) leave off contention before it be
meddled with. This caveat should keep the banks and sluices firm and
strong, that strife, like a breach of waters, break not in upon the sons
of men.

Yet strife must be distinguished: it is necessary or unnecessary,
godly or ungodly, Christian or unchristian, etc.

It is unnecessary, unlawful, dishonorable, ungodly, unchristian in
most cases in the world, for there is a possibility of keeping sweet
peace in most cases, and if it be possible, it is the express command
of God that peace be kept (Rom. 13).

Again, it is necessary, honorable, godly, etc. with civil and earthly
weapons to defend the innocent and to rescue the oppressed from

the violent paws and jaws of oppressing, persecuting Nimrods (Psalm 73, Job 29).

It is as necessary, yea more honorable, godly, and Christian, to fight the fight of faith with religious and spiritual artillery, and to contend earnestly for the faith of Jesus, once delivered to the saints, against all opposers, and the gates of earth and Hell, men or devils, yea against Paul himself or an angel from Heaven, if he bring any other faith or doctrine (Jude 4, Gal. 1:8).

Peace. With the clashing of such arms am I never wakened. Speak once again (dear Truth) to my second complaint of bloody persecution and devouring wars marching under the colors of upright justice and holy zeal, etc.

Truth. My ears have long been filled with a threefold doleful outcry.

First, of one hundred forty-four thousand virgins (Rev. 14) forced and ravished by emperors, kings, and governors to their beds of worship and religion, set up (like Absoloms) on high in their several states and countries.

Secondly, the cry of those precious souls under the altar (Rev. 6), the souls of such as have been persecuted and slain for the testimony and witness of Jesus, whose blood has been spilt like water upon the earth, and that because they have held fast the truth and witness of Jesus, against the worship of the states and times, compelling to an uniformity of state religion.

These cries of murdered virgins—who can sit still and hear? Who can but run with zeal inflamed to prevent the deflowering of chaste souls and spilling of the blood of the innocent? Humanity stirs up and prompts the sons of men to draw material swords for a virgin's chastity and life against a ravishing murderer! And piety and Christianity must needs awaken the sons of God to draw the spiritual sword (the Word of God) to preserve the chastity and life of spiritual virgins, who abhor the spiritual defilements of false worship (Rev. 14).

Thirdly, the cry of the whole earth made drunk with the blood of its inhabitants, slaughtering each other in their blinded zeal, for conscience, for religion, against the Catholics, against the Lutherans, etc.

What fearful cries within these twenty years of hundred thousands men, women, children, fathers, mothers, husbands, wives, brethren, sisters, old and young, high and low—plundered, ravished, slaughtered, murdered, famished! And hence these cries that men fling away the spiritual sword and spiritual artillery (in spiritual and religious causes) and rather trust for the suppression of each other's God, conscience, and religion (as they suppose) to an arm of flesh and a sword of steel.

Truth. Sweet Peace, what have you there?

Peace. Arguments against persecution for cause of conscience.

Truth. And what there?

Peace. An answer to such arguments, contrarily maintaining such persecution for cause of conscience.

Truth. These arguments against such persecution, and the answer pleading for it, written (as love hopes) from godly intentions, hearts, and hands, yet in a marvellous different style and manner. The arguments against persecution in milk, the answer for it (as I may say) in blood.

The author of these arguments [against persecution] (as I have been informed) being committed by some then in power, close prisoner to Newgate, for the witness of some truths of Jesus, and having not the use of pen and ink, wrote these arguments in milk, in sheets of paper, brought to him by the woman his keeper, from a friend in London, as the stopples of his milk bottle.

In such paper written with milk nothing will appear, but the way of reading it by fire being known to this friend who received the papers, he transcribed and kept together the papers, although the author himself could not correct, nor view what himself had written.

It was in milk, tending to soul nourishment, even for babes and sucklings in Christ.

It was in milk, spiritually white, pure and innocent, like those white horses of the word of truth and meekness, and the white linen or armor of righteousness, in the army of Jesus (Rev. 6 and 19).

It was in milk, soft, meek, peaceable and gentle, tending both to the peace of souls, and the peace of States and Kingdoms.

Peace. The answer (though I hope out of milky pure intentions) is returned in blood: bloody and slaughterous conclusions; bloody to the souls of all men, forced to the religion and worship which every civil state or commonweal agrees on, and compels all subjects to in a dissembled uniformity.

Bloody to the bodies, first of the holy witnesses of Christ Jesus, who testify against such invented worships.

Secondly, of the nation and peoples slaughtering each other for their several respective religions and consciences.

. . .

Peace. Pass on, holy Truth, to that similitude whereby they illustrate that negative assertion: "The prince in the ship," they say, "is governor over the bodies of all in the ship; but he has no power to govern the ship or the mariners in the actions of it. If the pilot manifestly err in his action, the prince may reprove him," and so, say they may any passenger; "if he offend against the life or goods of any, the prince may in due time and place punish him, which no private person may."

Truth. Although, dear Peace, we both agree that civil powers may not enjoin such devices, no nor enforce on any God's institutions, since Christ Jesus's coming, yet, for further illustration, I shall propose some queries concerning the civil magistrate's passing in the ship of the church, wherein Christ Jesus has appointed his ministers and officers as governors and pilots, etc.

If in a ship at sea, wherein the governor or pilot of a ship undertakes to carry the ship to such a port, the civil magistrate (suppose a king or emperor) shall command the master such and such a course, to steer upon such or such a point, which the master knows is not their course, and which if they steer he shall never bring the ship to that port or harbor: what shall the master do? Surely all men will say, the master of the ship or pilot is to present reasons and arguments from his mariner's art, if the prince be capable of them, or else in humble and submissive manner to persuade the prince not to interrupt them in their course and duty properly belonging to them, to wit, governing of the ship, steering of the course, etc.

If the master of the ship command the mariners thus and thus, in running the ship, managing the helm, trimming the sail, and the prince command the mariners a different or contrary course, who is to be obeyed?

It is confessed that the mariners may lawfully disobey the prince, and obey the governor of the ship in the actions of the ship.

Thirdly, what if the prince have as much skill, which is rare, as the pilot himself? I conceive it will be answered, that the master of the ship and pilot, in what concerns the ship, are chief and above, in respect of their office, the prince himself, and their commands ought to be attended by all the mariners, unless it be in manifest error, wherein it is granted any passenger may reprove the pilot.

Fourthly, I ask, if the prince and his attendants be unskillful in the ship's affairs, whether every sailor and mariner, the youngest and lowest, be not, so far as concerns the ship, to be preferred before the prince's followers, and the prince himself? And their counsel and advice more to be attended to, and their service more to be desired and respected, and the prince to be requested to stand by and let the business alone in their hands?

Fifthly, in case a willful king and his attendants, out of opinion of their skill, or willfulness of passion, would so steer the course, trim sail, etc., as that in the judgment of the master and seamen the ship and lives shall be endangered: whether, in case humble persuasions prevail not, ought not the ship's company to refuse to act in such a course, yea, and, in case power be in their hands, resist and suppress these dangerous practices of the prince and his followers, and so save the ship?

Lastly, suppose the master, out of base fear and cowardice, or covetous desire of reward, shall yield to gratify the mind of the prince, contrary to the rules of art and experience, etc., and the ship come in danger, and perish, and the prince with it: if the master get to shore, whether may he not be justly questioned, yea, and suffer as guilty of the prince's death, and those that perished with him? These

cases are clear, wherein, according to this similitude, the prince ought
not to govern and rule the actions of the ship, but such whose office,
and charge, and skill it is.

The result of all is this: the church of Christ is the ship, wherein
the prince—if a member, for otherwise the case is altered—is a
passenger. In this ship the officers and governors, such as are appointed by the Lord Jesus, they are the chief, and in those respects
above the prince himself, and are to be obeyed and submitted to in
their works and administrations, even before the prince himself.

In this respect every Christian in the church, man or woman, if of
more knowledge and grace of Christ, ought to be of higher esteem,
concerning religion and Christianity, than all the princes in the world
who have either none or less grace or knowledge of Christ, although
in civil things all civil reverence, honor, and obedience ought to be
yielded by all men.

Therefore, if in matters of religion the king command what is
contrary to Christ's rule, though according to his persuasion and
conscience, who sees not that, according to the similitude, he ought
not to be obeyed? Yea, and (in case) boldly, with spiritual force and
power, he ought to be resisted. And if any officer of the church of
Christ shall out of baseness yield to the command of the prince, to
the danger of the church and souls committed to his charge, the souls
that perish, notwithstanding the prince's command, shall be laid to
his charge.

If so, then I rejoin thus: how agree these truths of this similitude
with those former positions, viz., that the civil magistrate is keeper of
both tables, that he is to see the church do her duty, that he ought
to establish the true religion, suppress and punish the false, and so
consequently must discern, judge, and determine what the true gathering and governing of the church is, what the duty of every minister
of Christ is, what the true ordinances are, and what the true administrations of them; and where men fail, correct, punish, and reform
by the civil sword? I desire it may be answered, in the fear and
presence of Him whose eyes are as a flame of fire, if this be
not—according to the similitude, though contrary to their scope in
proposing of it—to be governor of the ship of the church, to see the
master, pilot, and mariners do their duty, in setting the course,
steering the ship, trimming the sails, keeping the watch etc., and
where they fail, to punish them; and therefore, by undeniable consequence, to judge and determine what their duties are, when they do
right, and when they do wrong: and this is not only to manifest
error, (for then they say every passenger may reprove) but in their
ordinary course and practice.

The similitude of a physician obeying the prince in the body
politic, but prescribing to the prince concerning the prince's body,
wherein the prince, unless the physician manifestly err, is to be
obedient to the physician, and not to be judge of the physician in his

art, but to be ruled and judged as touching the state of his body by the physician: I say this similitude and many others suiting with the former of a ship, might be alleged to prove the distinction of the civil and spiritual estate, and that according to the rule of the Lord Jesus in the gospel, the civil magistrate is only to attend the calling of the civil magistracy concerning the bodies and goods of the subjects, and is himself, if a member of the church and within, subject to the power of the Lord Jesus therein, as any member of the church is (I Cor. 5). . . .

from CIVIL DISOBEDIENCE

H. D. Thoreau

I heartily accept the motto, "That government is best which governs least;" and I should like to see it acted up to more rapidly and systematically. Carried out, it finally amounts to this, which also I believe—"That government is best which governs not at all;" and when men are prepared for it, that will be the kind of government which they will have. Government is at best but an expedient; but most governments are usually, and all governments are sometimes, inexpedient. The objections which have been brought against a standing army, and they are many and weighty, and deserve to prevail, may also at last be brought against a standing government. The standing army is only an arm of the standing government. The government itself, which is only the mode which the people have chosen to execute their will, is equally liable to be abused and perverted before the people can act through it. Witness the present Mexican war, the work of comparatively a few individuals using the standing government as their tool; for, in the outset, the people would not have consented to this measure.

This American government—what is it but a tradition, though a recent one, endeavoring to transmit itself unimpaired to posterity, but each instant losing some of its integrity? It has not the vitality and force of a single living man; for a single man can bend it to his will. It is a sort of wooden gun to the people themselves. But it is not the less necessary for this; for the people must have some complicated machinery or other, and hear its din, to satisfy that idea of government which they have. Governments show thus how success-fully men can be imposed on, even impose on themselves, for their own advantage. It is excellent, we must all allow. Yet this govern-ment never of itself furthered any enterprise, but by the alacrity with which it got out of its way. *It* does not keep the country free. *It* does not settle the West. *It* does not educate. The character inherent in the American people has done all that has been accomplished; and it would have done somewhat more, if the government had not sometimes got in its way. For government is an expedient by which men would fain succeed in letting one another alone; and, as has been said, when it is most expedient, the governed are most let alone by it. Trade and commerce, if they were not made of india-rubber, would never manage to bounce over the obstacles which legislators are continually putting in their way; and, if one were to judge these men wholly by the effects of their actions and not partly by their intentions, they would deserve to be classed and punished with those mischievous persons who put obstructions on the railroads.

But, to speak practically and as a citizen, unlike those who call themselves no-government men, I ask for, not at once no government, but *at once* a better government. Let every man make known what kind of government would command his respect, and that will be one step toward obtaining it.

After all, the practical reason why, when the power is once in the hands of the people, a majority are permitted, and for a long period continue, to rule is not because they are most likely to be in the right, nor because this seems fairest to the minority, but because they are physically the strongest. But a government in which the majority rule in all cases cannot be based on justice, even as far as men understand it. Can there not be a government in which majorities do not virtually decide right and wrong, but conscience?—in which majorities decide only those questions to which the rule of expediency is applicable? Must the citizen ever for a moment, or in the least degree, resign his conscience to the legislator? Why has every man a conscience, then? I think that we should be men first, and subjects afterward. It is not desirable to cultivate a respect for the law, so much as for the right. The only obligation which I have a right to assume is to do at any time what I think right. It is truly enough said that a corporation has no conscience; but a corporation of conscientious men is a corporation *with* a conscience. Law never made men a whit more just; and, by means of their respect for it, even the well-disposed are daily made the agents of injustice. A common and natural result of an undue respect for law is, that you may see a file of soldiers, colonel, captain, corporal, privates, powder-monkeys, and all, marching in admirable order over hill and dale to the wars, against their wills, ay, against their common sense and consciences, which makes it very steep marching indeed, and produces a palpitation of the heart. They have no doubt that it is a damnable business in which they are concerned; they are all peaceably inclined. Now, what are they? Men at all? or small movable forts and magazines, at the service of some unscrupulous man in power? Visit the Navy-Yard, and behold a marine, such a man as an American government can make, or such as it can make a man with its black arts—a mere shadow and reminiscence of humanity, a man laid out alive and standing, and already, as one may say, buried under arms with funeral accompaniments, though it may be,

> Not a drum was heard, not a funeral note,
> As his corse to the rampart we hurried;
> Not a soldier discharged his farewell shot
> O'er the grave where our hero we buried.

The mass of men serve the state thus, not as men mainly, but as machines, with their bodies. They are the standing army, and the militia, jailers, constables, *posse comitatus*, etc. In most cases there is no free exercise whatever of the judgment or of the moral sense; but they put themselves on a level with wood and earth and stones; and wooden men can perhaps be manufactured that will serve the purpose as well. Such command no more respect than men of straw or a lump of dirt. They have the same sort of worth only as horses and dogs. Yet such as these even are commonly esteemed good citizens. Others—as most legislators, politicians, lawyers, ministers, and office-holders—serve the state chiefly with their heads; and, as they rarely make any moral distinctions, they are as likely to serve the devil, without *intending* it, as God. A very few—as heroes, patriots, martyrs, reformers in the great sense, and *men*—serve the state with their consciences also, and so necessarily resist it for the most part; and they are commonly treated as enemies by it. A wise man will only be useful as a man, and will not submit to be "clay," and "stop a hole to keep the wind away," but leave that office to his dust at least:

> I am too high-born to be propertied,
> To be a secondary at control,
> Or useful serving-man and instrument
> To any sovereign state throughout the world.

He who gives himself entirely to his fellow-men appears to them useless and selfish; but he who gives himself partially to them is pronounced a benefactor and philanthropist.

How does it become a man to behave toward this American government today? I answer, that he cannot without disgrace be associated with it. I cannot for an instant recognize that political organization as *my* government which is the *slave's* government also.

All men recognize the right of revolution; that is, the right to refuse allegiance to, and to resist, the government, when its tyranny or its inefficiency are great and unendurable. But almost all say that such is not the case now. But such was the case, they think, in the Revolution of '75. If one were to tell me that this was a bad government because it taxed certain foreign commodities brought to its ports, it is most probable that I should not make an ado about it, for I can do without them. All machines have their friction; and possibly this does enough good to counterbalance the evil. At any rate, it is a great evil to make a stir about it. But when the friction comes to have its machine, and oppression and robbery are organized, I say, let us not have such a machine any longer. In other words, when a sixth of the population of a nation which has undertaken to be the refuge of liberty are slaves, and a whole country is unjustly overrun and conquered by a foreign army, and subjected to military law, I think that it is not too soon for honest men to rebel and revolutionize. What makes this duty the more urgent is the fact that the country so overrun is not our own, but ours is the invading army.

Paley, a common authority with many on moral questions, in his chapter on the "Duty of Submission to Civil Government," resolves all civil obligation into expediency; and he proceeds to say that "so long as the interest of the whole society requires it, that is, so long as the established government cannot be resisted or changed without public inconveniency, it is the will of God ... that the established government be obeyed—and no longer. This principle being admitted, the justice of every particular case of resistance is reduced to a computation of the quantity of the danger and grievance on the one side, and of the probability and expense of redressing it on the other." Of this, he says, every man shall judge for himself. But Paley appears never to have contemplated those cases to which the rule of expediency does not apply, in which a people, as well as an individual, must do justice, cost what it may. If I have unjustly wrested a plank from a drowning man, I must restore it to him though I drown myself. This, according to Paley, would be inconvenient. But he that would save his life, in such a case, shall lose it. This people must cease to hold slaves, and to make war on Mexico, though it cost them their existence as a people.

In their practice, nations agree with Paley; but does any one think that Massachusetts does exactly what is right at the present crisis?

> A drab of state, a cloth-o'-silver slut,
> To have her train borne up, and her soul trail in the dirt.

Practically speaking, the opponents to a reform in Massachusetts are not a hundred thousand politicians at the South, but a hundred thousand merchants and farmers here, who are more interested in commerce and agriculture than they are in humanity, and are not prepared to do justice to the slave and to Mexico, *cost what it may*. I quarrel not with far-off foes, but with those who, near at home, cooperate with, and do the bidding of, those far away, and without whom the latter would be harmless. We are accustomed to say, that the mass of men are unprepared; but improvement is slow, because the few are not materially wiser or better than the many. It is not so important that many should be as good as you, as that there be some absolute goodness somewhere; for that will leaven the whole lump. There are thousands who are *in opinion* opposed to slavery and to statistics are at fault: the population has been returned too large. How many *men* are there to a square thousand miles in this country? Hardly one. Does not America offer any inducement for men to settle here? The American has dwindled into an Odd Fellow—one who may be known by the development of his organ of gregariousness, and a manifest lack of intellect and cheerful self-reliance; whose first and chief concern, on coming into the world, is to see that the almshouses are in good repair; and, before yet he has lawfully donned the virile garb, to collect a fund for the support of the widows and orphans that may be; who, in short, ventures to live only by the aid of the Mutual Insurance company, which has promised to bury him decently.

It is not a man's duty, as a matter of course, to devote himself to the eradication of any, even the most enormous, wrong; he may still properly have other concerns to engage him; but it is his duty, at least, to wash his hands of it, and, if he gives it no thought longer, not to give it practically his support. If I devote myself to other pursuits and contemplations, I must first see, at least, that I do not pursue them sitting upon another man's shoulders. I must get off him first, that he may pursue his contemplations too. See what gross inconsistency is tolerated. I have heard some of my townsmen say, "I should like to leave them order me out to help put down an insurrection of the slaves, or to march to Mexico;—see if I would go;" and yet these very men have each, directly by their allegiance, and so indirectly, at least, by their money, furnished a substitute. The soldier is applauded who refuses to serve in an unjust war by those who do not refuse to sustain the unjust government which makes the war; is applauded by those whose own act and authority he disregards and sets at naught; as if the state were penitent to that degree that it hired one to scourge it while it sinned, but not to that degree that it left off sinning for a moment. Thus, under the name of Order and Civil Government, we are all made at last to pay homage to and support our own meanness. After the first blush of sin comes its indifference; and from immoral it becomes, as it were, *un*moral, and not quite unnecessary to that life which we have made.

The broadest and most prevalent error requires the most disinterested virtue to sustain it. The slight reproach to which the virtue of patriotism is commonly liable, the noble are most likely to incur. Those who, while they disapprove of the character and measures of a government, yield to it their allegiance and support are undoubtedly its most conscientious supporters, and so frequently the most serious obstacles to reform. Some are petitioning the State to dissolve the Union, to disregard the requisitions of the President. Why do they not dissolve it themselves—the union between themselves and the State—and refuse to pay their quota into its treasury? Do not they stand in the same relation to the State that the State does to the Union? And have not the same reasons prevented the State from the war, who yet in effect do nothing to put an end to them; who, esteeming themselves children of Washington and Franklin, sit down with their hands in their pockets, and say that they know not what to do, and do nothing; who even postpone the question of freedom to the question of free trade, and quietly read the prices-current along with the latest advices from Mexico, after dinner, and, it may be, fall asleep over them both. What is the price-current of an honest man and patriot today? They hesitate, and they regret, and sometimes they petition; but they do nothing in earnest and with effect. They will wait, well disposed, for others to remedy the evil, that they may no longer have it to regret. At most, they give only a cheap vote, and a feeble countenance and God-speed, to the right, as it goes by them. There are nine hundred and ninety-nine patrons of virtue to one virtuous man. But it is easier to deal with the real possessor of a thing than with the temporary guardian of it.

All voting is a sort of gaming, like checkers or backgammon, with a slight moral tinge to it, a playing with right and wrong, with moral questions; and betting naturally accompanies it. The character of the voters is not staked. I cast my vote, perchance, as I think right; but I am not vitally concerned that that right should prevail. I am willing to leave it to the majority. Its obligation, therefore, never exceeds that of expediency. Even voting *for the right* is *doing* nothing for it. It is only expressing to men feebly your desire that it should prevail. A wise man will not leave the right to the mercy of chance, nor wish it to prevail through the power of the majority. There is but little virtue in the action of masses of men. When the majority shall at length vote for the abolition of slavery, it will be because they are indifferent to slavery, or because there is but little slavery left to be abolished by their vote. *They* will then be the only slaves. Only *his* vote can hasten the abolition of slavery who asserts his own freedom by his vote.

I hear of a convention to be held at Baltimore, or elsewhere, for the selection of a candidate for the Presidency, made up chiefly of editors, and men who are politicians by profession; but I think, what is it to any independent, intelligent, and respectable man what decision they may come to? Shall we not have the advantage of his wisdom and honesty, nevertheless? Can we not count upon some independent votes? Are there not many individuals in the country who do not attend conventions? But no: I find that the respectable man, so called, has immediately drifted from his position, and despairs of his country, when his country has more reason to despair of him. He forthwith adopts one of the candidates thus selected as the only *available* one, thus proving that he is himself *available* for any purposes of the demagogue. His vote is of no more worth than that of any unprincipled foreigner or hireling native, who may have been bought. O for a man who is a *man*, and, as my neighbor says, has a bone in his back which you cannot pass your hand through! Our resisting the Union which have prevented them from resisting the State?

How can a man be satisfied to entertain an opinion merely, and enjoy *it*? Is there any enjoyment in it, if his opinion is that he is aggrieved? If you are cheated out of a single dollar by your neighbor, you do not rest satisfied with knowing that you are cheated, or with saying that you are cheated, or even with petitioning him to pay you your due; but you take effectual steps at once to obtain the full amount, and see that you are never cheated again. Action from principle, the perception and the performance of right, changes things and relations; it is essentially revolutionary, and does not consist wholly with anything which was. It not only divides States and churches, it divides families; ay, it divides the *individual*, separating the diabolical in him from the divine.

Unjust laws exist: shall we be content to obey them, or shall we endeavor to amend them, and obey them until we have succeeded, or shall we transgress them at once? Men generally, under such a government as this, think that they ought to wait until they have persuaded the majority to alter them. They think that, if they should resist, the remedy would be worse than the evil. But it is the fault of the government itself that the remedy *is* worse than the evil. *It* makes it worse. Why is it not more apt to anticipate and provide for reform? Why does it not cherish its wise minority? Why does it cry and resist before it is hurt? Why does it not encourage its citizens to be on the alert to point out its faults, and *do* better than it would have them? Why does it always crucify Christ, and excommunicate Copernicus and Luther, and pronounce Washington and Franklin rebels?

One would think, that a deliberate and practical denial of its authority was the only offence never contemplated by government; else, why has it not assigned its definite, its suitable and proportionate, penalty? If a man who has no property refuses but once to earn nine shillings for the State, he is put in prison for a period unlimited by any law that I know, and determined only by the discretion of those who placed him there; but if he should steal ninety times nine shillings from the State, he is soon permitted to go at large again.

If the injustice is part of the necessary friction of the machine of government, let it go, let it go: perchance it will wear smooth—certainly the machine will wear out. If the injustice has a spring, or a pulley, or a rope, or a crank, exclusively for itself, then perhaps you may consider whether the remedy will not be worse than the evil; but if it is of such a nature that it requires you to be the agent of injustice to another, then, I say, break the law. Let your life be a counter-friction to stop the machine. What I have to do is to see, at any rate, that I do not lend myself to the wrong which I condemn.

As for adopting the ways which the State has provided for remedying the evil, I know not of such ways. They take too much time, and a man's life will be gone. I have other affairs to attend to. I came into this world, not chiefly to make this a good place to live in, but to live in it, be it good or bad. A man has not everything to do, but something; and because he cannot do *everything*, it is not necessary that he should do *something* wrong. It is not my business to be petitioning the Governor or the Legislature any more than it is theirs to petition me; and if they should not hear my petition, what should I do then? But in this case the State has provided no way: its very Constitution is the evil. This may seem to be harsh and stubborn and unconciliatory; but it is to treat with the utmost kindness and consideration the only spirit that can appreciate or deserves it. So is all change for the better, like birth and death, which convulse the body.

I do not hesitate to say, that those who call themselves Abolitionists should at once effectually withdraw their support, both in person and property, from the government of Massachusetts, and not wait till they constitute a majority of one, before they suffer the right to prevail through them. I think that it is enough if they have God on their side, without waiting for that other one. Moreover, any man more right than his neighbors constitutes a majority of one already....

Under a government which imprisons any unjustly, the true place for a just man is also a prison. The proper place today, the only place which Massachusetts has provided for her freer and less desponding spirits, is in her prisons, to be put out and locked out of the State by her own act, as they have already put themselves out by their principles. It is there that the fugitive slave, and the Mexican prisoner on parole, and the Indian come to plead the wrongs of his race should find them; on that separate, but more free and honorable, ground, where the State places those who are not *with* her, but *against* her—the only house in a slave State in which a free man can abide with honor. If any think that their influence would be lost there, and their voices no longer afflict the ear of the State, that they would not be as an enemy within its walls, they do not know by how much truth is stronger than error, nor how much more eloquently and effectively he can combat injustice who has experienced a little in his own person. Cast your whole vote, not a strip of paper merely, but your whole influence. A minority is powerless while it conforms to the majority; it is not even a minority then; but it is irresistible when it clogs by its whole weight. If the alternative is to keep all just men in prison, or give up war and slavery, the State will not hesitate which to choose. If a thousand men were not to pay their tax-bills this year, that would not be a violent and bloody measure, as it would be to pay them, and enable the State to commit violence and shed innocent blood. This is, in fact, the definition of a peaceable revolution, if any such is possible. If the tax-gatherer, or any other public officer, asks me, as one has done, "But what shall I do?" my answer is, "If you really wish to do anything, resign your office." When the subject has refused allegiance, and the officer has resigned his office, then the revolution is accomplished. But even suppose blood should flow. Is there not a sort of blood shed when the conscience is wounded? Through this would a man's real manhood and immortality flow out, and he bleeds to an everlasting death. I see this blood flowing now. . . .

The authority of government, even such as I am willing to submit to—for I will cheerfully obey those who know and can do better than I, and in many things even those who neither know nor can do so well—is still an impure one: to be strictly just, it must have the sanction and consent of the governed. It can have no pure right over my person and property but what I concede to it. The progress from an absolute to a limited monarchy, from a limited monarchy to a democracy, is a progress toward a true respect for the individual. Even the Chinese philosopher was wise enough to regard the individual as the basis of the empire. Is a democracy, such as we know it, the last improvement possible in government? Is it not possible to take a step further towards recognizing and organizing the rights of man? There will never be a really free and enlightened State until the State comes to recognize the individual as a higher and independent power, from which all its own power and authority are derived, and treats him accordingly. I please myself with imagining a State at least which can afford to be just to all men, and to treat the individual with respect as a neighbor; which even would not think it inconsistent with its own repose if a few were to live aloof from it, not meddling with it, nor embraced by it, who fulfilled all the duties of neighbors and fellow-men. A State which bore this kind of fruit, and suffered it to drop off as fast as it ripened, would prepare the way for a still more perfect and glorious State, which also I have imagined, but not yet anywhere seen.

MAXIMS FOR REVOLUTIONISTS

George Bernard Shaw

THE GOLDEN RULE

Do not do unto others as you would that they should do unto you. Their tastes may not be the same.

Never resist temptation: prove all things: hold fast that which is good.

Do not love your neighbor as yourself. If you are on good terms with yourself it is an impertinence: if on bad, an injury.

The golden rule is that there are no golden rules.

ROYALTY

Kings are not born: they are made by artificial hallucination. When the process is interrupted by adversity at a critical age, as in the case of Charles II, the subject becomes sane and never completely recovers his kingliness.

The Court is the servant's hall of the sovereign.

Vulgarity in a king flatters the majority of the nation.

The flunkeyism propagated by the throne is the price we pay for its political convenience.

IDOLATRY

The art of government is the organization of idolatry.

The bureaucracy consists of functionaries; the aristocracy, of idols; the democracy, of idolaters.

The populace cannot understand the bureaucracy: it can only worship the national idols.

The savage bows down to idols of wood and stone: the civilized man to idols of flesh and blood.

A limited monarchy is a device for combining the inertia of a wooden idol with the credibility of a flesh and blood one.

When the wooden idol does not answer the peasant's prayer, he beats it: when the flesh and blood idol does not satisfy the civilized man, he cuts its head off.

He who slays a king and he who dies for him are alike idolaters.

DEMOCRACY

If the lesser mind could measure the greater as a footrule can measure a pyramid, there would be finality in universal suffrage. As it is, the political problem remains unsolved.

Democracy substitutes selection by the incompetent many for appointment by the corrupt few.

Democratic republics can no more dispense with national idols than monarchies with public functionaries.

Government presents only one problem: the discovery of a trustworthy anthropometric method.

IMPERIALISM

Excess of insularity makes a Briton an Imperialist.

Excess of local self-assertion makes a colonist an Imperialist.

A colonial Imperialist is one who raises colonial troops, equips a colonial squadron, claims a Federal Parliament sending its measures to the Throne instead of to the Colonial Office, and, being finally brought by this means into insoluble conflict with the insular British Imperialist, "cuts the painter" and breaks up the Empire.

LIBERTY AND EQUALITY

He who confuses political liberty with freedom and political equality with similarity has never thought for five minutes about either.

Nothing can be unconditional: consequently nothing can be free.

Liberty means responsibility. That is why most men dread it.

The duke inquires contemptuously whether his gamekeeper is the equal of the Astronomer Royal; but he insists that they shall both be hanged equally if they murder him.

The notion that the colonel need be a better man than the private is as confused as the notion that the keystone need be stronger than the coping stone.

Where equality is undisputed, so also is subordination.

Equality is fundamental in every department of social organization.

The relation of superior to inferior excludes good manners.

EDUCATION

When a man teaches something he does not know to somebody else who has no aptitude for it, and gives him a certificate of proficiency, the latter has completed the education of a gentleman.

A fool's brain digests philosophy into folly, science into superstition, and art into pedantry. Hence University education.

The best brought-up children are those who have seen their parents as they are. Hypocrisy is not the parent's first duty.

The vilest abortionist is he who attempts to mould a child's character.

At the University every great treatise is postponed until its author attains impartial judgment and perfect knowledge. If a horse could wait as long for its shoes and would pay for them in advance, our blacksmiths would all be college dons.

He who can, does. He who cannot, teaches.

A learned man is an idler who kills time with study. Beware of his false knowledge: it is more dangerous than ignorance.

Activity is the only road to knowledge.

Every fool believes what his teachers tell him, and calls his credulity science or morality as confidently as his father called it divine
revelation.

No man fully capable of his own language ever masters another.

No man can be a pure specialist without being in the strict sense an
idiot.

Do not give your children moral and religious instruction unless
you are quite sure they will not take it too seriously. Better be the
mother of Henri Quatre and Nell Gwynne than of Robespierre and
Queen Mary Tudor.

MARRIAGE

Marriage is popular because it combines the maximum of temptation
with the maximum of opportunity.

Marriage is the only legal contract which abrogates as between the
parties all the laws that safeguard the particular relation to which it
refers.

The essential function of marriage is the continuance of the race, as
stated in the Book of Common Prayer.[1]

The accidental function of marriage is the gratification of the
amoristic sentiment of mankind.

The artificial sterilization of marriage makes it possible for marriage
to fulfil its accidental function whilst neglecting its essential one.

The most revolutionary invention of the XIX century was the
artificial sterilization of marriage.

Any marriage system which condemns a majority of the population
to celibacy will be violently wrecked on the pretext that it outrages
morality.

Polygamy, when tried under modern democratic conditions, as by
the Mormons, is wrecked by the revolt of the mass of inferior men
who are condemned to celibacy by it; for the maternal instinct leads
a woman to prefer a tenth share in a first rate man to the exclusive
possession of a third rate one. Polyandry has been tried under these
conditions.

The minimum of national celibacy (ascertained by dividing the
number of males in the community by the number of females, and
taking the quotient as the number of wives or husbands permitted to
each person) is secured in England (where the quotient is 1) by the
institution of monogamy.

The modern sentimental term for the national minimum of celibacy
is Purity.

[1] The Prayer Book of the Church of England, but the Prayer Book of
the Protestant Episcopal Church in the United States does not contain the
statement.

Marriage, or any other form of promiscuous amoristic monogamy, is fatal to large States because it puts its ban on the deliberate breeding of man as a political animal.

CRIME AND PUNISHMENT

All scoundrelism is summed up in the phrase "Que Messieurs les Assassins commencent!"[2]

The man who has graduated from the flogging block at Eton to the bench from which he sentences the garotter to be flogged is the same social product as the garotter who has been kicked by his father and cuffed by his mother until he has grown strong enough to throttle and rob the rich citizen whose money he desires.

Imprisonment is as irrevocable as death.

Criminals do not die by the hands of the law. They die by the hands of other men.

The assassin Czolgosz made President McKinley a hero by assassinating him. The United States of America made Czolgosz a hero by the same process.

Assassination on the scaffold is the worst form of assassination, because there it is invested with the approval of society.

It is the deed that teaches, not the name we give it. Murder and capital punishment arc not opposites that cancel one another, but similars that breed their kind.

Crime is only the retail department of what, in wholesale, we call penal law.

When a man wants to murder a tiger he calls it sport: when the tiger wants to murder him he calls it ferocity. The distinction between Crime and Justice is no greater.

Whilst we have prisons it matters little which of us occupy the cells.

The most anxious man in a prison is the governor.

It is not necessary to replace a guillotined criminal: it is necessary to replace a guillotined social system.

TITLES

Titles distinguish the mediocre, embarrass the superior, and are disgraced by the inferior.

Great men refuse titles because they are jealous of them.

---

[2] From an article published in January, 1849, by Alphonse Karr, defending capital punishment. He made the point that if it were desirable to abolish the death penalty, "Let the murderers begin!"

HONOR

There are no perfectly honorable men; but every true man has one main point of honor and a few minor ones.

You cannot believe in honor until you have achieved it. Better keep yourself clean and bright: you are the window through which you must see the world.

Your word can never be as good as your bond, because your memory can never be as trustworthy as your honor.

PROPERTY

Property, said Proudhon, is theft. This is the only perfect truism that has been uttered on the subject.

SERVANTS

When domestic servants are treated as human beings it is not worth while to keep them.

The relation of master and servant is advantageous only to masters who do not scruple to abuse their authority, and to servants who do not scruple to abuse their trust.

The perfect servant, when his master makes humane advances to him, feels that his existence is threatened, and hastens to change his place.

Masters and servants are both tyrannical; but the masters are the more dependent of the two.

A man enjoys what he uses, not what his servants use.

Man is the only animal which esteems itself rich in proportion to the number and voracity of its parasites.

Ladies and gentlemen are permitted to have friends in the kennel, but not in the kitchen.

Domestic servants, by making spoiled children of their masters, are forced to intimidate them in order to be able to live with them.

In a slave state, the slaves rule; in Mayfair, the tradesman rules.

HOW TO BEAT CHILDREN

If you strike a child, take care that you strike it in anger, even at the risk of maiming it for life. A blow in cold blood neither can nor should be forgiven.

If you beat children for pleasure, avow your object frankly, and play the game according to the rules, as a foxhunter does; and you will do comparatively little harm. No foxhunter is such a cad as to pretend that he hunts the fox to teach it not to steal chickens, or that he suffers more acutely than the fox at the death. Remember that even in childbeating there is the sportsman's way and the cad's way.

RELIGION

Beware of the man whose god is in the skies.

What a man believes may be ascertained, not from his creed, but from the assumptions on which he habitually acts.

VIRTUES AND VICES

No specific virtue or vice in a man implies the existence of any other specific virtue or vice in him, however closely the imagination may associate them.

Virtue consists, not in abstaining from vice, but in not desiring it.

Self-denial is not a virtue: it is only the effect of prudence on rascality.

Obedience simulates subordination as fear of the police simulates honesty.

Disobedience, the rarest and most courageous of the virtues, is seldom distinguished from neglect, the laziest and commonest of the vices.

Vice is waste of life. Poverty, obedience, and celibacy are the canonical vices.

Economy is the art of making the most of life.

The love of economy is the root of all virtue.

FAIRPLAY

The love of fairplay is a spectator's virtue, not a principal's.

GREATNESS

Greatness is only one of the sensations of littleness.

In heaven an angel is nobody in particular.

Greatness is the secular name for Divinity: both mean simply what lies beyond us.

If a great man could make us understand him, we should hang him.

We admit that when the divinity we worshipped made itself visible and comprehensible we crucified it.

To a mathematician the eleventh means only a single unit: to the bushman who cannot count further than his ten fingers it is an incalculable myriad.

The difference between the shallowest routineer and the deepest thinker appears, to the latter, trifling; to the former, infinite.

In a stupid nation the man of genius becomes a god: everybody worships him and nobody does his will.

BEAUTY AND HAPPINESS, ART AND RICHES

Happiness and Beauty are by-products.

Folly is the direct pursuit of Happiness and Beauty.

Riches and Art are spurious receipts for the production of Happiness and Beauty.

He who desires a lifetime of happiness with a beautiful woman desires to enjoy the taste of wine by keeping his mouth always full of it.

The most intolerable pain is produced by prolonging the keenest pleasure.

The man with toothache thinks everyone happy whose teeth are sound. The poverty-stricken man makes the same mistake about the rich man.

The more a man possesses over and above what he uses, the more careworn he becomes.

The tyranny that forbids you to make the road with pick and shovel is worse than that which prevents you from lolling along it in a carriage and pair.

In an ugly and unhappy world the richest man can purchase nothing but ugliness and unhappiness.

In his efforts to escape from ugliness and unhappiness the rich man intensifies both. Every new yard of West End creates a new acre of East End.[3]

The XIX century was the Age of Faith in Fine Art. The results are before us.

THE PERFECT GENTLEMAN

The fatal reservation of the gentleman is that he sacrifices everything to his honor except his gentility.

A gentleman of our days is one who has money enough to do what every fool would do if he could afford it: that is, consume without producing.

The true diagnostic of modern gentility is parasitism.

No elaboration of physical or moral accomplishment can atone for the sin of parasitism.

[3]London's rich live in the West End; her poor in the East End.

A modern gentleman is necessarily the enemy of his country. Even in war he does not fight to defend it, but to prevent his power of preying on it from passing to a foreigner. Such combatants are patriots in the same sense as two dogs fighting for a bone are lovers of animals.

The North American Indian was a type of the sportsman warrior gentleman. The Periclean Anthenian was a type of the intellectually and artistically cultivated gentleman. Both were political failures. The modern gentleman, without the hardihood of the one or the culture of the other, has the appetite of both put together. He will not succeed where they failed.

He who believes in education, criminal law, and sport, needs only property to make him a perfect modern gentleman.

MODERATION

Moderation is never applauded for its own sake.

A moderately honest man with a moderately faithful wife, moderate drinkers both, in a moderately healthy house: that is the true middle class unit.

THE UNCONSCIOUS SELF

The unconscious self is the real genius. Your breathing goes wrong the moment your conscious self meddles with it.

Except during the nine months before he draws his first breath, no man manages his affairs as well as a tree does.

REASON

The reasonable man adapts himself to the world: the unreasonable one persists in trying to adapt the world to himself. Therefore all progress depends on the unreasonable man.

The man who listens to Reason is lost: Reason enslaves all whose minds are not strong enough to master her.

DECENCY

Decency is Indecency's Conspiracy of Silence.

EXPERIENCE

Men are wise in proportion, not to their experience, but to their capacity for experience.

If we could learn from mere experience, the stones of London would be wiser than its wisest men.

TIME'S REVENGES

Those whom we call brutes had their revenge when Darwin shewed us that they are our cousins.

The thieves had their revenge when Marx convicted the bourgeoisie of theft.

GOOD INTENTIONS

Hell is paved with good intentions, not bad ones.

All men mean well.

NATURAL RIGHTS

The Master of Arts, by proving that no man has any natural rights, compels himself to take his own for granted.

The right to live is abused whenever it is not constantly challenged.

FAUTE DE MIEUX

In my childhood I demurred to the description of a certain young lady as "the pretty Miss So and So." My Aunt rebuked me by saying "Remember always that the least plain sister is the family beauty."

No age or condition is without its heroes. The least incapable general in a nation is its Caesar, the least imbecile stateman its Solon, the least confused thinker its Socrates, the least commonplace poet its Shakespear.

CHARITY

Charity is the most mischievous sort of pruriency.

Those who minister to poverty and disease are accomplices in the two worst of all the crimes.

He who gives money he has not earned is generous with other people's labor.

Every genuinely benevolent person loathes almsgiving and mendicity.

FAME

Life levels all men: death reveals the eminent.

DISCIPLINE

Mutiny Acts are needed only by officers who command without authority. Divine right needs no whip.

WOMEN IN THE HOME

Home is the girl's prison and the woman's workhouse.

CIVILIZATION

Civilization is a disease produced by the practice of building societies with rotten material.

Those who admire modern civilization usually identify it with the steam engine and the electric telegraph.

Those who understand the steam engine and the electric telegraph spend their lives in trying to replace them with something better.

The imagination cannot conceive a viler criminal than he who should build another London like the present one, nor a greater benefactor than he who should destroy it.

GAMBLING

The most popular method of distributing wealth is the method of the roulette table.

The roulette table pays nobody except him that keeps it. Nevertheless a passion for gaming is common, though a passion for keeping roulette tables is unknown.

Gambling promises the poor what Property performs for the rich: that is why the bishops dare not denounce it fundamentally.

THE SOCIAL QUESTION

Do not waste your time on Social Questions. What is the matter with the poor is Poverty: what is the matter with the rich is Uselessness.

STRAY SAYINGS

We are told that when Jehovah created the world he saw that it was good. What would he say now?

The conversion of a savage to Christianity is the conversion of Christianity to savagery.

No man dares say so much of what he thinks as to appear to himself an extremist.

Mens sana in corpore sano is a foolish saying. The sound body is a product of the sound mind.

Decadence can find agents only when it wears the mask of progress.

In moments of progress the noble succeed, because things are going their way: in moments of decadence the base succeed for the same reason: hence the world is never without the exhilaration of contemporary success.

The reformer for whom the world is not good enough finds himself shoulder to shoulder with him that is not good enough for the world.

Every man over forty is a scoundrel.

Youth, which is forgiven everything, forgives itself nothing: age, which forgives itself everything, is forgiven nothing.

When we learn to sing that Britons never will be masters we shall make an end of slavery.

Do not mistake your objection to defeat for an objection to fighting, your objection to being a slave for an objection to slavery, your objection to not being as rich as your neighbor for an objection to poverty. The cowardly, the insubordinate, and the envious share your objections.

Take care to get what you like or you will be forced to like what you get. Where there is no ventilation fresh air is declared unwholesome. Where there is no religion hypocrisy becomes good taste. Where there is no knowledge ignorance calls itself science.

If the wicked flourish and the fittest survive, Nature must be the God of rascals.

If history repeats itself, and the unexpected always happens, how incapable must Man be of learning from experience!

Compassion is the fellow-feeling of the unsound.

Those who understand evil pardon it: those who resent it destroy it.

Acquired notions of propriety are stronger than natural instincts. It is easier to recruit for monasteries and convents than to induce an Arab woman to uncover her mouth in public, or a British officer to walk through Bond Street in a golfing cap on an afternoon in May.

It is dangerous to be sincere unless you are also stupid.

The Chinese tame fowls by clipping their wings, and women by deforming their feet. A petticoat round the ankles serves equally well.

Political Economy and Social Economy are amusing intellectual games; but Vital Economy is the Philosopher's Stone.

When a heretic wishes to avoid martyrdom he speaks of "Orthodoxy, True and False" and demonstrates that the True is his heresy.

Beware of the man who does not return your blow: he neither forgives you nor allows you to forgive yourself.

If you injure your neighbor, better not do it by halves.

Sentimentality is the error of supposing that quarter can be given or taken in moral conflicts.

Two starving men cannot be twice as hungry as one; but two rascals can be ten times as vicious as one.

Make your cross your crutch; but when you see another man do it, beware of him.

SELF-SACRIFICE

Self-sacrifice enables us to sacrifice other people without blushing.

If you begin by sacrificing yourself to those you love, you will end by hating those to whom you have sacrificed yourself.

THE STATE: ITS HISTORIC ROLE

Peter Kropotkin

If you look still deeper into all the facts which I have touched upon, if you see the State as it was in history and as it is in essence to-day, and if you consider moreover that a social institution cannot serve *all* aims indiscriminately, because, like every other organ, it is developed for a certain purpose, and not for all purposes, you will understand why we desire the abolition of the State.

We see in it an institution developed in the history of human societies to hinder union among men, to obstruct the development of local initiative, to crush existing liberties and prevent their restoration.

And we know that an institution, which has a past dating back some thousands of years cannot lend itself to a function opposed to that for which it was developed in the course of history.

To this argument, unassailable to anyone who has reflected on history, what replies do we receive?

We are answered by an almost childish argument: "The State is there, it exists, it represents a ready-made powerful organisation. Why destroy it instead of making use of it? Admittedly it works for ill, but that is due to its being in the hands of exploiters. In the hands of the people, why should it not be utilised for a better end and for the good of men?"

Always the same dream, the dream of Schiller's Marquis of Posa trying to make autocracy an instrument of enfranchisement, the dream of the gentle priest Peter in Zola's *Rome*, wishing to make the Church a lever of Socialism!

Those who reason in this way either have not the least notion of the real historical rôle of the State, or else conceive the Social Revolution under such a tame and insignificant form, that it has nothing more in common with Socialist aspirations.

Take a concrete example, France.

All of us have perceived that the Third Republic, in spite of its republican form of government, has remained monarchical in its essence. Everyone has reproached it with not having republicanised France. I do not speak of its not having done anything for the Social Revolution, but of its not having even introduced the simple republican habits and customs and spirit. For the little that *has* been done during the last twenty-five years to democratize customs, or to spread a little enlightenment, has been done everywhere—even in the European monarchies—under the pressure of the times through which we are passing. Whence comes then the strange anomaly that we have in France—a Republican Monarchy?

It comes from France having remained as much a State as it was thirty years ago. The holders of power have changed their name; but all the immense scaffolding of centralised organisation, the imitation of the Rome of the Caesars which had been elaborated in France, has remained. The wheels of this huge machinery continue to exchange their fifty documents when the wind has blown down a tree on the national route. The stamp on the documents has changed; but the State, its spirit, its organs, its territorial centralisation, and its centralisation of functions, have remained unaltered. Worse than that; they extend from day to day over the country.

Sincere Republicans nourished the illusion that the State organisation could be utilised to operate a change in a republican sense; and here is the result. When they ought to have destroyed the old organisation, destroyed the *State*, and constructed a *new* organisation, by beginning at the very basis of society—the free village commune, the free workers' union, and so on—they thought to utilise "the organisation that already existed." And for not having understood that you cannot make an historical institution go in any direction you would have it, that it must go its own way, they were swallowed up by the institution.

Yet in this case there was no question of modifying the whole of the economic relations of society, as is the case with us. It was merely a question of reforming certain points in the political relations among men!

But, after this complete failure and in face of such a conclusive experience, they obstinately continue to say that the conquest of power in the State by the people will suffice to accomplish the Social Revolution; that the old machine, slowly elaborated in the course of history to mangle liberty, to crush the individual, to seat oppression on a legal basis, to lead the brain astray in accustoming it to servitude, will lend itself marvellously to new functions; that it will become the means of making a new life germinate, that it will seat liberty and equality on an economic basis, awaken society, and march to the conquest of a better future! What an absurd miscomprehension of history!

To give free scope to Socialism, it is necessary to reconstruct society, based to-day on the narrow individualism of the shopkeeper, from top to bottom. It is not only, as they said sometimes in a vague metaphysical way, a question of returning to the worker "the integral product of his work," but a question of re-modelling in their entirety all relations among men, from those existing to-day between every individual and his churchwarden or his station master, to those existing between trades, hamlets, cities and regions. In every street, in every hamlet, in every group of men assembled about a factory or along a railroad, we must awaken the creative, constructive, organising spirit, in order to reconstruct the whole of life in the factory, on the railroad, in the village, in the stores, in taking supplies, in production, in distribution. All relations between individuals and between human agglomerations must begin to be remodelled as soon as we begin to reform any part of the present commercial or administrative organisation.

And they expect this immense work, demanding the full and free exercise of popular genius, to be carried out within the frame-work of the State, within the pyramidal scale of organisation that constitutes the essence of each State! They want the State, whose very reason for existence lies in the crushing of the individual, in the destruction of all free grouping and free creation, in the hatred of initiative and in the triumph of *one* idea (which must necessarily be that of the mediocrity), to become the lever of this immense transformation! They want to govern a newborn society by decrees and electoral majorities! What childishness!

Throughout the history of our civilisation, two traditions, two opposed tendencies, have been in conflict: the Roman tradition and the popular tradition, the imperial tradition and the federalist tradition, the authoritarian tradition and the libertarian tradition.

Again, on the eve of the great Social Revolution these two traditions stand face to face.

Between these two currents, always alive, always struggling in humanity—the current of the people and the current of the minorities which thirst for political and religious domination—our choice is made.

We again take up the current which led men in the twelfth century to organise themselves on the basis of free understanding, of free initiative of the individual, of free federation. We leave others to cling to the Roman, Canonic, and Imperial tradition.

History has not been an uninterrupted evolution. At different intervals evolution has been broken in a certain region, to begin again elsewhere. Egypt, Asia, the banks of the Mediterranean, Central Europe have in turn been the scene of historical development. But in every case, the first phase of the evolution has been the primitive tribe, passing on into a village commune, then into that of the free city, and finally dying out when it reached the phase of the state.

In Egypt, civilization began with the primitive tribe. It reached the village community phase, and later the period of free cities; still later that of the State, which, after a flourishing period, resulted in the death of the civilisation.

The evolution began again in Assyria, in Persia, in Palestine. Again it traversed the same phase: the tribe, the village community, the free city, the all-powerful State, and finally the result was—death!

A new civilization then sprang up in Greece. Always beginning by the tribe, it slowly reached the village commune, then the period of republican cities. In these cities, civilization reached its highest summits. But the East brought to them it poisoned traditions of despotism. Wars and conquests created Alexander's empire of Macedonia. The state enthroned itself, the parasite grew, killed all civilization, and then came—death!

Rome in its turn restored civilization. Again we find the primitive tribe at its origin; then, the village commune; then, the free city. At that stage, it reached the apex of its civilization. But then came the State, the Empire, and then—death!

On the ruins of the Roman Empire, Celtic, Germanic, Slavonian and Scandinavian tribes began civilization anew. Slowly the primitive tribe elaborated its institutions and reached the village commune. It remained at that stage till the twelfth century. Then rose the Republican cities which produced the glorious expansion of the human mind, attested by the monuments of architecture, the grand development of arts, the discoveries that laid the basis of natural sciences. But then came the State.

Will it again produce death? It will, unless we reconstitute society on a libertarian and anti-State basis. Either the State will be destroyed and a new life will begin in thousands of centres, on the principle of an energetic initiative of the individual, of groups, and of free agreement; or else the State must crush the individual and local life, it must become the master of all the domains of human activity, must bring with it wars and internal struggles for the possession of

power, surface-revolutions which only change one tyrant for another, and inevitably, at the end of this evolution—death!
Choose yourselves which of the two issues you prefer.

THE CHILDREN OF RIMBAUD: THRUST OF THE UNDERCULTURE

Kingsley Widmer

Recently, a former student who had been last year's archetypal hippy again confronted me. Still bearded and rebellious but now minus Indian regalia, and apparently on parole from a long term "high," he had a new thing: politics. His latest costuming included Neomarxist headgear and a good many decorative political gestures "to liven the scene in the streets of America." "You see," he concluded with a disingenuous smile, "you could turn on to me as living out the distinction you used to make between, first, a rebel who goes after a different life style, and, then, a radical who wants to fundamentally change the life of the system." He recited the lesson mockingly well; but, as with many another teacher who puts an abstract definition up against a hairy reality, I had for some time doubted my own text. Cultural rebelliousness and political radicalism come together.

From the underculture (the "marginals," the "dissident sub-cultures," the "generation in revolt," the "bohemian-beat-hippy tradition") comes much of the impetus for change in social values. But many intelligent people still disdain the rebels as "not authentically radical" and "not genuinely creative." So let me make the counter-argument. It seems that the "reasonable liberal" is quicker to put down the rebels than is the raging reactionary. He charges them with a lack of politics, a drugged mindlessness, a self-indulgent sensuality, messy ways, a lack of high art and, in sum, for not being reasonable liberals. This comfortingly dismisses our major social revolt as mere titillation and delinquency. Yet the custodians of the ideology of affluence, who almost had us thought-rinsed into believing that everyone was well washed and well subdued, seem alarmed by the rise of the inner barbarians. A Chicago cop, a Texas politician, or a California real estate broker violently defending American Civilization against underground poets and pacifists makes good farce. But in their righteous simplicity they may also rightly perceive the way their society is going under.

Is the rebellious underculture the radical force of major social change? No, insists the usual educated response, and snobbishly shrugs off the rebellious culture as offering nothing "new." True, but that should also suggest the relevant history. Take any of the major motifs of the rebellious, such as the ecstatic consciousness, the self-chosen alienation from the mainstream society, the syncretistic religiousness, the "action" arts, the polymorphous sexuality, the flamboyant costume, the utopian communalism, the tribal poetry-music, the "loving" anti-competitive personal code, and the outrageous life styles (including reversed "standards of living") as ways of protest. All repeatedly appear, with only secondary variations in manner, in the Beats of the 1950s, in their bohemian and utopian predecessors, and in a long tradition of rebellious modern culture. Any student of the more extreme literature of the last century, of Blake and Rimbaud, of Céline and Miller, of Nietzsche and Lawrence, knows where the ideas come from, though not all the young rebels do. What were once the solitary musings of the enraged poets and nihilistic critics now become the tangible style of the ten thousands who march up country from the mainline society. The small bohemian coteries of the past now become large ghettos of the dissident. The defiant styles of the outcast become the fancy uniforms of the fashionable in-class. In sum, the imaginative assault on middle-class life, a major effort of serious modern culture, becomes a literal social reality.

But are the effects of the rebellious culture really radical? Partly, of course, they get twisted by the exploitative society. Rebellion gets plagiarized for the amusement of the bored, commercialized for the solace of moral cripples, and neutralized into a mannered game for the protection of the powerful. I believe this process occurs less through a conspiracy by the custodians of our society than as an almost inevitable result of the emptiness of the mainline culture. Middle-class life produces many things, including commerce and efficiency and comfort, but it does not produce much significant art and thought, or new sensitivities and moral passions. Yet the society hungers for these, too, and the brokers of culture and manipulators of disguised ideology must come up with intriguing styles, both as protective coloration for their profit and power and as substitute gratifications for needed social changes.

From religion to footwear, from political revulsion to personal decoration, from erotic techniques to communal visions, the margins of the rebellious culture must be plundered for the sustenance of a disoriented and voracious society. It obtains not only much of its culture but also its moral sensitivity and social awareness from the rebels—peace and blackness as well as beads and rock. The cannibalizing of the rebellious may have accelerated, out of desperation, but the process is not new. Earlier in this century, reform movements drew heavily on bohemianism, as in past centuries moral and political awareness was strongly nourished by radical religious sectarians. The civil rights movement of the late fifties cannot fully be separated from the preceding Beat Generation's ethnic responsiveness and revulsion from the society's moral apathy. And anyone active in the anti-war and campus protests of the last four years must grant that the legions of dissent cannot be visualized apart from the beatnik-hippy-Yippy styles. Middle-class America seems aesthetically and morally unthinkable without its revitalization from outside and underneath. Hence the tolerance by way of guilt by many solid citizens for deviant behavior. Our social order inherently destroys aesthetic and moral sensibility, and so must repeatedly disguise and humanize itself by consuming the art and rebellion of subcultures.

Commonplace sophistication holds that the generations of revolt are mostly symptoms of social failures. In fact, they equally serve as agents of social change. The point needs stressing because it is a "liberal" rationalization—that minority culture is but another topical problem, like juvenile delinquency or the unemployment of the semi-skilled, to be cured by dosages of money, education, organization and intellectual hygiene. But these often exacerbate white cultural rebellion as much as they inflame black racial revolt. The rebellious culture, like blackness, is for real. Genuinely different, and subversive, it cannot be so easily ameliorated away. Dissident culture, like primitive Christianity, can become a self-generating social force and unreasonably powerful. As political and cultural extremity accelerate, co-opting partly defeats itself. Millions of Americans, for example, cannot stomach the underground styles which the culture brokers would peddle to them, and so start raging against the diet of "anarchists." That produces counter-revulsions, followed by punitive reactions which result in politicalization of the rebellious culture.

When one tries to weigh the significance for radical change of what develops out of the underculture, it appears that the most exalted offerings merit the least consideration. Such are drugs. Many of the recent studies of the hippy scene can see little else, mistaking a ritual for the total reality. Political militants may correctly judge the psychedelics as counterrevolutionary, the opiates of the elite. More importantly, and in spite of the glad tidings of the hallucinogenic gurus, drugs are not news. We have been there before, with the romantic and symbolist poets who ended testifying that drugs fail to maintain an intensified and enlarged awareness. Drugs but short-circuit what requires a whole way of life. Exoticism and defiance and desperation led to the exaggerated poetry and politics of pot until a minor indulgence was sometimes taken to be a revolutionary metaphysic. Ecstatic devices, chemical or mystical, might sometimes vault one into a different awareness and response, but to live there requires the more arduous creation of a different culture and society, which is what the drug scene finally demands.

Youth is another current opiate. Both Paul Goodman and J. Edgar Hoover indulge in this "generation hang-up," though from opposite sides. Any inherent correlation between age and radicalism seems dubious, though our Populist anti-intelectualism intentionally exaggerates the biology of discontent. Of course the young take major roles in the legions of the military. No doubt certain current conditions, including fatuous indoctrination disguised as education, totalitarian military conscription, and the exploitative meaninglessness of the corporate and public bureaucracies at whose gates they stand, fall especially heavy on the young and anger them. Then ideologues (such as those of the Peace and Freedom Party) borrow from an underculture mystique and draft revolutionary programs for the exact date in the 1970s when 50 per cent, plus one, of the American population will be under 25. Charming, but the law of demographic radicalism doesn't seem to apply to a number of countries in the world more youthful than ours. Even if there were a political biology with a rule that the young join the legions of change, which legions and which changes would they be? Perhaps some demogogue can work up the youth religiosity into a nasty political reality. Until then, we should remain skeptical of the pathetic American cultism of adolescence. Generation gap ideology merely disguises a radical dissatisfaction in the whole of our society that is naturally more visible among the young.

To take up another charge against the rebellious: their marginal ways reveal no monopoly on messy lives and destructive ambivalences. The individual origins of rebellious choices may, of course, sometimes be located in psychic and social disorders, and certainly rebellious styles can be ritualized into obsessional conformity. What can't? But the rebellious attempts at tribal life contain a relevant protest against a widely painful and perhaps finally unviable social form: the small, competitive suburban family. Though continuing with psychiatric crutches, and relieved by serial polygamy, the narrow and anxious nuclear family is socially regressive, and cruel to many. The awareness of this is a staple of our intellectual culture, and novels about domesticity, from Flaubert to Roth, have long provided devastating attacks on the tightly predatory family. And sexual experimentation and efforts toward broader families, now endemic in marginal groups, may often be poignant or messy, but they criticize a basic social form and attempt to restructure it. This search for new groupings, and not the post-Puritan permissiveness that is usually trumpeted, point the current direction of the continuing sexual revolution. The turn to trivial relatedness may forecast the crucial community sense of the future. Now social values, and their politics, require a changed libidinal and communal order.

Similarly, the culture from down under and outside does not aim at the competive connoisseurship of the high art of bourgeois society. The posters, the newspapers, the beads, the lyrics, the tribal decorations, the free-form psychodramas and the rest, also point to the communal. The underground arts mostly demand group rather than private responsiveness. Such communion criticizes what we may now recognize as the elitist and aggrandizing roles of much accepted modern art. Not the "artistic career" but the group art-action becomes the essential focus. The predecessors of today's underculture still yoked rebellion with the unique role of the artist; the current self-sanctification of the dissident and declassed by "creativity" operates quite outside the traditional roles of the poet and the painter. Masterpieces, or the attempt at drastically individualized art, are largely irrelevant to working on a communal style.

Besides, traditional high culture competes quite inadequately with the high decibel and hallucinatory pseudo-culture of technology, which empties most art and thought. The current underground may have created the best popular arts since the technological media smashed folk culture. They, too, may go to pieces in the processing and peddling—the present experience of rock musicians, now no longer local and communal but major product lines, rather sadly confirms this. But the deep longing for a culture of communal involvement remains. The drive toward more directly engaging arts includes considerable rejection of the debased culture-of-the-word, which now less serves intellectual and individualizing motives than technological and bureaucratic rationalization. The limited hippy interest in literature tended to fantasy (Tolkien, Heinlein, the sutras, science fiction, etc.). Perhaps the major novelist linked to the underculture, Ken Kesey, long ago gave up that middle-class form for more direct arts and rebellious-communal living. No doubt standards other than those of "high" literature and art and criticism need to be applied to this new neolithic culture. Most basically, the arts of the underculture should be recognized both as protest against the dominant culture and as ritual for subcommunities which symbolically enact dreams of a different society.

Increasingly, the cultural rebellions go beyond mere consciousness, and the private practice of art, to dress and ritual and family and community. Since our bankrupt humanism (and "liberal arts" education) depends on a nurtured distinction between learned culture and social existence, we are shocked when the underculture does not make the same separation. (The same alarm is expressed when "minorities" attack "pure" and "objective" institutions and students revolt against "scholarly disinterest" and "impersonal" education.) Generally in our society, "sophisticated" and "cultivated"—and even "educated"—are terms used to praise the ability to lead a schizophrenic life, to separate culture and politics, consciousness and social function. Much of the rebellion is about that forced and painful disparity between awareness and daily activity. Social necessity once seemed to mandate that fragmentation, the opposing styles of dress and morality and ideas in public and private. No more schizophrenia, say the cultural rebels, who thus simultaneously became social radicals.

Is this a way to make a revolution? It may not be the way that the traditional Left, usually quasi-Marxist or at least Jacobin, would choose to force transformations of economic and political power. But we must take the forces of change where we find them rather than fantasize rising proletariats or progressive bureaucracies. Today's rebels may be partly characterized by their refusal to compete directly for economic and political power. Instead, they attempt to withdraw from or circumvent power by resistant and contrasting ways of behavior. In our technically overpowered systems, this may be practical as well as principled. Compare the terrible pathos of most contemporary political revolutionaries caught up in their easily corruptible, and destructive, fantasies of the usurpation of power. Those from the underculture no more choose parliamentarianism, manipulating interests and structural repression—politics as legitimacy—than they do the revolutionary variants of movement organizing, ideological polemicizing and the break into sustained violence. The contemporary rebels do not elect to man the barricades or the bureaucracies; they insist instead upon a different consciousness, resistance, and alternate life styles as the way toward true change.

From the underculture comes the politics of "anti-politics" as both protest and communal creation. Their dancing in the streets may be a more significant public action than voting in elections devoid of alternatives. Their dissident manners may have more effect than a library of pedantic position papers. And their love games may create more vitality than the political games which reinforce the deadening current structures of response. It may even be more socially effective to attempt a lively different life style than to organize a variant political ideology. Yet, strangely, many who take pleasure in what they call politics rather vehemently resent any politics of pleasure. Given our actual cities, we must suspect the political dogmatists and pragmatists who become contemptuous about aspirations to the city of love.

And given the power of modern institutions and states, the rebellious styles of undermining and resisting and transforming just might lead to more effective as well as more humane ways of change than the expediency and bureaucratization of reform and the violence and authoritarianism of revolution. That, anyway, seems to be the inherent logic of the rebellious underculture and it seems to be widely, though not very clearly, adopted in increasing areas of society. Historically, these must be viewed as radical phenomena, proper offspring of the antinomian heretics and the enlightenment utopians and the modern literature of rage. Critically, the efforts toward new communities and life styles highlight our inadequacies. Morally, the sensuality, color and responsiveness, the anti-authoritarianism and almost violent pacifism, and the attempts to break out of the usual institutional labors and faiths—these are sufficient in and of themselves. Without further art or ideology or politics, they make authentic and radical demands on our culture and society. We may, of

course, deplore the ritual drugs, the protective cultishness about
youth, the Populist anti-intellectualism, and all sorts of other devia-
tions from middle-class and middle-aged good sense. But such changes
in ways of feeling and living and being, not just changes in doctrines
and institutions and powers, are what change the world. The reso-
nance of the underculture may carry much further than usually
reported, and a truly liberal or radical politics must now relate to it.

THE NEW FORMS OF CONTROL

Herbert Marcuse

A comfortable, smooth, reasonable, democratic unfreedom prevails in
advanced industrial civilization, a token of technical progress. Indeed,
what could be more rational than the suppression of individuality in
the mechanization of socially necessary but painful performances; the
concentration of individual enterprises in more effective, more productive corporations; the regulation of free competition among unequally equipped economic subjects; the curtailment of prerogatives
and national sovereignties which impede the international organization of resources. That this technological order also involves a political and intellectual coordination may be a regrettable and yet
promising development.
   The rights and liberties which were such vital factors in the origins
and earlier stages of industrial society yield to a higher stage of this
society: they are losing their traditional rationale and content. Freedom of thought, speech, and conscience were—just as free enterprise,
which they served to promote and protect—essentially *critical* ideas,
designed to replace an obsolescent material and intellectual culture by
a more productive and rational one. Once institutionalized, these
rights and liberties shared the fate of the society of which they had
become an integral part. The achievement cancels the premises.
   To the degree to which freedom from want, the concrete substance
of all freedom, is becoming a real possibility, the liberties which
pertain to a state of lower productivity are losing their former
content. Independence of thought, autonomy, and the right to political opposition are being deprived of their basic critical function in a
society which seems increasingly capable of satisfying the needs of
the individuals through the way in which it is organized. Such a
society may justly demand acceptance of its principles and institutions, and reduce the opposition to the discussion and promotion of
alternative policies *within* the status quo. In this respect, it seems to
make little difference whether the increasing satisfaction of needs is
accomplished by an authoritarian or a non-authoritarian system.

Under the conditions of a rising standard of living, non-conformity with the system itself appears to be socially useless, and the more so when it entails tangible economic and political disadvantages and threatens the smooth operation of the whole. Indeed, at least in so far as the necessities of life are involved, there seems to be no reason why the production and distribution of goods and services should proceed through the competitive concurrence of individual liberties.

Freedom of enterprise was from the beginning not altogether a blessing. As the liberty to work or to starve, it spelled toil, insecurity, and fear for the vast majority of the population. If the individual were no longer compelled to prove himself on the market, as a free economic subject, the disappearance of this kind of freedom would be one of the greatest achievements of civilization. The technological processes of mechanization and standardization might release individual energy into a yet uncharted realm of freedom beyond necessity. The very structure of human existence would be altered; the individual would be liberated from the work world's imposing upon him alien needs and alien possibilities. The individual would be free to exert autonomy over a life that would be his own. If the productive apparatus could be organized and directed toward the satisfaction of the vital needs, its control might well be centralized; such control would not prevent individual autonomy, but render it possible.

This is a goal within the capabilities of advanced industrial civilization, the "end" of technological rationality. In actual fact, however, the contrary trend operates: the apparatus imposes its economic and political requirements for defense and expansion on labor time and free time, on the material and intellectual culture. By virtue of the way it has organized its technological base, contemporary industrial society tends to be totalitarian. For "totalitarian" is not only a terroristic political coordination of society, but also a nonterroristic economic-technical coordination which operates through the manipulation of needs by vested interests. It thus precludes the emergence of an effective opposition against the whole. Not only a specific form of government or party rule makes for totalitarianism, but also a specific system of production and distribution which may well be compatible with a "pluralism" of parties, newspapers, "countervailing powers," etc.

Today political power asserts itself through its power over the machine process and over the technical organization of the apparatus. The government of advanced and advancing industrial societies can maintain and secure itself only when it succeeds in mobilizing, organizing, and exploiting the technical, scientific, and mechanical productivity available to industrial civilization. And this productivity mobilizes society as a whole, above and beyond any particular individual or group interests. The brute fact that the machine's physical (only physical?) power surpasses that of the individual, and of any particular group of individuals, makes the machine the most effective political instrument in any society whose basic organization is that of the machine process. But the political trend may be reversed; essentially the power of the machine is only the stored-up and projected power of man. To the extent to which the work world is conceived of as a machine and mechanized accordingly, it becomes the *potential* basis of a new freedom for man.

Contemporary industrial civilization demonstrates that it has reached the stage at which "the free society" can no longer be adequately defined in the traditional terms of economic, political, and intellectual liberties, not because these liberties have become insignificant, but because they are too significant to be confined within the traditional forms. New modes of realization are needed, corresponding to the new capabilities of society.

Such new modes can be indicated only in negative terms because they would amount to the negation of the prevailing modes. Thus economic freedom would mean freedom *from* the economy—from being controlled by economic forces and relationships; freedom from the daily struggle for existence, from earning a living. Political freedom would mean liberation of the individuals *from* politics over which they have no effective control. Similarly, intellectual freedom would mean the restoration of individual thought now absorbed by mass communication and indoctrination, abolition of "public opinion" together with its makers. The unrealistic sound of these propositions is indicative, not of their utopian character, but of the strength of the forces which prevent their realization. The most effective and enduring form of warfare against liberation is the implanting of material and intellectual needs that perpetuate obsolete forms of the struggle for existence.

The intensity, the satisfaction and even the character of human needs, beyond the biological level, have always been preconditioned. Whether or not the possibility of doing or leaving, enjoying or destroying, possessing or rejecting something is seized as a *need* depends on whether or not it can be seen as desirable and necessary for the prevailing societal institutions and interests. In this sense, human needs are historical needs and, to the extent to which the society demands the repressive development of the individual, his needs themselves and their claim for satisfaction are subject to overriding critical standards.

We may distinguish both true and false needs. "False" are those which are superimposed upon the individual by particular social interests in his repression: the needs which perpetuate toil, aggressiveness, misery, and injustice. Their satisfaction might be most gratifying to the individual, but this happiness is not a condition which has to be maintained and protected if it serves to arrest the development of the ability (his own and others) to recognize the disease of the whole and grasp the chances of curing the disease. The result then is euphoria in unhappiness. Most of the prevailing needs to relax, to have fun, to behave and consume in accordance with the advertisements, to love and hate what others love and hate, belong to this category of false needs.

Such needs have a societal content and function which are determined by eternal powers over which the individual has no control; the development and satisfaction of these needs is heteronomous. No matter how much such needs may have become the individual's own, reproduced and fortified by the conditions of his existence; no matter how much he identifies himself with them and finds himself in their satisfaction, they continue to be what they were from the beginning—products of a society whose dominant interest demands repression.

The prevalence of repressive needs is an accomplished fact, accepted in ignorance and defeat, but a fact that must be undone in the interest of the happy individual as well as all those whose misery is the price of his satisfaction. The only needs that have an unqualified claim for satisfaction are the vital ones—nourishment, clothing, lodging at the attainable level of culture. The satisfaction of these needs is the prerequisite for the realization of *all* needs, of the unsublimated as well as the sublimated ones.

For any consciousness and conscience, for any experience which does not accept the prevailing societal interest as the supreme law of thought and behavior, the established universe of needs and satisfactions is a fact to be questioned—questioned in terms of truth and falsehood. These terms are historical throughout, and their objectivity is historical. The judgment of needs and their satisfaction, under the given conditions, involves standards of *priority*—standards which refer to the optimal development of the individual, of all individuals, under the optimal utilization of the material and intellectual resources available to man. The resources are calculable. "Truth" and "falsehood" of needs designate objective conditions to the extent to which the universal satisfaction of vital needs and, beyond it, the progressive alleviation of toil and poverty, are universally valid standards. But as historical standards, they do not only vary according to area and stage of development, they also can be defined only in (greater or lesser) *contradiction* to the prevailing ones. What tribunal can possibly claim the authority of decision?

In the last analysis, the question of what are true and false needs must be answered by the individuals themselves, but only in the last analysis; that is, if and when they are free to give their own answer. As long as they are kept incapable of being autonomous, as long as they are indoctrinated and manipulated (down to their very instincts), their answer to this question cannot be taken as their own. By the same token, however, no tribunal can justly arrogate to itself the right to decide which needs should be developed and satisfied.

Any such tribunal is reprehensible, although our revulsion does not do away with the question: how can the people who have been the object of effective and productive domination by themselves create the conditions of freedom?

The more rational, productive, technical, and total the repressive administration of society becomes, the more unimaginable the means and ways by which the administered individuals might break their servitude and seize their own liberation. To be sure, to impose Reason upon an entire society is a paradoxical and scandalous idea— although one might dispute the righteousness of a society which ridicules this idea while making its own population into objects of total administration. All liberation depends on the consciousness of servitude, and the emergence of this consciousness is always hampered by the predominance of needs and satisfactions which, to a great extent, have become the individual's own. The process always replaces one system of preconditioning by another; the optimal goal is the replacement of false needs by true ones, the abandonment of repressive satisfaction.

The distinguishing feature of advanced industrial society is its effective suffocation of those needs which demand liberation—liberation also from that which is tolerable and rewarding and comfortable— while it sustains and absolves the destructive power and repressive function of the affluent society. Here, the social controls exact the overwhelming need for the production and consumption of waste; the need for stupefying work where it is no longer a real necessity; the need for modes of relaxation which soothe and prolong this stupefication; the need for maintaining such deceptive liberties as free competition at administered prices, a free press which censors itself, free choice between brands and gadgets.

Under the rule of a repressive whole, liberty can be made into a powerful instrument of domination. The range of choice open to the individual is not the decisive factor in determining the degree of human freedom, but *what* can be chosen and what *is* chosen by the individual. The criterion for free choice can never be an absolute one, but neither is it entirely relative. Free election of masters does not abolish the masters or the slaves. Free choice among a wide variety of goods and services does not signify freedom if these goods and services sustain social controls over a life of toil and fear—that is, if they sustain alienation. And the spontaneous reproduction of super- imposed needs by the individual does not establish autonomy; it only testifies to the efficacy of the controls.

Our insistence on the depth and efficacy of these controls is open to the objection that we overrate greatly the indoctrinating power of the "media," and that by themselves the people would feel and satisfy the needs which are now imposed upon them. The objection misses the point. The preconditioning does not start with the mass production of radio and television and with the centralization of their control. The people enter this stage as preconditioned receptacles of long standing; the decisive difference is in the flattening out of the contrast (or conflict) between the given and the possible, between the satisfied and the unsatisfied needs. Here, the so-called equalization of class distinctions reveals its ideological function. If the worker and his boss enjoy the same television program and visit the same resort places, if the typist is as attractively made up as the daughter of her employer, if the Negro owns a Cadillac, if they all read the same newspaper, then this assimilation indicates not the disappearance of classes, but the extent to which the needs and satisfactions that serve the preservation of the Establishment are shared by the underlying population.

Indeed, in the most highly developed areas of contemporary society, the transplantation of social into individual needs is so effective that the difference between them seems to be purely theoretical. Can one really distinguish between the mass media as instruments of information and entertainment, and as agents of manipulation and indoctrination? Between the automobile as nuisance and as convenience? Between the horrors and the comforts of functional architecture? Between the work for national defense and the work for corporate gain? Between the private pleasure and the commercial and political utility involved in increasing the birth rate?

We are again confronted with one of the most vexing aspects of advanced industrial civilization: the rational character of its irrationality. Its productivity and efficiency, its capacity to increase and spread comforts, to turn waste into need, and destruction into construction, the extent to which this civilization transforms the object world into an extension of man's mind and body makes the very notion of alienation questionable. The people recognize themselves in their commodities; they find their soul in their automobile, hi-fi set, split-level home, kitchen equipment. The very mechanism which ties the individual to his society has changed, and social control is anchored in the new needs which it has produced.

The prevailing forms of social control are technological in a new sense. To be sure, the technical structure and efficacy of the productive and destructive apparatus has been a major instrumentality for subjecting the population to the established social division of labor thoughout the modern period. Moreover, such integration has always been accompanied by more obvious forms of compulsion: loss of livelihood, the administration of justice, the police, the armed forces. It still is. But in the contemporary period, the technological controls appear to be the very embodiment of Reason for the benefit of all social groups and interests—to such an extent that all contradiction seems irrational and all counteraction impossible.

No wonder then that, in the most advanced areas of this civilization, the social controls have been introjected to the point where even individual protest is affected at its roots. The intellectual and emotional refusal "to go along" appears neurotic and impotent. This is the socio-psychological aspect of the political event that marks the contemporary period: the passing of the historical forces which, at the preceding stage of industrial society, seemed to represent the possibility of new forms of existence.

But the term "introjection" perhaps no longer describes the way in which the individual by himself reproduces and perpetuates the external controls exercised by his society. Introjection suggests a variety of relatively spontaneous processes by which a Self (Ego) transposes the "outer" into the "inner." Thus introjection implies the existence of an inner dimension distinguished from and even antagonistic to the external exigencies—an individual consciousness and an individual unconscious *apart from* public opinion and behavior.[1] The idea of "inner freedom" here has its reality: it designates the private space in which man may become and remain "himself."

Today this private space has been invaded and whittled down by technological reality. Mass production and mass distribution claim the *entire* individual, and industrial psychology has long since ceased to be confined to the factory. The manifold processes of introjection seem to be ossified in almost mechanical reactions. The result is, not adjustment but *mimesis*: an immediate identification of the individual with *his* society and, through it, with the society as a whole.

This immediate, automatic identification (which may have been characteristic of primitive forms of association) reappears in high industrial civilization; its new "immediacy," however, is the product of a sophisticated, scientific management and organization. In this process, the "inner" dimension of the mind in which opposition to the status quo can take root is whittled down. The loss of this dimension, in which the power of negative thinking the critical power of Reason—is at home, is the ideological counterpart to the very material process in which advanced industrial society silences and reconciles the opposition. The impact of progress turns Reason into submission to the facts of life, and to the dynamic capability of producing more and bigger facts of the same sort of life. The efficiency of the system blunts the individuals' recognition that it contains no facts which do not communicate the repressive power of the whole. If the individuals find themselves in the things which shape their life, they do so, not by giving, but by accepting the law of things—not the law of physics but the law of their society.

I have just suggested that the concept of alienation seems to become questionable when the individuals identify themselves with the existence which is imposed upon them and have in it their own

[1] The change in the function of the family here plays a decisive role: its "socializing" functions are increasingly taken over by outside groups and media. See my *Eros and Civilization* (Boston: Beacon Press, 1955), p. 96 ff.

development and satisfaction. This identification is not illusion but reality. However, the reality constitutes a more progressive stage of alienation. The latter has become entirely objective; the subject which is alienated is swallowed up by its alienated existence. There is only one dimension, and it is everywhere and in all forms. The achievements of progress defy ideological indictment as well as justification; before their tribunal, the "false consciousness" of their rationality becomes the true consciousness.

This absorption of ideology into reality does not, however, signify the "end of ideology." On the contrary, in a specific sense advanced industrial culture is *more* ideological than its predecessor, inasmuch as today the ideology is in the process of production itself.[2] In a provocative form, this proposition reveals the political aspects of the prevailing technological rationality. The productive apparatus and the goods and services which it produces "sell" or impose the social system as a whole. The means of mass transportation and communication, the commodities of lodging, food, and clothing, the irresistible output of the entertainment and information industry carry with them prescribed attitudes and habits, certain intellectual and emotional reactions which bind the consumers more or less pleasantly to the producers and, through the latter, to the whole. The products indoctrinate and manipulate; they promote a false consciousness which is immune against its falsehood. And as these beneficial products become available to more individuals in more social classes, the indoctrination they carry ceases to be publicity; it becomes a way of life. It is a good way of life—much better than before—and as a good way of life, it militates against qualitative change. Thus emerges a pattern of *one-dimensional thought and behavior* in which ideas, aspirations, and objectives that, by their content, transcend the establish universe of discourse and action are either repelled or reduced to terms of this universe. They are redefined by the rationality of the given system and of its quantitative extension.

The trend may be related to a development in scientific method: operationalism in the physical, behaviorism in the social sciences. The common feature is a total empiricism in the treatment of concepts; their meaning is restricted to the representation of particular operations and behavior. The operational point of view is well illustrated by P. W. Bridgman's analysis of the concept of length.[3]

We evidently know what we mean by length if we can tell what the length of any and every object is, and for the physicist nothing more is required. To find the length of an object, we have to perform certain physical operations. The

[2]Theodor W. Adorno, *Prismen. Kulturkritik und Gesellschaft.* (Frankfurt: Suhrkamp, 1955), p. 24 f.
[3]P. W. Bridgman, *The Logic of Modern Physics* (New York: Macmillan, 1928), p. 5. The operational doctrine has since been refined and qualified.

concept of length is therefore fixed when the operations by which length is measured are fixed: that is, the concept of length involves as much and nothing more than the set of operations by which length is determined. In general, we mean by any concept nothing more than a set of operations; *the concept is synonymous with the corresponding set of operations.*

Bridgman has seen the wide implications of this mode of thought for the society at large.[4]

To adopt the operational point of view involves much more than a mere restriction of the sense in which we understand 'concept,' but means a far-reaching change in all our habits of thought, in that we shall no longer permit ourselves to use as tools in our thinking concepts of which we cannot give an adequate account in terms of operations.

Bridgman's prediction has come true. The new mode of thought is today the predominant tendency in philosophy, psychology, sociology, and other fields. Many of the most seriously troublesome concepts are being "eliminated" by showing that no adequate account of them in terms of operations or behavior can be given. The radical empiricist onslaught . . . thus provides the methodological justification for debunking of the mind by the intellectuals—a positivism which, in its denial of the transcending elements of Reason, forms the academic counterpart of the socially required behavior.

Outside the academic establishment, the "far-reaching change in all our habits of thought" is more serious. It serves to coordinate ideas and goals with those exacted by the prevailing system, to enclose them in the system, and to repel those which are irreconcilable with system. The reign of such a one-dimensional reality does not mean that materialism rules, and that the spiritual, metaphysical, and bohemian occupations are petering out. On the contrary, there is a great deal of "Worship together this week," "Why not try God," Zen, existentialism, and beat ways of life, etc. But such modes of protest and transcendence are no longer contradictory to the status quo and no longer negative. They are rather the ceremonial part of practical behaviorism, its harmless negation, and are quickly digested by the status quo as part of its healthy diet.

One-dimensional thought is systematically promoted by the makers of politics and their purveyors of mass information. Their universe of discourse is populated by self-validating hypotheses which, incessantly and monopolistically repeated, become hypnotic definitions or dictations. For example, "free" are the institutions which operate (and are

Bridgman himself has extended the concept of "operation" to include the "paper-and-pencil" operations of the theorist (in Philipp J. Frank, *The Validation of Scientific Theories* [Boston: Beacon Press, 1954], Chap. II). The main impetus remains the same: it is "desirable" that the paper-and-pencil operations "be capable of eventual contact, although perhaps indirectly, with instrumental operations."

[4]P. W. Bridgman, *The Logic of Modern Physics,* loc. cit., p. 31.

operated on) in the countries of the Free World; other transcending modes of freedom are by definition either anarchism, communism, or propaganda. "Socialistic" are all encroachments on private enterprises not undertaken by private enterprise itself (or by government contracts), such as universal and comprehensive health insurance, or the protection of nature from all too sweeping commercialization, or the establishment of public services which may hurt private profit. This totalitarian logic of accomplished facts has its Eastern counterpart. There, freedom is the way of life instituted by a communist regime, and all other transcending modes of freedom are either capitalistic, or revisionist, or leftist sectarianism. In both camps, non-operational ideas are non-behavioral and subversive. The movement of thought is stopped at barriers which appear as the limits of Reason itself.

Such limitation of thought is certainly not new. Ascending modern rationalism, in its speculative as well as empirical form, shows a striking contrast between extreme critical radicalism in scientific and philosophic method on the one hand, and an uncritical quietism in the attitude toward established and functioning social institutions. Thus Descartes' *ego cogitans* was to leave the "great public bodies" untouched, and Hobbes held that "the present ought always to be preferred, maintained, and accounted best." Kant agreed with Locke in justifying revolution *if and when* it has succeeded in organizing the whole and in preventing subversion.

However, these accommodating concepts of Reason were always contradicted by the evident misery and injustice of the "great public bodies" and the effective, more or less conscious rebellion against them. Societal conditions existed which provoked and permitted real dissociation from the established state of affairs; a private as well as political dimension was present in which dissociation could develop into effective opposition, testing its strength and the validity of its objectives.

With the gradual closing of this dimension by the society, the self-limitation of thought assumes a larger significance. The interrelation between scientific-philosophical and societal processes, between theoretical and practical Reason, asserts itself "behind the back" of the scientists and philosophers. The society bars a whole type of oppositional operations and behavior; consequently, the concepts pertaining to them are rendered illusory or meaningless. Historical transcendence appears as metaphysical transcendence, not acceptable to science and scientific thought. The operational and behavioral point of view, practiced as a "habit of thought" at large, becomes the view of the established universe of discourse and action, needs and aspirations. The "cunning of Reason" works, as it so often did, in the interest of the powers that be. The insistence on operational and behavioral concepts turns against the efforts to free thought and behavior *from* the given reality and *for* the suppressed alternatives. Theoretical and practical Reason, academic and social behaviorism meet on common ground: that of an advanced society which makes scientific and technical progress into an instrument of domination.

"Progress" is not a neutral term; it moves toward specific ends, and these ends are defined by the possibilities of ameliorating the human condition. Advanced industrial society is approaching the stage where continued progress would demand the radical subversion of the prevailing direction and organization of progress. This stage would be reached when material production (including the necessary services) becomes automated to the extent that all vital needs can be satisfied while necessary labor time is reduced to marginal time. From this point on, technical progress would transcend the realm of necessity, where it served as the instrument of domination and exploitation which thereby limited its rationality; technology would become subject to the free play of faculties in the struggle for the pacification of nature and of society.

Such a state is envisioned in Marx's notion of the "abolition of labor." The term "pacification of existence" seems better suited to designate the historical alternative of a world which—through an international conflict which transforms and suspends the contradictions within the established societies—advances on the brink of global war. "Pacification of existence" means the development of man's struggle with man and with nature, under conditions where the competing needs, desires, and aspirations are no longer organized by vested interests in domination and scarcity—an organization which perpetuates the destructive forms of this struggle.

Today's fight against this historical alternative finds a firm mass basis in the underlying population, and finds its ideology in the rigid orientation of thought and behavior to the given universe of facts. Validated by the accomplishments of science and technology, justified by its growing productivity, the status quo defies all transcendence. Faced with the possibility of pacification on the grounds of its technical and intellectual achievements, the mature industrial society closes itself against this alternative. Operationalism, in theory and practice, becomes the theory and practice of *containment.* Underneath its obvious dynamics, this society is a thoroughly static system of life: self-propelling in its oppressive productivity and in its beneficial coordination. Containment of technical progress goes hand in hand with its growth in the established direction. In spite of the political fetters imposed by the status quo, the more technology appears capable of creating the conditions for pacification, the more are the minds and bodies of man organized against this alternative.

The most advanced areas of industrial society exhibit throughout these two features: a trend toward consummation of technological rationality, and intensive efforts to contain this trend within the established institutions. Here is the internal contradiction of this civilization: the irrational element in its rationality. It is the token of its achievements. The industrial society which makes technology and science its own is organized for the ever-more-effective domination of man and nature, for the ever-more-effective utilization of its resources. It becomes irrational when the success of these efforts opens new dimensions of human realization. Organization for peace is different from organization for war; the institutions which served the struggle for existence cannot serve the pacification of existence. Life as an end is qualitatively different from life as a means.

Such a qualitatively new mode of existence can never be envisaged as the mere by-product of economic and political changes, as the more or less spontaneous effect of the new institutions which constitute the necessary prerequisite. Qualitative change also involves a change in the *technical* basis on which this society rests—one which sustains the economic and political institutions through which the "second nature" of man as an aggressive object of administration is stabilized. The techniques of industrialization are political techniques; as such, they prejudge the possibilities of Reason and Freedom.

To be sure, labor must precede the reduction of labor, and industrialization must precede the development of human needs and satisfactions. But as all freedom depends on the conquest of alien necessity, the realization of freedom depends on the *techniques* of this conquest. The highest productivity of labor can be used for the perpetuation of labor, and the most efficient industrialization can serve the restriction and manipulation of needs.

When this point is reached, domination—in the guise of affluence and liberty—extends to all spheres of private and public existence, integrates all authentic opposition, absorbs all alternatives. Technological rationality reveals its political character as it becomes the great vehicle of better domination, creating a truly totalitarian universe in which society and nature, mind and body are kept in a state of permanent mobilization for the defense of this universe.

PRAGMATIC ANARCHISM

Herbert Read

... while it is true that the conclusion of a syllogism follows from the premises in quite a different sense from that in which a knee-jerk follows from the doctor's tap, it seems reasonable to say that, just as I cannot help jerking my knee once I have been tapped, so I cannot help assenting to the conclusion once I have grasped the premisses.

                              D. H. Monro: *Godwin's Moral Philosophy*

The appearance of a comprehensive collection of writings on the anarchist tradition[1] gives me an opportunity to review my own anarchist convictions, which have now lasted for more than fifty years. I date my conversion to the reading of a pamphlet by Edward Carpenter with the title *Non-Governmental Society*, which took place in 1911 or 1912, and immediately opened up to me a whole new range of thought—not only the works of professed anarchists such as Kropotkin, Bakunin and Proudhon, but also those of Nietzsche, Ibsen, and Tolstoy which directly or indirectly supported the anarchist philosophy, and those of Marx and Shaw which directly attacked it.

I use the word "conversion" to describe the experience because it was undoubtedly quasi-religious; I was at the same time slipping away from the Christian faith I had acquired from a pious family background. And yet my new beliefs were not idealistic—in spite of all appearances to the contrary, I am not an idealist, but rather, in the sense defined by Unamuno, a quixotist, and a practical rather than a speculative or meditative quixotist. Unamuno tells us that "the philosophy of Don Quixote cannot strictly be called idealism: he did not fight for ideas. It was of the spiritual order; he fought for the spirit." In exactly the same way the type of anarchist I am does not fight for ideas: he is not an ideologist of any kind, but rather a pragmatist. The editors of *Patterns of Anarchy* recognise this: "The positive goal of anarchism, then, can be regarded as a consistently individualised pragmatism." Philosophically anarchists are nearer to deflaters of idealism such as John Dewey and Karl Popper than to Utopian socialists such as Karl Marx or Lenin. All forms of historicism are profoundly repugnant to the true anarchist.[2]

Nevertheless, anarchism is a social or political philosophy, and the editors of this anthology, as they proceeded, became "more and more amazed at how many perceptive social theorists have spoken in the anarchist tradition." They present 57 selections from 41 writers, including 8 critics of anarchism. There are many other writers they might have quoted, including some who have made important contributions to anarchist thought, such as H. B. Brewster, Gustav Landauer, and Martin Buber, and they perhaps rightly exclude those many writers who have expressed an anarchist philosophy though they may never have used the word anarchism—Zeno, Lao Tse, Chuang Tse, Thoreau, Shelley, Nietzsche, Morris, Ibsen, Gandhi, Vinoba, Wilde, Camus, Silone, A. S. Neill, and Lewis Mumford. Personally, just for the fun of it, I would have included Marx's

---

[1] *Patterns of Anarchy*, edited by Leonard I. Krimerman and Lewis Perry (New York, Anchor Books).
[2] Bakunin made this clear in his criticism of Marx's "idealism." The only universal law in human history, said Bakunin, is the struggle for existence. Historicism arises from the fallacy that thought is prior to life, and abstract theory prior to social practice.

famous statement about "the withering away of the state."

There is perhaps only one belief on dogma common to all professed anarchists, the fundamental one that is indicated by the word itself in its literal meaning—a way of life *without government*. But this is a negative definition, a fact from which the movement has always suffered, though its critics should have recognised that the assertion of a negation always implies, not only a prior thesis, but a leap forward to a synthesis, which in the case of anarchism is the "consistently individualised pragmatism" mentioned by our anthologists. This positive doctrine requires far more explanation than will be found in *Patterns of Anarchy*, and my present intention is to contribute to such further explanation. But before doing so I would like to mention some legitimate points of difference among anarchists, all of which, however, are resolved in the final synthesis.

The anarchist is committed to the decentralisation of power in the political sense. Does this also imply decentralisation in the economic sense, the reversal of those processes that have led to the big city, the giant factory, the multiple store, and other concentrations of human activity? I believe it does, for reasons not essentially anarchist, reasons which are given in one of the contributions to *Patterns of Anarchism*, namely, that such a tendency is

much more in consonance with the basic trends of modern technics than the centralised State economics of the Marxists. . . . Specialisation of industry and gigantic units are a liability under conditions demanding flexibility and ease of adaptation. And they will become superfluous with the growing mobility of power, its wider distribution from central energy stations.

The writer ("Senex") gives many other reasons which favour this process of decentralisation, and in this respect architects such as Frank Lloyd Wright, sociologists such as Lewis Mumford, and contemporary planning experts generally, have come to conclusions similar to those that have always been advocated by anarchists.

But do anarchists accept what is in effect a technological civilisation, or are they, as so many people suspect, instinctive Luddites, opposed to the whole concept of mechanisation, yearning for a return to a more primitive pattern of life?

There is a certain justification for this suspicion if one confuses anarchism with the medievalism of William Morris and the romantic distributivism of Catholics such as Hilaire Belloc and G. K. Chesterton. But actually most of the leading anarchists have been scientific in their outlook—Kropotkin, who did so much to establish anarchism as a political philosophy, notably so. For Kropotkin (as Krimerman and Perry point out) the justification of anarchism is primarily an empirical task,

to be carried out by close and comprehensive observation of such facts as might be gathered by a biologist or anthropologist. Human culture manifests an evolving pattern and direction, which it is the function of the anarchist philosopher to record, much as celestial motions and patterns are recorded by the astronomer. And when this is accomplished, so Kropotkin maintains, it will be clear that anarchist communism is the conclusion towards which all the data of biology, anthropology, and history are directed.

As political "gradualism" this seems to lag behind even the extreme Fabianism of Karl Popper. Kropotkin's ultimate appeal as a scientific anarchist, according to Krimerman and Perry, is not to what ought to be, but to what is or what is steadily evolving. Kropotkin himself renounced all forms of utopianism. The following extract from one of his little-known pamphlets makes this clear:

> The anarchist thinker does not resort to metaphysical concepts (like "natural rights," the "duties of the state," and so on) to establish what are, in his opinion, the best conditions for realising the greatest happiness of humanity. He follows, on the contrary, the course traced by the modern philosophy of evolution.... He merely considers society as an aggregation of organisms trying to find out the best ways of combining the wants of the individual with those of cooperation for the welfare of the species. He studies society and tries to discover its *tendencies*, past and present, its growing needs, intellectual and economic, and in his ideal he merely points out in which direction evolution goes. He distinguishes between the real needs and tendencies of human aggregations and the accidents (want of knowledge, migrations, wars, conquests) which have prevented these tendencies from being satisfied. And he concludes that the two most prominent, although often unconscious, tendencies throughout our history have been: first, a tendency towards integrating labour for the production of all riches in common, so as finally to render it impossible to discriminate the part of the common production due to the separate individual; and second, a tendency towards the fullest freedom of the individual in the prosecution of all aims, beneficial both for himself and for society at large. The ideal of the anarchist is thus a mere summing-up of what he considers to be the next phase of evolution. It is no longer a matter of faith; it is a matter of scientific discussion....

This doctrine might not seem to differ in any respect from the aims of *laissez-faire* liberalism or democratic socialism, but the anarchist differs profoundly from these political parties in his conception of means. Any form of government, and particularly representative government, he sees as a perpetuation of class-rule, and therefore as conflicting with the necessary evolution of the individual towards greater potentialities of consciousness and fullness of life—what Kropotkin called "the natural growth of altruistic feelings, which develop as soon as the conditions of life favour their growth." That this prospect involved profound problems of ethics and individual psychology was evident to Kropotkin: his last work, unfinished, was a treatise on ethics. Its purpose was to demonstrate that "the moral sense is a natural faculty in us like the sense of smell or of touch." This moral sense arises in the course of evolution, even within the animal kingdom, and can be expressed by the one word *solidarity*, that instinct without which, in times of danger, society would perish.

Kropotkin's insights into the origins of morality have been powerfully reinforced by the scientific observations of Dr. Konrad Lorenz, one of the most distinguished of contemporary ethologists. The following passage from his most recent book, *On Aggression* might have been written by Kropotkin:

Left to itself, reason is like a computer into which no relevant information conducive to an important answer has been fed; logically valid though all its operations may be, it is a wonderful system of wheels within wheels, without a motor to make them go round. The motor power that makes them do so stems from instinctive behaviour mechanisms much older than reason and not directly accessible to rational self-observation. They are the source of love and friendship, of all warmth of feeling, of appreciation of beauty, of the urge to artistic creativeness, of insatiable curiosity striving for scientific enlightenment. These deepest strata of the human personality are, in their dynamics, not essentially different from the instincts of animals, but on their basis human culture has erected all the enormous superstructures of social norms and rites whose function is so closely analogous to that of phylogenetic ritualisation.

The phylogentically determined principle of mutual aid has been perverted again and again in the course of history, always in the name of some abstract principle—"the abstract trinity of law, religion, and authority." The anarchist recognises the danger of all such abstractions. I repeat, he is a pragmatist, or more specifically, a pragmatic realist. He does not believe in any philosophical or political doctrine (not even in anarchism) except in so far as it results in actions that are in accordance with the creative or positive tendencies in human evolution. Ideas and knowledge are instruments in the service of a communal solidarity: aspects of mutual aid. Mutual aid is the only "phylogenetically adapted mechanism of behaviour" (Lorenz) of a progressive and self-preservative tendency in an evolutionary situation that otherwise is predatory and destructive. It is the predatory tendency, regressive from an evolutionary point of view, that is expressed in the capitalist and *laissez-faire* philosophies of politics.

Anarchism, nevertheless, is highly critical of the scientific attitude as it is usually expressed in politics, which is seen as a threat to liberty. A distinction is made, already by Bakunin, between the exact or natural sciences and "such sciences as history, philosophy, politics, and economic science, which are falsified by being deprived of their true basis, natural science." With uncanny prescience Bakunin saw the future development of a State in which the scientist would be enthroned as a despot far more restrictive of the people's liberties than any military despot of the past. "A scientific body entrusted with the government of society would soon end by devoting itself not to science but to quite another interest. And that, as in the case

with all established powers, would consist in its endeavour to perpetuate itself in power and consolidate its position by rendering the
society placed in its care even more stupid and consequently ever
more in need of being governed and directed by such a body." In
this connection Bakunin makes an interesting comparison of science
and art:

Science cannot go outside the realm of abstractions. In this respect it is vastly
inferior to art, which, properly speaking, has to do with general types and
general situations, but which, by the use of its own peculiar methods, embodies
them in forms which, though not living forms in the sense of real life, none the
less arouse in our imagination the feeling and recollection of life. In a certain
sense it individualises types and situations which it has conceived; and by
means of those individualities without flesh and blood—and consequently
permanent and immortal—which it has the power to create, it recalls to our
minds living, real individuals who appear and disappear before our eyes.
Science, on the contrary, is the perpetual immolation of fugitive and passing,
but real life on the altar of eternal abstraction.[3]

Much that Bakunin wrote about science seems to anticipate Orwell's *1984*. He accepted science, but he feared scientism, which he
saw as almost a branch of Marxism. "So long as it forms a separate
domain, specially represented by a corporation of savants, this ideal
world threatens to take the place of the Eucharist in relation to the
real world, reserving for its licensed representatives the duties and
functions of priests." This danger could only be avoided "by means
of general education, equally available to all, to dissolve the segregated social organisation of science, in order that the masses, ceasing
to be a mere herd, led and shorn by privileged shepherds, may take
into their own hands their historic destinies." But writing in 1871
Bakunin did not foresee the immense distance that, nearly a hundred
years later, would separate any conceivable form of general education
from the specialised arcana of modern science. The sinister combination of scientism and statism can now be broken only by the
abolition of the state.

In spite of Bakunin's deep interest in science Kropotkin remains the
greatest exponent of a scientific anarchism, but since Kropotkin's
time his ideas have been immensely reinforced by the development of
individual psychology. To appreciate the relevance of this psychology
to anarchism we must return to the philosophical foundations of
anarchism and to certain "stated or assumed premisses" of anarchism.
They occupy "a pivotal position" in the Krimerman-Perry anthology,
and they are nothing less than the perennial problems of ethical and
political philosophy.

[3] Bakunin's writings are not easily accessible in English. Unless otherwise
stated my quotations come from the excellent anthology compiled and edited
by G. P. Maximoff: *The Political Philosophy of Bakunin: Scientific Anarchism*
(Glencoe, Illinois, The Free Press, 1953).

These problems—questions of what sort of life men *ought* to live and the sort of society that will permit them to live a life that is both morally imperative and intrinsically desirable—all resolve into the one question of personal freedom. (Questions of rights and duties, of authority and coercion, are all subordinate to this one concept.)

Our anthologists begin by pointing out that Hobbes' definition of liberty as the absence of external impediments would not be acceptable to the anarchist thinkers they present in this section of their book (they include Godwin, Kropotkin, Max Stirner, Nicholas Berdyeav, Adin Ballou, and Stephen Pearl Andrews). The anarchist standard of what is ultimately desirable, and of what society should preserve,

resides in a more constructive ideal which they alternatively designate as "the sovereignty of the individual" (Andrews), "personality" (Berdyaev), "independent judgment" (Godwin), "self-ownership" (Stirner), and so on. Correct or not, this unanimous rejection of the Hobbesian notion of freedom for a more positive chief good provides a unifying theme in anarchist thought.

None of the writers quoted in this section of the anthology is specifically a psychologist, unless Max Stirner's deep and original analysis of the ego is to be called psychological (Freud may have owed something to it). *Der Einzige und sein Eigentum (The Ego and his Own*[4]*)* is a work of considerable power and originality. Marx was so impressed by its threat to his position that he devoted hundreds of pages in *The German Ideology* to its refutation. His attack was so effective that the work has been unjustly neglected ever since, except in Germany (in the margin of Marxist studies) and in France where Victor Basch devoted a comprehensive study to it and, more recently, Albert Camus paid tribute to it in *L'homme revolte*.[5] Stirner attacks all ideologies, all concepts and abstractions, all of which without exception demand a surrender of the individual will. The state, of course, above all, for whatever its constitution it is always a despotism, above all when it assumes power in the name of "the people." Even freedom is a delusion. "Who is it that is to become free?" Stirner asks. "You, I, we. Free from what? From everything that is not you, not I, not we. . . . What is left when I have been freed from everything that is not I? Only I; nothing but I. But

[4] A translation by Steven I. Byington was originally published in 1913. It was reprinted by the Libertarian Press, New York, in 1962.

[5] A new work on Stirner has been published in Germany: *Die Ideologie des anonyme Gesellschaft*, by Hans G. Helms (Cologne, Dumont Schauberg Verlag). It runs to more than 600 pages, including a bibliography of 90 pages. Helms sees in Stirner an "apostle of the middle classes" and a forerunner of fascism, a point of view which can be maintained only by ignoring what is must fundamental in Stirner—his rejection of every kind of ideology. A more balanced view of Stirner's significance may be found in Martin Buber's *Between Man and Man* (Collins, Fontana Library, 1961), pp. 60-108.

freedom has nothing to offer to this I himself." Why not proclaim
your own identity without further ado? "Freedom" merely awakens
your *rage* against everything that is not you; "egoism" calls you to
joy over yourself, to self-enjoyment. "Freedom" is and remains a
longing, a romantic plaint, a Christian hope for unearthliness and
futurity; "ownness" is a reality, which of *itself* removes just so much
unfreedom as by barring your own way hinders you. What does not
disturb you you will not want to renounce; and, if it begins to
disturb you, why, you know that "you must obey yourselves rather .
than men!"

Again we see the realism, the anti-idealism that is at the base of the
anarchist position. Stirner's attack on the State, which is fierce and
sustained (and the source of Nietzsche's similar attack) is motivated
by this intense feeling that it establishes and legalises a mythical
entity that deprives the individual of his uniqueness, of his very self.

What is called a State is a tissue and plexus of dependence and adherence; it is
a *belonging together*, a holding together, in which those who are placed
together fit themselves to each other; or in short mutually depend on each
other; it is the *order* of this *dependence*. . . . The State seeks to hinder every
free activity by its censorship, its supervision, its police, and holds this hin-
dering to be its duty, because it is in truth a duty of self-preservation. The
State wants to make something out of man, therefore there live in it only *made*
men; every one who wants to be his own self is its opponent. . . .

What remained in Stirner an affirmation of selfhood and a stubborn
opposition to the State in all its collective and repressive aspects has
now become a characteristic of the good bourgeois. The modern
anarchist tends to ignore the State as an anachronism which, powerful and intrusive as it is, is destined not so much to wither away, but
to become the obvious and indefensible instrument of tyranny, and
in this sense it is no longer worth arguing about. The millenary
statists, the scientific "experts," the professional economists and
career politicians, will continue to support it and to extend its
powers, but by the people at large the State is now universally hated
and from the State's point of view we are all impenitent criminals,
tax-evaders and delinquents, or witless citizens waiting to be penned
in various social categories or houses of correction—municipal estates,
comprehensive schools, hospitals, defence corps, peace corps, collec-
tives of every kind. Against this conception of man has arisen (or
rather, has been revived, for in the East it is an ancient doctrine) the
conception of man as an individual who becomes whole and even
"god-like" by deliberate dissociation from the collective psyche.

The literature of individual psychology is now immense, and none
of it, from Freud and Adler to Jung, Piaget, Rank, Burrow and
Fromm can be neglected if we would arrive at an appreciation of its
range, its therapeutic pretensions and its effectiveness. It would serve
no purpose to discuss here the therapeutic aspects of individual
psychology; what is relevant is the description of the personal psyche
in relation to the collective psyche, and the distinction which Jung in

particular makes between the undifferentiated ego instincts and the achieved personality or "Self." For the sake of simplicity I shall take Jung's description of the process of "individuation," which is that part of individual psychology that has most relevance to a philosophy of anarchism.

The individual has, of course, always stood in opposition to the group—to the family group, the environmental group, the tribe, and the nation. All psychologists agree that most if not all of the individual's troubles come from maladjustment to one or more of these groups, and psycho-therapy has been concerned largely with techniques of reconciliation.

In one direction an extreme maladjustment leads to complete alienation and narcissism; in the opposite direction to loss of identity and participation in various forms of mass hysteria. The ideal to be achieved is not so much an uneasy balance between these two tendencies as the achievement of a separate indivisible unity or "whole," with firm foundations in education and creative activity.

Jung is the best guide to the process because his knowledge is the most eclectic and his exposition the most detailed. An acceptance of the hypothesis of the unconscious (which is the basis of all con-temporary psycho-analytic theory and practice) is of course neces-sary, but the evidence for this is so manifest (in dream activities, for example) and has for so long been the common assumption of all religions and philosophies that we need not pay particular attention to those few mechanists or behaviourists such as J. H. Eysenck who deny its realities. I believe it could be shown that they are merely using a different language to describe identical phenomena.

Jung wrote many (not always consistent) descriptions of the indi-viduation process. The following,[6] long as it is, is the shortest that gives an adequate account of it:

For the development of personality, then, strict differentiation from the collec-tive psyche is absolutely necessary, since partial or blurred differentiation leads to an immediate melting away of the individual in the collective. There is now a danger that in the analysis of the unconscious the collective and the personal psyche may be fused together, with, as I have intimated, highly unfortunate results. These results are injurious both to the patient's life-feeling and to his fellow men, if he has any influence at all on his environment. Through his identification with the collective psyche he will infallibly try to force the demands of his unconscious upon others, for identity with the collective psyche always brings with it a feeling of universal validity—"godlikeness"—which com-pletely ignores all differences in the personal psyche of his fellows. (The feeling of universal validity comes, of course, from the universality of the collective psyche.) A collective attitude naturally presupposes this same collective psyche in others. But that means a ruthless disregard not only of individual differences but also of differences of a more general kind within the collective psyche

[6]From *Two Essays on Analytical Psychology*, trans. by R. F. C. Hull, §240. New York (Bollingen Series); London (Routledge & Kegan Paul), 1953.

itself, as for example differences of race. This disregard for individuality obviously means the suffocation of the single individual, as a consequence of which the element of differentiation is obliterated from the community. *The element of differentiation is the individual. All the highest achievements of virtue, as well as the blackest villainies, are individual. The larger a community is, and the more the sum total of collective factors peculiar to every large community rests on conservative prejudices detrimental to individuality, the more will the individual be morally and spiritually crushed*, and, as a result, the one source of moral and spiritual progress for society is choked up. Naturally the only thing that can thrive in such an atmosphere is sociality and whatever is collective in the individual. Everything individual in him goes under, *i.e.*, is doomed to repression. The individual elements lapse into the unconscious, where, by the law of necessity, they are transformed into something essentially baleful, destructive, and anarchical. Socially, this evil principle shows itself in the spectacular crimes—regicide and the like—perpetrated by certain prophetically-minded individuals; but in the great mass of the community it remains in the background, and only manifests itself indirectly in the inexorable moral degeneration of society. *It is a notorious fact that the morality of society as a whole is in inverse ratio to its size; for the greater the aggregation of individuals, the more the individual factors are blotted out, and with them morality, which rests entirely on the moral sense of the individual and the freedom necessary for this.* Hence every man is, in a certain sense, unconsciously a worse man when he is in society than when acting alone; for he is carried by society and to that extent relieved of his individual responsibility. Any large company composed of wholly admirable persons has the morality and intelligence of an unwieldy, stupid and violent animal. The bigger the organisation, the more unavoidable is its immorality and blind stupidity (*Senatus bestia, senatores boni viri*). Society, by automatically stressing all the collective qualities in its individual representatives, puts a premium on mediocrity, on everything that settles down to vegetate in an easy, irresponsible way. Individuality will inevitably be driven to the wall. This process begins in school, continues at the university, and rules all departments in which the State has a hand. In a small social body, the individuality of its members is better safeguarded; and the greater is their relative freedom and the possibility of conscious responsibility. *Without freedom there can be no morality. Our admiration for great organisations dwindles when once we become aware of the other side of the wonder: the tremendous piling up and accentuation of all that is primitive in man, and the unavoidable destruction of his individuality in the interests of the monstrosity that every great organisation in fact is.* The man of today, who resembles more or less the collective ideal, has made his heart into a den of murderers, as can easily be proved by the analysis of his unconscious, even though he himself is not in the least disturbed by it. And in so far as he is normally "adapted" to his environment, it is true that the greatest infamy on the part of his group will not disturb him, so long as the majority of his fellows steadfastly believe in the exalted morality of their social organisation.

I have italicised three passages in this long quotation which seem to have a particular relevance to anarchism—indeed, they might have come from the writings of an anarchist, as might many other passages in Jung's works.[7] There are just one or two further points that need emphasis if we are to understand the process of individuation.

For example, the emancipated individual cannot wholly escape from the collective psyche, nor is it desirable that he should. Jung confesses that he is always astonished to find how much of so-called individual psychology is really collective—"so much', indeed, that the individual traits are completely overshadowed by it. Since, however, individuation is an ineluctable psychological requirement, we can see from the superior force of the collective what very special attention must be paid to this delicate plant 'individuality' if it is not to be completely smothered." But this is just to admit that the process of individuation is a long and severe discipline.

Secondly, it should be emphasised that individuation does not imply isolation. Jung himself has said: "Since the individual is not only a single entity, but also, by his very existence, presupposes a collective relationship, the process of individuation does not lead to isolation, but to an intenser and more universal collective solidarity." This brings us back to Kropotkin and to mutual aid (and to Martin Buber and his concept of "dialogue"). The ego, we might say, achieves his own in order to offer it, in mutual trust to "the other."

The psychologist (more particularly the psycho-therapist) thinks in terms of a situation that needs correction: his concern is "the cure of souls." From a more general sociological point of view the anarchist must think of the process of individuation as an educational one. Krimerman and Perry recognise that anarchism has distinctive and revolutionary implications for education and, indeed, assert that "no other movement whatever has assigned to educational principles, concepts, experiments, and practices a more significant place in its writings and activities." Tolstoy is seminal in this respect, but the eleven extracts on education make the most impressive of all the contributions to this anthology, from Godwin to Paul Goodman.

Education has been my own particular concern. It is not often realised how deeply anarchist in its orientation a work such as

[7] Indeed, Jung sometimes seems to echo Stirner's very words—*e.g.*: "Individuation means becoming a single, homogeneous being, and, in so far as 'individuality' embrases *our innermost, last, and incomparable uniqueness*, it also implies becoming one's own self. We could therefore translate individuation as 'coming to selfhood' or 'self-realisation.'" (*Two Essays*, §266.) The similarity is, of course, all the more striking in the original German of both writers. It is also interesting to observe that Kropotkin used the word "individuation" (or "invividualisation") long before Jung. Man in an anarchist society, he wrote, "would be enabled to obtain the full development of all his faculties, intellectual, artistic, and moral, without being hampered by overwork for the monopolists, or by the servility and inertia of mind of the great number. He would thus be able to reach full *individualisation* which is not possible either under the present system of *individualism*, or under any system of state-socialism in the so-called *Volkstaat* (popular state). . . ."

Education through Art is and was intended to be. It is of course humiliating to have to confess that its success (and it is by far the most influential book I have written) has been in spite of this fact. I must conclude that I did not make my intention clear enough, but I still hope that the message has been most effective in the degree that it has been most innocently received. My stress in that book was precisely on the individuation of a self—a whole chapter was devoted to "Unconscious Modes of Integration" and in the first chapter I stated that in my view an answer to the question: *What is the purpose of education?* could only be given within the terms of a libertarian conception of democracy. (I should have said "of socialism," for democracy implies a governmental exercise of power.) I then went on to define this purpose as the concurrent development of the "uniqueness" and the "social consciousness or reciprocity" of the individual. "As a result of the infinite permutations of heredity the individual will inevitably be unique, and this uniqueness, because it is something not possessed by anyone else, will be of value to the community." Uniqueness, I declared, has no *practical* value in isolation. "One of the most certain lessons of modern psychology, and of recent historical experiences, is that education must be a process, not only of individuation, but also of *integration*, which is the reconciliation of individual uniqueness with social unity."

I still believe that individuation must process *pari passu* with integration, and that an anarchist philosophy must include this concept of reconciliation. Both processes are implicit in Kropotkin's concept of mutual aid, and in Buber's concept of reciprocity (the instinct for communion, *Verbundenheit*). Stirner would have rejected a word like *Verbundenheit*, with its implication of a bond, of a chain on the ego's liberty. Anarchism owes much to Stirner's realism, and we feel that his philosophical importance has been ignored. (Krimerman and Perry point out that it offers "a possible, and largely ignored, approach to the philosophical problem of free will. . . . If a man does not own the acts he performs, can these be counted as voluntary actions or are they simply responses to factors over which he himself has no control? Can one be held to account for conduct which stems from beliefs and goals, or ideals and interests, of which one is not the owner?") Nevertheless, we must recognise that the individual is inexorably compelled to find a place in society and undergo some process of integration simply because otherwise he will lapse into schizophrenia. The individual may possess his self, become his "own," only to find that the result is an intolerable sense of isolation.

All objections to anarchism reduce to the one of impracticality. But none of its critics has considered anarchism as a long-term process of individuation, accomplished by general education and personal discipline—that is to say: from a socio-psychological point of view. I have already noted that Krimerman and Perry come to the conclusion that anarchism must now be regarded as *a consistently individualised pragmatism*, and objections on the score of innate human depravity or selfishness are thus obviated by the anarchist's insistence on reformative education and environmental transformation.

The new interpretation of anarchism now put forward may not seem to differ much from the rational liberalism of Karp Popper, but I think it does so in two ways. In the first place, the anarchist cannot abandon the revolutionary myth, much as he may realise with Popper that revolutionary *methods* can only make things worse. Rebellion, as Camus has said, is still today "at the basis of the struggle. Origin of form, source of real life, it keeps us always erect in the savage formless movement of history." But rebellion, Camus argued, always demands, defends and re-creates moderation. "Moderation, born of rebellion, can only live by rebellion. It is a perpetual conflict, continually created and mastered by the intelligence." We cannot do without that tension, that dynamic equilibrium.

In the second place, anarchism differs profoundly from liberalism in its attitude to institutions. The liberal regards institutions as the safeguard of personal liberty. Popper points out, quite truly, that Marxists have been taught to think in terms not of institutions but of classes. "Classes, however, never rule, any more than nations. The rulers are always certain persons. And, whatever class they may once have belonged to, once they are rulers they belong to the ruling class." True enough. But what guarantee do we have that the same persons will not exercise a stronger and more tyrannical power under the cover of institutions? Is not that precisely the kind of tyranny we are experiencing now, the tyranny of "the backroom boys," the faceless "experts" who control our institutions, our civil service departments, merchant banks, economic councils. Institutions in the modern world are megalomanic, self-perpetuating, and viviparous. They do not protect personal liberty: they legalise tyranny and spread its invisible tentacles into every cell of life.

That is why anarchism, however much it may have changed its methods or strategy, remains committed to the non-governmental principle, which implies the breakdown of all centralised institutions—of nations, of federations, of constitutions, of conglomerations of every kind. Not only does the anarchist believe that that government is best that governs least; he does not accept any form of external coercion that prevents the free development of the fully integrated personality.

My own belief is that such a development of the personality will never conflict with what Popper calls "the authority of objective truth." But finally I must insist with Paul Goodman ("no other contemporary anarchist rivals Paul Goodman in imagination and scholarship") that freedom is not the same thing as *laissez-faire*. Freedom must be understood in a very positive sense: "it is *the condition of initiating activity*.... The justification for freedom is that initiation is essential to *any* high-grade human behaviour. Only free action has grace and force." But free *action*! There is nothing in the anarchist philosophy to justify indifference, complacency, or anything but a pragmatic activity patiently and consistently directed to a revolutionary end.

Counterrhetoric

THE NEW "CONFRONTATION POLITICS" IS A DANGEROUS GAME

Irving Howe

A new term has entered the American language—"confrontation politics," the equivalent in public life of Russian roulette in private life. Some who play this new political game are authentic desperadoes, mostly young Negro militants; others are white middle-class students acting—or acting out—a fantasy-wish of revolution.

For the black desperadoes, "confrontation politics" can bring large risks: prison, violence, death. For the white students, the risks until recently were small; but now, after the ghastliness of Chicago and the growing popular obsession with "law and order," they will surely increase. For the country as a whole, the problem is perplexing. At a time of social disorder, when gross injustices continue to plague us, there arise combative minorities charged with moral idealism and apocalyptic emotion, which have developed tactics of protest going beyond the usual democratic methods yet short of the usual insurrectionary ones.

Like many other New-Left notions, "confrontation politics" has not been well articulated as a theory. It is a kind of politics that grows up through improvisation, and it has been improvised as a way of getting around the sense of futility which has usually beset

American radicalism. It has been choreographed as an out-of-doors explosion, a sort of real-life theater.

The purpose is to prod and incite a dormant, insensitive society into recognizing its moral failures. No longer committed, as were the Marxists, to the idea that the proletariat would be the crucial lever for the transformation of history, the young semi-anarchists who practice "confrontation" see themselves as a minority probably doomed to remain one for a long time. They have no expectation of creating new electoral majorities and small expectation of persuading large numbers of people; for they see the mass of Americans as brainwashed by "the media" (the very media which give them vast amounts of publicity). Their politics is a politics of desperation, at best moral shock and at worst nihilist irritation. They assign to themselves the task of sacrifice and assault, as a self-chosen vanguard which must destroy the complacence of "corporate liberalism."

What makes this task seem especially urgent is the feeling that in Vietnam the U.S. is conducting an immoral war which the ordinary democratic process is too slow and cumbersome to cope with.

One source of confrontation politics, seldom acknowledged, is the strategy worked out by the civil-rights movement in the South during the fifties. Under strong pacifist guidance at that point, the civil-rights movement "confronted" Southern institutions through direct action—that is, through demonstrations, parades, lunch-counter sit-ins. Conceived as a way to force the South into recognizing that Negroes would no longer be dormant, these actions involved a degree of "obstruction" (Jim Crow arrangements in stores were upset) and a kind of "confrontation" (nonviolent minorities exposed themselves to beatings by police and mobs).

The success of such actions depended on the following conditions:

The demonstrators were demanding rights which had already been recognized, both in law and moral consensus, by the nation as a whole. Despite failures by the Federal Government to enforce anti-discrimination laws, the demonstrators could count on at least some practical help from the Kennedy and Johnson Administrations, as well as large amounts of support from many Northerners. And while the Southern police often remained brutal, it was no longer possible for municipal and state governments in the South to destroy Negro protest through sheer terror.

The demonstrations came at a time when there were growing differences of response among Southern whites. A majority may still have remained convinced that Jim Crow was a practical convenience, but a growing minority seems to have felt it was morally indefensible. Even if that minority did not always act with courage, it did begin to break the monolithic front which the white South had put up for decades. Doubt and guilt pierced the hard shell of white superiority.

The unconditional nonviolence practiced by Dr. King and his friends was a principle that sections of the middle-class South had to respect—indeed, to respect almost as much as white Northerners came to admire. The sight of men willing to turn the other cheek is one that must move, or at least disturb, people who retain even the flimsiest connections with Christianity. Tactically, it bewildered the Southern police who would have been delighted to trade 100 blows for one, but didn't know how to cope with men going limp under beatings.

While the Southern demonstrators sometimes broke local ordinances, their actions were justifiable by democratic standards. For they had long been deprived of the right to vote and thereby participate in changing policies through peaceful means—which meant they now had a certain sanction for resorting to partly coercive but completely nonviolent forms of direct action. Furthermore, they were struggling for the enforcement of national laws superceding local ordinances, many of which were deliberately contrived to circumvent Federal legislation and were commonly felt to be of dubious constitutionality. Indeed, one reason for breaking local ordinances was to challenge their constitutionality.

The power of Southern protest derived partly from its alliance with major forces in the North: liberals, unionists, churches and academicians, all pressing for civil-rights legislation. One reason the Selma march proved to be so valuable was that it came just at the moment when it could most dramatically induce popular support for the Voting Rights Act. By contrast, demonstrations leading only to other demonstrations, or demonstrations lacking clearly defined goals (e.g., "justice") or demonstrations with hopelessly unrealizable goals (e.g., a "black republic" in the South) will result in a dissipation of energies. The civil-rights marches during the fifties and early sixties, however, were directed toward concrete local aims and in support of proposed national legislation.

Now, all of these favorable circumstances were special to the South, and it would be naive to suppose they can now be duplicated on a national scale. When certain kinds of demonstrations are held by anti-Vietnam protestors—especially if they are feckless enough to include Vietcong banners—it can hardly be said that they act in behalf of moral-political opinions shared by a large majority of the people but thwarted by a sectional minority; or that they have been significantly deprived of their right to organize and protest; or that they act out of a principled devotion to nonviolence.

These are not new problems, either in the development of radical movements or the history of democratic states. There are historical precedents, and something can be learned from glancing at them.

Shortly after the Russian Revolution there appeared tendencies within the Communist movement, opposed by Lenin and Trotsky, which led to a strategy of constant assault: endless demonstrations, unremitting "offensives," indeed a precursor of confrontation politics. Some ultra-left German Communists even gave this strategy a name, the "theory of electrification." Through reckless self-sacrifice, the party would "electrify" the masses into revolution. Predictably, this led to disasters in Germany and elsewhere during the early twenties—brave but suicidal coups by Communist combat groups which failed to gain the support of the workers. About the "theory of electrification" Trotsky remarked with asperity that the probable consequence was that the electrifiers would burn themselves.

In the immediate pre-Hitler period, there was an even more senseless turn toward a kind of confrontation politics. The Communists came up with the insane notion of "social fascism," according to which the Social Democrats, and not the Nazis, were the main danger in Germany. (Today, it is "the liberals" who are the main danger. . . .) The Communists kept staging endless demonstrations which, in Trotsky's phrase, "succeeded only in irritating all classes without winning over any." They antagonized the middle classes; they wore out the patience of the workers; they exhausted their own cadres. They made loud noises about "taking power" but never came within reach of power. Inevitably there appeared a force calling for the restoration of "law and order," behind which a large segment of the population united, actively or passively. It would be an exaggeration to say that the Communist tactics caused the rise of Hitlerism, but no exaggeration at all to say that they helped the Nazis come to power.

Taken simply as a syndrome of going into the streets (what has been called the "Theory of Permanent Demonstrations"), the politics of confrontation would not be a very serious matter. Demonstrations can be useful; demonstrations can be self-defeating. Opposition to the Vietnam war was surely rallied and increased through demonstrations; but some of them, by allowing themselves to be linked with the Vietcong and overtaken by anti-American hatreds not at all essential to the cause of peace, had a counterproductive effect, stiffening the hostility felt by millions of Americans toward dissent. About such matters we can only make estimates based partly on our sense of what this country is like. There is, finally, no science for measuring the consequences of going into the streets.

Far more serious is the political overlook which inspires confrontationist acts. As developed by Herbert Marcuse, the current New-Left guru, this political outlook advances the following propositions: We live in an advanced stage of capitalism, a mass society providing bread, circuses and technology, which has tamed the forces of opposition and thereby undercut hopes for "transcendence." There is no great likelihood, in Marcuse's view, that we will soon witness an end to a social oppression sustained by material plenty but yielding no spiritual gratification. Efforts at reform tend to be superficial, and many of the values of liberalism—tolerance, free speech, electoral activity—are depreciated as devices for adjusting people to the status quo.

Revolution thus being declared all but impossible and reform all but ineffectual, Marcuse's doctrines justify those radicals who turn away from both traditional Leninism and social democracy, in order to launch a series of adventures or "raids," perhaps to usurp, perhaps to unsettle established power, but clearly without much concern for democratic processes. The claim here is that the society can be shaken into change, if shaken at all, only through attacks by marginal groups: the outraged poor, alienated hippies, rebellious students.

Whatever one may think about the analytical portions of Marcuse's thought, his political conclusions offer a simultaneous rationalization for withdrawal and wildness, copping-out and turning-on. Precisely insofar as numbers of students have come under Marcuse's influence, the picture of society he draws seems less and less valid. Men are not slipping into apathy and somnolence, at least not yet; they are disturbed, restless, worried. In the last decade the U.S. has not become stultified, immobile and indifferent. The *cul-de-sac* of historical stagnation posited by Marcuse is indeed a nightmare haunting every sensitive man, but one must be able to distinguish between the fears of the dark and the facts of day.

Still, if you hold a version of Marcuse's ideas and believe liberalism is exhausted or corrupt or inseparable from "racist imperialism;" if you further conclude that no major social classes within society can be expected significantly to transform it; you then have no serious alternative to either a Salinger-like withdrawal or the political equivalent of guerrilla raids. By this last phrase I don't mean literally shooting it out—though there are a few freelance lunatics advocating as much—but rather a series of actions, dramatic, desperate and provocative, which keep the society in a state of constant turmoil and the university in a state of constant chaos.

This strategy, in my view, can lead only to disaster and a backlash of terrifying proportions. The signs of it are everywhere about us.

A tacit premise behind "confrontation politics" is that the university largely resembles the surrounding society, or is even identical in nature with it. The result is to damage academic life and distort political action.

Within the university the New Left students engage with more or less liberal faculties, and behind these engagements there is often the assumption that, finally, the university will behave like a middle-class parent. When sometimes it does not, there follow among students considerable shock and rage. At Columbia the students who seized buildings and declared "communes," were engaged in a quasi-revolutionary action—or so some of them said. But when the Columbia administration (quite stupidly, I think) retaliated with the police force which New Left theory says is inevitable but which New Left feelings are often not really prepared for, the students cried foul. They invoked the traditional view of the university as a cloister of intellect from which police should be barred.

At this point they were caught in a dilemma. If they believed it proper to transform the campus into a training ground for revolutionary action, they could hardly complain when the powers-that-be retaliated with force. If they genuinely believed (as I, for one, believe) that the campus should be a center of learning from which the police are barred, then they could hardly treat the university as if it were *no more than* a microcosm of capitalist society. True, they might argue with much cogency that many universities have been contaminated and should be returned to their true purposes of scholarship and teaching; but to say that would be to accept—O, dreadful prospect!—a view of the university close to that of liberalism.

The analogy between university and society breaks down in a still more serious way. One reason the tactics of the Students for a Democratic Society have worked on certain campuses is that implicitly they count on that mixture of affection and irritation many faculty people feel toward "the students." In good measure the politics of confrontation as practiced on the campus depends on a benevolent or indecisive response from the liberal professors whom the New Left treats with such contempt. But once such tactics are transferred to the society at large, the result is going to be very different. The professors, who count for a good deal on the campus, count for fairly little in the society; and the society itself is not nearly so pacific or indulgent as are most professors. One needs a talent for self-delusion to say that in the United States liberalism—for all its many faults and failures—represents the main danger to humane aspirations.

No; this society retains large potentials of hatred and violence, its capacities for tolerating what it regards as disruption have a visible limit, and its response to confrontation tactics could well be a crushing display of force which would harm many people who have nothing to do with the New Left. I say none of this by way of approval, only by way of describing hard facts which those of us who believe in radical politics must take into account.

If anything should give the New Left pause, it is the fact that according to the polls, a clear majority of the American people approved of Mayor Daley's treatment of the Chicago demonstrators. I don't mean it should give them pause in their opposition to the Vietnam war, an opposition I share; but that it should stir them into rethinking the value of confrontation methods.

Now, when arguments of this kind are put forward in debates with the New Left, one of the usual replies goes like this: "You liberals, you Social Democrats are always trying to hamstring protest by raising the specter of backlash. But where is the backlash? Is it perhaps just a bogy with which you're trying to frighten us? And if we pay attention to it, how can we ever mount an effective protest?"

The backlash is everywhere. Some of us, raised on memories of earlier decades, carry a mental picture of reactionary mobs and American Legionnaires assaulting radicals in the street: that was true in the twenties and thirties; it may yet prove true in the next few years. But just as everything else in modern society becomes bureaucratized, so has backlash. Instead of swarming mobs, there are now trained police. The white workers of Italian or Polish or Slavic origin who have managed to save up enough money to buy themselves little homes in the suburbs aren't likely to organize mobs to invade the black ghettos—at least not yet; but they are inclined, many of them, to vote for George Wallace in the name of "law and order." That some 20 per cent of the American electorate could even consider voting for Wallace—surely that's a sufficient sign of backlash.

Is the answer, then, for dissidents to crawl into holes and keep silent? Of course not. But in order to protest the Vietnam war it isn't necessary to rouse all the prejudices millions of Americans hold, and it isn't even necessary to outrage their sincere patriotic sentiments. In order to fight for Negro rights, it isn't necessary to talk blood or to call white men "honkies" and policemen "pigs." That's a way of blowing off steam, and the resulting profit goes to George Wallace.

One aim of confrontation politics is the "polarization" of society. In plain English, this means that by constant assault the activists hope to drive a segment of the liberals into radicalism; thereupon the "mushy middle" of the country will be broken up; and we can then look forward to an apocalypse, with two extremes hardened and ready for a final conflict.

When they invoke this vision the confrontationists are drawing upon political emotions that have been very powerful in the 20th century—emotions concerning "the seizure of power," a political Second Coming. Having shared these emotions and still being susceptible to them, I can appreciate their force. But I must nevertheless ask: what, in the present circumstances, would be the likely outcome of such a "polarization" in the United States?

Were anything of the sort to happen, millions of ordinary Americans—for whom student protest-drugs-hippiedom-Negro rioting forms a stream of detested association—would also be activated. Lower-class white ethnic groups would be stirred up. *Lumpen* elements would be emboldened. Both respectable and marginal classes would turn to demagogues promising order in the streets.

Despite its talk about "the power élite" and the idiotic notion it sometimes proposes that we live under "liberal fascism," the New Left clings to an excessively optimistic view of American society. Its spokesmen have neither memory nor awareness of what fascism—the real thing, *fascist* fascism—would be like. They fail to recognize that there are sleeping dogs it would be just as well to let lie. And they are shockingly indifferent to the likelihood that the first victim of a new reaction in America would be the universities in which they now find shelter.

Only in terms of a theory of "polarization" can one explain the peculiar intensity with which New Left students kept trying to break up the meetings of Hubert Humphrey, while virtually ignoring those of Richard Nixon. (I am against breaking up anyone's meetings.) They were acting on the premise that liberalism is their main enemy, and some of them have even said that they would find attractive an alliance between far left and far right.

Such notions tacitly continue the old Stalinist tradition of "the worse, the better" and *"Nach Hitler, uns."* Yet all of recent history enforces the lesson that misery cannot be the seedbed of progress or · chaos of freedom. Polarization helps, not the left, but the right; not those with grievances, but those with guns. In any case, is the prospect of "polarization" an attractive one? How many of us would like to face a choice between an America symbolized by George Wallace and an America symbolized by Tom Hayden? Morally, because he is against racism, Hayden is superior; but politically, neither has much respect for democracy. I for one would fear for my safety almost as much with one as with the other. Wallace might have me pistol-whipped as a Communist, and Hayden have me sent to a labor camp as a Social Democrat. Hayden would be more accurate politically, but what sort of consolation would that be?

For a while confrontation politics seems to work. Caught off balance, the enemy panics. College administrators aren's sure how to cope with students who seize buildings. But in time, for better or worse, they are going to figure out a way of dealing with this problem.

There is some truth in the claim—it constitutes a damning criticism of our society—that provocative demonstrations spilling over into violence have a way of gaining attention, certainly from TV, which programmatic and disciplined protest does not. But it is a truth easily overstated. The ghetto riots in Detroit and Watts have not brought notable improvements to their communities; they have not led to those increased Federal appropriations which are the only serious way of starting to clear the slums. At best they have enabled these communities, at enormous cost to themselves, to gain a slightly larger share of the funds already available. And as the California election of Ronald Reagan showed, the violence helped set off an electoral trend which can only signify a tight-fisted and mean-spirited policy toward the blacks.

Concerning this, let me quote from a discussion between Bayard Rustin, the Negro leader, and myself in the November Dissent:

Howe: I keep encountering the argument in regard to riots: "We know in principle it's not a good thing. But when you have a society that is not susceptible to pressure or moral appeals, the only way you can get them to pay attention is through raising hell."

Rustin: There are two tragedies here. One is that to some extent they're right. You don't get concessions until there's been trouble . . . The second tragedy is that although we receive minor concessions from the establishment, once the rioting reaches a certain point there will be repression against the entire Negro community.

Howe: Raising the ante indefinitely isn't going to work . . .

Rustin: Right. To repress one-tenth of the population will require an assault on the civil liberties of everyone. And in such an atmosphere, no genuine progress in the redistribution of wealth can take place . . . There's another factor. Sooner or later the unity of the Negroes, small as it is, in making demands on the whole society will be splintered, because the Negro community gets into a debate—are you or are you not for violence?—instead of uniting around a fight for political and economic objectives.

The advocates of "confrontation" seem undisturbed by the fact that they are setting precedents which could lead to a major crisis for democracy. If it is permissible for opponents of the war to burn Government records, why may not neo-Fascists do the same thing a few years later? If it is permissible for left-wing students to seize buildings in behalf of virtuous ends, why may not their action become a precedent for doing the same thing in behalf of detestable ends? At the very least, such problems must be discussed.

Some will say that violence and illegality are already rampant in the society, and that they are merely responding to its official use. This has a measure of truth. But I would reply that democratic procedures, incomplete as they may still be, have been established only after decades of struggle, and that it would be feckless to dismiss them as mere sham. Those of us who see the need for radical change have the most interest in preserving democracy.

A few years ago, Staughton Lynd wrote about an anti-war demonstration in Washington: "It was unbearably moving to watch the sea of banners moving out . . . toward the Capitol . . . Still more poignant was the perception that as the crowd moved toward the seat of Government . . . our forward movement was irresistibly strong . . . nothing could have stopped that crowd from taking possession of its Government. Perhaps next time we should keep going, occupying for a time the rooms from which orders issue."

One must ask Staughton Lynd: under whose mandate were the marchers to occupy the Government? And if they did "perhaps next time" arrogate to themselves the privilege of a *coup d'état*, even a symbolic one lasting five minutes, how will they keep other crowds, other causes—equally sincere, equally "moving"—from doing the same "perhaps the time after next?"

The politics of confrontation bears an inherent drift toward antidemocratic élitism. Electoral processes are declared irrelevant, majorities mere formalities. Once such notions are indulged, the choice is either to sink back into apathy with pot or to plunge into a desperate élitism which dismisses the people as boobs and assigns the "tasks of history" to a self-appointed vanguard. And in the current atmosphere, it isn't hard to drift from elitism to talk of violence. Mostly, so far, it is talk.

But there are troubling signs. This past summer the office of Stanford University's president was set afire, an event that followed in time a season of student sit-ins. I see no reason to connect these two, and would never have dreamed of doing so had I not read the following in a New-Left paper, The Midpeninsula Observer:

"Most leftists in this area seem to feel that the fire was politically motivated, and a split of opinion has developed with regard to the tactical efficacy of the act. Some believe that the fire was an effective attack on state power and that it was a logical extension of the leftist activity that has been going on at and around Stanford. Others think that the fire itself was a mistake ... since it is not clearly connected with a political movement and since most of the people who might be educated by such an act are gone for the summer."

Significant here is not the speculation that the fire was politically motivated—a speculation I refuse to accept—but the argument offered by those leftists opposed to setting fires. They seem to have a seasonal theory of the revolutionary uses of arson. In the winter, apparently, when more people can be "educated" by such an act, these critics would find arson more acceptable. The whole thing, I must say, reminds one of Dostoyevsky's "The Possessed"—as also of George Orwell's caustic remark that a certain kind of infantile leftism is "playing with fire on the part of people who don't even know that fire is hot."

Or here, to cite another instance, is an Aug. 25 report by Robert Maynard in The Washington Post about a feud between S.N.C.C. and the Black Panthers. At a meeting between leaders of the two groups, writes Maynard, there was a sharp dispute which "resulted in Panthers drawing guns on James Forman," the S.N.C.C. leader. Another S.N.C.C. leader, Julius Lester, is quoted by Maynard as having written: "The shoot-out was averted, fortunately, but there was no doubt ... that whatever merger or alliance may have existed was finished."

As a sign of the fraternal spirit induced by Black Power, this isn't much more convincing than the civil war in Nigeria. No doubt, much of this gun-drawing is a kind of play-acting; but play-acting can lead to acting.

Nor is the rhetoric of violence likely to diminish soon. The New Left will continue to talk blithely about revolution, but the police will do most of the shooting. Might it not, therefore, be in order to plead with the young confrontationists that if the ethic of democracy seems to them hollow or irrelevant, they at least think in terms of common prudence? And perhaps that they take off an hour to read Lenin's "Left-Wing Communism: An Infantile Disorder" in which the great revolutionist explains why compromise and even retreat is sometimes necessary?

One defense sometimes offered for confrontation politics is that, effective or not, it provides a dramatic way of releasing emotions. Of all the arguments, this seems to me the least tolerable. It means that in behalf of self-indulgence one is ready to bring down on oneself and others the forces of repression, of which the first victims would surely be the Negroes about whom the New Left declares itself so deeply concerned. This is a form of middle-class frivolity; a politics of the kindergarten. About such carryings-on (Yippies' trippies) I would cite a remarkable statement recently made by the English writer, David Caute, himself a New Left sympathizer, after his return from Czechoslovakia:

"These observations reveal to me a certain perversity in my own attitude. Nostalgia for student riots, clashes with the police, and totally exposed thighs suggests a false romanticism, an irritable desire to inflict on an ostensibly sane society a form of chaos which, as a way of life, is superficial and nihilistic. The manner in which the young Czechs are conducting themselves is really a model of civic control and enlightenment, whereas we have become alcoholic on sensation and violence."

Far more serious are those who advance the view that as a matter of conscience and regardless of consequences, they must break a given law. If a man finds the Vietnam war a moral crime and says he cannot serve in the Army even though the result be his imprisonment, then I think he merits respect and, often, admiration. He is ready to accept punishment for his behavior, ready to pay the price of his convictions. His violation of the law is undertaken in behalf of a higher principle and out of respect for law in general; he hopes to stir the conscience of society or, failing that, to live according to his own. Such a version of civil disobedience, Spiro Agnew notwithstanding, is a legitimate act when seriously undertaken in a democratic society.

What is not legitimate is to use tactics that look like civil disobedience but are meant to further "revolutionary" ends (e.g., blocking draft boards), since these can only lead to displays of impotence and are likely to harm those who genuinely care about civil disobedience. Nor is it legitimate to resort to civil disobedience, or a tactic easily confused with it, every Monday and Thursday morning. Acts of conscience violating the law can be taken seriously only if they are concerned with the most fundamental moral issues. And there is also, I think, an obligation to obey many laws one dislikes, in order to preserve the possibility for peacefully changing them.

This is a bad moment in American politics. The Vietnam war is a scandal and a disaster; social obligations pile up shamefully in the cities; radical measures are called for; the exploited cannot remain silent. Militant protest is therefore needed. Yet we must try to make certain that the methods we use to fight against injustice do not give the opponents of liberty an occasion for destroying both the struggle for justice and the procedures of liberty. That would be to invite disaster through a celebration of mindlessness.

THE RHETORIC OF CONFRONTATION

Robert L. Scott and Donald K. Smith

"Confront" is a simple enough verb meaning to stand or to come in front of. Like many simple words, however, it has been used in diverse contexts for varied purposes and has developed complex meanings. Among these the most interesting, and perhaps the strongest, is the sense of standing in front of as a barrier or a threat. This sense is especially apparent in the noun "confrontation."

Repeatedly in his book *Essays in the Public Philosophy*, Walter Lippmann uses the word "confrontation" in the sense of face-to-face coming together of spokesmen for disparate views. Confrontation, as he saw it then, was the guarantee of open communication and fruitful dissent. But Lippmann's book was copyrighted in 1955. Today, his phrase "because the purpose of the confrontation is to discern truth" sounds a bit archaic. If so, the remainder of his sentence, "there are rules of evidence and parliamentary procedure, there are codes of fair dealing and fair comment, by which a loyal man will consider himself bound when he exercises the right to publish opinion,"[1] seems absolutely irrelevant to the notion of "confrontation" as we live with it in marches, sit-ins, demonstrations, and discourse featuring disruption, obscenity, and threats.

Although certainly some use the word "confrontation" moderately, we shall be concerned here with the radical and revolutionary suggestion which the word carries more and more frequently. Even obviously moderate circumstances today gain some of the revolutionary overtones when the word is applied, as it might be for example, in announcing a church study group as the "confrontation of sacred and secular morality."

Acts of confrontation are currently at hand in such profusion that no one will lack evidence to prove or disprove the generalizations we make.[2]

Confrontation crackles menacingly from every issue in our country

[1] (New York, 1955), p. 128.

[2] Readers will find our generalizations more or less in harmony with other discussions of racial rhetoric which have appeared in the *QJS* recently, e.g., Parke G. Burgess, "The Rhetoric of Black Power: A Moral Demand?" LIV (April 1968), 122-133; Leland M. Griffin, "The Rhetorical Structure of the 'New Left' Movement: Part I," L (April 1964), 113-135; and Franklyn S. Haiman, "The Rhetoric of the Streets: Some Legal and Ethical Considerations," LIII (April 1967), 99-114.

These writers sense a corporate wholeness in the messages and methods of various men. An attempt to explain the combination of message and method which forms the wholeness gives rise in each case to a *rhetoric*. All these efforts seem to us impulses to examine the sufficiency of our traditional concepts in

(Black Power and Student Power, as examples), hemisphere (Castro-ism, for example), and globe (Radical Nationalism everywhere). But primary to every confrontation in any setting, radical or moderate, is the impulse to confront. From what roots does that impulse spring?

RADICAL DIVISION

Radical confrontation reflects a dramatic sense of division. The old language of the "haves" and the "have-nots" scarcely indicates the basis of the division, nor its depth. The old language evokes the history of staid, well-controlled concern on the part of those who have, for those who have not. It suggests that remedy can come from traditional means—the use of some part of the wealth and talent of those who have to ease the burden of those who have not, and perhaps open opportunities for some of them to enter the main-stream of traditional values and institutions. It recalls the missionary spirit of the voluntary associations of those who have—the legislative charity of the New Deal, the Fair Deal, the Welfare State, and the whole spectrum of international development missions.

A benevolent tone characterizes the old rhetoric of social welfare. The tone assumes that all men seek and should increasingly have more of the available wealth, or education, or security, or culture, or opportunities. The values of those who "have" are celebrated as the goals to which all should aspire, and effective social policy becomes a series of acts to extend opportunity to share in those values. If those who have can provide for others more of their own perquisites—more of the right to vote, or to find employment, or to go to college, or to consume goods—then progress is assured.

Although the terms "have" and "have not" are still accurate enough descriptions of the conditions that divide people and groups, their evocation of a traditional past hides the depth and radical nature of current divisions. Those on the "have not" side of the division, or at least some of their theorists and leaders, no longer accept designation as an inert mass hoping to receive what they lack

dealing with phenomena which are becoming characteristic of contemporary dissent. In seeing rhetoric as an amalgam of meaning and method, these writers break with a tradition that takes rhetoric to be amoral techniques of manipu-lating a message to fit various contexts.

Rhetoric has always been response-oriented, that is, the rationale of practical discourse, discourse designed to gain response for specific ends. But these writers see response differently. For them, the response of audiences is an integral part of the message-method that makes the rhetoric. Thus, rhetoric is shifted from a focus of reaction to one of interaction or transaction. (See especially Burgess, 132-133; Griffin, 121; and Haiman, 113.)

Although we believe we share the sense of *rhetoric* which permeates these essays, we claim to analyze a fundamental level of meaning which underlies them.

through action by the "haves." Neither do they accept any assumption that what they wish is membership in the institutions of those who have, or an opportunity to learn and join their value system. Rather the "have nots" picture themselves as radically divided from traditional society, questioning not simply the limitations of its benevolence but more fundamentally its purposes and modes of operation. Whether they experience deprivation as poverty, or lack of political power, or disaffection from traditional values, the "have not" leaders and theorists challenge existing institutions. This radical challenge, and its accompanying disposition toward confrontation, marks the vague attitudinal web that links revolutionaries in emerging nations to Black Power advocates in America or to students and intellectuals of the New Left. Three statements will illustrate the similar disposition of men who serve rather different causes in varied circumstances.

For Frantz Fanon, Algerian revolutionary and author of *The Wretched of the Earth*, the symbol of deprivation is the term "colonisation," and the end of confrontation is "decolonisation": "In decolonisation there is therefore the need of a complete calling in question of the colonial situation. If we wish to describe it precisely, we might find it in the well-known words 'The last shall be first and the first last.' Decolonisation is the putting into practice of this statement. That is why, if we try to describe it, all decolonisation is successful."[3]

For Black Power advocate Stokely Carmichael, the enemy is white racism, which is to be confronted, not joined: "Our concern for black power addresses itself directly to this problem, the necessity to reclaim our history and our identity from the cultural terrorism and depredation of self-justifying white guilt. To do this we shall have to struggle for the right to create our own terms through which to define ourselves and our relationship to the society, and to have these terms recognized. This is the first necessity of a free people, and the first right that any oppressor must suspend."[4]

For students in the New Left, the enemy to be confronted is simply "the establishment," or often in the United States, "technocracy." As student Frederick Richman sees the division:

The world in which the older generation grew up, and which the political systems support, is no longer one which youth can accept. In a world of rampaging technology, racial turmoil, and poverty, they see a President whose program is constituted largely of finishing touches to the New Deal, and a Congress unwilling to accept even that. In a time when personal freedom is of increasing concern, they see a republic operated by an immense bureaucratic structure, geared more to cold war adventures than to domestic needs, stifling

[3] Tr. Constance Farrington (New York, 1963), p. 30.
[4] "Toward Black Liberation," *Massachusetts Review*, VII (Autumn 1966), 639-640.

individual initiative along with that of states and cities. Finally, they see a political system obsessed with stability and loyalty instead of with social justice.[5]

Those have-nots who confront established power do not seek to share; they demand to supplant.

They must demand to supplant for they live in a Manichean world. Fanon, who features the term, argues that the settler (we may translate "settler" into other words, e.g., racist, establishment, or power structure) is responsible for the situation in which he must now suffer: "The colonial world is a Manichean world."[6] Those who rule and take the fruit of the system as their due create an equation that identifies themselves with the force of good (order, civilization, progress) which struggles with evil (chaos, the primitive, retrogression). In such a circumstance, established authority often crusades to eliminate the vessels of evil by direct action; but often its leaders work benignly and energetically to transform the others into worthy copies of themselves. At best, the process of transformation is slow, during which time the mass of the others must be carefully held apart to keep them from contaminating the system. Only a few can cross the great gulf to be numbered among the good. Claiming to recognize the reality of this process, which is always masked under exalted labels, black radicals in America cry that the traditional goal of integration masks and preserves racism. In an analogous posture, Students for a Democratic Society picture their educational system as a vast machine to recruit servants for a traditional society, perpetuating all of the injustices of that society.

Whether the force of "good" works energetically and directly or indirectly and somewhat benignly, those without caste must strive to supplant such holders of power. Forced to accept a Manichean struggle, they must reverse the equation, not simply to gain food, land, power, or whatever, but to survive. Reversing the equation will deny the justice of the system that has dehumanized them.

The process of supplanting will be violent for it is born of a violent system. To complete the long quotation introduced above from Fanon: "The naked truth of decolonisation evokes for us the searing bullets and booodstained knives which emanate from it. For if the last shall be first, this will only come to pass after a murderous and decisive struggle between the two protagonists. That affirmed intention to place the last at the head of things . . . can only triumph if we use all means to turn the scale, including, of course, that of violence."[7]

 [5]"The Disenfranchised Majority," *Students and Society*, report on a conference, Vol. 1, No. 1; an occasional paper published by the Center for the Study of Democratic Institutions (Santa Barbara, Calif., 1967), p. 4.
 [6]Fanon, p. 33. The book is replete with references to "Manicheanism."
 [7]*Ibid.*, p. 30.

As Eric Hoffer concludes in his study of mass movements, those who make revolutions are apt to see themselves as spoiled, degraded, and without hope as things exist. But they locate the genesis of their degradation in things, in others, in the world as it is organized around them.[8]

THE RITE OF THE KILL

The enemy is obvious, and it is he who has set the scene upon which the actors must play out the roles determined by the cleavage of exploitation. The situation shrieks kill-or-be-killed. "From here on in, if we must die anyway, we will die fighting back and we will not die alone," Malcolm X wrote in his "Appeal to African Heads of State." "We intend to see that our racist oppressors also get a taste of death."[9]

Judgments like "the oppressor" cannot be made without concomitant judgments. If there are those who oppress, there are those who are oppressed. This much seems obvious, but beneath that surface is the accusation that those oppressed have been something less than men ought to be. If one stresses the cunning, tenacious brutality of the oppressor, he suggests that the oppressed has been less than wise, alert, and strong. If one feels the heritage of injustice, then he senses the ignominy of his patrimony. The blighted self must be killed in striking the enemy. By the act of overcoming his enemy, he who supplants demonstrates his own worthiness, effacing the mark, whatever it may be—immaturity, weakness, subhumanity—that his enemy has set upon his brow.

To satisfy the rite that destroys the evil self in the act of destroying the enemy that has made the self evil, the radical may work out the rite of kill symbolically.[10] Harassing, embarrassing, and disarming the enemy may suffice, especially if he is finally led to admit his impotence in the face of the superior will of the revolutionary. Symbolic destruction of some manifestation of evil is well illustrated by the outbursts on campuses across America directed toward Dow Chemical. As far as we know in every confrontation of authority centering around the presence on the campus of a recruiter from Dow Chemical, the demonstrators early announced their intention of paralyzing the process until the recruiter agrees on behalf of the company to contaminate the scene no further with his presence.

Michael Novak, a Stanford University professor, pictures student disruption as a tactic to remove the mask of respectability worn by the establishment and kept in place both by the centralized control

---

[8] *The True Believer* (New York, 1951), pp. 19-20 and *passim*.
[9] *Malcolm X Speaks*, ed. George Breitman (New York, 1966), p. 77.
[10] See Fanon, p. 73.

of communication processes and the traditional canons of free speech.

The balance of power in the formation of public opinion has been altered by the advent of television. The society of independent, rational individuals envisaged by John Stuart Mill does not exist. The fate of all is bound up with the interpretation of events given by the mass media, by the image projected, and by the political power which results. . . . In a society with respect for its political institutions, officials have only to act with decorum and energy in order to benefit by such respect and to have their views established as true until proven false. . . .

What, then, does freedom of speech mean in a technological society? How can one defend oneself against McCarthyism on the one hand and official newspeak on the other? The solution of the students has been to violate the taboos of decorum and thus embrace Vice President Humphrey, the CIA, Dow Chemical, and other enemies in an ugly scene, hoping that the unpopularity of the radicals will rub off on those embraced. They want to make the heretofore bland and respectable wear that tag which most alarms American sensibilities: "controversial."[11]

Student Stephen Saltonstall of Yale University views coercive disruption as the obvious tactic by which "a small concentrated minority" group can bring society to heel and proposes use of this tactic by students to "destroy the university's capability to prop up our political institutions. By stalemating America's intellectual establishment," he continues, "we may be able to paralyze the political establishment as well." Saltonstall's specific recommendations are far-ranging: "A small, disciplined group of shock troops could pack classes, break up drills, and harass army professors. . . . Students could infiltrate the office staffs on the electronic accelerators and foreign policy institutes and hamper their efficiency. The introduction of a small quantity of LSD in only five or six government department coffee-urns might be a highly effective tactic. Students should prevent their universities from being used as forums for government apologists. Public figures like Humphrey and McNamara, when they appear, should be subject to intimidation and humiliation."[12]

Some who confront the oppressive authority seek to transform its representatives as well as themselves, working to wipe out the Manichean world. Such a stance is typical of the strongly Christian representatives of the Civil Rights Movement in this country. But those who advocate killing the enemy or degrading him symbolically act out more simply and more directly the dynamics dictated by the sense of radical division.

[11] "An End of Ideology?" *Commonweal*, LXXXVII (March 8, 1968), 681-682.

[12] "Toward a Strategy of Disruption," from *Students and Society*, p. 29.

CONFRONTATION AS A TOTALISTIC STRATEGY

Part of the attraction of confrontation is the strong sense of success, so strong that it may be a can't-lose strategy. After all in the Christian text Fanon cites ironically, "The last *shall be* first." The last shall be first precisely because he is last. The feeling is that one has nowhere to go but up, that he has nothing to lose, that after having suffered being down so long, he deserves to move up. Aside from the innate logic of the situation, four reasons for success seem apparent. In them we can imagine the radical voice speaking.

a. *We are already dead.* In the world as it is, we do not count. We make no difference. We are not persons. "Baby, it don't mean shit if I burn in a rebellion, because my life ain't worth shit. Dig?"[13] There is no mistaking that idiom, nor the sense behind it. Some radicals take oaths, changing their names, considering themselves as dead, without families, until the revolution succeeds. It is difficult to cow a dead orphan.

b. *We can be reborn.* Having accepted the evaluation of what is, agreeing to be the most worthless of things, we can be reborn. We have nothing to hang on to. No old identity to stop us from identifying with a new world, no matter how horrifying the prospect may seem at the outset; and a new world will certainly be born of the fire we shall create. You, the enemy, on the other hand, must cling to what is, must seek to stamp out the flames, and at best can only end sorrowing at a world that cannot remain the same. Eventually you will be consumed.

c. *We have the stomach for the fight; you don't.* Having created the Manichean world, having degraded humanity, you are overwhelmed by guilt. The sense of guilt stops your hand, for what you would kill is the world you have made. Every blow you strike is suicide and you know it. At best, you can fight only delaying actions. We can strike to kill for the old world is not ours but one in which we are already dead, in which killing injures us not, but provides us with the chance of rebirth.

d. *We are united and understand.* We are united in a sense of a past dead and a present that is valuable only to turn into a future free of your degrading domination. We have accepted our past as past by willing our future. Since you must cling to the past, you have no future and cannot even understand.

CONFRONTATION AS A NON-TOTALISTIC TACTIC

Radical and revolutionary confrontation worries and bleeds the enemy to death or it engulfs and annihilates him. The logic of the

[13]Quoted by Jack Newfield, "The Biggest Lab in the Nation," *Life*, LXIV (March 8, 1968), 87.

situation that calls it forth bids it be total. But undoubtedly confrontation is brought about by those who feel only division, not radical division. For these the forces of good and evil pop in and out of focus, now clearly perceived, now not; now identified with this manifestation of established power and now that. These radicals may stop short of revolution because they have motives that turn them into politicians who at some point will make practical moves rather than toss every possible compromise and accommodation into the flaming jaws that would destroy the old order.

Student activists in the New Left vacillate in their demands between calls for "destruction" of universities as they are now known and tactical discussions of ways of "getting into the system" to make it more responsive to student goals.[14]

Drift toward non-totalistic goals seems consistent with both the general affluence of this group and its position as a small minority in a large student population generally committed to establishment goals and values. It may also reflect a latent response to the embarrassment of affluent students, beneficiaries of the establishment, who claim the language and motivations of the truly deprived.[15]

Similarly, the perception of confrontation as a tactic for prying apart and thus remodeling the machines of established power seems evident in many adherents of the Black Power movement. In many ways, the power Stokely Carmichael and Charles V. Hamilton forecast in their book is quite conventional, drawing analogies from past, thoroughly American experiences.[16]

Finally, one should observe the possible use of confrontation as a tactic for achieving attention and an importance not readily attainable through decorum. In retiring temporarily from his task of writing a regular newspaper column, Howard K. Smith complained bitterly of a press which inflated Stokely Carmichael from a "nobody who . . . had achieved nothing and represented no one" into "a factor to be reckoned with."[17] But Carmichael knows, from bitter experience, the art of confrontation. Martin Luther King writes of meeting a group of small boys while touring Watts after the riot. "We won!" they shouted joyously. King says his group asked them, "How can you say you won when thirty-four Negroes are dead, your community is destroyed, and whites are using the riot as an excuse for

---

[14]*Students and Society.* A full reading of the conference proceedings reveals clearly this split among the most vocal and militant of New Left students.

[15]For an analysis of the structure and characteristics of the student left, see Richard E. Peterson, "The Student Left in American Higher Education," *Daedalus,* XCVII (Winter 1968), 293-317.

[16]*Black Power: The Politics of Liberation in America* (New York, 1967), see especially Chap. 5.

[17]"Great Age of Journalism Gone?" *Minneapolis Star,* February 19, 1968, p. 5B.

inaction?" The reply was, "We won because we made them pay attention to us."[18]

Without doubt, for many the act of confrontation itself, the march, sit-in, or altercation with the police is enough. It is consummatory. Through it the radical acts out his drama of self-assertion and writes in smeary, wordless language all over the establishment, "We know you for what you are. And you know that we know." Justifying the sense of rightness and, perhaps, firing a sense of guilt in the other is the hopeful outcome of the many coy confrontations of some shy radicals.[19]

CONFRONTATION AND RHETORICAL THEORY

We have talked of the *rhetoric* of confrontation, not merely confrontation, because this action, as diverse as its manifestations may be, is inherently symbolic. The act carries a message. It dissolves the lines between marches, sit-ins, demonstrations, acts of physical violence, and aggressive discourse. In this way it informs us of the essential nature of discourse itself as human action.

The rhetoric of confrontation also poses new problems for rhetorical theory. Since the time of Aristotle, academic rhetorics have been for the most part instruments of established society, presupposing the "goods" of order, civility, reason, decorum, and civil or theocratic law. Challenges to the sufficiency of this theory and its presuppositions have been few, and largely proposed either by elusive theologians such as Kierkegaard or Buber, or by manifestly unsavory revolutionaries such as Hitler, whose degraded theories of discourse seemed to flow naturally from degraded values and paranoid ambitions.

But the contemporary rhetoric of confrontation is argued by theorists whose aspirations for a better world are not easily dismissed, and whose passion for action equals or exceeds their passion for theory. Even if the presuppositions of civility and rationality underlying the old rhetoric are sound, they can no longer be treated as self-evident.[20] A rhetorical theory suitable to our age must take into

[18] *Where Do We Go From Here: Chaos or Community?* (New York, 1967), p. 112.

[19] See Norman Mailer, "The Steps of the Pentagon," *Harper's Magazine*, CCXXXVI (March 1968), 47-142 [published in book form as *Armies of the Night* (New York, 1968)]. It may seem difficult to believe but Mailer, who calls himself a "right radical," fits our adjectives, coy and shy.

[20] Herein lies a major problem for rhetorical theory. In a sense Haiman's essay (note 2) is a defense of these values accepting the responsibility implied by his analysis which shows a significant case made by the very existence of "A Rhetoric of the Streets" which demands a rebuttal. Burgess' essay (note 2) sees Black Power as a unique method of forcing conventional thought to take seriously its own criterion of rationality.

account the charge that civility and decorum serve as masks for the preservation of injustice, that they condemn the dispossessed to non-being, and that as transmitted in a technological society they become the instrumentalities of power for those who "have."

A broader base for rhetorical theory is also needed if only as a means of bringing up to date the traditional status of rhetoric as a theory of managing public symbolic transactions. The managerial advice implicit in current theories of debate and discussion scarcely contemplates the possibility that respectable people should confront disruption of reasonable or customary actions, obscenity, threats of violence, and the like. Yet the response mechanisms turned to by those whose presuppositions could not contemplate confrontation often seem to complete the action sought by those who confront, or to confirm their subjective sense of division from the establishment. The use of force to get students out of halls consecrated to university administration or out of holes dedicated to construction projects seems to confirm the radical analysis that the establishment serves itself rather than justice. In this sense, the confronter who prompts violence in the language or behavior of another has found his collaborator. "Show us how ugly you really are," he says, and the enemy with dogs and cattle prods, or police billies and mace, complies. How can administrators ignore the insurgency of those committed to jamming the machinery of whatever enterprise is supposed to be ongoing? Those who would confront have learned a brutal art, practiced sometimes awkwardly and sometimes skillfully, which demands response. But that art may provoke the response that confirms its presuppositions, gratifies the adherents of those presuppositions, and turns the power-enforced victory of the establishment into a symbolic victory for its opponents.

As specialists interested in communication, we who profess the field of rhetoric need to read the rhetoric of confrontation, seek understanding of its presuppositions, tactics, and purposes, and seek placement of its claim against a just accounting of the presuppositions and claims of our tradition. Often as we read and reflect we shall see only grotesque, childish posturings that vaguely act out the deeper drama rooted in radical division. But even so, we shall understand more, act more wisely, and teach more usefully if we open ourselves to the fundamental meaning of radical confrontation.

TOWARDS THE NEW MORALITY

Charles B. Ketcham

Because the humanist revolution in thought, expression, and act has been so widespread, the effects are everywhere noticeable. One cannot be exposed daily to our new art forms, new literary forms, new musical expressions, and new theologies and philosophies without being profoundly concerned about and affected by the radical changes they present and symbolize. Though one may reject many of these changes as immature, incomprehensible, irrational, or just plain phony, they have made an impressive impact on our society and, for that matter, on the world. Our electronics revolution—radio, films, television, computers—has only served to intensify and accelerate this impact by making possible and accessible an audio-visual exposure to these radical changes. We are, according to Marshall McLuhan, tribalizing the world.

The theologian Paul Tillich puts the end of the nineteenth century at World War I, but this event is not just the end of that century. It is, Tillich rightly claims, the end of one era and the beginning of another. Surely the course of our study thus far substantiates such a judgment. The whole fabric of our culture is being worked over by some very visible weavers, and it is difficult to establish at this point whether they are merely patching or actually re-weaving a whole new cloth. Consequently, what has been celebrated recently under the simplistic banner of "The New Morality" tends to be a representative mixture of destruction and reformation.

With the ending of an era comes the collapse of old standards, old values, old norms—in short, the old morality. In our own situation, when Absolutes are called into question, when Form itself is questioned, the result is an accelerated deterioration of traditional moral standards which have been variously labeled "the Victorian ethic," "the Protestant ethic," "middle class values," "the American way," and so on. Stability, particularly in terms of predictability, has disappeared. We no longer know what is "right" for us to do as individuals or as a nation. For example, the ethical principles and simple, straight-forward injunctions once thought central and adequate for the national ideal—liberty, justice, equality, freedom of press, freedom of speech, freedom of opportunity—have crumbled under the pressures of the complexities of twentieth-century life. One can no longer realistically expect that all emergent nations will have the American form of democracy any more than one can realistically respond to a Wilsonian plea to "make the world safe for democracy." What we now know is that no one nation can totally and effectively control its own destiny let alone the destiny of the world. *Pax*

Americana may be a glorious wish, but it is certainly not a realistic picture of the political realities of the late twentieth century.

Since discovering that we as Americans have not cornered or monopolized the truth market and have had to compete with other viable political and economic systems, our self-righteousness and our assurance have been shaken. Our national posture has gradually sagged into an expediency relative to self-interest, as the struggle in South-East Asia indicates. The traditional words, though still used, are all too often not attempts at redefinition but, rather, totem terms invoked by confused or frightened citizens in the desperate hope that sheer repetition of the words themselves will somehow reestablish the power of the principle; or such words are often calculated cliches in the mouths of some "superpatriots," politicians and laymen alike, who want to justify injustice and their own self-interests. The growing "credibility gap" (as a two-way gap) between the government and the people is the result. Such civil sickness can only increase, with dissident groups of all kinds becoming increasingly self-seeking and militant, if the loss of national integrity continues. The growing polarities in America over the issues of race and war are evidence of such a trend.

Other examples of the moral confusion of this transition period are not hard to find. We no longer know what is "right" for us to do about the relations among labor, management, and government. The interests of all three are so interlocking that any deviation can cause a national crisis. The old rules about hard work and honest bargaining just do not apply: one cannot bargain with the boss or "catch his eye" when one's point of contact is a management time study or a union quota system; individual unions and industries must abandon much local bargaining for "industry-wide" sessions; labor and management together must now face a government which not only controls and limits their activities to a degree but, in some cases, even becomes a competitor; the government can no longer simply concern itself with domestic issues, for foreign markets and common markets make economics a world problem. So the economic problem and its accompanying moral dilemmas become acute. The coal miner in West Virginia feels the impact of the world, but his credit is still calculated by the local grocery store.

We no longer know what is "right" to do about the problems of interpersonal relations, particularly in the area of sex. Education, population problems, the "pill," and loss of the sacramental nature of marriage all have eaten away at the traditional cultural patterns. Taboos once observed for no other reason than that they were "right and proper" for generations cannot persuade or convince the contemporary questioning mind. Extravagant theological threats ("God will make you impotent!") no longer strike fear into hearts of teenagers or anyone else. Social ostracism for, or legal restraint of, so-called "deviant behavior" is no longer an unavoidable threat. The

fear of pregnancy has been removed from sexual intercourse so that
this physical expression of "love" has been freed from the moral
restraints of responsible paternity or maternity. The questions then
are posed: "Why not love with the body as completely as with the
heart?" and "Must such physical love necessarily be confined to
marriage?" In an age of transition when new values are being established, the emotional, physical, and spiritual strains of the existing
value void are often tragically evident in broken hearts, broken
homes, and broken lives. Loss of authority has left a legacy of
anxiety. The search for the New Morality is the search for new
directions, not the repudiation of direction.

The citation of these three areas of acute moral concern as examples is enough to suggest the complexity of the problem. Old patterns
are either inadequate or discarded, and, without new expressions,
genuine confusion ensues. Some people courageously cling to the old
values, the proverbial "good old days," terrified at what might happen if they abandoned them. Others courageously search for new
patterns, new values which would provide a meaningful life, frightened that their experimentation may bring irremedial tragedy rather
than fulfillment. Still others simply exploit the confusion to gratify
their own self-interests, confident that there are no values other than
one's own.

When one hears the term "New Morality," one is apt to find
reference to any one of the above three possibilities, but particularly
the latter two. The very last alternative, however, is representative of
the ethics of nihilism and offers little that is constructive for us to
consider. It is certainly not an expression of what we have termed
the New Humanism.

The "New Morality" has been a catch-all phrase for all activity
deviating from pre-World-War-I ethical norms. Yet it should be clearly
understood that the breakdown of traditional standards we are wit-
nessing about us, the seemingly inevitable disenchantment and frustration which results when the basis for a once-meaningful life has been
threatened, is really only the prelude to the New Morality. But if
there is to be a genuine New Morality, it will have to emerge not
from the least common denominator of such moral decadence, but
rather from some understanding of the implication, the contours, the
nature of the New Humanism. Chaos alone can never be the matrix
for spontaneous generation. Passive acceptance of the destructive
forces at work in society is not the rôle of the New Humanist. What
is urgently needed is the thoughtful creation of new and significant
value structures. Until this affirmative response is made, the moral
dilemma in which we find ourselves can only be intensified.

Before going further, terminology ought to be clarified. Normally
the word "morality" is used to describe the value designation inherent or assumed in any specific human act or generally accepted
custom. By contrast, the word "ethics" usually denotes a rational

system of values which is both prescriptive and adjudicative. Thus to call an act "immoral" or "unethical" is really to misuse both terms. What we mean when we misuse such terms is quite clear: it is *not* that the act has no value at all; it is rather that the act is wrong or harmful either according to custom (morality) or according to system (ethics). Much of the confused talk about the New Morality reveals such a misunderstanding of these basic terms. What most people mean by the search for the New Morality is the search for a New Ethic. However, I have retained the term New Morality not only because of its popular acceptance but, more importantly, for the fact that we are discussing not so much an ethic as an ethos, a context, within which several ethical systems may coexist.

If the New Humanism, in both its secular and religious forms, is to give rise to a New Morality, then it should be possible to determine, on the basis of our study, some of the directions or contours of that morality. Taking as normative the ambiguity we have observed governing all human existence, capacities, and relationships, the New Morality should expect no exemption from such a limitation.

Our understanding of *Being* in terms of self-awareness is limited and elusive; our knowledge of God through the *I-Thou* encounter is private and hidden; our relationship to others is limited by the degree of our authenticity as well as theirs; our information about the physical world is provisional as well as being an apparent one-way rational appropriation; and all these relationships are further limited by the time-fullness of *Being* in which we all participate here-and-now.

Under these circumstances, any New Morality must reflect such limitations in its rejection of absolute prescriptive ends—*the* Good, *the* Right, *the* Truth, *the* Kingdom—as well as absolute prescriptive laws—"obey the government without question," "obey the Bible without question," "obey the parent without question." Any expression of these goals or laws as absolutely inviolable would not only falsely deny the reality of ambiguity but would also establish a priority of abstract principle or law over self, an error Western tradition has made all too often. In the New Humanist's understanding of integrity, there are times when my integrity, or truth of *Being*, is contrary to, or cannot be limited to, the world of objectively verifiable facts, *i.e.*, I do not always tell the medical patient of his condition, or my hostess of her indigestible meal.

But having acknowledged this, one must immediately affirm that life can be *reasonably* lived only if goals or ends or standards such as "the good," "the right," "the truth," "the kingdom," are provisionally accepted; and that chaos can be averted in an inescapably social world only if one does, for example, intelligently obey the government and/or does imaginatively follow the ethical insights of Scripture.

The difference, of course, is immediately evident, for under these

latter conditions such goals and such laws become *authoritative for
our lives' but do not function as Absolutes.* Times, insights, and
contexts change and, therefore, so must laws, means, and ends. I
must so live in the condition of freedom that my authenticity as a
self may be maintained even at the risk of defying the existing
external authorities. This is not to plead for anarchy but for the
constant reevaluation and restatement of that penultimate authority
which would permit a continuous authentic expression of self and
society. Such is my responsibility to the continuing demands of
ambiguity.

The instances of civil disobedience in the American civil rights
struggle are a case in point. As opposed to the anarchy and lawlessness of the ghetto riots, civil disobedience challenges the authority
and effective justice of the existing laws by the deliberate violation of
such laws and the self-surrender of the violators to the government.
Such action brings the inadequacy of the laws or customs in question
to the attention of society, and a fitting reform can be made.
However, when such reforms prove empty or resulting legislation is
powerless to enforce the reform, then more serious disobedience,
even violence, can result—as we see in the urban riots. Human
desperation does not recognize the authority of abstract Absolutes;
pleas for sanity at such times appear to the desperate only as
rejection, a banishment to futility and meaningless existence.

It is not at all amiss to note here that democracy as a form of
government is structured on the reality of ambiguity as a human
condition. The three-branch structure of the U.S. Government serves
to preserve and honor that ambiguity so that an absolute rule can
never be established while responsible authority is always maintained.
This recognition of human limitation is reflected in Reinhold
Niebuhr's celebrated dictum from *The Children of Light and the
Children of Darkness*: "Man's capacity for justice makes democracy
possible; but man's inclination to injustice makes democracy necessary."[1] Ambiguity as a human condition of *Being* must be reflected
in the condition of social and political organization.

The use of the descriptive term "penultimate" is questionable, a
case of ambiguity in point. "Penultimate" conveys the idea of next-
to-final in principle, power, or purpose and implies that there is an
ultimate which *is*, even though such an ultimate is unknown or
unknowable, not yet attained or attainable. But this is not what the
New Humanist wants to convey by such a word, for such usage
brings metaphysical absolutism in by the semantic back door.
"Penultimate" authority should suggest for us the natural, reasonable,
authentic expression of *Being*—more specifically of my *Being* and the
correlated objective world of "Things" which reveal themselves to me

[1] Reinhold Niebuhr, *The Children of Light and the Children of Darkness*, Nisbet and Company, Ltd., London, p. vi.

and are related to me in terms of *Being Itself*. Thus my relationship to fire or water carries its own natural authority or expression which I violate at my own peril. In other words, the "penultimate" authority, those rules and laws by which I partially govern my existence, is simply the natural expression of the *I-It* world about which Martin Buber writes. Such rules and laws are discerned through experience, by experimentation, not through Platonic metaphysical speculation.

The issue becomes more complicated when one adds to the *I-It* relation the relational world of *Thou*. Three things are immediately discernible. First, authority is established, as in the relation to *Its*, by experience; that is, the relationship establishes its own authenticity and is thereby self-governed. Second, the authority of the *I-Thou* relationship takes priority over the *I-It* relationship, a priority not only of origin but also in *Being*. This priority, for example, is the implicit justification behind the appealing lyrics of "I can't give you anything but love. . . ." And third, the world of potential *Thous* forms and constitutes a particular world of *Its* (businesses, organizations, communities we call society, and this world—as in the other relational situations—forms its own laws, principles, goals, and relational structures, natural to the *I-It* context. As before, experience, which we call history, informs us of the general nature of that relationship, and does so with enough accuracy that we speak of it (and of such related disciplines as economics and sociology) as social science.

The problem is further complicated by the fact that any of these *I-It* relationships with other people who constitute society, can at any moment become an *I-Thou* relationship, and when this occurs, the priorities which govern my decision-making undergo significant change. As an American businessman I know that only law, order, and stability can provide the climate for commercial growth and prosperity, but as a man with intimate friends within some American minority group, I may choose to defy the "City Council" and march in the streets to secure equality for my friends, to the detriment of my own business. Though I have a profound respect for equality and justice, what really sends me into the streets is not the thought of future financial benefits but the love of my friend.

As priorities change, so do my actions and so do those of all men. Thus the picture of human society is continuously being refocused. All men need to act in such a way that personal and public responsibilities, personal and public actions do not countermand each other. To ignore public responsibility (the world of *It*) is to end with anarchy; to ignore personal responsibility (the world of *Thou*) is to end with dehumanizing conformity. The answer is not merely compromise, for compromise implies that there is some unifying identity between the nature of the *It* world and the nature of the *Thou* world. But this is simply not the case. The "laws, principles, and ends" peculiar to society and the physical world are not those "laws, principles, and ends" peculiar to my personal life. The former we characterized by impersonally ordered relations, the latter by freedom, spontaneity, and decision.

This is part of the ambiguity of human existence. The limitation I experience in comprehension and action, "in *Being*," means that my life must be lived not in compromise, which itself hints at finality, but in tension and risk. Both *Thou* and *It* loyalties make their claims upon me; more important, both relationships help "define" me. To honor one may be to dishonor the other. But this is the risk which a time-full, ambiguous life runs. In the act of decision, I can use the word "compromise" only if by that word I imply a genuine consideration of the tensions upon me—not their resolution. My decision is made in tension and is carried out (for better or for worse) as a decision-intension. The security of finality is a luxury which ambiguity cannot afford and a snare which authenticity must avoid.

If ambiguity, as evidence in the New Humanism, is normative for the New Morality, then it follows that some form of contextual ethic will emerge. The very fact that such divergent contemporary thinkers as Joseph Fletcher, Karl Barth, Joseph Sitler, Paul Lehmann, and H. Richard Niebuhr all propose some form of contextual ethic is reason enough to take seriously such a contention.

The "contextual ethic" obviously receives its name from the fact that ethical decisions are determined by assessing the context, the various forces—social, political, physical, economic, intellectual, spiritual—past, present, and future, which impose themselves upon us in our deliberations prior to or during any "value" decision. But to describe such an ethic is not to justify its use. A contextual ethic suggests itself as one natural expression for the New Humanism because it does take the ambiguity of existence into account; because it is totally inclusive of all those factors, deliberative and active, which constitute *Being*-in-the-world-here-and-now whether such *Being* is secular or religious; and because we note that the very process of decision-making involves all these factors—attention to our total self within its total orientation of meaning.

It follows, then, that although we acknowledge our dependence upon historical guidance, precedent, and wisdom no one standard or set of standards can be final for a contextual ethic which tries to take into account all the limiting factors involved in any given new context. In each decision one must ask, "What am I trying to achieve?" "What is known?" "What are the limits?" "What are the priorities?" "What will be the response to my decision?" "What act will, in fact, give the fullest expression to *Being*?" In any given situation, therefore, what we expect from one man we might not expect from another who is politically more powerful, or another better educated, or yet another who is mentally retarded. Likewise, the patterns of response and reward for the twentieth-century American are likely to be quite different from those of a contemporary man of a less advanced culture, though variations within any given culture complex are apt to be limited because of the focus of common forces.

A problem, of course, arises when the contextual ethic provides the opportunity for willful, selfish action. For both secularist and religionist such action, as noted in Chapter 5, is apostasy. For the secularist, it is the forsaking of the authentic expression of *Being*, the penalty for which is a self-inflicted isolation and loss of meaning. For the religionist, apostasy is the forsaking of God, the Eminent *Thou*, which carries a comparable penalty. For the secularist, restitution of authenticity within the *I-It* relationship is a matter of new insight which informs him of the ignorance and destructiveness of previous acts. For secularist and religionist alike, forgiveness alone can provide the possibility of a resumption and renewal of the *I-Thou* relationship. Restitution involved in the *I-Thou* apostasy is more difficult to achieve than in the *I-It*, of course, for it involves the necessity both of forgiveness (renewed acceptance and trust) and of repentence (acknowledgement of betrayal and regret).

For some Cassandras the loss of absolute standards, principles, and goals can result only in destructive forces being indiscriminately released against an idyllic heritage. Yet "The backward look behind the assurance/Of recorded history, the backward half-look/Over the shoulder" does not, as Mr. T. S. Eliot reminds us in "The Dry Salvages," convince most of us of the unqualified sanctity of the past. The inhumanity of human behavior seems to be the expression more of allegiance to nonhuman Absolutes than of authentic response to the nature of *Being*—as God or man. Certainly the last fifty years of war, suffering, and growing disenchantment with Absolute demands have served to strengthen this conviction. This is not to resurrect the "noble savage" of Rousseau. It *is* to bring into question the assumption in Western thought that morality and ethics can be meaningfully expressed only with the context of, and as reflections of, an Absolute. One of the things which contemporary interest in the New Humanism seems to be displaying is a growing belief that metaphysical Absolutes such as *the* Good, *the* Truth, *the* Beautiful have really hampered man's free and open expression of *Being*—whether that be in art, music, literature, or morality—and that health can only be achieved when the *I-Thou* and *I-It* can time-fully express themselves. We cannont avoid the ambiguities of human existence, and we are tragically mislead if we believe that some ethical system can resolve them for us. Our present "sickness unto death" certainly is no witness for those who deprecate this contemporary revolution in the name of past holiness or of moral perfectionism.

For the contextual ethic, the ambiguities involved are both its strength and limitation. One of the finest of the contextualists, H. R. Niebuhr, brings this sharply into focus: decisions "are made, it appears, on the basis of relative insight and faith, but they are not relativistic. They are individual decisions, but not individualistic. They are made in freedom, but not in independence; they are made in the moment, but are not nonhistorical."[2] Each of these qualifications deserves further explication.

Niebuhr indicates that the decisions which we reach are relative in four ways: First, they are relative to our limited fragmentary knowledge—as anyone who has contemplated marriage, tried to discipline children effectively, or endeavored constructively to criticize government policy on international affairs surely knows. Second, decisions are relative to the extent of our belief and unbelief—as anyone recognizes who has hedged his commitments to God or man with mental reservations, hidden alternatives, or flight insurance. Third, decisions are relative to our historical and social context—as any first-generation American, any Vista or Peace Corps volunteer, or any Depression-age father and his hippie-age child dazedly admit. Finally, decisions are made relative to the values of our time—as most Victorians admit, gazing wonderingly at the guiltless sexual freedom of the present generation. Niebuhr makes these qualifications about our relative decisions within the Christian heritage, but as already indicated, such qualifications could equally well apply to secular humanism, though "belief" in such a case would be understood in terms of the affirmation of *Being* rather than faith in God.

The reasons that such decisions are relative and not relativistic are that they each find points of orientation, i.e., *Being* or God, from which all else is understood. But what is found is not an ultimate point of orientation nor is it a point of ultimate orientation. As we have noted earlier, both of these considerations, i.e., my understanding and my appropriation of Absolute Truth, are finally ambiguous. Decisions are only possible under such conditions; otherwise action would be a matter of resignation to either fate or chance. What we have found is a context which offers its own coherence within which my authenticity may be expressed. Thus as a Jew or a Christian, my authenticity is bound up with justice, mercy, and humility—all expressive of my belief, hedged as it is, by my unbelief or doubt. I do not make the claim that all life must be Judeo-Christian, but I do make the claim that my understanding of life is Judeo-Christian. Such an affirmation on my part does not necessitate a denial of the meaningfulness of all other contexts, Buddhist, for example, but it does demand that we search for some common ground for genuine encounter. If our contention about *Being* is correct, then its revelation must be evident in all contextual encounters.

The reason my decisions are individual but not individualistic is that my individuality is the result of my involvement, the *I-Thou* encounter. I can only know myself in terms of my social context,

[2] H. Richard Niebuhr, *Christ and Culture*, Harper & Row, Incorporated, New York, p. 234.

therefore I can act only out of that context. While I am responsible for my deliberate act, I am not equally responsible for my cultural context. If I display signs of prejudice, it is in part a response to existing elements in my society by which I have been conditioned. Anyone who has tried to overcome a sectional or racial prejudice knows with what difficulty and with how many relapses such a victory is won. If I am an advocate for new sexual mores, or for a radically New Humanism, these must be defined and explained in terms of traditional expression, even if that amounts to a disavowal of that older tradition. Anyone who recognizes the statement, "I know the words you're using but I can't understand what you're saying" is aware of the problem. The individualistic decision simply does not exist; the reality of the here-and-now in which I live involves me with my contemporaries and links me to the past and to the future. But the confusion persists because the linkage is ambiguous; it is not simply the expression of some efficient cause.

My decisions are made in freedom but not in independence because of similar ambiguities. The reason that I use to come to a decision is not only fragmented and partial, it is also schooled by my society, my historical position, and my cultural stance. The time-full limitation of my existence brings my known, historical life continuously into contact with the unknown and the not-yet, so that I am continually impelled to be that which is new, even if it be only a new interpretation of the old. Both authentic and inauthentic acts express my freedom now in terms of my continuity with the past and my dependence upon my cultural conditioning. The freedom of the twentieth-century technocrat is quite different from the freedom of the early twentieth-century industrialist. Ford Motor Company can no longer be the private domain of Henry Ford, yet the corporation's freedom to affect the economic health of the United States is far greater than Henry Ford I ever dreamed.

That decisions are made *now*, but are at the same time not nonhistorical, has been discussed before. The time-fullness of existence not only ensures that meaningfulness is now, it also assures us that one aspect of that meaningfulness is the continuity with past meaningful moments out of which our understanding (ambiguous as that is) of *this* moment arises. Again, the time-fulness of existence assures us that though our decision is *now*, that *now* will have a continuous influence upon future decisions. The commitment I make on my wedding day is part of the now-commitment I must continue making one, ten, or thirty-seven years later.

In each of these aspects of decision, one thing becomes clear: there is no such thing as the guaranteed, absolute, or final "right" decision, as any parent can affirm without analytical justification. Any decision is in some significant part a leap into the unknown, a commitment beyond proof or evidence for which we can only prepare ourselves as responsibly as possible. For the secularist, this means a responibility to self in terms of *Being*; for the religionist, it means a responsibility to self and to God. In either case, the self is involved in his community of encounter.

In terms of the New Humanism, this means that any New Morality must be a responsible expression of *Being*-inaction. Such an action begins in encounter and ends in enactment, which is another way of stating that my response begins in authenticity and ends in an affirmation grounded in freedom. The standards, laws, and goals we establish for ourselves as secularists, or in keeping with our response to God as men of faith, are always tentative and subject to change, but on the other hand authoritative and demanding of our resolute loyalty. A rational, meaningful existence demands that accuracy and clarity exist, that effective order and coherence prevail. It is the ambiguity of these norms which makes change possible, but only when the risk of rebellion seems less than the risk of meaninglessness. Such an imbalance of risks is the case when the *I-It* world assumes the authority of or priority over the *I-Thou* world, when principle becomes more important than person, law more important than love. When reform is found to be impossible, then rebellion is necessary. Albert Camus, writing about the liberation of Paris in 1944, makes this point perfectly evident:

Four years ago men rose up amid ruins and despair and calmly declared that nothing was lost. They said we had to carry on and that the forces of good could always overcome the forces of evil if we were willing to pay the price. They paid the price. And, to be sure, that price was heavy; it had all the weight of blood and the dreadful heaviness of prisons. Many of those men are dead, whereas others have been living for years surrounded by windowless walls. That was the price that had to be paid. But those same men, if they could, would not blame us for this terrible and marvelous joy that sweeps us off our feet like a high tide. For our joy has not broken faith with them. On the contrary, it justifies them and declares that they were right. . . . Nothing is given to men, and the little they can conquer is paid for with unjust deaths. But man's greatness lies elsewhere. It lies in his decision to be stronger than his condition. And if his condition is unjust, he has only one way of overcoming it, which is to be just himself.[3]

Needless to say, relatively trivial changes require commensurately trivial risks. Customs change through defiance more quickly than laws, laws more quickly than cultural myths, and cultural myths more quickly than faith or belief. For example, the risk a boy takes in defying the contemporary masculine image by wearing his hair long, growing a beard, or wearing bright colorful clothing, is really not great—a Victorian school board or school principal may demand that he "shape up" or "ship out," or his peers may jeer that he is really a g-i-r-l. Styles and customs have always been changed by those

[3] Albert Camus, *Resistance, Rebellion, and Death*, translated by Justin, O'Brien, Alfred A. Knopf, Inc., New York, 1961, pp. 38-40.

with the courage to defy the acceptable for the sake of the new. What proves creative and expressive remains; what is simply defiant and destructive soon disappears.

Laws, on the other hand, change more slowly. They themselves are the product of established and, usually, honored customs, enacted to protect society from specific abuses. Defiance here is more costly and more complicated. The threat of official public reprimand, fine, or imprisonment usually insures that defiance is more than just a whim. Because this type of change applies to everyone, an extended example may be warranted.

In the United States, certain laws govern legalized abortion. Defiance has arisen in the form of a general disregard for the law, with one exception: the *official* Roman Catholic community. For Roman Catholics, the issue revolves about the Church's belief that "life" begins not at birth but at conception. Abortion is therefore the arbitrary taking of a life intended by God—to any Catholic, of course, a heinous sin. The act of abortion is not simply defiance of the State, it is defiance of God. Consequently, there is no pressure for change from official quarters.

For some Catholics, the majority of Protestants, and secularists, however, the situation is different. These groups recognize neither the "natural law" tradition nor any other authoritative or definitive ruling about prenatal life. Other human factors have assumed greater importance. Arguments in favor of abortion usually begin by the loaded question: "Would it not be more humane to end the existence of a foetus which has been damaged by thalidimide or German measles?" Why bring a disfigured, handicapped, or retarded child into the world when it is unnecessary, and cruel for the child? Such arguments are persuasive, but the ethical-legal problem becomes more subtle and more difficult when one anticipates a normal pregnancy.

Many concerned people believe that the life of an unwanted child is jeopardized from the beginning. If, as many child psychologists maintain, the basic attitude of the child toward the world is framed, if not fixed, within the first six months of its life, there is little weight to the counter argument that the unwanted child could win its way into the hearts of recalcitrant parents, if indeed it has "parents" to win. To believe this is to romanticize child-care in the first place, and to ignore the clinical evidence of "disturbed children" who are conditioned by such tension-situations in the second place. It might also be the case that the physical or mental health of the mother would be endangered by pregnancy and birth, a situation for which abortion is the obvious solution. Fortunately, some parts of the world already acknowledge this condition as reason enough for the operation. Or it may be the case that the two people involved in the conception are truly not in love and should not be married. Perhaps they are simply too young for marriage. Must placing the child up for adoption be the only way out?

These and a host of similar "humane" considerations compel people to seek out an illegal abortionist who, for several hundred dollars or more, "takes care of things." If one is not convinced that the official Roman Catholic position concerning the beginning of "life" can be maintained, then the case for possible abortion can be reasonably argued in terms of the merits surrounding each individual situation, so that the result may truly represent that affirmation of life characteristic of the New Humanism. If life is here-and-now, and life is threatened by a pregnancy which is determined deleterious to those involved, then one hopes that laws (which are to protect life) will enable abortion to occur. To deny it categorically under any conditions others than those official Roman Catholicism has established, would seem far too restrictive and punitive. If the reason for denial is that the participants were "bad" or irresponsible and should pay for their folly, then such a primitive denial is not responsive—and, perhaps psychologically irresponsible—to the situation and is possibly sadistic. Nor should abortion be denied because then "everyone would do it"—as though it were done for a lark at lunchtime break. No one who has agonized over the decision, had the standard "dilation and curettage," experienced the emotional strain, and paid the bill, believes it to be so inconsequential.

The above arguments are incomplete, oversimplified, and themselves riddled with ambiguity; but they do at least give some sense of the dilemmas that many people face. Such dilemmas, in turn, provide motivation for action, both legal and illegal, which could change the laws of a nation. The price of such change is high; but the price of no change is higher. It cannot be otherwise for life characterized by ambiguity, for meaning dependent upon encounter here-and-now.

The change in cultural myths or ethos, e.g., the change from a rural mentality to an urban mentality in America, is even more complicated, more risky, more costly, and more lengthy. The technical and financial crises in the major cities of the world are only one phase of the great human problem caused by the change. Politicians whose responsibility it is to administer city governments know the problems in terms of power, representation, and financial apportionments on the local, state, and federal levels. But we all know that there are poignant human problems involving poverty, waste, exploitation, hunger, and so forth, where the risk of the search for meaning has become worth the risk of defiance. Responsible organizational leaders of American minority groups—Charles Evers, Roy Wilkins, Cesar Chavez—and responsible government advisors Sargent Shriver, Abraham Ribicoff, Otto Kerner—all suggest that it would take a crash program involving tens of billions of dollars to begin to rectify the hardships and inequities of a technological society trying to function with a rural mind-set. Unfortunately, as we have observed, even in such enlightened cities as New Haven, Connecticut, money—even were it available—is not enough. In terms of law, it means constitutional revisions; in terms of society, it means a redistribution of power, apportionments, and aid programs. None of this can happen without working hardships on the existing Establishment or at least depriving it of its position of authority and importance. Such a transition cannot take place without struggle and without changes of heart and mind in the citizenry itself. Money cannot buy peace for long and can never provide meaning. The recent organization of militant poverty groups, of Black Power groups, and their concomitant refusal of Establishment help and Establishment dollars are all evidences of the colossal struggle going on in the United States. One can only hope, in spite of grave doubts, that reforms will come quickly and reasonably enough that the risk for meaning will not necessitate any greater acts of defiance. Such is the tension of cultural ambiguity which necessarily and continuously juxtaposes one's responsibilities to the *It* and *Thou* worlds.

The change in faith and belief is even more traumatic, for here the point of our orientation, the very center of meaning, is shaken. Despite the fact that we recognize and know the ambiguity of belief, we resist such changes with great tenacity. The change in belief means not only a change in our understanding of *Being* or God, but also a consequent change in our own identity. Is it any wonder, then, that men and women of the older generations, set in their religious ways, become the conservatives of the community? Superior wisdom does not make them so adament; their fear of change, loss of power, loss of understanding, and loss of meaning does. Is it any wonder that the recent innovations initiated by the Second Vatican Council and by the theological turmoil within Protestantism have produced powerful reactions among all churchmen, laymen and clergy alike? For some, the changes are signs of apostasy—sin in its most subtle form; for others, these changes signal the rebirth without which Christianity is a quaint cultural curiosity. Not since the reformation itself has the Church experienced such change. It is our privilege and peril to live in an age when the need for meaning has produced radical reforms. But, radical reforms in religious expression take generations for effective assimilation. Meanwhile, they occasion profound spiritual anxiety which is often expressed as massive resistance to change.

We are concerned here with all of these changes. We are engaged in a genuine search for a new sense of our humanity and a more relevant morality. The old lights have gone out; the old gods have died; the old ways are inadequate. Life lived meaningfully in the *now*, in terms of our *Being* or in terms of our God, is beginning to emerge, but the patterns are not yet distinct. What is distinct, however, is the overall pattern which includes the presence of the ambiguity of encounter. It is something like this that I believe E. E. Cummings had in mind when he wrote:

are world's collapsing? any was a glove
but i'm and you are actual either hand
is when for sale? forever is to give
and on forever's very now we stand[4]

Thus the delicate balance is sought between structure and freedom, stability and change. As in any fragile human situation, too much weight on one side brings a compensatory reaction to restore the ambiguity necessary for free and meaningful human existence. The danger is that the compensation will be excessive: too much structure brings too much indeterminism; too much objectivity results in too much subjectivism; too much order invites too much chaos. The times in which we live, on all the levels we have discussed, exhibit such contending forces as indeterminism, subjectivism, and irrationality. But, in the gradual emergence of the New Humanism, order and reason will again begin to reassert their authority hopefully, creatively, freely, and affirmatively, yet never absolutely. The awareness of ambiguity adds a new dimension to our understanding of our responsibility for life here-and-now.

The humanist revolution in the arts, in philosophy, and in religion is really an expression of man's authenticity. He takes the risk of defying both inhuman absolutism and ahuman chaos in order to establish communities of meaning. In such communities, *Being* can express itself freely in the integrity of its own existence or in its acknowledgment of the love of God. Within such communities, relative standards of value and behavior exist and are changed only through risk and cost. And such costs must be paid. For such communities the meaningfulness of the moment is the ground of genuine eventfulness, the recognition of the importance of the fullness of the present, of history, of time.

That such meaningfulness points beyond itself to some final resolution is an assertion of faith, not of knowledge. Ambiguity permits no finality. Consequently such issues remain secondary for the New Morality. What does concern us is the quality of lives we determine within the determining context. For the secularist, that is enough. For the man of faith, if heaven—some new context of *Being*—be the later wish of God, so be it. Meaning is not then. It is *now*.

[4] E. E. Cummings, "what freedom's not some under's mere above," *100 Selected Poems*, Grove Press, Inc., New York, p. 84.

IV

Revolution and the Young

"O my son Absalom, my son, my son Absalom! Would God I had
died for thee, O Absalom, my son, my son!"

Old Testament

CORDELIA'S SILENT DEFIANCE*

William Shakespeare

King Lear's palace.

[*Enter* Kent, Gloucester, *and* Edmund.]

Kent. I thought the King had more affected the Duke of Albany than Cornwall.

Gloucester. It did always seem so to us; but now, in the division of the kingdom, it appears not which of the Dukes he values most; for equalities are so weigh'd, that curiosity in neither can make choice of either's moiety.

Kent. Is not this your son, my lord?

Gloucester. His breeding, sir, hath been at my charge. I have so often blushed to acknowledge him, that now I am brazed to't.

Kent. I cannot conceive you.

Gloucester. Sir, this young fellow's mother could; whereupon she grew round-wombed, and had, indeed, sir, a son for her cradle ere she had a husband for her bed. Do you smell a fault?

Kent. I cannot wish the fault undone, the issue of it being so proper.

Gloucester. But I have a son, sir, by order of law, some year older than this, who yet is no dearer in my account. Though this knave came something saucily into the world before he was sent for, yet was his mother fair; there was good sport at his making, and the whoreson must be acknowledged. Do you know this noble gentleman, Edmund?

Edmund. No, my lord.

Gloucester. My Lord of Kent. Remember him hereafter as my honourable friend.

Edmund. My services to your lordship.

Kent. I must love you, and sue to know you better.

Edmund. Sir, I shall study deserving.

Gloucester. He hath been out nine years, and away he shall again.

*From *King Lear,* Act I, Scene i.

229

The King is coming.
> [*Sennet. Enter one bearing a coronet, then* King Lear, *then
> the* Dukes *of* Albany *and* Cornwall, *next* Goneril, Regan,
> Cordelia, *with followers.*]

Lear. Attend the lords of France and Burgundy, Gloucester.

Gloucester. I shall, my liege. [*Exeunt* Gloucester *and* Edmund.]

Lear. Meantime we shall express our darker purpose.
Give me the map there. Know that we have divided
In three our kingdom; and't is our fast intent
To shake all cares and business from our age,
Conferring them on younger strengths, while we
Unburden'd crawl toward death. Our son of Cornwall,
And you, our no less loving son of Albany,
We have this hour a constant will to publish
Our daughters' several dowers, that future strife
May be prevented now. The Princes, France and Burgundy,
Great rivals in our youngest daughter's love,
Long in our court have made their amorous sojourn,
And here are to be answer'd. Tell me, my daughters,—
Since now we will divest us both of rule,
Interest of territory, cares of state,—
Which of you shall we say doth love us most,
That we our largest bounty may extend
Where nature doth with merit challenge? Goneril,
Our eldest-born, speak first.

Goneril. Sir, I do love you more than words can wield the matter;
Dearer than eye-sight, space, and liberty:
Beyond what can be valued, rich or rare;
No less than life, with grace, health, beauty, honour;
As much as child e'er lov'd, or father found;
A love that makes breath poor, and speech unable:
Beyond all manner of so much I love you.

Cordelia [*aside*]. What shall Cordelia speak? Love and be silent.

Lear. Of all these bounds, even from this line to this,
With shadowy forest and with champains rich'd,
With plenteous rivers and wide-skirted meads,
We make thee lady. To thine and Albany's issues
Be this perpetual. What says our second daughter,
Our dearest Regan, wife of Cornwall? Speak.

Regan. I am made of that self metal as my sister,
And prize me at her worth. In my true heart
I find she names my very deed of love;
Only she comes too short, that I profess
Myself an enemy to all other joys
Which the most precious square of sense possesses;
And find I am alone felicitate
In your Highness' love.

Cordelia [*aside*]. Then poor Cordelia!

And yet not so; since, I am sure, my love's
More ponderous than my tongue.
　Lear. To thee and thine hereditary ever
Remain this ample third of our fair kingdom;
No less in space, validity, and pleasure,
Than that conferr'd on Goneril. Now, our joy,
Although our last and least, to whose young love
The vines of France and milk of Burgundy
Strive to be interess'd, what can you say to draw
A third more opulent than your sisters? Speak.
　Cordelia. Nothing, my lord.
　Lear. Nothing!
　Cordelia. Nothing.
　Lear. Nothing will come of nothing. Speak again.
　Cordelia. Unhappy that I am, I cannot heave
My heart into my mouth. I love your Majesty
According to my bond; nor more nor less.
　Lear. How, how, Cordelia! Mend your speech a little,
Lest you may mar your fortune.
　Cordelia. Good my lord,
You have begot me, bred me, lov'd me: I
Return those duties back as are right fit;
Obey you, love you, and most honour you.
Why have my sisters husbands, if they say
They love you all? Haply, when I shall wed,
That lord whose hand must take my plight shall carry
Half my love with him, half my care and duty.
Sure, I shall never marry like my sisters
To love my father all.
　Lear. But goes thy heart with this?
　Cordelia. Ay, my good lord.
　Lear. So young, and so untender?
　Cordelia. So young, my lord, and true.
　Lear. Let it be so; thy truth, then, be thy dower!
For, by the sacred radiance of the sun,
The mysteries of Hecate, and the night;
By all the operation of the orbs
From whom we do exist, and cease to be;
Here I disclaim all my paternal care,
Propinquity and property of blood,
And as a stranger to my heart and me
Hold thee, from this, for ever. The barbarous Scythian,
Or he that makes his generation messes

To gorge his appetite, shall to my bosom
Be as well neighbour'd, piti'd, and reliev'd,
As thou my sometime daughter.
　Kent. Good my liege,—

Lear. Peace, Kent!
Come not between the dragon and his wrath.
I lov'd her most, and though to set my rest
On her kind nursery. [*To* Cordelia] Hence, and avoid my sight!—
So be my grave my peace, as here I give
Her father's heart from her! Call France.—Who stirs?
Call Burgundy. Cornwall and Albany,
With my two daughters' dowers digest this third;
Let pride, which she calls plainness, marry her.
I do invest you jointly in my power,
Pre-eminence, and all the large effects
That troop with majesty. Ourself, by monthly course,
With reservation of an hundred knights,
By you to be sustain'd, shall our abode
Make with you by due turn. Only we still retain
The name, and all th' additions to a king;
The sway, revénue, execution of the rest,
Beloved sons, be yours; which to confirm,
This coronet part betwixt you.
      Kent. Royal Lear,
Whom I have ever honour'd as my king,
Lov'd as my father, as my master follow'd,
As my great patron thought on in my prayers,—
      Lear. The bow is bent and drawn; make from the shaft.
      Kent. Let it fall rather, though the fork invade
The region of my heart: be Kent unmannerly
When Lear is mad. What wouldst thou do, old man?
Think'st thou that duty shall have dread to speak
When power to flattery bows? To plainness honour's bound,
When majesty falls to folly. Reserve thy state;
And, in thy best consideration, check
This hideous rashness. Answer my life my judgement,
Thy youngest daughter does not love thee least;
Nor are those empty-hearted whose low sounds
Reberb no hollowness.
      Lear. Kent, on thy life, no more.
      Kent. My life I never held but as a pawn
To wage against thine enemies, nor fear to lose it,
Thy safety being the motive.
      Lear. Out of my sight!
      Kent. See better, Lear; and let me still remain
The true blank of thine eye.
      Lear. Now, by Apollo,—
      Kent. Now, by Apollo, king,
Thou swear'st thy gods in vain.
      Lear. O, vassal! miscreant!
            [*Laying his hand on his sword.*]

Albany.
Cornwall.   Dear sir, forbear.

Kent. Kill thy physician, and thy fee bestow
Upon the foul disease. Revoke thy doom;
Or, whilst I can vent clamour from my throat,
I'll tell thee thou dost evil.

Lear. Hear me, recreant!
On thine allegiance, hear me!
That thou hast sought to make us break our vows,
Which we durst never yet, and with strain'd pride
To come betwixt our sentence and our power,
Which nor our nature nor our place can bear,
Our potency made good, take thy reward.
Five days we do allot thee, for provision
To shield thee from diseases of the world;
And on the sixth to turn thy hated back
Upon our kingdom. If, on the tenth day following,
Thy banish'd trunk be found in our dominions,
The moment is thy death. Away! By Jupiter,
This shall not be revok'd.

Kent. Fare thee well, king! Sith thus thou wilt appear,
Freedom lives hence, and banishment is here.
[*To* Cordelia.] The gods to their dear shelter take thee, maid,
That justly think'st, and hast most rightly said!
[*To* Regan *and* Goneril.]
And your large speeches may your deeds approve,
That good effects may spring from words of love.
Thus Kent, O princes, bids you all adieu;
He'll shape his old course in a country new. [*Exit.*]
> [*Flourish. Enter* Gloucester, *with* France *and* Burgundy, *Attendants.*]

Gloucester. Here's France and Burgundy, my noble lord.

Lear. My Lord of Burgundy,
We first address toward you, who with this king
Hath rivall'd for our daughter. What, in the least,
Will you require in present dower with her,
Or cease your quest of love?

Burgundy. Most royal Majesty.
I crave no more than hath your Highness offer'd,
Nor will you tender less.

Lear. Right noble Burgundy,
When she was dear to us, we did hold her so;
But now her price is fal'n. Sir, there she stands:
If aught within that little-seeming substance,
Or all of it, with our displeasure piec'd,
And nothing more, may fitly like your Grace,
She's there, and she is yours.

Burgundy. I know no answer.

Lear. Will-you, with those infirmities she owes,
Unfriended, new-adopted to our hate,
Dower'd with our curse, and stranger'd with our oath,
Take her, or leave her?

Burgundy. Pardon me, royal sir;
Election makes not up in such conditions.

Lear. Then leave her, sir; for, by the power that made me,
I tell you all her wealth. [*To* France.] For you, great king,
I would not from your love make such a stray,
To match you where I hate; therefore beseech you
T' avert your liking a more worthier way
Than on a wretch whom Nature is asham'd
Almost t' acknowledge hers.

France. This is most strange,
That she, that even but now was your best object,
The argument of your praise, balm of your age,
Most best, most dearest, should in this trice of time
Commit a thing so monstrous, to dismantle
So many folds of favour. Sure, her offence
Must be of such unnatural degree,
That monsters it, or your fore-vouch'd affection
Fall'n into taint; which to believe of her,
Must be a faith that reason without miracle
Should never plant in me.

Cordelia. I yet beseech your Majesty,—
If for I want that glib and oily art,
To speak and purpose not; since what I well intend,
I'll do't before I speak,—that you make known
It is no vicious blot, murder, or foulness,
No unchaste action, or dishonoured step,
That hath depriv'd me of your grace and favour;
But even for want of that for which I am richer,
A still-soliciting eye, and such a tongue
That I am glad I have not, though not to have it
Hath lost me in your liking.

Lear. Better thou
Hadst not been born than not to have pleas'd me better.

France. It is but this,—a tardiness in nature
Which often leaves the history unspoke
That it intends to do? My Lord of Burgundy,
What say you to the lady? Love is not love
When it is mingled with regards that stands
Aloof from th' entire point. Will you have her?
She is herself a dowry.

Burgundy. Royal Lear,
Give but that portion which yourself propos'd,

And here I take Cordelia by the hand,
Duchess of Burgundy.
   Lear. Nothing. I have sworn; I am firm.
   Burgundy. I am sorry, then, you have so lost a father
That you must lose a husband.
   Cordelia. Peace be with Burgundy!
Since that respects of fortune are his love,
I shall not be his wife.
   France. Fairest Cordelia, that art most rich being poor,
Most choice forsaken, and most lov'd despis'd!
Thee and thy virtues here I seize upon,
Be it lawful I take up what's cast away.
Gods, gods! 't is strange that from their cold'st neglect
My love should kindle to inflam'd respect.
Thy dowerless daughter, king, thrown to my chance,
Is queen of us, of ours, and our fair France.
Not all the dukes of waterish Burgundy
Shall buy this unpriz'd precious maid of me.
Bid them farewell, Cordelia, though unkind;
Thou losest here, a better where to find.
   Lear. Thou hast her, France. Let her be thine; for we
Have no such daughter, nor shall ever see
That face of hers again. [*To* Cordelia.] Therefore be gone
Without our grace, our love, our benison.
Come, noble Burgundy. [*Flourish. Exeunt* Lear *and* Burgundy.]
   France. Bid farewell to your sisters.
   Cordelia. The jewels of our father, with wash'd eyes
Cordelia leaves you. I know you what you are;
And like a sister am most loath to call
Your faults as they are named. Use well our father,
To your professed bosoms I commit him;
But yet, alas, stood I within his grace,
I would prefer him to a better place.
So, farewell to you both.
   Regan. Prescribe not us our duties.
   Goneril. Let your study
Be to content your lord, who hath receiv'd you
At fortune's alms. You have obedience scanted,
And well are worth the want that you have wanted.
   Cordelia. Time shall unfold what plighted cunning hides;
Who covers faults, at last shame them derides.
Well may you prosper!
   France. Come, my fair Cordelia. [*Exeunt* France *and* Cordelia.]
   Goneril. Sister, it is not little I have to say of what most nearly
appertains to us both. I think our father will hence tonight.
   Regan. That's most certain, and with you; next month with us.
   Goneril. You see how full of changes his age is; the observation we

have made of it hath not been little. He always loved our sister most; and with what poor judgement he hath now cast her off appears too gross.

Regan. 'T is the infirmity of his age; yet he hath ever but slenderly known himself.

Goneril. The best and soundest of his time hath been but rash; then must we look to receive from his age not alone the imperfections of long-engrafted condition, but therewithal the unruly waywardness that infirm and choleric years bring with them.

Regan. Such unconstant starts are we like to have from him as this of Kent's banishment.

Goneril. There is further compliment of leave-taking between France and him. Pray you, let's hit together; if our father carry authority with such disposition as he bears, this last surrender of his will but offend us.

Regan. We shall further think on 't.

Goneril. We must do something, and i' th' heat. [*Exeunt.*]

YOU CAN'T PRAY A LIE

Mark Twain

We dasn't stop again at any town for days and days; kept right along down the river. We was down south in the warm weather now, and a mighty long ways from home. We begun to come to trees with Spanish moss on them, hanging down from the limbs like long, gray beards. It was the first I ever see it growing, and it made the woods look solemn and dismal. So now the frauds reckoned they was out of danger, and they begun to work the villages again.

First they done a lecture on temperance; but they didn't make enough for them both to get drunk on. Then in another village they started a dancing-school; but they didn't know no more how to dance than a kangaroo does; so the first prance they made the general public jumped in and pranced them out of town. Another time they tried to go at yellocution; but they didn't yellocute long till the audience got up and give them a solid good cussing, and made them skip out. They tackled missionarying, and mesmerizing, and doctoring, and telling fortunes, and a little of everything; but they couldn't seem to have no luck. So at last they got just about dead broke, and laid around the raft as she floated along, thinking and thinking, and never saying nothing, by the half a day at a time, and dreadful blue and desperate.

And at last they took a change and begun to lay their heads together in the wigwam and talk low and confidential two or three hours at a time. Jim and me got uneasy. We didn't like the look of it. We judged they was studying up some kind of worse deviltry than ever. We turned it over and over, and at last we made up our minds they was going to break into somebody's house or store, or was going into the counterfeit-money business, or something. So then we was pretty scared, and made up an agreement that we wouldn't have nothing in the world to do with such actions, and if we ever got the least show we would give them the cold shake and clear out and leave them behind. Well, early one morning we hid the raft in a good, safe place about two mile below a little bit of a shabby village named Pikesville, and the king he went ashore and told us all to stay hid whilst he went up to town and smelt around to see if anybody had got any wind of the "Royal Nonesuch" there yet. ("House to rob, you *mean*," says I to myself; "and when you get through robbing it you'll come back here and wonder what has become of me and Jim and the raft—and you'll have to take it out in wondering.) And he said if he warn't back by midday the duke and me would know it was all right, and we was to come along.

So we stayed where we was. The duke he fretted and sweated around, and was in a mighty sour way. He scolded us for everything, and we couldn't seem to do nothing right; he found fault with every little thing. Something was a-brewing, sure. I was good and glad when midday come and no king; we could have a change, anyway—and maybe a chance for *the* chance on top of it. So me and the duke went up to the village, and hunted around there for the king, and by and by we found him in the back room of a little low doggery, very tight, and a lot of loafers bullyragging him for sport, and he a-cussing and a-threatening with all his might, and so tight he couldn't walk, and couldn't do nothing to them. The duke he begun to abuse him for an old fool, and the king begun to sass back, and the minute they was fairly at it I lit out and shook the reefs out of my hind legs, and spun down the river road like a deer, for I see our chance; and I made up my mind that it would be a long day before they ever see me and Jim again. I got down there all out of breath but loaded up with joy, and sung out:

"Set her loose, Jim; we're all right now!"

But there warn't no answer, and nobody come out of the wigwam. Jim was gone! I set up a shout—and then another—and then another one; and run this way and that in the woods, whooping and screeching; but it warn't no use—old Jim was gone. Then I set down and cried; I couldn't help it. But I couldn't set still long. Pretty soon I went out on the road, trying to think what I better do, and I run across a boy walking, and asked him if he'd seen a strange nigger dressed so and so, and he says:

"Yes."

"Whereabouts?" says I.

"Down to Silas Phelps's place, two mile below here. He's a runaway nigger, and they've got him. Was you looking for him?"

"You bet I ain't! I run across him in the woods about an hour or two ago, and he said if I hollered he'd cut my livers out—and told me to lay down and stay where I was; and I done it. Been there ever since; afeared to come out."

"Well," he says, "you needn't be afeared no more, becuz they've got him. He run off f'm down South, som'ers."

"It's a good job they got him."

"Well, I *reckon*! There's two hundred dollars' reward on him. It's like picking up money out'n the road."

"Yes, it is—and *I* could 'a' had it if I'd been big enough; I see him *first*. Who nailed him?"

"It was an old fellow—a stranger—and he sold out his chance in him for forty dollars, becuz he's got to go up the river and can't wait. Think o' that, now! You bet *I'd* wait if it was seven year."

"That's me, every time," says I. "But maybe his chance ain't worth no more than that, if he'll sell it so cheap. Maybe there's something ain't straight about it."

"But it *is*, though—straight as a string. I see the handbill myself. It tells all about him, to a dot—paints him like a picture, and tells the plantation he's frum, below New*rleans*. No-sirree-*bob*, they ain't no trouble 'bout *that* speculation, you bet you. Say, gimme a chaw tobacker, won't ye?"

I didn't have none, so he left. I went to the raft, and set down in the wigwam to think. But I couldn't come to nothing. I thought till I wore my head sore, but I couldn't see no way out of the trouble. After all this long journey, and after all we'd done for them scoundrels, here it was all come to nothing, everything all busted up and ruined, because they could have the heart to serve Jim such a trick as that, and make him a slave again all his life, and amongst strangers, too, for forty dirty dollars.

Once I said to myself it would be a thousand times better for Jim to be a slave at home where his family was, as long as he'd *got* to be a slave, and so I'd better write a letter to Tom Sawyer and tell him to tell Miss Watson where he was. But I soon give up that notion for two things: she'd be mad and disgusted at his rascality and ungratefulness for leaving her, and so she'd sell him straight down the river again; and if she didn't, everybody naturally despises an ungrateful nigger, and they'd make Jim feel it all the time, and so he'd feel ornery and disgraced. And then think of *me*! It would get all around that Huck Finn helped a nigger to get his freedom; and if I was ever to see anybody from that town again I'd be ready to get down and lick his boots for shame. That's just the way: a person does a low-down thing, and then he don't want to take no consequences of it. Thinks as long as he can hide, it ain't no disgrace. That was my fix exactly. The more I studied about this the more my conscience

went to grinding me, and the more wicked and low-down and ornery
I got to feeling. And at last, when it hit me all of a sudden that here
was the plain hand of Providence slapping me in the face and letting
me know my wickedness was being watched all the time from up
there in heaven, whilst I was stealing a poor old woman's nigger that
hadn't ever done me no harm, and now was showing me there's One
that's always on the lookout, and ain't a-going to allow no such
miserable doings to go only just so fur and no further, I most
dropped in my tracks I was so scared. Well, I tried the best I could
to kinder soften it up somehow for myself by saying I was brung up
wicked, and so I warn't so much to blame; but something inside of
me kept saying, "There was the Sunday-school, you could 'a' gone to
it; and if you'd 'a' done it they'd 'a' learnt you there that people
that acts as I'd been acting about that nigger goes to everlasting fire."

It made me shiver. And I about made up my mind to pray, and see
if I couldn't try to quit being the kind of a boy I was and be better.
So I kneeled down. But the words wouldn't come. Why wouldn't
they? It warn't no use to try and hide it from Him. Nor from *me*,
neither. I knowed very well why they wouldn't come. It was because
my heart warn't right; it was because I warn't square; it was because
I was playing double. I was letting *on* to give up sin, but away inside
of me I was holding on to the biggest one of all. I was trying to
make my mouth *say* I would do the right thing and the clean thing,
and go and write to that nigger's owner and tell where he was; but
deep down in me I knowed it was a lie, and He knowed it. You can't
pray a lie—I found that out.

So I was full of trouble, full as I could be; and didn't know what
to do. At last I had an idea; and I says, I'll go and write the
letter—and *then* see if I can pray. Why, it was astonishing, the way I
felt as light as a feather right straight off, and my troubles all gone.
So I got a piece of paper and a pencil, all glad and excited, and set
down and wrote:

*Miss Watson, your runaway nigger Jim is down here two mile below Pikesville,
and Mr. Phelps has got him and he will give him up for the reward if you send.*
                                                                    Huck Finn.

I felt good and all washed clean of sin for the first time I had ever
felt so in my life, and I knowed I could pray now. But I didn't do it
straight off, but laid the paper down and set there thinking—thinking
how good it was all this happened so, and how near I come to being
lost and going to hell. And went on thinking. And got to thinking
over our trip down the river; and I see Jim before me all the time: in
the day and in the night-time, sometimes moonlight, sometimes
storms, and we a-floating along, talking and singing and laughing. But
somehow I couldn't seem to strike no places to harden me against
him, but only the other kind. I'd see him standing my watch on top
of his'n, 'stead of calling me, so I could go on sleeping; and see him
how glad he was when I come back out of the fog; and when I come

to him again in the swamp, up there where the feud was; and such-like times; and would always call me honey, and pet me, and do everything he could think of for me, and how good he always was; and at last I struck the time I saved him by telling the men we had smallpox aboard, and he was so grateful, and said I was the best friend old Jim ever had in the world, and the *only* one he's got now; and then I happened to look around and see that paper.

It was a close place. I took it up, and held it in my hand. I was a-trembling, because I'd got to decide, forever, betwixt two things, and I knowed it. I studied a minute, sort of holding my breath, and then says to myself:

"All right, then, I'll *go* to hell"—and tore it up.

It was awful thoughts and awful words, but they was said. And I let them stay said; and never thought no more about reforming. I shoved the whole thing out of my head, and said I would take up wickedness again, which was in my line, being brung up to it, and the other warn't. And for a starter I would go to work and steal Jim out of slavery again; and if I could think up anything worse, I would do that, too; because as long as I was in, and in for good, I might as well go the whole hog.

Then I set to thinking over how to get at it, and turned over some considerable many ways in my mind; and at last fixed up a plan that suited me. So then I took the bearings of a woody island that was down the river a piece, and as soon as it was fairly dark I crept out with my raft and went for it, and hid it there, and then turned in. I slept the night through, and got up before it was light, and had my breakfast, and put on my store clothes, and tied up some others and one thing or another in a bundle, and took the canoe and cleared for shore. I landed below where I judged was Phelps's place, and hid my bundle in the woods, and then filled up the canoe with water, and loaded rocks into her and sunk her where I could find her again when I wanted her, about a quarter of a mile below a little steam-sawmill that was on the bank.

Then I struck up the road, and when I passed the mill I see a sign on it, "Phelps's Sawmill," and when I come to the farm-houses, two or three hundred yards further along, I kept my eyes peeled, but didn't see nobody around, though it was good day-light now. But I didn't mind, because I didn't want to see nobody just yet—I only wanted to get the lay of the land. According to my plan, I was going to turn up there from the village, not from below. So I just took a look, and shoved along, straight for town. Well, the very first man I see when I got there was the duke. He was sticking up a bill for the "Royal Nonesuch"—three-night performance—like that other time. *They* had the cheek, them frauds! I was right on him before I could shirk. He looked astonished, and says:

"Hel-*lo*! where'd *you* come from?" Then he says, kind of glad and eager, "Where's the raft?—got her in a good place?"

I says:

"Why, that's just what I was going to ask your grace."

Then he didn't look so joyful, and says:

"What was your idea for asking *me*?" he says.

"Well," I says, "when I see the king in that doggery yesterday I says to myself, we can't get him home for hours, till he's soberer; so I went a-loafing around town to put in the time and wait. A man up and offered me ten cents to help him pull a skiff over the river and back to fetch a sheep, and so I went along; but when we was dragging him to the boat, and the man left me a-holt of the rope and went behind him to shove him along, he was too strong for me and jerked loose and run, and we after him. We didn't have no dog, and so we had to chase him all over the country till we tired him out. We never got him till dark; then we fetched him over, and I started down for the raft. When I got there and see it was gone, I says to myself, 'They've got into trouble and had to leave; and they've took my nigger, which is the only nigger I've got in the world, and now I'm in a strange country, and ain't got no property no more, nor nothing, and no way to make my living'; so I set down and cried. I slept in the woods all night. But what *did* become of the raft, then?—and Jim—poor Jim!"

"Blamed if *I* know—that is, what's become of the raft. That old fool had made a trade and got forty dollars, and when we found him in the doggery the loafers had matched half-dollars with him and got every cent but what he'd spent for whisky; and when I got him home late last night and found the raft gone, we said, 'That little rascal has stole our raft and shook us, and run off down the river.' "

"I wouldn't shake my *nigger*, would I?—the only nigger I had in the world, and the only property."

"We never thought of that. Fact is, I reckon we'd come to consider him *our* nigger; yes, we did consider him so—goodness knows we had trouble enough for him. So when we see the raft was gone and we flat broke, there warn't anything for it but to try the 'Royal Nonesuch' another shake. And I've pegged along ever since, dry as a powder-horn. Where's that ten cents? Give it here."

I had considerable money, so I give him ten cents, but begged him to spend it for something to eat, and give me some, because it was all the money I had, and I hadn't had nothing to eat since yesterday. He never said nothing. The next minute he whirls on me and says:

"Do you reckon that nigger would blow on us? We'd skin him if he done that!"

"How can he blow? Hain't he run off?"

"No! That old fool sold him, and never divided with me, and the money's gone."

"*Sold* him?" I says, and begun to cry; "why, he was *my* nigger, and that was my money. Where is he?—I want my nigger."

"Well, you can't *get* your nigger, that's all—so dry up your blubbering. Looky here—do you think *you'd* venture to blow on us? Blamed if I think I'd trust you. Why, if you *was* to blow on us—"

He stopped, but I never seen the duke look so ugly out of his eyes before. I went on a-whimpering, and says:

"I don't want to blow on nobody; and I ain't got no time to blow, nohow; I got to turn out and find my nigger."

He looked kinder bothered, and stood there with his bills fluttering on his arm, thinking, and wrinkling up his forehead. At last he says:

"I'll tell you something. We got to be here three days. If you'll promise you won't blow, and won't let the nigger blow, I'll tell you where to find him."

So I promised, and he says:

"A farmer by the name of Silas Ph—" and then he stopped. You see, he started to tell me the truth; but when he stopped that way, and begun to study and think again, I reckoned he was changing his mind. And so he was. He wouldn't trust me; he wanted to make sure of having me out of the way the whole three days. So pretty soon he says:

"The man that brought him is named Abram Foster—Abram G. Foster—and he lives forty mile back here in the country, on the road to Lafayette."

"All right," I says, "I can walk it in three days. And I'll start this very afternoon."

"No you won't, you'll start *now*; and don't you lose any time about it, neither, nor do any gabbling by the way. Just keep a tight tongue in your head and move right along, and then you won't get into trouble with *us*, d'ye hear?"

That was the order I wanted, and that was the one I played for. I wanted to be left free to work my plans.

"So clear out," he says; "and you can tell Mr. Foster whatever you want to. Maybe you can get him to believe that Jim *is* your nigger— some idiots don't require documents—least-ways I've heard there's such down South here. And when you tell him the handbill and the reward's bogus, maybe he'll believe you when you explain to him what the idea was for getting 'em out. Go 'long now, and tell him anything you want to; but mind you don't work your jaw any *between* here and there."

So I left, and struck for the back country. I didn't look around, but I kinder felt like he was watching me. But I knowed I could tire him out at that. I went straight out in the country as much as a mile before I stopped; then I doubled back through the woods towards Phelps's. I reckoned I better start in on my plan straight off without fooling around, because I wanted to stop Jim's mouth till these fellows could get away. I didn't want to trouble with their kind. I'd seen all I wanted to of them, and wanted to get entirely shut of them.

BAZAROV'S NIHILISM

Ivan Turgenev

About two weeks went by. Life at Maryino flowed along much as usual: Arcadii sybaritized, Bazarov worked away. Everybody in the house had become accustomed to him, to his easygoing ways, his laconic and abrupt speech. To Phenechka especially he had become so such like one of the household that one night she had him awakened when Mitya went into convulsions; Bazarov had come and, half-yawning, half-joking as usual, had sat up with her for a couple of hours and relieved the baby. Pavel Petrovich, though, had come to loathe Bazarov with all his soul: he considered him arrogant, brazen, a cynic, a plebeian; he suspected that Bazarov had no respect for him, that he all but held him in contempt—him, Pavel Kirsanov! Nicholai Petrovich was somewhat apprehensive about the young "nihilist" and had doubts as to whether his influence on Arcadii was a beneficial one, but he listened to his talks willingly and willingly attended his experiments in physics and chemistry. Bazarov had brought his microscope along and would fuss with it for hours at a stretch. The servants also had become attached to him, even though he twitted them: they felt that, when you came right down to it, he was a man and brother and not one of the masters. Dunyasha giggled readily enough when he was around and would cast meaningful sidelong glances at him whenever she dashed by like a little hen partridge; Peter, a fellow extremely conceited and stupid, with forehead perpetually wrinkled from strain, a fellow whose worth consisted, all in all, of his air of civility, his being able to read by syllables and his frequent cleaning of his small frock coat with a little brush—even he would smirk and brighten the moment Bazarov bestowed any attention upon him; the urchins about the place ran after the "doc" like so many puppies. Procophich, that old man, was the only one who had no liking for him; he served him at table with a surly air, referring to him as "knacker" and "scalawag" and maintained that Bazarov with those side whiskers of his looked like nothing else than a pig stuck in a bush. Procophich, after his fashion, was no less an aristocrat than Pavel Petrovich.

The best days of the year—the first days of June—set in. The weather was consistently fine; true, there was a remote threat of cholera recurring, but the people inhabiting this particular province had by now become accustomed to its visitations. Bazarov would get up very early and set out for a hike of two or three miles; not for the sake of pleasure, however, since he could not abide idle jaunts, but to collect herbs and insects. Now and then he would take Arcadii along. On the way back they would usually get into an argument—

with Arcadii most often winding up as the loser even though he had
more to say than his companion.

On one occasion their return had been somehow long delayed;
Nicholai Petrovich came out into the garden to meet them and, as he
came abreast of the arbor, he suddenly caught the voices and quick
steps of the two young men. They were following a path on the
other side of the arbor and could not see him.

"You don't know my father sufficiently well," Arcadii was saying.
Nicholai Petrovich held his breath.

"Your father is a kindhearted fellow," Bazarov declared, "but he's
a has-been—his act is over."

The father was all ears. Arcadii did not answer anything.

The has-been stood there without stirring for two minutes or so
and then plodded homeward.

"A couple of days ago I came upon him reading Pushkin," Bazarov
went on. "Do explain to him, please, that this sort of thing is utterly
useless. After all, he isn't a little boy; it's time to abandon all this
twaddle. Why should he hanker to be a romantic in this day and age!
Give him something worth while to read."

"What should I give him?" asked Arcadii.

"Why, Büchner's *Stoff und Kraft* for a starter, I think."

"That's what I think," Arcadii remarked with approval. "*Stoff und
Kraft* is written in popular language."

"And that's how you and I happened to find ourselves among the
has-beens," Nicholai Petrovich was saying the same day after dinner
to his brother, sitting in the latter's study. "Our act is over. Oh,
well—Bazarov may be right, at that; one thing does hurt me, however—I had hopes, precisely now, of getting on close and friendly
terms with Arcadii, yet it turns out that I have been left behind; he
has advanced and we can't understand each other."

"Come, just how has he advanced? And what makes him so very
different from us by now?" Pavel Petrovich exclaimed impatiently.
"It's that seigneur, that nihilist, who has stuffed his head with all
this. I abominate this wretched little pillroller; he's simply a charla-
tan, to my way of thinking. I feel certain that, with all his frogs, he
hasn't made much headway even in physics."

"No, don't say that, brother—Bazarov is intelligent and knowing."

"And what disgusting self-conceit!" Pavel again broke in.

"Yes," Nicholai commented, "he is conceited. But it looks as if one
couldn't do without that. There's only one thing I can't grasp. I'm
doing everything, it seems, not to fall behind the times; I've arranged
things for the peasants, I have started a farm—why, they actually
style me a Red all over the province; I read, I study, I strive—on the
whole—to keep up with the demands of the times, yet they're saying
my act is over. There, brother, I myself am starting in to think that
it is over, sure enough."

"But why?"

"Well, here's why. Today I was sitting reading Pushkin. It happened to be "The Gypsies," I remember. Suddenly Arcadii walked up to me and without a word, his face betraying a compassion that was ever so tender, took the book away from me ever so gently, as if I were a baby, and placed another one before me, a German one. Then he smiled and left—and carried Pushkin off with him."

"Well, now! But just what sort of a book did he give you?"

"This one." And Nicholai Petrovich drew Büchner's celebrated brochure, a copy of the ninth edition, out of his coattail pocket.

Pavel Kirsanov emitted a rumbling "Hm!" as he turned the book in his hands. "Arcadii is concerned about your education. Well, now, did you make a try at reading it?"

"I certainly did."

"And what was the upshot?"

"Either I'm stupid or all this is twaddle. Probably I'm stupid."

"You haven't forgotten your German, have you?" asked Pavel.

"I understand German."

Pavel again turned the book in his hands and glanced at his brother from under his brows. There was a short silence between them.

"And, by the way," Nicholai began, evidently desirous of shifting the conversation, "I've received a letter from Kolyazin."

"Matvei Ilyich?"

"The very same. He's in town on an inspection tour of the province. He has become a bigwig now and writes me that, as a kinsman, he desires to see us and invites both of us, as well as Arcadii, to visit him in town."

"Are you going?" asked Pavel.

"No. What about you?"

"No; I'm not going either. No great need to drag oneself forty miles or more for a mouthful of cranberry sauce. *Mathieu* wants to show himself in all his glory before us; to the devil with him. Let the incense the whole province will be burning before him suffice him; he'll manage to do without ours. And what a grand personage—a Privy Councilor! If I had gone on in the service, staying in the stupid harness, I would have been an adjutant general by now. Besides, you and I are has-beens."

"Yes, brother; the way things look it's time to get measured for a coffin and fold one's hands on one's breast," Nicholai commented with a sigh.

"Well, I'm not giving in so fast," his brother muttered. "I have a premonition that that pillroller and I are going to tangle yet."

Tangle they did that same day, at evening tea. Pavel Kirsanov came down into the drawing room all set for battle, irritated and determined. All he was waiting for was a pretext for falling upon the enemy, but for a long time the pretext did not materialize. Bazarov generally had little to say in the presence of the "little Kirsanov

ancients," as he dubbed both brothers, while on this evening he felt
out of sorts and drank off cup after cup of tea in silence. Pavel
Petrovich was being utterly consumed by impatience; his wishes
found fulfillment at last.

The talk turned to one of the neighboring landed proprietors.
"Trash; a wretched little aristocrat," Bazarov, who had met this
fellow in Petersburg, commented apathetically.

"Permit me to ask you," Pavel Petrovich began, and his lips started
quivering, "according to your conceptions the words 'trash' and
'aristocrat' have one and the same significance?"

"I said 'wretched little aristocrat,' " Bazarov let drop, lazily sipping
and swallowing some tea.

"Precisely so, sir; yet I suppose that you hold to the same opinion
of aristocrats as of wretched little aristocrats. I consider it my duty
to declare to you that I do not share that opinion. I venture to say
that everybody knows me as a liberal and a man who loves progress;
but it is precisely for that reason that I respect aristocrats—the real
ones. Recall, my dear sir"—at these words Bazarov looked up and
eyed Pavel Petrovich—"recall, my dear sir," the speaker repeated
acrimoniously, "the English aristocrats. They do not yield an iota of
their rights, and therefore respect the rights of others; they demand
the fulfillment of the obligations due them, and therefore they
themselves fulfill *their* obligations. The aristocracy has given freedom
to England and it supports that freedom."

"We've heard that song, many's the time," Bazarov retorted. "However, what do you wish to prove by that?"

"What I want to prove by *that there*"—Pavel Petrovich, whenever
he was in an angry mood, intentionally resorted to such turns of
speech, even though he knew well enough that they were not gram-
matically permissible; this whim evinced a vestige of the traditions of
the time of Alexander I: some of the gallants of that day, on the
infrequent occasions when they spoke their native tongue, used *that
there*, while others preferred *this here*, as if to say they were Russians
from 'way back, and grandees on top of that, having the license to
disdain rules laid down by scholars—"what I want to prove by that
there is that without a feeling of one's own worth, without respect
for one's own self—and in an aristocrat these two feelings are
thoroughly developed—there is no firm basis for the social *bien
public*, the public good, the social structure. Personality, my dear sir,
that's the main thing; man's personality must be as firm as a rock,
for everything is built upon it. I know very well, for example, that it
pleases you to find amusement in my habits, my dress—my personal
neatness, if it comes to that; all this, however, emanates from a sense
of self-respect, from a sense of duty—yes sir, yes sir: duty. I live in
the country, in the backwoods, but I do not let myself sink, I respect
the man within me."

"Just a moment, Pavel Petrovich," Bazarov spoke up. "So you

respect yourself and sit there twiddling your thumbs. What good does that do the *bien public*? You still would be doing the same thing, even if you didn't respect yourself."

Pavel Petrovich paled.

"That's something else entirely. I am not at all constrained to explain to you at present why I sit twiddling my thumbs, as it pleases you to express it. All I want to say is that aristocracy is a principle, and that it is solely immoral or frivolous people who can live without principles in our time. I told that to Arcadii the day after his arrival, and I repeat it to you now. Didn't I say that, Nicholai?"

Nicholai nodded.

"Aristocracy, liberalism, progress, principles," Bazarov was saying in the meantime. "My, what a batch of foreign—and useless—words! No Russian needs them, even gratis."

"What does he need then, according to you? To hear you tell it, why, we're outside humanity, outside its laws. The logic of history, if you please, demands—"

"Why, what do we need that logic for? We manage even without it."

"How so?"

"Why, just so. You have no need of logic, I trust, to pop a hunk of bread in your mouth when you feel hungry? Who are we to bother with those abstractions!"

Pavel Kirsanov flung up his hands. "I don't understand you after this. You're insulting the Russian people. I don't understand—how is it possible not to acknowledge principles, rules? By virtue of what do you act, then?"

"I've already told you, dear uncle, that we don't acknowledge authorities," Arcadii broke in.

"We act by virtue of that which we acknowledge to be useful. At the present time repudiation is the most useful of all. We repudiate."

"Everything?"

"Everything."

"What! Not only art, poetry . . . but also—one dreads to say it—"

"Everything," Bazarov repeated with inexpressible calm.

Pavel Petrovich stared at him. He had not expected this; as for Arcadii, he actually glowed with satisfaction.

"However, permit me to say something," Nicholai Petrovich spoke up. "You're repudiating everything, or, to put it more exactly, you're demolishing everything. But then, it is necessary to be constructive as well."

"That, now, is no business of ours. The ground must be cleared, first of all."

"That's what the present state of the people demands," Arcadii added with a pompous air. "We are obligated to fulfill these demands; we haven't the right to indulge in personal egoism."

Bazarov, it seemed, found this last phrase displeasing; there was a whiff of philosophy—of romanticism, that is—about it, since Bazarov dubbed philosophy, too, as romanticism; however, he did not deem it necessary to controvert his youthful disciple.

"No, no!" Pavel Kirsanov exclaimed with unrestrained impulsiveness. "I don't want to believe that you gentlemen have a true knowledge of the Russian people, that you are representatives of its needs, its aspirations! No, the Russian people is not such as you imagine it. It considers its traditions sacred; it is patriarchal, it cannot live without faith—"

"I'm not going to argue against that," Bazarov cut him short. "I am even prepared to agree that *as far as that goes* you are right."

"Well, if I am right—"

"But, just the same, that doesn't prove a thing."

"Precisely—that doesn't prove a thing," Arcadii echoed, with the assurance of an experienced chess-player who had anticipated an apparently dangerous move of an opponent and therefore had not been at all at a loss.

"Just how doesn't it prove a thing?" muttered the astonished Pavel Petrovich. "You must be opposing your own people, in that case?"

"Well, and what if that is so?" Bazarov exclaimed. "Whenever it thunders the common folk think it's Elijah the prophet out for a ride through the sky in his chariot. Well, now—am I supposed to agree with them? And suppose the common folk are Russian, so what? Am I not Russian too?"

"No, you're not Russian—not after all you've just told me! I can't acknowledge you as a Russian."

"My grandfather ploughed the soil," Bazarov answered with a pride that bordered on superciliousness. "Ask any peasant you like—even one of your own—whom he would rather acknowledge as a fellow-countryman—you or me. Why, you don't even know how to talk to a peasant."

"Well, you talk to him—and hold him in contempt at the same time."

"What of that, if he deserves contempt! You disparage my attitude, yet who told you that it isn't accidental in my case, that it wasn't provoked by that self-same national spirit in the name of which you are contending so strenuously?"

"Oh, to be sure! As if there were any great need of nihilists!"

"Whether there is need of them or no is not up to us to decide. Why, you too consider yourself as not useless."

"Gentlemen, gentlemen—please, no personalities!" Nicholai Petrovich called out and rose from his seat.

Pavel Kirsanov smiled and, putting a hand on his brother's shoulder, made him sit down again. "Don't be alarmed," he remarked. "I shan't forget myself, precisely as a consequence of that sense of dignity which this gentleman, this doctor gentleman pokes such cruel fun at. Allow me to ask you," he went on, addressing Bazarov once more, "are you possibly thinking that your teaching is a novelty? You imagine so in vain. The materialism you are preaching has already been all the rage, more than once, and turned out to be insolvent—"

"Another foreign word!" Bazarov cut him short. He was turning rancorous and his face had taken on a coppery and coarse hue. "First of all, we aren't preaching a thing—that's not one of our ways—"

"What is it you're doing, then?"

"Well, here's what we're doing. Hitherto, still quite recently, we used to say that our bureaucrats took bribes, that we had neither roads, nor commerce, nor real justice—"

"Why, yes, yes—you're denouncers: that's the term, I believe. I, too, am in agreement with many of your denunciations, but—"

"However, in time we wised up to the fact that blather, nothing but perpetual blather about our social sores wasn't worth the effort, that it led to nothing but banality and doctrinarism; we perceived that even the clever fellows among us, the so-called vanguard people and denunciators, weren't good for anything, that we were taken up with twaddle, spouting about some art or other, about unconscious creativeness, about parliamentarism, about the legal profession, and about the devil knows what else, when the real business at hand has to do with our daily bread, when the crassest superstition is suffocating us, when all our stock-issuing companies are going up the chimney solely because it turns out that there aren't enough honest men to go around, when that very emancipation which the government is going to such bother about will hardly be of any benefit to us, since our mouzhik is eager to rob his own self if only it will enable him to stupefy himself with rotgut at a pothouse."

"Exactly," Pavel Petrovich interposed. "Exactly; you've become convinced of all this and have resolved not to take on anything seriously yourselves."

"And we resolved not to take on anything," Bazarov repeated dourly. He had suddenly become vexed with himself: why had he become so expansive before this seigneur?

"But only to go in for abuse?"

"And to go in for abuse."

"And that's what they call nihilism?"

"And that's what they call nihilism," Bazarov repeated once more, this time with especial rudeness.

Pavel Kirsanov puckered up his eyes slightly. "So that's how things stand!" he uttered in a strangely calm voice. "Nihilism is bound to help in everything that's wrong, and you—you!—are our redeemers and heroes. So! But why are you tongue-lashing others now—even though they may be the same sort of denouncers as yourselves? Aren't you going in for the same sort of blather as everybody else?"

"Whatever else we may be guilty of, this is one sin of which we're innocent," Bazarov got out through clenched teeth.

"Well, then? Are you taking action, or what? Are you getting ready to act?"

Bazarov did not answer anything. Pavel Petrovich plainly shuddered but immediately controlled himself. "Hm! Taking action, wrecking," he continued. "Yet how can one wreck without as much as knowing why?"

"We wreck because we are a force," Arcadii remarked. Pavel Petrovich gave his nephew a look and smiled slightly. "Yes, and a force simply does not give any accounting of itself," Arcadii declared, straightening up.

"You poor unfortunate!" Pavel Petrovich vociferated; he was utterly incapable of restraining himself any longer. "If you would only reflect just *what* it is you're supporting in Russia by your blatant sententiousness! No, this could make an angel lose his patience. Force! You'll find force even in the savage Kalmuck, even in the Mongol, but what's the good of it to us? It is civilization that we hold dear—yes, yes, my dear sir; we hold dear its fruits. And don't tell me those fruits are trifling: the last dauber, *un barbouilleur*, or the professor who gets five kopecks for pounding a piano all evening—why, even they are more useful than you, because they are representatives of civilization and not of naked Mongolian force! You imagine that you are in the vanguard, but where you really belong is squatting in a Kalmuck tent. Force! And finally, my forceful gentlemen, the fact remains that there are only four and a half of you, all in all, whereas there are millions of the others who won't allow you to trample down their most sacred beliefs, who will crush you!"

"If they crush us, that will be that. Only thing is, you may have another guess coming. There aren't as few of us as you seem to think."

"What! Are you thinking, in all seriousness, that you can come out on top—come out on top against all the people?"

"It took only a kopeck candle to burn down all of Moscow," Bazarov retorted.

"Exactly, exactly. Pride, almost satanic, first; then jeering. There, that's what infatuates youth, there's what vanquishes the callow hearts of schoolboys! There, take a look—there's one of them sitting right beside you; why, he's all but worshiping you—feast your eyes on him." Arcadii turned his face away and assumed a deep frown. "And by now this pestilence is widespread. In Rome—so they've told me—our artists won't as much as set foot in the Vatican. Raphael they consider as but little short of an ass because, it seems, he is authoritative, yet they themselves are so impotent and sterile that they are abominable, while their own imagination cannot reach beyond some Girl at a Fountain, no matter what you do to them! And even that girl is drawn most execrably. Fine fellows, according to you, aren't they?"

"According to me," Bazarov retorted, "Raphael isn't worth a sou marquee, and as for those artists, they're no better than he is."

"Bravo, bravo! Just listen, Arcadii, that's how young people of today should express themselves! And, if one stops to think of it, how can they do otherwise than follow you! Formerly young people were faced with having to study; they were averse to becoming known as ignoramuses; so, like it or not, they worked hard. But now all they have to do is to say 'Everything in the world is bosh!'—and that does it. The young people rejoiced. And for good cause—up to that time they had been simply blockheads, but now they have, all of a sudden, become nihilists."

"There, now, your vaunted sense of personal dignity has failed you," Bazarov observed phlegmatically, while Arcadii brightened altogether and his eyes glittered. "Our disputation has gone too far. Apparently it would be better to break it off. As for me, I'll be ready to agree with you," he added as he stood up, "whenever you confront me with even one factuality in our present way of life, either domestic or social, which would not provoke total and merciless repudiation."

"I'll confront you with millions of such factualities!" Pavel Kirsanov exclaimed. "Millions of them! Why, take the village commune, for example—"

A chill smile distorted Bazarov's lips. "Well, as far as the village commune is concerned," he said, "you'd better have a talk with your own brother. The way things look, he has by now had a real taste of the village commune, mutual responsibility, temperance and suchlike pretty doodads."

"The family, then—the family, as one finds it among our peasants!" Pavel Petrovich was by now shouting.

"And that question too, I opine, it would be better for your own sake not to go into in detail. You've heard, I guess, about patriarchs who have the first go at their daughters-in-law? You listen to me, Pavel Petrovich—give yourself time for a couple of days; you're hardly likely to come up with anything right off. Go over all our social classes and give quite a bit of thought to each one, and in the meantime Arcadii and I will—"

"Mock at everything!" Pavel Petrovich broke in on him.

"No; we'll be cutting up frogs. Come on, Arcadii; we'll be seeing you, gentlemen!"

The two friends left the room. The brothers were left by themselves, and all they could do at first was to exchange occasional glances.

"There," Pavel Kirsanov began at last, "there is modern youth for you! There they are—our heirs!"

"Our heirs," his brother echoed with a despondent sigh. Throughout the dispute he had been sitting as if on a bed of live coals and could only cast furtive and pained glances at his son from time to time. "Do you know what I've recalled, brother? I had a quarrel once with our dear mother? she kept screaming, wouldn't listen to me. Well, now, I told her at last: 'you are incapable of understanding me; you and I, now, belong to two different generations.' She was horribly hurt by that, whereas I thought to myself, What can one do? The pill is a bitter one, yet it must be swallowed. Well, our turn has come now, and our inheritors are in a position to say to us 'You now don't belong to our generation; go ahead and swallow that pill!' "

"You're really too magnanimous and unassuming," Pavel Kirsanov retorted. "I, on the contrary, am convinced that you and I are considerably more right than these young *gentlemen*, even though we do, possibly, express ourselves in somewhat antiquated language, *vieilli*, and do not possess their impudent self-reliance. And how pompous the young people of today are! If you happen to ask one of them 'What wine do you want—red or white?' he answers in a bass and with a face as grave as if all Creation were regarding him at that moment 'A preference for red wine is a habit of mine!' "

"Don't you want some more tea?" asked Phenechka, with her head in the doorway: she had hesitated about entering the drawing room as long as the voices issuing from it had sounded disputatious.

"No; you can tell them to remove the samovar," Nicholai Petrovich answered and got up to meet her. Pavel Kirsanov bade him "*Bon soir!*" abruptly and withdrew to his study.

THE HANG-LOOSE ETHIC

J. J. Simmons and Barry Winograd

Happenings are the concrete manifestations of an emerging new ethos in American society, which seems most aptly called "the hang-loose ethic." It is cool and irreverent and it reflects a good deal of disaffection toward many of our more traditional roots. For this reason, it is perhaps more worrisome to parents, educators, and officials than the mere wildness or deviant flirtations of youth.

A barefooted man with a beard and a surplus Navy jacket that had "Love IS" written on the back of it was walking down the main street of a small midwestern city, digging the sunlight and thinking that the heat was really pleasant when you got out into it. A group of high school kids rode by him in a car and began shouting to him. "Hey beatnik." "Hey, you're high man." "what color's your dingy?" And, from one of the less imaginative boys, "Why don't you go fly a kite?"

The man looked up musingly, jaywalked across the street to a dime store, bought a kite and some luminous paint and two thousand feet of string. He took them to his battered car and drove around the adjacent suburbs for awhile, rounding up kids to fly the kite with him. Some parents looked him over and scurried their kids away, shaking their heads about the invasion of perverts; others looked into his face and saw nothing evil there, so consented. They drove to the top of a hill overlooking the town, painted the kite with bright psychedelic colors, sent it up and flew it all afternoon. Toward sunset, they cut loose the string and watched their *objet d'art* disappear into the aerial world above them.

The thing about this story is that the young man didn't turn upon his assailants and by opposing them become their likes. Nor did he go into a foetal crouch over a beer, pitying himself as a sensitive and misunderstood soul (which he is) and condemning the society which trains even its children to put down the unusual. He transcended the harassment, rather than succumbing to it by being roused to self-pity or anger.

The emerging ethic is hang-loose in a number of senses, but, its deep-running feature is that things once taken for granted as God-given or American Constitution-given—those basic premises about the world and the way it works—are no longer taken for granted or given automatic allegiance. In other words, many Americans are hanging a bit loose from traditional Americana.

This new ethos is still in the process of forming and emerging; the adherents themselves are mostly unaware of the credo they are participating in making and are already living by. For instance, if you went up to many of the likely young people about town and said, "Say, are you an adherent of the hang-loose ethic?", many of them would look at you oddly and wonder what the hell you were talking about.

Well, if this thing is still so amorphous and you can only speculate about it, and the supposed followers are hardly even aware of it, why bother?

Because we want to see what lies beneath the legion of different concrete happenings. A society can be portrayed in a number of different ways and each gives a different picture of what the society is. It can be done by sketching the material objects, the streets, the buildings, the childhood and adult toys. It can be done by describing the typical behavior, the activities, the rituals, the average life-course of an ordinary member. It can also be done by trying to ferret out the underlying ideology or ethos, which comes forth in a thousand and one different ways and which is the wellspring from which flows the other things, the toys, the scenes, the lives, the typical attitudes and responses. Our attempt to ferret out the ideology behind the happenings is an attempt, then, to dive beneath the trappings and veneers down to the basic world view of the people who are making them happen.

At first glance, it might seem as if the hang-loose ethic is the absence of any morality, that it rejects every ideology, that the followers have no rudder and no star except the swift gratification of all impulses. At a second glance it appears only as a bewildering melange of scenes in various locales. But upon closer examination, one can see that it does embody some values and some guiding principles which, although still ill-formed and vaguely expressed, shape the attitudes and actions of the followers. However, to convey a fuller picture of this ethos, we must sketch the previous American ethics from which it emerged.

Europeans and Americans of the past few centuries have been characterized by most writers as human beings who subscribed to and lived by what is called the Protestant Ethic. This Protestant Ethic was a way of life and a view of life which stressed the more somber virtues, like the quiet good feeling of a hard day's work well done, the idea that the good man always more than earned his pay, and a kind of fierce pragmatism in which the hard and fast, here and now, seeable, touchable, aspects of reality were the only things given the name of reality.

Another thing about the Protestant Ethic was a kind of positive moderatism. Moderation wasn't just a safe course between extremes; moderation was an optimum, positive, good in-and-of-itself thing. Moderation was raised almost to a first principle of ethics. It was a mandate on how to conduct your life.

Anything which veered very far from this somber dignity in oneself and one's accumulations was thought of as bad and suspect. We will see, for example, when we discuss "tripping" that whereas most of the world has regarded exceptional behavior that strays beyond the mundane with an awe combining wonder and terror, in the Western world the wonder has until very recently dropped away and it was suppressed as altogether dangerous. Western man neglected what other times and places made a good deal of, the positive aspects which exceptional experiences might have.

This moderatism carried over into virtually every aspect of the lives of the people. Even in religion and young love, anything smacking too much of mysticism was suspect. The West has relied mostly upon dogma rather than experience in its religious institutions and, despite our hungry romanticism, most of our marriages and other sexual liasons have been made largely by arrangement.

This Protestant Ethic seems to have characterized the majority of our forefathers although there was always a "lunatic" fringe and a subterranean stratum composed of those at the bottom of the social ladder and of outsiders. And, like all people everywhere, the adherents didn't entirely live up to their own ideals. But, the Protestants ran the schools and the courts and the country and the fringe was contained and circumscribed, largely kept at the fringe.

Then, as the decades passed and we moved into the present century, America began to undergo a secularization which involved not only a dwindling of the force of religion but also a dwindling of the force of the work ethic and the rather stiff personal code which surrounded it. Particularly in the mushrooming urban areas after the Second World War, something grew up which William F. Whyte termed "the Social Ethic."

The Social Ethic (or perhaps more aptly, the Sociable Ethic) was a kind of jocular, benign, superficial, "we're all in the same boat," goodwill. But it shared many things with the Protestant Ethic from which it evolved under the impact of modern times. It was still taken for granted that getting ahead in the Establishment was the thing to do, and that the accumulation of material wealth was a good thing in and of itself. Whyte used the "organization man" living in the new suburbs as his prototypic example and he made a good argument that this was tending to become the overweening American ethos. Work and play, family and politics, each of these were supposed to be a good thing, a fun thing, a comfortable thing. The Sociable Ethic was a secularization of the Protestant ideology combined with a feeling of comfort and goodwill which is easy to generate in a luxuriant society such as ours.

Risk is minimized in the Sociable Ethic. All parties join in a collusion which reduces the chance of great failure and great success once you've been hooked into the system. Of course, there were some dark counterthemes in this portrait: those thirty percent of the people who were not in any real sense beneficiaries of the luxuriant system. And it certainly was not a comfortable place for them—it was as Baldwin has suggested, another country. This didn't just mean the Negro of the South; it also included most Northern Negroes, the uneducated, the abysmally poor, those who lacked the skills to sell themselves, to make themselves an attractive enough package to get recruited into the system.

But the majority of Americans were in it and were doing fairly well. And the continuities with the earlier ethic remained. There still existed a kind of blandness, a real distrust for the exceptional and the bizarre, and there still remained a real distrust for doing something, let's say, "just for kicks." We had in the fifties almost the Utopian culmination of the principle of moderation. Moderate in politics, moderate in work—not too much because it doesn't really pay, not too little because you might get dropped. Moderate in family which involved a kind of thing where you were moderately attached to your spouse and children and moderately concerned with their welfare and you were moderately unfaithful and moderately blasphemous. But you also gave a moderate allegiance to your family and your company and your country.

This was not a picture window nightmare. Most of those involved were probably moderately comfortable and moderately happy.

Does this mean that these people were apathetic and uninvolved, just going through some motions?

No. They were moderately involved in many things. They cried a little and they cared a little and they strove a little and were proud a little and ashamed a little. You see, these people were veterans of hard times; a world depression which was tough, a world war which was tough, an uncertain time afterwards which was tough. And so at last they arrived in their ranch houses and they could afford cocktails on the way home without much worrying about the price. It was, in a sense, the indulgence of a dream, the dream of building an affluent society. Because in the fifties that's exactly what we had—fantastically affluent compared with anything that had ever existed before.

Certainly, there were a few hot social movements and protests about the thirty percent who weren't "in." But, we must realize that in most times and countries it's been 90% or 98%. So only thirty percent left out is pretty damn good and something brand new in history. And the first scattered appearance of the beats and the freedom cats must not obscure the fact that the vast majority were (moderately) good Americans in the small sense of not rocking any boats.

Yet even as the sociable ideology was crystallizing and taking hold and Eisenhower was virtually proclaiming moderation the cornerstone of our national policy, a new kind of feeling was beginning to stir across the land—a feeling which had many ties with the past but which was also new.

Although there were precursors in the late fifties when Ginsberg was telling people he'd seen the best minds of his generation driven mad, and hip talk (and an inevitable bit of the philosophy behind it) was being picked up by teenagers, the hang-loose ethos really belongs to the sixties because this is the decade in which it is emerging and spreading throughout our society.

When we search for the "philosophy" which is the common denominator running through the variety of happenings—the implicit code of values pushing those involved toward some things and away from other things—some of the characteristics of this yet crystallizing view can be discerned.

One of the fundamental characteristics of the hang-loose ethic is that it is *irreverent*. It repudiates, or at least questions, such cornerstones of conventional society as Christianity, "my country right or wrong," the sanctity of marriage and premarital chastity, civil obedience, the accumulation of wealth, the right and even competence of parents, the schools, and the government to head and make decisions for everyone—in sum, the Establishment. This irreverence is probably what most arouses the ire and condemnation of the populace. Not only are the mainstream institutions and values violated, but their very legitimacy is challenged and this has heaped insult upon moral injury in the eyes of the rank and file.

Sin, as the violation of sacred beliefs and practices, is nothing new and most of us have had at least a few shamefully delightful adventures somewhere along the way. But what is qualitatively new is that the very truth and moral validity of so many notions and practices, long cherished in our country, are being challenged. When caught by parents or authorities, youths are no longer hanging their heads in shame. Instead, they are asserting the rightness, at least for themselves, of what they're doing. And they are asking what right do their elders have to put them down?

And not infrequently the irreverence takes a form which goes beyond this openly aggressive challenging. An increasing number of happeners have reached a level of disrespect so thoroughgoing that they don't even bother to "push their cause." Not only have they dropped their defensive posture, but their own assertiveness has become quiet, even urbane, in its detachment and indifference toward the "other morality." This withdrawal has aroused some of the greatest resentment and opposition since it is perhaps the gravest affront to an established ethic not to be taken seriously. To be defied is one thing; to be simply ignored and dismissed out of hand is something else. The spread of this more fullblown irreverence testifies to the fact that a good many happeners are managing to set up a life that is relatively independent of conventional society.

Another basic aspect of the hang-loose ethic is a diffuse and pervasive *humanism* which puts great store upon the value of human beings and human life. Adherents don't necessarily proclaim the rationality of men or their inherent "goodness," but they do claim that people are precious and that their full development is perhaps the most worthwhile of all things.

Killing is a heinous violation of this ethos and so is any action which puts others down, except under extreme circumstances. The most approved method of defense and retaliation is to turn one's oppressors onto the good life they're condemning and to help them resolve hangups which prevent this from happening. If this fails, one may attempt to "blow their minds," to shock their preconceptions and prejudices in some way and hence force them to open their eyes, to re-evaluate, and hopefully to grow. The happeners refuse under most circumstances to employ the weapons of their adversaries because they feel that by so doing they would merely become like them. Instead, they try to transform their adversaries into fellows. The only really endorsed aggression is to try and force your enemies to become your friends. Only in extreme cases is putting down—the main strategy of the Establishment—even partly acceptable.

Ideally, the happeners do not fill the role of modern missionaries, though their practice in conversation and contact reminds one of historical attempts at persuasion and conversion. When approaching others, they welcome acceptance as well as adoption, but this does not imply that happeners resemble the adventurous, pioneering missionaries of established religions or ideologies. The few actual organizations existing in the happening world are there, first, to serve their "constituents" and, second, to espouse and inform.

This humanism, combined as it is with irreverence, produces a passive resistance toward the Establishment and the persuasive efforts of straights, rather than an active rebellion. The happeners are more transcendent than antagonistic; more indifferent and benevolently contemptuous than negative and bitter. Bitterness does occur over concrete immediate cases of harassment or "for your own good" busts, commitments, and putdowns. But it fades rather quickly again into the more general mood of simple wariness. The mood is not grim, although there is a diffuse paranoia toward the established social order which waxes and wanes as the scene gets hot and cools down again.

Another basic aspect of the hang-loose ethic is the pursuit of *experience* both as a thing in itself and as a means of learning and growing. The idea is that a great variety and depth of experience is beneficial and not at all harmful as long as you can handle it. This entails a heightened attention to the present ongoing moment and far less concern with the past or future. It also involves a mistrust of dogmas and principles which tend to obscure the richness of life. For this reason, they also often reject the categorizing and generalizing which is so rampant in our educational system. Within the drug scenes, for instance, there is full awareness that LSD-25 can trigger "bad trips," for some people. But, again the fact of experience alone, whether guided officially by researchers or informally by "guides," overrides the application of a generalized rule about the possible detrimental effects of such drugs.

This courting of raw experience is what gives many people the impression that those participating in the happenings are without any morals whatsoever; that they are selfishly pursuing swift gratification of their impulses. And it is true that the unabashed seeking of experiences will frequently lead the seeker to violate what other people consider proper. But such judgments are one-sided. Although they see that swingers are breaking standards, they entirely miss the point that swingers are following another, different set of standards; so that arguments between the camps are in reality debates between conflicting ideologies.

As part and parcel of the importance placed on directly experiencing oneself and the world, we find that *spontaneity,* the ability to groove with whatever is currently happening, is a highly valued personal trait. Spontaneity enables the person to give himself up to the existential here and now without dragging along poses and hang-ups and without playing investment games in hopes of possible future returns. The purest example of spontaneity is the jazz musician as he stands up and blows a cascade of swinging sounds.

Another facet of the hang-loose ethic is an untutored and unpretentious *tolerance*. Do whatever you want to as long as you don't step on other people while doing it. A girl is free to wet her pants or play with herself openly while she's up on an acid trip and no one will think less of her for it. A man can stand and stare at roadside grass blowing in the wind and no one will accuse him of being the village idiot. If you like something that I don't like, that's fine, that's your bag; just don't bring me down.

The swingers, when you come down to it, are anarchists in the fullest sense. They chafe at virtually all restrictions because they see most every restriction that modern man has devised as a limitation on directions people can travel and grow. They feel that the irony of contemporary society is that the very restrictions necessary to curb an immature populace prevent that same populace from becoming mature enough to live without restrictions, just as a girdle weakens the muscles it supports.

Even clothes are regarded by some as mostly a nuisance and swingers have led the whole Western world toward simplicity and ease in styles and makeup. And over weekends and vacations, small groups will often go up together to back country retreats where whoever wants to can run around naked.

Without the fuss or the self-righteousness so common among Establishment liberals, the happeners have come closer to integrating the races, religions, and the sexes than any other group one can think of. A fierce equality is practiced among them, which is appreciative of differences in backgrounds and temperaments. Equality and tolerance aren't abject attempts to make people feel comfortable or wanted; they are dispositions that permit things and relationships to just happen without deliberate forethought and planning. In most happening circles, a Negro is not the recipient of conscious liberal acceptance, but an individual in and of himself who may or may not be a "good" person. Acceptance and participation is based more on how the individual presents himself within the context of the scene, not by preconceived and nurtured stereotypes about the way he is expected to be.

One's past is not held against one and one's reputation is not spoiled by the fact that one might have served time in a prison or mental institution, had an abortion, or perhaps a homosexual affair.

This doesn't mean that the swingers will indiscriminately associate with anyone. Like everybody else, they choose their friends, their lovers, their acquaintances and the people they avoid by how well they get along with one another and enjoy doing things together. But they are less down on the people they don't choose to associate with than others generally are.

But the tolerance stops if somebody is stepping on other people.

For instance, if a guy shows up in a particular scene and starts tooling around with other people's minds or bum tripping them just for his own kicks, several people are likely to get together and elect themselves to deal with him by busting *his* mind. And such a guy can quickly be shut out of virtually the entire happenings in that specific scene.

The ideal person in the hang-loose view embodies traits that are difficult to combine. Being as spontaneous as a child yet being sophisticated and worldwise; being fully self-expressive yet being always in control of oneself. This is the ambiguity of being cool. Being able to dig the on-going present as it unfolds yet being able to get things done and maintain a competent life of fulfilled commitments and involvements. Being hang-loose from any constraining orthodoxy, yet being courageous enough to follow your own path wherever it may lead and whatever the travails it plunges you into.

The heroes are those who have managed to swing in some eminent way especially if they did so in spite of tough conditions. The distinguished outsiders of history, avant-garde artists, the leaders of unpopular social movements. The list of admirable people would include figures such as Aldous Huxley, Allen Ginsberg, Gandhi, John F. Kennedy, Fidel Castro, Alpert and Leary, and Bob Dylan. But such people are not so much heroes in the ordinary sense because, although they are much admired, they are not so much worshipped, and because they are critically discussed as well as fondly quoted.

The fact that swingers operate at least partly outside the Establishment and often even outside the law produces a certain admiration and sympathy among them for other categories of alienated and disaffiliated people, such as the Negroes, the poor, the mentally disturbed, the delinquent, the sexual deviant, and the peoples of under-developed countries. They do not necessarily approve of what these people do, but they do see them as victims of Establishments.

These sympathies, coupled with their tolerance and opposition to restrictiveness lead the happeners to take a "liberal" stand on almost every question and issue, from welfare measures to disarmament, to the legalization of pot and abortions, to racial integration and civil liberties generally, to recognition of Red China and negotiations with the Viet Cong, to sexual permissiveness and progressive education, to socialized medicine and the exploration of space.

But most of them are not self-conscious "liberals." They take these stands for granted as the only reasonable and sensible ones, but they usually don't work within organized political parties to bring them about and they are not very happy with the compromising Establishment liberals who do. They support such men as Governor Brown, Clark Kerr and Bobby Kennedy only as the best of the poor choices available, all of whom are really more alike than different, and none of whom are really worth a good God damn.

But they are not pro-Communist either, although sympathetic

toward revolutionaries in under-developed countries. They see Communism as at least as odious and repressive as the societies of the West and probably a good deal more so.

The hang-loose people are not joiners; indeed this is one of their defining attributes. They tend to shy away from any kind of conventional ideologies or fanaticisms, seeing them as unfree compulsions and obsessions rather than noble dedications. They regard those who are too intensely and doggedly involved in even such highly approved causes as integration and peace, a little askance and happeners will sometimes describe their own past involvements in these movements as something of a psychological hangup.

The villains in the hang-loose view are people and social forces which put other people down and hang them up, which teach people to be stolid and dignified rather than swinging, self-righteous and moralistic rather than responsible, dutiful rather than devoted. Those who, for the sake of some ideology, will set fire to other peoples' kids; who, for the sake of some ideology, will slap their own children into becoming something less than they might have been. The villains are those who pass their own hangups onto those around them and thus propagate a sickness, "for your own good."

This seems to be the still amorphous and emerging ethos which is the basis of the happenings we're concerned with. Admirable in some ways, perhaps a bit idealistic and innocent and even silly in others, still in the process of forming and changing, and creating many problems for everyone. And perhaps as inevitable, given current conditions, as the spring winds which stir its adherents.

And it is a set of ideals which, like all people, the adherents are not able to live up to. Sometimes when things get uptight, they betray themselves and each other. Sometimes, they can't resist selling out for a better package deal. Sometimes, despite their utterances they can become as provincial and arrogant as any tribesman who thinks he has the monopoly on truth. And sometimes they are driven by other motives to cheat and exploit one another. But such shortcomings are panhuman and can be leveled at any group including the United States Senate or the medical profession. And this should not obscure the fact that ideals are a potent social force which have a major hand in making people what they are. Ideals, aside from having a part in making individual attitudes, attachments and adjustments, also serve to categorize people as runners along certain tracks of life. What is today called deviant is tomorrow only eccentric. What harps upon and tortures the older ethics and ideologies, can eventually become an accepted, if not generally followed, belief system.

Like all ideologies, this ethos is sometimes used as a rationalization and justification. Irresponsibility can be excused as freedom. Apathy can be called being cool. Lack of dependability can be called spontaneity and so can boorishness and sloth. And virtually any behavior can be justified on the grounds that it is experience and will lead in some way to personal growth.

But then pointing out these blindspots may be a pot calling a kettle black for all ideologies are so misused and the misuse doesn't destroy the fact that they are also faithfully followed.

Those following under the banner of the hang-loose ethic are not of one stripe. Sometimes it is the spontaneous pose of a youth who is drunk on his own vaulting life-energy. Sometimes it is the final vision which has resulted from long training in some Eastern philosophy. Sometimes it is the whimsical realization that your hard work has produced a degree of comfort and success but that you're growing older and that things are perhaps just too uncertain to lay too much store upon the alleged joys of the future or the hereafter. Sometimes it is a temporary fling in what will prove to be an otherwise pedestrian life. Sometimes it is a later stage in a journey which has led a youth through romantic idealism, folksong clubs and science fiction, protest movements, a period of disenchantment, wandering, and psychedelic drugs while still in his teens. And sometimes it is the stony and even vicious hipsterism of the slum ghetto.

The hang-loose attitude is simply not a uniform thing. One can hang-loose happily or bitterly, stoicly or desperately, wisely or floundering, as a posing actor or as a blithe spirit. Sometimes it is mixed with defiance; sometimes loving tolerance; and sometimes it embodies an indifference which smacks of callous unconcern for the fate of others. And sometimes it is tinged with the pathos of the feeling that in another, better world things would be different.

This ethos will have a somewhat different flavor in different groups and in different regions of the country. On the Eastern seaboard, it is likely to be more cosmopolitan and European in temperament. In the midwest it is more likely to be a reaction to the stolid Dirksonesque environment. In the South, it tends to combine the effete with the rustic. And in the West it is likely to be more gaudy and mystical. Among students it tends to be more self-reflective and among dropouts it tends to be more starkly hedonistic. Among the lower classes it tends to be a proletarian disaffiliation, among the middle and upper classes it tends to combine the *Playboy* hipsterism with psychoanalytic self-realization. Among teenagers it is likely to be the following of fads, among youth it is more likely to be a search for meanings and recipes, among adults it is likely to be more cautious and more straight, and among older people it is likely to be hobbies and vitriolic conversations in the sun.

Among Negroes, Mexicans and Puerto Ricans it will tend to be more angry and physical and immediate, among whites it will probably be more sedentary and compromising and tolerant because it is more their society. Among Catholics it will involve "soul trouble"; among Protestants, a Nietzschean debate over whether God is dead;

among Jews, an agnostic urbanity; and among the uncommitted, a search for alternative faiths.

In the urban slums it is explosive and a source of constant potential violence. Among middle class youth it is a source of scandals, a recruiting ground for protests of all kinds, and a susceptibility toward the milder, unharmful forms of deviance, and personal problems. And among suburban adults it is a careful but sometimes determined minority voice within the Establishment, and an "aw, come on!" ambivalence toward the Great Society bit.

American suburbs aren't the places of otherdirected conformity as Whyte and Reisman depicted them in the fifties. Perhaps they never altogether were. But the stereotype of the jovial empty-spirited organization man which may have had a good deal of truth a decade ago, now fits only a plurality at most—and a plurality that is no longer in the center of things, but off to the side as a disinherited conservatism.

In today's suburbs one finds a widespread diffidence toward job, background, and other external tags and badges. People are unwilling to think of themselves or others as merely the sum of their statuses and nothing more. A few years ago you might ask "what do you do?"; be answered, "I'm an accountant"; and say, "Oh, that's nice." But now you'd say, "Well, yes, but what do you do, who are you?"

Fromm's classic thesis that contemporary people are only using their freedom from the chains of tradition to package and sell their external selves until the package becomes the person and there's nothing left but a gaudy shell, is no longer so true either. In almost any neighborhood gathering, one can find plenty of evidence for a growing disaffection with external symbols (which were the main unit of currency in the heyday of the Sociable Ethic). Expressions of a certain distance from one's job and other positions and a conspiratorial show of fellow humanness have in fact become the newest gambit in advertising, salesmanship and interpersonal relations generally.

There is of course a good deal of the older ideologies still around and certain facets of them still ring faintly even among the most far out followers of the hang-loose view. Among those followers who are working within the Establishment there is still moderate disapproval of doing things just for kicks. Swinging should be "constructive," either by refreshing you so that you can return zestfully to the playful fray of your workaday world, or by helping you resolve psychoanalytic hangups so that you can move on to the next stage of growth.

And with a bit of pendulum swinging from the gregarious outwardness of the Sociable Ethic to the fierce individualism of our puritan predecessors, the current swingers in schools and suburbs are less concerned with courting the offhand opinions and tepid acceptance of the crowds they encounter. They are not immune to the smiles and frowns of others, especially people they like, but they are not enslaved by them either, and much of the time they groove along with an inner-directedness that would delight Reisman.

There is also an appreciation of affluence as with the Sociable Ethic, and in fairly sharp distinction to the self-conscious poverty of most of the Beats during the fifties. But this is more of a taken-for-granted that the world is full of material baubles which can be very useful, than a deliberate striving to accumulate them. The current swingers take national affluence for granted and only strive to have it distributed more widely and with less necessity of selling oneself to get a part of it.

The modern happeners like many of the things which our shopping-center society produces in so great a quantity, such as cars and clothes and stereos and prints and books, and they do not share the anti-television stance of the intellectuals during the last decade. But they don't want to struggle too hard to get them and they will freely loan and borrow them. So this shared appreciation of affluence shouldn't lead us to neglect what is now so different—namely that swingers have broken away from the high valuation of property which has been the cornerstone of every Western society since the Reformation and the rise of the middle classes. Property is not something designed to dominate an individual's life; it is something to be lived with and used, not as a focus of existence, but as incidental to the fact that humans are alive and dynamic. A young man, who like many others is only involved in some of the happening scenes, once commented, "do you realize that legally we can kill for the sake of property? What gives us the right to say that if a burglar is stealing a damned TV set we can go ahead and blow his brains out. Property, not human life, has become the most sacred thing in our society."

Along with the repudiation of property as something to work and live for, the hang-loose people feel less honor bound to fulfill commitments unless they are coupled with personal involvements and attachments. This makes them less dependable workers and spouses, and their lack of steadfastness creates part of their bad reputation in a society which still harkens to the Calvinist idea of duty. But swingers will not discharge their duties as students, workers, lovers, or citizens just because someone else says they *should*. "Should" isn't good enough unless it is coupled with "want to," stemming either from personal desire or personal convictions. Concretely, this means that they will break a law they disagree with, will desert a spouse or friend they no longer love, will cheat on a test they feel is unjust, will walk off a job they find odious, and will speak against a war they feel is dishonorable. The swingers will, because of expediency, often cool if by fulfilling obligations they do not feel personally bound to, but if they don't have to, they frequently won't.

Hence, an obvious strategy for those in the opposition wishing the demise of happening scenes and their tangential attributes, would involve making these people "want to" do something or discharge some particular responsibility. Sadly it is too infrequently recognized that unless those with the hang-loose philosophy are, at a minimum, tolerated, little progress in the above direction can be made. You can't call somebody a lunatic, beatnik, dope addict, or radical and expect them to jump to your beck and call. Regardless of how much reason and substance are part of the opposition doctrines, they will get nowhere until debate goes beyond mutual debasement and vilification.

In the hang-loose view, the main problems besides hassles with the Establishment and its blue-frocked representatives, are the personal hang-ups which prevent people from living as fully and spontaneously as they otherwise might. This is a more general and extreme form of the ideals of individualism, self-determination and self-realization which have been kicking around Western Civilization for several centuries and which have been such a prominent part of psychoanalysis. These ideals, when carried to their logical extreme by the swingers, however, put them in opposition to a good many of the rules and practices of the Establishment, which, like societies everywhere grants personal freedom only within limits and which labels those who go beyond these limits, deviant.

And this is the dilemma of the swinger. In the very process of attempting to resolve his hang-ups, he will usually move further outside the pale of conventional society and will become more deviant, immoral and dangerous in the eyes of the general populace.

Happeners are aware of this dilemma and spend long hours talking with each other about how it might be resolved. An individual solution is to become exceedingly cool—to develop the skills and habits to swing yet evade the eye of the Establishment by being discreet and by being able to play straight when necessary.

But this is only a makeshift solution, temporary and high in personal cost. The longterm solution almost all swingers agree is to turn the world on. Their dream is to live in a world of beautiful people in which everyone grooves on their own things and doesn't interfere with anyone else in doing it. Where people will say "no" only because they want to and not because of fear or tie-ups. Where people don't make it their business to screw each other up over some decrepit dogma. Where children aren't stunted by "education" and "training" into growing up absurd, sad caricatures of their possible selves. Where people are free enough and fearless enough to grow their own trees.

If you think this dream is a little naive and foolish and fantastic, you are right. If you think it neglects and glosses over many of the realities of present world conditions and that it is a bit pretentious and unlikely, given the facts of history, you are right again. And if you find nothing good or true or beautiful about it, you can go to hell.

There is a storm of violent opposition to the hang-loose ethos and the behavior that stems from it. This storm of opposition seems to be of two kinds, and the first kind is moral.

A good many people feel that those participating in the happenings are morally depraved. Bratty overgrown kids crying for the freedom to play with each other underneath the streetlights. Arrogant but innocent youngsters who think they know more than they do and who are easy prey for dope peddlers, sexual perverts, and Communist agitators. A few more rapped knuckles, stiffer curfews and supervision, a few more jail sentences to set examples, and a stint in the army might make men (and women) out of them. But right now they're spoiled, oversexed, smart aleck brats who aren't worth their pay on a job of work and who are unfit to inherit our great country.

In the rush of controversy and opposition to what's happening, the swingers become *objects* for explanation, condescending sympathy, or condemnation. But because the happeners don't themselves own or have much access to communication channels for reaching the general public, the fact that they are active *subjects* who are in turn evaluating their evaluators is lost sight of. So their turnabout indictments seldom reach the ears of the general public, although they are widely circulated and discussed among the swingers themselves. When they are quoted by officials or the mass media, it is usually only to illustrate their alienation, willfulness, or delinquency. The quotes are treated only as graphic evidence of their sickness and depravity. Attempts, for example to legalize the use of marijuana receive the sarcastic and superior attention of smiling commentators on the 11 o'clock news. But, for those even partially involved in the drug world such activity is serious business that is a frequent subject of conversation, if not direct action. Although they might discuss it with a measure of frivolity, fearful of taking themselves *too* seriously, marijuana legalization has become a meaningful aspect of personal commitment and not some deviant's practical joke.

Parents and other concerned adults are discussing and fretting over what is becoming of today's youth and turning to each other, to experts (usually self-proclaimed) and to their officials for advice.

And youth are discussing and fretting over their elders and they turn to each other and to those rare experts and officials who are in any sense "where it's at" for advice. Restless and uncertain they are; unsure of themselves, of their beliefs, and of their futures. But they are more self-assured in their feelings that parents and mentors, neighbors and newscasters, officials and Presidents of the United States cannot be taken at face-value. They suspect—dimly or consciously—that their elders are not altogether honest, wise or competent to run the world and give advice, though many sincerely wish they were.

To the widespread charges that they are being immoral, irresponsible, and irreverent, they turn about and reply: "Look at you, blowing up whole countries for the sake of some crazy ideologies that you

don't live up to anyway. Look at you, mindfucking a whole generation of kids into getting a revolving charge account and buying your
junk. (Who's a junkie?) Look at you, needing a couple of stiff drinks
before you have the balls to talk with another human being. Look at
you, making it with your neighbor's wife on the sly just to try and
prove that you're really alive. Look at you, hooked on *your* cafeteria
of pills, and making up dirty names for anybody who isn't in your
bag, and screwing up the land and the water and the air for profit,
and calling this nowhere scene the Great Society! *And you're gonna
tell us how to live?* C'mon, man, you've got to be kidding!"

(This collage was made from a multitude of remarks dropped in a
wide variety of different scenes. The remarks were usually reactions
to specific events such as McNamara's proposal to draft the world or
Reagan's promises of suppression, Dirkson's Biblical pronouncements
or the sentencing of a youth for smoking a casual weekend joint.
Ill-will is more of a temporary reaction than an intrinsic attitude
among happeners.)

And the oldsters in their turn reply: "Well what are you doing
that's so meaningful? Aren't you maybe on a hundred roads to
nowhere too?" And the host of individual debates that go to make
up the Great Debate continue all over our country.

The other kind of opposition is a practical concern. Who's going to
be left to run the world if everybody turns on? This question bothers
many people who are otherwise not so concerned about the morality
or immorality of what's happening. They fear that nobody will be
left to mind the store, to do those thousand-and-one routine but
necessary things that keep society's wheels turning, her goods flowing
and her children growing. Who will hold the world together?

Maybe nobody will hold the *present* world together. Who wants to?
How much of it do we really need? How many of our proud items
are only consolation prizes? Maybe a newer social order could evolve
in which we would have the real things that we talk about on rainy
nights but never quite seem to achieve?

The worry that the present social order cannot continue unless the
happenings are checked is counter-balanced by the worry among
happeners that the present social order may well persist in spite of
their wishes and efforts to change things, and that the current social
order at the worst may destroy the world in a thermo-nuclear light
that would dim any prospect of an enlightened future. Here we find
a true opposition and conflict between those who want to preserve
the present moral order and those who wish to transform it.

Many among the older cohort worry whether today's youth are
training and preparing themselves for the adult roles they are soon to
occupy. This worry contains some validity, for many swingers are
pretty unimpressive even judged in terms of their own values and
ideals. A three year collection of *Wonder Woman* comics is perhaps
trippy but it doesn't make the world a cleaner, greener land.

But the worry is also ethnocentric and historically arrogant because the young needn't accept or strive to fill adult roles as the oldsters choose to define them—and it might even be best if they didn't. On this issue youth *is* rebellious as it tries to revamp the more traditional conceptions of a "man," a "woman," a "career," a "citizen," a "human being." In their uncertain experimentations some swingers are probably stumbling toward what will prove to be more realistic and effective roles which may better fit the upcoming times.

Perhaps the most curious irony about the hang-loose ethic is that it is distilled from many of the highest ideals of Western man and our national heritage, carried out to their logical conclusion. America, is now, in a sense, confronted by a legion of youths who are trying in their own fumbling way to practice what generations of fatuous graduation speakers have been preaching. This emerging ethos which seems so heretical at first glance is partly a restatement of some of the highest ideals and values which the great middle classes struggled for during the Industrial Revolution and which have since served all-too-often as a covering rationalization for self-seeking exploitation; the ideals we learn to bend and compromise in the process of "growing up" and "learning the ropes" and becoming "mature." The irony is not that Americans have failed to teach the upcoming generation but that they have been perhaps too successful in their training and must now confront their fervent pupils.

THE NANTERRE MANIFESTO—JUNE 11, 1968

(Translated from the French by Peter Brooks)

Henceforth social reality and the University's function in relation to it shall be the object of permanent criticism and questioning. To the limit of our possibilities, we will have to subvert the whole academic institution from the functions assigned to it by the ruling class and by our deepest repressions, to make of it a place where we can

Translator's Note: The "May Revolution" in France was first of all, and perhaps most lastingly, a revolution of the word. With the proliferation of flamboyant tracts composed, mimeographed and distributed almost instantaneously, with the stark and beautiful posters of the *atelier populaire* of Beaux-Arts, perhaps most of all with the graffiti that appeared on walls everywhere to give voice to the individual's participation in the new order of things, the students achieved a redistribution of the power of the word, and of the word as power. They seized and exercised a language which had belonged to the "others," to the forces of alienation, to the government, to official sources of information, to propaganda and advertising, gave it a new vitality and originality, and made it serve imagination in power.

elaborate the means of a critical understanding and expression of reality. The return to classes in 1968 at Nanterre will not be a return to normal, the normal being cultural oppression. Our task is not simply to make the Faculty run: for whom? to what ends? etc. It is rather to criticize and deconstruct the institution, to determine the orientation that we wish to give to our work, to determine a program for this work and to realize it.

I. MAY 1968

1) The crisis begun in May, 1968, is not a "crisis": through it, we enter into a new period of history. What has been aimed at and shaken, through criticism and through struggle, is not only the political regime, but the social system; and not only capitalist private property, but the entire organization of life, all the "values" that modern societies, whether of the West or the East, use or fabricate, impose or insinuate, to disarm desire. You have understood nothing about our movement if you do not see this: what swept across France—to the point of creating a power vacuum—was not the spirit of professional demands, nor the wish for a political change, but the desire for other relations among men. The force of this desire has shaken the edifice of exploitation, oppression and alienation; it has frightened all the men, the organizations, the parties directly or indirectly interested in the exercise of power, and they are attempting by all means to suppress it. They will never have done with doing so.

2) The political oppression of the citizen, the socioeconomic exploitation of labor, have been denounced in word and act. But the movement has attacked cultural alienation with the same vigor. Thus it has brought the revolutionary critique into the whole of the sphere to which the modern ruling classes have extended their empire. Within the University, this critique has been directed above and beyond the old hierarchical relations, to the exteriority of knowledge in relation to life, its connivance with power; within society, to the monopoly of knowledge by one social class, to the mercantilization and deproblematization of the information distributed to the other

When, in the occupied Faculties, the "paritary committees"—the soviets of students and teachers—sat down to transform the movement of revolt into the constitution of a new University, this revolution of the word informed their efforts, determined content and style. The committee reports were to be the first texts in a Cultural Revolution which would end repression, in both the Marxist and Freudian senses. One of the most remarkable of these reports was that produced by the "Interdisciplinary Committee" of the Faculty of Letters and Social Sciences of Nanterre, where the "movement" first began. Translated here is the general preamble, which was followed by reports in the specific areas of "Culture and Critique," "Structure and Organization of the Faculty," "Form and Content of Teaching."

classes, to the proffering of cultural objects favoring only those identifications willed by the ruling powers, to the exclusion of the working classes from the means of understanding and expression. What the movement wishes to destroy is the separation between culture and social experience (the division between intellectual and manual labor); and also the separation between decision and practice (the division between managers and executors); and finally the defamation and recuperation of creative force.

3) Our critique is not merely verbal, it is criticism-as-practice: the offensive blockage of the academic institution and its subversion to revolutionary ends, physical combat against so-called order, transgressions. By its forms of struggle, the movement makes manifest the weakness of the overall system. It breathes new life into the workers' struggle, which had been channeled and absorbed into the verbal and legal forms of protest that the system imposed on it. To the continuous violence of oppression in the factories, in the pursuit of leisure, in the family, in the establishments called "educational," the movement opposes liberty to speak from equal to equal, ridicule of all hierarchy, courage to pose all questions, destruction of forced solitude, dialogue and initiative. Our violence consists in reestablishing the word and the expressive gesture, for the violence that opposes us sets up reflections. That we are judged for our violence is simply droll.

4) The radical and practical nature of our critique calls forth an echo from among the workers, especially the young workers. Questioning begins to come out from the university ghetto; the critique of cultural alienation begins to merge with the critique of socioeconomic exploitation and political oppression. An embryonic union of the workers' and students' struggles is formed. It is weak in the face of the enemy to be overthrown; it is formidable if one compares it to the isolation and despair which presided over the class struggle before May, 1968.

5) The future of the revolution under way depends entirely on the reinforcement of the union of students and workers. The students bring to the struggle their denunciation of culture and values; isolated, their critique would be recuperated by the system, for nothing prevents the ruling classes from entertaining themselves with the spectacle of the cultural revolution. The workers contribute their experience and their denunciation of exploitation; isolated, and in the absence of a revolutionary sector, their struggle loses its dimension of global questioning, and remains confined to professional demands. In modern society, where technical progress increases the importance of intellectual labor, the student is no longer a young bohemian bourgeois, he is a fraction in training of the social forces of production. That is why his desertion from the camp of the ruling class can take on decisive importance.

6) If it is to achieve this union, the movement must not let itself be intimidated by defamation, wherever it may come from, especially

must not let itself be disarmed from within by self-censorship. That we are called provocateurs and adventurers[1] would not merit a second's attention did the insult not mask a dangerous attempt to cut the student movement off from the worker movement, and to maintain the latter within the social order and established politics. We must counterattack by consolidating our union with the workers on the basis of a critique of this "order" in its entirety. But this union is not a subordination, either of workers to students or students to workers. The student movement has brought to the revolution a dimension that the workers movement, such as it is today, had lost. The student movement is far more than a detonator in the class struggle; it is a constituent element in theory and practice. For the real problem posed by modern societies is no longer simply that of the suppression of the boss as the owner of capital, but that of the separation between those who give directives and those who carry them out. By placing this problem in the foreground, the student movement has shown that this point of the revolutionary program, representing the most radical content of socialism, is the only valid reply to the contradictions of modern societies.

II. THE FACULTY

1) The Faculty is not an independent institution consecrated to the elaboration and transmission of a knowledge for its own sake. A society like ours, which can subsist only by striving ceaselessly for the complete integration of all its functions, cannot maintain within itself a zone of free knowledge and free expression. The Faculty is at the center of two grand operations directed at the means of understanding and expression: their defusing and their recuperation. Their defusing is the Faculty of Dead Letters; their recuperation, the Faculty of Human Relations. In the first case, intelligence and inventiveness are subverted from practice toward fetishism of the finished work, of the past, of what is established; in the second case, these qualities are employed to condition the work force, to increase its efficiency. Defusing creates erudition, recuperation expertise. All the imagination of which the ruling class is capable can go no further than this: to arrange for the Faculty to produce experts rather than esthetes. . . .

2) Not only are the means of understanding and expression reserved to a few; *by this very fact* they cease to be means of

[1]The reference is to the French Communist Party (and the Communist-led trade unions) which originally denounced the student activists as a *groupuscle* of provocateurs and adventurers, and throughout the May crisis maneuvered to foil any revolutionary union of students and workers outside Party structures, to preserve intact the traditional policy of "no enemies to the Left" and to maintain its claim to be the exclusive spokesman of the proletariat. Daniel Cohn-Bendit in turn denounced the Party as a bunch of "Stalinist slobs."

comprehension and creation, they become a culture which is separated, barricaded behind pure enjoyment or efficiency, denatured. It is a fact that expression and understanding are most often doomed to find their field of development outside the University. It would be vain to democratize admission to the University if the alienation of the spirit which reigns within its walls were to remain intact. The Faculty must become the smithy of tools and works.

3) The University will not indeed be revolutionary; all that we do and will do can always be recuperated by the ruling powers so long as the whole of society has not been reconstructed. Yet the task to be accomplished within the Faculty is not vulgarly reformist. We must impose institutions and modes of teaching and research that permit critical understanding of reality in all its forms and liberation of the power of expression. We must not let the reform be made by the existing powers and their allies, middle-of-the-road students and teachers: they would not accomplish anything at all, and by their failure we would once again be faced with the preexisting University conditions. Between the critique of a University judged wrong because it is *unadapted* to the demands of modern capitalism and the critique of a University which would be wrong precisely because *adapted* to these demands, the distinction would not always be made, and the revolutionary critique would become confused with reformism. The movement would be led to close itself off within the University, instead of fighting side by side with the workers. Essentially, it would be recuperated.

4) In attacking not only political oppression and socioeconomic exploitation, but also cultural alienation, the movement has revealed this: that repression is not only a question of police clubs or electoral trickery, nor even exclusively a question of pressures on salaries and work outputs, but that it permeates the content and forms of culture, what the ruling class diffuses through television, press, vacation clubs, organized tours, films, periodicals, as well as university culture. In particular, it appears that repressive systems operate at the heart of the cultural relationship (in the first examples above: distributor/cultural product/consumer; in the last: teachers/knowledge/students)—systems which are more primitive and basic than those of class society, and which nourish the newer forms of repression. The drama of desire and its repression, anxiety and the reflexive search for security—here is the silent mechanism which the managerial classes play upon more and more openly to maintain their domination, and here is the level to which our critique must pierce in order to be true. The truth is what transforms; it alone is revolutionary; with it alone there can be no compromise. We must try to be the wound of truth in the side of alienation.

5) We must keep open and available to the critical consciousness, the pedagogical triangle in its fullness.[2] The dynamic between teacher

[2] On this conception of the relation between teacher and taught, and the relation of both to knowledge, see Paul Ricoeur, "Réforme et révolution

and taught must be permanently preserved from retrogression into the old hierarchical relation of master and disciple, and from the demagogy of a symmetry between teacher and taught, or the transformation of the former into a simple expert-counselor. Knowledge must also ceaselessly be rescued from falling into the status of a thing known; its compartmentalization (in departments or fields of specialization within the Faculty, for example) must be thrown into question; its ultimate goal must be under constant suspicion. In this society, knowledge is ever compromised by power.

6) May those who fear the "politicization" of instruction and wish for "serious work" to be possible in this Faculty be entirely reassured: we too fear the politicization of the University by Fouchet or Ortoli, we too want to pursue true work, that is, the work of the truth. We have no catechism to make others recite, no dogma to insinuate, no conviction to suggest. We desire that in all the seminars, workshops, committees of this Faculty be raised and debated the questions which are posed to Humanity.

THE NEW RADICALS IN THE MULTIVERSITY

AN ANALYSIS AND STRATEGY FOR THE STUDENT MOVEMENT

Carl Davidson

INTRODUCTION

The student movement has come under criticism from both the right and the left for its lack of a coherent ideology and strategy for social change. While there is certainly a great deal of truth in this criticism, my sensibilities tell me that this lack may be more to our advantage than to our disadvantage. To my mind, the great strength of the New Left has been its unconscious adherence to Marx's favourite motto—doubt everything. The student movement is young and inexperienced; yet, it has shown great wisdom in maintaining the principle that political truth must come from political experience. Ideology is not something sucked out of thumbs, nor found in this or that set of political catechisms. Rather, political analysis and strategy is something that grows slowly out of years of political experience and struggle. It must find its beginnings and maintain its deepest roots in

dans l'université," which originally appeared in *Le Monde* in early June and has been reprinted in *Esprit*, No. 6-7 (June-July, 1968). Ricoeur is Professor of Philosophy at Nanterre.

people's day-to-day life-activity, for it is social reality that we are trying to understand and change.

In deepening that understanding of social reality, we must always remember that "The dispute over the reality or non-reality of thinking that is isolated from practice is a purely *scholastic* question."[1] Too often we are bogged down in theoretical disputes when the only way we can answer those questions is in *practice*, in political experimentation, in action. This is why we must remain open on many political questions. But this is not to say that we should only "do what the spirit say do." The concept of practical-critical activity (i.e. praxis) is three-sided: we must *act*, then *reflect* on the activity, and finally *criticize* the activity. The process of action, reflection, and criticism must be repeated again and again. The body of knowledge, ever changing and expanding, that grows from this process emerges as an ideology. Finally, the process is historical; it develops over a period of time.

It is for these reasons, as well as the fact that we are young and politically inexperienced, that we must emphasize an ongoing *practical-critical activity* over and above any allegiance to theoretical certitude. I hope that my following remarks on theory, strategy, and tactics will be taken in this context. All my assertions come from a limited experience; and, as such, are open to criticism, revision, and the acid-test of political practice.

PART 1

THE PRESENT MALAISE OF EDUCATION

"Happiness Is Student Power" was the most catching slogan emblazoned on the many banners and picket signs during the Berkeley Student Strike in December, 1966. But, as most college administrators know only too well, Berkeley and its rebellious student body is not an isolated phenomenon among the vast variety of American campuses. Far from being an exception, Berkeley has become the paradigm case of the educational malaise in the United States; and, in the last few years, that malaise has been transformed into a movement. Indeed a spectre is haunting our universities—the spectre of a radical and militant nationally co-ordinated movement for *student power*.

Students began using the slogan "student power" soon after black people in the civil rights movement made the demand for "black power." Are students niggers? After studying the history of the Wobblies and labour syndicalism, students started thinking about student syndicalism. Are students workers? Power for what? Just any old kind of power? The university is a clumsy and uncoordinated

[1] Marx: *Theses on Feuerbach*.

machine, engulfing and serving thousands of people. Do students want to be administrators?

Obviously the cry for "power" in and of itself is a vacuous demand. Student power is not so much something we are fighting *for*, as it is something we must have in order to gain specific objectives. Then what are the objectives? What is our program? There is much variety and dispute on these questions. But there is one thing that seems clear. However the specific forms of our immediate demands and programs may vary, the long-range goal and the daily drive that motivates and directs us is our intense longing for our liberation. In short, what the student power movement is about: *freedom.*

But aren't students free? Isn't America a democracy, even if it is a little manipulative? To answer those kinds of questions and many others that are more serious, it is important to look more closely and come to an understanding of the malaise motivating the movement.

What do American students think of the educational institutions in which they live an important part of their lives? The most significant fact is that most of them don't think about them. Such young men and women made up that apathetic majority we called the "beat generation" in the 1950's. While the last few years has shown a marked and dramatic growth of a new radicalism, we should not forget that the apathetic and the cynical among the student population are still in the majority. But this need not be discouraging. In fact, we should view that apparent apathy among the majority of students with a certain qualified optimism.

What makes people apathetic? My feeling is that apathy is the *unconscious* recognition students make of the fact that they are *powerless.* Despite all the machinations and rhetoric used by hot-shot student politicos within administration-sponsored student governments, people's experience tells them that nothing changes. Furthermore, if and when change does occur, students fully recognize that they were powerless to effect those changes in one way or another. If this is in fact the case, then why shouldn't students be apathetic? The administration rules, despite the facade of student governments, of dorm councils, and of student judicials. And when *they* give us ex-officio seats on *their* academic committees, the result among most students is that deeper, more hardened kind of apathy—cynicism.

The apathetic students are correct *as far as they go.* They are powerless. The forms given us for our self-government are of the Mickey Mouse, sand-box variety. I would only be pessimistic if a majority of students really accepted the illusion that those institutions had meaning in their lives, or that they could significantly alter those institutions. But the opposite is the case. The apathy reflects the *reality* of their powerlessness. When that reality confronts the lie of the official rhetoric, the contradiction is driven home—then the apathetic become the cynical. What that contradiction—the daily living with a lie—all adds up to is a *dynamic* tension and alienation.

And that, fellow organizers, is the necessary subjective condition for any revolution.

It is important to understand that students are alienated from much more than the social and extracurricular aspect of their education. In fact, their deepest alienation is directed at the education process itself. The excerpts that follow are from a letter written to the New York Times by a young woman student:

I came to this school not thinking I could even keep up with the work. I was wrong. I can keep up. I can even come out on top. My daily schedule's rough. I get up at 6:30.... After dinner I work until midnight or 12:30. In the beginning, the first few weeks or so, I'm fine. Then I begin to wonder just what this is all about: am I educating myself? I have that one answered ... I'm educating myself the way *they* want. So I convince myself the real reason I'm doing all this is to prepare myself; meantime I'm wasting those years of preparation. I'm not learning what I want to learn ... I don't care about the feudal system. I want to know about life. I want to think and read. When? ... My life is a whirlpool. I'm caught up in it, but I'm not conscious of it. I'm what *you* call living, but somehow I can't find life ... So maybe I got an A ... but when I get it back I find that A means nothing. It's a letter *you* use to keep me going ... I wonder what I'm doing here. I feel phony. I don't belong ... You wonder about juvenile delinquents. If I ever become one, I'll tell why it will be so. I feel cramped. I feel like I'm in a coffin and can't move or breathe ... My life is worth nothing. It's enclosed in a few buildings on a campus; it goes no further. I've got to bust.[2]

Tell the truth. Every American student knows that's the way it is. Even our administrators recognize what is going on. In 1962, a year or so *before* the first Berkeley insurrection, Clark Kerr emphasized, "...the undergraduate students are restless. Recent changes in the American university have done them little good ... There is an incipient revolt ..."[3] Kerr is not only concerned about the students. He also casts a worried glance at the faculty. "Knowledge is now in so many bits and pieces and administration so distant that faculty members are increasingly figures in a 'lonely crowd,' intellectually and institutionally."[4] The academic division of labour and depersonalization among the faculty is more than apparent to the students. Incoming freshmen scratch their heads, trying to understand *any* possible relevance of many of the courses in the catalogue, some of which they are required to take. Also, some of the best belly-laughs are had by reading the titles of master's and doctoral theses, like one granted a Ph.Ed. at Michigan State University: "An Evaluation of Thirteen Brands of Football Helmets on the Basis of Certain Impact Measures."[5] What's worse, even if a course seems as though it might be relevant to our lives, like Psychology or Political Science, we are

[2]*New York Times*, November 29, 1964.
[3]Kerr, Clark: *Uses of the University*, p. 103.
[4]Ibid, p. 101.
[5]Baran and Sweezy: *Monopoly Capital*.

soon told by our prof that what we'll learn only has to do with the laboratory behavior of rats, and that "political science" has nothing to do with day-to-day politics. A student from Brandeis sums it up nicely, "By the time we graduate, we have been painstakingly trained in separating facts from their meaning . . . No wonder that our classes, with few exceptions, seem irrelevant to our lives. No wonder they're so boring. Boredom is the necessary condition of any education which teaches us to manipulate the facts and suppress their meaning."[6] Irrelevancy, meaninglessness, boredom, and fragmentation are the kinds of attributes that are becoming more and more applicable to mass education in America. We are becoming a people required to know more and more about less and less. This is true not only for our students, but also for our teachers; not only in our universities, but also in our secondary and primary schools—private as well as public.

What should education be about in America? The official rhetoric seems to offer an answer: education should be the process of developing the free, autonomous, creative and responsible *individual*—the "citizen," in the best sense of that word. Furthermore, higher education ought to encourage and enable the individual to turn his personal concerns into social issues, open to rational consideration and solution. C. Wright Mills put it clearly: "The aim of the college, for the individual student, is to eliminate the need in his life for the college; the task is to help him become a self-educating man. For only that will set him free."[7]

But what is the reality of American education? Contrary to our commitment to individualism, we find that the day-to-day practice of our schools is authoritarian, conformist, and almost entirely status oriented. We find the usual relationship between teacher and student to be a disciplined form of dominance and subordination. We are told of the egalitarianism inherent in our school system, where the classroom becomes the melting-pot for the classless society of America's "people's capitalism," where everyone has the opportunity to climb to the top. Again, the opposite is the case. Our schools are more racially segregated now (1967) than ever before. There is a clear class bias contained both within and among the public schools—not even considering the clear class nature of the private schools and colleges. Within the secondary schools, students are quickly channelled—usually according to the class background of their parents—into vocational, commercial, or academic preparatory programs. Concerning the class differences among our public schools, James Conant remarks in *Slums and Suburbs*, ". . .I cannot imagine the possibility of a wealthy suburban district deliberately consolidating with other districts to achieve a truly comprehensive high school in which students of all abilities and socio-economic backgrounds will study together."[8]

[6] Golin, Steve: *New Left Notes*, October 7, 1966, p. 3.
[7] Mills, C. Wright: *Power, Politics and People*, p. 368.
[8] Conant, James: *Slums and Suburbs*, p. 77.

Even if they did consolidate the problem would only be rationalized, rather than solved. Who knows? Maybe the class struggle would break out on the playground.

Finally, what about that traditional American ideal that we were all taught to honour—the legend of the self-educated and self educating man? It seems to me that rather than enabling an individual to initiate and engage himself in a continual and coherent life-long educational process, our public programs are the sort where an individual is merely subjected to a random series of isolated training situations.

From individual freedom to national service, from egalitarianism to class and racial hierarchical ossification, from self-reliance to institutional dependence—we have come to see education as the mechanistic process of homogeneous, uncritical absorption of "data" and development of job skills. But it is something more than that. The socialization and acculturation that goes on within American educational institutions is becoming increasingly central in the attempts to mold and shape American youth. This is mainly the result of the declining influence and, in some cases, the collapse of other traditional socializing institutions such as the church and the family. The schools, at all levels, end up with the job of maintaining, modifying, and transmitting the dominant themes of the national culture.

Quantitatively education has been rapidly increasing in the last few decades; but, as it grows in size, it decreases *qualitatively*. Rickover states in *Education and Freedom*: "We end up where we began a hundred years ago—with an elementary vocational education for the majority, and a poor college preparatory course for a minority of students."[9] Conant, who is quite concerned with the plight of the 80-85% of urban non-college bound high school students who are "social dynamite," places as a primary goal of education, giving these students "...the kind of zeal and dedication ... to withstand the relentless pressures of communism."[10]

What about our school teachers? How is the nation faring on that front? Over 30% of the students in U.S. colleges and universities are going into primary and secondary education. However, despite the quantity, Mortimer Smith remarks in *The Diminished Mind*, "...the teacher-training institutions ... are providing us with teachers who are our most poorly educated citizens."[11] While the job of teacher should command the highest respect in any society, many of us are well aware of the fact that in relation to other parts of the university, the college or school of education is considered to be the intellectual slum of the campus.

[9] Rickover, Hyman: *Education and Freedom*, p. 145.
[10] Conant, James: *Slums and Suburbs*, p. 34.
[11] Smith, Mortimer: *The Diminished Mind*, p. 87.

It seems clear that bourgeois education in the U.S. is in its historically most irrational and decadent state. Primary, secondary, and university systems are fusing together, thoroughly rationalizing and dehumanizing their internal order, and placing themselves in the service of the state, industry, and the military. Kerr is quite clear about this when he speaks of the "multiversity" making a common-law marriage with the federal government. John Hannah, president of Michigan State, was even more clear in a speech given in September, 1961, "Our colleges and universities must be regarded as bastions of our defence, as essential to the preservation of our country and our way of life as super-sonic bombers, nuclear powered submarines and intercontinental ballistics missiles."[12] The fact that none of the three weapons systems Hannah mentioned could have been designed, constructed, or operated without college-educated men proves that this is not just Fourth of July rhetoric. Hannah gives us an even better look at his idea of education in an article entitled, "The Schools Responsibility in National Defense," where he comments: "I believe the primary and secondary schools can make education serve the individual and national interest by preparing youngsters for military service and life under conditions of stress as well as preparing them for college, or for a job or profession . . . I would not even shrink from putting the word 'indoctrination' to the kind of education I have in mind. If we do not hesitate to indoctrinate our children with a love of truth, a love of home, and a love of God, then I see no justification for balking at teaching them love of country and love of what this country means."[13]

. . .

Despite the crass attitudes of so many of our educators, or the dehumanization of the form and content of our educational institutions, it would be a mistake to think the problems are only within the educational system. While is it true that education has been stripped of any meaning it once had, and Dr. Conant is reduced to defining education as ". . . what goes on in schools and colleges,"[14] yet our system of schools and colleges are far from a point of collapse. In fact, they are thriving. The "knowledge industry," as Kerr puts it, accounts for 30% of the Gross National Product; and, it is expanding at *twice* the rate of any sector of the economy. School teachers make up the largest single occupational group of the labor force—some 3 million workers.

[12] Hannah, John: Speech given at Parents' Convocation at Michigan State University, September, 1961.
[13] Hannah, John: "The Schools' Responsibility in National Defense", May 5, 1955, quoted in *The Paper*, November 17, 1966, p. 1.
[14] Conant, James: Bulletin of the Council for Basic Education, January, 1960, p. 3.

Twenty-five years ago, the government and industry were hardly interested in education. But [in the immediate post-war period] the aggregate national outlay, public and private, amounted to 20 billions. As Kerr says, ". . . the university has become a prime instrument of national purpose. This is new. This is the essence of the transformation now engulfing our universities."[15] In short, our education institutions are becoming appendages to, and transformed by, U.S. corporate capitalism.

Education is not being done away with in favour of something called training. Rather, education is being transformed from a quasi-aristocratic classicism and petty-bourgeois romanticism into something quite new. These changes are apparent in ways other than the quantitative statistics given above. For example, we can examine the social sciences and the humanities. The social and psychological "reality" that we are given to study is "objectified" to the point of sterility. The real world, we are to understand, is "valuefree" and pragmatically bears little or no relation to the actual life-activity of men, classes, and nations. In one sense, we are separated from life. In another, we are being conditioned for life in a lifeless, stagnant, and sterile society.

For another example, there is more than a semantic connection between the academic division of labour and specialization we are so aware, of, and the corresponding division of labour that has gone on in large-scale industry. But it is important to understand what this connection is. It does *not* follow that because technology becomes diversified and specialized, then academic knowledge and skills must follow suit. André Gorz makes the relevant comment, "It is completely untrue that modern technology demands specialization: quite the reverse. It demands a basic 'polyvalent' education, comprising not of fragmentary, pre-digested and specialized knowledge, but an imagination—or, put more precisely, a faculty of self-initiation—new methods of scientifico-technological research and discovery."[16] If it is not the new technological production that deems necessary, this kind of isolated specialization we know so well, then what is responsible? Gorz spells it out again, "Capitalism actually needs shattered and atomized men . . ."[17] in order to maintain its system of centralized, bureaucratized and militarized hierarchies, so as ". . . to perpetuate its domination over men, not only as workers, but also as consumers and citizens."[18]

From this perspective, we can begin to understand that the educational malaise we as students and faculty have felt so personally and intensely is no aberration, but firmly rooted in the American political

[15] Kerr, Clark: *Uses of the University*, p. 87.
[16] Gorz, Andre: "Capitalism and the Labour Force", *International Socialist Journal*, p. 423.
[17] Ibid, p. 428.
[18] Ibid, p. 428.

economy. In fact, the Organized System which Paul Goodman calls "compulsory mis-education" may mis-educate us, but it certainly serves the masters of that system, the U.S. ruling class, quite well. As Edgar Z. Friedenberg wrote. "Educational evils are attributed to *defective* schools. In fact, they are as likely to be the work of *effective* schools that are being directed toward evil ends by the society that supports and controls them."[19] Furthermore, he continues later in the same article, "Schools are a definite indication that a society is divisible into a dominant and a subordinate group, and that the dominant group want to teach the subordinate group something they could not be trusted to learn if left to themselves."[20] Clark Kerr would accept this, both for the society in general, which he divides into the "managers" and the "managed," and for the university. Kerr states: "The intellectuals (including university students) are a particularly volatile element . . . They are by nature irresponsible . . . They are, as a result, never fully trusted by anybody, including themselves."[21] But Kerr doesn't dismiss us. Even if we are by nature irresponsible (perhaps because we can perceive the contradictions?) he considers us essential. ". . . It is important who best attracts or captures the intellectuals and who uses them most effectively, for they may be a tool as well as a source of danger."[22]

I think we can conclude that the American educational system is a coherent, well-organized, and—to the extent that the rulers are still ruling—effective mechanism. However, it has turned our humanitarian values into their opposites and at the same time, given us the potential to understand and critically evaluate both ourselves and the system itself. To that extent the system is fraught with internal contradictions. Furthermore, the events comprising the student revolt in the last few years demonstrate the likelihood that those contradictions will continue to manifest themselves in an open and protracted struggle. As Kerr predicted, we *are* a source of danger and incipient revolt. And the fact that Kerr was fired and the police used in the face of that revolt only goes to prove that those contradictions are irreconcilable within the structure of corporate capitalism. As Quintin Hoare remarked in *New Left Review No. 32*, "*. . . a reform of the educational system involves a reform of the educators as well, and this is a political task, which immediately ricochets back to the question of transforming consciousness and ideology throughout society.*"[23] The central problem of radically transforming the educa-

---

[19]Friedenberg, Edgar Z.: *The Nation*, September 20, 1965, p. 72.
[20]Ibid.
[21]Kerr, Clark: "Industrialism and Industrial Man", quoted in "The Mind of Clark", in Draper, Hal (ed.): *Berkeley: The New Student Revolt*, p. 211.
[22]Ibid.

[23]Hoare, Quintin: "Education: Programs and Men", *New Left Review* #32, pp. 50-51.

tional system is that of the transformation of the teaching and learning body—the faculty and students. And this transformation while it *begins* with the demands of the students' and teachers' work situation, cannot take place unless it occurs *within* and is organically connected *to* the practice of a mass radical *political* movement. . . .

PART 3

THE PRAXIS OF STUDENT POWER STRATEGY AND TACTICS

Socialism on One Campus . . . an Infantile Disorder Perhaps the single most important factor for the student power movement to keep in mind is the fact that the university is intimately bound up with the society in general. Because of this, we should always remember that we cannot liberate the university without radically changing the rest of society. The lesson to be drawn is that any attempt to build a student movement based on "on-campus" issues only is inherently conservative and ultimately reactionary. Every attempt should be made to connect campus issues with off-campus questions. For example, the question of ranking and university complicity with the Selective Service System needs to be tied to a general anti-draft and "No Draft for Vietnam" movement. The question of the presence of the military on the campus in all its forms needs to be tied to the question of what that military is used for—fighting aggressive wars of oppression abroad—and not just to the question of secret research being poor academic policy. Furthermore, the student movement must actively seek to join off-campus struggles in the surrounding community. For example, strikes by local unions should be supported if possible. This kind of communication and understanding with the local working class is essential if we are ever going to have community support for student strikes.

Radicalizing the New Working Class If there is a single over-all purpose for the student power movement, it wouldbe the development of a radical political consciousness among those students who will later hold jobs in strategic sectors of the political economy. This means that we should reach out to engineers and technical students rather than to business administration majors, education majors rather than to art students. From a national perspective, this strategy would also suggest that we should place priorities on organizing in certain *kinds* of universities—the community colleges, junior colleges, state universities, and technical schools, rather than religious colleges or the Ivy League.

One way to mount political action around this notion is to focus on the placement offices—the nexus between the university and industry. For example, when DOW Chemical comes to recruit, our main approach to junior and senior chemical engineering students who are being interviewed should not only be around the issue of the immorality of napalm. Rather, our leaflets should say that one of the main faults of DOW and all other industries as well is that their workers *have no control* over content or purposes of their work. In other words, DOW Chemical is bad, not only because of napalm, but mainly because it renders its workers *powerless*, makes them *unfree*. In short, DOW and all American industry oppresses *its own workers* as well as the people of the Third World. DOW in particular should be run off the campus and students urged not to work for them because of their complicity in war crimes. But when other industries are recruiting, our leaflets should address themselves to the interviewees' instincts of workmanship, his desires to be free and creative, to do humane work, rather than work for profit. We should encourage him, if he takes the job, to see himself in this light—as a skilled worker—and of his self-interest of organizing on his future job with his fellow workers, skilled and unskilled, for control of production and the end to which his work is directed. The need for control, for the power, on and off the job, to affect the decisions shaping one's life in all arenas; developing this kind of consciousness, on and off the campus, is what we should be fundamentally all about.

Practical, Critical Activity: Notes on Organizing There are three virtues necessary for successful radical organizing: honesty, patience, and a sense of humour. First of all if the students we are trying to reach can't trust us, who can they trust? Secondly it takes time to build a movement. Sometimes several years of groundwork must be laid before a student power movement has a constituency. It took most of us several years before we had developed a radical perspective. Why should it be any different for the people we are trying to reach? This is not to say that everyone must repeat all the mistakes we have gone through, but there are certain *forms* of involvement and action that many students will have to repeat. Finally, by a sense of humour, I mean we must be life-affirming. Lusty passionate people are the only kind of men who have the enduring strength to motivate enough people to radically transform a life-negating system.

Che Guevara remarked in *Guerrilla Warfare* that as long as people had faith in certain institutions and forms of political activity, then the organizer must work *with* the people *through* those institutions, even though we might think those forms of action are dead ends.[24] The point of Che's remark is that people must learn that those forms are stacked against them through their *own experience* in attempting

---

[24]Guevara, Ernest "Che": *Guerrilla Warfare.*

change. The role of the organizer at this point is crucial. He or she should neither passively go along with the student government "reformer" types nor stand apart from the action denouncing it as "sell-out." Rather, his task is that of *constant criticism* from within the action. When the reformers fail, become bogged down, or are banging their heads against the wall, the organizer should be there as *one who has been with them throughout their struggle* to offer the relevant analysis of *why* their approach has failed and to indicate future strategies and tactics.

However, we also need to be discriminating. There are certain forms of political action, like working within the Democratic Party, that are so obviously bankrupt, that we need not waste our time. In order to discern these limits, an organizer has to develop a sensitivity to understand where people are. Many radical actions have failed on campuses because the activists have failed in laying a base for a particular action. It does no good to sit in against the CIA if a broad educational campaign, petitions, and rallies on the nature of the CIA have not been done for several days before the sit-in. It is not enough that we have a clear understanding of the oppressiveness of institutions like the CIA and HUAC before we act in a radical fashion. We must make our position clear to the students, faculty, and the surrounding community.

The Cultural Apparatus and the Problem of False Consciousness In addition to its role in the political economy, it is important to deal with the university as the backbone of what Mills called "the cultural apparatus."[25] He defined this as all those organizations and *milieux* in which artistic, scientific and intellectual work goes on, as well as the means by which that work is made available to others. Within this apparatus, the various vehicles of communication—language, the mass arts, public arts, and design arts—stand between a man's consciousness and his material existence. At present, the bulk of the apparatus is centralized and controlled by the corporate rulers of America. As a result, their use of the official communications has the effect of limiting our experience and, furthermore, expropriates much of that potential experience that we might have called our own. What we need to understand is that the cultural apparatus, properly used, has the ability both to transform power into authority and transform authority into mere overt coercion.

At present, the university's role in acculturation and socialization is the promulgation of the utter mystification of "corporate consciousness." Society is presented to us as a kind of caste system in which we are to see ourselves as a "privileged elite"—a bureaucratic man channelled into the proper bureaucratic niche. In addition to

[25] Mills, C. Wright: *Power, Politics and People*, p. 386.

strengthening the forms of social control off the campus, the administration uses the apparatus on campus to legitimize its own power over us.

On the campus, the student press, underground newspapers, campus radio and television, literature tables, posters and leaflets, artist and lecture series, theaters, films, and the local press make up a good part of the non-academic cultural media. Most of it is both actively and passively being used against us. Any student power movement should (1) try to gain control as much of the *established* campus cultural apparatus as possible, (2) if control is not possible, we should try to influence and/or resist it when necessary and (3) organize and develop a new counter-apparatus of our own. In short, we need our people on the staff of the school newspapers, and radio stations. We need our own local magazines. We need sympathetic contacts on local off-campus new media. Finally, we all could use some training in graphic and communicative arts.

What this all adds up to is strengthening our ability to wage an effective "de-sanctification" program against the authoritarian institutions controlling us. The purpose of de-sanctification is to strip institutions of their legitimizing authority, to have them reveal themselves to the people under them for what they are—raw coercive power. This is the purpose of singing the Mickey Mouse Club jingle at student government meetings, of ridiculing and harrassing student disciplinary hearings and tribunals, of burning the Dean of Men and/or Women in effigy. People will not move *against* institutions of power until the legitimizing authority has been stripped away. On many campuses this has already happened; but for those remaining, the task remains. And we should be forewarned: it is a tricky job and often can backfire, de-legitimizing us.

The Correct Handling of Student Governments While student governments vary in form in the United States, the objective reasons for their existence are the containment, or pacification and manipulation of the student body. Very few of our student governments are autonomously incorporated or have any powers or rights apart from those sanctioned by the regents or trustees of the university. Furthermore, most administrations hold a veto power over anything done by the student governments. Perhaps the worst aspect of this kind of manipulation and repression is that the administration uses students to control other students. Most student government politicos are lackeys of the worst sort. That is, they have internalized and embraced all the repressive mechanisms the administration has designed for use *against* them and their fellow students.

With this in mind, it would seem that we should ignore student governments and/or abolish them. While this is certainly true in the final analysis, it is important to relate to student governments dif-

ferently during the earlier stages of on-campus political struggles. The
question we are left with is how do we render student governments
ineffective in terms of what they are designed to do, while at the
same time, using them effectively in building the movement?

Do we work inside the system? Of course we do. The question is
not one of working "inside" or "outside" the system. Rather, the
question is do we play by the established rules? Here, the answer is
an emphatic no. The established habits of student politics—popularity
contest elections, disguising oneself as a moderate, working for "better communications and dialogue" with administrators, watering
down demands before they are made, going through channels—all of
these gambits are stacked against us. If liberal and moderate student
politicians really believe in them, then we should tell *them* to try it
with all they have. But if they continue to make this ploy after they
have learned from their own experience that these methods are
dead-ends, then they should be soundly denounced as opportunists or
gutless administration puppets.

We should face the fact that student governments are *powerless* and
designed to stay that way. From this perspective, all talk about
"getting into power" is so much nonsense. The only thing that
student governments are useful for is their ability to be a *temporary
vehicle* in building a grass-roots student power movement. This means
that student elections are useful as an arena for raising real issues,
combatting and exposing administration apologists, and involving new
people, rather than getting elected. If our people do happen to get
elected *as radicals* (this is becoming increasingly possible) then the
seats won should be used as a focal point and sounding board for
demonstrating the impotence of student government *from within*. A
seat should be seen as a soap-box, where our representatives can
stand, gaining a kind of visibility and speaking to the student body as
a whole, over the heads of the other student politicians.

Can anything positive be gained through student government? Apart
from publicity, one thing it can be used for is money. Many student-
activities funds are open for the kinds of things we would like to see
on campus: certain speakers, films, sponsoring conferences. Money,
without strings, is always a help. Also, non-political services, such as
non-profit used-book exchanges, are helpful to many students. But in
terms of radical changes, student government can do nothing apart
from a mass, radical student power movement. Even then, student
government tends to be a conservative force within those struggles. In
the end, meaningful changes can only come through a radical transformation of both the consciousness of large numbers of students and
the forms of student self-government.

Reform or Revolution: What Kinds of Demand? Fighting for reforms
and making a revolution should not be seen as mutually exclusive
positions. The question should be: what kind of reforms move us
toward a radical transformation of both the university and the

society in general? First of all, we should avoid the kinds of reforms which leave the basic *rationale* of the system unchallenged. For instance, a bad reform to work for would be getting a better grading system, because the underlying rationale—the need for grades at all—remains unchallenged.

Secondly, we should avoid certain kinds of reform that divide students from each other. For instance, trying to win certain privileges for upper classmen but not for freshmen or sophomores. Or trying to establish non-graded courses for students above a certain grade-point average. In the course of campus political activity, the administration will try a whole range of "divide and rule" tactics such as fostering the "Greek-Independent Split," sexual double standards, intellectual vs. "jocks," responsible vs. irresponsible leaders, red-baiting and "non-student" vs. students. We need to avoid falling into these traps ahead of time, as well as fighting them when used against us.

Finally, we should avoid all of the "co-management" kinds of reforms. These usually come in the form of giving certain "responsible" student leaders a voice or influence in certain decision-making processes, rather than abolishing or winning effective control over those parts of the governing apparatus. One way to counter administration suggestions for setting up "tripartite" committees (1/3 student, 1/3 faculty, 1/3 administration, each with an equal number of votes) is to say, "OK, but once a month the committee must hold an all-university plenary session—one man, one vote." The thought of being outvoted 1000 to 1 will cause administrators to scrap that co-optive measure in a hurry.

We have learned the hard way that the reformist path is full of pitfalls. What, then, are the kinds of reformist measures that do make sense? First of all, there are the civil libertarian issues. We must always fight, dramatically and quickly, for free speech and the right to organize, advocate, and mount political action—of all sorts. However, even here, we should avoid getting bogged down in "legalitarianism." We cannot count on this society's legal apparatus to guarantee our civil liberties: and, we should not organize around civil libertarian issues *as if it could.* Rather, when our legal rights are violated, we should move as quickly as possible, without losing our base, to expand the campus libertarian moral indignation into a multi-issues *political* insurgency, exposing the repressive character of the administration and the corporate state in general.

The second kind of partial reform worth fighting for and possibly winning is the abolition of on-campus repressive mechanisms, i.e., student courts, disciplinary tribunals, deans of men and women, campus police, and the use of civil police on campus. While it is true that "abolition" is a negative reform, and while we will be criticized for not offering "constructive" criticisms, we should reply that the only constructive way to deal with an inherently destructive apparatus is to destroy it. We must curtail the ability of administrators to repress our *need to refuse* their way of life—the regimentation and bureaucratization of existence.

When our universities are already major agencies for social change in the direction of *1984*, our initial demands must, almost of necessity, be negative demands. In this sense, the first task of a student power movement will be the organization of a holding action or a resistance. Along these lines, one potentially effective tactic for resisting the university's disciplinary apparatus would be the formation of a Student Defence League. The purpose of the group would be to make its services available to any student who must appear before campus authorities for infractions of repressive (or just plain stupid) rules and regulations. The defence group would then attend the student's hearings *en masse*. However, for some cases, it might be wise to include law students or local radical lawyers in the group for the purpose of making legal counter-attacks. A student defence group would have three major goals: 1) saving as many students as possible from punishment, 2) de-sanctifying and rendering disfunctional the administration's repressive apparatus, and 3) using 1) and 2) as tactics in reaching other students for building a movement to abolish the apparatus as a whole.

When engaging in this kind of activity, it is important to be clear in our rhetoric as to what we are about. We are not trying to *liberalize* the existing order, but trying to win our *liberation* from it. We must refuse the administrations' rhetoric of "responsibility." To their one-dimensional way of thinking, the concept of responsibility has been reduced to its opposite, namely, be nice, don't rock the boat, do things according to *our* criteria of what is permissible. In actuality their whole system is geared toward the inculcation of the values of a planned irresponsibility. We should refuse *their* definitions, *their* terms, and even refuse to engage in *their* semantic hassles. We only need to define for *ourselves and other students* our notions of what it means to be free, constructive, and responsible. Too many campus movements have been co-opted for weeks or even permanently by falling into the administrations' rhetorical bags.

Besides the abolition of repressive disciplinary mechanisms within the university, there are other negative reforms that radicals should work for. Getting the military off the campus, abolishing the grade system, and abolishing universal compulsory courses (i.e., physical education) would fit into this category. However, an important question for the student movement is whether or not *positive* radical reforms can be won within the university short of making a revolution in the society as a whole. Furthermore, would the achievement of these kinds of partial reforms have the cumulative effect of weakening certain aspects of corporate capitalism, and, in their small way, make that broader revolution more likely?

At present, my feeling is that these kinds of anti-capitalist positive reforms are almost as hard to conceive intellectually as they are to win. To be sure, there has been a wealth of positive educational reforms suggested by people like Paul Goodman. But are they anti-capitalist as well? For example, we have been able to organize several good free universities. Many of the brightest and most sensitive students on American campuses, disgusted with the present state of education, left the campus and organized these counter-institutions. Some of their experiments were successful in an immediate internal sense. A few of these organizers were initially convinced that the sheer moral force of their work in these free institutions would cause the existing educational structure to tremble and finally collapse like a house of IBM cards. But what happenned? What effect did the free universities have on the established educational order? At best, they had no effect. But it is more likely that they had the effect of strengthening the existing system. How? First of all, the best of our people left the campus, enabling the existing university to function more smoothly, since the "troublemakers" were gone. Secondly, they gave liberal administrators the rhetoric, the analysis, and sometimes the man-power to co-opt their programs and establish elitist forms of "experimental" colleges inside of, although quarantined from, the existing educational system. This is not to say that free universities should not be organized, both on and off the campus. They can be valuable and useful. But they should not be seen as a primary aspect of a strategy for change.

What then is open to us in the area of positive anti-capitalist reforms? For the most part, it will be difficult to determine whether or not a reform has the effect of being anti-capitalist until it has been achieved. Since it is both difficult and undesirable to attempt to predict the future, questions of this sort are often best answered in practice. Nevertheless, it would seem that the kind of reforms we are looking for are most likely to be found within a strategy of what I would call "encroaching control." There are aspects of the university's administrative, academic, financial-physical, and social apparatus that are potentially, if not actually, useful and productive. While we should try to abolish the repressive mechanisms of the university; our strategy should be to gain *control*, piece by piece, of its positive aspects.

What would that control look like? To begin, all aspects of the non-academic life of the campus should either be completely under the control of the students as individuals or embodied in the institutional forms *they* establish for their collective government. For example, an independent union of students should have the final say on the form and content of *all-university* political, social, and cultural events. Naturally, individual students and student organizations would be completely free in organizing events of their own.

Second, only the students and the teaching faculty, individually and through their organizations, should control the academic affairs of the university. One example of a worthwhile reform in this area would be enabling all history majors and history professors to meet jointly at the beginning of each semester and shape the form, content, and direction of their departmental curriculum. Another partial reform in this area would be enabling an independent union of students to hire additional professors of their choice and establish additional accredited courses of their choice independently of the faculty or administration.

Finally, we should remember that control should be sought *for some specific purpose*. One reason we want this kind of power is to enable us to meet the *self-determined* needs of students and teachers. But another objective that we should see as radicals is to put as much of the university's resources as possible into the hands of the underclass and the working class. We should use the student press to publicize and support local strikes. We should use campus facilities for meeting the educational needs of insurgent organizations of the poor, and of rank and file workers. Or we could mobilize the universities' research facilities for serving projects established and controlled by the poor and worker, rather than projects established and controlled by the government, management, and labour bureaucrats. The conservative nature of American trade unions makes activity of this sort very difficult, although not impossible. But we should always be careful to make a distinction between the American working class itself and the labour bureaucrats.

The Faculty Question: Allies or Finks? One question almost always confronts the student movement on the campus. Do we try to win faculty support before we go into action? Or do we lump them together with the administration? What we have learned in the past seems to indicate that both of these responses are wrong. Earlier in this paper, I remarked on the kinds of divisions that exist among the faculty. What is important to see is that this division is not just between good and bad guys. Rather, the faculty is becoming more and more divided in terms of the objective functions of their jobs. To make the hard case on one hand, the function of the lower level of the faculty is to teach—a potentially creative and useful activity; on the other hand, the function of most administrative and research faculty is manipulation, repression, and—for the defence department hirelings—destruction. In general, we should develop our strategies so that our lot falls with the teaching faculty and theirs with ours. As for the research and administrative faculty, we should set both ourselves and the teaching faculty against them. Also, during any student confrontation with the administration, the faculty can do one of four things *as a group*. They can 1) support the administration, 2) remain neutral, 3) split among themselves, and 4) support us. In any situation, we should favor the development of one of the last three alternatives rather than the first. Furthermore, if it seems likely that the faculty will split on an issue, we should try to encourage the division indicated above. While it is important to remain open to the faculty, we should not let their support or non-support become an issue in determining whether or not we begin to mount political action. Finally, we should encourage the potentially radical sectors of the faculty to organize among themselves around their own grievances, hopefully being able to *eventually* form a radical alliance with us.

The Vital Issue of Teaching Assistants' Unions Probably the most exploited and alienated group of people on any campus *are* the graduate student teaching assistants. The forces of the multiversity hit them from two directions—both as students and as teachers. As students, they have been around long enough to have lost their awe of academia. As faculty, they are given the worst jobs for the lowest pay. For the most part, they have no illusions about their work. Their working conditions, low pay, and the fact that their futures are subject to the whimsical machinations of their department chairmen, make them a group ripe for radical organization. Furthermore, their strategic position within the university structure—makes them potentially powerful as a group if they should decide to organize and strike. If they go out, a large part of the multiversity comes grinding to a halt. The kinds of demands they are most likely to be organized around naturally connect them with a radical student power movement and with the potentially radical sector of the faculty. Furthermore, these considerations make the organization of a radical trade union of TAs a crucial part of any strategy for change. We should see this kind of labour organizing as one of our first priorities in building the campus movement.

Non-Academic Employes: On-Campus Labor Organizing Almost all colleges and especially the multiversities have a large number of blue-collar maintainance workers on campus. Within the state supported institutions in particular, these people are often forbidden to organize unions, have terrible working conditions, and are paid very low wages. Their presence on the campus offers a unique opportunity for many students to become involved in blue-collar labour organizing at the same time that they are in school. Secondly, since these workers usually live in the surrounding community, their friends and relatives will come from other sectors of the local working class. Quite naturally, they will carry their ideas, opinions, and feelings toward the radical student movement home with them. In this sense, they can be an important link connecting us with other workers, and our help in enabling them to organize a local independent and radical trade union would help tremendously. Finally, if we should ever strike as students, they could be an important ally. For instance, after SDS at the University of Missouri played a major role in organizing a militant local of non-academic employees, they learned that, were the union to strike for its own demands in sympathy with student demands, the university as a physical plant would cease to function after four days. It is obviously important to have that kind of power.

The Knowledge Machinery and Sabotage: Striking on the Job One mistake radical students have been making in relating to the worst aspects of the multiversity's academic apparatus has been their avoidance of it. We tend to avoid large classes, lousy courses, and reactionary professors like the plague. At best, we have organized counter-courses outside the class-room and off the campus. My suggestion is that we should do the opposite. Our brightest people should sign up for the large freshman and sophomore sections with the worst profs in *strategic* courses in history, political science, education, and even the ROTC counter-insurgency lectures. From this position, they should then begin to take out their frustrations with the work of the course while they are on the job, i.e., inside the classroom. Specifically, they should be constant vocal critics of the form and content of the course, the prof, class size, the educational system, and corporate capitalism in general. Their primary strategy, rather than winning debating points against the prof, should be to reach other students in the class. Hopefully, our on-the-job organizer will begin to develop a radical caucus in the class. This group could then meet outside of the class, continue to collectively develop a further radical critique of the future class-work, to be presented at the succeding sessions. If all goes well with the prof, and perhaps his department as well, they will have a full-scale academic revolt on their hands by the end of the semester. Finally, if this sort of work were being done in a variety of courses at once, the local radical student movement would have the makings of an underground educational movement that was actively engaged in mounting an effective resistance to the educational *status quo.*

Provo Tactics: Radicalization or Sublimation? There is little doubt that the hippy movement has made its impact on most American campuses. It is also becoming more clear that the culture of advanced capitalist society is becoming more sterile, dehumanized and one-dimensional. It is directed toward a passive mass, rather than an active public. Its root value is consumption. We obviously need a cultural revolution, along with a revolution in the political economy. But the question remains: where do the hippies fit in? At the present time, their role seems ambivalent.

On the one hand, they thoroughly reject the dominant culture and seem to be life-affirming. On the other hand, they seem to be for the most part, passive consumers of culture, rather than active creators of culture. For all their talk of community, the nexus of their relations with each other seems to consist only of drugs and a common jargon.

With all their talk of love, one finds little deep-rooted passion. Yet, they are there; and they are a major phenomenon. Their relevance to the campus scene is evidenced by the success of the wave of "Gentle Thursdays" that swept the country. Through this approach, we have been able to reach and break loose a good number of people. Often, during the frivolity of Gentle Thursday, the life-denying aspects of corporate capitalism are brought home to many people with an impact that could never be obtained by the best of all of our anti-war demonstrations.

However, the hippy movement has served to make many of our people withdraw into a personalistic, passive cult of consumption. These aspects need to be criticized and curtailed. We should be clear about one thing: the *individual* liberation of man, the most social of animals, is a dead-end—an impossibility. And even if individual liberation were possible, would it be desirable? The sublimation of reality within the individual consciousness neither destroys nor transforms the objective reality of other men.

Nevertheless, the excitement and imagination of some aspects of hippydom can be useful in building critiques of the existing culture. Here, I am referring to the provos and the diggers. Gentle Thursday, when used as a provo (provocative) tactic on campus, can cause the administration to display some of its most repressive characteristics. Even something as blunt as burning a television set in the middle of campus can make a profound statement about the life styles of many people. However, people engaging in this kind of action should 1) not see the action as a substitute for serious revolutionary activity and 2) read up on the Provos and Situationists rather than the Haight-Ashbury scene.

From Soap-box to Student Strikes: The Forms of Protest During the development of radical politics on the campus, the student movement will pass through a multitude of organizational forms. I have already mentioned several: Student Defence League, Teaching Assistants' Unions, Non-Academic Employees' Unions, and of course, SDS chapters. Another important development on many campuses has been the formation of Black Student Unions, or Afro-American cultural groups. All of these groups are vital, although some are more important than others at different stages of the struggle. However, for the purpose of keeping a radical and multi-issue focus throughout the growth of the movement, it is important to begin work on a campus by organizing an SDS chapter.

From this starting point, how does SDS see its relation to the rest of the campus? I think we have learned that we should not look upon ourselves as an intellectual and political oasis, hugging each other in a wasteland. Rather, our chapters should see themselves as *organizing committees* for reaching out to the majority of the student population. Furthermore, we are organizing for something—the power to effect change. With this in mind, we should be well aware of the fact that the kind of power and changes we would like to have and achieve are not going to be given to us gracefully. Ultimately, we have access to only one source of power within the knowledge factory. And that power lies in our potential ability to stop the university from functioning, to render the system disfunctional for limited periods of time. Throughout all our on-campus organizing efforts we should keep this one point in mind: that sooner or later we are going to have to strike—or at least successfully threaten to strike. Because of this, our constant strategy should be the preparation of a mass base for supporting and participating in this kind of action.

What are the organizational forms, other than those mentioned above, that are necessary for the development of this kind of radical constituency? The first kind of extra-SDS organization needed is a Hyde Park or Free Speech Forum. An area of the campus, centrally located and heavily travelled, should be selected and equipped with a P.A. system. Then, on a certain afternoon one day a week, the platform would be open to anyone to give speeches on anything they choose. SDS people should attend regularly and speak regularly, although they should encourage variety and debate, and not monopolize the platform. To begin, the forum should be weekly, so that students don't become bored with it. Rather, we should try to give it the aura of a special event. Later on, when political activity intensifies, the forum could be held every day. In the early stages, publicity, the establishment of a mood and climate for radical politics, is of utmost importance. We should make our presence felt everywhere—in the campus news media, leafletting and poster displays, and regular attendance at the meetings of all student political, social, and religious organizations. We should make all aspects of our politics as visible and open as possible.

Once our presence has become known, we can begin to organize on a variety of issues. One arena that it will be important to relate to at this stage will be student government elections. The best organizational form for this activity would be the formation of a Campus Freedom Party for running radical candidates. It is important that the party be clear and open as to its radical consciousness, keeping in mind that our first task is that of building radical consciousness, rather than winning seats. It is also important that the party take positions on off-campus questions as well, such as the war in Vietnam. Otherwise, if we only relate to on-campus issues, we run the risk of laying the counter-revolutionary groundwork for an elitist, conservative and corporatist student movement. As many people as possible should be involved in the work of the party, with SDS people having the function of keeping it militant and radical in a non-manipulative and honest fashion. The party should permeate the campus with speeches, films, and leaflets, as well as a series of solidly intellectual and radical position papers on a variety of issues. Furthermore, we should remember that an election campaign should be fun. Campus Freedom Parties should organize Gentle Thursdays, jug bands, rock groups, theater groups for political skits, and homemade 8mm. campaign films. Finally, during non-election periods, the Campus Freedom Party should form a variety of CFP *ad hoc* committees for relating to student government on various issues throughout the year.

The next stage of the movement is the most crucial and delicate in the formation of a Student Strike Coordinating Committee. There are two pre-conditions necessary for its existence. First, there must be a quasi-radical base of some size that has been developed from past activity. Secondly, either a crisis situation provoked by the administration or a climate of active frustration with the administration and/or the ruling class it represents must exist. The frustration should be centered around a set of specific demands that have been unresolved through the established channels of liberal action. If this kind of situation exists, then a strike is both possible and desirable. A temporary steering committee should be set up, consisting of representatives of radical groups (SDS, Black Student Union, TA's Union). This group would set the initial demands and put out the call for a strike within a few weeks time. Within that time, they would try to bring in as many other groups and individuals as possible without seriously watering down the demands. This new coalition would then constitute itself as the Student Strike Coordinating Committee, with the new groups adding members to the original temporary steering committee. Also, a series of working committees and a negotiating committee should be established. Finally, the strike committee should attempt to have as many open mass plenary sessions as possible.

What should come out of a student strike? First, the development of a radical consciousness among large numbers of students. Secondly, we should try to include within our demands some issues on which we can win partial victories. Finally, the organizational form that should grow out of strike or series of strikes is an independent, radical, and political Free Student Union that would replace the existing student government. I have already dealt with the general political life of radical movements. But some points need to be repeated. First of all, a radical student union *must* be in alliance with the radical sectors of the underclass and working class. Secondly, the student movement has the additional task of radicalizing the sub-sector of the labour force that some of us in SDS have come to call the new working class. Thirdly, a radical union of students should have an anti-imperialist critique of U.S. foreign policy. Finally, local student unions, if they are to grow and thrive, must become federated on regional, national, and international levels. However, we should be careful not to form a national union of students lacking in a grass-roots constituency that actively and democratically participates in all aspects of the organization's life. One NSA is enough. On the international level, we should avoid both the CIA and Soviet Union sponsored International Unions. We would be better off to establish informal relations with groups like the Zengakuren in Japan, the German SDS, the French Situationists, the Spanish Democratic Student Syndicate, and the third world revolutionary student organizations. Hopefully, in the not too distant future, we may be instrumental in forming a new International Union of Revolutionary Youth. But there is much work to be done between now and then. And even greater tasks remain to be done before we can begin to build the conditions for human liberation.

Counterrhetoric

THE SDS TRIP: FROM VISION TO EGO SHRIEK

Albert H. Hobbs

THE SDS BIRTHRIGHT

Our ideal is a university, a community of scholars bound together by the search for knowledge and truth and feeling a sense of responsibility to their society. That ideal declares that teaching and learning are more important than economic self-interest, and where that ideal has been a reality, men have been able to face the future with self-confidence and hope. We believe in the defense of this ideal, but this vision of the university is being extinguished by a general social process of which Kerr (Clark Kerr, then President of the U. of California) is both analyst and advocate.

The three Berkeley students who expressed these ideals and this fear[1] described the society of which President Kerr was both analyst and advocate[2] as one which is fundamentally identical with the managerialism of Saint-Simon and the militarized capitalism of Edward Bellamy; one in which the government of persons is replaced by the administration of things—because under its beneficent aegis persons are reduced to things—and in it the university will be handmaiden to this new industrial state, with higher education centered around the production of technicians and managers.

Writing in 1962, two years before the Berkeley rioting, these students were aware that it would be difficult to prevent the degradation of universities into knowledge factories, but they proposed to resist this trend, hoping thereby to postpone the Kerr-Orwell 1984 to perhaps 2025 rather than trying to establish it, as they accused Kerr of attempting to do, by 1975.

Similar reasoned objection to ". . . the greatest problem of our time—depersonalized, unresponsive, bureaucracy" was expressed by the leader of the 1964 Berkeley revolt, Mario Savio,[3] and one finds the 1962 Port Huron Statement of Students for a Democratic Society (SDS) well-sprinkled with stress on idealistically motivated intellectual analysis, emphasizing that the new left should be ". . . committed to deliberativeness, honesty, and reflection." SDS leader Tom Hayden, now a fanatic and somewhat ludicrous proponent of violence, then insisted that radicalism meant intellectual penetration of a social problem to its roots; the real causes which hid beneath the delusive surface appearance.[4]

THE FOCUS OF PROTEST

A good case can be made that during 1962-64, SDS members seriously attempted to make reasoned protest against the bureaucratized Pluralistic Industrial Society of which Clark Kerr was both analyst and advocate, and against the multiversity which was to be the creature of this new corporate state. Most people, I believe, would agree with their protest because there is much that is unlovely and

[1] Bruce Payne, David Walls, and Jerry Berman, "Theodicy of 1984: The Philosophy of Clark Kerr," in *The New Student Left*, Mitchell Cohen and Dennis Hale, eds. (Boston: Beacon, 1966). First published in *The Activist*, Vol. 2, 1962.

[2] Clark Kerr, John T. Dunopp, F. Harbison, and Charles A. Myers, *Industrialism and Industrial Man* (Cambridge: Harvard Univ. Press, 1960), (New York: Oxford Univ. Press, 1964).

[3] Mario Savio, "An End to History," *Humanity*, December, 1964. Also in *Revolution at Berkeley*, Michael V. Miller and Susan Gilmore, eds. (New York: Dell, 1965).

[4] In Cohen and Hale.

soul-shrinking in both of the conceptualized structures which these youths then protested against.

As technology continues to evolve, Kerr believes that the conflict of ideologies—such as differences between Communism and capitalism—will become blunted, fade, and be replaced by consensus as the cultural patterns of the world intermingle and merge. Distinctions between private and public managers "... will decrease just as the distinction between the private and the public enterprise will diminish. . . . There will be a controlled market as well as a controlled budget. The middle class and the middle bureaucracy will be very much alike."[5] This new, all-powerful state will unite its diverse elements under *a web of rules* and, with conflict now taking the form of bureaucratic gamemanship, "... the battles will be in the corridors instead of in the streets, and memos will flow instead of blood."[6] Social classes will disappear, but status differences will persist in the distinctions between *the managers and the managed*.

As handmaiden to Kerr's Pluralistic Industrial Society, the university would become the multiversity, a creature of the state, with its incompatible purposes "...kept as confused as possible for the preservation of the whole uneasy balance."[7] Such deliberate duplicity as a necessary aspect of university administration is to be conjoined with a deterioration in undergraduate education as training replaces general education.[8]

A particularly ominous aspect of this change is the rapidity with which the federal government is already taking control of our universities. In "To Probe the Academic Conscience," I noted that federal funds to universities rose from $415 million in 1956 to $2 billion in 1965. At the 1968 meeting of the Association of American Universities, the leading administrators from all over America insisted that such federal grants be increased to $8 billion. At the 1968 trial of Columbia students for seizing university buildings, their lawyer argued that they could not be prosecuted for trespassing upon private property because Columbia, as of 1966, had 770 contracts with federal agencies totalling $58 million, which constituted 45 percent of its budget. In addition to such grants, he pointed out, Columbia received federal funds for scholarships, for student loans, and operated on a tax-exempt status making it a public, not a private, institution.

In "*E Multis Universitatibus Una*,"[9] I parodied this federal take-

[5]Clark Kerr, *et al.*, Oxford Univ. edition, p. 234.

[6]Clark Kerr, *et al.*, Oxford Univ. edition, p. 235.

[7]Clark Kerr, *The Uses of the University* (Cambridge: Harvard Univ. Press, 1963).

[8]A. H. Hobbs, "To Probe the Academic Conscience," *The Intercollegiate Review*, November, 1967.

[9]A. H. Hobbs, *"E Multis Universitatibus Una,"* *The Intercollegiate Review*, December, 1966.

over of universities, hinting that someday college students might be admitted on the basis of ethnic and religious quota, regardless of ability. Parody quickly became sordid truth: by 1968, City University of New York callously dictated that the percentage of Negro and Puerto Rican students would be increased from 12 to 26 within the year. To do this, entrance requirements would be sharply reduced, but the president fatuously announced that such reduction ". . . would not affect the traditional academic excellence."[10]

Much additional evidence could be adduced to support the new left contention that America is rapidly becoming a bureaucratic corporate state and that the multiversity is increasingly its slavish creature, and students who look upon these changes as a threat to the integrity of the individual as well as a degradation of the ideal of the university (several of the left-wing Berkeley protestors were embarrassed to realize that they were using the same phrases as Barry Goldwater) deserve the sympathy and merit the support of their fellows in an endeavor to uphold their preference for education rather than training and their desire to foster a higher degree of independence of the citizenry than would be permitted in Clark Kerr's Pluralistic Industrial Society.

THE FOCUS BLURS

Tempting as it was to believe that the protest of SDS was motivated by reasoned idealism, as time went on even highly sympathetic observers, myself among them, found it increasingly difficult to reconcile verbal idealism with behavior which ranged from lack of consideration for the rights of others to downright hooliganism.

Mario Savio's shining enunciation of principle was soon tarnished, as numerous qualified observers, most of them sympathetic, regretfully concluded that the Berkeley pleas for free speech would not stand the test of critical analysis and the appeals for student participation to improve the educational functions of the university conflicted with factual indifference to opportunities to do so.

In their analysis of university trends, Jencks and Riesman[11] point out that at Berkeley, questionnaires showed that students involved in the Free Speech Movement were as satisfied with classroom teaching as students who remained aloof, and neither group had many complaints. When Acting Chancellor Martin Meyerson called a meeting to discuss students' ideas about improving the academic program, almost nobody showed up. Similar experiences on other campuses indicate that many students who talked loudest about the need for educa-

[10] New York *Times*, August 3, 1968.
[11] Christopher Jencks and David Riesman, *The Academic Revolution* (New York: Doubleday, 1968), p. 541.

tional reform actually showed little real interest in doing anything about it.

Soon after the riots a considerable number of competent observers, with reason, concluded that the Free Speech Movement at Berkeley was only an excuse for an attempt on the part of malcontents to seize power, without any clear idea—or at least without any clearly enunciated idea—of what to do with it if they got it.[12]

THE VISION DIMMED,
BUT STILL GLIMMERING

Despite their failure to respond in mature fashion to opportunities to correct at least some of the many abuses of the multiversity, and although it became increasingly difficult to reconcile their verbal protestations with their behavior, many people, sympathetic because of the youth of the protestors, still hoped that they would bring the flickering vision of reform into clear focus. They clung to a belief that the ostensible motives of the new left were the real ones: that these youths were bravely trying to postpone Kerr's corporate state even though they knew they were unable to prevent it; that they were engaged in a Ruddite rebellion to smash the machines (universities) which were needed to produce the new corporate state in much the same futile but nonetheless romantic sense that the Luddites, many years ago in England,[13] tried to smash the machines that were needed to create the Industrial Revolution.[14] It was hoped that they really believed in participatory democracy—democracy in actual practice instead of just in name—and that they wished to participate actively and responsibly in the functioning of universities.

Though it increasingly stretched their credulity, such sympathetic observers tried to believe that when the youthful protestors were unable to express themselves in relation to their goals, they were Rebels Without a Cause. Their long hair, their careful disregard for appearance—except that their appearance must contrast with that of

[12] Nathan Glazer, in *Revolution at Berkeley*; Sidney Hook, in *Revolution at Berkeley*; William Peterson, in *The Berkeley Student Revolt*, Seymour M. Lipset and S. S. Wolin, eds. (New York: Anchor, 1965); and Professors Lipset and Seabury in *The Berkeley Student Revolt*.
[13] London *Times*, "The Times of London Looks at the Student Global War," May 27-29, 1968.
[14] This romantic concept of Luddite-Ruddite rebellion could be elaborated to include Herman Melville's Billy Budd, the epitome of innocent virtue whose speech impediment prevented him from answering the lies of the mate (Claggert) who epitomized evil and led him to last out physically. As part of such elaboration it would be primly noted that Billy was impressed from the civilian vessel, *The Rights of Man*, onto a warship, but a Luddite-Ruddite-Buddite syndrome would be a bit too much, don't you think?

members of the establishment—contributed to their romantic appeal; and they wore poverty as though it were a halo. In her perceptive analysis, *On Revolution* (1963, p. 76), Hannah Arendt described how, during the French Revolution, numerous intellectuals behaved according to the same assumption that many new leftists do today: They observe the vices of the rich (or the nobles, or the Whites) and thereupon assume that virtue must reside in the poor (or commoners, or Blacks). Then, mostly unwittingly, they conclude that if they mimic the appearance of poverty and parrot semi-literate jargon and lower class obscenities they will be flooded so fully with virtue that its only escape is to gush forth in incoherence.

Similarly, Aleksandr I. Solzhenitsyn in *The First Circle* (1968, pp. 388-389) recounts the manner in which his protagonist, Nerzhin, while serving time in a Russian forced-labor camp reserved for intellectuals—thus the reference in the title to Dante's first circle— mused upon his former belief in the intrinsic and limitless virtue of The People, a belief which sustained his allegiance to Communism until, as an equal with The People at an earlier forced-labor camp, he learned that The People not only possessed no intrinsic superiority but were more prone to crude deception, more sycophantic to their bosses, more selfishly materialistic than the middle and upper classes. This perennial fallacy, now revived by the new left, is also, of course, the lesson of Dostoevsky's allegory, The Grand Inquisitor.

But this idealized, romantic version of dedicated, selfless, youthful intellectuals began to conflict ever more sharply with their deeds, and conflicted also with the irresponsible violence espoused by their mentors, such as Che Guevara, Frantz Fanon, Fidel Castro, Ho Chi Minh, Mao, Paul Goodman, and their "Professor" *Master of Syntactical Violence*, Herbert Marcuse.

DON'T TELL ME WHAT YOU ARE, I'M WATCHING WHAT YOU DO

New leftists, with the student members clustered mostly around SDS, soon abandoned their ideals of reasoned argument and sober intellectual criticism and increasingly resorted to violence. By 1966 a campus survey conducted by New York *Times* reporter Nan Robertson[15] indicated that formerly sympathetic professors, as well as most students, were being alienated:

At Wisconsin and Berkeley . . . radicals of the left shout down opposition, stifle debate over the war, or student power, or faculty power, and call for the destruction of the "corporate-military system," which, they say, includes the university.

The editor of the Wisconsin *Daily Cardinal* said: "the extremists have broken

[15] N.Y. *Times*, January 20, 1967.

down, intellectually and psychologically. Instead of asking themselves 'What is the problem? What can be done about it?' they're asking 'What is the most radical thing to do?' "

On all five campuses visited, the new leftists were beginning to argue that the "Higher Morality" of their protest against an unjust war superceded individual rights such as free speech. The most radical among them displayed total scorn for individual liberties.

Prof. John Silber, a liberal philosopher from U. of Texas, described them as "The new Fascisti" and said: "They are indistinguishable from the far right. They share a contempt for rational political discussion and constitutional, legal solutions. . ."

At Wisconsin, Professor Williams, a socialist, whose stinging critiques of American foreign policy are read eagerly by new leftists, said of them: "They are the most selfish people I know. They just terrify me. They are acting out a society I'd like to live in only if I were an orangutan.

To indicate the degree of change which took place in SDS after the 1962 Port Huron statement, Gregory Calvery, former National Secretary, said, in 1967: "We are working to build a guerrilla force in an urban environment. We are actively organizing sedition."[16] In such manner, SDS nonviolent dissent was quickly abandoned and replaced by the tactic of deliberate provocation, sometimes called (after Frantz Fanon) *Fanonization*. SDS leader Robert Gottlieb (who organized the protest against Secretary of State Rusk's visit to New York City during which steer's blood was splashed upon automobiles and slogans sprayed upon buildings) boasted that the new tactics of deliberate provocation would be used to pursue Americans who are influential in foreign policy decisions into their homes and offices.[17]

Richard Arvedon, another SDS worker, said of the arrest which followed as he and his cohorts burned a Nazi flag in Rockefeller Plaza and pushed and jostled people until stopped by the police, "We didn't let them get anyone peacefully. It broke into fighting in each case."[18]

Such hooliganism alienated increasing numbers of sympathizers including some members of the League for Industrial Democracy, parent organization of SDS. By 1967, a member of L.I.D. described[19] them as "Panic disguised as moral superiority."

Irresponsibility and total disregard for the rights of others led the authors of a *New Republic* analysis of the seizure of buildings at Columbia to conclude:[20]

[16]N.Y. *Times*, May 6, 1967.
[17]N.Y. *Times*, November 16, 1967.
[18]N.Y. *Times*, April 18 1968.
[19]N.Y. *Times*, May 7, 1967.
[20]Dotson Rader and Craig Anderson, "Rebellion at Columbia," *The New Republic*, May 11, 1968.

The . . . issues were pretexts. The point of the game was power. And in the broadest sense, to the most radical members of the SDS Steering Committee, Columbia itself was not the issue. It was revolution, and if it could be shown that a great university could literally be taken over in a matter of days by a well-organized group of students then no university was secure. Everywhere the purpose was to destroy institutions of the American establishment.

One of the members of the SDS defense committee in Math Hall, when approached by moderate students in opposition to his instruction to the commune that it use clubs and gasoline against the police, retorted, "You fucking liberals don't understand what the scene's about. It's about power and disruption. The more blood the better."

Mark Rudd, Leader of SDS at Columbia, boasted in an open letter to President Grayson Kirk:[21]

If we win, we will take control of your world, your corporation, your university, and attempt to mold a world in which we and other people can live as human beings. Your power is directly threatened, since we shall have to destroy that power before we take over.

REASONS OR EXCUSES?

When Columbia professor of psychology Eugene Galanter brought together SDS members with Vice President Truman in an effort to resolve the issues raised by SDS, Mark Rudd admits[22] that he refused to listen to any resolution of the difficulties, telling Vice President Truman that SDS insisted on nothing less than running the entire university, and that the only action for the administration to take was to ". . . give us the bursar's office so we can pay the people."

In a letter to the Columbia *Spectator*, and in a speech at Harvard,[23] Rudd admitted that the Institute of Defense Analysis was not an important issue, not a real reason for student protest, only an SDS excuse to politicize students into leftist activism. He also stated that he opposed, rather than supported, student participation in reform of the university. He designated both the IDA and the issue of the construction of the Harlem gym as "bull." In his own words,[24] "The essence of the matter is that we are out for social and political revolution, nothing less."

Carl Davidson, interorganizational secretary of SDS, similarly referred to the lack of interest in student participation in university reform, advising those SDS members who do win influence in student

[21] N.Y. *Times*, May 19, 1968.
[22] Jerry L. Avorn, ed., *Up Against the Ivy Wall: A History of the Columbia Crisis* (New York: Atheneum, 1969), pp. 228-229.
[23] *Up Against the Ivy Wall*, p. 151; and Sophy Burnham, "Twelve Rebels of the Student Right," *New York Times Magazine*, March 9, 1969.
[24] *Up Against the Ivy Wall*, p. 291.

organizations to ". . . use this position to denounce and destroy."[25]

When SDS demands at Columbia were pusillanimously acceded to, and President Kirk resigned, they immediately attacked his successor, Acting President Andrew W. Cordier, as being implicated in the murder of Congo rebel Patrice Lumumba because he had been associated with the U.N. during its efforts to establish peace in the Congo![26] The first chant was "Cordier must go!" Soon it became "Hey, hey, Cordier, assassin for the C.I.A."[27]

From this and other evidence it would appear that the reasons for student protest advanced by SDS are quite often merely excuses for an opportunity to politicize gullible students.[28]

As the hypocrisy of SDS demands seeped through their thin veneer of righteousness, other students began to burlesque them. A group of Columbia students, falsely identifying themselves as Manhattan Indians, demanded:[29]

1. Give Manhattan back to the Indians.
2. Destroy all buildings on Manhattan so the buffalo can roam again.
3. Reserve the state of Indiana for Indians only.
4. Reinstate the Indian head nickel.
5. Halt classes on Sitting Bull's birthday.
6. Grant complete amnesty for Geronimo.

If these demands were not met, they threatened to hold Mark Rudd hostage.

A group of Queens College students, calling themselves Irish Students Interested in Scholastic Help[30] demanded:

1. All students be compelled to march in the St. Patrick's Day parade.
2. Only Irish coffee be served in the cafeteria.
3. All college identification cards be green.
4. An exchange program with Dublin University.
5. The establishment of the Michael J. Quill Irish Studies Program.
6. Admission of 200 deserving Irish students next fall.

Between the first of January and the middle of June, 1968, there were 221 major demonstrations at 101 colleges and universities.[31]

---

[25] George Charles Keller, ed., "Six Weeks that Shook Morningside," *Columbia College Today*, Spring, 1968.

[26] *Time*, August 30, 1968.

[27] N.Y. *Times*, September 19, 1968.

[28] John R. Searle, "A Foolproof Scenario for Student Revolts," *New York Times Magazine*, December 29, 1968.

[29] "Six Weeks that Shook Morningside," p. 56.

[30] N.Y. *Times*, February 23, 1969.

[31] N.Y. *Times*, August 27, 1968.

Black Power was a factor in 97 of the demonstrations, but 50 involved student power, 26 involved Vietnam protests, and attempts to prevent recruiting by Dow Chemical Company accounted for 14. In 59 cases demonstrators took over a building; there were 42 sleep-ins or sit-ins, 11 boycotts, eight incidents of blocking or resisting arrest—and five of these were associated with a charge of attempting to destroy life or property.

Events which took place at Columbia University were not included in the above compilation made by the National Student Association, but the white students at Columbia, led by SDS, seized five buildings, barricaded the Dean of Men in his office, put up posters bearing the likenesses of Lenin, Che Guevara, and Malcolm X, and proclaimed, "Lenin won, Fidel won, we'll win."[32] Private papers of President Grayson Kirk were stolen from his files and reproduced, obscenities were written on a portrait of his family; papers representing ten years of research by a professor who had questioned their violent methods were taken from his files and burned, some police were bitten by girls, others were kicked in the groin, most were spat upon, and all were subjected to obscene abuse.

During the short time it took for the idealistic vision of SDS to become senseless vandalism, the Free Speech Movement was transmuted into the Foul Speech Movement, with obscenities long associated with gutter language, and quite commonly used by 12-year-old boys as they smoke their first cigarette, came into usage among youths who long since should have out-grown them. One of the more widely used expressions, "Fuck the Draft" attests that their knowledge of physiological possibilities is as deficient as their sense of decency. Their only rationale is "We are not obscene; Vietnam is obscene."

BOYS WHO WORE PINK BOOTIES

When analysing the appeal of SDS activities, one should remember that, while they sometimes attract fairly large numbers of students in support of specific protests, most students disagree with them on most counts. Zealous activists are few. It is necessary to remember, also, that there are many sound reasons for protesting the deterioration of the university into the knowledge-factory multiversity and the drift of the society into a corporate state in which people are divided into the managers and the managed. It is well to remember that the structure of the American university was a jerry-built bundle of paradoxes embedded in tradition and held together mostly by platitudes and, as such, invited attack. Too, Communists in their various shades of red were eager to exploit any protest against the multiversity or against the society, especially those protests which were related—as many were—to military affairs.

[32] N.Y. *Times*, May 1, 1968.

While all of these and other factors should be included in an analysis of the motives of student protest, the types of hooliganism encouraged by SDS activists requires other interpretation as well. When youths protest the existing American order, the wonder about their motives is often put in the form of a question as to whether their protest is a generational revolt or a predictable response from Red Diaper Babies. I believe that the form of violence espoused by SDS activists involves something else—it is mostly engendered by boys who wore pink booties.

A generational revolt would be exemplified by the rakehell son of a Calvinist clergyman or by the wastrel son of a stingy father. As for Red Diaper Babies, Bettina Aptheker, daughter of Communist theoretician Herbert Aptheker, would be an example, and so would Staughton Lynd, son of leftist sociologist parents Robert and Helen Lynd. The meaning of the Pink Bootie Boys is derived in part from Kenneth Keniston's sympathetic analysis[33] which he derived from his lengthy interviews with activist new leftists.

Keniston found that these activists came from middle-class or upper-middle-class homes; most of their parents had attended college, and all of the radicals had attended "good" colleges. Economically, all were well off. Some came from Communist backgrounds, but ". . . most of the remainder were Democrats, often of a 'Stevensonian' persuasion." The idea of a generational revolt is negated by Keniston, who learned that, while the political beliefs of parents and children differ in detail, they do not differ in principle.[34]

. . . each of those interviewed was brought up in a family whose core values were fully congruent with his present radical activities . . . the great majority of these radical parents currently applaud, approve or accept their activities . . . Especially for those from radical families, the process of radicalization involves a return to the fundamental values of the family.

Nathan Glazer, in "The Jewish Role in Student Activism" (*Fortune*, Jan., 1969), also favors the Red Diaper interpretation over the Generational Revolt, citing a study of University of Chicago Jewish student militants, 60 percent of whose parents were either "highly liberal" or "socialist" while only six percent of a control group of students put their parents in such categories.

While, according to Keniston,[35] both parents seem to have been frustrated or dissatisfied, the fathers became crushed and alienated from the home ". . . withdrawn, detached, embittered and distant." While "the mothers of alienated students seem to have turned their drives and perhaps their own frustrated needs for love onto their sons . . . Often these mothers deprecated or disparaged their husband . . .

[33]Kenneth Keniston, *Young Radicals* (New York: Harvest, 1968). But the "Pink Booties" phrase is mine, not his.
[34] *Young Radicals*, p. 113.
[35] *Young Radicals*, p. 337.

leaving mother and son locked in a special alliance of mutual under-standing and maternal control."

Growing up in a mother-dominated, liberal-left family during an era when parents were so influenced by pseudo-scientific theories about child rearing that they were afraid to discipline their children seems to be a factor in producing undisciplined activists who grew up in pink booties and now frantically try to find their identity—their manhood.

This pattern of parental approval and (at least implied) maternal dominance is illustrated in an interview with Mark Rudd's mother:[36]

Mrs. Jacob Rudd pointed out the picture window of her brick ranch house to a colorful rock garden. "My revolutionary helped me plant those tulips last November, my rebel," she said with motherly pride.

Mama's approval of Mark's activities is obvious, but please note, also, the reference to *my* revolutionary, *my* rebel—not *our* revolu-tionary, *our* rebel.

SIZE OF STUDENT GROUP AS A FACTOR

Any analysis of motives of the SDS of the 1960's should take into consideration the recency of change in student behavior, for while the university began to deteriorate into the multiversity and the society into the corporate state in the 1930's and 1940's, the college students of the 1950's were commonly called "The Silent Genera-tion," and were widely criticized for their apathy and for their readiness to fit into the materialistic economic system.

As for the influence of the size of a group: When you enter a building as most people are leaving it, or get off a bus when a crowd is trying to get on, don't you feel just a bit apologetic and on the defensive? Don't you, conversely, feel righteous and somewhat more powerful than usual when you join with 50,000 others to cheer the winning home team? While it is easy to exaggerate the importance of belonging to a large group in an endeavor, it is foolish to ignore the possible influence of the size of a group upon the behavior of its members.

The history of nations indicates that they tend to expand in both power and territory when they undergo a period of rapid growth of population, and that they not only cease growing but tend to shrink in both territory and prestige when their rate of population growth slows. England, first major country to benefit by the improvements of the Industrial Revolution, experienced a population spurt and grew into the mighty British Empire. But as her rate of population growth declined so did her status as a world power. She relinquished most of

[36]N.Y. *Times*, May 19, 1968.

her foreign territories, and now even Scotland and Wales are restive under her moderate control. France went through a similar expansion followed by similar decline, and when Germany's turn came, her efforts to expand conflicted with British and French claims and World Wars I and II followed. Japan similarly expanded and then contracted in territory when her population underwent rapid growth which was followed by a sharp decline in her birth rate. During and after World War II, Russia pushed her control into much of Europe and now, with a much slower rate of growth, this hold is increasingly being challenged. America expanded similarly during the years of her rapid population growth, but in recent years our hold on extra-continental territories has weakened, and in Korea and Vietnam our vaunted military might has shown itself to be mostly talk as our population growth slowed to the lowest rate in our history.

In student revolts also, one factor may involve the fact that the current student generation is the one which was born soon after the end of World War II—when birth rates were very high. The peak rate was in 1947, when 3,834,000 babies were born. Though the rate immediately began to decline, the larger population base brought increased numbers of births to a peak of 4,350,000 in 1960, after which both the rate and the number declined, with the rate in 1967 and 1968 being the lowest in our history and the number of births going down from the 1960 peak of 4,350,000 to 3,496,000 in 1967—many fewer babies than were born 20 years ago.

The influence of numbers as such is clearly a significant aspect of student revolts in countries such as France, Japan, and Mexico, where sheer lack of facilities to accommodate the flood of new students is a provocative issue. Mexican students revolt even though they have long possessed most of the rights now demanded by American students. But perhaps the best indication that much of the revolt is muscle-flexing by a large population group which is looking for excuses rather than reacting to reason is found in the fact that while American students often idolize Che Guevara, students in Cuba (N.Y. *Times* 10/20/68), ". . . have been roaming the streets of Havana burning Cuban flags and destroying portraits of Ernesto Che Guevara. . . ."

As another aspect of the possible influence of the effect of unusually large or unusually small population groups, consider the plight of females born in post World War II years. Females, on average, marry men who are two years older than they are, so the large group of girls born in the first couple of years after World War II must draw its husbands from a small group (the deficit would be close to a million) of men born before the end of the war. The demand for eligible males far exceeds the supply; hence, in the form of bikinis and mini-skirts, females advertise their products in a frantic and shameless manner. With keener competition, they become more aggressive, sexually and otherwise, and the males, especially the insecure ones who grew up in pink booties, have their already shaky masculine status further threatened.[37]

Coupled with their "mama's boy" insecurity and shrinking from aggressive females, these youths who got too much, too soon, too easy, must feel guilty about Vietnam. After all, most of them are evading the draft and if they have any sense of decency at all they must feel badly about the preferred status which protects them from the draft while others must run the risk of death. Instead of facing up to their insecurity and their guilt and trying to make up for it, they blame everybody and everything else. They embody A. E. Housman's plaint, "I, a stranger and afraid / In a world I never made," when they should feel

> I, a man, alone but not lonely
> My world made by me,
> Me only.

While there is merit to some of their complaints, there is only squawking cacophony in their everlasting whining. On page 48 of their recent analysis of students and universities quoted above, Jencks and Riesman describe the magnitude of their squawks:

Some among the current generation of students are in revolt against all authority and obsessively test all limits. Clothes are a constraint; razors are a constraint; courses and examinations are constraints; intervisitation hours are a constraint; refined language is a constraint. This revolt is supported by developments in the arts and also in the bohemias of the world—developments that are readily visible to undergraduates ... On many campuses the rebels can also count on the tolerance of their fellow students, who fear to be thought square or chaste or fearful or finks.

George Kennan[38] argues that these play-acting revolutionaries refuse to face the fact that the "... decisive seat of evil in this world is not in the social and political institutions but ... in the weakness of the human soul itself. Their vision is apocalyptic—a final upheaval to cleanse the human race." Karl Jaspers makes the same point, though in a somewhat different context,[39] in his analysis of the future of Germany.

The many and cavernous omissions in their responses join with the inexcusable excesses of their behavior to make it increasingly difficult to accept the verbal protests of SDS at their face value.

[37]Vance Packard, *The Sexual Wilderness* (New York: McKay, 1968). Also, Charles L. Winick, *The New People: Desexualization in American Life* (New York: Pegasus, 1968).
[38]George F. Kennan, *Democracy and the Student Left* (Boston: Little-Brown, 1968), pp. 9-10.
[39]Karl Jaspers, *The Future of Germany* (Chicago: Univ. of Chicago Press, 1967).

If the SDS is really dedicated to participatory democracy, to civil rights, to responsible student participation in universities, to intellectual analysis of trends in society, to freedom of the individual from the total oppression of the total state, why do they fail to develop specific proposals for improvement of the university, as other students have done? Why do they fail to look for inspiration in the works of the Yugoslav, Milovan Djilas, whose analyses of bureaucracy describe intelligently and precisely what they pretend to detest? Why do they fail to turn to the works of the Russians—Pasternak, Alexsandr I. Solzhenitsyn, and Mikhail Bulgakov? Why did they fail to respond with all their considerable fury to the Russian invasion of Czechoslovakia? Why don't they credit Barry Goldwater specifically and conservatives generally for first discovering the problems they now shout about? Instead of discriminate and intelligent analysis, why do they select mentors who do little more than shriek about the desirability of violence; whose level of intellectual analysis, for the most part, is laughably childish.

Add to all this their disregard for the rights of others, including the rights of their fellow-students, their senseless and sometimes vicious destruction of property, their frequent use of puerile obscenities which they should have outgrown years ago; their fake poverty and inappropriate affectation of purity and innocence; their babyish fascination with their physical excretions and their general dirtiness, now that mama isn't around to wash them, their cops-and-robbers play-acting at being guerillas, and it becomes reasonable, I believe, to conclude that in large measure the ostensible reasons for the activities of SDS are only excuses, and that a major factor in their behavior is a childish effort to postpone growing up, a frantic effort to delay the acceptance of adult responsibility.

Daniel James, editor of the diaries of Che Guevara[40] expresses this idea generally about one of their mentors, saying, "He needed a revolution far more than the revolution needed him."

New York *Times* reporter Tom Buckley describes those youths who engaged in violence in Chicago during the National Convention of the Democratic Party by saying that[41] ". . . these young men were playing a game—in which the maximum penalties were not the torture, death or endless imprisonment faced by a real revolutionary but a possible crack on the head, a night in jail and their pictures in the papers." SDSers Tom Hayden and Rennie Davis ". . . appeared to think of themselves as hardened revolutionaries in some way comparable to Che Guevara in the Sierra Maestra, Ho Chi Minh in the jungles of Tonkin and Mao Tse-tung in the caves of Yunan. But they

[40]Daniel James, ed., *Complete Bolivian Diaries of Che Guevara and Other Captured Documents* (New York: Stein and Day, 1968).
       [41]Tom Buckley, "The Battle of Chicago: From the Yippies' Side," *New York Times Magazine*, September 15, 1968.

used the revolutionary lingo and little else." One thirty-year-old "kid" said, "My goal is at the age of 35 to act like I'm 15."

So strange as to be difficult to believe is the continuance of such play-acting into adult years. A new left graduate student, interviewed by Lionel Abel,[42] when asked how Che Guevara would differ from the pacifism of Paul Goodman, mimed what he thought Guevara's answer would be:

Amigo, I want there to be more Vietnams, as many Vietnams as possible. Wars without number, murders, executions, surprise raids, night attacks, bombings and burnings and beatings. . .

How can people take such clowns seriously? And this question is the most disquieting one which arises out of the antics of SDS—What is the basis for the guillibility of students who take them seriously enough to support their shenanigans, what is lacking in such students, in their parents, in the educational system which fails so completely to instill respect for reason?

The primary rationale which SDS employs to defend its seizure of buildings, destruction of property, its disruption of the proper business of the university and its immediate demand for amnesty prior to any discussion, is that its members are engaged in civil disobedience and are hence entitled to protection under the First Amendment. Associate Justice Abe Fortas negates this contention:[43]

By calling criminal acts "civil disobedience," they seek to persuade us that offenses against public and private security should be immune from punishment and even commended. They seek to excuse physical attacks upon police; assaults upon recruiters for munitions firms and for the armed services . . . trespassing on private and official premises; occupying academic offices . . . and promiscuous violence.

We are urged to accept these as part of the First Amendment freedoms. We are asked to agree that freedom to speak and write, to protest and to persuade, and to assemble provides a sanctuary for this sort of conduct. But that is nonsense.

The Supreme Court of the United States has said, over and over, that the words of the First Amendment mean what they say. But they mean what they say and not something else.

They guarantee freedom to speak and freedom of the press—not freedom to club people or to destroy property. The First Amendment protects the right to assemble and to petition, but it requires—in plain words—that the right be peaceably exercised.

[42] Lionel Abel, "Seven Heroes of the New Left," *New York Times Magazine*, May 5, 1968.
[43] Abe Fortas, *Concerning Dissent and Civil Disobedience* (New York: New American Library, 1968).

IN SUMMARY

Student protest is a legitimate form of activity which is badly needed as the ideals of the university are bartered away by professors and administrators for foundation grants and federal contracts but— following the principles laid down by Sidney Hook[44] —such protest should be truly nonviolent (to provoke police to react violently and then to whine about police brutality is, in my judgment, more contemptible than outright violence). Civil disobedience is never morally legitimate when other means to remedy the evil are avilable, and those who resort to it are conscience-bound to accept the punishment imposed by law (to mewl for amnesty is unmanly, and raises serious question about the conviction of the protestor). A moral issue should be clearly at stake, and the protestors should recognize that men of good will sometimes differ on such issues, making discussion more appropriate than action.

When civil disobedience is done there should be a clear relation between the disobedience and the situation which needs correction (scrawling obsenities on a family portrait and stealing materials from private files is hardly appropriate conduct for those who say that they want to reform the university). Those who engage in civil disobedience to obtain redress for what they believe to be wrong should know that their precedent may be followed by those who believe the opposite.

Though the SDS began with high ideals, many of its representatives soon began to violate some of the most fundamental rules of proper intellectual protest, and they chose to ignore the many mentors who could provide them with an adequate intellectual rationale and selected mentors whose principal stress was anti-intellectual violence.

Thus members of a large population group want to throw their weight around without paying the price. They represent a group which had too much, too soon, too easy; its male members feel guilty about the unearned draft preference they receive and, in some cases at least, their already shaky "mama's boy" masculinity is further rudely jostled by aggressive females. Influenced by Communism and socialism, but with sufficient knowledge of Russia and England to reject the drab bureaucratic greyness which characterizes countries which have put Communism and socialism into practice, they turn to variants which are remote enough (Chinese Maoism, Ho Chi Minh) or exotic enough (Frantz Fanon, Che Guevara) to romanticize their inchoate yearnings and their unanalysed fears, and now their credo may be expressed in the following doggerel:[45]

[44] Sidney Hook, "Neither Blind Obedience nor Civil Disobedience," *New York Times Magazine*, June 5, 1966.
[45] The blame for the doggerel is mine, but the idea was derived from Bugs Baer as reported by columnist Paul Jones in The Philadelphia *Evening Bulletin*, June 27, 1968.

The Credo of SDS

Obeying rules I did not pass
   Thwarts my ego.
So, alas:

I'll drink no beer
   I did not brew,
Nor smoke the pot
   I never grew.

Nor drive the car
   I did not build,
Or eat the meat
   I have not killed.

While awaiting chaos
   (for which I yearn),
I'll spend no money
   I did not earn.

SDS has
   Set me free,
To hell with
   Newton's gravity!

THE CLICHES OF THE RADICAL STUDENTS

James Reston

Q—The meeting of the RRS (Revolutionaries for a Radical Society) will now come to order, if I may use that word. What is the matter with our universities today?

A—They are irrelevant, arrogant and unresponsive.

Q—Precisely. And what is missing?

A—Meaningful interpersonal relationships.

Q—Very good. Now in dealing with irrelevant, arrogant and unresponsive universities where there is no meaningful interpersonal relationships, what happens?

A—A lack of communications.

Q—Leading to?

A—Separation and alienation of the individual.
Q—What is the remedy for this?
A—A dialogue.
Q—Of course, but what kind of dialogue?
A—A *meaningful* dialogue between people under thirty.
Q—How can this be achieved?
A—By radicalizing the moderates in the student body through the process of participatory democracy.
Q—Who participates in participatory democracy?
A—Everybody participates in participatory democracy: it is the tribune of the people, the foe of the imperialist machine, the scourge of the military-industrial complex, the enemy of. . . .
Q—Wait a minute! You are confusing our clichés. Try again: Who participates in participatory democracy? Now be careful.
A—We do. The majority must be manipulated for its own good and, we know what that is.
Q—That's better. Now, suppose the moderates just go on dating, studying and attending classes, what do we do?
A—We force them to pay attention. We have a confrontation with the Establishment.
Q—How do we do it?
A—We occupy and liberate a university building. We evacuate the deans, and capture and Xerox the files, and publish carefully selected documents thereof, and wait for the cops.
Q—So?
A—So the cops arrive and crack a few skulls and clear the joint, and then we're in business. The moderates wake up and are appalled and come over to our side, and the press comes running and dramatizes the confrontation.
Q—Good. You are getting the point. Please define and explain the press.
A—It is a capitalist tool, the agent of the ruling class, the voice of the Establishment, but it is useful.
Q—Please explain.
A—It dramatizes the confrontation. We feed its hunger for excitement and conflict. We hate its objectivity but we can use it.
Q—How so?
A—It nationalizes our struggle. It escalates the confrontation. It mobilizes the student power and black power and it divides and confuses the faculty.
Q—How so?
A—The faculty seldom likes the administration of the university, or the students, and it hates to choose between them; but it loves to argue about the decision-making process, and while the faculty members argue, we can shut the place down.
Q—And then?
A—We have a meaningful dialogue, and meaningful interpersonal

relationships, and a confrontation with the incompetent and illegitimate power-holders and the Establishment press.

Q—And after that?

A—We put forward our demands.

Q—How do we at RRS describe our demands?

A—They are non-negotiable.

Q—What do we mean by that?

A—We don't want a negative peace, we want a positive peace. We want what we want and to the wall with the opposition, and amnesty for our warriors. The Establishment is wrecking the university, but we will inherit the wreckage.

Q—And what will we do when we inherit it?

A—We'll think about that later.

WHAT THE REBELLIOUS STUDENTS WANT

Stephen Spender

What do the students want? Statements have been made by students, reports by committees, books have been written by journalists, to answer this question. When one has read a few of these one begins to wonder—which is the student movement about, the society or the university? For it soon becomes clear that the students have two sets of complaints, two sets of demands, one about the university, one about the "society." Sometimes the two are merged and the university is seen as "a microcosm of the society."

By now all the complaints have been thoroughly gone into, and there is (if one reads, for example, the reports set up by the University of California and Columbia University) a plea of partial guilt from the universities, and much excusing and explaining. Since the war, we are reminded, there has been an immense expansion of university education all over the world. The consequent increase in the university population, with corresponding increases in courses, tests and examinations, and in practical arrangements about dormitories, housing, etc., has been so great that personal relations between teachers and taught have largely broken down. The university has become a faceless education factory. Lectures are given through TV to overflow audiences, tests are made by mechanical systems, professors are unapproachable, the student thinks of himself (or thinks that he is thought of or likes people to think that he thinks that he is thought of) as a number on a computer card.

In addition to the depersonalization of the student-teacher relationship, the teachers themselves have begun to think that they are in a similar, depersonalized relationship with the university: with the regents, chancellors, vice-chancellors, presidents, alumni and the immensely overgrown administration. Indeed, younger members of the faculty often identify with the student in thinking that both are dealing with an impersonal machinery of administration and knowledge distribution.

All this is a bit exaggerated, but one can see it being built up into the great historical explanation of why the university went wrong (like those accounts of the burial grounds full of bones of nameless illegitimate babies next to convents, which explain the decadence of the monasteries). There are, of course, good professors who are friendly to their students and there are small seminars, just as there were monks who didn't cohabit with nuns.

There are similar complaints, partly true and partly exaggerated, in France and West Germany. There is the absurd centralization of French education, all directed from the ministry, so that the minister can sit in his office knowing exactly what every student in a certain class studying a certain subject is reading at any hour of that day (exaggeration, of course). In most West German universities, professors remain the unapproachable old princelings, hedged round by their assistants, they always have been. An attempt was made with the founding of the new Freie Universität in West Berlin after the war to alter this and form a new democratic university, "a community of teachers and taught," but it largely collapsed through a combination of overcrowding, political complications and internecine disputes. In Italy, matters are still worse. Professors are so badly paid that most of them, to be able to afford to teach, have to take other jobs. I have no space here to discuss universities in Asia, but they are slums for students who know that without a university degree they won't get jobs and that with it the chances are enormous that they won't do so either. Perpetual revolt here reflects perpetual despair.

In America the stated demands of the students are that they should have voices in deciding who teaches them, what they study, how they are governed. They demand, on the university level, participation— that is to say, sitting with faculty members on committees where decisions are made, and having a student senate or parliament that can debate university policies.

Another complaint of the student militants is against the relations of the university with the power structures of the surrounding society and the representation, in American universities, of governmental, military and industrial interests: Dow Chemical, the Institute for Defense Analyses, the C.I.A. and the R.O.T.C.—which are bound up with militant policies the militant students detest. Today these are symbolized by Vietnam. The presence of these organizations is resented not only because of what they are and what they stand for, but also because, the students feel, they cast ideological shadows across the university and "prove" that its ultimate purpose is to instill in them the attitudes of the military and industry.

In France the militants also suspect the state of infusing capitalist ideology into the university. Daniel Cohn-Bendit in his book, "Obsolete Communism: the Left-Wing Alternative," writes about his fellow students of sociology at Nanterre forming the opinion that the American industrial psychology they were taught was a weapon for helping the world *bourgeoisie*. In being trained as sociologists the students were being enlisted to support the system. (Apart from this there was the worry as to whether they would get any employment anyway.) Alain Touraine, one of the teachers at Nanterre sympathetic to the students, remarked in an interview: "If the study of sociology didn't make one sensitive to social problems, it would be a bit surprising." So the Nanterre students of sociology and political science formed groups (*groupuscules*), which approached their subjects with the idea of interpreting them as two-edged instruments that they were being taught to use in defense of the society but that could also be turned against it and used for the defense of "*la révolution*."

There is a problem special to American universities that has greatly preoccupied the students, and that is racialism. This is a problem that certainly cannot be dissolved in "participation" or, as might happen in cases of recruiting for industry or military purposes, simply be removed from the campus. The blacks are there on the campus, and even if they segregate themselves from the whites, their absence is felt. It is a problem that involves the students more than the administration, for ultimately its solution lies in the relations between black and white students. The importance of racialism as a new element in the life of the campus was evident during the Columbia uprising, when the question of building or not building the proposed gymnasium on Morningside Heights—which involved the racial problem—became a central issue. As every reader will know, the university had arranged that the blacks of neighboring Harlem would be able to use the gymnasium; but at the same time the students disputed the conditions under which they were to do so, and they charged that the administration had been high-handed in its relations with the neighborhood.

I am not concerned here with the rights or wrongs of this. What far outweighs them is the importance of the black-white confrontation that they symbolize. The white students at Columbia, in opposing the building of the gymnasium, had shown their eagerness to join with the black students in a situation that made black and white one community.

As most readers will recall, the white students were rebuffed, their advances rejected by the black students. There is a parallel here to the relation of the Sorbonne students with the young workers. At the time of the general strike in France following on the student revolt, the students marched to the Renault factories on the outskirts of Paris and asked the young workers to join them. Like the white students at Hamilton Hall who, after joining the blacks were then asked to leave, the Sorbonne students were coldly received by the workers and then asked to go home.

Yet, rebuffed as they were, I think that the attempt to form a community of the young who shared their ideals was what American and French students most deeply wanted. Their "demands" and "confrontations" were real, but they were improvised, and shifting, and always had the look of symbolic causes that referred to issues beyond themselves. One could not move among the students who had "liberated" buildings at Columbia and at the Sorbonne without realizing that what most closely answered their "demands" was the communal life they had temporarily achieved. When they called the "liberated" buildings "ours," they indicated what they meant by the revolution: the commune.

The authors of the Cox Commission Report, "Crisis at Columbia," quoted from an eyewitness of the events during the occupation of Low Library:

". . . Always meetings and more meetings lasting long into the night. Participatory democracy. There was a real community spirit; everything belonged to everybody; the building was 'liberated'. . . . Here was a single commune in which adult hypocrisies did not apply any longer, where people shared and shared alike, where democracy decided everything. . . ."

With their Gallic intensity, the students occupying the Sorbonne, with their discussions in the Grand Amphithéâtre and many classrooms spilling over into the "liberated" Odéon Theatre, diffused a similar excitement. A professor at Paris who had little sympathy with the "movement" told me that he had never seen his students so beautiful, so inspired. Students who were stupid and silent in class suddenly became eloquent and comprehending.

In his famous interview with Jean-Paul Sartre, Daniel Cohn-Bendit was surprisingly modest about the political achievements of the students, declaring, at the headiest moment of their success, that they could not possibly achieve any revolution, and might at most be instrumental in tipping over the Gaullist regime. In fact, at one moment it looked as if they would do this. He said that all they had done was to "launch an experiment that completely breaks" with the surrounding society, "an experiment which will not last but which allows a glimpse of a possibility; something which is revealed for a moment and then vanishes. But that is enough to prove that something could exist."

This strikes to the truth of the "movement of March 22nd" (as the Nanterre students called themselves), and is perhaps more revealing of their aims than were their stated demands. What they wanted was to perpetuate the revelation of that moment, which was the revolution.

Their dilemma was that they could not perpetuate it without real political revolution, but that real revolution would probably destroy it.

Norman Mailer and Diana Trilling have commented on the "existential" character of the marchers on the White House in the spring of 1967, and the students of the Columbia uprising. What both the American and the French students wanted was to realize a state of being within a political form of such a kind that it would not blight or destroy that state of being. They were not ignorant of the fact that most revolutions of the present century have first frozen and then killed the original revolutionary impulse. Hence, their desperate invocations of Castro, Che Guevara and Mao as upholders of the revolution that remains in a state of liquefaction, *"la révolution permanente."* Hence, also, the insistence on "spontaneity"; the refusal of the outstanding figures in the movement to accept the idea that they were "leaders"; the repudiation of any suggestion that they should put forward a "program"; their distrust of all existing political movements (apart from Castro's) of the left as well as the right; their insistence on youth, because the young are physically and mentally alive to the possibilities of combining the greatest release of their subjectivity with the greatest degree of objective action. They have not yet become enclosed in either public or private worlds, and can fervently echo the paradoxical sentiment conveyed in a delightful slogan on the walls of the Sorbonne: "The more I make revolution the more I make love, the more I make love the more I make revolution."

It might be misleading to say that the true aims of the student movement are religious rather than political. Nevertheless, one finds oneself constantly forced back onto religious example to describe them. For it is in religion rather than politics that the revolution precedes the goal, and that the aim of the revolutionaries is—when they have gained power and have overthrown the conflicting systems—to retain the original vision, the *élan* of the first demonstrations and manifestoes which were, in the existence of the revolutionaries, the already accomplished revolution. The "glimpse of a possibility; something which is revealed for a moment and then vanishes" describes not so much the Marxist revolution as the Christian vision of the "kingdom of heaven which is within."

I do not mean by this that the students who burned automobiles on the barricades and those who "liberated" the private papers of a university president and then published them are saints. What I do mean is that their protest is ultimately that of their idea of "life," upheld against a society which to them spells death. Their slogans ("Imagination seizes power," etc.), their insistence on the values of a total self-awareness merged into political consciousness and the epithets that they use to describe the powers that be—sclerotic, paternalistic, bureaucratic, etc.—all dramatize a conflict between the living forces and the social death. If the students of the spring of 1968 had to choose between political necessity and personal self-realization they would have chosen self-realization. Everything they did, I think, showed that.

The revolt of the students at Nanterre began with demonstrations in favor of the rights of boys and girls to enter one another's dormitories. In this the students were not just asserting their sexual needs. They could easily have got round any rules frustrating them. They were demonstrating the identity of personal values with public rights. Sex meant "life" in their political-existential revolution. More dubiously than with sex, "pot" is revolutionary to students because it stimulates awareness of the sensation of being alive.

The grievances and demands of the students, the issues and con-frontations—reasonable or unreasonable as they may in themselves be, excusable or deplorable—express their total rejection of the deper-sonalizing forces of modern society. The feeling of the young is that the aims, the powers, the "production" of this world are opposed to the spirit, flesh, imagination, instincts and spontaneous self-realization that are life.

To avoid the embarrassing connotations of that word "life," I would have preferred to substitute some such phrase as "individual self-awareness." But in fact the students are not great upholders of individualism. They are communalists—rather than communists—believing essentially in the shared consciousness of the group that accepts their life values and rejects the death ones. The individualist, with his self-cultivation and his development of his intellectual or aesthetic sensibility, seems to them to seek after a superiority that cuts him off from the group. Here again the student movement is closer to a religious than to an aesthetic or intellectualist outlook.

In all this, however, the students are far less original than they look. Their protest is only the most recent manifestation of the idea of a struggle of those who have chosen to reject the riches of the world (which the students call the advertised products of the con-sumer society), in favor of a psychically and spiritually richer com-munity of the chosen, which is recurrent through history. One need not regard their movement as a throwback to chiliastic revolts. Ever since the industrial revolution at the end of the 18th century, there has been an underground struggle between the "life forces" and the immensely powerful inhuman and impersonal ones of the scientif-ically equipped modern state. Ever since the Romantic movement, literature has been schizoid with this struggle. It continues in an unbroken line from William Blake, to Nietzche, Carlyle and Ruskin, to D. H. Lawrence and Henry Miller, to the beatniks—to mention only a few names. It is significant, too, that critics of the students, when not attacking them for being communistic or anarchistic, attack them for being fascist. For the most revolutionary and the most reactionary movements do have this in common: their starting point is usually condemnation of materialistic, modern, bourgeois civilization.

So far I have only described what the students want in terms of what they are against, which they call "the consumer society." Since they refuse to put forward a program, or to have leaders, or to support a party, it is difficult to say what they are *for*. But some students at the Sorbonne could be quite forthcoming when I asked them about this. In fact, one of them, over coffee, took out pen and paper and made me a diagram of the society of the future. It consisted of little boxes that were autonomous groups of people running their own lives, by democratic discussion, in industries, factories, villages, universities, etc., and sending representatives to a center where those responsible, instead of giving orders to the autonomous groups, received information from them as to their plans, and related it to the plans of other similar groups.

When I went to Israel a few weeks later and asked at the *kibbutzim* how the community of a *kibbutz*—where there was an industry or an agricultural settlement—coordinated its plans with other *kibbutzim* and with the state, the picture I was given of the members of the group discussing their plans and then coordinating them with the plans of other settlements, through a center, seemed to me close to the kind of society of which the French students would approve (though Israel is too exceptional in its structures and economy to be taken as a model).

The students had this vision of their goal but little idea how they get there. However, they were confident that just because they were a different generation they would avoid the mistakes of young people in the thirties who fell into the traps of Fascism or of Communism. I am not so sure.

I was in Czechoslovakia in July, 1968, and I found the attitudes of the Czech students very different from those of their French, West German and American colleagues.

The Czech students do not care for the revolutionary talk of their Western colleagues. As some of them explained to me, they have lived through the euphoria, the horror, and finally the boredom, of revolution. What they want is to have, within the context of a socialism that they have no wish to overthrow, some individual freedom. They feel, rather bitterly, that American, French and West German students have been glutted with too much democracy, so that they are fed up with it. One of them remarked to me drily that the Czech students, during the past 10 years, would have been grateful for only a few of the freedoms that the Western students complain so much about. Recently, in Ramparts, a Czech student leader, Jan Kavan, declared: "For us, the classic liberties are of the utmost importance. . . . I have often been told by my friends in

Western Europe that we are only fighting for bourgeois-democratic freedom. But somehow I cannot seem to distinguish between capitalist freedoms and socialist freedoms. What I recognize are basic human freedoms."

The Czech students also criticize the French students for their burning of automobiles on barricades, their destructiveness, their professed contempt for the consumer goods with which—as with freedom—the Czech students feel that the Westerners are glutted, so that they cannot draw a line between having too much and having too little. As one of them said: "The French students want to remodel the whole society according to patterns of the inner life, but in doing this they neglect the material means which are needed in order that one may enjoy an inner life."

All this is anathema to the Western students, and meetings between them and their Czech colleagues have ended without much mutual understanding. This is a pity, for under the rhetoric there is a great deal that they might learn from one another. The real cause of the misunderstanding is that the Westerners are Haves, the Czechs are Have-nots. The Westerners have the freedoms and the material goods, which the Czechs are extremely short of. But even on the crude level of having or not having, here, with goodwill and a genuine desire to understand, there is much to discuss. For instance, to what extent are the Western freedoms real, and to what extent are they illusory? Those who have no freedoms are certainly in a position to explain to those who have them, and treat them so lightly, their reasons for thinking that students in Eastern Europe could benefit from Western freedoms, which do not seem illusory to them. On the other hand, there are certainly reasons why Western students feel their freedoms to be illusory. The same goes for a discussion about consumer goods. Those who have almost none are in a position to explain why, up to a certain point, labor-saving devices can be accessories to a better life. Perhaps what is wrong in the West is not that freedom is illusory and consumer goods destructive of values of living, but that people do not know how to use either in order to extend the values of living.

A Czech student, commenting on the methods used by the Western students, said to me: "They occupy their liberated buildings on the campus—so what? When they are in them what can they do except play table tennis?" Under the rather sneering tone, a real question is being posed here. Supposing—to press the question further—the student extremists succeeded in wrecking the universities, which they consider microcosms of the society. What then do they do? The students in Paris left the university and tried to join the workers, but the workers, some of whom—the young ones—were interested when they were invited into the university, were not interested when the students who had traded their mess of pottage for a pottage of mess asked to join them. Students who give up being students to become revolutionaries immediately put themselves into competition with professional politicians, trade unionists, etc., who have their own plans for a better society.

Obviously, the student revolution, after the phase of occupying buildings—which might be called the phase of demonstration—has now reached a turning point. It is likely that it will become split between those students who accept participation from the university as the answer to their demands, and those students who remain "revolutionary." There will be student senates and parliaments where topics of general university policy will be debated, as they have been at the *Konvent*, the student parliament at the Freie Universität of West Berlin. There will be student-faculty committees to arrange courses, and perhaps even to appoint teachers.

Having gone far to meet the student demands, the university will take steps to protect itself from extremists who regard it as a microcosm of the society, and who think it reasonable to begin their revolution by attacking the society at its weakest point, the university itself, without reflecting that in doing so they are also destroying their own base.

The combination of participation, self-protection by the university and wrecking tactics by the extremists, seems likely to lead to increasing concentration of the university on itself and its own problems. A type of student who likes attending committees and managing the affairs of whatever institution or family he belongs to, is likely to emerge. He is just as likely to be a Republican as a revolutionary.

If this happens it will be because the students could not answer the question put by the Czech student: So what happens after you take the buildings? At Columbia, when this question was asked, the answer, if not "Play table tennis," was "Take another building."

Although the problems of the Czech students are different from those of the Westerners, I think that what happened in Czechoslovakia still might provide a model for students elsewhere to reflect on. The Czech students did not seek to overthrow the society. They did, though, stand for values—in their case, human freedom—which the government did not grant. Proof of their seriousness about these objective demands was that they did not insist on the making of them as a monopoly of their youth. They supported whoever made them—for example, senior members of the university faculties and intellectuals of the Writers' Union. They had a clear program of aims within the university, and other aims within the society, which they pressed. In fact, they defined themselves quite consciously as a pressure group. Beyond this, they regarded the university as an institution that was inside the society—in the sense of not attempting to disrupt it—but outside it, in the sense of being independent and of maintaining standards critical of the society.

Put like this, it seems to me that there might be a parallel development of universities in the West. To try to convert the university into an instrument for wrecking the society is totally self-destructive. But there are plenty of things in the society of which the university might be critical and on which it might exercise influence as a pressure group. There are even causes that seem peculiarly the concern of youth, in which the students might really make their pressure felt (for example, the mass media and the commercialization of means of communication). The young, considered as a social group, have every right to claim that they are the section of society most open to corruption by the mass media and advertising. In the same way the young, being the inheritors of the earth, have a particular interest in exercising pressure to oppose the destruction and pollution of the earth. It seems to me curious that, during the weeks when miles of the California coast near Santa Barbara were being polluted by oil from undersea wells, the students, busy making life impossible on their campuses, made no protest against the desecration of the most beautiful coast in the world, their world.

Beyond issues such as the corruption of the mind, the destruction of the landscape and the pollution of the atmosphere—which are more the concern of the young than of the old—there lies the world. There are reasons quite other than those of understanding one another's tactics that the students of America, Eastern Europe, Asia and Latin America should try to understand one another. The attitude of the students toward problems of freedom and productivity should be discussed internationally because they are really world problems. The students should surely ask to send representatives as observers to meetings of United Nations organizations, which have bearing on the fact that while the standard of life is going up in one half of the world, it is going down in the other half. Problems of population, feeding, youth, education and illiteracy vitally and immediately concern the young. One could wish that rebellious students showed more interest in them.

The universities are extremely vulnerable, if either governments that pay for them or students who belong to them choose to destroy them. If they are not destroyed, they are extremely strong—so much so that it sometimes seems to me that, in America, one begins to see on the campuses, which resemble city states, the emergence of an alternative civilization. It is nonsense to be misguided by the "presence" on the campus of vested and governmental interests into thinking that the university is simply a reflection of the society. The university is the students, the young, and in some way their life is much in advance of the society from which they come. The students lead a life, not just as a result of their own efforts but as an effect of the institution, that is more egalitarian, more open to "direct democracy," more communal and certainly more civilized than that of the surrounding society. The universities are probably the institutions in our society in which freedom is most truly felt. It is just for this reason that some students realize that the freedoms in the democracy outside the university are so largely deceptive.

The power of the universities lies, then, essentially in their position as centers of a life more disinterested, more democratic, more critical than that of the society. The problem for the present generation of students is to exercise this power—the power of criticism—within the limits of what is possible, without destroying the university. It is an immense responsibility; for on the one hand they have more power than they realize, on the other hand they may well throw it away, not just for themselves but for future generations.

THE WAR AGAINST THE DEMOCRATIC PROCESS

Sidney Hook

In the past we used to believe that we could turn for intellectual guidance to our colleges and universities as relatively disinterested centers of inquiry in matters of law and liberty. But alas! Colleges and universities have themselves become embattled storm centers of controversy not only about the presuppositions of the democratic process but about the nature and goals of the university. A few years ago a movement in educational circles advocated that the study of communism, fascism, and other forms of totalitarianism be incorporated into the curriculum of our colleges, that we teach in a scholarly and objective fashion about the fighting faiths and subversive stratagems of the enemies of a free society. Judging by the behavior of student bodies from one end of the country to the other in refusing to give a hearing to points of view which they do not share, and their resort to direct, often violent, action to impose their demands on the academic community, we have failed for the most part to teach students properly even about the meaning of democracy—its logic, ethics, and discipline.

What I wish to consider is some misconceptions both of the democratic process and of the educational process which have contributed to current confusions, darkened counsel, and lamed effective action. Indeed, there is a real danger that unless they are exposed, they may inflame disorders in both school and society. The disconcerting thing is that these misconceptions are being circulated not by demagogues and rabble-rousers, appealing to the vigilante spirit, but by members of the intellectual establishment, individuals in a position of influence and power both in the academy and judiciary. It was said of Florence Nightingale that she began her great reforms of the hospitals of her day with the maxim that whatever hospitals accomplish, they should at least not become centers for the spread of disease. Similarly, it is not too much to expect that one who professes to live by the word of reason should not encourage propaganda by the deed, that educators not apologize for or extenuate violence on the campus, and members of the judiciary not incite to lawlessness.

It is dismaying, for example, to hear Dr. Harvey Wheeler of the Center for the Study of Democratic Institutions characterize rioting as "an American way of life" and speak of its "creative uses."

"Direct action," he says in the *Saturday Review* (May 11, 1968), "the sort that now issues in violence too often [no objection is voiced to its often issuing in violence] —must be given fuller Constitutional protection."

What does this talk about "direct action" mean for which constitutional protection is demanded? Mr. Wheeler is saying that if students, impatient with the refusal of the faculty and/or administration to grant their demands, seize a building and bar access to classes by other students and teachers, they should have *legal* protection for their action. "Violence" would be the attempt to prevent lawless students from preventing other students from carrying on their legitimate educational business. In Wheeler's view, if the faculty or students invite a speaker of whom some other students disapprove, who bar his access to the campus or physically harass him until he leaves, the disrupters should have legal protection against any disciplinary measures.

"Direct action" clearly goes far beyond the expression of orderly dissent and protest. It may be too much to expect that dissent and protest be reasoned or reasonable. But is it too much to ask that it be orderly and peaceful? If so, it is as obvious as anything can be that this call for the constitutional protection of "direct action" is an invitation to chaos. Suppose one group of students resorted to "direct action" against the "direct action" of another group of students. Since the law must be equitably enforced, it could not prevent any group from preventing those who would prevent others from carrying on. What we would have is a kind of academic Hobbesian war of all against all, with the police standing idly by as those in pursuit of the good, the true, and the beautiful pursue and decimate each other.

In a democratic society in which the legal process has not broken down, to advise citizens to resort to "direct action" to get their way is to employ a calculatedly ambiguous expression. It is a covert appeal to the use of violence. When anyone urges "direct action" on students in a university, in which due process cannot be strictly legal but must be interpreted as the use of rational procedures, he is in effect urging the substitution of mob action for the rule of reason.

After all, what is "direct action" as distinct from "indirect action"? It is action which shortcuts deliberation and consultation in order to produce confrontation. Even when passive, its consequences may be harmful to person and property. Union picketing is a right under the

First Amendment only when it is *peaceful*. But direct action is not necessarily peaceful any more than resistance is. That is why it is a clear evasion, and further evidence of confusion, when Mr. Wheeler equates his new constitutional right to direct action with the demand that "we must have a new Constitutional right to civil disobedience." A constitutional right, like any legal right, is a claim made by an individual or group which the state must be ready to enforce. Would the state then protect the "direct action" of Southern racists standing in the doorway of integrated school buildings to prevent Negro children from entering? How then could the law enforce the constitutional rights of these children? The law itself would suffer a breakdown from a new disease—legal schizophrenia.

It is a striking phenomenon that more has been written about civil disobedience in the last few years than in the entire period of American history which preceded it. But the nature of civil disobedience in the political democratic process has been radically misunderstood by many, and when these misunderstandings are applied to the academic world, the results border on the grotesque.

There are two fundamental misapprehensions about civil disobedience in general which have seriously misled many. The first is the assumption that each law in a democratic community posits as a legitimate question to every citizen whether to obey that law or to disobey it.

What is overlooked is the fact that, except on rare occasions, the prior allegiance of the *democrat* is to the legitimacy of the process by which the law is adopted. There is always, to be sure, a moral right to reject the whole democratic process on revolutionary or counter-revolutionary grounds, but we are now speaking of civil disobedience in a *democracy*. The democrat cannot make an issue of obeying or not obeying *every* law without repudiating the principle of majority rule and the democratic process to which that rule is integral. It is only on a matter of the gravest moral importance that he will be civilly disobedient, and the limits of his civil disobedience, *if he wishes to remain a democrat and operate within the democratic system*, will be drawn at that point in which the consequences of civil disobedience threaten to destroy the democratic system. That is why there is a presumption that a good citizen will obey the law which passes by majority vote of his fellow citizens or their representatives, even if he happens to be on the losing side. Why else have a vote? The implicit obligation is that the decision, freely made, after discussion, is *prima facie* binding. It is also clear that despite this *prima facie* obligation, any democrat may find *some* decision so unjust that he publicly refuses to obey it, and confident that he is not destroying the democratic system, he accepts the legal consequences of his refusal. But he cannot make *every* law of which he disapproves, *every* vote which has gone against him, a matter of

conscientious brooding, of potential commitment to civil disobedience or defiance.

An analogy may make this clear. In the ethical universe of discourse and behavior, we assume that the truth must be told. But only
a fanatic will assume that we must tell the truth all the time; and we
can all conceive of circumstances in which a moral man will tell a lie.
Yet, if anyone therefore inferred that as a moral man he must *always*
grapple with the option to speak the truth or not to speak the truth
whenever a question is put to him, he would either be the victim of
doubting mania or would be disclosing the fact that he was not a
moral man, but a confidence man. There is a *prima facie* obligation
to speak the truth, even if, in order to save a human life or a
woman's honor (to use an old-fashioned phrase), one must sometimes
lie.

The trouble with much of the literature on civil disobedience is
that in recognizing that it is *sometimes* justifiable, it does not recognize the presumptive validity (not wisdom) to a democrat of laws
passed by means of the democratic process. (Whoever, like Thoreau,
says that as an individual he will obey society's laws when he can
benefit by them but will not accept its laws when they limit his
freedom of action or offend his conscience is a freeloader.)

The second misconception of civil disobedience has far more
dangerous fruits. The civilly disobedient democrat violates the law
and accepts punishment in order to bear witness, to re-educate the
majority by provoking them to second thoughts. Having failed to
persuade his fellow citizens about the wisdom or justice of some
measure by using all the methods open to him through the democratic process, he cannot honestly use civil disobedience as a strategy
to prevent the majority of his fellow citizens from achieving their
ends. A citizen may refuse to pay a tax which he regards as morally
objectionable and go to jail to bring about the repeal of the tax; he
has no right to prevent others from paying it. A student may refuse
to take a course required of him and may suffer the consequences; he
has no right to prevent other students who wish to take it from
doing so. He may even strike and urge other students to join him,
but he has no right to prevent his fellow students from attending
class if they so desire.

What I particularly wish to challenge is the application of the
principles of civil disobedience to the university as fundamentally
misconceived. The university is not a political community. Its business is not government but primarily the discovery, publication, and
teaching of the truth. Its authority is based *not* on numbers or the
rule of the majority, but on knowledge. Although it can function in a
spirit of democracy, it cannot be organized on the principle of one,
one vote, or, if it takes its educational mission seriously, of equal
vote for student and faculty in the affairs of the mind or even with
respect to organizational and curricular continuity. The fact that a

society is politically organized as a democracy does not entail that all its other institutions be so organized—its families, its orchestras, museums, theaters, churches, and professional guilds.

I think that we may expect that all the institutions in a political democracy function in a *democratic spirit*, and by that I mean that all participants of any institution should be regarded as persons, should be heard, listened to, consulted with. But the responsibility for *decision* cannot be shared equally without equating inexperience with experience, ignorance with expertness, childishness with maturity. The assumption of a political democracy is that there are no experts in wisdom, that each citizen's vote is as good as any other's. If we make the same assumption about universities, and define a citizen of that community as anyone who functions in any capacity on the campus, we may as well shut up educational shop.

All this is denied, directly or indirectly, by the president since 1966 of the State University of New York New College at Old Westbury, Mr. Harris Wofford, Jr., who in a recent address to the American Bar Association maintained that our chief danger in college and country is not civil disobedience, but "undue obedience to law."

Why does Mr. Wofford believe that our students suffer from undue obedience and that they should be encouraged to accept "the theory and practice of civil disobedience"? He admits that "speech, lawful assembly or peaceful petition for the redress of grievances . . . [is] permitted in most of our colleges and universities." He asserts that "the right of students or faculties or visitors to advocate anything on our campuses—Nazism, Communism, sexual freedom, the legalization of marijuana, black supremacy, the war in Viet Nam, the victory of the Viet Cong . . . is generally accepted by academic administrators."

Surely this takes in a lot of ground. Why isn't this enough? Why, if students have the right to speech—which, in effect, means they can talk to faculty and administration about anything—and can make a reasonable case, do they need to be encouraged to resort to direct action? Speech means the possibility of communication. Reasonable speech means the likelihood that procedures can be established in which grievances can be heard and settled. What academic rules exist, and where, comparable with the Nazi laws against Jews and Alabama laws against Negroes, which, as Mr. Wofford claims, an "increasing number of our students feel a basic need to destroy"? Certainly not at Berkeley or Columbia.

Mr. Wofford fails to cite any. But with respect to both the community and the academy, he does say, "We need to develop a different and stronger dialectic than mere words and periodic elections." What can this mean except, when a thorny issue arises, a resort to direct action that corrupts words by making them merely "mere" and by defeating the popular will? What can this mean except a resort to violence in order to get one's way after mere words have proved unavailing? Mr. Wofford wants "to encourage civil disobedience and discourage violence." But having justified civil disobedience as a method of resisting or *preventing* the occurrence of what is regarded as evil, rather than as a self-sacrificial educational act of *teaching* what is evil, he is in effect countenancing student violence, although he claims he is not.

There are some ritualistic liberals, Mr. Wofford among them, who make a sharp distinction between humanrights and property rights, and profess relative unconcern about illegal interference with property rights, especially the lawless occupation of public premises. In some contexts this distinction may be illuminating, particularly in legislative decisions where the public interest sometimes conflicts with large vested interests in corporate property. But in the educational context it is misleading and specious. Is the right to learn a human right or a property right? When a handful of students seize buildings at Berkeley or Columbia and prevent the great mass of other students from learning, is a property right or a human right being violated? When a teacher's or administrator's office is being occupied and vandalized, is not this a grave violation of his human right to exercise his profession, an arrogant abridgment of his freedom of movement? When his files are rifled and his letters are destroyed or published, is not this the gravest violation of the personal right of privacy?

The democratic spirit in institutions of higher education has its locus not in any specific mechanisms of voicing ideas, opinions, judgments, or requests on any relevant matter of educational concern, but in the realities of participation. I know of few institutions in which participation of students in the discussion of issues is not welcomed—and where it is not, it seems to me to be elementary educational wisdom as well as discretion on the part of the faculty to see that the situation is remedied as soon as possible. But once it is present, there is no place for the violence and lawlessness which paralyzed Columbia University last spring and which are currently being prepared for other universities.

We have noted an understandable uneasiness about the presence of violence on university campuses on the part of Mr. Wheeler and Mr. Wofford, betrayed by their ambiguous and inconsistent remarks about direct action. We must, however, consider finally a more forthright defense of violence in the academy, recently presented by, of all people, a leading figure in the federal judiciary, Judge Charles Wyzanski, Jr., apropos of his discussion of the Columbia imbroglio in the *Saturday Review* (July 20, 1968). Judge Wyzanski begins his discussion by expressing agreement with Harold Howe II, former U.S. Commissioner of Education, that "the colleges were to blame, not the students, for what has been going on at Ohio State, Columbia, Boston University, in Paris and Italy." This is not an auspicious beginning, for to couple such disparate events and to imply that colleges at home and abroad are equally to blame, or are blame-worthy in the same way, is to overlook the fact that European students revolted against conditions of squalor and material scarcities not found anywhere in the United States except perhaps in small denominational colleges in the South. On no important American college campus that has spawned violence have students suffered the material deprivations and the rigid authoritarian rules of the French and Italian university systems.

Justice Wyzanski in his specific reference to Columbia University asserts that the students were right in resenting the proposed gymnasium in Harlem. Let us grant *arguendo* that students were justified in feeling resentment, although no poll was taken at the time to determine whether they wanted a new gymnasium; nor was a poll of Harlem residents taken to determine whether they preferred the existence of the stone outcropping in its barren uselessness to the presence of the gymnasium with its impressive, even if limited, facilities. The pertinent question is not whether the students were justified in feeling resentment, but whether they were justified in expressing their resentment as they did. To mention just a few things, were they justified in (1) invading and seizing five university build-ings, (2) holding an assistant dean captive and threatening him with violence, (3) pillaging the personal files of the president, (4) com-mitting acts of arson, (5) carrying out widespread vandalism costing in the neighborhood of $350,000, (6) destroying records as well as valuable research papers, (7) publicly denouncing the dean of Colum-bia College before the assembled students with some of the choicest gutter obscenities, and (8) to cite only one action symbolic of the practices of the gutter as well as its languages, spitting in the face of Vice President David Truman, who, as dean of the college the previous year, had received a standing ovation from both students and faculty for opening up new lines of communication between the administration and the student body?

Suppose for a moment that Judge Wyzanski were to make an important legal decision that some citizens of the community re-sented. This is not an unusual occurrence. What would we normally say if they expressed their resentment at Judge Wyzanski's decision in a manner comparable with the behavior of the resentful students toward the Columbia administrators? Would we content ourselves in saying that these citizens were justified in feeling resentment—as well they may!—and remain silent, as Judge Wyzanski has, about the horrendous method of expressing it? Grant that the dignity of the academic process cannot be compared with the awful majesty of the judicial process. But in either case, is not the basic or paramount issue not the fact of the resentment, however justified, but the violent disruption of the educational or legal process? Whatever the alleged grievances of the small group of students at Columbia, did they warrant the flagrant violence and other forms of lawlessness of which Judge Wyzanski seemingly approved? This is the issue of transcendent educational, political, and moral importance. It is disregarded when he asks about violence not whether it was morally justified or historically necessary but merely whether it was futile or successful. The student violence was obviously successful at Columbia. Is this all we need to know to judge it?

One final word about responsibility. There are those who dismiss the entire concept of responsibility as meaningless on the ground that all causation is ultimately reducible to the influence of objective conditions on human behavior. I know of no one who can consistently exclude reference to responsibility from his talk and thought. At the time of Little Rock, Arkansas, had someone blamed the riotous behavior of the white racists against Negro women and children on the conditions in which they were nurtured, we would have dismissed such an explanation as evasive apologetics. Not all brought up under the same conditions rioted. Sometimes conditions reduce men to a state of being which makes moral judgment on human behavior irrelevant. But whoever would explain away the assaults against academic due process as the result not of deliberate action, but merely of the state of the world or the nation, of the Vietnam War or the draft, has barred his own way to understanding the problems we face in attempting to extend human freedom under law both in schools and in society. Whatever the conditions are, so long as we are recognizably human we are all responsible for our actions; and sometimes for the conditions under which we act, too, but, of course, not in the same way, and not to the same degree.

One sign of responsibility is the making of an intelligent response not only to events that have occurred but to the possibilities of what might occur. The faculties and student bodies of this country can measure up to their responsibilities only by addressing themselves now, separately and cooperatively, not so much to the conquest of power in the academy or general community but primarily to the problems of achieving the best liberal education possible under the imperfect conditions of American society.

THE PUMP HOUSE GANG

Tom Wolfe

Our boys never hair out. The black panther has black feet. Black feet on the crumbling black panther, Pan-thuh. Mee-dah. Pam Stacy, 16 years old, a cute girl here in La Jolla, California, with a pair of orange bell-bottom hip-huggers on, sits on a step about four steps down the stairway to the beach and she can see a pair of revolting black feet without lifting her head. So she says it out loud, "The black panther."

Somebody farther down the stairs, one of the boys with the *major* hair and khaki shorts, says, "The black feet of the black panther."

"Mee-dah," says another kid. This happens to be the cry of a, well, *underground* society known as the Mac Meda Destruction Company.

"The pan-thuh."

"The poon-thuh."

All these kids, 17 of them, members of the Pump House crowd, are lollygagging around the stairs down to Windansea Beach, La Jolla, California, about 11 A.M., and they all look at the black feet, which are a woman's pair of black street shoes, out of which stick a pair of old veiny white ankles, which lead up like a senile cone to a fudge of tallowy, edematous flesh, her thighs, squeezing out of her bathing suit, with old faded yellow bruises on them, which she probably got from running eight feet to catch a bus or something. She is standing with her old work-a-hubby, who has on *san*dals: you know, a pair of navy-blue anklet socks and these sandals with big, wide, new-smelling tan straps going this way and that, *for keeps.* Man, they look like orthopedic sandals, if one can imagine that. Obviously, these people come from Tucson or Albuquerque or one of those hincty adobe towns. All these hincty, crumbling black feet come to La Jolla-by-the-sea from the adobe towns for the weekend. They even drive in cars all full of thermos bottles and mayonnaisey sandwiches and some kind of latticework wooden-back support for the old crock who drives and Venetian blinds on the back window.

"The black panther."

"Pan-thuh."

"Poon-thuh."

"Mee-dah."

Nobody says it to the two old crocks directly. God, they must be practically 50 years old. Naturally, they're carrying every piece of garbage imaginable: the folding aluminum chairs, the newspapers, the lending-library book with the clear plastic wrapper on it, the sunglasses, the sun ointment, about a vat of goo—

It is a Mexican standoff. In a Mexican standoff, both parties narrow their eyes and glare but nobody throws a punch. Of course, nobody in the Pump House crowd would ever even jostle these people or say anything right to them; they are too cool for that.

Everybody in the Pump House crowd looks over, even Tom Coleman, who is a cool person. Tom Coleman, 16 years old, got thrown out of his garage last night. He is sitting up on top of the railing, near the stairs, up over the beach, with his legs apart. Some nice long willowy girl in yellow slacks is standing on the sidewalk but leaning into him with her arms around his body, just resting. Neale Jones, 16, a boy with great lank perfect surfer's hair, is standing nearby with a Band-aid on his upper lip, where the sun has burnt it raw.

Little Vicki Ballard is up on the sidewalk. Her older sister, Liz, is down the stairs by the pump house itself, a concrete block, 15 feet high, full of machinery for the La Jolla water system. Liz is wearing her great "Liz" styles, a hulking rabbit-fur vest and black-leather boots over her Levis, even though it is about 85 out here and the sun is plugged in up there like God's own dentist lamp and the Pacific is heaving in with some fair-to-middling surf. Kit Tilden is lollygagging around, and Tom Jones, Connie Carter, Roger Johnson, Sharon Sandquist, Mary Beth White, Rupert Fellows, Glenn Jackson, Dan Watson from San Diego, they are all out here, and everybody takes a look at the panthers.

The old guy, one means, you know, he must be practically 50 years old, he says to his wife, "Come on, let's go farther up," and he takes her by her fat upper arm as if to wheel her around and aim her away from here.

But she says, "No! We have just as much right to be here as they do."

"That's *not the point—*"

"Are you going to—"

"*Mrs. Roberts,*" the work-a-day hubby says, calling his own wife by her official married name, as if to say she took a vow once and his word is law, even if he is not testing it with the blonde kids here—"farther up, *Mrs. Roberts.*"

They start to walk up the sidewalk, but one kid won't move his feet, and, oh, god, her work-a-hubby breaks into a terrible shaking Jello smile as she steps over them, as if to say, Excuse me, sir, I don't mean to make trouble, please, and don't you and your colleagues rise up and jump me, screaming *Gotcha—*

Mee-dah!

But exactly! This beach *is* verboten for people practically 50 years old. This is a segregated beach. They can look down on Windansea Beach and see nothing but lean tan kids. It is posted "no swimming" (for safety reasons), meaning surfing only. In effect, it is segregated by age. From Los Angeles on down the California coast, this is an era of age segregation. People have always tended to segregate themselves by age, teenagers hanging around with teenagers, old people with old people, like the old men who sit on the benches up near the Bronx Zoo and smoke black cigars. But before, age segregation has gone on within a larger community. Sooner or later during the day everybody has melted back into the old community network that embraces practically everyone, all ages.

But in California today surfers, not to mention rock and roll kids and the hot-rodders or Hair Boys, named for their fanciful pompadours—all sorts of sets of kids—they don't merely hang around together. They establish whole little societies for themselves. In some cases they live with one another for months at a time. The "Sunset

Strip" on Sunset Boulevard used to be a kind of Times Square for
Hollywood hot dogs of all ages, anyone who wanted to promenade in
his version of the high life. Today "The Strip" is almost completely
the preserve of kids from about 16 to 25. It is lined with go-go clubs.
One of them, a place called It's Boss, is set up for people 16 to 25
and won't let in anybody over 25, and there are some terrible
I'm-dying-a-thousand-deaths scenes when a girl comes up with her
boyfriend and the guy at the door at It's Boss doesn't think she
looks under 25 and tells her she will have to produce some identification proving she is young enough to come in here and live The Strip
kind of life and—she's *had* it, because she can't get up the I.D. and
nothing in the world is going to make a woman look stupider than to
stand around trying to argue *I'm younger than I look, I'm younger
than I look*. So she practically shrivels up like a Peruvian shrunken
head in front of her boyfriend and he trundles her off, looking for
some place you can get an old doll like this into. One of the few
remaining clubs for "older people," curiously, is the Playboy Club.
There are apartment houses for people 20 to 30 only, such as the
Sheri Plaza in Hollywood and the E'Questre Inn in Burbank. There
are whole suburban housing developments, mostly private developments, where only people over 45 or 50 can buy a house. Whole
towns, meantime, have become identified as "young": Venice, Newport Beach, Balboa—or "old": Pasadena, Riverside, Coronado Island.
    .... That is what makes it so weird when all these black pan-thuhs
come around to pick up "surfing styles," like the clothing manufacturers. They don't know what any of it means. It's like arche-
ologists discovering hieroglyphics or something, and they, god, that's
neat—Egypt!—but they don't know what the hell it is. They don't
know anything about ... *The Life*. It's great to think of a lot of old
emphysematous pan-thuhs in the Garment District in New York City
struggling in off the street against a gummy 15-mile-an-hour wind full
of soot and coffee-brown snow and gasping in the elevator to clear
their old nicotine-phlegm tubes on the way upstairs to make out the
invoices on a lot of surfer stuff for 1966, the big nylon windbreakers
with the wide, white horizontal competition stripes, nylon swimming
trunks with competition stripes, bell-bottom slacks for girls, the big
hairy sleeveless jackets, vests, the blue "tennies," meaning tennis
shoes, and the ... *look*, the Major Hair, all this long lank blonde
hair, the plain face kind of tanned and bleached out at the same
time, but with big eyes. It all starts in a few places, a few strategic
groups, the Pump House gang being one of them, and then it moves
up the beach, to places like Newport Beach and as far up as Malibu.

Well, actually there is a kind of back-and-forth thing with some of
the older guys, the old heroes of surfing, like Bruce Brown, John
Severson, Hobie Alter and Phil Edwards. Bruce Brown will do one of
those incredible surfing movies and he is out in the surf himself

filming Phil Edwards coming down a 20-footer in Hawaii, and Phil has on a pair of nylon swimming trunks, which he has had made in Hawaii, because they dry out fast—and it is like a grapevine. Everybody's got to have a pair of nylon swimming trunks, and then the manufacturers move in, and everybody's making nylon swimming trunks, boxer trunk style, and pretty soon every kid in Utica, N. Y., is buying a pair of them, with the competition stripe and the whole thing, and they never heard of Phil Edwards. So it works back and forth—but so what? Phil Edwards is part of it. He may be an old guy, he is 27 years old, but he and Bruce Brown, who is even older, 29, and John Severson, 31, and Hobie Alter, 28, never haired out to the square world even though they make thousands. Hair refers to courage. A guy who "has a lot of hair" is courageous; a guy who "hairs out" is yellow.

Bruce Brown and Severson and Alter are known as the "surfing millionaires." They are not millionaires, actually, but they must be among the top businessmen south of Los Angeles. Brown grossed something around $500,000 in 1965 and he has only about three people working for him. He goes out on a surfboard with a camera encased in a plastic shell and takes his own movies and edits them himself and goes around showing them himself and narrating them at places like the Santa Monica Civic Auditorium, where 24,000 came in eight days once, at $1.50 a person, and all he has to pay is for developing the film and hiring the hall. John Severson has the big surfing magazine, *Surfer*. Hobie Alter is the biggest surfboard manufacturer, all hand-made boards. He made 5000 boards in 1965 at $140 a board. He also designed the "Hobie" skate boards and gets 25 cents for every one sold. He grossed between $900,000 and $1 million in 1964.

God, if only everybody could grow up like these guys and know that crossing the horror dividing line, 25 years old, won't be the end of everything. One means, keep on living *The Life* and not get sucked into the ticky-tacky life with some insurance salesman sitting forward in your stuffed chair on your wall-to-wall telling you that life is like a football game and you sit there and take that stuff. The hell with that! Bruce Brown has the money and *The Life*. He has a great house on a cliff about 60 feet above the beach at Dana Point. He is married and has two children, but it is not that hubby-mommy you're-breaking-my-gourd scene. His office is only two blocks from his house and he doesn't even have to go on the streets to get there. He gets on his Triumph scrambling motorcycle and cuts straight across a couple of vacant lots and one can see him . . . *bounding* to work over the vacant lots. The Triumph hits ruts and hummocks and things and Bruce Brown bounces into the air with the motor—*thragggggh*—moaning away, and when he gets to the curbing in front of his office, he just leans back and pulls up the front wheel and hops its and gets

off and walks into the office barefooted. *Barefooted*; why not? He
wears the same things now that he did when he was doing nothing
but surfing. He has on a faded gray sweatshirt with the sleeves cut
off just above the elbows and a pair of faded corduroys. His hair is
the lightest corn yellow imaginable, towheaded, practically white,
from the sun. Even his eyes seem to be bleached. He has a rain-barrel
old-apple-tree Tom-Sawyer little-boy roughneck look about him, like
Bobby Kennedy.

Sometimes he carries on his business right there at the house. He
has a dugout room built into the side of the cliff, about 15 feet
down from the level of the house. It is like a big pale green box set
into the side of the cliff, and inside is a kind of upholstered bench or
settee you can lie down on if you want to and look out at the
Pacific. The surf is crashing like a maniac on the rocks down below.
He has a telephone in there. Sometimes it will ring, and Bruce Brown
says hello, and the surf is crashing away down below, roaring like
mad, and the guy on the other end, maybe one of the TV networks
calling from New York or some movie hair-out from Los Angeles,
says:

"What is all that noise? It sounds like you're sitting out in the
surf."

"That's right," says Bruce Brown, "I have my desk out on the
beach now. It's nice out here."

The guy on the other end doesn't know what to think. He is
another Mr. Efficiency who just got back from bloating his colon up
at a three-hour executive lunch somewhere and now he is Mr.-Big-
Time-Let's-Get-This-Show-on-the-Road.

"On the beach?"

"Yeah. It's cooler down here. And it's good for you, but it's not so
great for the desk. You know what I have now? A warped leg."

"A warped leg?"

"Yeah, and this is an $800 desk."

Those nutball California kids—and he will still be muttering that
five days after Bruce Brown delivers his film, on time, and Mr.
Efficiency is still going through memo thickets or heaving his way
into the bar car to Darien—in the very moment that Bruce Brown
and Hobie Alter are both on their motorcycles out on the vacant lot
in Dana Point. Hobie Alter left his surf board plant about two in the
afternoon because the wind was up and it would be good cata-
maranning and he wanted to go out and see how far he could tip his
new catamaran without going over, and he did tip it over, about half
a mile out in high swells and it was hell getting the thing right side
up again. But he did, and he got back in time to go scrambling on
the lot with Bruce Brown. They are out there, roaring over the ruts,
bouncing up in the air, and every now and then they roar up the
embankment so they can ... fly, going up in the air about six feet

off the ground as they come up off the embankment—*thraaagggggh*—
all these people in the houses around there come to the door and
look out. These two ... nuts are at it again. Well, they can only fool
around there for 20 minutes, because that is about how long it takes
the cops to get there if anybody gets burned up enough and calls,
and what efficient business magnate wants to get hauled off by the
Dana Point cops for scrambling on his motorcycle in a vacant lot.

Bruce Brown has it figured out so no one in the whole rubber-
bloated black pan-thuh world can trap him, though. He bought a
forest in the Sierras. There is nothing on it but trees. His own wilds:
no house, no nothing, just Bruce Brown's forest. Beautiful things
happen up there. One day, right after he bought it, he was on the
edge of his forest, where the road comes into it, and one of these big
rancher king motheroos with the broad belly and the $70 lisle Safari
shirt comes tooling up in a Pontiac convertible with a funnel of dust
pouring out behind. He gravels it to a great flashy stop and yells:

"Hey! You!"

Of course, what he sees is some towheaded barefooted kid in a
torn-off sweatshirt fooling around the edge of the road.

"Hey! You!"

"Yeah?" says Bruce Brown.

"Don't you know this is private property?"

"Yeah," says Bruce Brown.

"Well, then, why don't you get yourself off it?"

"Because it's mine, it's my private property," says Bruce Brown.
"Now you get *your*self off it."

And Safari gets a few rays from that old appletree rain-barrel
don't-cross-that-line look and doesn't say anything and roars off,
slipping gravel, the dumb crumbling pan-thuh.

But ... perfect! It is like, one means, you know, poetic justice for
all the nights Bruce Brown slept out on the beach at San Onofre and
such places in the old surfing days and would wake up with some old
crock's black feet standing beside his head and some phlegmy black
rubber voice saying:

"All right, kid, don't you know this is private property?"

And he would prop his head up and out there would be the Pacific
Ocean, a kind of shadowy magenta-mauve, and one thing, *that* was
nobody's private property—

But how many Bruce Browns can there be? There is a built-in
trouble with age segregation. Eventually one *does* reach the horror
age of 25, the horror dividing line. Surfing and the surfing life have
been going big since 1958, and already there are kids who—well, who
aren't kids anymore, they are pushing 30, and they are stagnating on
the beach. Pretty soon the California littoral will be littered with
these guys, stroked out on the beach like beached white whales, and
girls, too, who can't give up the mystique, the mysterioso mystique.

Oh Mighty Hulking Sea, who can't *conceive* of living any other life. It is pathetic when they are edged out of groups like the Pump House gang. Already there are some guys who hang around with the older crowd around the Shack who are stagnating on the beach. Some of the older guys, like Gary Wickham, who is 24, are still in *The Life*, they still have it, but even Gary Wickham will be 25 one day and then 26 and then. . . . and then even pan-thuh age. Is one really going to be pan-thuh age one day? Watch those black feet go. And Tom Coleman still snuggles with Yellow Slacks, and Liz still roosts moodily in her rabbit fur at the bottom of the Pump House and Pam still sits on the steps contemplating the mysterioso mysteries of Pump House ascension and John and Artie still bob, tiny pink porcelain shells, way out there waiting for godsown bitchen *set*, and godsown sun is still turned on like a dentist's lamp and so far—

—the panthers scrape on up the sidewalk. They are at just about the point Leonard Anderson and Donna Blanchard got that day, December 6, 1964, when Leonard said, Pipe it, and fired two shots, one at her and one at himself. Leonard was 18 and Donna was 21—21!—god, for a girl in the Pump House gang that is almost the horror line right there. But it was all so mysterioso. Leonard was just lying down on the beach at the foot of the Pump House, near the stairs, just talking to John K. Weldon down there, and then Donna appeared at the top of the stairs and Leonard got up and went up the stairs to meet her, and they didn't say anything, they weren't *angry* over anything, they never had been, although the police said they had, they just turned and went a few feet down the sidewalk, away from the Pump House and—blam blam!—these two shots. Leonard fell dead on the sidewalk and Donna died that afternoon in Scripps Memorial Hospital. Nobody knew what to think. But one thing it seemed like—well, it seemed like Donna and Leonard thought they had lived *The Life* as far as it would go and now it was running out. All that was left to do was—but that is an *insane* idea. It can't be like that, *The Life* can't run out, people can't change all that much just because godsown chronometer runs on and the body packing starts deteriorating and the fudgy tallow shows up at the thighs where they squeeze out of the bathing suit—

Tom, boy! John, boy! Gary, boy! Neale, boy! Artie, boy! Pam, Liz, Vicki, Jackie Haddad! After all this—just a pair of bitchen black panther bunions inching down the sidewalk away from the old Pump House stairs?

V

The Black Man's Revolution

"To carve out a place for itself in the politico-social order a new group may have to fight for reorientation of many of the values of the old order."

V. O. Key, Jr., *Politics, Parties and Pressure Groups*

NAT TURNER'S INSURRECTION

Thomas Wentworth Higginson

During the year 1831, up to the twenty-third of August, the Virginia newspapers were absorbed in the momentous problems which then occupied the minds of intelligent American citizens:—What General Jackson should do with the scolds, and what with the disreputables, —Should South Carolina be allowed to nullify? and would the wives of Cabinet Ministers call on Mrs. Eaton? It is an unfailing opiate, to turn over the drowsy files of the "Richmond Enquirer," until the moment when those dry and dusty pages are suddenly kindled into flame by the torch of Nat Turner. Then the terror flares on increasing, until the remotest Southern States are found shuddering at nightly rumors of insurrection,—until far-off European colonies, Antigua, Martinique, Caraccas, Tortola, recognize by some secret sympathy the same epidemic alarms,—until the very boldest words of freedom are reported as uttered in the Virginia House of Delegates with unclosed doors,—until an obscure young man named Garrison is indicted at Common Law in North Carolina, and has a price set upon his head by the Legislature of Georgia. The insurrection revived in one agonizing reminiscence all the distresses of Gabriel's Revolt, thirty years before; and its memory endures still fresh, now that thirty added years have brought the more formidable presence of General Butler. It is by no means impossible that the very children or even confederates of Nat Turner may be included at this moment among the contraband articles of Fort Monroe.

Near the southeastern border of Virginia, in Southampton County, there is a neighborhood known as "The Cross Keys." It lies fifteen miles from Jerusalem, the county-town or "court-house," seventy miles from Norfolk, and about as far from Richmond. It is some ten or fifteen miles from Murfreesboro' in North Carolina, and about twenty-five from the Great Dismal Swamp. Up to Sunday, the twenty-first of August, 1831, there was nothing to distinguish it from any other rural, lethargic, slipshod Virginia neighborhood, with the due allotment of mansion-houses and log-huts, tobacco-fields and "old-fields," horses, dogs, negroes, "poor white folks," so called, and other

white folks, poor without being called so. One of these last was
Joseph Travis, who had recently married the widow of one Putnam
Moore, and had unfortunately wedded to himself her negroes also.

In the woods on the plantation of Joseph Travis, upon the Sunday
just named, six slaves met at noon for what is called in the Northern
States a picnic and in the Southern a barbecue. The bill of fare was
to be simple: one brought a pig, and another some brandy, giving to
the meeting an aspect so cheaply convivial that no one would have
imagined it to be the final consummation of a conspiracy which had
been for six months in preparation. In this plot four of the men had
been already initiated,—Henry, Hark or Hercules, Nelson, and Sam.
Two others were novices, Will and Jack by name. The party had
remained together from twelve to three o'clock, when a seventh man
joined them,—a short, stout, powerfully built person, of dark mulatto
complexion and strongly-marked African features, but with a face full
of expression and resolution. This was Nat Turner.

He was at this time nearly thirty-one years old, having been born
on the second of October, 1800. He had belonged originally to
Benjamin Turner,—whence his last name, slaves having usually no
patronymic,—had then been transferred to Putnam Moore, and then
to his present owner. He had, by his own account, felt himself
singled out from childhood for some great work; and he had some
peculiar marks on his person, which, joined to his great mental
precocity, were enough to occasion, among his youthful companions,
a superstitious faith in his gifts and destiny. He had great mechanical
ingenuity also, experimentalized very early in making paper, gun-
powder, pottery, and in other arts which in later life he was found
thoroughly to understand. His moral faculties were very strong, so
that white witnesses admitted that he had never been known to swear
an oath, to drink a drop of spirits, or to commit a theft. And in
general, so marked were his early peculiarities, that people said "he
had too much sense to be raised, and if he was, he would never be of
any use as a slave." This impression of personal destiny grew with his
growth;—he fasted, prayed, preached, read the Bible, heard voices
when he walked behind his plough, and communicated his revelations
to the awe-struck slaves. They told him in return that, "if they had
his sense, they would not serve any master in the world."

The biographies of slaves can hardly be individualized; they belong
to the class. We know bare facts; it is only the general experience of
human beings in like condition which can clothe them with life. The
outlines are certain, the details are inferential. Thus, for instance, we
know that Nat Turner's young wife was a slave; we know that she
belonged to a different master from himself; we know little more
than this, but this is much. For this is equivalent to saying that by
day or by night that husband had no more power to protect her than
the man who lies bound upon a plundered vessel's deck has power to
protect his wife on board the pirate-schooner disappearing in the
horizon; she may be reverenced, she may be outraged; it is in the

powerlessness that the agony lies. There is, indeed, one thing more which we do know of this young woman: the Virginia newspapers state that she was tortured under the lash, after her husband's execution, to make her produce his papers: this is all.

What his private experiences and special privileges or wrongs may have been, it is therefore now impossible to say. Travis was declared to be "more humane and fatherly to his slaves than any man in the county"; but it is astonishing how often this phenomenon occurs in the contemporary annals of slave insurrections. The chairman of the county court also stated, in pronouncing sentence, that Nat Turner had spoken of his master as "only too indulgent"; but this, for some reason, does not appear in his printed Confession, which only says, "He was a kind master, and placed the greatest confidence in me." It is very possible that it may have been so, but the printed accounts of Nat Turner's person look suspicious: he is described in Governor Floyd's proclamation as having a scar on one of his temples, also one on the back of his neck, and a large knot on one of the bones of his right arm, produced by a blow; and although these were explained away in Virginia newspapers as being produced by fights with his companions, yet such affrays are entirely foreign to the admitted habits of the man. It must, therefore, remain an open question, whether the scars and the knot were produced by black hands or by white.

Whatever Nat Turner's experiences of slavery might have been, it is certain that his plans were not suddenly adopted, but that he had brooded over them for years. To this day there are traditions among the Virginia slaves of the keen devices of "Prophet Nat." If he was caught with lime and lamp-black in hand, conning over a half-finished county-map on the barn-door, he was always "planning what to do, if he were blind," or "studying how to get to Mr. Francis's house." When he had called a meeting of slaves, and some poor whites at once became the subjects for discussion; he incidentally mentioned that the masters had been heard threatening to drive them away; one slave had been ordered to shoot Mr. Jones's pigs, another to tear down Mr. Johnson's fences. The poor whites, Johnson and Jones, ran home to see to their homesteads, and were better friends than ever to Prophet Nat.

He never was a Baptist preacher, though such vocation has often been attributed to him. The impression arose from his having immersed himself, during one of his periods of special enthusiasm, together with a poor white man named Brantley. "About this time," he says in his Confession, "I told these things to a white man, on whom it had a wonderful effect, and he ceased from his wickedness, and was attacked immediately with a cutaneous eruption, and the blood oozed from the pores of his skin, and after praying and fasting nine days he was healed. And the Spirit appeared to me again, and said, as the Saviour had been baptized, so should we be also; and when the white people would not let us be baptized by the Church, we went down into the water together, in the sight of many who reviled us, and were baptized by the Spirit. After this I rejoiced greatly and gave thanks to God."

The religious hallucinations narrated in his Confession seem to have been as genuine as the average of such things, and are very well expressed. It reads quite like Jacob Behmen. He saw white spirits and black spirits contending in the skies, the sun was darkened, the thunder rolled. "And the Holy Ghost was with me, and said, 'Behold me as I stand in the heavens!' And I looked and saw the forms of men in different attitudes. And there were lights in the sky, to which the children of darkness gave other names than what they really were; for they were the lights of the Saviour's hands, stretched forth from east to west, even as they were extended on the cross on Calvary, for the redemption of sinners." He saw drops of blood on the corn: this was Christ's blood, shed for man. He saw on the leaves in the woods letters and numbers and figures of men,—the same symbols which he had seen in the skies. On May 12, 1828, the Holy Spirit appeared to him and proclaimed that the yoke of Jesus must fall on him, and he must fight against the Serpent when the sign appeared. Then came an eclipse of the sun in February, 1831: this was the sign; then he must arise and prepare himself, and slay his enemies with their own weapons; then also the seal was removed from his lips, and then he confided his plans to four associates.

When he came, therefore, to the barbecue on the appointed Sunday, and found, not these four only, but two others, his first question to the intruders was, How they came thither. To this Will answered manfully, that his life was worth no more than the others, and "his liberty was as dear to him." This admitted him to confidence, and as Jack was known to be entirely under Hark's influence, the strangers were no bar to their discussion. Eleven hours they remained there, in anxious consultation: one can imagine those terrible dusky faces, beneath the funereal woods, and amid the flickering of pine-knot torches, preparing that stern revenge whose shuddering echoes should ring through the land so long. Two things were at last decided: to begin their work that night, and to begin it with a massacre so swift and irresistible as to create in a few days more terror than many battles, and so spare the need of future bloodshed. "It was agreed that we should commence at home on that night, and, until we had armed and equipped ourselves and gained sufficient force, neither age nor sex was to be spared: which was invariably adhered to."

John Brown invaded Virginia with nineteen men, and with the avowed resolution to take no life but in self-defence. Nat Turner attacked Virginia from within, with six men, and with the determination to spare no life until his power was established. John Brown intended to pass rapidly through Virginia, and then retreat to the mountains. Nat Turner intended to "conquer Southampton County as the white men did in the Revolution, and then retreat, if necessary,

Nat Turner's Insurrection   347

to the Dismal Swamp." Each plan was deliberately matured; each was
in its way practicable; but each was defeated by a single false step, as
will soon appear.

We must pass over the details of horror, as they occurred during
the next twenty-four hours. Swift and stealthy as Indians, the black
men passed from house to house,—not pausing, not hesitating, as
their terrible work went on. In one thing they were humaner than
Indians or than white men fighting against Indians,—there was no
gratuitous outrage beyond the death-blow itself, no insult, no mutila-
tion; but in every house they entered, that blow fell on man, woman,
and child,—nothing that had a white skin was spared. From every
house they took arms and ammunition, and from a few, money; on
every plantation they found recruits: those dusky slaves, so obsequi-
ous to their master the day before, so prompt to sing and dance
before his Northern visitors, were all swift to transform themselves
into fiends of retribution now; show them sword or musket and they
grasped it, though it were an heirloom from Washington himself. The
troop increased from house to house,—first to fifteen, then to forty,
then to sixty. Some were armed with muskets, some with axes, some
with scythes; some came on their masters' horses. As the numbers
increased, they could be divided, and the awful work was carried on
more rapidly still. The plan then was for an advanced guard of
horsemen to approach each house at a gallop, and surround it till the
others came up. Meanwhile what agonies of terror must have taken
place within, shared alike by innocent and by guilty! what memories
of wrongs inflicted on those dusky creatures, by some,—what innocent participation, by others, in the penance! The outbreak lasted for
but forty-eight hours; but during that period fifty-five whites were
slain, without the loss of a single slave.

One fear was needless, which to many a husband and father must
have intensified the last struggle. These negroes had been systematically brutalized from childhood; they had been allowed no legalized
or permanent marriage; they had beheld around them an habitual
licentiousness, such as can scarcely exist except in a Slave State; some
of them had seen their wives and sisters habitually polluted by the
husbands and the brothers of these fair white women who were now
absolutely in their power. Yet I have looked through the Virginia
newspapers of that time in vain for one charge of an indecent outrage
on a woman against these triumphant and terrible slaves. Wherever
they went, there went death, and that was all. Compare this with
ordinary wars; compare it with the annals of the French Revolution.
No one, perhaps, has yet painted the wrongs of the French populace
so terribly as Dickens in his "Tale of Two Cities"; yet what man,
conversant with slave-biographies, can read that narrative without
feeling it weak beside the provocations to which fugitive slaves
testify? It is something for human nature that these desperate insurgents revenged such wrongs by death alone. Even that fearful penalty
was to be inflicted only till the object was won. It was admitted in

the "Richmond Enquirer" of the time, that "indiscriminate massacre was not their intention, after they obtained foothold, and was resorted to in the first instance to strike terror and alarm. Women and children would afterwards have been spared, and men also who ceased to resist."

It is reported by some of the comtemporary newspapers, that a portion of this abstinence was the result of deliberate consultation among the insurrectionists; that some of them were resolved on taking the white women for wives, but were overruled by Nat Turner. If so, he is the only American slave-leader of whom we know certainly that he rose above the ordinary level of slave vengeance, and Mrs. Stowe's picture of Dred's purposes is then precisely typical of his. "Whom the Lord saith unto us, 'Smite,' them will we smite. We will not torment them with the scourge and fire, nor defile their women as they have done with ours. But we will slay them utterly, and consume them from off the face of the earth."

When the number of adherents had increased to fifty or sixty, Nat Turner judged it time to strike at the county-seat, Jerusalem. Thither a few white fugitives had already fled, and couriers might thence be despatched for aid to Richmond and Petersburg, unless promptly intercepted. Besides, he could there find arms, ammunition, and money; though they had already obtained, it is dubiously reported, from eight hundred to one thousand dollars. On the way it was necessary to pass the plantation of Mr. Parker, three miles from Jerusalem. Some of the men wished to stop here and enlist some of their friends. Nat Turner objected, as the delay might prove dangerous; he yielded at last, and it proved fatal.

He remained at the gate with six or eight men; thirty or forty went to the house, half a mile distant. They remained too long, and he went alone to hasten them. During his absence a party of eighteen white men came up suddenly, dispersing the small guard left at the gate; and when the main body of slaves emerged from the house, they encountered, for the first time, their armed masters. The blacks halted, the whites advanced cautiously within a hundred yards and fired a volley; on its being returned, they broke into disorder, and hurriedly retreated, leaving some wounded on the ground. The retreating whites were pursued, and were saved only by falling in with another band of fresh men from Jerusalem, with whose aid they turned upon the slaves, who in their turn fell into confusion. Turner, Hark, and about twenty men on horseback retreated in some order; the rest were scattered. The leader still planned to reach Jerusalem by a private way, thus evading pursuit; but at last decided to stop for the night, in the hope of enlisting additional recruits.

During the night the number increased again to forty, and they encamped on Major Ridley's plantation. An alarm took place during the darkness,—whether real or imaginary does not appear,—and the men became scattered again. Proceeding to make fresh enlistments with the daylight, they were resisted at Dr. Blunt's house, where his slaves, under his orders, fired upon them, and this, with a later attack from a party of white men near Captain Harris's, so broke up the whole force that they never reunited. The few who remained together agreed to separate for a few hours to see if anything could be done to revive the insurrection, and meet again that evening at their original rendezvous. But they never reached it.

Sadly came Nat Turner at nightfall into those gloomy woods where forty-eight hours before he had revealed the details of his terrible plot to his companions. At the outset all his plans had succeeded; everything was as he predicted: the slaves had come readily at his call, the masters had proved perfectly defenceless. Had he not been persuaded to pause at Parker's plantation, he would have been master before now of the arms and ammunition at Jerusalem; and with these to aid, and the Dismal Swamp for a refuge, he might have sustained himself indefinitely against his pursuers.

Now the blood was shed, the risk was incurred, his friends were killed or captured, and all for what? Lasting memories of terror, to be sure, for his oppressors; but on the other hand, hopeless failure for the insurrection, and certain death for him. What a watch he must have kept that night! To that excited imagination, which had always seen spirits in the sky and blood-drops on the corn and hieroglyphic marks on the dry leaves, how full the lonely forest must have been of signs and solemn warnings! Alone with the fox's bark, the rabbit's rustle, and the screech-owl's scream, the self-appointed prophet brooded over his despair. Once creeping to the edge of the wood, he saw men stealthily approach on horseback. He fancied them some of his companions; but before he dared to whisper their ominous names, "Hark" or "Dred,"—for the latter was the name, since famous, of one of his more recent recruits,—he saw them to be white men, and shrank back stealthily beneath his covert.

There he waited two weary days and two melancholy nights,—long enough to satisfy himself that no one would rejoin him, and that the insurrection had hopelessly failed. The determined, desperate spirits who had shared his plans were scattered forever, and longer delay would be destruction for him also. He found a spot which he judged safe, dug a hole under a pile of fence-rails in a field, and lay there for six weeks, only leaving it for a few moments at midnight to obtain water from a neighboring spring. Food he had previously provided, without discovery, from a house near by.

Meanwhile an unbounded variety of rumors went flying through the State. The express which first reached the Governor announced that the militia were retreating before the slaves. An express to Petesburg further fixed the number of militia at three hundred, and of blacks at eigh hundred, and invented a convenient shower of rain to explain the dampened ardor of the whites. Later reports described the slaves as making three desperate attempts to cross the bridge over the Nottoway between Cross Keys and Jerusalem, and stated that the leader had been shot in the attempt. Other accounts put the number of negroes at three hundred, all well mounted and armed, with two or three white men as leaders. Their intention was supposed to be to reach the Dismal Swamp, and they must be hemmed in from that side.

Indeed, the most formidable weapon in the hands of slave-insurgents is always this blind panic they create, and the wild exaggerations which follow. The worst being possible, every one takes the worst for granted. Undoubtedly a dozen armed men could have stifled this insurrection, even after it had commenced operations; but it is the fatal weakness of a slaveholding community, that it can never furnish men promptly for such a purpose. "My first intention was," says one of the most intelligent newspaper narrators of the affair, "to have attacked them with thirty or forty men; but those who had families here were strongly opposed to it."

As usual, each man was pinioned to his own hearth-stone. As usual, aid had to be summoned from a distance, and, as usual, the United States troops were the chief reliance. Colonel House, commanding at Fort Monroe, sent at once three companies of artillery under Lieutenant-Colonel Worth, and embarked them on board the steamer Hampton for Suffolk. These were joined by detachments from the United States ships Warren and Natchez, the whole amounting to nearly eight hundred men. Two volunteer companies went from Richmond, four from Petersburg, one from Norfolk, one from Portsmouth, and several from North Carolina. The militia of Norfolk, Nansemond, and Princess Anne Counties, and the United States troops at Old Point Comfort, were ordered to scour the Dismal Swamp, where it was believed that two or three thousand fugitives were preparing to join the insurgents. It was even proposed to send two companies from New York and one from New London to the same point.

When these various forces reached Southampton County, they found all labor paralyzed and whole plantations abandoned. A letter from Jerusalem, dated August 24th, says, "The oldest inhabitant of our county has never experienced such a distressing time as we have had since Sunday night last. . . . . Every house, room, and corner in this place is full of women and children, driven from home, who had to take the woods until they could get to this place." "For many miles around their track," says another, "the county is deserted by women and children." Still another writes, "Jerusalem is full of women, most of them from the other side of the river,—about two hundred at Vix's." Then follow descriptions of the sufferings of these persons, many of whom had lain night after night in the woods. But the immediate danger was at an end, the short-lived insurrection was finished, and now the work of vengeance was to begin. In the frank phrase of a North Carolina correspondent,—"The massacre of the whites was over, and the white people had commenced the destruction of the negroes, which was continued after our men got there, from time to time, as they could fall in with them, all day yesterday." A postscript adds, that "passengers by the Fayetteville stage say, that, by the latest accounts, one hundred and twenty negroes had been killed,"—this being little more than one day's work.

These murders were defended as Nat Turner defended his: a fearful blow must be struck. In shuddering at the horrors of the insurrection, we have forgotten the far greater horrors of its suppression.

The newspapers of the day contain many indignant protests against the cruelties which took place. "It is with pain," says a correspondent of the "National Intelligencer," September 7, 1831, "that we speak of another feature of the Southampton Rebellion; for we have been most unwilling to have our sympathies for the sufferers diminished or affected by their misconduct. We allude to the slaughter of many blacks without trial and under circumstances of great barbarity. . . . . We met with an individual of intelligence who told us that he himself had killed between ten and fifteen. . . . . We [the Richmond troop] witnessed with surprise the sanguinary temper of the population, who evinced a strong disposition to inflict immediate death on every prisoner."

There is a remarkable official document from General Eppes, the officer in command, to be found in the "Richmond Enquirer" for September 6, 1831. It is an indignant denunciation of precisely these outrages; and though he refuses to give details, he supplies their place by epithets: "revolting,"—"inhuman and not to be justified,"—"acts of barbarity and cruelty,"—"acts of atrocity,"—"this course of proceeding dignifies the rebel and the assassin with the sanctity of martyrdom." And he ends by threatening martial law upon all future transgressors. Such general orders are not issued except in rather extreme cases. And in the parallel columns of the newspaper the innocent editor prints equally indignant descriptions of Russian atrocities in Lithuania, where the Poles were engaged in active insurrection, amid profuse sympathy from Virginia.

The truth is, it was a Reign of Terror. Volunteer patrols rode in all directions, visiting plantations. "It was with the greatest difficulty," said General Brodnax before the House of Delegates, "and at the hazard of personal popularity and esteem, that the coolest and most judicious among us could exert an influence sufficient to restrain an indiscriminate slaughter of the blacks who were suspected." A letter from the Rev. G. W. Powell declares, "There are thousands of troops searching in every direction, and many negroes are killed every day: the exact number will never be ascertained." Petition after petition was subsequently presented to the legislature, asking compensation for slaves thus assassinated without trial.

Men were tortured to death, burned, maimed, and subjected to nameless atrocities. The overseers were called on to point out any slaves whom they distrusted, and if any tried to escape, they were shot down. Nay, worse than this. "A party of horsemen started from Richmond with the intention of killing every colored person they saw in Southampton County. They stopped opposite the cabin of a free colored man, who was hoeing in his little field. They called out, 'Is this Southampton County?' He replied, 'Yes, Sir, you have just crossed the line, by yonder tree.' They shot him dead and rode on." This is from the narrative of the editor of the "Richmond Whig," who was then on duty in the militia, and protested manfully against these outrages. "Some of these scenes," he adds, "are hardly inferior in barbarity to the atrocities of the insurgents."

These were the masters' stories. If even these conceded so much, it would be interesting to hear what the slaves had to report. I am indebted to my honored friend, Lydia Maria Child, for some vivid recollections of this terrible period, as noted down from the lips of an old colored woman, once well known in New York, Charity Bowery. "At the time of the old Prophet Nat," she said, "the colored folks was afraid to pray loud; for the whites threatened to punish 'em dreadfully, if the least noise was heard. The patrols was low drunken whites, and in Nat's time, if they heard any of the colored folks praying or singing a hymn, they would fall upon 'em and abuse 'em and sometimes kill 'em afore master or missis could get to 'em. The brightest and best was killed in Nat's time. The whites always suspect such ones. They killed a great many at a place called Duplon. They killed Antonio, a slave of Mr. J. Stanley, whom they shot; then they pointed their guns at him, and told him to confess about the insurrection. He told 'em he didn't know anything about any insurrection. They shot several balls through him, quartered him, and put his head on a pole at the fork of the road leading to the court." (This is exaggeration, if the Virginia newspapers may be taken as evidence.) "It was there but a short time. He had no trial. They never do. In Nat's time, the patrols would tie up the free colored people, flog 'em, and try to make 'em lie against one another, and often killed them before anybody could interfere. Mr. James Cole, High Sheriff, said, if any of the patrols came on his plantation, he would lose his life in defence of his people. One day he heard a patroller boasting how many niggers he had killed. Mr. Cole said, 'If you don't pack up, as quick as God Almighty will let you, and get out of this town, and never be seen in it again, I'll put you where dogs won't bark at you.' He went off, and wasn't seen in them parts again."

These outrages were not limited to the colored population; but other instances occurred which strikingly remind one of more recent times. An Englishman, named Robinson, was engaged in selling books at Petersburg. An alarm being given, one night, that five hundred blacks were marching towards the town, he stood guard, with others, on the bridge. After the panic had a little subsided, he happened to remark, that "the blacks, as men, were entitled to their freedom, and ought to be emancipated." This led to great excitement, and he was warned to leave town. He took passage in the stage, but the stage was intercepted. He then fled to a friend's house; the house was broken open, and he was dragged forth. The civil authorities, being applied to, refused to interfere. The mob stripped him, gave him a great

number of lashes, and sent him on foot, naked, under a hot sun, to
Richmond, whence he with difficulty found a passage to New York.

Of the capture or escape of most of that small band who met with
Nat Turner in the woods upon the Travis plantation little can now be
known. All appear among the list of convicted, except Henry and
Will. General Moore, who occasionally figures as second in command,
in the newspaper narratives of that day, was probably the Hark or
Hercules before mentioned; as no other of the confederates had
belonged to Mrs. Travis, or would have been likely to bear her
previous name of Moore. As usual, the newspapers state that most, if
not all the slaves, were "the property of kind and indulgent masters."
Whether in any case they were also the sons of those masters is a
point ignored; but from the fact that three out of the seven were at
first reported as being white men by several different witnesses,—the
whole number being correctly given, and the statement therefore
probably authentic,—one must suppose that there was an admixture
of patrician blood in some of these conspirators.

The subordinate insurgents sought safety as they could. A free
colored man, named Will Artist, shot himself in the woods, where his
hat was found on a stake and his pistol lying by him; another was
found drowned; others were traced to the Dismal Swamp; others
returned to their homes, and tried to conceal their share in the
insurrection, assuring their masters that they had been forced, against
their will, to join,—the usual defence in such cases. The number shot
down at random must, by all accounts, have amounted to many
hundreds, but it is past all human registration now. The number who
had a formal trial, such as it was, is officially stated at fifty-five; of
these, seventeen were convicted and hanged, twelve convicted and
transported, twenty acquitted, and four free colored men sent on for
further trial and finally acquitted. "Not one of those known to be
concerned escaped." Of those executed, one only was a woman:
"Lucy, slave of John T. Barrow": that is all her epitaph, shorter even
that that of Wordsworth's more famous Lucy;—but whether this one
was old or young, pure or wicked, lovely or repulsive, octroon or
negro, a Cassy, an Emily, or a Topsy, no information appears; she
was a woman, she was a slave, and she died.

There is one touching story, in connection with these terrible
retaliations, which rests on good authority, that of the Rev. M. B.
Cox, a Liberian missionary, then in Virginia. In the hunt which
followed the massacre, a slaveholder went into the woods accompanied by a faithful slave, who had been the means of saving his life
during the insurrection. When they had reached a retired place in the
forest, the man handed his gun to his master, informing him that he
could not live a slave any longer, and requesting him either to free
him or shoot him on the spot. The master took the gun, in some
trepidation, levelled it at the faithful negro, and shot him through the
heart. It is probable that this slaveholder was a Dr. Blunt,—his being
the only plantation where the slaves were reported as thus defending

their masters. "If this be true," said the "Richmond Enquirer," when it first narrated this instance of loyalty, "great will be the desert of these noble-minded Africans." This "noble-minded African," at least, estimated his own desert at a high standard: he demanded freedom, —and obtained it.

Meanwhile the panic of the whites continued; for, though all others might be disposed of, Nat Turner was still at large. We have positive evidence of the extent of the alarm, although great efforts were afterwards made to represent it as a trifling affair. A distinguished citizen of Virginia wrote three months later to the Hon. W. B. Seabrook of South Carolina,—"From all that has come to my knowledge during and since that affair, I am convinced most fully that every black preacher in the country east of the Blue Ridge was in the secret." "There is much reason to believe," says the Governor's message on December 6th, "that the spirit of insurrection was not confined to Southampton. Many convictions have taken place elsewhere, and some few in distant counties." The withdrawal of the United States troops, after some ten days' service, was a signal for fresh excitement, and an address, numerously signed, was presented to the United States Government, imploring their continued stay. More than three weeks after the first alarm, the Governor sent a supply of arms into Prince William, Fauquier, and Orange Counties. "From examinations which have taken place in other counties," says one of the best newspaper historians of the affair, (in the "Richmond Enquirer" of September 6th,) "I fear that the scheme embraced a wider sphere than I at first supposed." Nat Turner himself, intentionally or otherwise, increased the confusion by denying all knowledge of the North Carolina outbreak, and declaring that he had communicated his plans to his four confederates within six months; while, on the other hand, a slave-girl, sixteen or seventeen years old, belonging to Solomon Parker, testified that she had heard the subject discussed for eighteen months, and that at a meeting held during the previous May some eight or ten had joined the plot.

It is astonishing to discover, by laborious comparison of newspaper files, how vast was the immediate range of these insurrectionary alarms. Every Southern State seems to have borne its harvest of terror. On the Eastern shore of Maryland great alarm was at once manifested, especially in the neighborhood of Easton and Snowhill; and the houses of colored men were searched for arms even in Baltimore. In Deleware, there were similar rumors through Sussex and Dover Counties; there were arrests and executions; and in Somerset County great public meetings were held, to demand additional safeguards. On election-day, in Seaford, Del., some young men, going out to hunt rabbits, discharged their guns in sport; the men being absent, all the women in the vicinity took to flight; the alarm spread like the "Ipswich Fright"; soon Seaford was thronged with armed men; and when the boys returned from hunting, they found cannon drawn out to receive them.

In North Carolina, Raleigh and Fayetteville were put under military defence, and women and children concealed themselves in the swamps for many days. The rebel organization was supposed to include two thousand. Forty-six slaves were imprisoned in Union County, twenty-five in Sampson County, and twenty-three at least in Duplin County, some of whom were executed. The panic also extended into Wayne, New Hanover, and Lenoir Counties. Four men were shot without trial in Wilmington,—Nimrod, Abraham, Prince, and "Dan the Drayman," the latter a man of seventy,—and their heads placed on poles at the four corners of the town. Nearly two months afterwards the trials were still continuing; and at a still later day, the Governor in his proclamation recommended the formation of companies of volunteers in every county.

In South Carolina, General Hayne issued a proclamation "to prove the groundlessness of the existing alarms,"—thus implying that serious alarms existed. In Macon, Georgia, the whole population were roused from their beds at midnight by a large force of armed negroes five miles off. In an hour, every woman and child was deposited in the largest building of the town, and a military force hastily collected in front. The editor of the Macon "Messenger" excused the poor condition of his paper, a few days afterwards, by the absorption of his workmen in patrol duties, and describes "dismay and terror" as the condition of the people, of "all ages and sexes." In Jones, Twiggs, and Monroe Counties, the same alarms were reported; and in one place "several slaves were tied to a tree, while a militia captain hacked at them with his sword."

In Alabama, at Columbus and Fort Mitchell, a rumor was spread of a joint conspiracy of Indians and negroes. At Claiborne the panic was still greater; the slaves were said to be thoroughly organized through that part of the State, and multitudes were imprisoned; the whole alarm being apparently founded on one stray copy of the "Liberator."

In Tennessee, the Shelbyville "Freeman" announced that an insurrectionary plot had just been discovered, barely in time for its defeat, through the treachery of a female slave. In Louisville, Kentucky, a similar organization was discovered or imagined, and arrests were made in consequence. "The papers, from motives of policy, do not notice the disturbance," wrote one correspondent to the Portland "Courier." "Pity us!" he added.

But the greatest bubble burst in Louisiana. Captain Alexander, an English tourist, arriving in New Orleans at the beginning of September, found the whole city in tumult. Handbills had been issued, appealing to the slaves to rise against their masters, saying that all men were born equal, declaring that Hannibal was a black man, and that they also might have great leaders among them. Twelve hundred stand of weapons were said to have been found in a black man's house; five hundred citizens were under arms, and four companies of regulars were ordered to the city, whose barracks Alexander himself visited.

If such were the alarm in New Orleans, the story, of course, lost nothing by transmission to other Slave States. A rumor reached Frankfort, Kentucky, that the slaves already had possession of the coast, both above and below New Orleans. But the most remarkable circumstance is, that all this seems to have been a mere revival of an old terror, once before excited and exploded. The following paragraph had appeared in the Jacksonville (Georgia) "Observer," during the spring previous:—

"FEARFUL DISCOVERY. We were favored, by yesterday's mail, with a letter from New Orleans, of May 1st, in which we find that an important discovery had been made a few days previous in that city. The following is an extract:—'Four days ago, as some planters were digging under ground, they found a square room containing eleven thousand stand of arms and fifteen thousand cartridges, each of the cartridges containing a bullet.' It is said the negroes intended to rise as soon as the sickly season began, and obtain possession of the city by massacring the white population. The same letter states that the mayor had prohibited the opening of Sunday-schools for the instruction of blacks, under a penalty of five hundred dollars for the first offence, and for the second, death."

Such were the terrors that came back from nine other Slave States, as the echo of the voice of Nat Turner; and when it is also known that the subject was at once taken up by the legislatures of other States, where there was no public panic, as in Missouri and Tennessee,—and when, finally, it is added that reports of insurrection had been arriving all that year from Rio Janeiro, Martinique, St. Jago, Antigua, Caraccas, and Tortola, it is easy to see with what prolonged distress the accumulated terror must have weighed down upon Virginia, during the two months that Nat Turner lay hid.

True, there were a thousand men in arms in Southampton County, to inspire security. But the blow had been struck by only seven men before; and unless there were an armed guard in every house, who could tell but any house might at any moment be the scene of new horrors? They might kill or imprison unresisting negroes by day, but could they resist their avengers by night? "The half cannot be told," wrote a lady from another part of Virginia, at this time, "of the distresses of the people. In Southampton County, the scene of the insurrection, the distress beggars description. A gentleman who has been there says that even here, where there has been great alarm, we have no idea of the situation of those in that county. . . . . I do not hesitate to believe that many negroes around us would join in a massacre as horrible as that which has taken place, if an opportunity should offer."

Meanwhile the cause of all this terror was made the object of desperate search. On September 17th the Governor offered a reward of five hundred dollars for his capture, and there were other rewards swelling the amount to eleven hundred dollars,—but in vain. No one could track or trap him. On September 30th a minute account of his capture appeared in the newspapers, but it was wholly false. On October 7th there was another, and on October 18th another; yet all without foundation. Worn out by confinement in his little cave, Nat Turner grew more adventurous, and began to move about stealthily by night, afraid to speak to any human being, but hoping to obtain some information that might aid his escape. Returning regularly to his retreat before daybreak, he might possibly have continued this mode of life until pursuit had ceased, had not a dog succeeded where men had failed. The creature accidentally smelt out the provisions hid in the cave, and finally led thither his masters, two negroes, one of whom was named Nelson. On discovering the terrible fugitive, they fled precipitately, when he hastened to retreat in an opposite direction. This was on October 15th, and from this moment the neighborhood was all alive with excitement, and five or six hundred men undertook the pursuit.

It shows a more than Indian adroitness in Nat Turner to have escaped capture any longer. The cave, the arms, the provisions were found; and lying among them the notched stick of this miserable Robinson Crusoe, marked with five weary weeks and six days. But the man was gone. For ten days more he concealed himself among the wheat-stacks on Mr. Francis's plantation, and during this time was reduced almost to despair. Once he decided to surrender himself, and walked by night within two miles of Jerusalem before his purpose failed him. Three times he tried to get out of that neighborhood, but in vain: travelling by day was, of course, out of the question, and by night he found it impossible to elude the patrol. Again and again, therefore, he returned to his hiding-place, and during his whole two months' liberty never went five miles from the Cross Keys. On the 25th of October, he was at last discovered by Mr. Francis, as he was emerging from a stack. A load of buckshot was instantly discharged at him, twelve of which passed through his hat as he fell to the ground. He escaped even then, but his pursuers were rapidly concentrating upon him, and it is perfectly astonishing that he could have eluded them for five days more.

On Sunday, October 30th, a man named Benjamin Phipps, going out for the first time on patrol duty, was passing at noon a clearing in the woods where a number of pine-trees had long since been felled. There was a motion among their boughs; he stopped to watch it; and through a gap in the branches he saw, emerging from a hole in the earth beneath, the face of Nat Turner. Aiming his gun instantly, Phipps called on him to surrender. The fugitive, exhausted with watching and privation, entangled in the branches, armed only with a sword, had nothing to do but to yield; sagaciously reflecting, also, as he afterwards explained, that the woods were full of armed men, and that he had better trust fortune for some later chance of escape, instead of desperately attempting it then. He was correct in the first impression, since there were fifty armed scouts within a circuit of two miles. His insurrection ended where it began; for this spot was only a mile and a half from the house of Joseph Travis.

Torn, emaciated, ragged, "a mere scarecrow," still wearing the hat perforated with buckshot, with his arms bound to his sides, he was driven before the levelled gun to the nearest house, that of a Mr. Edwards. He was confined there that night; but the news had spread so rapidly that within an hour after his arrival a hundred persons had collected, and the excitement became so intense "that it was with difficulty he could be conveyed alive to Jerusalem." The enthusiasm spread instantly through Virginia; Mr. Trezvant, the Jerusalem postmaster, sent notices of it far and near; and Governor Floyd himself wrote a letter to the "Richmond Enguirer" to give official announcement of the momentous capture.

When Nat Turner was asked by Mr. T. R. Gray, the counsel assigned him, whether, although defeated, he still believed in his own Providential mission, he answered, as simply as one who came thirty years after him, "Was not Christ crucified?" In the same spirit, when arraigned before the court, "he answered, 'Not guilty,' saying to his counsel that he did not feel so." But apparently no argument was made in his favor by his counsel, nor were any witnesses called,—he being convicted on the testimony of Levi Waller, and upon his own confession, which was put in by Mr. Gray, and acknowledged by the prisoner before the six justices composing the court, as being "full, free, and voluntary." He was therefore placed in the paradoxical position of conviction by his own confession, under a plea of "Not guilty." The arrest took place on the thirtieth of October, 1831, the confession on the first of November, the trial and conviction on the fifth, and the execution on the following Friday, the eleventh of November, precisely at noon. He met his death with perfect composure, declined addressing the multitude assembled, and told the sheriff in a firm voice that he was ready. Another account says that he "betrayed no emotion, and even hurried the executioner in the performance of his duty." "Not a limb nor a muscle was observed to move. His body, after his death, was given over to the surgeons for dissection."

This last statement merits remark. There would be no evidence that this formidable man was not favored during his imprisonment with that full measure of luxury which slave-jails afford to slaves, but for a rumor which arose after the execution, that he was compelled to sell his body in advance, for purposes of dissection, in exchange for food. But it does not appear probable, from the known habits of Southern anatomists, that any such bargain could have been needed. For in the circular of the South Carolina Medical School for that very year I find this remarkable suggestion:—"Some advantages of a peculiar character are connected with this institution. No place in the United States affords so great opportunities for the acquisition of medical knowledge, subjects being obtained among the colored population in sufficient number for every purpose, and proper dissections carried on without offending any individual." What a convenience, to possess for scientific purposes a class of population sufficiently human to be dissected, but not human enough to be supposed to take offence at it! And as the same arrangement may be supposed to have existed in Virginia, Nat Turner would hardly have gone through the formality of selling his body for food to those who claimed its control at any rate.

The Confession of the captive was published under authority of Mr. Gray, in a pamphlet, at Baltimore. Fifthy thousand copies of it are said to have been printed, and it was "embellished with an accurate likeness of the brigand, taken by Mr. John Crawley, portrait-painter, and lithographed by Endicott & Swett, at Baltimore." The newly published "Liberator" said of it, at the time, that it would "only serve to rouse up other leaders, and hasten other insurrections," and advised grand juries to indict Mr. Gray. I have never seen a copy of the original pamphlet, it is not to be found in any of our public libraries, and I have heard of but one as still existing, although the Confession itself has been repeatedly reprinted. Another small pamphlet, containing the main features of the outbreak, was published at New York during the same year, and this is in my possession. But the greater part of the facts which I have given were gleaned from the contemporary newspapers.

Who now shall go back thirty years and read the heart of this extraordinary man, who, by the admission of his captors, "never was known to swear an oath or drink a drop of spirits,"—who, on the same authority, "for natural intellignece and quickness of apprehension was surpassed by few men," "with a mind capable of attaining anything,"—who knew no book but his Bible, and that by heart,— who devoted himself soul and body to the cause of his race, without a trace of personal hope or fear,—who laid his plans so shrewdly that they came at last with less warning than any earthquake on the doomed community around,—and who, when that time arrived, took the life of man, woman, and child, without a throb of compunction, a word of exultation, or an act of superfluous outrage? Mrs. Stowe's "Dred" seems dim and melodramatic beside the actual Nat Turner. De Quincey's Avenger" is his only parallel in imaginative literature: similar wrongs, similar retribution. Mr. Gray, his self-appointed confessor, rises into a sort of bewildered enthusiasm, with the prisoner before him. "I shall not attempt to describe the effect of his narrative, as told and commented on by himself, in the condemned-hole of the prison. The calm, deliberate composure with which he spoke of his late deeds and intentions, the expression of his fiend-like face when excited by enthusiasm, still bearing the stains of the blood of helpless innocence about him, clothed with rags and covered with chains, yet daring to raise his manacled hands to heaven, with a spirit soaring above the attributes of man,—I looked on him, and the blood curdled in my veins."

But the more remarkable the personal character of Nat Turner, the greater the amazement felt that he should not have appreciated the extreme felicity of his position as a slave. In all insurrections, the standing wonder seems to be that the slaves most trusted and best used should be most deeply involved. So in this case, as usual, they resorted to the most astonishing theories of the origin of the affair. One attributed it to Free-Masonry, and another to free whiskey, —liberty appearing dangerous, even in these forms. The poor whites charged it upon the free colored people, and urged their expulsion, forgetting that in North Carolina the plot was betrayed by one of this class, and that in Virginia there were but two engaged, both of whom had slave-wives. The slaveholding clergymen traced it to want of knowledge of the Bible, forgetting that Nat Turner knew scarcely anything else. On the other hand, "a distinguished citizen of Virginia" combined in one sweeping denunciation "Northern incendiaries, tracts, Sunday-schools, religion, reading, and writing."

But whether the theories of its origin were wise or foolish, the insurrection made its mark, and the famous band of Virginia emancipationists who all that winter made the House of Delegates ring with unavailing eloquence—till the rise of slave-exportation to new cotton regions stopped their voices—were but the unconscious mouth-pieces of Nat Turner. In January, 1832, in reply to a member who had called the outbreak a "petty affair," the eloquent James McDowell thus described the impression it left behind:—

"Now, Sir, I ask you, I ask gentlemen, in conscience to say, was that a 'petty affair' which startled the feelings of your whole population,—which threw a portion of it into alarm, a portion of it into panic,—which wrung out from an affrighted people the thrilling cry, day after day, conveyed to your executive, *'We are in peril of our lives; send us an army for defence'*? Was that a 'petty affair' which drove families from their homes,—which assembled women and children in crowds, without shelter, at places of common refuge, in every condition of weakness and infirmity, under every suffering which want and terror could inflict, yet willing to endure all, willing to meet death from famine, death from climate, death from hardships, preferring anything rather than the horrors of meeting it from a domestic assassin? Was that a 'petty affair' which erected a peaceful and confiding portion of the State into a military camp,—which outlawed from pity the unfortunate beings whose brothers had offended,—which barred every door, penetrated every bosom with fear or suspicion,—which so banished every sense of security from every man's dwelling, that, let but a hoof or horn break upon the silence of the night, and an aching throb would be driven to the heart, the husband would look to his weapon, and the mother would shudder and weep upon her cradle? Was it the fear of Nat Turner, and his deluded, drunken handful of followers, which produced such effects? Was it this that induced distant counties, where the very name of

Southampton was strange, to arm and equip for a struggle? No, Sir, it was the suspicion eternally attached to the slave himself,—the suspicion that a Nat Turner might be in every family,—that the same bloody deed might be acted over at any time and in any place,—that the materials for it were spread through the land, and were always ready for a like explosion. Nothing but the force of this withering apprehension,—nothing but the paralyzing and deadening weight with which it falls upon and prostrates the heart of every man who has helpless dependants to protect,—nothing but this could have thrown a brave people into consternation, or could have made any portion of this powerful Commonwealth, for a single instant, to have quailed and trembled."

While these things were going on, the enthusiasm for the Polish Revolution was rising to its height. The nation was ringing with a peal of joy, on hearing that at Frankfort the Poles had killed fourteen thousand Russians. "The Southern Religious Telegraph" was publishing an impassioned address to Kosciusko; standards were being consecrated for Poland in the larger cities; heroes, like Skrzynecki, Czartoryski, Rozyski, Kaminski, were choking the trump of Fame with their complicated patronymics. These are all forgotten now; and this poor negro, who did not even possess a name, beyond one abrupt monosyllable,—for even the name of Turner was the master's property,—still lives a memory of terror and a symbol of retribution triumphant.

NAT TURNER'S CONFESSION

You have asked me to give a history of the motives which induced me to undertake the late insurrection, as you call it—To do so I must go back to the days of my infancy, and even before I was born. I was thirty-one years of age the 2nd of October last, and born the property of Benj. Turner, of this county. In my childhood a circumstance occurred which made an indelible impression on my mind, and laid the ground work of that enthusiasm, which has terminated so fatally to many, both white and black, and for which I am about to atone at the gallows. It is here necessary to relate this circumstance— trifling as it may seem, it was the commencement of that belief which has grown with time, and even now, sir, in this dungeon, helpless and forsaken as I am, I cannot divest myself of. Being at play with other children, when three or four years old, I was telling them something, which my mother overhearing, said it had happened

before I was born—I stuck to my story, however, and related some-
things which went, in her opinion, to confirm it—others being called
on were greatly astonished, knowing that these things had happened,
and caused them to say in my hearing, I surely would be a prophet,
as the Lord had shewn me things that had happened before my birth.
And my father and mother strengthened me in this my first impression, saying in my presence, I was intended for some great
purpose, which they had always thought from certain marks on my
head and breast—[a parcel of excrescences which I believe are not at
all uncommon, particularly among negroes, as I have seen several with
the same. In this case he has either cut them off or they have nearly
disappeared]—My grandmother, who was very religious, and to whom
I was much attached—my master, who belonged to the church, and
other religious persons who visited the house, and whom I often saw
at prayers, noticing the singularity of my manners, I suppose, and my
uncommon intelligence for a child, remarked I had too much sense to
be raised, and if I was, I would never be of any service to any one as
a slave—To a mind like mine, restless, inquisitive and observant of
every thing that was passing, it is easy to suppose that religion was
the subject to which it would be directed, and although this subject
principally occupied my thoughts—there was nothing that I saw or
heard of to which my attention was not directed—The manner in
which I learned to read and write, not only had great influence on
my own mind, as I acquired it with the most perfect ease, so much
so, that I have no recollection whatever of learning the alphabet—but
to the astonishment of the family, one day, when a book was shewn
to me to keep me from crying, I began spelling the names of
different objects—this was a source of wonder to all in the neighborhood, particularly the blacks—and this learning was constantly improved at all opportunities—when I got large enough to go to work,
while employed, I was reflecting on many things that would present
themselves to my imagination, and whenever an opportunity occurred
of looking at a book, when the school children were getting their
lessons, I would find many things that the fertility of my own
imagination had depicted to me before; all my time, not devoted to
my master's service, was spent either in prayer, or in making experiments in casting different things in moulds made of earth, in attempting to make paper, gun-powder, and many other experiments,
that although I could not perfect, yet convinced me of its practica-
bility if I had the means.* I was not addicted to stealing in my
youth, nor have ever been—Yet such was the confidence of the
negroes in the neighborhood, even at this early period of my life, in
my superior judgment, that they would often carry me with them
when they were going on any roguery, to plan for them. Growing up

*When questioned as to the manner of manufacturing those different
articles, he was found well informed on the subject.

among them, with this confidence in my superior judgment, and
when this, in their opinions, was perfected by Divine inspiration,
from the circumstances already alluded to in my infancy, and which
belief was ever afterwards zealously inculcated by the austerity of my
life and manners, which became the subject of remark by white and
black.—Having soon discovered to be great, I must appear so, and
therefore studiously avoided mixing in society, and wrapped myself
in mystery, devoting my time to fasting and prayer—By this time,
having arrived to man's estate, and hearing the scriptures commented
on at meetings, I was struck with that particular passage which says:
"Seek ye the kingdom of Heaven and all things shall be added unto
you." I reflected much on this passage, and prayed daily for light on
this subject As I was praying one day at my plough, the spirit spoke
to me, saying "Seek ye the kingdom of Heaven and all things shall be
added unto you." *Question*—what do you mean by the Spirit. *Ans.*
The Spirit that spoke to the prophets in former days—and I was
greatly astonished, and for two years prayed continually, whenever
my duty would permit—and then again I had the same revelation,
which fully confirmed me in the impression that I was ordained for
some great purpose in the hands of the Almighty. Several years rolled
round, in which many events occurred to strengthen me in this my
belief. At this time I reverted in my mind to the remarks made of me
in my childhood, and the things that had been shewn me—and as it
had been said of me in my childhood by those by whom I had been
taught to pray, both white and black, and in whom I had the greatest
confidence, that I had too much sense to be raised, and if I was, I
would never be of any use to any one as a slave. Now finding I had
arrived to man's estate, and was a slave, and these revelations being
made known to me, I began to direct my attention to this great
object, to fulfill the purpose for which, by this time, I felt assured I
was intended. Knowing the influence I had obtained over the minds
of my fellow servants, (not by the means of conjuring and such like
tricks—for to them I always spoke of such things with contempt) but
by the communion of the Spirit whose revelations I often communicated to them, and they believed and said my wisdom came from
God. I now began to prepare them for my purpose, by telling them
something was about to happen that would terminate in fulfilling the
great promise that had been made to me—About this time I was
placed under an overseer, from whom I ranaway—and after remaining
in the woods thirty days, I returned, to the astonishment of the
negroes on the plantation, who thought I had made my escape to
some other part of the country, as my father had done before. But
the reason of my return was, that the Spirit appeared to me and said
I had my wishes directed to the things of this world, and not to the
kingdom of Heaven, and that I should return to the service of my
earthly master—"For he who knoweth his Master's will, and doeth it
not, shall be beaten with many stripes, and thus have I chastened

you." And the negroes found fault, and murmured against me, saying that if they had my sense they would not serve any master in the world. And about this time I had a vision—and I saw white spirits and black spirits engaged in battle, and the sun was darkened—the thunder rolled in the Heavens, and blood flowed in streams—and I heard a voice saying, "Such is your luck, such you are called to see, and let it come rough or smooth, you must surely bare it." I now withdrew myself as much as my situation would permit, from the intercourse of my fellow servants, for the avowed purpose of serving the Spirit more fully—and it appeared to me, and reminded me of the things it had already shown me, and that it would then reveal to me the knowledge of the elements, the revolution of the planets, the operation of tides, and changes of the seasons. After this revelation in the year of 1825, and the knowledge of the elements being made known to me, I sought more than ever to obtain true holiness before the great day of judgment should appear, and then I began to receive the true knowledge of faith. And from the first steps of righteousness until the last, was I made perfect; and the Holy Ghost was with me, and said, "Behold me as I stand in the Heavens"—and I looked and saw the forms of men in different attitudes—and there were lights in the sky to which the children of darkness gave other names than what they really were—for they were the lights of the Savior's hands, stretched forth from east to west, even as they were extended on the cross on Calvary for the redemption of sinners. And I wondered greatly at these miracles, and prayed to be informed of a certainty of the meaning thereof—and shortly afterwards, while laboring in the field, I discovered drops of blood on the corn as though it were dew from heaven—and I communicated it to many, both white and black, in the neighborhood—and I then found on the leaves in the woods hieroglyphic characters, and numbers, with the forms of men in different attitudes, portrayed in blood, and representing the figures I had seen before in the heavens. And now the Holy Ghost had revealed itself to me, and made plain the miracles it had shown me—For as the blood of Christ had been shed on this earth, and had ascended to heaven for the salvation of sinners, and was now returning to earth again in the form of dew—and as the leaves on the trees bore the impression of the figures I had seen in the heavens, it was plain to me that the Savior was about to lay down the yoke he had borne for the sins of men, and the great day of judgment was at hand. About this time I told these things to a white man, (Etheldred T. Brantley) on whom it had a wonderful effect—and he ceased from his wickedness, and was attacked immediately with a cutaneous eruption, and blood oozed from the pores of his skin, and after praying and fasting nine days, he was healed, and the Spirit appeared to me again, and said, as the Savior had been baptised so should we be also—and when the white people would not let us be baptised by the church, we went down into the water together, in the sight of many who reviled us, and were baptised by the Spirit—After this I rejoiced greatly, and gave thanks to God. And on the 12th of May, 1828, I heard a loud noise in the heavens, and the Spirit instantly appeared to me and said the Serpent was loosened, and Christ had laid down the yoke he had borne for the sins of men, and that I should take it on and fight against the Serpent, for the time was fast approaching when the first should be last and the last should be first. *Ques.* Do you not find yourself mistaken now? *Ans.* Was not Christ crucified? And by signs in the heavens that it would make known to me when I should commence the great work—and until the first sign appeared, I should conceal it from the knowledge of men—And on the appearance of the sign, (the eclipse of the sun last February) I should arise and prepare myself, and slay my enemies with their own weapons. And immediately on the sign appearing in the heavens, the seal was removed from my lips, and I communicated the great work laid out for me to do, to four in whom I had the greatest confidence, (Henry, Hark, Nelson, and Sam)—It was intended by us to have begun the work of death on the 4th July last—Many were the plans formed and rejected by us, and it affected my mind to such a degree, that I fell sick, and the time passed without our coming to any determination how to commence—Still forming new schemes and rejecting them, when the sign appeared again, which determined me not to wait longer.

Since the commencement of 1830, I had been living with Mr. Joseph Travis, who was to me a kind master, and placed the greatest confidence in me; in fact, I had no cause to complain of his treatment to me. On Saturday evening, the 20th of August, it was agreed between Henry, Hark and myself, to prepare a dinner the next day for the men we expected, and then to concert a plan, as we had not yet determined on any. Hark, on the following morning, brought a pig, and Henry brandy, and being joined by Sam, Nelson, Will and Jack, they prepared in the woods a dinner, where, about three o'clock, I joined them.

Q. Why were you so backward in joining them.

A. The same reason that had caused me not to mix with them for years before.

I saluted them on coming up, and asked Will how came he there, he answered, his life was worth no more thanothers, and his liberty as dear to him. I asked him if he thought to obtain it? He said he would, or lose his life. This was enough to put him in full confidence. Jack, I knew, was only a tool in the hands of Hark, it was quickly agreed we should commence at home (Mr. J. Travis') on that night, and until we had armed and equipped ourselves, and gathered sufficient force, neither age nor sex was to be spared, (which was invariably adhered to). We remained at the feast, until about two hours in the night, when we went to the house and found Austin; they all went to the cider press and drank, except myself. On returning to the house, Hark went to the door with an axe, for the purpose of breaking it open, as we knew we were strong enough to murder the family, if they were awaked by the noise; but reflecting that it might create an alarm in the neighborhood, we determined to enter the house secretly, and murder them whilst sleeping. Hark got a ladder and set it against the chimney, on which I ascended, and hoisting a window, entered and came down stairs, unbarred the door, and removed the guns from their places. It was then observed that I must spill the first blood. On which, armed with a hatchet, and accompanied by Will, I entered my master's chamber, it being dark, I could not give a death blow, the hatchet glanced from his head, he sprang from the bed and called his wife, it was his last word, Will laid him dead, with a blow of his axe, and Mrs. Travis shared the same fate, as she lay in bed. The murder of this family, five in number, was the work of a moment, not one of them awoke; there was a little infant sleeping in a cradle, that was forgotten, until we had left the house and gone some distance, when Henry and Will returned and killed it; we got here, four guns that would shoot, and several old muskets, with a pound or two of powder. We remained some time at the barn, where we paraded; I formed them in a line as soldiers, and after carrying them through all the manoeuvres I was master of marched them off to Mr. Salathul Francis', about six hundred yards distant. Sam and Will went to the door and knocked. Mr. Francis asked who was there, Sam replied it was him, and he had a letter for him, on which he got up and came to the door; they immediately seized him, and dragging him out a little from the door, he was dispatched by repeated blows on the head; there was no other white person in the family. We started from there for Mrs. Reese's, maintaining the most perfect silence on our march, where finding the door unlocked, we entered, and murdered Mrs. Reese in her bed, while sleeping; her son awoke, but it was only to sleep the sleep of death, he had only time to say who is that, and he was no more. From Mrs. Reese's we went to Mrs. Turner's, a mile distant, which we reached about sunrise, on Monday morning. Henry, Austin, and Sam, went to the still, where, finding Mr. Peebles, Austin shot him, and the rest of us went to the house; as we approached, the family discovered us, and shut the door. Vain hope! Will, with one stroke of his axe, opened it, and we entered and found Mrs. Turner and Mrs. Newsome in the middle of a room, almost frightened to death. Will immediately killed Mrs. Turner, with one blow of his axe. I took Mrs. Newsome by the hand, and with the sword I had when I was apprehended, I struck her several blows over the head, but not being able to kill her, as the sword was dull. Will turning around and discovering it, despatched her also. A general destruction of property and search for money and ammunition, always succeded the murders. By this time my company amounted to fifteen, and nine men mounted, who started for Mrs. Whitehead's, (the other six were to go through a by way to Mr. Bryant's, and rejoin us at Mrs. Whitehead's,) as we approached the house we discovered Mr. Richard Whitehead standing in the cotton patch, near the lane fence; we called him over into the lane, and Will, the executioner, was near at hand, with his fatal axe, to send him to an untimely grave. As we pushed on to the house, I discovered some one run round the garden, and thinking it was some of the white family, I pursued them, but finding it was a servant girl belonging to the house, I returned to commence the work of death, but they whom I left, had not been idle; all the family were already murdered, but Mrs. Whitehead and her daughter Margaret. As I came round to the door I saw Will pulling Mrs. Whitehead out of the house, and at the step he nearly severed her head from her body, with his broad axe. Miss Margaret, when I discovered her, had concealed herself in the corner, formed by the projection of cellar cap from the house; on my approach she fled, but was soon overtaken, and after repeated blows with a sword, I killed her by a blow on the head, with a fence rail. By this time, the six who had gone by Mr. Bryant's, rejoined us, and informed me they had done the work of death assigned them. We again divided, part going to Mr. Richard Porter's, and from thence to Nathaniel Francis', the others to Mr. Howell Harris', and Mr. T. Doyles. On my reaching Mr. Porter's, he had escaped with his family. I understood there, that the alarm had already spread, and I immediately returned to bring up those sent to Mr. Doyles, and Mr. Howell Harris'; the party I left going on to Mr. Francis', having told them I would join them in that neighborhood. I met these sent to Mr. Doyles' and Mr. Harris' returning, having met Mr. Doyle on the road and killed him; and learning from some who joined them, that Mr. Harris was from home, I immediately pursued the course taken by the party gone on before; but knowing they would complete the work of death and pillage, at Mr. Francis' before I could get there, I went to Mr. Peter Edwards', expecting to find them there, but they had been here also. I then went to Mr. John T. Barrow's, they had been here and murdered him. I pursued on their track to Capt. Newit Harris', where I found the greater part mounted, and ready to start; the men now amounting to about forty, shouted and hurraed as I rode up, some were in the yard, loading their guns, others drinking. They said Captain Harris and his family had escaped, the property in the house they destroyed, robbing him of money and other valuables. I ordered them to mount and march instantly, this was about nine or ten o'clock, Monday morning. I proceeded to Mr. Levi Waller's, two or three miles distant. I took my station in the rear, and as it was my object to carry terror and devastation wherever we went, I placed fifteen or twenty of the best armed and most relied on, in front, who generally approached the houses as fast as their horses could run; this was for two purposes, to prevent escape and strike terror to the inhabitants—on this account I never got to the houses, after leaving Mrs. Whitehead's, until the murders were committed, except in one case. I sometimes got in sight in time to see the work of death completed, viewed the mangled bodies as they lay, in silent satisfaction, and immediately started in quest of other victims—Having murdered Mrs. Waller and ten children, we started for Mr. William Williams'—having killed him and two little boys that were there; while engaged in this, Mrs. Williams fled and got some distance from the house, but she was pursued, overtaken, and compelled to get up behind one of the company, who brought her back, and after showing her the mangled body of her lifeless husband, she was told to get down and lay by his side, where she was shot dead. I then started for Mr. Jacob Williams, where the family were murdered—Here he found a young man named Drury, who had come on business with Mr. Williams—he was pursued, overtaken and shot. Mrs. Vaughan was the next place we visited—and after murdering the family here, I determined on starting for Jerusalem—Our number amounted now to fifty or sixty, all mounted and armed with guns, axes, swords and clubs—On reaching Mr. James W. Parker's gate, immediately on the road leading to Jerusalem, and about three miles distant, it was proposed to me to call there, but I objected, as I knew he was gone to Jerusalem, and my object was to reach there as soon as possible; but some of the men having relations at Mr. Parker's it was agreed that they might call and get his people. I remained at the gate on the road, with seven or eight; the others going across the field to the house, about half a mile off. After waiting some time for them, I became impatient, and started to the house for them, and on our return we were met by a party of white men, who had pursued our blood-stained track, and who had fired on those at the gate, and dispersed them, which I knew nothing of, not having been at that time rejoined by any of them—Immediately on discovering the whites, I ordered my men to halt and form, as they appeared to be alarmed—The white men, eighteen in number, approached us in about one hundred yards, when one of them fired, (this was against the positive orders of Captain Alexander P. Peete, who commanded, and who had directed the men to reserve their fire until within thirty paces)—And I discovered about half of them retreating, I then ordered my men to fire and rush on them; the few remaining stood their ground until we approached within fifty yards, when they fired and retreated. We pursued and overtook some of them who we thought we left dead; (they were not killed) after pursuing them about two hundred yards, and rising a little hill, I discovered they were met by another party, and had halted, and were reloading their guns, (this was a small party from Jerusalem who knew the negroes were in the field, and had just tied their horses to await their return to the road, knowing that Mr. Parker and family were in Jerusalem, but knew nothing of the party that had gone in with Captain Peete; on hearing the firing they immediately rushed to the spot and arrived just in time to arrest the progress of these barbarous villians, and save the lives of their friends and fellow citizens). Thinking that those who retreated first, and the party who fired on us at fifty or sixty yards distant, had all fallen back to meet others with ammunition. As I saw them reloading their guns, and more coming up than I saw at first, and several of my bravest men being wounded, the others became panick struck and squandered over the field; the white men pursued and fired on us several times. Hark had his horse shot under him, and I caught another for him as it was running by me; five or six of my men were wounded, but none left on the field; finding myself defeated here I instantly determined to go through a private way, and cross the Nottoway river at the Cypress Bridge, three miles below Jerusalem, and attack that place in the rear, as I expected they would look for me on the other road, and I had a great desire to get there to procure arms and ammunition. After going a short distance in this private way, accompanied by about twenty men, I overtook two or three who told me the others were dispersed in every direction. After trying in vain to collect a sufficient force to proceed to Jerusalem, I determined to return, as I was sure they would make back to their old neighborhood, where they would rejoin me, make new recruits, and come down again. On my way back, I called at Mrs. Thomas's, Mrs. Spencer's, and several other places, the white families having fled, we found no more victims to gratify our thirst for blood, we stopped at Maj. Ridley's quarter for the night, and being joined by four of his men, with the recruits made since my defeat, we mustered now about forty strong. After placing out sentinels, I laid down to sleep, but was quickly roused by a great racket; starting up, I found some mounted, and others in great confusion; one of the sentinels having given the alarm that we were about to be attacked, I ordered some to ride round and reconnoitre, and on their return the others being more alarmed, not knowing who they were, fled in different ways, so that I was reduced to about twenty again; with this I determined to attempt to recruit, and proceed on to rally in the neighborhood, I had left. Dr. Blunt's was the nearest house, which we reached just before day; on riding up the yard, Hark fired a gun. We expected Dr. Blunt and his family were at Maj. Ridley's, as I knew there was a company of men there; the gun was fired to ascertain if any of the family were at home; we were immediately fired upon and retreated, leaving several of my men. I do not know what became of them, as I never saw them afterwards. Pursuing our course back and coming in sight of Captain Harris', where we had been the day before, we discovered a party of white men at the house, on which all deserted me but two, (Jacob and Nat), we concealed ourselves in the woods until near night, when I sent them in search of Henry, Sam, Nelson, and Hark, and directed them to rally all they could, at the place we had had our dinner the Sunday before, where they would find me, and I accordingly returned there as soon as it was dark and remained until Wednesday evening, when discovering white men riding around the place as though they were looking for some one, and none of my men joining me, I concluded Jacob and Nat had been taken, and compelled to betray me. On this I gave up all hope for the present; and on Thursday night after having supplied myself with provisions from Mr. Travis's, I scratched a hole under a pile of fence rails in a field, where I concealed myself for six weeks, never leaving my hiding place but for a few minutes in the dead of night to get water which was very near; thinking by this time I could venture out, I began to go about in the night and eaves drop the houses in the neighborhood; pursuing this course for about a fortnight and gathering little or no intelligence, afraid of speaking to any human being, and returning every morning to my cave before the dawn of day. I know not how long I might have led this life, if accident had not betrayed me, a dog in the neighborhood passing by my hiding place one night while I was out, was attracted by some meat I had in my cave, and crawled in and stole it, and was coming out just as I returned. A few nights after, two negroes having started to go hunting with the same dog, and passed that way, the dog came again to the place, and having just gone out to walk about, discovered me and barked, on which thinking myself discovered, I spoke to them to beg concealment. On making myself known they fled from me. Knowing then they would betray me, I immediately left my hiding place, and was pursued almost incessantly until I was taken a fortnight afterwards by Mr. Benjamin Phipps, in a little hole I had dug out with my sword, for the purpose of concealment, under the top of a fallen tree. On Mr. Phipps' discovering the place of my concealment, he cocked his gun and aimed at me. I requested him not to shoot and I would give up, upon which he demanded my sword. I delivered it to him, and he brought me to prison. During the time I was pursued, I had many hair breadth escapes, which your time will not permit you to relate. I am here loaded with chains, and willing to suffer the fate that awaits me.

A LETTER TO HIS MASTER

Frederick Douglass

Thomas Auld:

Sir—The long and intimate, though by no means friendly relation which unhappily subsisted between you and myself, leads me to hope that you will easily account for the great liberty which I now take in addressing you in this open and public manner. The same fact may possibly remove any disagreeable surprise which you may experience on again finding your name coupled with mine, in any other way than in an advertisement, accurately describing my person, and offering a large sum for my arrest. In thus dragging you again before the public, I am aware that I shall subject myself to no inconsiderable amount of censure. I shall probably be charged with an unwarrantable, if not a wanton and reckless disregard of the rights and proprieties of private life. There are those North as well as South who entertain a much higher respect for rights which are merely conventional, than they do for rights which are personal and essential. Not a few there are in our country, who, while they have no scruples against robbing the laborer of the hard earned results of his patient industry, will be shocked by the extremely indelicate manner of bringing your name before the public. . . .

I have selected this day on which to address you, because it is the anniversary of my emancipation; and knowing of no better way, I am led to this as the best mode of celebrating that truly important event. Just ten years ago this beautiful September morning, yon bright sun beheld me a slave—a poor, degraded chattel—trembling at the sound of your voice, lamenting that I was a man, and wishing myself a brute. The hopes which I had treasured up for weeks of a safe and successful escape from your grasp, were powerfully confronted at this last hour by dark clouds of doubt and fear, making my person shake and my bosom to heave with the heavy contest between hope and fear. I have no words to describe to you the deep agony of soul which I experienced on that never to be forgotten morning—(for I left by daylight). I was making a leap in the dark. The probabilities, so far as I could by reason determine them, were stoutly against the undertaking. The preliminaries and precautions I had adopted previously, all worked badly. I was like one going to war without weapons—ten chances of defeat to one of victory. One in whom I had confided, and one who had promised me assistance, appalled by fear at the trial hour, deserted me, thus leaving the responsibility of success or failure solely with myself. You, sir, can never know my feelings. As I look back to them, I can scarcely realize that I have passed through a scene so trying. Trying however as they were, and gloomy as was the prospect, thanks be to the Most High, who is ever the God of the oppressed, at the moment which was to determine my whole earthly career. His grace was sufficient, my mind was made up, I embraced the golden opportunity, took the morning tide at the flood, and a free man, young, active and strong, is the result. . . .

Since I left you, I have had a rich experience. I have occupied stations which I never dreamed of when a slave. Three out of the ten years since I left you, I spent as a common laborer on the wharves of New Bedford, Massachusetts. It was there I earned my first free dollar. It was mine. I could spend it as I pleased. I could buy hams or herring with it, without asking any odds of any body. That was a precious dollar to me. You remember when I used to make seven or eight, or even nine dollars a week in Baltimore, you would take every cent of it from me every Saturday night, saying that I belonged to you, and my earnings also. I never liked this conduct on your part—to say the best, I thought it a little mean. I would not have served you so. But let that pass. I was a little awkward about counting money in New England fashion when I first landed in New Bedford. I like to have betrayed myself several times. I caught myself saying phip, for fourpence; and at one time a man actually charged me with being a runaway, whereupon I was silly enough to become one by running away from him, for I was greatly afraid he might adopt measures to give me again into slavery, a condition I then dreaded more than death.

I soon, however, learned to count money, as well as to make it, and got on swimmingly. I married soon after leaving you; in fact, I was engaged to be married before I left you; and instead of finding my companion a burden, she was truly a helpmeet. She went to live at service, and I to work on the wharf, and though we toiled hard the first winter, we never lived more happily. After remaining in New Bedford for three years, I met with Wm. Lloyd Garrison, a person of whom you have *possibly* heard, as he is pretty generally known among slave-holders. He put it into my head that I might make myself serviceable to the cause of the slave by devoting a portion of my time to telling my own sorrows, and those of other slaves which had come under my observation. This was the commencement of a higher state of existence than any to which I had ever aspired. I was thrown into society the most pure, enlightened and benevolent that the country affords. Among these I have never forgotten you, but have invariably made you the topic of conversation—thus giving you all the notoriety I could do. I need not tell you that the opinion formed of you in these circles, is far from being favorable. They have little respect for your honesty, and less for your religion.

But I was going on to relate to you something of my interesting experience. I had not long enjoyed the excellent society to which I have referred, before the light of its excellence exerted a beneficial influence on my mind and heart. Much of my early dislike of white persons was removed, and their manners, habits and customs, so entirely unlike what I had been used to in the kitchen-quarters on the plantations of the South, fairly charmed me, and gave me a strong disrelish for the coarse and degrading customs of my former condition. I therefore made an effort so to improve my mind and deportment as to be somewhat fitted to the station to which I seemed almost providentially called. The transition from degradation to respectability was indeed great, and to get from one to the other without carrying some marks of one's former condition, is truly a difficult matter. I would not have you think that I am now entirely clear of all plantation peculiarities, but my friends here, while they entertain the strongest dislike to them, regard me with that charity to which my past life somewhat entitles me, so that my condition in this respect is exceedingly pleasant. So far as my domestic affairs are concerned, I can boast of as comfortable a dwelling as your own. I have an industrious and neat companion, and four dear children—the oldest a girl of nine years, and three fine boys, the oldest eight, the next six, and the youngest four years old. The three oldest are now going regularly to school—two can read and write, and the other can spell with tolerable correctness words of two syllables: Dear fellows! they are all in comfortable beds, and are sound asleep, perfectly secure under my own roof. There are no slaveholders here to rend my heart by snatching them from my arms, or blast a mother's dearest hopes by tearing them from her bosom. These dear children are ours—not to work up into rice, sugar and tobacco, but to watch over, regard, and protect, and to rear them up in the nurture and admonition of the gospel—to train them up in the paths of wisdom and virtue, and, as far as we can to make them useful to the world and to themselves. Oh! sir, a slaveholder never appears to me so completely an agent of hell, as when I think of and look upon my dear children. It is then that my feelings rise above my control. I meant to have said more with respect to my own prosperity and happiness, but thoughts and feelings which this recital has quickened unfit me to proceed further in that direction. The grim horrors of slavery rise in all their ghastly terror before me, the wails of millions pierce my heart, and chill my blood. I remember the chain, the gag, the bloody whip, the death-like gloom overshadowing the broken spirit of the fettered bondman, the appalling liability of his being torn away from wife and children, and sold like a beast in the market. Say not that this is a picture of fancy. You well know that I wear stripes on my back inflicted by your direction; and that you, while we were brothers in the same church, caused this right hand, with which I am now penning this letter, to be closely tied to my left, and my person dragged at the pistol's mouth, fifteen miles, from the Bay side to Easton to be sold like a beast in the market, for the alleged crime of intending to escape from your possession. All this and more you remember, and know to be perfectly true, not only of yourself, but of nearly all of the slaveholders around you.

At this moment, you are probably the guilty holder of at least three of my own dear sisters, and my only brother in bondage. These you regard as your property. They are recorded on your ledger, or perhaps have been sold to human flesh mongers, with a view to filling your own ever-hungry purse. Sir, I desire to know how and where these dear sisters are. Have you sold them? or are they still in your possession? What has become of them? are they living or dead? And my dear old grand-mother, whom you turned out like an old horse, to die in the woods—is she still alive? Write and let me know all about them. If my grandmother be still alive, she is of no service to you, for by this time she must be nearly eighty years old—too old to be cared for by one to whom she has ceased to be of service, send

her to me at Rochester, or bring her to Philadelphia, and it shall be
the crowning happiness of my life to take care of her in her old age.
Oh! she was to me a mother, and a father, so far as hard toil for my
comfort could make her such. Send me my grandmother! that I may
watch over and take care of her in her old age. And my sisters, let
me know all about them. I would write to them, and learn all I want
to know of them, without disturbing you in any way, but that,
through your unrighteous conduct, they have been entirely deprived
of the power to read and write. You have kept them in utter
ignorance, and have therefore robbed them of the sweet enjoyments
of writing or receiving letters from absent friends and relatives. Your
wickedness and cruelty committed in this respect on your fellow-
creatures, are greater than all the stripes you have laid upon my back,
or theirs. It is an outrage upon the soul—a war upon the immortal
spirit, and one for which you must give account at the bar of our
common Father and Creator. . . .

I will now bring this letter to a close, you shall hear from me again
unless you let me hear from you. I intend to make use of you as a
weapon with which to assail the system of slavery—as a means of
concentrating public attention on the system, and deepening their
horror of trafficking in the souls and bodies of men. I shall make use
of you as a means of exposing the character of the American church
and clergy—and as a means of bringing this guilty nation with yourself to repentance. In doing this I entertain no malice towards you
personally. There is no roof under which you would be more safe
than mine, and there is nothing in my house which you might need
for your comfort, which I would not readily grant. Indeed, I should
esteem it a privilege, to set you an example as to how mankind ought
to treat each other.

I am your fellow man, but not your slave,

Frederick Douglass

FROM THE NEGRO FOLK TRADITION . . .

JOHN GETS THE BETTER OF OLD MARSTER

OLD BOSS AND JOHN AT THE PRAYING TREE

This also happened back in the old days too. It was one year on a
plantation when crops were bad. There wasn't enough food for all
the slave hands, no flour at all; all they had to eat was fatback and
cornbread. John and his buddy was the only slickers on the farm.

They would have two kinds of meat in the house, all the lard they could use, plenty flour and plenty sugar, biscuits every morning for breakfast. (They was rogues.) The Boss kept a-missing meat, but they was too slick for him to catch 'em at it.

Every morning, he'd ask John, "How you getting along over there with your family?" John said, "Well, I'm doing all right, Old Marster. (*High-pitched, whiny*) I'm fair's a middling and spick as a ham, coffee in the kittle, bread on the fire, if that ain't living I hope I die."

The Old Boss checked on John. And he saw his hams and lard and biscuits all laid up in John's place. (In those days people branded their hams with their own name.) He said, "John, I can see why you're living so high. You got all my hams and things up there." "Oh, no," John told him, "those ain't none of your ham, Boss. God give me them ham. God is good, just like you, and God been looking out for me, because I pray every night."

Boss said, "I'm still going to kill you John, because I know that's my meat."

Old John was real slick. He asked his Marster, "Tonight meet me at the old 'simmon tree. I'm going to show you God is good to me. I'm going to have some of your same ham, some of your same lard, and some of your same flour."

So that night about eight o'clock (it was dark by then in the winter), John went for his partner. They get everything all set up in the tree before John goes for Old Boss. They go out to the tree. Old Boss brings along his double-barreled shotgun, and he tells John, "Now if you don't get my flour and stuff, just like you said you would, you will never leave this tree."

So John gets down on his knees and begins to pray. "Now, Lord, I never axed you for nothing that I didn't get. You know Old Marster here is about to kill me, thinking I'm stealing. Not a child of yours would steal, would he, Lord?" He says, "Now I'm going to pat on this tree three times. And I want you to rain down persimmons." John patted on the tree three times and his partner shook down all the persimmons all over Old Boss. Boss shakes himself and says, "John, Old Boss is so good to you, why don't you have God send my meat down?"

John said, "Don't get impatient; I'm going to talk to him a little while longer for you." So John prayed, "Now Lord, you know me and I know you. Throw me down one of Old Boss's hams with his same brand on it."

Just at that time the ham hit down on top of Old Boss's head. Old Boss grabbed the ham, and said, "John, I spec you better not pray no more." (Old Boss done got scared.) But John kept on praying and the flour fell. Old Boss told John, "Come on John, don't pray no more." "I just want to show you I'm a child of God," John tells him, and he prays again. "Send me down a sack of Old Boss's sugar, the same weight and the same name like on all his sacks."

"John, if you pray any more no telling what might happen to us,"

Boss said. "I'll give you a forty-acre farm and a team of mules if you just don't pray no more." John didn't pay no attention; he prayed some more. "Now God, I want you to do me a personal favor. That's to hop down out of the tree and horsewhip the hell out of Old Boss." So his buddy jumped out with a white sheet and laid it on Old Boss.

Boss said, "You see what you gone done, John; you got God down on me. From now on you can go free."

CHARLIE AND PAT

The two mules, Charlie and Pat, were talking in the barn. Charlie says to Pat: "We're working so hard, working so hard. What are we going to do tomorrow?" Pat says, "Well, it's nearly the end. Tomorrow we're going to haul Old Marster to the cemetery."

Sam, who was out in the barn, heard 'em talking, and ran to the house and told Old Marsa. "Pat and Charlie are talking; they say they're working so hard—and tomorrow they're going to haul you to the cemetery." Old Marsa wouldn't believe it. Sam says, "Come down to the barn and hear for yourself." Old Marsa says, "If you're telling a lie, I'll take all your clothes off and put a mulehide on you."

So he went down to the barn, and when he got near there he could hear something talking. He peeped through the crack and looked in their mouths, and heard Charlie say to Pat, "We're working so hard, so hard." And Pat says, "Well, it's about over; tomorrow we haul Old Marster to the cemetery." Marster jumped up and ran for the house, jumped over the fence, got his foot caught in the paling, fell, and broke his neck.

So old Missie had to get him ready, because they didn't keep him out then like they do now (they didn't embalm you). Next day Pat and Charlie hauled him to the cemetery.

OLD MASTER EATS CROW

John was hunting on Old Marster's place, shooting squirrels, and Old Marster caught him, and told him not to shoot there any more. "You can keep the two squirrels you got but don't be caught down here no more." John goes out the next morning and shoots a crow. Old Marster went down that morning and caught him, and asked John to let him see the gun. John gave him the gun, and then Marster told him to let him see the shell. And Old Marster put the shell in the gun. Then he backed off from John, pointing the gun, and told John to pick the feathers off the crow, halfway down. "Now start at his head, John, and eat the crow up to where you stopped picking the feathers at." When John finished eating, Marster gave him the gun back and throwed him the crow. Then he told John to go on and not let him be caught there no more.

John turned around and started off, and got a little piece away. Then he stopped and turned and called Old Marster. Old Marster said, "What you want, John?" John pointed the gun and says, "Lookee here, Old Marster," and throwed Old Marster the half a crow. "I want you to start at his ass and eat all the way, and don't let a feather fly from your mouth."

OF THE DAWN OF FREEDOM

W. E. B. DuBois

Careless seems the great Avenger;
  History's lessons but record
One death-grapple in the darkness
  'Twixt old systems and the Word;
Truth forever on the scaffold,
  Wrong forever on the throne;
Yet that scaffold sways the future,
  And behind the dim unknown
Standeth God within the shadow
  Keeping watch above His own.

Lowell

The problem of the twentieth century is the problem of the color-line—the relation of the darker to the lighter races of men in Asia and Africa, in America and the islands of the sea. It was a phase of this problem that caused the Civil War; and however much they who marched South and North in 1861 may have fixed on the technical points of union and local autonomy as a shibboleth, all nevertheless knew, as we know, that the question of Negro slavery was the real cause of the conflict. Curious it was, too, how this deeper question ever forced itself to the surface despite effort and disclaimer. No sooner had Northern armies touched Southern soil than this old question, newly guised, sprang from the earth—What shall be done with Negroes? Peremptory military commands, this way and that, could not answer the query; the Emancipation Proclamation seemed but to broaden and intensify the difficulties; and the War Amendments made the Negro problems of to-day.

It is the aim of this essay to study the period of history from 1861 to 1872 so far as it relates to the American Negro. In effect, this tale of the dawn of Freedom is an account of that government of men called the Freedmen's Bureau,—one of the most singular and interesting of the attempts made by a great nation to grapple with vast problems of race and social condition.

The war has naught to do with slaves, cried Congress, the President, and the Nation; and yet no sooner had the armies, East and West, penetrated Virginia and Tennessee than fugitive slaves appeared within their lines. They came at night, when the flickering camp-fires shone like vast unsteady stars along the black horizon: old men and thin, with gray and tufted hair; women, with frightened eyes, dragging whimpering hungry children; men and girls, stalwart and gaunt—a horde of starving vagabonds, homeless, helpless, and pitiable, in their dark distress. Two methods of treating these newcomers seemed equally logical to opposite sorts of minds. Ben Butler, in Virginia, quickly declared slave property contraband of war, and put the fugitives to work; while Fremont, in Missouri, declared the slaves free under martial law. Butler's action was approved, but Fremont's was hastily countermanded, and his successor, Halleck, saw things differently. "Hereafter," he commanded, "no slaves should be allowed to come into your lines at all; if any come without your knowledge, when owners call for them deliver them." Such a policy was difficult to enforce; some of the black refugees declared themselves freemen, others showed that their masters had deserted them, and still others were captured with forts and plantations. Evidently, too, slaves were a source of strength to the Confederacy, and were being used as laborers and producers. "They constitute a military resource," wrote Secretary Cameron, late in 1861; "and being such, that they should not be turned over to the enemy is too plain to discuss." So gradually the tone of the army chiefs changed; Congress forbade the rendition of fugitives, and Butler's "contrabands" were welcomed as military laborers. This complicated rather than solved the problem, for now the scattering fugitives became a steady stream, which flowed faster as the armies marched.

Then the long-headed man with care-chiselled face who sat in the White House saw the inevitable, and emancipated the slaves of rebels on New Year's, 1863. A month later Congress called earnestly for the Negro soldiers whom the act of July, 1862, had half grudgingly allowed to enlist. Thus the barriers were levelled and the deed was done. The stream of fugitives swelled to a flood, and anxious army officers kept inquiring: "What must be done with slaves, arriving almost daily? Are we to find food and shelter for women and children?"

It was a Pierce of Boston who pointed out the way, and thus became in a sense the founder of the Freedmen's Bureau. He was a firm friend of Secretary Chase; and when, in 1861, the care of slaves and abandoned lands developed upon the Treasury officials, Pierce was specially detailed from the ranks to study the conditions. First, he cared for the refugees at Fortress Monroe; and then, after Sherman had captured Hilton Head, Pierce was sent there to found his Port Royal experiment of making free workingmen out of slaves. Before his experiment was barely started, however, the problem of the fugitives had assumed such proportions that it was taken from the hands of the over-burdened Treasury Department and given to the army officials. Already centres of massed freedmen were forming at Fortress Monroe, Washington, New Orleans, Vicksburg and Corinth, Columbus, Ky., and Cairo, Ill., as well as at Port Royal. Army chaplains found here new and fruitful fields; "superintendents of contrabands" multiplied, and some attempt at systematic work was made by enlisting the able-bodied men and giving work to the others.

Then came the Freedmen's Aid societies, born of the touching appeals from Pierce and from these other centres of distress. There was the American Missionary Association, sprung from the *Amistad*, and now full-grown for work; the various church organizations, the National Freedmen's Relief Association, the American Freedmen's Union, the Western Freedmen's Aid Commission—in all fifty or more active organizations, which sent clothes, money, school-books, and teachers southward. All they did was needed, for the destitution of the freedmen was often reported as "too appalling for belief," and the situation was daily growing worse rather than better.

And daily, too, it seemed more plain that this was no ordinary matter of temporary relief, but a national crisis; for here loomed a labor problem of vast dimensions. Masses of Negroes stood idle, or, if they worked spasmodically, were never sure of pay; and if perchance they received pay, squandered the new thing thoughtlessly. In these and other ways were camp—life and the new liberty demoralizing the freedmen. The broader economic organization thus clearly demanded sprang up here and there as accident and local conditions determined. Here it was that Pierce's Port Royal plan of leased plantations and guided workmen pointed out the rough way. In Washington the military governor, at the urgent appeal of the superintendent, opened confiscated estates to the cultivation of the fugitives, and there in the shadow of the dome gathered black farm villages. General Dix gave over estates to the freedmen of Fortress Monroe, and so on, South and West. The government and benevolent societies furnished the means of cultivation, and the Negro turned again slowly to work. The systems of control, thus started, rapidly grew, here and there, into strange little governments, like that of General Banks in Louisiana, with its ninety thousand black subjects, its fifty thousand guided laborers, and its annual budget of one hundred thousand dollars and more. It made out four thousand pay-rolls a year, registered all freedmen, inquired into grievances and redressed them, laid and collected taxes, and established a system of public schools. So, too, Colonel Eaton, the superintendent of Tennessee and Arkansas, ruled over one hundred thousand freedmen, leased and cultivated seven thousand acres of cotton land, and fed ten thousand paupers a year. In South Carolina was General Saxton, with his deep interest in black folk. He succeeded Pierce and the Treasury officials, and sold forfeited estates, leased abandoned plantations, encouraged schools, and received from Sherman, after that terribly picturesque march to the sea, thousands of the wretched camp followers.

Three characteristic things one might have seen in Sherman's raid through Georgia, which threw the new situation in shadowy relief: the Conqueror, the Conquered, and the Negro. Some see all significance in the grim front of the destroyer, and some in the bitter sufferers of the Lost Cause. But to me neither soldier nor fugitive speaks with so deep a meaning as that dark human cloud that clung like remorse on the rear of those swift columns, swelling at times to half their size, almost engulfing and choking them. In vain were they ordered back, in vain were bridges hewn from beneath their feet; on they trudged and writhed and surged, until they rolled into Savannah, a starved and naked horde of tens of thousands. There too came the characteristic military remedy: "The islands from Charleston south, the abandoned rice-fields along the rivers for thirty miles back from the sea, and the country bordering the St. John's River, Florida, are reserved and set apart for the settlement of Negroes now made free by act of war." So read the celebrated "Field-order Number Fifteen."

All these experiments, orders, and systems were bound to attract and perplex the government and the nation. Directly after the Emancipation Proclamation, Representative Eliot had introduced a bill creating a Bureau of Emancipation; but it was never reported. The following June a committee of inquiry, appointed by the Secretary of War, reported in favor of a temporary bureau for the "improvement, protection, and employment of refugee freedmen," on much the same lines as were afterwards followed. Petitions came in to President Lincoln from distinguished citizens and organizations, strongly urging a comprehensive and unified plan of dealing with the freedmen, under a bureau which should be "charged with the study of plans and execution of measures for easily guiding, and in every way judiciously and humanely aiding, the passage of our emancipated and yet to be emancipated blacks from the old condition of forced labor to their new state of voluntary industry."

Some half-hearted steps were taken to accomplish this, in part, by putting the whole matter again in charge of the special Treasury agents. Laws of 1863 and 1864 directed them to take charge of and lease abandoned lands for periods not exceeding twelve months, and to "provide in such leases, or otherwise, for the employment and general welfare" of the freedmen. Most of the army officers greeted this as a welcome relief from perplexing "Negro affairs," and Secretary Fessenden, July 29, 1864, issued an excellent system of regulations, which were afterward closely followed by General Howard. Under Treasury agents, large quantities of land were leased in the Mississippi Valley, and many Negroes were employed; but in August, 1864, the new regulations were suspended for reasons of "public policy," and the army was again in control.

Meanwhile Congress had turned its attention to the subject; and in March the House passed a bill by a majority of two establishing a Bureau for Freedmen in the War Department. Charles Sumner, who had charge of the bill in the Senate, argued that freedmen and abandoned lands ought to be under the same department, and reported a substitute for the House bill attaching the Bureau to the Treasury Department. This bill passed, but too late for action by the House. The debates wandered over the whole policy of the administration and the general question of slavery, without touching very closely the specific merits of the measure in hand. Then the national election took place; and the administration, with a vote of renewed confidence from the country, addressed itself to the matter more seriously. A conference between the two branches of Congress agreed upon a carefully drawn measure which contained the chief provisions of Sumner's bill, but made the proposed organization a department independent of both the War and the Treasury officials. The bill was conservative, giving the new department "general superintendence of all freedmen." Its purpose was to "establish regulations" for them, protect them, lease them lands, adjust their wages, and appear in civil and military courts as their "next friend." There were many limitations attached to the powers thus granted, and the organization was made permanent. Nevertheless, the Senate defeated the bill, and a new conference committee was appointed. This committee reported a new bill, February 28, which was whirled through just as the session closed, and became the act of 1865 establishing in the War Department a "Bureau of Refugees, Freedmen, and Abandoned Lands."

This last compromise was a hasty bit of legislation, vague and uncertain in outline. A Bureau was created, "to continue during the present War of Rebellion, and for one year thereafter," to which was given "the supervision and management of all abandoned lands and the control of all subjects relating to refugees and freedmen," under "such rules and regulations as may be presented by the head of the Bureau and approved by the President." A Commissioner, appointed by the President and Senate, was to control the Bureau, with an office force not exceeding ten clerks. The President might also appoint assistant commissioners in the seceded States, and to all these offices military officials might be detailed at regular pay. The Secretary of War could issue rations, clothing, and fuel to the destitute, and all abandoned property was placed in the hands of the Bureau for eventual lease and sale to ex-slaves in forty-acre parcels.

Thus did the United States government definitely assume charge of the emancipated Negro as the ward of the nation. It was a tremendous undertaking. Here at a stroke of the pen was erected a government of millions of men—and not ordinary men either, but black men emasculated by a peculiarly complete system of slavery, centuries old; and now, suddenly, violently, they come into a new birthright, at a time of war and passion, in the midst of the stricken and embittered population of their former masters. Any man might well have hesitated to assume charge of such a work, with vast responsibilities, indefinite powers, and limited resources. Probably no one but a soldier would have answered such a call promptly; and, indeed, no one but a soldier could be called, for Congress had appropriated no money for salaries and expenses.

Less than a month after the weary Emancipator passed to his rest, his successor assigned Major-Gen. Oliver O. Howard to duty as Commissioner of the new Bureau. He was a Maine man, then only thirty-five years of age. He had marched with Sherman to the sea, had fought well at Gettysburg, and but the year before had been assigned to the command of the Department of Tennessee. An honest man, with too much faith in human nature, little aptitude for business and intricate detail, he had had large opportunity of becoming acquainted at first hand with much of the work before him. And of that work it has been truly said that "no approximately correct history of civilization can ever be written which does not throw out in bold relief, as one of the great landmarks of political and social progress, the organization and administration of the Freedmen's Bureau."

On May 12, 1865, Howard was appointed; and he assumed the duties of his office promptly on the 15th, and began examining the field of work. A curious mess he looked upon: little despotisms, communistic experiments, slavery, peonage, business speculations, organized charity, unorganized almsgiving—all reeling on under the guise of helping the freedmen, and all enshrined in the smoke and blood of war and the cursing and silence of angry men. On May 19 the new government—for a government it really was—issued its constitution; commissioners were to be appointed in each of the seceded states, who were to take charge of "all subjects relating to refugees and freedmen," and all relief and rations were to be given by their consent alone. The Bureau invited continued coöperation with benevolent societies, and declared: "It will be the object of all commissioners to introduce practicable systems of compensated labor," and to establish schools. Forthwith nine assistant commissioners were appointed. They were to hasten to their fields of work; seek gradually to close relief establishments, and make the destitute self-supporting; act as courts of law where there were no courts, or where Negroes were not recognized in them as free; establish the institution of marriage among ex-slaves, and keep records; see that freedmen were free to choose their employers, and help in making fair contracts for them; and finally, the circular said: "Simple good faith, for which we hope on all hands for those concerned in the passing away of slavery, will especially relieve the assistant commissioners in the discharge of their duties toward the freedmen, as well as promote the general welfare."

No sooner was the work thus started, and the general system and local organization in some measure begun, than two grave difficulties appeared which changed largely the theory and outcome of Bureau work. First, there were the abandoned lands of the South. It had long been the more or less definitely expressed theory of the North that all the chief problems of Emancipation might be settled by establishing the slaves on the forfeited lands of their masters—a sort of poetic justice, said some. But this poetry done into solemn prose meant either wholesale confiscation of private property in the South, or vast appropriations. Now Congress had not appropriated a cent, and no sooner did the proclamations of general amnesty appear than the eight hundred thousand acres of abandoned lands in the hands of the Freedmen's Bureau melted quickly away. The second difficulty lay in perfecting the local organization of the Bureau throughout the wide field of work. Making a new machine and sending out officials of duly ascertained fitness for a great work of social reform is no child's task; but this task was even harder, for a new central organization had to be fitted on a heterogeneous and confused but already existing system of relief and control of ex-slaves; and the agents available for this work must be sought for in an army still busy with war operations—men in the very nature of the case ill fitted for delicate social work—or among the questionable camp followers of an invading host. Thus, after a year's work, vigorously as it was pushed, the problem looked even more difficult to grasp and solve than at the beginning. Nevertheless, three things that year's work did, well worth the doing: it relieved a vast amount of physical suffering; it transported seven thousand fugitives from congested centres back to the farm; and, best of all, it inaugurated the crusade of the New England schoolma'am.

The annals of this Ninth Crusade are yet to be written—the tale of a mission that seemed to our age far more quixotic than the quest of St. Louis seemed to his. Behind the mists of ruin and rapine waved the calico dresses of women who dared, and after the hoarse mouthings of the field guns rang the rhythm of the alphabet. Rich and poor they were, serious and curious. Bereaved now of a father, now of a brother, now of more than these, they came seeking a life work in planting New England schoolhouses among the white and black of the South. They did their work well. In that first year they taught one hundred thousand souls, and more.

Evidently, Congress must soon legislate again on the hastily organized Bureau, which had so quickly grown into wide significance and vast possibilities. An institution such as that was well-nigh as difficult to end as to begin. Early in 1866 Congress took up the matter, when Senator Trumbull, of Illinois, introduced a bill to extend the Bureau and enlarge its powers. This measure received, at the hands of Congress, far more thorough discussion and attention than its predecessor. The war cloud had thinned enough to allow a clearer conception of the work of Emancipation. The champions of the bill argued that the strengthening of the Freedmen's Bureau was still a military necessity; that it was needed for the proper carrying out of the Thirteenth Amendment, and was a work of sheer justice to the ex-slave, at a trifling cost to the government. The opponents of the measure declared that the war was over, and the necessity for war measures past; that the Bureau, by reason of its extraordinary powers, was clearly unconstitutional in time of peace, and was destined to irritate the South and pauperize the freedmen, at a final cost of possibly hundreds of millions. These two arguments were unanswered, and indeed unanswerable: the one that the extraordinary powers of the Bureau threatened the civil rights of all citizens; and the other that the government must have power to do what manifestly must be done, and that present abandonment of the freedmen meant their practical re-enslavement. The bill which finally passed enlarged and made permanent the Freedmen's Bureau. It was promptly vetoed by President Johnson as "unconstitutional," "unnecessary," and "extrajudicial," and failed of passage over the veto. Meantime, however, the breach between Congress and the President began to broaden, and a modified form of the lost bill was finally passed over the President's second veto, July 16.

The act of 1866 gave the Freedmen's Bureau its final form—the form by which it will be known to posterity and judged of men. It extended the existence of the Bureau to July, 1868; it authorized additional assistant commissioners, the retention of army officers mustered out of regular service, the sale of certain forfeited lands to freedmen on nominal terms, the sale of Confederate public property for Negro schools, and a wider field of judicial interpretation and cognizance. The government of the unreconstructed South was thus put very largely in the hands of the Freedmen's Bureau, especially as in many cases the departmental military commander was now made also assistant commissioner. It was thus that the Freedmen's Bureau became a full-fledged government of men. It made laws, executed them and interpreted them: it laid and collected taxes, defined and punished crime, maintained and used military force, and dictated such mueasures as it thought necessary and proper for the accomplishment of its varied ends. Naturally, all those powers were not exercised continuously nor to their fullest extent; and yet, as General Howard has said, "scarcely any subject that has to be legislated upon in civil society failed, at one time or another, to demand the action of this singular Bureau."

To understand and criticise intelligently so vast a work, one must not forget an instant the drift of things in the later sixties. Lee had surrendered, Lincoln was dead, and Johnson and Congress were at loggerheads; the Thirteenth Amendment was adopted, the Fourteenth pending, and the Fifteenth declared in force in 1870. Guerrilla raiding, the ever-present flickering after-flame of war, was spending its forces against the Negroes, and all the Southern land was awakening as from some wild dream to poverty and social revolution. In a time of perfect calm, amid willing neighbors and streaming wealth, the social uplifting of four million slaves to an assured and self-sustaining place in the body politic and economic would have been a herculean task; but when to the inherent difficulties of so delicate and nice a social operation were added the spite and hate of conflict, the hell of war; when suspicion and cruelty were rife, and gaunt Hunger wept beside Bereavement—in such a case, the work of any instrument of social regeneration was in large part foredoomed to failure. The very name of the Bureau stood for a thing in the South which for two centuries and better men had refused even to argue—that life amid free Negroes was simply unthinkable, the maddest of experiments.

The agents that the Bureau could command varied all the way from unselfish philanthropists to narrow-minded busybodies and thieves; and even though it be true that the average was far better than the worst, it was the occasional fly that helped spoil the ointment.

Then amid all crouched the freed slave, bewildered between friend and foe. He had emerged from slavery—not the worst slavery in the world, not a slavery that made all life unbearable, rather a slavery that had here and there something of kindliness, fidelity, and happiness—but withal slavery, which, so far as human aspiration and desert were concerned, classed the black man and the ox together. And the Negro knew full well that, whatever their deeper convictions may have been, Southern men had fought with desperate energy to perpetuate this slavery under which the black masses, with half-articulate thought, had writhed and shivered. They welcomed freedom with a cry. They shrank from the master who still strove for their chains; they fled to the friends that had freed them, even though those friends stood ready to use them as a club for driving the recalcitrant South back into loyalty. So the cleft between the white and black South grew. Idle to say it never should have been; it was as inevitable as its results were pitiable. Curiously incongruous elements were left arrayed against each other—the North, the government, the carpet-bagger, and the slave, here; and there, all the South that was white, whether gentleman or vagabond, honest man or rascal, lawless murderer or martyr to duty.

Thus it is doubly difficult to write of this period calmly, so intense was the feeling, so mighty the human passions that swayed and blinded men. Amid it all, two figures ever stand to typify that day to coming ages—the one, a gray-haired gentleman, whose fathers had quit themselves like men, whose sons lay in nameless graves; who bowed to the evil of slavery because its abolition threatened untold ill to all; who stood at last, in the evening of life, a blighted, ruined form, with hate in his eyes; and the other, a form hovering dark and mother-like; her awful face black with the mists of centuries, had aforetime quailed at that white master's command, had bent in love over the cradles of his sons and daughters, and closed in death the sunken eyes of his wife—aye, too, at his behest had laid herself low to his lust, and borne a tawny man-child to the world, only to see her dark boy's limbs scattered to the winds by midnight marauders riding after "damned Niggers." These were the saddest sights of that woeful day; and no man clasped the hands of these two passing figures of the present-past; but, hating, they went to their long home, and, hating, their children's children live to-day.

Here, then, was the field of work for the Freedmen's Bureau; and since, with some hesitation, it was continued by the act of 1868 until 1869, let us look upon four years of its work as a whole. There were, in 1868, nine hundred Bureau officials scattered from Washington to Texas, ruling, directly and indirectly, many millions of men. The deeds of these rulers fall mainly under seven heads: the relief of physical suffering, the overseeing of the beginnings of free labor, the buying and selling of land, the establishment of schools, the paying of bounties, the administration of justice, and the financiering of all these activities.

Up to June, 1869, over half a million patients had been treated by Bureau physicians and surgeons, and sixty hospitals and asylums had been in operation. In fifty months twenty-one million free rations were distributed at a cost of over four million dollars. Next came the difficult question of labor. First, thirty thousand black men were transported from the refuges and relief stations back to the farms, back to the critical trial of a new way of working. Plain instructions went out from Washington: the laborers must be free to choose their employers, no fixed rate of wages was prescribed, and there was to be no peonage or forced labor. So far, so good; but where local agents differed *toto coelo* in capacity and character, where the *personnel* was continually changing, the outcome was necessarily varied. The largest element of success lay in the fact that the majority of the freedmen were willing, even eager, to work. So labor contracts were written—fifty thousand in a single State—laborers advised, wages guaranteed, and employers supplied. In truth, the organization became a vast labor bureau—not perfect, indeed, notably defective here and there, but on the whole successful beyond the dreams of thoughtful men. The two great obstacles which confronted the officials were the tyrant and the idler—the slaveholder who was determined to perpetuate slavery under another name; and the freedman who regarded freedom as perpetual rest—the Devil and the Deep Sea.

In the work of establishing the Negroes as peasant proprietors, the Bureau was from the first handicapped and at last absolutely checked. Something was done, and larger things were planned; abandoned lands were leased so long as they remained in the hands of the Bureau, and a total revenue of nearly half a million dollars derived from black tenants. Some other lands to which the nation had gained title were sold on easy terms, and public lands were opened for settlement to the very few freedmen who had tools and capital. But the vision of "forty acres and a mule"—the righteous and reasonable ambition to become a landholder, which the nation had all but categorically promised the freedmen—was destined in most cases to bitter disappointment. And those men of marvellous hindsight who are today seeking to preach the Negro back to the present peonage of the soil know well, or ought to know, that the opportunity of binding the Negro peasant willingly to the soil was lost on that day when the Commissioner of the Freedmen's Bureau had to go to South Carolina and tell the weeping freedmen, after their years of toil, that their land was not theirs, that there was a mistake—somewhere. If by 1874 the Georgia Negro alone owned three hundred and fifty thousand acres of land, it was by grace of his thrift rather than by bounty of the government.

The greatest success of the Freedmen's Bureau lay in the planting of the free school among Negroes, and the idea of free elementary education among all classes in the South. It not only called the school-mistresses through the benevolent agencies and built them school-houses, but it helped discover and support such apostles of human culture as Edmund Ware, Samuel Armstrong and Erastus Cravath. The opposition to Negro education in the South was at first bitter, and showed itself in ashes, insult, and blood; for the South believed an educated Negro to be a dangerous Negro. And the South was not wholly wrong; for education among all kinds of men always has had, and always will have, an element of danger and revolution, of dissatisfaction and discontent. Nevertheless, men strive to know. Perhaps some inkling of this paradox, even in the unquiet days of the Bureau, helped the bayonets allay an opposition to human training which still to-day lies smouldering in the South, but not flaming. Fisk, Atlanta, Howard, and Hampton were founded in these days, and six million dollars were expended for educational work, seven hundred and fifty thousand dollars of which the freedmen themselves gave of their poverty.

Such contributions, together with the buying of land and various other enterprises, showed that the ex-slave was handling some free capital already. The chief initial source of this was labor in the army, and his pay and bounty as a soldier. Payments to Negro soldiers were at first complicated by the ignorance of the recipients, and the fact that the quotas of colored regiments from Northern States were largely filled by recruits from the South, unknown to their fellow soldiers. Consequently, payments were accompanied by such frauds that Congress, by joint resolution in 1867, put the whole matter in the hands of the Freedmen's Bureau. In two years six million dollars was thus distributed to five thousand claimants, and in the end the sum exceeded eight million dollars. Even in this system fraud was frequent; but still the work put needed capital in the hands of practical paupers, and some, at least, was well spent.

The most perplexing and least successful part of the Bureau's work lay in the exercise of its judicial functions. The regular Bureau court consisted of one representative of the employer, one of the Negro, and one of the Bureau. If the Bureau could have maintained a perfectly judicial attitude, this arrangement would have been ideal, and must in time have gained confidence; but the nature of its other activities and the character of its *personnel* prejudiced the Bureau in favor of the black litigants, and led without doubt to much injustice and annoyance. On the other hand, to leave the Negro in the hands of Southern courts was impossible. In a distracted land where slavery had hardly fallen, to keep the strong from wanton abuse of the weak, and the weak from gloating insolently over the half-shorn strength of the strong, was a thankless, hopeless task. The former masters of the land were peremptorily ordered about, seized, and imprisoned, and punished over and again, with scant courtesy from army officers. The former slaves were intimidated, beaten, raped, and butchered by angry and revengeful men. Bureau courts tended to become centres simply for punishing whites, while the regular civil courts tended to become solely institutions for perpetuating the slavery of blacks. Almost every law and method ingenuity could devise was employed by the legislatures to reduce the Negroes to serfdom—to make them the slaves of the State, if not of individual owners; while the Bureau officials too often were found striving to put the "bottom rail on top," and gave the freedmen a power and independence which they could not yet use. It is all well enough for us of another generation to wax wise with advice to those who bore the burden in the heat of the day. It is full easy now to see that the man who lost home, fortune, and family at a stroke, and saw his land ruled by "mules and niggers," was really benefited by the passing of slavery. It is not difficult now to say to the young freedman, cheated and cuffed about who has seen his father's head beaten to a jelly and his own mother namelessly assaulted, that the meek shall inherit the earth. Above all, nothing is more convenient than to heap on the Freedmen's Bureau all the evils of that evil day, and damn it utterly for every mistake and blunder that was made.

All this is easy, but it is neither sensible nor just. Some one had blundered, but that was long before Oliver Howard was born; there was criminal aggression and heedless neglect, but without some system of control there would have been far more than there was. Had that control been from within, the Negro would have been re-enslaved, to all intents and purposes. Coming as the control did from without, perfect men and methods would have bettered all things; and even with imperfect agents and questionable methods, the work accomplished was not undeserving of commendation.

Such was the dawn of Freedom; such was the work of the Freedmen's Bureau, which, summed up in brief, may be epitomized thus: for some fifteen million dollars, beside the sums spent before 1865, and the dole of benevolent societies, this Bureau set going a system of free labor, established a beginning of peasant proprietorship, secured the recognition of black freedmen before courts of law, and founded the free common school in the South. On the other hand, it failed to begin the establishment of good-will between ex-masters and freedmen, to guard its work wholly from paternalistic methods which discouraged self-reliance, and to carry out to any considerable extent its implied promises to furnish the freedmen with land. Its successes were the result of hard work, supplemented by the aid of philanthropists and the eager striving of black men. Its failures were the result of bad local agents, the inherent difficulties of the work, and national neglect.

Such an institution, from its wide powers, great responsibilities, large control of moneys, and generally conspicuous position, was naturally open to repeated and bitter attack. It sustained a searching Congressional investigation at the instance of Fernando Wood in 1870. Its archives and few remaining functions were with blunt discourtesy transferred from Howard's control, in his absence, to the supervision of Secretary of War Belknap in 1872, on the Secretary's recommendation. Finally, in consequence of grave intimations of wrong-doing made by the Secretary and his subordinates. General Howard was court-martialed in 1874. In both of these trials the Commissioner of the Freedmen's Bureau was officially exonerated from any willful misdoing, and his work commended. Nevertheless, many unpleasant things were brought to light—the methods of transacting the business of the Bureau were faulty; several cases of defalcation were proved, and other frauds strongly suspected; there were some business transactions which savored of dangerous speculation, if not dishonesty; and around it all lay the smirch of the Freedmen's Bank.

Morally and practically, the Freedmen's Bank was part of the Freedmen's Bureau, although it had no legal connection with it. With the prestige of the government back of it, and a directing board of unusual respectability and national reputation, this banking institution had made a remarkable start in the development of that thrift among black folk which slavery had kept them from knowing. Then in one sad day came the crash—all the hard-earned dollars of the freedmen disappeared; but that was the least of the loss—all the faith in saving went too, and much of the faith in men; and that was a loss that a Nation which to-day sneers at Negro shiftlessness has never yet made good. Not even ten additional years of slavery could have done so much to throttle the thrift of the freedmen as the mismanagement and bankruptcy of the series of savings banks chartered by the Nation for their especial aid. Where all the blame should rest, it is hard to say; whether the Bureau and the Bank died chiefly by reason of the blows of its selfish friends or the dark machinations of its foes, perhaps even time will never reveal, for here lies unwritten history.

Of the foes without the Bureau, the bitterest were those who attacked not so much its conduct or policy under the law as the necessity for any such institution at all. Such attacks came primarily from the Border States and the South; and they were summed up by Senator Davis, of Kentucky, when he moved to entitle the act of 1866 a bill "to promote strife and conflict between the white and black races . . . by a grant of unconstitutional power." The argument gathered tremendous strength South and North; but its very strength was its weakness. For, argued the plain common-sense of the nation, if it is unconstitutional, unpractical, and futile for the nation to stand guardian over its helpless wards, then there is left but one alternative—to make those wards their own guardians by arming them with the ballot. Moreover, the path of the practical politician pointed the same way; for, argued this opportunist, if we cannot peacefully reconstruct the South with white votes we certainly can with black votes. So justice and force joined hands.

The alternative thus offered the nation was not between full and restricted Negro suffrage; else every sensible man, black and white, would easily have chosen the latter. It was rather a choice between suffrage and slavery, after endless blood and gold had flowed to sweep human bondage away. Not a single Southern legislature stood ready to admit a Negro, under any conditions, to the polls; not a single Southern legislature believed free Negro labor was possible without a system of restrictions that took all its freedom away; there was scarcely a white man in the South who did not honestly regard emancipation as a crime, and its practical nullification as a duty. In such a situation, the granting of the ballot to the black man was a necessity, the very least a guilty nation could grant a wronged race, and the only method of compelling the South to accept the results of the war. Thus Negro suffrage ended a civil war by beginning a race feud. And some felt gratitude toward the race thus sacrificed in its swaddling clothes on the altar of national integrity; and some felt and feel only indifference and contempt.

Had political exigencies been less pressing, the opposition to government guardianship of Negroes less bitter, and the attachment to the slave system less strong, the social seer can well imagine a far better policy—a permanent Freedmen's Bureau, with a national system of Negro schools; a carefully supervised employment and labor office; a system of impartial protection before the regular courts; and such institutions for social betterment as savings-banks, land and building associations, and social settlements. All this vast expenditure of money and brains might have formed a great school of prospective citizenship, and solved in a way we have not yet solved the most perplexing and persistent of the Negro problems.

That such an institution was unthinkable in 1870 was due in part to certain acts of the Freedmen's Bureau itself. It came to regard its work as merely temporary, and Negro suffrage as a final answer to all present perplexities. The political ambition of many of its agents and *protégés* led it far afield into questionable activities, until the South, nursing its own deep prejudices, came easily to ignore all the good deeds of the Bureau and hate its very name with perfect hatred. So the Freedmen's Bureau died, and its child was the Fifteenth Amendment.

The passing of a great human insitituion before its work is done, like the untimely passing of a single soul, but leaves a legacy of striving for other men. The legacy of the Freedmen's Bureau is the heavy heritage of this generation. To-day, when new and vaster problems are destined to strain every fibre of the national mind and soul, would it not be well to count this legacy honestly and carefully? For this much all men know: despite compromise, war, and struggle, the Negro is not free. In the backwoods of the Gulf States, for miles and miles, he may not leave the plantation of his birth; in well-nigh the whole rural South the black farmers are peons, bound by law and custom to an economic slavery, from which the only escape is death or the penitentiary. In the most cultured sections and cities of the South the Negroes are a segregated servile caste, with restricted rights and privileges. Before the courts, both in law and custom, they stand on a different and peculiar basis. Taxation without representation is the rule of their political life. And the result of all this is, and in nature must have been, lawlessness and crime. That is the large legacy of the Freedmen's Bureau, the work it did not do because it could not.

I have seen a land right merry with the sun, where children sing, and rolling hills lie like passioned women wanton with harvest. And there in the King's Highway sat and sits a figure veiled and bowed, by which the traveller's footsteps hasten as they go. On the tainted air broods fear. Three centuries' thought has been the raising and unveiling of that bowed human heart, and now behold a century new for the duty and the deed. The problem of the Twentieth Century is the problem of the color-line.

DEAR DR. BUTTS

Langston Hughes

"Do you know what has happened to me?" said Simple.

"No."

"I'm out of a job."

"That's tough. How did that come about?"

"Laid off—they're converting again. And right now, just when I am planning to get married this spring, they have to go changing from civilian production to war contracts, installing new machinery. Manager says it might take two months, might take three or four. They'll send us mens notices. If it takes four months, that's up to June, which is no good for my plans. To get married a man needs money. To stay married he needs more money. And where am I? As usual, behind the eight-ball."

"You can find another job meanwhile, no doubt."

"That ain't easy. And if I do, they liable not to pay much. Jobs that pay good money nowadays are scarce as hen's teeth. But Joyce says she do not care. She is going to marry me, come June, anyhow—even if she has to pay for it herself. Joyce says since I paid for the divorce, she can pay for the wedding. But I do not want her to do that."

"Naturally not, but maybe you can curtail your plans somewhat and not have so big a wedding. Wedlock does not require an elaborate ceremony."

"I do not care if we don't have none, just so we get locked. But you know how womens is. Joyce has waited an extra year for her great day. Now here I am broke as a busted bank."

"How're you keeping up with your expenses?"

"I ain't. And I don't drop by Joyce's every night like I did when I was working. I'm embarrassed. Then she didn't have to ask me to eat. Now she does. In fact, she insists. She says, 'You got to eat somewheres. I enjoy your company. Eat with me.' I do, if I'm there when she extends the invitation. But I don't go looking for it. I just sets home and broods, man, and looks at my four walls, which gives me plenty of time to think. And do you know what I been thinking about lately?"

"Finding work, I presume."

"Besides that?"

"No. I don't know what you've been thinking about."

"Negro leaders, and how they're talking about how great democracy is—and me out of a job. Also how there is so many leaders I don't know that white folks know about, because they are always in the white papers. Yet *I'm* the one they are supposed to be leading. Now, you take that little short leader named Dr. Butts, I do not know him, except in name only. If he ever made a speech in Harlem

392

it were not well advertised. From what I reads, he teaches at a white college in Massachusetts, stays at the Commodore when he's in New York, and ain't lived in Harlem for ten years. Yet he's leading me. He's an article writer, but he does not write in colored papers. But lately the colored papers taken to reprinting parts of what he writes—otherwise I would have never seen it. Anyhow, with all this time on my hands these days, I writ him a letter last night. Here, read it."

Harlem, U.S.A.
One Cold February Day

Dear Dr. Butts,

I seen last week in the colored papers where you have writ an article for The New York Times *in which you say America is the greatest country in the world for the Negro race and Democracy the greatest kind of government for all, but it would be better if there was equal education for colored folks in the South, and if everybody could vote, and if there were not Jim Crow in the army, also if the churches was not divided up into white churches and colored churches, and if Negroes did not have to ride on the back seats of busses South of Washington.*

Now, all this later part of your article is hanging onto your but. *You start off talking about how great American democracy is, then you* but *it all over the place. In fact, the* but *end of your see-saw is so far down on the ground I do not believe the other end can ever pull it up. So me myself, I would not write no article for no* New York Times *if I had to put in so many* buts. *I reckon maybe you come by it naturally, though, that being your name, dear Dr. Butts.*

I hear tell that you are a race leader, but I do not know who you lead because I have not heard tell of you before and I have not laid eyes on you. But if you are leading me, make me know it, because I do not read the New York Times *very often, less I happen to pick up a copy blowing around in the subway, so I did not know you were my leader. But since you are my leader, lead on, and see if I will follow behind your* but—*because there is more behind that* but *than there is in front of it.*

Dr. Butts, I am glad to read that you writ an article in The New York Times, *but also sometime I wish you would write one in the colored papers and let me know how to get out from behind all these* buts *that are staring me in the face. I know America is a great country* but—*and it is that* but *that has been keeping me where I is all these years. I can't get over it, I can't get under it, and I can't get around it, so what am I supposed to do? If you are leading me, lemme see. Because we have too many colored leaders now that nobody knows until they get from the white papers to the colored papers and from the colored papers to me who has never seen hair nor hide of you. Dear Dr. Butts, are you hiding from me—and leading me, too?*

From the way you write, a man would think my race problem was made out of nothing but buts. But *this,* but *that, and, yes, there is Jim Crow in Georgia* but–. *America admits they bomb folks in Florida*–but *Hitler gassed the Jews. Mississippi is bad*–but *Russia is worse. Detroit slums are awful*–but *compared to the slums in India, Detroit's Paradise Valley is Paradise.*

Dear Dr. Butts, Hitler is dead. I don't live in Russia. India is across the Pacific Ocean. And I do not hope to see Paradise no time soon. I am nowhere near some of them foreign countries you are talking about being so bad. I am here! *And you know as well as I do, Mississippi is hell. There ain't no* but *in the world can make it out different. They tell when Nazis gas you, you die slow. But when they put a bomb under you like in Florida, you don't have time to say your prayers. As for Detroit, there is as much difference between Paradise Valley and Paradise as there is between heaven and Harlem. I don't know nothing about India, but I been in Washington, D.C. If you think there ain't slums there, just take your* but *up Seventh Street late some night, and see if you still got it by the time you get to Howard University.*

I should not have to be telling you these things. You are colored just like me. To put a but *after all this Jim Crow fly-papering around our feet is just like telling a hungry man, "But Mr. Rockefeller has got plenty to eat." It's just like telling a joker with no overcoat in the winter time, "But you will be hot next summer." The fellow is liable to haul off and say, "I am hot now!" And bop you over your head.*

Are you in your right mind, dear Dr. Butts? Or are you just writing? Do you really think a new day is dawning? Do you really think Christians are having a change of heart? I can see you now taking your pen in hand to write, "But just last year the Southern Denominations of Hell-Fired Salvation resolved to work toward Brotherhood." In fact, that is what you already writ. Do you think Brotherhood means colored *to them Southerners?*

Do you reckon they will recognize you *for a brother, Dr. Butts, since you done had your picture taken in the Grand Ballroom of the Waldorf-Astoria shaking hands at some kind of meeting with five hundred white big-shots and* five *Negroes,* all five of them Negro leaders, *so it said underneath the picture? I did not know any of them Negro leaders by sight, neither by name, but since it says in the white papers that they are leaders, I reckon they are. Anyhow, I take my pen in hand to write you this letter to ask you to make yourself clear to me. When you answer me, do not write no "so-and-so-and-so* but–." *I will not take* but *for an answer. Negroes have been looking at Democracy's* but *too long. What we want to know is how to get rid of that* but.

Do you dig me, dear Dr. Butts?

Sincerely very truly,
Jesse B. Simple

NEGROES WITH GUNS

Robert F. Williams

Why do I speak to you from exile?

Because a Negro community in the South took up guns in self-defense against racist violence and used them. I am held responsible for this action, that for the first time in history American Negroes have armed themselves as a group, to defend their homes, their wives, their children, in a situation where law and order had broken down, where the authorities could not, or rather would not, enforce their duty to protect Americans from a lawless mob. I accept this responsibility and am proud of it. I have asserted the right of Negroes to meet the violence of the Ku Klux Klan by armed self-defense—and have acted on it. It has always been an accepted right of Americans, as the history of our Western states proves, that where the law is unable, or unwilling, to enforce order, the citizens can, and must, act in self-defense against lawless violence. I believe this right holds for black Americans as well as whites.

Many people will remember that in the summer of 1957 the Ku Klux Klan made an armed raid on an Indian community in the South and were met with determined rifle fire from the Indians acting in self-defense. The nation approved of the action and there were widespread expressions of pleasure at the defeat of the Kluxers, who showed their courage by running away despite their armed superiority. What the nation doesn't know, because it has never been told, is that the Negro community in Monroe, North Carolina, had set the example two weeks before when we shot up an armed motorcade of the Ku Klux Klan, *including two police cars*, which had come to attack the home of Dr. Albert E. Perry, vice-president of the Monroe chapter of the National Association for the Advancement of Colored People. The stand taken by our chapter resulted in the official re-affirmation by the NAACP of the right of self-defense. The Preamble to the resolution of the 50th Convention of the NAACP, New York City, July 1959, states: ". . . we do not deny, but reaffirm, the right of an individual and collective self-defense against unlawful assaults."

Because there has been much distortion of my position, I wish to make it clear that I do not advocate violence for its own sake, or for the sake of reprisals against whites. Nor am I against the passive resistance advocated by the Reverend Martin Luther King and others. My only difference with Dr. King is that I believe in flexibility in the freedom struggle. This means that I believe in non-violent tactics where feasible and the mere fact that I have a Sit-In case pending before the U.S. Supreme Court bears this out. Massive civil disobedience is a powerful weapon under civilized conditions, where the law safeguards the citizens' right of peaceful demonstrations. In civilized society the law serves as a deterrent against lawless forces that would destroy the democratic process. But where there is a breakdown of the law, the individual citizen has a right to protect his person, his family, his home and his property. To me this is so simple and proper that it is self-evident.

When an oppressed people show a willingness to defend themselves, the enemy, who is a moral weakling and coward is more willing to grant concessions and work for a respectable compromise. Psychologically, moreover, racists consider themselves superior beings and they are not willing to exchange their superior lives for our inferior ones. They are most vicious and violent when they can practice violence with impunity. This we have shown in Monroe. Moreover, when because of our self-defense there is a danger that the blood of whites may be spilled, the local authorities in the South suddenly enforce law and order when previously they had been complaisant toward lawless, racist violence. This too we have proven in Monroe. It is remarkable how easily and quickly state and local police control and disperse lawless mobs when the Negro is ready to defend himself with arms.

Furthermore, because of the international situation, the Federal Government does not want racial incidents which draw the attention of the world to the situation in the South. Negro self-defense draws such attention, and the federal government will be more willing to enforce law and order if the local authorities don't. When our people become fighters, our leaders will be able to sit at the conference table as equals, not dependent on the whim and the generosity of the oppressors. It will be to the best interests of both sides to negotiate just, honorable and lasting settlements.

The majority of white people in the United States have literally no idea of the violence with which Negroes in the South are treated daily—nay, hourly. This violence is deliberate, conscious, condoned by the authorities. It has gone on for centuries and is going on today, every day, unceasing and unremitting. It is our way of life. Negro existence in the South has been one long travail, steeped in terror and blood—our blood. The incidents which took place in Monroe, which I witnessed and which I suffered, will give some idea of the conditions in the South, such conditions that can no longer be borne. That is why, one hundred years after the Civil War began, we Negroes in Monroe armed ourselves in self-defense and used our weapons. We showed that our policy worked. The lawful authorities of Monroe and North Carolina acted to enforce order *only after, and as a direct result of, our being armed.* Previously they had connived with the Ku Klux Klan in the racist violence against our people. Self-defense prevented bloodshed and forced the law to establish order. This is the meaning of Monroe and I believe it marks a historic change in the life of my people. This is the story of that change.

The tactics of non-violence will continue and should continue. We too believed in non-violent tactics in Monroe. We've used these tactics; we've used all tactics. But we also believe that any struggle for liberation should be a flexible struggle. We shouldn't take the attitude that one method alone is the way to liberation. This is to become dogmatic. This is to fall into the same sort of dogmatism practiced by some of the religious fanatics. We can't afford to develop this type of attitude.

We must use non-violence as a means as long as this is feasible, but the day will come when conditions become so pronounced that non-violence will be suicidal in itself. The day is surely coming when we will see more violence on the same American scene. The day is surely coming when some of the same Negroes who have denounced our using weapons for self-defense will be arming themselves. There are those who pretend to be horrified by the idea that a black veteran who shouldered arms for the United States would willingly take up weapons to defend his wife, his children, his home, and his life. These same people will one day be the loud advocates of self-defense. When violent racism and fascism strike at their families and their homes, not in a token way but in an all-out bloody campaign, then they will be among the first to advocate self-defense. They will justify their position as a question of survival. When it is no longer some distant Negro who's no more than a statistic, no more than an article in a newspaper; when it is no longer their neighbors, but it means them and it becomes a matter of personal salvation, then will their attitude change.

As a tactic, we use and approve non-violent resistance. But we also believe that a man cannot have human dignity if he allows himself to be abused; to be kicked and beaten to the ground, to allow his wife and children to be attacked, refusing to defend them and himself on the basis that he's so pious, so self-righteous, that it would demean his personality if he fought back.

We know that the average Afro-American is not a pacifist. He's not a pacifist and he has never been a pacifist and he's not made of the type of material that would make a good pacifist. Those who doubt that the great majority of Negroes are not pacifists, just let them slap one. Pick any Negro on any street corner in the U.S.A. and they'll find out how much he believes in turning the other cheek.

All those who dare to attack are going to learn the hard way that the Afro-American is not a pacifist; that he cannot forever be counted on not to defend himself. Those who attack him brutally and ruthlessly can no longer expect to attack him with impunity.

The Afro-American cannot forget that his enslavement in this country did not pass because of pacifist moral force or noble appeals to the Christian conscience of the slaveholders.

Henry David Thoreau is idealized as an apostle of non-violence, the writer who influenced Gandhi, and through Gandhi, Martin Luther King, Jr. But Thoreau was not dogmatic; his eyes were open and he saw clearly. I keep with me a copy of Thoreau's *Plea For Captain John Brown*. There are truths that are just as evident in 1962 as they were in 1859 when he wrote:

... It was his [John Brown's] peculiar doctrine that a man has a perfect right to interfere by force with the slaveholder, in order to rescue the slave. I agree with him. They who are continually shocked by slavery have some right to be shocked by the violent death of the slaveholder, but such will be more shocked by his life than by his death. I shall not be forward to think him mistaken in his method who quickest succeeds to liberate the slave.

I speak for the slave when I say, that I prefer the philanthropy of Captain Brown to that philanthropy which neither shoots me nor liberates me. . . . I do not wish to kill nor to be killed, but I can foresee circumstances in which both these things would be by me unavoidable. We preserve the so-called peace of our community by deeds of petty violence every day. Look at the policeman's billy and handcuffs! Look at the jail! . . . We are hoping only to live safely on the outskirts of this provisional army. So we defend ourselves and our hen-roosts, and maintain slavery. I know that the mass of my countrymen think that the only righteous use that can be made of Sharpe's rifles and revolvers is to fight duels with them, when we are insulted by other nations, or to hunt Indians, or shoot fugitive slaves with them or the like. I think that for once the Sharpe's rifles and the revolvers were employed in a righteous cause. The tools were in the hands of one who could use them.

The same indignation that is said to have cleared the temple once will clear it again. The question is not about the weapon, but the spirit in which you use it. No man has appeared in America, as yet, who loved his fellowman so well, and treated him so tenderly. He [John Brown] lived for him. He took up his life and he laid it down for him. What sort of violence is that which is encouraged, not by soldiers, but by peaceable citizens, not so much by laymen as by ministers of the Gospel, not so much by the fighting sects as by the Quakers, and not so much by Quaker men as by Quaker women?

This event advertises me that there is such a fact as death; the possibility of a man's dying. It seems as if no man had ever died in America before; for in order to die you must first have lived.

It is in the nature of the American Negro, the same as all other men, to fight and try to destroy those things that block his path to a greater happiness in life. . . .

NOTES ON A NATIVE SON

Eldridge Cleaver

After reading a couple of James Baldwin's books, I began experiencing that continuous delight one feels upon discovering a fascinating, brilliant talent on the scene, a talent capable of penetrating so profoundly into one's own little world that one knows oneself to have been unalterably changed and *liberated*, liberated from the frustrating grasp of whatever devils happen to possess one. Being a Negro, I have found this to be a rare and infrequent experience, for few of my black brothers and sisters here in America have achieved the power, which James Baldwin calls his revenge, which outlasts kingdoms: the power of doing whatever cats like Baldwin do when combining the alphabet with the volatile elements of his soul. (And, like it or not, a black man, unless he has become irretrievably "white-minded," responds with an additional dimension of his being to the articulated experience of another black—in spite of the universality of human experience.)

I, as I imagine many others did and still do, lusted for anything that Baldwin had written. It would have been a gas for me to sit on a pillow beneath the womb of Baldwin's typewriter and catch each newborn page as it entered this world of ours. I was delighted that Baldwin, with those great big eyes of his, which one thought to be fixedly focused on the macrocosm, could also pierce the microcosm. And although he was so full of sound, he was not a noisy writer like Ralph Ellison. He placed so much of my own experience, which I thought I had understood, into new perspective.

Gradually, however, I began to feel uncomfortable about something in Baldwin. I was disturbed upon becoming aware of an aversion in my heart to part of the song he sang. Why this was so, I was unable at first to say. Then I read *Another Country*, and I knew why my love for Baldwin's vision had become ambivalent.

Long before, I had become a student of Norman Mailer's *The White Negro*, which seemed to me to be prophetic and penetrating in its understanding of the psychology involved in the accelerating confrontation of black and white in America. I was therefore personally insulted by Baldwin's flippant, schoolmarmish dismissal of *The White Negro*. Baldwin committed a literary crime by his arrogant repudiation of one of the few gravely important expressions of our time. *The White Negro* may contain an excess of esoteric verbal husk, but one can forgive Mailer for that because of the solid kernel of truth he gave us. After all, it is the baby we want and not the blood of afterbirth. Mailer described, in that incisive essay, the first important chinks in the "mountain of white supremacy"—important because it shows the depth of ferment, on a personal level, in the white world. People are feverishly, and at great psychic and social expense, seeking *fundamental and irrevocable liberation*—and, what is more important, *are succeeding in escaping*—from the big white lies that compose the monolithic myth of White Supremacy/Black Inferiority, in a desperate attempt on the part of a new generation of white Americans to enter into the cosmopolitan egalitarian spirit of the twentieth century. But let us examine the reasoning that lies behind Baldwin's attack on Mailer.

There is in James Baldwin's work the most grueling, agonizing, total hatred of the blacks, particularly of himself, and the most shameful, fanatical, fawning, sycophantic love of the whites that one can find in the writings of any black American writer of note in our time. This is an appalling contradiction and the implications of it are vast.

A rereading of *Nobody Knows My Name* cannot help but convince the most avid of Baldwin's admirers of the hatred for blacks permeating his writings. In the essay "Princes and Powers," Baldwin's antipathy toward the black race is shockingly clear. The essay is Baldwin's interpretation of the Conference of Black Writers and Artists which met in Paris in September 1956. The portrait of Baldwin that comes through his words is that of a mind in unrelenting opposition to the efforts of solemn, dedicated black men who have undertaken the enormous task of rejuvenating and reclaiming the shattered psyches and culture of the black people, a people scattered over the continents of the world and the islands of the seas, where they exist in the mud of the floor of the foul dungeon into which the world has been transformed by the whites.

In his report of the conference, Baldwin, the reluctant black, dragging his feet at every step, could only ridicule the vision and efforts of these great men and heap scorn upon them, reserving his compliments—all of them lefthanded—for the speakers at the conference who were themselves rejected and booed by the other conferees because of their reactionary, sycophantic views. Baldwin felt called upon to pop his cap pistol in a duel with Aimé Césaire, the big gun from Martinique. Indirectly, Baldwin was defending his first love—the white man. But the revulsion which Baldwin felt for the blacks at this conference, who were glorying in their blackness, seeking and showing their pride in Negritude and the African Personality, drives him to self-revealing sortie after sortie, so obvious in "Princes and Powers." Each successive sortie, however, becomes more expensive than the last one, because to score each time he has to go a little farther out on the limb, and it takes him a little longer each time to hustle back to the cover and camouflage of the perfumed smoke screen of his prose. Now and then we catch a glimpse of his little jive ass—his big eyes peering back over his shoulder in the mischievous retreat of a child sneak-thief from a cookie jar.

In the autobiographical notes of *Notes of a Native Son*, Baldwin is frank to confess that, in growing into his version of manhood in Harlem, he discovered that, since his African heritage had been wiped out and was not accessible to him, he would appropriate the white man's heritage and make it his own. This terrible reality, central to the psychic stance of all American Negroes, revealed to Baldwin that he hated and feared white people. Then he says: "This did not mean that I loved black people; on the contrary, I despised them, possibly because they failed to produce Rembrandt." The psychic distance between love and hate could be the mechanical difference between a smile and a sneer, or it could be the journey of a nervous impulse from the depths of one's brain to the tip of one's toe. But this impulse in its path through North American nerves may, if it is honest, find the passage disputed: may find the leap from the fiber of hate to that of love too taxing on its meager store of energy—and so the long trip back may never be completed, may end in a reconnaissance, a compromise, and then a lie.

Self-hatred takes many forms; sometimes it can be detected by no one, not by the keenest observer, not by the self-hater himself, not by his most intimate friends. Ethnic self-hate is even more difficult to detect. But in American Negroes, this ethnic self-hatred often takes the bizarre form of a racial death-wish, with many and elusive manifestations. Ironically, it provides much of the impetus behind the motivations of integration. And the attempt to suppress or deny such drives in one's psyche leads many American Negroes to become ostentatious separationists, Black Muslims, and back-to-Africa advocates. It is no wonder that Elijah Muhammad could conceive of the process of controlling evolution whereby the white race was brought into being. According to Elijah, about 6300 years ago all the people of the earth were Original Blacks. Secluded on the island of Patmos, a mad black scientist by the name of Yacub set up the machinery for grafting whites out of blacks through the operation of a birth-control system. The population on this island of Patmos was 59,999 and whenever a couple on this island wanted to get married they were only allowed to do so if there was a difference in their color, so that by mating black with those in the population of a brownish color and brown with brown—but never black with black—all traces of the black were eventually eliminated; the process was repeated until all the brown was eliminated, leaving only men of the red race; the red was bleached out, leaving only yellow; then the yellow was bleached out, and only white was left. Thus Yacub, who was long since dead, because this whole process took hundreds of years, had finally succeeded in creating the white devil with the blue eyes of death.

This myth of the creation of the white race, called "Yacub's history," is an inversion of the racial death-wish of American Negroes. Yacub's plan is still being followed by many negroes today.

Quite simply, many Negroes believe, as the principle of assimilation into white America implies, that the race problem in America cannot be settled until all traces of the black race are eliminated. Toward this end, many Negroes loathe the very idea of two very dark Negroes mating. The children, they say, will come out ugly. What they mean is that the children are sure to be black, and this is not desirable. From the widespread use of cosmetics to bleach the black out of one's skin and other concoctions to take Africa out of one's hair, to the extreme, resorted to by more Negroes than one might wish to believe, of undergoing nose-thinning and lip-clipping operations, the racial death-wish of American Negroes—Yacub's goal—takes its terrible toll. What has been happening for the past four hundred years is that the white man, through his access to black women, has been pumping his blood and genes into the blacks, has been diluting the blood and genes of the blacks—i.e., has been fulfilling Yacub's plan and accelerating the Negroes' racial death-wish.

The case of James Baldwin aside for a moment, it seems that many Negro homosexuals, acquiescing in this racial death-wish, are outraged and frustrated because in their sickness they are unable to have a baby by a white man. The cross they have to bear is that, already bending over and touching their toes for the white man, the fruit of their miscegenation is not the little half-white offspring of their dreams but an increase in the unwinding of their nerves—though they redouble their efforts and intake of the white man's sperm.

In this land of dichotomies and disunited opposites, those truly concerned with the resurrection of black Americans have had eternally to deal with black intellectuals who have become their own opposites, taking on all of the behavior patterns of their enemy, vices and virtues, in an effort to aspire to alien standards in all respects. The gulf between an audacious, bootlicking Uncle Tom and an intellectual buckdancer is filled only with sophistication and style. On second thought, Uncle Tom comes off much cleaner here because usually he is just trying to survive, choosing to pretend to be something other than his true self in order to please the white man and thus receive favors. Whereas the intellectual sycophant does not pretend to be other than he actually is, but hates what he is and seeks to redefine himself in the image of his white idols. He becomes a white man in a black body. A self-willed, automated slave, he becomes the white man's most valuable tool in oppressing other blacks.

The black homosexual, when his twist has a racial nexus, is an extreme embodiment of this contradiction. The white man has deprived him of his masculinity, castrated him in the center of his burning skull, and when he submits to this change and takes the white man for his lover as well as Big Daddy, he focuses on "whiteness" all the love in his pent up soul and turns the razor edge of hatred against "blackness"—upon himself, what he is, and all those

who look like him, remind him of himself. He may even hate the
darkness of night.

The racial death-wish is manifested as the driving force in James
Baldwin. His hatred for blacks, even as he pleads what he conceives
as their cause, makes him the apotheosis of the dilemma in the ethos
of the black bourgeoisie who have completely rejected their African
heritage, consider the loss irrevocable, and refuse to look again in
that direction. This is the root of Baldwin's violent repudiation of
Mailer's *The White Negro*.

To understand what is at stake here, and to understand it in terms
of the life of this nation, is to know the central fact that the
relationship between black and white in America is a power equation,
a power struggle, and that this power struggle is not only manifested
in the aggregate (civil rights, black nationalism, etc.) but also in the
interpersonal relationships, actions, and reactions between blacks and
whites where taken into account. When those "two lean cats," Baldwin and Mailer, met in a French living room, it was precisely this
power equation that was at work.

It is fascinating to read (in *Nobody Knows My Name*) in what
terms this power equation was manifested in Baldwin's immediate
reaction to that meeting: "And here we were, suddenly, circling
around each other. We liked each other at once, but each was
frightened that the other would pull rank. He could have pulled rank
on me because he was more famous and *had more money* and also
because he was white; but I could have pulled rank on him precisely
because I was black and knew more about that periphery he so
helplessly maligns in *The White Negro* than he could ever hope to
know." [Italics added.]

Pulling rank, it would seem, is a very dangerous business, especially
when the troops have mutinied and the basis of one's authority, or
rank, is devoid of that interdictive power and has become suspect.
One would think that for Baldwin, of all people, these hues of black
and white were no longer armed with the power to intimidate—and if
one thought this, one would be exceedingly wrong: for behind the
structure of the thought of Baldwin's quoted above, there lurks the
imp of Baldwin's unwinding, of his tension between love and hate—
love of the white and hate of the black. And when we dig into this
tension we will find that when those "two lean cats" crossed tracks
in that French living room, one was a Pussy Cat, the other a Tiger.
Baldwin's purr was transmitted magnificently in *The Fire Next Time*.
But his work is the fruit of a tree with a poison root. Such succulent
fruit, such a painful tree, what a malignant root!

It is ironic, but fascinating for what it reveals about the ferment in
the North American soul in our time, that Norman Mailer, the white
boy, and James Baldwin, the black boy, encountered each other in
the eye of a social storm, traveling in opposite directions; the white

404	The Black Man's Revolution

boy, with knowledge of white Negroes, was traveling toward a confrontation with the black, with Africa; while the black boy, with a white mind, was on his way to Europe. Baldwin's nose, like the North-seeking needle on a compass, is forever pointed toward his adopted fatherland, Europe, his by intellectual osmosis and in Africa's stead. What he says of Aimé Césaire, one of the greatest black writers of the twentieth century, and intending it as an ironic rebuke, that "he had penetrated into the heart of the great wilderness which was Europe and stolen the sacred fire ... which ... was ... the assurance of his power," seems only too clearly to speak more about Peter than it does about Paul. What Baldwin seems to forget is that Césaire explains that fire, whether sacred or profane, burns. In Baldwin's case, though the fire could not burn the black off his face, it certainly did burn it out of his heart.

I am not interested in denying anything to Baldwin. I, like the entire nation, owe a great debt to him. But throughout the range of his work, from *Go Tell It on the Mountain*, through *Notes of a Native Son*, *Nobody Knows My Name*, *Another Country*, to *The Fire Next Time*, all of which I treasure, there is a decisive quirk in Baldwin's vision which corresponds to his relationship to black people and to masculinity. It was this same quirk, in my opinion, that compelled Baldwin to slander Rufus Scott in *Another Country*, venerate André Gide, repudiate *The White Negro*, and drive the blade of Brutus into the corpse of Richard Wright. As Baldwin has said in *Nobody Knows My Name*, "I think that I know something about the American masculinity which most men of my generation do not know because they have not been menaced by it in the way I have been." O.K., Sugar, but isn't it true that Rufus Scott, the weak, craven-hearted ghost of *Another Country*, bears the same relation to Bigger Thomas of *Native Son*, the black rebel of the ghetto and a man, as you yourself bore to the fallen giant, Richard Wright, a rebel and a man?

Somewhere in one of his books, Richard Wright describes an encounter between a ghost and several young Negroes. The young Negroes rejected the homosexual, and this was Wright alluding to a classic, if cruel, example of a ubiquitous phenomenon in the black ghettos of America: the practice by Negro youths of going "punk-hunting." This practice of seeking out homosexuals on the prowl, rolling them, beating them up, seemingly just to satisfy some savage impulse to inflict pain on the specific target selected, the "social outcast," seems to me to be not unrelated, in terms of the psychological mechanisms involved, to the ritualistic lynchings and castrations inflicted on Southern blacks by Southern whites. This was, as I recall, one of Wright's few comments on the subject of homosexuality.

I think it can safely be said that the men in Wright's books, albeit shackled with a form of impotence, were strongly heterosexual. Their

heterosexuality was implied rather than laboriously stated or emphasized; it was taken for granted, as we all take men until something
occurs to make us know otherwise. And Bigger Thomas, Wright's
greatest creation, was a man in violent, though inept, rebellion against
the stifling, murderous, totalitarian white world. There was no trace
in Bigger of a Martin Luther King-type self-effacing love for his
oppressors. For example, Bigger would have been completely baffled,
as most Negroes are today, at Baldwin's advice to his nephew (*The
Fire Next Time*), concerning white people: "You must accept them
and accept them with love. For these innocent people have no other
hope." [Italics added.]

Rufus Scott, a pathetic wretch who indulged in the white man's
pastime of committing suicide, who let a white bisexual homosexual
fuck him in his ass, and who took a Southern Jezebel for his woman,
with all that these tortured relationships imply, was the epitome of a
black eunuch who has completely submitted to the white man. Yes,
Rufus was a psychological freedom rider, turning the ultimate cheek,
murmuring like a ghost, "*You took the best so why not take the
rest,*" which has absolutely nothing to do with the way Negroes have
managed to survive here in the hells of North America! This all
becomes very clear from what we learn of Erich, the arch-ghost of
Another Country, of the depths of his alienation from his body and
the source of his need. "And it had taken him almost until this very
moment, on the eve of his departure, to begin to recognize that part
of Rufus' great power over him had to do with the past which Erich
had buried in some deep, dark place; was connected with himself, in
Alabama, *when I wasn't nothing but a child*; with the cold white
people and the warm black people, warm at least for him. . . ."

So, too, who cannot wonder at the source of such audacious
madness as moved Baldwin to make this startling remark about
Richard Wright, in his ignoble essay "Alas, Poor Richard": "In my
own relations with him, I was always exasperated by his notions of
society, politics, and history, for they seemed to me utterly fanciful.
I never believed that he had any real sense of how a society is put
together."

Richard Wright is dead and Baldwin is alive with us. Baldwin says
that Richard Wright held notions that were utterly fanciful, and
Baldwin is an honorable man.

> O judgment; thou art fled to
>   brutish beasts,
> And men have lost their reason!

Wright has no need, as Caesar did, of an outraged Antony to plead
his cause: his life and his work are his shield against the mellow
thrust of Brutus' blade. The good that he did, unlike Caesar's, will
not be interred with his bones. It is, on the contrary, only the living
who can be harmed by Brutus.

Baldwin says that in Wright's writings violence sits enthroned where

sex should be. If this is so, then it is only because in the North
American reality hate holds sway in love's true province. And it is
only through a rank perversion that the artist, whose duty is to tell
us the truth, can turn the two-dollar trick of wedding violence to
love and sex to hate—if, to achieve this end, one has basely to
transmute rebellion into lamblike submission—"*You took the best,*"
sniveled Rufus, "*so why not take the rest?*" Richard Wright was not
ghost enough to achieve his cruel distortion. With him, sex, being not
a spectator sport or a panacea but the sacred vehicle of life and love,
is itself sacred. And the America which Wright knew and which *is*, is
not the Garden of Eden but its opposite. Baldwin, embodying in his
art the self-flagellating policy of Martin Luther King, and giving out
falsely the news that the Day of the Ghost has arrived, pulled it off
in *Another Country.*

Of all black American novelists, and indeed of all American novelists of any hue. Richard Wright reigns supreme for his profound
political, economic, and social reference. Wright had the ability, like
Dreiser, of harnessing the gigantic, overwhelming environmental forces
and focusing them, with pinpoint sharpness, on individuals and their
acts as they are caught up in the whirlwind of the savage, anarchistic
sweep of life, love, death, and hate, pain, hope, pleasure, and despair
across the face of a nation and the world. But, ah! "O masters," it is
Baldwin's work which is so void of a political, economic, or even a
social reference. His characters all seem to be fucking and sucking in
a vacuum. Baldwin has a superb touch when he speaks of human
beings, when he is inside of them—especially his homosexuals—but he
flounders when he looks beyond the skin; whereas Wright's forte, it
seems to me, was in reflecting the intricate mechanisms of a social
organization, its functioning as a unit.

Baldwin's essay on Richard Wright reveals that he despised—not
Richard Wright, but his masculinity. He cannot confront the stud in
others—except that he must either submit to it or destroy it. And he
was not about to bow to a *black* man. Wright understood and lived
the truth of what Norman Mailer meant when he said ". . . for being
a man is the continuing battle of one's life, and one loses a bit of
manhood with every stale compromise to the authority of any power
in which one does not believe." Baldwin, compromised beyond
getting back by the white man's *power*, which is real and which has
nothing to do with *authority*, but to which Baldwin has ultimately
succumbed psychologically, is totally unable to extricate himself from
that horrible pain. It is the scourge of his art, because the only way
out for him is psychologically to embrace Africa, the land of his
fathers, which he utterly refuses to do. He has instead resorted to a
despicable underground guerrilla war, waged on paper, against black
masculinity, playing out the racial death-wish of Yacub, reaching, I
think, a point where Mailer hits the spot: "Driven into defiance, it is
natural if regrettable, that many homosexuals go to the direction of

assuming that there is something intrinsically superior in homosexuality, and carried far enough it is a viewpoint which is as stultifying, as ridiculous, and as anti-human as the heterosexual's prejudice."

I, for one, do not think homosexuality is the latest advance over heterosexuality on the scale of human evolution. Homosexuality is a sickness, just as are baby-rape or wanting to become the head of General Motors.

A grave danger faces this nation, of which we are as yet unaware. And it is precisely this danger which Baldwin's work conceals; indeed, leads us away from. We are engaged in the deepest, the most fundamental revolution and reconstruction which men have ever been called upon to make in their lives, and which they absolutely cannot escape or avoid except at the peril of the very continued existence of human life on this planet. The time of the sham is over, and the cheek of the suffering saint must no longer be turned twice to the brute. The titillation of the guilt complexes of bored white liberals leads to doom. The grotesque hideousness of what is happening to us is reflected in this remark by Murray Kempton, quoted in *The Realist*: "When I was a boy Stepin Fetchit was the only Negro actor who worked regularly in the movies. . . . The fashion changes, but I sometimes think that Malcolm X and, to a degree, even James Baldwin are *our* Stepin Fetchits."

Yes, the fashion does change. "Will the machinegunners please step forward," said LeRoi Jones in a poem. "The machine gun on the corner," wrote Richard Wright, "is the symbol of the twentieth century." The embryonic spirit of kamikaze, real and alive, grows each day in the black man's heart and there are dreams of Nat Turner's legacy. The ghost of John Brown is creeping through suburbia. And I wonder if James Chaney said, as Andrew Goodman and Michael Schwerner stood helplessly watching, as the grizzly dogs crushed his bones with savage blows of chains—did poor James say, after Rufus Scott—"*You took the best, so why not take the rest?*" Or did he turn to his white brothers, seeing their plight, and say, after Baldwin, "That's your problem, baby!"

I say, after Mailer, "There's a shit-storm coming."

THE BLACK ARTIST AND THE REVOLUTION

LeRoi Jones

I. THE REVOLUTIONARY THEATRE

The Revolutionary Theatre should force change; it should be change. (All their faces turned into the lights and you work on them black nigger magic, and cleanse them at having seen the ugliness. And if the beautiful see themselves, they will love themselves.) We are preaching virtue again, but by that to mean NOW, toward what seems the most constructive use of the world.

The Revolutionary Theatre must EXPOSE! Show up the insides of these humans, look into black skulls. White men will cower before this theatre because it hates them. Because they themselves have been trained to hate. The Revolutionary Theatre must hate them for hating. For presuming with their technology to deny the supremacy of the Spirit. They will all die because of this.

The Revolutionary Theatre must teach them their deaths. It must crack their faces open to the mad cries of the poor. It must teach them about silence and the truths lodged there. It must kill any God anyone names except Common Sense. The Revolutionary Theatre should flush the fags and murders out of Lincoln's face.

It should stagger through our universe correcting, insulting, preaching, spitting craziness—but a craziness taught to us in our most rational moments. People must be taught to trust true scientists (knowers, diggers, oddballs) and that the holiness of life is the constant possibility of widening the consciousness. And they must be incited to strike back against *any* agency that attempts to prevent this widening.

The Revolutionary Theatre must Accuse and Attack anything that can be accused and attacked. It must Accuse and Attack because it is a theatre of Victims. It looks at the sky with the victims' eyes, and moves the victims to look at the strength in their minds and their bodies.

Clay, in *Dutchman*, Ray in *The Toilet*, Walker in *The Slave*, all are victims. In the Western sense they could be heroes. But the Revolutionary Theatre, even if it is Western, must be anti-Western. It must show horrible coming attractions of *The Crumbling of the West*. Even as Artaud designed *The Conquest of Mexico*, so we must design *The Conquest of White Eye*, and show the missionaries and wiggly Liberals dying under blasts of concrete. For sound effects, wild screams of joy, from all the peoples of the world.

408

The Revolutionary Theatre must take dreams and give them a reality. It must isolate the ritual and historical cycles of reality. But it must be food for all those who need food, and daring propaganda for the beauty of the Human Mind. It is a political theatre, a weapon to help in the slaughter of these dim-witted fatbellied white guys who somehow believe that the rest of the world is here for them to slobber on.

This should be a theatre of World Spirit. Where the spirit can be shown to be the most competent force in the world. Force. Spirit. Feeling. The language will be anybody's, but tightened by the poet's backbone. And even the language must show what the facts are in this consciousness epic, what's happening. We will talk about the world, and the preciseness with which we are able to summon the world will be our art. Art is method. And art, "like any ashtray or senator," remains in the world. Wittgenstein said ethics and aesthetics are one. I believe this. So the Broadway theatre is a theatre of reaction whose ethics, like its aesthetics, reflect the spiritual values of this unholy society, which sends young crackers all over the world blowing off colored people's heads. (In some of these flippy Southern towns they even shoot up the immigrants' Favorite Son, be it Michael Schwerner or JFKennedy.)

The Revolutionary Theatre is shaped by the world, and moves to reshape the world, using as its force the natural force and perpetual vibrations of the mind in the world. We are history and desire, what we are, and what any experience can make us.

It is a social theatre, but all theatre is social theatre. But we will change the drawing rooms into places where real things can be said about a real world, or into smoky rooms where the destruction of Washington can be plotted. The Revolutionary Theatre must function like an incendiary pencil planted in Curtis Lemay's cap. So that when the final curtain goes down brains are splattered over the seats and the floor, and bleeding nuns must wire SOS's to Belgians with gold teeth.

Our theatre will show victims so that their brothers in the audience will be better able to understand that they are the brothers of victims, and that they themselves are victims if they are blood brothers. And what we show must cause the blood to rush, so that pre-revolutionary temperaments will be bathed in this blood, and it will cause their deepest souls to move, and they will find themselves tensed and clenched, even ready to die, at what the soul has been taught. We will scream and cry, murder, run through the streets in agony, if it means some soul will be moved, moved to actual life understanding of what the world is, and what it ought to be. We are preaching virtue and feeling, and a natural sense of the self in the world. All men live in the world, and the world ought to be a place for them to live.

What is called the imagination (from image, magi, magic, magician, etc.) is a practical vector from the soul. It stores all data, and can be called on to solve all our "problems." The imagination is the projection of ourselves past our sense of ourselves as "things." Imagination (Image) is all possibility, because from the image, the initial circumscribed energy, any use (idea) is possible. And so begins that image's use in the world. Possibility is what moves us.

The popular white man's theatre like the popular white man's novel shows tired white lives, and the problems of eating white sugar, or else it herds bigcaboosed blondes onto huge stages in rhinestones and makes believe they are dancing or singing. WHITE BUSINESSMEN OF THE WORLD, DO YOU WANT TO SEE PEOPLE REALLY DANCING AND SINGING??? ALL OF YOU GO UP TO HARLEM AND GET YOURSELF KILLED, THERE WILL BE DANCING AND SINGING, THEN, FOR REAL!! (In *The Slave*, Walker Vessels, the black revolutionary, wears an armband, which is the insignia of the attacking army—a big red-lipped minstrel, grinning like crazy.)

The liberal white man's objection to the theatre of the revolution (if he is "hip" enough) will be on aesthetic grounds. Most white Western artists do not need to be "political," since usually, whether they know it or not, they are in complete sympathy with the most repressive social forces in the world today. There are more junior birdmen fascists running around the West today disguised as Artists than there are disguised as fascists. (But then, that word, *Fascist*, and with it, *Fascism*, has been made obsolete by the words *America*, and *Americanism*.) The American Artist usually turns out to be just a super-Bourgeois, because, finally, all he has to show for his sojourn through the world is "better taste" than the Bourgeois—many times not even that.

Americans will hate the Revolutionary Theatre because it will be out to destroy them and whatever they believe is real. American cops will try to close the theatres where such nakedness of the human spirit is paraded. American producers will say the revolutionary plays are filth, usually because they will treat human life as if it were actually happening. American directors will say that the white guys in the plays are too abstract and cowardly ("don't get me wrong . . . I mean aesthetically . . .") and they will be right.

The force we want is of twenty million spooks storming America with furious cries and unstoppable weapons. We want actual explosions and actual brutality: AN EPIC IS CRUMBLING and we must give it the space and hugeness of its actual demise. The Revolutionary Theatre, which is now peopled with victims, will soon begin to be peopled with new kinds of heroes—not the weak Hamlets debating whether or not they are ready to die for what's on their minds, but men and women (and minds) digging out from under a thousand years of "high art" and weak-faced dalliance. We must make an art that will function so as to call down the actual wrath of world spirit.

We are witch doctors and assassins, but we will open a place for the true scientists to expand our consciousness. This is a theatre of assault. The play that will split the heavens for us will be called THE DESTRUCTION OF AMERICA. The heroes will be Crazy Horse, Denmark Vesey, Patrice Lumumba, and not history, not memory, not sad sentimental groping for a warmth in our despair; these will be new men, new heroes, and their enemies most of you who are reading this.

II. STATE/MENT

The Black Artist's role in America is to aid in the destruction of America as he knows it. His role is to report and reflect so precisely the nature of the society, and of himself in that society, that other men will be moved by the exactness of his rendering and, if they are black men, grow strong through this moving, having seen their own strength, and weakness; and if they are white men, tremble, curse, and go mad, because they will be drenched with the filth of their evil.

The Black Artist must draw out of his soul the correct image of the world. He must use this image to band his brothers and sisters together in common understanding of the nature of the world (and the nature of America) and the nature of the human soul.

The Black Artist must demonstrate sweet life, how it differs from the deathly grip of the White Eyes. The Black Artist must teach the White Eyes their deaths, and teach the black man how to bring these deaths about.

> We are unfair, and unfair.
> We are black magicians, black art
> s we make in black labs of the heart.

> The fair are
> fair, and death
> ly white.

> The day will not save them
> and we own
> the night.

Counterrhetoric

THE TROUBLE WITH BLACK POWER

Christopher Lasch

"In the place of a matured social vision there will always be those who will gladly substitute the catastrophic and glorious act of martyrdom and self-immolation for a cause."
                    Harold Cruse *The Crisis of the Negro Intellectual*

Whatever else "Black Power" means, the slogan itself indicates that the movement for racial equality has entered a new phase. Even those who argue that the change is largely rhetorical or that Black Power merely complements the struggle for "civil rights" would presumably not deny that "Black Power" articulates, at the very least, a new sense of urgency, if not a sense of impending crisis. Together with last summer's riots, it challenges the belief, until recently widespread, that the United States is making substantial progress toward racial justice and that it is only a matter of time and further effort before the color line is effectively obliterated.

Now even the opponents of Black Power issue warnings of apocalypse. "We shall overcome" no longer expresses the spirit of the struggle. Race war seems a more likely prospect. The Negro movement itself is splitting along racial lines. In the form in which it existed until 1963 or 1964, the civil rights movement is dead: this is not a conjecture but a historical fact. Whether the movement can be revived in some other form, or whether it will give way to something completely different, remains to be seen. Meanwhile time seems to be working on the side of an imminent disaster.

What has changed? Why did the civil rights movement, which seemed so confident and successful at the time of the Washington march in 1963, falter until now it seems to have reached the point of collapse? Why has "Black Power" displaced "freedom" as the rallying-point of Negro militancy?

There are several reasons for this change. The most obvious is that the apparent victories of the civil rights coalition have not brought about any discernible changes in the lives of most Negroes, at least not in the North. Virtually all the recent books and articles on Black Power acknowledge this failure or insist on it, depending on the point of view. Charles E. Fager's *White Reflections on Black Power*, for example, analyzes in detail the Civil Rights Act of 1964—the major legislative achievement of the civil rights coalition—and shows how the act has been systematically subverted in the South, title by title, and how, in the North, many of its provisions (such as voting safeguards and desegregation of public accommodations) were irrelevant to begin with. The inadequacy of civil rights legislation is not difficult to grasp. Even the most superficial accounts of the summer's riots see the connection between hopes raised by civil rights agitation and the Negroes' disappointing realization that this agitation, whatever its apparent successes, has nevertheless failed to relieve the tangible miseries of ghetto life.

Not only have the civil rights laws proved to be intrinsically weaker and more limited in their application than they seemed at the time they were passed, but the unexpectedly bitter resistance to civil rights, particularly in the North, has made it difficult to implement even these limited gains, let alone to win new struggles for open housing, an end to de facto segregation, and equal employment. Northern segregationists may not be strong enough to elect Mrs. Hicks mayor of Boston, but they can delay open housing indefinitely, it would seem, in Milwaukee as well as in every other Northern city—even those which have nominally adopted open housing. Everywhere in the North civil rights agitation, instead of breaking down barriers as expected, has met a wall of resistance. If anything, Negroes have made more gains in the South than in the North. The strategy of the civil rights movement, resting implicitly on the premise that the North was more enlightened than the South, was unprepared for the resistance it has encountered in the North.

The shifting focus of the struggle from the South to the North thus has contributed both to the weakening of the civil rights movement and to the emergence of Black Power. The implications of this change of scene go beyond what is immediately evident—that federal troops, for instance, appear on the side of the Negroes in Little Rock, whereas in Detroit they are the enemy. The civil rights movement in the South was the product of a set of conditions which is not likely to be repeated in the North: federal efforts to "reconstruct" the South; the tendency of Northern liberals to express their distaste for American society vicariously by attacking racism in the South, rather than by confronting racism at home; the revival of

Southern liberalism. Moreover, the civil rights movement, in its Southern phase, rested on the indigenous Negro subculture which has grown up since the Civil War under the peculiar conditions of Southern segregation—a culture separate and unequal but semi-autonomous and therefore capable of giving its own distinctive character to the movement for legal and political equality.

E. Franklin Frazier once wrote that the Negro's "primary struggle" in America "has been to acquire a culture"—customs, values, and forms of expression which, transmitted from generation to generation, provide a people with a sense of its own integrity and collective identity. Under slavery, African forms of social organization, family life, religion, language, and even art disintegrated, leaving the slave neither an African nor an American but a man suspended, as Kenneth Stampp has said, "between two cultures," unable to participate in either. After the Civil War, Southern Negroes gradually developed institutions of their own, derived from American sources but adapted to their own needs, and therefore capable of giving the Negro community the beginnings at least of cohesiveness and collective self-discipline. The Negro church managed to impose strict standards of sexual morality, thereby making possible the emergence of stable families over which the father—not the mother, as under slavery—presided.

Stable families, in turn, furnished the continuity between generations without which Negroes could not even have begun their slow and painful self-advancement—the accumulation of talent, skills, and leadership which by the 1950s had progressed to the point where Southern Negroes, together with their liberal allies, could launch an attack against segregation. The prominence of the Negro church in their struggle showed the degree to which the civil rights movement was rooted in the peculiar conditions of Negro life in the South—conditions which had made the church the central institution of the Negro subculture. Even radicals like Charles M. Sherrod of SNCC who condemned the passivity of the Negro church realized that "no one working in the South can expect to 'beat the box' if he assumes . . . that one does not need the church as it exists."

The breakdown of the Southern Negro subculture in the North has recreated one of the conditions that existed under slavery, that of dangling between two cultures. Unlike other rural people who have migrated over the last hundred and forty years to the cities of the North, Southern Negroes have not been able to transplant their rural way of life even with modifications. The church decays; the family reverts to the matricentric pattern. The schools, which are segregated but at the same time controlled by white people, hold up middle-class norms to which black children are expected to conform; if they fail they are written off as "unteachable." Meanwhile the mass media flood the ghetto with images of affluence, which Negroes absorb without absorbing the ethic of disciplined self-denial and postponement of gratification that has traditionally been a central component of the materialist ethic.

In the South, the Negro church implanted an ethic of patience, suffering, and endurance. As in many peasant or precapitalist societies, this kind of religion proved surprisingly conducive—once endurance was divorced from passive resignation—to effective political action. But the ethic of endurance, which is generally found among oppressed peoples in backward societies, cannot survive exposure to modern materialism. It gives way to an ethic of accumulation. Or, if real opportunities for accumulation do not exist, it gives way to hedonism, opportunism, cynicism, violence, and self-hatred—the characteristics of what Oscar Lewis calls the culture of poverty.

Lewis writes:

The culture of poverty is a relatively thin culture. . . . It does not provide much support or long-range satisfaction and its encouragement of mistrust tends to magnify helplessness and isolation. Indeed, the poverty of culture is one of the crucial aspects of the culture of poverty.

These observations rest on Lewis's studies of the ghettos of Mexico City and of the Puerto Rican ghettos of San Juan and New York, where the breakdown of traditional peasant cultures has created a distinctive type of culture which comes close to being no culture at all. Something of the same thing has happened to the Negro in the North; and this helps to explain what Frazier meant when he said that the Negro's primary struggle in America had been "to acquire a culture."

This analysis in turn makes it possible to see why nationalist sects like the Nation of Islam, which have never made much headway in the South, find the Northern ghetto a fertile soil; while the civil rights movement, on the other hand, has become progressively weaker as the focus of the Negroes' struggle shifts from the South to the North. The civil rights movement does not address itself to the question of how Negroes are to acquire a culture, or to the consequences of their failure to do so. It addresses itself to legal inequalities. In so far as it implies a cultural program of any kind, the civil rights strategy proposes to integrate Negroes into the culture which already surrounds them.

Now the real objection to this is not the one so often given by the advocates of Black Power—that Negroes have nothing to gain from integrating into a culture dominated by materialist values. Since most Negroes have already absorbed those values, this is a frivolous argument—especially so since it seems to imply that there is something virtuous and ennobling about poverty. What the assimilationist argument does overlook is that the civil rights movement owes its own existence, in part, to the rise of a Negro subculture in the South, and that the absence of a comparable culture in the ghetto changes the whole character of the Negro problem in the North. American history seems to show that a group cannot achieve "integration"—that is, equality—without first developing institutions which express and create a sense of its own distinctiveness. That is why black nationalism, which attempts to fill the cultural vacuum of the ghetto, has had a continuing attraction for Negroes, and why, even during the period of its eclipse in the Thirties, Forties, and Fifties, nationalism won converts among the most despised and degraded elements of the Negro community in spite of the low repute in which it was held by Negro leaders.

Nationalist sects like the Black Muslims, the Black Jews, and the Moorish Temple Science movement speak to the wretchedness of the ghetto, particularly to the wretchedness of the ghetto male, in a way that the civil rights movement does not. Thus while the free and easy sexual life of the ghetto may excite the envy of outsiders, the Black Muslims correctly see it as a disrupting influence and preach a strict, "puritanical" sexual ethic. In a society in which women dominate the family and the church, the Muslims stress the role of the male as provider and protector. "Protect your women!" strikes at the heart of the humiliation of the Negro male. Similarly, the Muslims attack the hedonism of the ghetto. "Stop wasting your money!" says Elijah Muhammad. ". . . Stop spending money for tobacco, dope, cigarettes, whiskey, fine clothes, fine automobiles, expensive rugs and carpets, idleness, sport and gambling. . . . If you must have a car, buy the low-priced car." Those who see in the Black Muslims no more than "the hate that hate produced" mistake the character of this movement, which joins to the mythology of racial glorification a practical program of moral rehabilitation. As Lawrence L. Tyler has noted (*Phylon*, Spring 1966), the Muslim style of life is "both mystical and practical," and it is the combination of the two that "has definitely provided an escape from degradation for lower-class Negroes." If anyone doubts this, he should consider the Muslims' well-documented success in redeeming, where others have failed, drug pushers, addicts, pimps, criminals of every type, the dregs of the slums. In subjecting them to a harsh, uncompromising, and admittedly authoritarian discipline, the Black Muslims and other sects have organized people who have not been organized by nonviolence, which presupposes an existing self-respect and a sense of community, or by any other form of Negro politics or religion.

Black Power represents, among other things, a revival of Negro-American nationalism and therefore cannot be regarded simply as a response to recent events. Black Power has secularized the separatist impulse which has usually (though not always) manifested itself in religious forms. Without necessarily abandoning the myth of the Negroes as a chosen people, the new-style nationalists have secularized this myth by identifying the American Negroes—whom many

of them continue to regard as in some sense Negroes of the dias-
pora—not with "the Asian Black Nation and the tribe of Shabazz," as
in Black Muslim theology, but with the contemporary struggle against
colonialism in the third world. Where earlier nationalist movements,
both secular and religious, envisioned physical separation from America and reunion with Islam or with Africa, many of the younger
nationalists propose to fight it out here in America, by revolutionary
means if necessary, and to establish—what? a black America? an
America in which black people can survive as a separate "nation"? an
integrated America?

Here the new-style nationalism begins to reveal underlying ambiguities which make one wonder whether it can properly be called
nationalist at all. Older varieties of black nationalism—Garveyism,
DuBois's Pan-Africanism, the Nation of Islam—whatever their own
ambiguities, consistently sought escape from America, either to Africa, to some part of America which might be set aside for black
people, or to some other part of the world. The new-style nationalists, however, view their movement as a revolution against American
"colonialism" and thereby embark on a line of analysis which leads
to conclusions that are not always consistent with the premise that
American Negroes constitute a "nation."

Clearly, the rhetoric of Black Power owes more to Frantz Fanon
and to Che Guevara than it owes to Marcus Garvey or DuBois, let
alone to Elijah Muhammad. Last August, Stokely Carmichael presented himself to the congress of the Organization of Latin American
Solidarity in Havana as a conscious revolutionary. Claiming to speak
for the black people of the United States, he is reported to have said:

> We greet you as comrades because it becomes increasingly clear to us each day
> that we share with you a common struggle; we have a common enemy. Our
> enemy is white Western imperialist society; our struggle is to overthrow the
> system which feeds itself and expands itself through the economic and cultural
> exploitation of non-white, non-Western peoples. We speak with you, comrades,
> because we wish to make clear that we understand that our destinies are
> inter-twined.

The advocates of Black Power, it should be noted, do not have a
monopoly on this type of rhetoric or on the political analysis, or lack
of it, which it implies. The New Left in general more and more
identifies itself with Castro, Guevara, Régis Debray, and Ho Chi
Minh; many of the new radicals speak of "guerrilla warfare" against
"colonialism" at home; and in fact they see the black militants, as
the black militants see themselves, as the revolutionary vanguard of
violent social change. The congruence of the rhetoric of Black Power
with the ideology of the more demented sections of the white Left
suggests that Black Power is more than a revival of Negro-American
nationalism, just as it is more than a response to the collapse of the
civil rights movement in the North. Black Power is itself, in part, a

manifestation of the New Left. It shares with the white Left not only
the language of romantic anarchism but several other features as well,
none of them (it must be said) conducive to its success—a pronounced distrust of people over thirty, a sense of powerlessness and
despair, for which the revolutionary rhetoric serves to compensate,
and a tendency to substitute rhetoric for political analysis and defiant
gestures for political action. Even as they seek to disentangle themselves from the white Left, of which they are understandably contemptuous, black militants continue to share some of its worst
features, the very tendencies that may indeed be destroying what
strength the New Left, during its brief career, has managed to
accumulate. The more these tendencies come to dominate Black
Power itself, the gloomier, presumably, will be the outlook for its
future.

Because Black Power has many sources, it abounds in contradictions. On the one hand Black Power derives from a tradition of
Negro separatism, self-discipline, and self-help, advocating traditional
"nationalist" measures ranging from cooperative businesses to proposals for complete separation. On the other hand, some of the
spokesmen for Black Power contemplate guerrilla warfare against
American "colonialism." In general, CORE is closer to the first
position, SNCC to the second. But the ambiguity of Black Power
derives from the fact that both positions frequently coexist—as in
Black Power, the new book by Stokely Carmichael and Charles V.
Hamilton, chairman of the political science department at Roosevelt
University.

This book is disappointing, first of all because it makes so few
concrete proposals for action, and these seem hardly revolutionary in
nature: black control of black schools, black-owned businesses, and
the like. Carmichael and Hamilton talk vaguely of a "major reorientation of the society" and of "the necessarily total revamping of the
society" (expressions they use interchangeably) as the "central goal"
of Black Power, and they urge black people not to enter coalitions
with groups not similarly committed to sweeping change. But they
never explain why their program demands such changes, or indeed
why it would be likely to bring them about.

In order to deal with this question, one would have to discuss the
relation of the ghetto to the rest of American society. To what
extent does American society *depend* on the ghetto? It is undoubtedly true, as the advocates of Black Power maintain, that there is no
immediate prospect that the ghettos will disappear. But it is still not
clear whether the ghettos in their present state of inferiority and
dependence are in some sense necessary for the functioning of American society—that is, whether powerful interests have a stake in perpetuating them—or whether they persist because American society
can get along so well without black people that there is no motive

either to integrate them by getting rid of the ghettos or to allow the ghettos to govern themselves. In other words, what interests have a stake in maintaining the present state of affairs? Does the welfare of General Motors depend on keeping the ghetto in a state of dependence? Would self-determination for the ghetto threaten General Motors? Carmichael and Hamilton urge black people to force white merchants out of the ghetto and to replace them with black businesses, but it is not clear why this program, aimed at businesses which themselves occupy a marginal place in American corporate capitalism, would demand or lead to a "total revamping of the society."

On this point the critics of Black Power raise what appears to be a telling objection, which can be met only by clarifying the Black Power position beyond anything Carmichael and Hamilton have done here. In a recent article in *Dissent* ("The Pathos of Black Power," January-February 1967), Paul Feldman writes:

A separatist black economy—unless it were to be no more than a carbon copy of the poverty that already prevails—would need black steel, black automobiles, black refrigerators. And for that, Negroes would have to take control of General Motors and US Steel: hardly an immediate prospect, and utter fantasy as long as Carmichael proposes to "go it alone."

But a related criticism of Black Power, that it merely proposes to substitute for white storekeepers black storekeepers who would then continue to exploit the ghetto in the same ways, seems to me to miss the point, since advocates of Black Power propose to replace white businesses with black *cooperatives*. In this respect Black Power does challenge capitalism, at least in principle; but the question remains whether a program aimed at small businessmen effectively confronts capitalism at any very sensitive point.

Still, small businessmen, whatever their importance outside, are a sensitive issue in the ghetto and getting rid of them might do wonders for Negro morale. Not only that, but Negro cooperatives would help to reduce the flow of capital out of the ghetto, contributing thereby, if only modestly, to the accumulation of capital as well as providing employment. A "separatist black economy" is not really what Black Power seems to point to, any more than it points to exploitive Negro shopkeepers in place of white ones. "In the end," Feldman writes, "the militant-sounding proposals for a build-it-yourself black economy (a black economy, alas, without capital) remind one of ... precisely those white moderates who preach self-help to the Negroes." But Black Power envisions (or seems to envision) *collective* self-help, which is not the same thing as individualist petty capitalism on the one hand, or, on the other hand, a separate black economy.

Black Power proposes, or seems to propose, that Negroes do for themselves what other ethnic groups, faced with somewhat similar conditions, have done—advance themselves not as individuals but as groups conscious of their own special interests and identity. The Irish advanced themselves by making politics their own special business, the Italians by making a business of crime. In both cases, the regular avenues of individual self-advancement were effectively closed, forcing ethnic minorities to improvise extra-legal institutions—the political machine in the one case, crime syndicates in the other. These were defined as illegitimate and resisted by the rest of society, but they were finally absorbed after protracted struggles. Those who urge Negroes to advance themselves through the regular channels of personal mobility ignore the experience of earlier minorities in America, the relevance of which is obscured both by the tendency to view the history of immigration as a triumph of assimilation and by the individualism which persistently blinds Americans to the importance of collective action, and therefore to most of history.

Carmichael and Hamilton mention the parallel with other ethnic groups, but only in passing, and without noticing that this analogy undermines the analogy with colonial people which they draw at the beginning of the book and wherever else their militant rhetoric appears to demand it. They observe, correctly, that on the evidence of ethnic voting "the American pot has not melted," politically at least, and they recognize that "traditionally, each new ethnic group in this society has found the route to social and political viability through the organization of its own institutions." But they do not explain how this analysis of the Negro's situation squares with the argument that "black people in this country form a colony and it is not in the interest of the colonial power to liberate them."

Quite apart from this inconsistency, the ethnic parallel, whether or not it finally proves useful, needs to be systematically explored. Did the struggles of other minorities contribute to a "major reorientation of the society"? Not if a "major reorientation" is equivalent to the "complete revision" of American institutions, which is the precondition, according to Carmichael and Hamilton, of black liberation. Perhaps the analogy is therefore misleading and should be abandoned. On the other hand, it may be that the special institutions created by other nationalities in America—like Tammany and the Mafia—do in fact represent "major reorientations," even though they fall somewhat short of a "total revamping" or "complete revision" of society. Perhaps it is confusing to think of "major reorientations" as synonymous with "complete revisions," particularly when the nature of the changes proposed remains so indeterminate. In that case it is the colonial analogy that should be dropped, as contributing to the confusion.

Black Power contains many other examples of sloppy analysis and the failure to pursue any line of reasoning through to its consequences. Basic questions are left in doubt. Is the Negro issue a class issue, a race issue, or a "national" (ethnic) issue? Treating it as a class issue—as the authors appear to do when they write that the "only coalition which seems acceptable to us," in the long run, is "a coalition of poor blacks and poor whites"—further weakens the ethnic analogy and blurs the concept of black people as a "nation"— the essential premise, one would think, of "Black Power."

Paul Feldman seems to me on the wrong track when he accuses SNCC of resorting to "what is primarily a racial rather than an economic approach." On the contrary, the advocates of Black Power tend, if anything, toward a class analysis, derived from popularized Marxism or from Castroism, which considers the American Negro as an exploited proletarian. Thus Carmichael and Hamilton try to sustain their analogy of the Negroes as a "colonial" people by arguing that the Negro communities "export" cheap labor. This may be true of the South, where Negroes do represent cheap labor (although mechanization is changing the situation even in the South) and where racism, accordingly, is functionally necessary as a way of maintaining class exploitation. Here the Negroes might be mobilized behind a program of class action designed to change society in fundamental ways.* In the North, however, the essential feature of the Negro's situation is precisely his dispensability, which is increasingly evident in the growing unemployment of Negro men, particularly young men. As Bayard Rustin has pointed out, ghetto Negroes do not constitute an exploited proletariat. They should be regarded not as a working class but as a lower class or *lumpenproletariat.*

The distinction [he writes] is important. The working class is employed. It has a relation to the production of goods and services; much of it is organized in unions. It enjoys a measure of cohesion, discipline and stability lacking in the lower class. The latter is unemployed or marginally employed. It is relatively unorganized, incohesive, unstable. It contains the petty criminal and antisocial elements. Above all, unlike the working class, it lacks the sense of a stake in society. When the slum proletariat is black, its alienation is even greater.

It is precisely these conditions, however, that make Black Power more relevant to the ghetto than "civil rights," if Black Power is understood as a form of ethnic solidarity which addresses itself to the instability and to the "antisocial" elements of ghetto life, and tries to organize and "socialize" those elements around a program of col-

*This does not mean, however, that Southern Negroes will be receptive to the rhetoric of alienation, which depicts Negroes as a revolutionary vanguard. On the contrary, the Northern radicals at the Conference for New Politics failed to stir the delegates from the Mississippi Freedom Democratic Party with their "easy talk about violence and guerrilla warfare," as Feldman notes in an unpublished report on the conference. The rhetoric of alienation addresses itself not to the actual class situation of the Southern Negro sharecropper or tenant but to the rootlessness and despair of the Northern Negro.

lective self-help. The potential usefulness of black nationalism, in other words, lies in its ability to organize groups which neither the church, the unions, the political parties, nor the social workers have been able to organize. Rustin's analysis, while it effectively refutes the idea that the Negro lower class can become a revolutionary political force in any conventional sense, does not necessarily lead one to reject Black Power altogether, as he does, or to endorse "coalitions." Actually it can be used as an argument *against* coalitions, on the grounds that a marginal lower class has no interests in common with, say, the labor movement. If the Negroes are a lower class as opposed to a working class, it is hard to see, theoretically, why the labor movement is "foremost among [the Negroes'] political allies," as Paul Feldman believes. Theory aside, experience does not bear out this contention.

Concerning the revolutionary potential of Black Power, however, Rustin seems to me absolutely right. "From the revolutionist point of view," he says, "the question is not whether steps could be taken to strengthen organization among the *lumpenproletariat* but whether that group could be a central agent of social transformation. Generally, the answer has been no." But these observations, again, do not necessarily lead to the conclusion that Black Power has no validity. Rather they suggest the need to divorce Black Power as a program of collective self-advancement from the revolutionary rhetoric of the New Left, while at the same time they remind us that other ethnic minorities, faced with somewhat similar conditions, created new institutions that had important (though not revolutionary) social consequences. Negro-Americans cannot be considered a "nation" and a revolutionary *class* at the same time. . . .

The nihilist tendencies latent in Black Power have been identified and analyzed not only by the advocates of "liberal" coalitions. The most penetrating study of these tendencies is to be found in Harold Cruse's *The Crisis of the Negro Intellectual*, which is also an analysis of integration and a defense of black nationalism. Cruse is a radical, but his book gives no comfort to the "radicalism" currently fashionable. It deals with real issues, not leftist fantasies. Cruse understands that radicals need clarity more than they need revolutionary purity, and he refuses to be taken in by loud exclamations of militancy which conceal an essential flabbiness of purpose. At a time when Negro intellectuals are expected to show their devotion to the cause by acting out a ritual and expiatory return to the dress and manners of their "people"—when intellectuals of all nationalities are held to be the very symbol of futility, and when even a respected journalist like Andrew Kopkind can write that "the responsibility of the intellectual is the same as that of the street organizer, the draft resister, the Digger: to talk *to* people, not *about* them"—Cruse feels no need to apologize for the intellectual's work, which is to clarify issues. It is because Negro intellectuals have almost uniformly failed in this work that he judges them, at his angriest and most impatient, a "colossal fraud"—a judgment that applies without much modification to white intellectuals, now as in the recent past.

The Crisis of the Negro Intellectual is a history of the Negro Left since the First World War. When all the manifestoes and polemics of the Sixties are forgotten, this book will survive as a monument of historical analysis—a notable contribution to the understanding of the American past, but more than that, a vindication of historical analysis as the best way, maybe the only way, of gaining a clear understanding of social issues.

As a historian, an intellectual, a Negro, and, above all perhaps, as a man who came of political age in the 1940s, Cruse sees more clearly than the young black nationalists of the Sixties how easily Negro radicals—integrationists and nationalists alike—become "disoriented prisoners of white leftists, no matter how militant they sound." Instead of devising strategies appropriate to the special situation of American Negroes, they import ideologies which have no relevance to that situation and which subordinate the needs of American Negroes to an abstract model of revolutionary change. Marxism is such a model, and a considerable portion of Cruse's book elaborates and documents the thesis that American Marxism has disastrously misled Negro intellectuals over a period of fifty years.

But the ideology of guerrilla warfare, which in some Black Power circles has replaced Marxism as the current mode, equally ignores American realities. According to Cruse,

> The black ghettoes are in dire need of new organizations or parties of a political nature, yet it is a fact that most of the leading young nationalist spokesmen are apolitical .,. . The black ghettoes are in even more dire need of every possible kind of economic and self-help organization, and a buyers and consumers council, but the most militant young nationalists openly ridicule such efforts as reformist and a waste of time. For them politics and economics are most unrevolutionary. What they do consider revolutionary are Watts-type uprisings—which lead nowhere.

Black Power—with or without the guerrilla rhetoric—is a "strategic retreat." "It proposes to change, not the white world outside, but the black world inside, by reforming it into something else politically or economically." The Muslims, Cruse points out, have "already achieved this in a limited way, substituting religion for politics"; and Malcolm X (whom the advocates of Black Power now list as one of their patron saints) quit the Black Muslims precisely because "this type of Black Power lacked a dynamic, was static and aloof to the broad struggle." By emphasizing "Psychological Warfare" as "Phase 1" of Black Power, as one of the new nationalists puts it, the advocates of Black Power have placed themselves "almost in the lap of the Nation of Islam." Moreover, they have reversed the proper order of priorities, according to Cruse, for "psychological equality" must be the product, not the precondition, of cultural regeneration and political power.

He thinks that integrationists, on the other hand, while they may have addressed themselves to the "broad struggle," conceive of the struggle in the wrong terms. They waste their strength fighting prejudice, when they ought to be organizing the ghetto so that it could exert more influence, say, over the use of anti-poverty funds. Instead of trying to change the Constitution in order to make it "reflect the social reality of America as a nation of nations, or a nation of ethnic groups," even advocates of violence like Robert Williams propose merely to "implement" the Constitution, with, in Williams's words, "justice and equality for all people." Cruse accuses integrationists of being taken in by the dominant mythology of American individualism and of failing to see the importance of collective action along ethnic lines, or—even worse—of mistakenly conceiving collective action in class terms which are irrelevant to the Negro's situation in America.

Cruse himself is a Marxist—that is, a historical materialist. But he opposes the obstinate effort to impose on the Negro problem a class analysis which sees Negroes as an oppressed proletariat. He thinks this obscures, among other things, the nature of the Negro middle class and the role it plays in American life. Actually "middle class" is a misnomer, because this class is not a real bourgeoisie. The most important thing about it is that "Negro businessmen must depend on the Negro group for their support," which according to Cruse means two things: Negro businessmen are more closely tied to the Negro nation than to their white middle-class counterparts, no matter how hard they may struggle against this identification; and they occupy a marginal position in American capitalism as a whole, since black capitalism can only function in limited areas—personal services to the Negro community, such as barbershops, insurance companies, etc.—which white capitalism does not choose to enter.

Because of its marginal position, the black bourgeoisie does not have the resources to support Negro institutions—a theater, for instance—which might help to give the Negro community some consciousness of itself. Negro intellectuals thus depend on white intellectuals—or white foundations—as much as Negro maids depend on white housewives, even though the intellectual world, according to Cruse, is the only realm in which genuine integration has taken place or is likely to take place. Even there, Negroes have been forced to compete at a disadvantage. They have had to regard their white counterparts not only as colleagues but as patrons. Hence the dominance of Jews in the Negro-Jewish coalition that has been characteristic of American Marxist movements.

The effort to explain how this coalition emerged and what it did to Negro radicalism occupies the better part of *The Crisis of the Negro Intellectual.* The history of the Negro intellectual from the 1920s to the present necessarily becomes a history of American Marxism as well. Cruse begins with the "Harlem renaissance," when Marcus Garvey's version of black nationalism was only one of many signs of cultural and political awakening among American Negroes, and he shows, step by step, how Negro intellectuals retreated from these promising beginnings and began to preach culturally sterile and politically futile doctrines of proletarian uplift. Thus in the Twenties and Thirties Negro intellectuals lent themselves to the Communists' efforts to convince Moscow that American Negroes could become the spearhead of a proletarian revolution. A delegation of Negro Communists in Moscow claimed in 1922 that "in five years we will have the American revolution"—just as Stokely Carmichael now carries a similar message to Havana. "I listened to the American delegates deliberately telling lies about conditions in America," wrote the poet Claude McKay, "and I was disgusted."

Thirty-eight years later Harold Cruse found himself in a somewhat similar position in Castro's Cuba, where he had gone with LeRoi Jones and other Americans "to 'see for ourselves' what it was all about." "The ideology of a new revolutionary wave in the world at large had lifted us out of the anonymity of the lonely struggle in the United States to the glorified rank of visiting dignitaries. . . . Nothing in our American experience had ever been as arduous and exhausting as this journey. Our reward was the prize of revolutionary protocol that favored those victims of capitalism away from home." But in the midst of this "ideological enchantment," none of the delegates bothered to ask: *"What did it all mean and how did it relate to the Negro in America?"*

The new-wave Negro militants, like their forerunners of the 1930s, "have taken on a radical veneer without radical substance" and have formulated "no comprehensive radical philosophy to replace either the liberalism they denounce or the radicalism of the past that bred them." In a chapter on "The Intellectuals and Force and Violence" - in some ways the most important chapter in the book—Cruse examines a notable instance of the prevailing confusion among Negro radicals (shared by white radicals): the cult of "armed self-defense" as a form of revolutionary action. Robert Williams, an officer of the NAACP, raised the issue of self-defense in Monroe, North Carolina, in 1959, when he armed his followers against the Ku Klux Klan. In the uproar following the NAACP's suspension of Williams and his deification by the new black Left, basic questions went unanswered. For one thing, violence in the South, where it is directed against the Klan, has been strategically different from violence in the North, where it has been directed against the National Guard. For another, the issue of armed self-defense does not touch the deep-rooted conditions that have to be changed if the Negro's position is to be changed. Violence, Cruse argues, becomes a meaningful strategy only in so far as American institutions resist radical change and resist it violently. Since the Negro movement has not yet even formulated a program for radical change, violence is tactically premature; and, in any case, "the *main* front of tactics must always be organizational and institutional."

Neither the black Left nor the white Left, however, understands that an American revolution (even if it were imminent, which it isn't) "would have very little in common with the foreign revolutions they have read about." Lacking a theory, lacking any understanding of history, confusing violent protest with radicalism, black radicals persist in yet another mistake—the equation of pro-blackness with hatred of whites. Violent hatred fills the vacuum left by the lack of an ideology and a program. Long before the new radicals came on the scene, Cruse writes, "this had been one of the Negro intellectual's most severe 'hang-ups' "—one that in our own time threatens to become the driving force of the Negro movement. "This situation results from a psychology that is rooted in the Negro's symbiotic 'blood-ties' to the white Anglo-Saxon. It is the culmination of that racial drama of love and hate between slave and master, bound together in the purgatory of plantations." The self-advancement of the Negro community, however, cannot rest on ambivalent hatreds. "All race hate is self-defeating in the long run because it distorts the critical faculties."

The complexity and richness of *The Crisis of the Negro Intellectual* is difficult to convey in a review. The book documents not only the failure of Negro radicalism in general, which lives off imported ideologies and myths of imminent revolution in which Negroes have always been assigned a leading part. Reading this book today, in the wake of such disasters as the Conference for New Politics, one realizes how little has changed, and how, in spite of its determination to avoid the mistakes of the radicals of the Thirties and Forties, the New Left remains trapped in the rhetoric and postures of its predecessors. The Left today should be concerned not only with the long-range problem of creating new institutions of popular democracy (a subject to which it has given very little thought) but with the immediate problem of saving what remains of liberalism—free speech, safeguards against arbitrary authority, separation of powers—without which further democratic experiments of any kind will come to an end.

The Left should take seriously the possibility which it rhetorically proclaims—that the crisis of American colonialism abroad, together with the failure of welfare programs to approve conditions in the ghetto, will generate a demand for thoroughgoing repression which, if it succeeded, would seal the fate of liberals and radicals alike. But instead of confronting the present crisis, the Left still babbles of revolution and looks to the Negroes, as before, to deliver the country from its capitalist oppressors. "We are just a little tail on the end of a very powerful black panther," says one of the delegates to the Conference for New Politics. "And I want to be on that tail—if they'll let me." In the next breath he urges white radicals to "trust the blacks the way you trust children."

In this atmosphere, Harold Cruse's book, quite apart from its intrinsic and enduring merits, might do much immediate good. It might help to recall American radicals to their senses (those that ever had any). Perhaps it is too late even for intelligent radicals to accomplish anything. *The Crisis of the Negro Intellectual* exposes the mistakes of the past at a time when the accumulated weight of those mistakes has become so crushing that it may be too late to profit from the lesson. Crises overlap crises. The defeat of liberal colonialism in Vietnam coincides with the defeat of liberalism in the ghetto, and the deterioration of the ghetto coincides with the deterioration of the city as a whole: the flight of industry and jobs from the city, the withdrawal of the middle class, the decay of public transportation and schools, the decay of public facilities in general, the pollution of the water, the pollution of the air.

In the 1930s an alarming crisis stirred enlightened conservatives like Franklin Roosevelt to measures which palliated the immediate effects of the crisis and thereby averted a general breakdown of the system. By throwing its support at a decisive moment behind the CIO, the New Deal made possible the organization of elements which, unorganized, threatened to become an immensely violent and disruptive force. One might imagine that the still graver crisis of the Sixties might lead conservatives to consider a similar approach to the more moderate black nationalists. Indeed some gestures have recently been made in this direction. But given the total lack of national political leadership at the present time, and given the decay of the city, the kind of "solution" which will seem increasingly attractive to many Americans is a solution that would merely carry existing historical trends to their logical culmination: abandon the cities completely, put up walls around them, and use them as Negro reservations. This could even be done under the cloak of Black Power—"self-determination for the ghetto." On their reservations, black people would be encouraged to cultivate their native handicrafts, songs, dances, and festivals. Tourists would go there, bringing in a little loose change. In American history there are precedents for such "solutions."

Not only have things reached the point where any program of radical reform may be inadequate, it is still not clear whether even Cruse's version of black nationalism, as it stands, points the way to such a program. That the book itself offers no program is not an objection—although the objection applies, it seems to me, to Carmichael and Hamilton's *Black Power* which claims to present "a political framework and ideology which represents the last reasonable opportunity for this society to work out its racial problems short of prolonged destructive guerrilla warfare." Cruse does not pretend to offer a "political framework"; his book attempts to clarify underlying issues. The question is whether his analysis clarifies those issues or obscures them.

That it clears up a great deal of confusion should already be evident. Certain questions, however, remain. One concerns the slippery concept of "nationalism," which may not be the best idea around which to organize a movement of Negro liberation. Cruse does not seem to me to confront the possibility that black nationalism, which he realizes has always been flawed by its "romantic and escapist" tendencies, may be *inherently* romantic and escapist—now looking wistfully back to Africa, now indulging in fantasies of global revolution. The analysis of American Negroes as an ethnic group should properly include a study of the role of other nationalist ideologies, like Zionism or Irish-American nationalism, in order to discover whether they played any important part in the successful efforts of those communities to organize themselves. From what I have been able to learn, Irish-American nationalism focused almost exclusively on Ireland and contributed nothing important to the political successes of the Irish in America. (See Thomas N. Brown, *Irish-American Nationalism*.) A study of other ethnic nationalisms might show the same thing. It is possible, in other words, that nationalist movements in America, even when they cease to be merely fraternal and convivial and actually involve themselves in the revolutionary politics of the homeland (as was true of some Irish-American movements), have had no practical bearing on ethnic group politics in America itself. In that case, nationalism may not serve Negroes as a particularly useful guide to political action, although it is clear that the Negroes' situation demands some sort of action along ethnic lines.

Even as a means of cultural regeneration, nationalism may be too narrowly based to achieve what Cruse wants it to achieve. Black nationalist movements in the United States are largely movements of young men—of all groups, the one least able to develop values that can be passed on to the next generation. According to C. Eric Lincoln's study of the Black Muslims, "up to 80 per cent of a typical congregation is between the ages of seventeen and thirty-five"; moreover, "the Muslim temples attract many more men than women, and men assume the full management of temple affairs." Frazier remarks, in another connection, "Young males, it will be readily agreed, are poor bearers of the cultural heritage of a people." Of course there is no reason, in theory, why black nationalism should remain a young man's movement. The chief exponents of Negro-American nationalism or of a point of view that could be called nationalist—Booker T. Washington, Garvey, and DuBois (when he was not swinging to the opposite pole of integration)—were themselves men of years and experience.

But historically the nationalist ideology has owed much of its appeal to the need of the young Negro male to escape from the stifling embrace of the feminine-centered family and church. The assertion of masculinity so obviously underlies the present manifestations of black nationalism that it is difficult, at times, to distinguish nationalist movements from neighborhood gangs. It is easy to see why black nationalism might be associated with riots, especially as nationalism becomes increasingly secularized and loses its capacity to instill inner discipline; but can it produce a culture capable of unifying the black community around values distinct from and superior to those of American society as a whole?

There is the further problem of what Cruse means by "culture." Sometimes he uses the word in its broad sense, sometimes narrowly, as when he asks Negro intellectuals to follow the lead of C. Wright Mills by formulating a theory of "cultural radicalism." In modern society, Cruse argues, "mass cultural communications is a basic industry," and "only the blind cannot see that whoever controls the cultural apparatus .,. . also controls the destiny of the United States and everything in it." This statement is open to a number of objections; but quite apart from that, it is not clear what it has to do with what Frazier called the Negro's "primary struggle"—to acquire a "culture" much more basic than the kind of culture Mills and Cruse, in this passage, have in mind. How are Negroes to get control of the "cultural apparatus" until they have solved their more immediately difficulties? And how would their efforts to control the culture industry differ from the efforts of Lorraine Hansberry and Sydney Poitier, whom Cruse criticizes on the grounds that their personal triumphs on Broadway and in Hollywood did nothing to advance Negro "culture"?

These questions aside, Cruse leaves no doubt of the validity of his main thesis: that intellectuals must play a central role in movements for radical change, that this role should consist of formulating "a new political philosophy," and that in twentieth-century American history they have failed in this work. They must now address themselves to a more systematic analysis of American society than they have attempted before, building on the social theory of the nineteenth century but scrapping those parts that no longer apply. This analysis will have to explain, among other things, how the situation of the Negro in America relates to the rest of American history—a problem on which Cruse has now made an impressive assault, without however solving the dilemma posed by W.E.B. DuBois: "There faces the American Negro ... an intricate and subtle problem of combining into one object two difficult sets of facts"—he is both a Negro and an American at the same time. The failure to grasp this point, according to Cruse, has prevented both integrationists and nationalists from "synthesizing composite trends." The pendulum swings back and forth between nationalism and integrationism, but as with so many discussions among American intellectuals, the discussion never seems to progress to a higher level of analysis. Today, riots, armed self-defense, conflicts over control of ghetto schools, efforts of CORE to move Negroes into cooperative communities in the South, and other uncoordinated actions, signify a reawakening of something that can loosely be called nationalism; but they express not a new synthesis but varying degrees of disenchantment with integration. The advocates of Black Power have so far failed to show why their brand of nationalism comes any closer than its predecessors to providing a long-range strategy not for escaping from America but for changing it. The dilemma remains; more than ever it needs to become the object of critical analysis.

In the meantime, will events wait for analysis? Immediate crises confront us, and there is no time, it seems, for long-range solutions, no time for reflection. Should we all take to the streets, then, as Andrew Kopkind recommends? In critical times militancy may appear to be the only authentic politics. But the very gravity of the crisis makes it all the more imperative that radicals try to formulate at least a provisional theory which will serve them as a guide to tactics in the immediate future as well as to long-range questions of strategy. Without such a perspective, militancy will carry the day by default; then, quickly exhausting itself, it will give way to another cycle of disillusionment, cynicism, and hopelessness.

I HAVE A DREAM

Martin Luther King, Jr.

Five score years ago, a great American, in whose symbolic shadow we stand, signed the Emancipation Proclamation. This momentous decree came as a great beacon light of hope to millions of Negro slaves who had been seared in the flames of withering injustice. It came as a joyous daybreak to end the long night of captivity.

But one hundred years later, we must face the tragic fact that the Negro is still not free. One hundred years later, the life of the Negro is still sadly crippled by the manacles of segregation and the chains of discrimination. One hundred years later, the Negro lives on a lonely island of poverty in the midst of a vast ocean of material prosperity. One hundred years later, the Negro is still languished in the corners of American society and finds himself an exile in his own land. So we have come here today to dramatize an appalling condition.

In a sense we have come to our nation's Capital to cash a check. When the architects of our republic wrote the magnificent words of the Constitution and the Declaration of Independence, they were signing a promissory note to which every American was to fall heir. This note was a promise that all men would be guaranteed the unalienable rights of life, liberty, and the pursuit of happiness.

It is obvious today that America has defaulted on this promisory note insofar as her citizens of color are concerned. Instead of honoring this sacred obligation, America has given the Negro people a bad check; a check which has come back marked "insufficient funds." But we refuse to believe that the bank of justice is bankrupt. We refuse to believe that there are insufficient funds in the great vaults of opportunity of this nation. So we have come to cash this check—a check that will give us upon demand the riches of freedom and the security of justice. We have also come to this hallowed spot to remind America of the fierce urgency of *now*. This is no time to engage in the luxury of cooling off or to take the tranquilizing drug of gradualism. *Now* is the time to make real the promises of Democracy. *Now* is the time to rise from the dark and desolate valley of segregation to the sunlit path of racial justice. *Now* is the time to open the doors of opportunity to all of God's children. *Now* is the time to lift our nation from the quicksands of racial injustice to the solid rock of brotherhood.

It would be fatal for the nation to overlook the urgency of the moment and to underestimate the determination of the Negro. This sweltering summer of the Negro's legitimate discontent will not pass until there is an invigorating autumn of freedom and equality. 1963 is not an end, but a beginning. Those who hope that the Negro needed to blow off steam and will now be content will have a rude awakening if the nation returns to business as usual. There will be neither rest nor tranquillity in America until the Negro is granted his citizenship rights. The whirlwinds of revolt will continue to shake the foundations of our nation until the bright day of justice emerges.

But there is something that I must say to my people who stand on the warm threshold which leads into the palace of justice. In the process of gaining our rightful place we must not be guilty of wrongful deeds. Let us not seek to satisfy our thirst for freedom by drinking from the cup of bitterness and hatred. We must forever conduct our struggle on the high plane of dignity and discipline. We must not allow our creative protest to degenerate into physical violence. Again and again we must rise to the majestic heights of meeting physical force with soul force. The marvelous new militancy which has engulfed the Negro community must not lead us to a distrust of all white people, for many of our white brothers, as evidenced by their presence here today, have come to realize that their destiny is tied up with our destiny and their freedom is inextricably bound to our freedom. We cannot walk alone.

And as we walk, we must make the pledge that we shall march ahead. We cannot turn back. There are those who are asking the devotees of civil rights, "When will you be satisfied?" We can never be satisfied as long as the Negro is the victim of the unspeakable horrors of police brutality. We can never be satisfied as long as our bodies, heavy with the fatigue of travel, cannot gain lodging in the motels of the highways and the hotels of the cities. We cannot be satisfied as long as the Negro's basic mobility is from a smaller ghetto to a larger one. We can never be satisfied as long as a Negro in Mississippi cannot vote and a Negro in New York believes he has nothing for which to vote. No, no, we are not satisfied, and we will not be satisfied until justice rolls down like waters and righteousness like a mighty stream.

I am not unmindful that some of you have come here out of great trials and tribulations. Some of you have come fresh from narrow jail cells. Some of you have come from areas where your quest for freedom left you battered by the storms of persecution and staggered by the winds of police brutality. You have been the veterans of creative suffering. Continue to work with the faith that unearned suffering is redemptive.

Go back to Mississippi, go back to Alabama, go back to South Carolina, go back to Georgia, go back to Louisiana, go back to the slums and ghettos of our northern cities, knowing that somehow this situation can and will be changed. Let us not wallow in the valley of despair.

I say to you today, my friends, that in spite of the difficulties and frustrations of the moment I still have a dream. It is a dream deeply rooted in the American dream.

I have a dream that one day this nation will rise up and live out the true meaning of its creed: "We hold these truths to be self-evident; that all men are created equal."

I have a dream that one day on the red hills of Georgia the sons of former slaves and the sons of former slaveowners will be able to sit down together at the table of brotherhood.

I have a dream that one day even the state of Mississippi, a desert state sweltering with the heat of injustice and oppression, will be transformed into an oasis of freedom and justice.

I have a dream that my four little children will one day live in a nation where they will not be judged by the color of their skin but by the content of their character.

I have a dream today.

I have a dream that one day the state of Alabama, whose governor's lips are presently dripping with the words of interposition and nullification, will be transformed into a situation where little black boys and black girls will be able to join hands with little white boys and white girls and walk together as sisters and brothers.

I have a dream today.

I have a dream that one day every valley shall be exalted, every hill and mountain shall be made low, the rough places will be made plain, and the crooked places will be made straight, and the glory of the Lord shall be revealed, and all flesh shall see it together.

This is our hope. This is the faith with which I return to the South. With this faith we will be able to hew out of the mountain of despair a stone of hope. With this faith we will be able to transform the jangling discords of our nation into a beautiful symphony of brotherhood. With this faith we will be able to work together, to pray together, to struggle together, to go to jail together, to stand up for freedom together, knowing that we will be free one day.

This will be the day when all of God's children will be able to sing with new meaning

> My country, 'tis of thee,
> Sweet land of liberty,
>   Of thee I sing:
> Land where my fathers died,
> Land of the pilgrims' pride,
> From every mountain-side
>   Let freedom ring.

And if America is to be a great nation this must become true. So let freedom ring from the prodigious hilltops of New Hampshire. Let freedom ring from the mighty mountains of New York. Let freedom ring from the heightening Alleghenies of Pennsylvania!

Let freedom ring from the snowcapped Rockies of Colorado!

Let freedom ring from the curvacious peaks of California!

But not only that; let freedom ring from Stone Mountain of Georgia!

Let freedom ring from Lookout Mountain of Tennessee!

Let freedom ring from every hill and molehill of Mississippi. From every mountainside, let freedom ring.

When we let freedom ring, when we let it ring from every village and every hamlet, from every state and every city, we will be able to speed up that day when all of God's children, black men and white men, Jews and Gentiles, Protestants and Catholics, will be able to join hands and sing in the words of the old Negro spiritual, "Free at last! free at last! thank God almighty, we are free at last!"

VI

The Empirical Eye: Revolution in Science, Technology and Method

"Slave, I before reasoned with you, but you have proved yourself unworthy of my condescension. Remember that I have power.... I can make you so wretched that the light of day will be hateful to you. You are my creator, but I am your master—obey!"

Mary Godwin Shelley, *Frankenstein*

From   THE METAPHYSICS:
NUMBERS AND THINGS

Aristotle

Contemporaneously with these philosophers and before them the so-called Pythagoreans, who were the first to take up mathematics not only advanced this study, but also having been brought up in it they thought its principles were the principles of all things. Since of these principles numbers are by nature the first, and in numbers they seemed to see many resemblances to the things that exist and come into being—more than in fire and earth and water (such and such a modification of numbers being justice, another being soul and reason, another being opportunity—and similarly almost all other things being numerically expressible); since, again, they saw that the modifications and the ratios of the musical scales were expressible in numbers;— since, then, all other things seemed in their whole nature to be modelled on numbers, and numbers seemed to be the first things in the whole of nature, they supposed the elements of numbers to be the elements of all things, and the whole heaven to be a musical scale and a number. And all the properties of numbers and scales which they could show to agree with the attributes and parts and the whole arrangement of the heavens, they collected and fitted into their scheme; and if there was a gap anywhere, they readily made additions so as to make their whole theory coherent. E.g. as the number 10 is thought to be perfect and to comprise the whole nature of numbers, they say that the bodies which move through the heavens are ten, but as the visible bodies are only nine, to meet this they invent a tenth—the 'counter-earth'. We have discussed these matters more exactly elsewhere.

But the object of our review is that we may learn from these philosophers also what they suppose to be the principles and how these fall under the causes we have named. Evidently, then, these thinkers also consider that number is the principle both as matter for things and as forming both their modifications and their permanent states, and hold that the elements of number are the even and the odd, and that of these the latter is limited, and the former unlimited;

and that the One proceeds from both of these (for it is both even and odd), and number from the One; and that the whole heaven, as has been said, is numbers.

Other members of this same school say there are ten principles, which they arrange in two columns of cognates—limit and unlimited, odd and even, one and plurality, right and left, male and female, resting and moving, straight and curved, light and darkness, good and bad, square and oblong. In this way Alcmaeon of Croton seems also to have conceived the matter, and either he got this view from them or they got it from him; for he expressed himself similarly to them. For he says most human affairs go in pairs, meaning not definite contrarieties such as the Pythagoreans speak of, but any chance contrarieties, e.g. white and black, sweet and bitter, good and bad, great and small. He threw out indefinite suggestions about the other contrarieties, but the Pythagoreans declared both how many and which their contrarieties are.

From both these schools, then, we can learn this much, that the contraries are the principles of things; and how many these principles are and which they are, we can learn from one of the two schools. But how these principles can be brought together under the causes we have named has not been clearly and articulately stated by them; they seem, however, to range the elements under the head of matter; for out of these as immanent parts they say substance is composed and moulded.

From these facts we may sufficiently perceive the meaning of the ancients who said the elements of nature were more than one; but there are some who spoke of the universe as if it were one entity, though they were not all alike either in the excellence of their statement or in its conformity to the facts of nature. The discussion of them is in no way appropriate to our present investigation of causes, for they do not, like some of the natural philosophers, assume being to be one and yet generate it out of the one as out of matter, but they speak in another way; those others add change, since they generate the universe, but these thinkers say the universe is unchangeable. Yet *this* much is germane to the present inquiry: Parmenides seems to fasten on that which is one in definition, Melissus on that which is one in matter, for which reason the former says that it is limited, the latter that it is unlimited; while Xenophanes, the first of these partisans of the One (for Parmenides is said to have been his pupil), gave no clear statement, nor does he seem to have grasped the nature of either of these causes, but with reference to the whole material universe he says the One is God. Now these thinkers, as we said, must be neglected for the purposes of the present inquiry—two of them entirely, as being a little too naive, viz. Xenophanes and Melissus; but Parmenides seems in places to speak with more insight. For, claiming that, besides the existent, nothing non-existent exists, he thinks that of necessity one thing exists, viz. the existent and nothing else (on this we have spoken more clearly in our work on nature), but being forced to follow the observed facts, and supposing the existence of that which is one in definition, but more than one according to our sensations, he now posits two causes and two principles, calling them hot and cold, i.e. fire and earth; and of these he ranges the hot with the existent, and the other with the non-existent.

From what has been said, then, and from the wise men who have now sat in council with us, we have got thus much—on the one hand from the earliest philosophers, who regard the first principle as corporeal (for water and fire and such things are bodies), and of whom some suppose that there is one corporeal principle, others that there are more than one, but both put these under the head of matter; and on the other hand from some who posit both this cause and besides this the source of movement, which we have got from some as single and from others as twofold.

Down to the Italian school, then, and apart from it, philosophers have treated these subjects rather obscurely, except that, as we said, they have in fact used two kinds of cause, and one of these—the source of movement—some treat as one and others as two. But the Pythagoreans have said in the same way that there are two principles, but added this much, which is peculiar to them, that they thought that finitude and infinity were not attributes of certain other things, e.g. of fire or earth or anything else of this kind, but that infinity itself and unity itself were the substance of the things of which they are predicated. This is why number was the substance of all things. On this subject, then, they expressed themselves thus; and regarding the question of essence they began to make statements and definitions, but treated the matter too simply. For they both defined superficially and thought that the first subject of which a given definition was predicable was the substance of the thing defined, as if one supposed that 'double' and '2' were the same, because 2 is the first thing of which 'double' is predicable. But surely to be double and to be 2 are not the same; if they are, one thing will be many—a consequence which they actually drew. From the earlier philosophers, then, and from their successors we can learn thus much.

THE NEW ORGANON, OR TRUE DIRECTIONS CONCERNING THE INTERPRETATION OF NATURE

APHORISMS/BOOK 1

Francis Bacon

XXXIX

There are four classes of Idols which beset men's minds. To these for distinction's sake I have assigned names, calling the first class *Idols of the Tribe*; the second, *Idols of the Cave*; the third, *Idols of the Market Place*; the fourth, *Idols of the Theater*.

XL

The formation of ideas and axioms by true induction is no doubt the proper remedy to be applied for the keeping off and clearing away of idols. To point them out, however, is of great use; for the doctrine of Idols is to the interpretation of nature what the doctrine of the refutation of sophisms is to common logic.

XLI

The Idols of the Tribe have their foundation in human nature itself, and in the tribe or race of men. For it is a false assertion that the sense of man is the measure of things. On the contrary, all perceptions as well of the sense as of the mind are according to the measure of the individual and not according to the measure of the universe. And the human understanding is like a false mirror, which, receiving rays irregularly, distorts and discolors the nature of things by mingling its own nature with it.

XLII

The Idols of the Cave are the idols of the individual man. For everyone (besides the errors common to human nature in general) has a cave or den of his own, which refracts and discolors the light of nature, owing either to his own proper and peculiar nature; or to his education and conversation with others; or to the reading of books, and the authority of those whom he esteems and admires; or to the

440

differences of impressions, accordingly as they take place in a mind preoccupied and predisposed or in a mind indifferent and settled; or the like. So that the spirit of man (according as it is meted out to different individuals) is in fact a thing variable and full of perturbation, and governed as it were by chance. Whence it was well observed by Heraclitus that men look for sciences in their own lesser worlds, and not in the greater or common world.

XLIII

There are also Idols formed by the intercourse and association of men with each other, which I call Idols of the Market Place, on account of the commerce and consort of men there. For it is by discourse that men associate, and words are imposed according to the apprehension of the vulgar. And therefore the ill and unfit choice of words wonderfully obstructs the understanding. Nor do the definitions or explanations wherewith in some things learned men are wont to guard and defend themselves, by any means set the matter right. But words plainly force and overrule the understanding, and throw all into confusion, and lead men away into numberless empty controversies and idle fancies.

XLIV

Lastly, there are Idols which have immigrated into men's minds from the various dogmas of philosophies, and also from wrong laws of demonstration. These I call Idols of the Theater, because in my judgment all the received systems are but so many stage plays, representing worlds of their own creation after an unreal and scenic fashion. Nor is it only of the systems now in vogue, or only of the ancient sects and philosophies, that I speak; for many more plays of the same kind may yet be composed and in like artificial manner set forth; seeing that errors the most widely different have nevertheless causes for the most part alike. Neither again do I mean this only of entire systems, but also of many principles and axioms in science, which by tradition, credulity, and negligence have come to be received.

But of these several kinds of Idols I must speak more largely and exactly, that the understanding may be duly cautioned.

XLVI

The human understanding when it has once adopted an opinion (either as being the received opinion or as being agreeable to itself) draws all things else to support and agree with it. And though there be a greater number and weight of instances to be found on the other side, yet these it either neglects and despises, or else by some distinction sets aside and rejects, in order that by this great and pernicious predetermination the authority of its former conclusions may remain inviolate. And therefore it was a good answer that was made by one who, when they showed him hanging in a temple a picture of those who had paid their vows as having escaped ship-wreck, and would have him say whether he did·not now acknowledge the power of the gods—"Aye," asked he again, "but where are they painted that were drowned after their vows?" And such is the way of all superstition, whether in astrology, dreams, omens, divine judg-ments, or the like; wherein men, having a delight in such vanities, mark the events where they are fulfilled, but where they fail, though this happen much oftener, neglect and pass them by. But with far more subtlety does this mischief insinuate itself into philosophy and the sciences; in which the first conclusion colors and brings into conformity with itself all that come after, though far sounder and better. Besides, independently of that delight and vanity which I have described, it is the peculiar and perpetual error of the human intellect to be more moved and excited by affirmatives than by negatives; whereas it ought properly to hold itself indifferently disposed toward both alike. Indeed, in the establishment of any true axiom, the negative instance is the more forcible of the two.

XLVII

The human understanding is moved by those things most which strike and enter the mind simultaneously and suddenly, and so fill the imagination; and then it feigns and supposes all other things to be somehow, though it cannot see how, similar to those few things by which it is surrounded. But for that going to and fro to remote and heterogeneous instances by which axioms are tried as in the fire, the intellect is altogether slow and unfit, unless it be forced thereto by severe laws and overruling authority.

XLVIII

The human understanding is unquiet; it cannot stop or rest, and still presses onward, but in vain. Therefore it is that we cannot conceive of any end or limit to the world, but always as of necessity it occurs to us that there is something beyond. Neither, again, can it be conceived how eternity has flowed down to the present day, for that distinction which is commonly received of infinity in time past and in time to come can by no means hold; for it would thence follow that one infinity is greater than another, and that infinity is wasting away and tending to become finite. The like subtlety arises touching the infinite divisibility of lines, from the same inability of thought to stop. But this inability interferes more mischievously in the discovery of causes; for although the most general principles in nature ought to be held merely positive, as they are discovered, and cannot with truth be referred to a cause, nevertheless the human understanding being unable to rest still seeks something prior in the order of nature. And then it is that in struggling toward that which is further off it falls back upon that which is nearer at hand, namely, on final causes, which have relation clearly to the nature of man rather than to the nature of the universe; and from this source have strangely defiled philosophy. But he is no less an unskilled and shallow philosopher who seeks causes of that which is most general, than he who in things subordinate and subaltern omits to do so.

XLIX

The human understanding is no dry light, but receives an infusion from the will and affections; whence proceed sciences which may be called "sciences as one would." For what a man had rather were true he more readily believes. Therefore he rejects difficult things from impatience of research; sober things, because they narrow hope; the deeper things of nature, from superstition; the light of experience, from arrogance and pride, lest his mind should seem to be occupied with things mean and transitory; things not commonly believed, out of deference to the opinion of the vulgar. Numberless, in short, are the ways, and sometimes imperceptible, in which the affections color and infect the understanding.

L

But by far the greatest hindrance and aberration of the human understanding proceeds from the dullness, incompetency, and deceptions of the senses; in that things which strike the sense outweigh things which do not immediately strike it, though they be more important. Hence it is that speculation commonly ceases where sight ceases; insomuch that of things invisible there is little or no observation. Hence all the working of the spirits enclosed in tangible bodies lies hid and unobserved of men. So also all the more subtle changes of form in the parts of coarser substances (which they commonly call alteration, though it is in truth local motion through exceedingly small spaces) is in like manner unobserved. And yet unless these two things just mentioned be searched out and brought to light, nothing great can be achieved in nature, as far as the production of works is concerned. So again the essential nature of our common air, and of all bodies less dense than air (which are very many), is almost unknown. For the sense by itself is a thing infirm and erring; neither can instruments for enlarging or sharpening the senses do much; but all the truer kind of interpretation of nature is effected by instances and experiments fit and apposite; wherein the sense decides touching the experiment only, and the experiment touching the point in nature and the thing itself.

LI

The human understanding is of its own nature prone to abstractions and gives a substance and reality to things which are fleeting. But to resolve nature into abstractions is less to our purpose than to dissect her into parts; as did the school of Democritus, which went further into nature than the rest. Matter rather than forms should be the object of our attention, its configurations and changes of configuration, and simple action, and law of action or motion; for forms are figments of the human mind, unless you will call those laws of action forms.

LIX

But the *Idols of the Market Place* are the most troublesome of all—idols which have crept into the understanding through the alliances of words and names. For men believe that their reason governs words; but it is also true that words react on the understanding; and this it is that has rendered philosophy and the sciences sophistical and inactive. Now words, being commonly framed and applied according to the capacity of the vulgar, follow those lines of division which are most obvious to the vulgar understanding. And whenever an understanding of greater acuteness or a more diligent observation would alter those lines to suit the true divisions of nature, words stand in the way and resist the change. Whence it comes to pass that the high and formal discussions of learned men end oftentimes in disputes about words and names; with which (according to the use and wisdom of the mathematicians) it would be more prudent to begin, and so by means of definitions reduce them to order. Yet even definitions cannot cure this evil in dealing with natural and material things, since the definitions themselves consist of words, and those words beget others. So that it is necessary to recur to individual instances, and those in due series and order, as I shall say presently when I come to the method and scheme for the formation of notions and axioms.

LXII

Idols of the Theater, or of Systems, are many, and there can be and perhaps will be yet many more. For were it not that now for many ages men's minds have been busied with religion and theology; and were it not that civil governments, especially monarchies, have been averse to such novelties, even in matters speculative; so that men labor therein to the peril and harming of their fortunes—not only unrewarded, but exposed also to contempt and envy—doubtless there would have arisen many other philosophical sects like those which in great variety flourished once among the Greeks. For as on the phenomena of the heavens many hypotheses may be constructed, so likewise (and more also) many various dogmas may be set up and established on the phenomena of philosophy. And in the plays of this philosophical theater you may observe the same thing which is found in the theater of the poets, that stories invented for the stage are more compact and elegant, and more as one would wish them to be, than true stories out of history.

In general, however, there is taken for the material of philosophy either a great deal out of a few things, or a very little out of many things; so that on both sides philosophy is based on too narrow a foundation of experiment and natural history, and decides on the authority of too few cases. For the Rational School of philosophers snatches from experience a variety of common instances, neither duly ascertained nor diligently examined and weighed, and leaves all the rest to meditation and agitation of wit.

There is also another class of philosophers who, having bestowed much diligent and careful labor on a few experiments have thence made bold to educe and construct systems, wresting all other facts in a strange fashion to conformity therewith.

And there is yet a third class, consisting of those who out of faith and veneration mix their philosophy with theology and traditions; among whom the vanity of some has gone so far aside as to seek the origin of sciences among spirits and genii. So that this parent stock of errors—this false philosophy—is of three kinds: the Sophistical, the Empirical, and the Superstitious.

LXIII

The most conspicous example of the first class was Aristotle, who corrupted natural philosophy by his logic: fashioning the world out of categories; assigning to the human soul, the noblest of substances, a genus from words of the second intention; doing the business of density and rarity (which is to make bodies of greater or less dimensions, that is, occupy greater or less spaces), by the frigid distinction of act and power; asserting that single bodies have each a single and proper motion, and that if they participate in any other, then this results from an external cause; and imposing countless other arbitrary restrictions on the nature of things; being always more solicitous to provide an answer to the question and affirm something positive in words, than about the inner truth of things; a failing best shown when his philosophy is compared with other systems of note among the Greeks. For the *homoeomera* of Anaxagoras; the Atoms of Leucippus and Democritus; the Heaven and Earth of Parmenides; the Strife and Friendship of Empedocles; Heraclitus' doctrine how bodies are resolved into the indifferent nature of fire, and remolded into solids, have all of them some taste of the natural philosopher— some savor of the nature of things, and experience, and bodies; whereas in the physics of Aristotle you hear hardly anything but the words of logic, which in his metaphysics also, under a more imposing name, and more forsooth as a realist than a nominalist, he has handled over again. Nor let any weight be given to the fact that in his books on animals and his problems, and other of his treatises, there is frequent dealing with experiments. For he had come to his conclusion before; he did not consult experience, as he should have done, for the purpose of framing his decisions and axioms, but having first determined the question according to his will, he then resorts to experience, and bending her into conformity with his placets, leads her about like a captive in a procession. So that even on this count he is more guilty than his modern followers, the schoolmen, who have abandoned experience altogether.

LXV

But the corruption of philosophy by superstition and an admixture of theology is far more widely spread, and does the greatest harm, whether to entire systems or to their parts. For the human understanding is obnoxious to the influence of the imagination no less than to the influence of common notions. For the contentious and sophistical kind of philosophy ensnares the understanding; but this kind, being fanciful and tumid and half poetical, misleads it more by flattery. For there is in man an ambition of the understanding, no less than of the will, especially in high and lofty spirits.

Of this kind we have among the Greeks a striking example in Pythagoras, though he united with it a coarser and more cumbrous superstition; another in Plato and his school, more dangerous and subtle. It shows itself likewise in parts of other philosophies, in the introduction of abstract forms and final causes and first causes, with the omission in most cases of causes intermediate, and the like. Upon this point the greatest caution should be used. For nothing is so mischievous as the apotheosis of error; and it is a very plague of the understanding for vanity to become the object of veneration. Yet in this vanity some of the moderns have with extreme levity indulged so far as to attempt to found a system of natural philosophy on the first chapter of Genesis, on the book of Job, and other parts of the sacred writings, seeking for the dead among the living; which also makes the inhibition and repression of it the more important, because from this unwholesome mixture of things human and divine there arises not only a fantastic philosophy but also a heretical religion. Very meet it is therefore that we be sober-minded, and give to faith that only which is faith's.

LXVIII

So much concerning the several classes of Idols and their equipage; all of which must be renounced and put away with a fixed and solemn determination, and the understanding thoroughly freed and cleansed; the entrance into the kingdom of man, founded on the sciences, being not much other than the entrance into the kingdom of heaven, whereinto none may enter except as a little child.

LXX

But the best demonstration by far is experience, if it go not beyond the actual experiment. For if it be transferred to other cases which are deemed similar, unless such transfer be made by a just and orderly process, it is a fallacious thing. But the manner of making experiments which men now use is blind and stupid. And therefore, wandering and straying as they do with no settled course, and taking counsel only from things as they fall out, they fetch a wide circuit and meet with many matters, but make little progress; and sometimes are full of hope, sometimes are distracted; and always find that there is something beyond to be sought. For it generally happens that men make their trials carelessly, and as it were in play; slightly varying experiments already known, and, if the thing does not answer, growing weary and abandoning the attempt. And even if they apply themselves to experiments more seriously and earnestly and laboriously, still they spend their labor in working out some one experiment, as Gilbert with the magnet, and the chemists with gold; a course of proceeding not less unskillful in the design than small in the attempt. For no one successfully investigates the nature of a thing in the thing itself; the inquiry must be enlarged so as to become more general.

And even when they seek to educe some science or theory from their experiments, they nevertheless almost always turn aside with overhasty and unseasonable eagerness to practice; not only for the sake of the uses and fruits of the practice, but from impatience to obtain in the shape of some new work an assurance for themselves that it is worth their while to go on; and also to show themselves off to the world, and so raise the credit of the business in which they are engaged. Thus, like Atalanta, they go aside to pick up the golden apple, but meanwhile they interrupt their course, and let the victory escape them. But in the true course of experience, and in carrying it on to the effecting of new works, the divine wisdom and order must be our pattern. Now God on the first day of creation created light only, giving to that work an entire day, in which no material substance was created. So must we likewise from experience of every kind first endeavor to discover true causes and axioms; and seek for experiments of Light, not for experiments of Fruit. For axioms rightly discovered and established supply practice with its instruments, not one by one, but in clusters, and draw after them trains and troops of works. Of the paths, however, of experience, which no less than the paths of judgment are impeded and beset, I will speak hereafter; here I have only mentioned ordinary experimental research as a bad kind of demonstration. But now the order of the matter in hand leads me to add something both as to those *signs* which I lately mentioned (signs that the systems of philosophy and contemplation in use are in a bad condition), and also as to the *causes* of what seems at first so strange and incredible. For a knowledge of the signs prepares assent; an explanation of the causes removes the marvel—which two things will do much to render the extirpation of idols from the understanding more easy and gentle.

XCVIII

Now for grounds of experience—since to experience we must come—we have as yet had either none or very weak ones; no search has been made to collect a store of particular observations sufficient either in number, or in kind, or in certainty, to inform the understanding, or in any way adequate. On the contrary, men of learning, but easy withal and idle, have taken for the construction or for the confirmation of their philosophy certain rumors and vague fames or airs of experience, and allowed to these the weight of lawful evidence. And just as if some kingdom or state were to direct its counsels and affairs not by letters and reports from ambassadors and trustworthy messengers, but by the gossip of the streets; such exactly is the system of management introduced into philosophy with relation to experience. Nothing duly investigated, nothing verified, nothing counted, weighed, or measured, is to be found in natural history; and what in observation is loose and vague, is in information deceptive and treacherous. And if anyone thinks that this is a strange thing to say, and something like an unjust complaint, seeing that Aristotle, himself so great a man, and supported by the wealth of so great a king, has composed so accurate a history of animals; and that others with greater diligence, though less pretense, have made many additions; while others, again, have compiled copious histories and descriptions of metals, plants, and fossils; it seems that he does not rightly apprehend what it is that we are now about. For a natural history which is composed for its own sake is not like one that is collected to supply the understanding with information for the building up of philosophy. They differ in many ways, but especially in this: that the former contains the variety of natural species only, and not experiments of the mechanical arts. For even as in the business of life a man's disposition and the secret workings of his mind and affections are better discovered when he is in trouble than at other times, so likewise the secrets of nature reveal themselves more readily under the vexations of art than when they go their own way. Good hopes may therefore be conceived of natural philosophy, when natural history, which is the basis and foundation of it, has been drawn up on a better plan; but not till then.

XCIX

Again, even in the great plenty of mechanical experiments, there is yet a great scarcity of those which are of most use for the information of the understanding. For the mechanic, not troubling himself with the investigation of truth, confines his attention to those things which bear upon his particular work, and will not either raise his mind or stretch out his hand for anything else. But then only will there be good ground of hope for the further advance of knowledge when there shall be received and gathered together into natural history a variety of experiments which are of no use in themselves but simply serve to discover causes and axioms, which I call *Experimenta lucifera*, experiments of *light*, to distinguish then from those which I call *fructifera*, experiments of *fruit*.

Now experiments of this kind have one admirable property and condition: they never miss or fail. For since they are applied, not for the purpose of producing any particular effect, but only of discovering the natural cause of some effect, they answer the end equally well whichever way they turn out; for they settle the question.

C

But not only is a greater abundance of experiments to be sought for and procured, and that too of a different kind from those hitherto tried; an entirely different method, order, and process for carrying on and advancing experience must also be introduced. For experience, when it wanders in its own track, is, as I have already remarked, mere groping in the dark, and confounds men rather than instructs them. But when it shall proceed in accordance with a fixed law, in regular order, and without interruption, then may better things be hoped of knowledge.

CI

But even after such a store of natural history and experience as is required for the work of the understanding, or of philosophy, shall be ready at hand, still the understanding is by no means competent to deal with it offhand and by memory alone; no more than if a man should hope by force of memory to retain and make himself master of the computation of an ephemeris. And yet hitherto more has been done in matter of invention by thinking than by writing; and experience has not yet learned her letters. Now no course of invention can be satisfactory unless it be carried on in writing. But when this is brought into use, and experience has been taught to read and write, better things may be hoped.

CII

Moreover, since there is so great a number and army of particulars, and that army so scattered and dispersed as to distract and confound the understanding, little is to be hoped for from the skirmishings and slight attacks and desultory movements of the intellect, unless all the particulars which pertain to the subject of inquiry shall, by means of Tables of Discovery, apt, well arranged, and, as it were, animate, be drawn up and marshaled; and the mind be set to work upon the helps duly prepared and digested which these tables supply.

CIII

But after this store of particulars has been set out duly and in order before our eyes, we are not to pass at once to the investigation and discovery of new particulars or works; or at any rate if we do so we must not stop there. For although I do not deny that when all the experiments of all the arts shall have been collected and digested, and brought within one man's knowledge and judgment, the mere transferring of the experiments of one art to others may lead, by means of that experience which I term literate, to the discovery of many new things of service to the life and state of man, yet it is no great matter that can be hoped from that; but from the new light of axioms, which having been educed from those particulars by a certain method and rule, shall in their turn point out the way again to new particulars, greater things may be looked for. For our road does not lie on a level, but ascends and descends; first ascending to axioms, then descending to works.

CIV

The understanding must not, however, be allowed to jump and fly from particulars to axioms remote and of almost the highest generality (such as the first principles, as they are called, of arts and things), and taking stand upon them as truths that cannot be shaken, proceed to prove and frame the middle axioms by reference to them; which has been the practice hitherto, the understanding being not only carried that way by a natural impulse, but also by the use of syllogistic demonstration trained and inured to it. But then, and then only, may we hope well of the sciences when in a just scale of ascent, and by successive steps not interrupted or broken, we rise from particulars to lesser axioms; and then to middle axioms, one above the other; and last of all to the most general. For the lowest axioms differ but slightly from bare experience, while the highest and most general (which we now have) are notional and abstract and without solidity. But the middle are the true and solid and living axioms, on which depend the affairs and fortunes of men; and above them again, last of all, those which are indeed the most general; such, I mean, as are not abstract, but of which those intermediate axioms are really limitations.

The understanding must not therefore be supplied with wings, but rather hung with weights, to keep it from leaping and flying. Now this has never yet been done; when it is done, we may entertain better hopes of the sciences.

CV

In establishing axioms, another form of induction must be devised than has hitherto been employed, and it must be used for proving and discovering not first principles (as they are called) only, but also the lesser axioms, and the middle, and indeed all. For the induction which proceeds by simple enumeration is childish; its conclusions are precarious and exposed to peril from a contradictory instance; and it generally decides on too small a number of facts, and on those only which are at hand. But the induction which is to be available for the discovery and demonstration of sciences and arts, must analyze nature by proper rejections and exclusions; and then, after a sufficient number of negatives, come to a conclusion on the affirmative instances—which has not yet been done or even attempted, save only by Plato, who does indeed employ this form of induction to a certain extent for the purpose of discussing definitions and ideas. But in order to furnish this induction or demonstration well and duly for its work, very many things are to be provided which no mortal has yet thought of; insomuch that greater labor will have to be spent in it than has hitherto been spent on the syllogism. And this induction must be used not only to discover axioms, but also in the formation of notions. And it is in this induction that our chief hope lies.

CVI

But in establishing axioms by this kind of induction, we must also examine and try whether the axiom so established be framed to the measure of those particulars only from which it is derived, or whether it be larger and wider. And if it be larger and wider, we must observe whether by indicating to us new particulars it confirm that wideness and largeness as by a collateral security, that we may not either stick fast in things already known, or loosely grasp at shadows and abstract forms, not at things solid and realized in matter. And when this process shall have come into use, then at last shall we see the dawn of a solid hope.

CVII

And here also should be remembered what was said above concerning the extending of the range of natural philosophy to take in the particular sciences, and the referring or bringing back of the particular sciences to natural philosophy, that the branches of knowledge may not be severed and cut off from the stem. For without this the hope of progress will not be so good.

CVIII

So much then for the removing of despair and the raising of hope through the dismissal or rectification of the errors of past time. We must now see what else there is to ground hope upon. And this consideration occurs at once—that if many useful discoveries have been made by accident or upon occasion, when men were not seeking for them but were busy about other things, no one can doubt but that when they apply themselves to seek and make this their business, and that too by method and in order and not by desultory impulses, they will discover far more. For although it may happen once or twice that a man shall stumble on a thing by accident which, when taking great pains to search for it, he could not find, yet upon the whole it unquestionably falls out the other way. And therefore far better things, and more of them, and at shorter intervals, are to be expected from man's reason and industry and direction and fixed application than from accident and animal instinct and the like, in which inventions have hitherto had their origin.

from THE SYSTEM OF THE WORLD

Isaac Newton

It was the antient opinion of not a few, in the earliest ages of philosophy, that the fixed stars stood immoveable in the highest parts of the world; that under the fixed stars the planets were carried about the sun; that the earth, as one of the planets, described an annual course about the sun, while by a diurnal motion it was in the mean time revolved about its own axis; and that the sun, as the common fire which served to warm the whole, was fixed in the centre of the universe. . . .

It is not to be denied but that *Anaxagoras, Democritus,* and others, did now and then start up, who would have it that the earth possessed the centre of the world, and that the stars of all sorts were revolved towards the west about the earth quiescent in the centre, some at a swifter, others at a slower rate.

However, it was agreed on both sides that the motions of the celestial bodies were performed in spaces altogether free and void of resistance. The whim of solid orbs was of a later date, introduced by *Eudoxus, Calippus* and *Aristotle*; when the antient philosophy began to decline, and to give place to the new prevailing fictions of the Greeks. . . .

Whence it was that the planets came to be retained within any certain bounds in these free spaces, and to be drawn off from the rectilinear courses, which, left to themselves, they should have pursued, into regular revolutions in curvilinear orbits, are questions which we do not know how the antients explained; and probably it was to give some sort of satisfaction to this difficulty that solid orbs were introduced.

The later philosophers pretend to account for it either by the action of certain vortices, as *Kepler* and *Des Cartes*; or by some other principle of impulse or attraction, as *Borelli, Hooke,* and others of our nation; for, from the laws of motion, it is most certain that these effects must proceed from the action of some force or other.

But our purpose is only to trace out the quantity and properties of this force from the phaenomena, and to apply what we discover in some simple cases as principles, by which, in a mathematical way, we may estimate the effects thereof in more involved cases; for it would be endless and impossible to bring every particular to direct and immediate observation.

We said, *in a mathematical way*, to avoid all questions about the nature or quality of this force, which we would not be understood to determine by any hypothesis; and therefore call it by the general name of a centripetal force, as it is a force which is directed towards some centre; and as it regards more particularly a body in that centre, we call it circum-solar, circum-terrestrial, circum-jovial; and in like manner in respect of other central bodies. . . .

That there are centripetal forces actually directed to the bodies of the sun, of the earth, and other planets, I thus infer.

The moon revolves about our earth, and by radii drawn to its centre describes areas nearly proportional to the times in which they are described, as is evident from its velocity compared with its apparent diameter; for its motion is slower when its diameter is less (and therefore its distance greater), and its motion is swifter when its diameter is greater.

The revolutions of the satellites of Jupiter about that planet are more regular; for they describe circles concentric with Jupiter by equable motions, as exactly as our senses can distinguish.

And so the satellites of Saturn are revolved about this planet with motions nearly circular and equable, scarcely disturbed by any eccentricity hitherto observed.

That Venus and Mercury are revolved about the sun, is demonstrable from their moon-like appearances: when they shine with a full face, they are in those parts of their orbs which in respect of the earth lie beyond the sun; when they appear half full, they are in those parts which lie over against the sun; when horned, in those parts which lie between the earth and the sun; and sometimes they pass over the sun's disk, when directly interposed between the earth and the sun.

And Venus, with a motion almost uniform, describes an orb nearly circular and concentric with the sun.

But Mercury, with a more eccentric motion, makes remarkable approaches to the sun, and goes off again by turns; but it is always swifter as it is near to the sun, and therefore by a radius drawn to the sun still describes areas proportional to the times.

Lastly, that the earth describes about the sun, or the sun about the earth, by a radius from the one to the other, areas exactly proportional to the times, is demonstrable from the apparent diameter of the sun compared with its apparent motion.

These are astronomical experiments; from which it follows, by prop. 1, 2, 3, in the first book of our *Principles*, and their corollaries, that there are centripetal forces actually directed (either accurately or without considerable error) to the centres of the earth, of Jupiter, of Saturn, and of the sun. In Mercury, Venus, Mars, and the lesser planets, where experiments are wanting, the arguments from analogy must be allowed in their place.

That those forces decrease in the duplicate proportion of the distances from the centre of every planet, appears by cor. 6, prop. 4, book 1; for the periodic times of the satellites of Juipter are one to another in the sesquiplicate proportion of their distances from the centre of this planet.

This proportion has been long ago observed in those satellites; and Mr. *Flamsted*, who had often measured their distances from Jupiter by the micrometer, and by the eclipses of the satellites, wrote to me, that it holds to all the accuracy that possibly can be discerned by our senses. And he sent me the dimensions of their orbits taken by the micrometer, and reduced to the mean distance of Jupiter from the earth, or from the sun, together with the times of their revolutions, as follows:

The greatest elongation of the satellites from the centre of Jupiter as seen from the sun.	*The periodic times of their revolutions.*			
	d.	h.		
1st ... 1' 48" or 108"	1	18	28'	36"
2nd ... 3 01 or 181	3	13	17	54
3rd ... 4 46 or 286	7	03	59	36
4th ... 8 13½ or 493½	16	18	5	13

Whence the sesquiplicate proportion may be easily seen. For example: the $16^{\text{d}\cdot} 18^{\text{h}\cdot} 05' 13''$ is to the time $1^{\text{d}\cdot} 18^{\text{h}\cdot} 28' 36''$ as $493\frac{1}{2}'' \times \sqrt{493\frac{1}{2}''}$ to $108'' \times \sqrt{108''}$, neglecting those small fractions which, in observing, cannot be certainly determined.

Before the invention of the micrometer, the same distances were determined in semi-diameters of Jupiter thus:

Distance of the 1st.	2d.	3d.	4th.
By *Galileo* 6	10	16	28
Simon Marius 6	10	16	26
Cassini 5	8	13	23
Borelli more exactly 5²/₃	8²/₃	14	24²/₃

After the invention of the micrometer.

By *Townley*	5,51	8,78	13,47	24,72
Flamsted	5,31	8,85	13,98	24,23
More accurately by the eclipses	5,578	8,876	14,159	24,903

And the periodic times of those satellites, by the observation of Mr. *Flamsted*, are

$$1^d. \ 18^h. \ 28' \ 36'' \ | \ 3^d. \ 17^h. \ 17' \ 54''$$
$$7^d. \ 3^h. \ 59' \ 36'' \ | \ 16^d. \ 18^h. \ 5' \ 13'',$$

as above.

And the distances thence computed are

$$5,578 \ | \ 8,878 \ | \ 14,168 \ | \ 24,968,$$

accurately agreeing with the distances by observation.

Cassini assures us (p. 164, 165) that the same proportion is observed in the circum-saturnal planets. But a longer course of observations is required before we can have a certain and accurate theory of those planets.

In the circum-solar planets, Mercury and Venus, the same proportion holds with great accuracy, according to the dimensions of their orbs, as determined by the observations of the best astronomers.

That Mars is revolved about the sun is demonstrated from the phases which it shows, and the proportion of its apparent diameters; for from its appearing full near conjunction with the sun, and gibbous in its quadratures, it is certain that it surrounds the sun.

And since its apparent diameter appears about five times greater when in opposition to the sun than when in conjunction therewith, and its distance from the earth is reciprocally as its apparent diameter, that distance will be about five times less when in opposition to than when in conjunction with the sun: but in both cases its distance from the sun will be nearly about the same with the distance which is inferred from its gibbous appearance in the quadratures. And as it encompasses the sun at almost equal distances, but in respect of the earth is very unequally distant, so by radii drawn to the sun it describes areas nearly uniform; but by radii drawn to the earth, it is sometimes swift, sometimes stationary, and sometimes retrograde. . . .

Kepler and *Bullialdus* have, with great care, determined the distances of the planets from the sun: and hence it is that their tables agree best with the heavens. And in all the planets, in Jupiter and Mars, in Saturn and the Earth, as well as in Venus and Mercury, the cubes of their distances are as the squares of their periodic times; and therefore (by cor. 6, prop. 4) the centripetal circum-solar force throughout all the planetary regions decreases in the duplicate proportion of the distances from the sun. In examining this proportion, we are to use the mean distances, or the transverse semi-axes of the orbits (by prop. 15), and to neglect those little fractions, which, in defining the orbits, may have arisen from the insensible errors of observation, or may be ascribed to other causes which we shall afterwards explain. And thus we shall always find the said proportion to hold exactly; for the distances of Saturn, Jupiter, Mars, the Earth, Venus, and Mercury, from the sun, drawn from the observations of astronomers, are, according to the computation of *Kepler*, as the numbers 951000, 519650, 152350, 100000, 72400, 38806; by the computation of *Bullialdus*, as the numbers 954198, 522520, 152350, 100000, 72398, 38585; and from the periodic times they come out 953806, 520116, 152399, 100000, 72333, 38710. Their distances, according to *Kepler* and *Bullialdus*, scarcely differ by any sensible quantity, and where they differ most the distances drawn from the periodic times fall in between them.

That the circum-terrestrial force likewise decreases in the duplicate proportion of the distances, I infer thus.

The mean distance of the moon from the centre of the earth, is, in semi-diameters of the earth, according to *Ptolomy*, *Kepler* in his *Ephemerides*, *Bullialdus*, *Hevelius* and *Ricciolus*, 59; according to *Flamsted*, $59\frac{1}{3}$; according to *Tycho*, 56½; to *Vendelin*, 60; to *Copernicus*, $60\frac{1}{3}$; to *Kircher*, 62½.

But *Tycho*, and all that follow his tables of refraction, making the refractions of the sun and moon (altogether against the nature of light) to exceed those of the fixed stars, and that by about four or five minutes in the horizon, did thereby augment the horizontal parallax of the moon by about the like number of minutes; that is, by about the 12th or 15th part of the whole parallax. Correct this error, and the distance will become 60 or 61 semi-diameters of the earth, nearly agreeing with what others have determined.

Let us, then, assume the mean distance of the moon 60 semi diameters of the earth, and its periodic time in respect of the fixed stars 27^d· 7^h· 43$'$, as astronomers have determined it. And (by cor. 6, prop. 4) a body revolved in our air, near the surface of the earth, supposed at rest, by means of a centripetal force which should be to the same force at the distance of the moon in the reciprocal dupli-cate proportion of the distances from the centre of the earth, that is, as 3600 to 1, would (secluding the resistance of the air) complete a revolution in 1^h· 24$'$ 27$''$.

Suppose the circumference of the earth to be 123249600 *Paris* feet, as has been determined by the late mensuration of the *French*, then the same body, deprived of its circular motion, and falling by the impulse of the same centripetal force as before, would, in one second of time, describe $15\frac{1}{12}$ *Paris* feet.

This we infer by a calculus formed upon prop. 36, and it agrees with what we observe in all bodies about the earth. For by the experiments of pendulums, and a computation raised thereon, Mr. *Huygens* has demonstrated that bodies falling by all that centripetal force with which (of whatever nature it is) they are impelled near the surface of the earth, do, in one second of time, describe $15\frac{1}{12}$ *Paris* feet. . . .

In such bodies as are found on our earth of very different sorts, I examine this analogy with great accuracy.

If the action of the circum-terrestrial force is proportional to the bodies to be moved, it will (by the second law of motion) move them with equal velocity in equal times, and will make all bodies let fall to descend through equal spaces in equal times, and all bodies hung by equal threads to vibrate in equal times. If the action of the force was greater, the times would be less; if that was less, these would be greater.

But it has long ago been observed by others, that (allowance being made for the small resistance of the air) all bodies descend through equal spaces in equal times; and, by the help of pendulums, that equality of times may be distinguished to great exactness.

I tried the thing in gold, silver, lead, glass, sand, common salt, wood, water, and wheat. I provided two equal wooden boxes. I filled the one with wood, and suspended an equal weight of gold (as exactly as I could) in the centre of oscillation of the other. The boxes, hung by equal threads of 11 feet, made a couple of pendulums perfectly equal in weight and figure, and equally exposed to the resistance of the air: and, placing the one by the other, I observed them to play together forwards and backwards for a long while, with equal vibrations. And therefore (by cor. 1 and 6, prop. 24, book 2) the quantity of matter in the gold was to the quantity of matter in the wood as the action of the motive force upon all the gold to the action of the same upon all the wood; that is, as the weight of one to the weight of the other.

And by these experiments, in bodies of the same weight, I could have discovered a difference of matter less than the thousandth part of the whole.

Since the action of the centripetal force upon the bodies attracted is, at equal distances, proportional to the quantities of matter in those bodies, reason requires that it should be also proportional to the quantity of matter in the body attracting.

For all action is mutual, and (by the third law of motion) makes the bodies mutually to approach one to the other, and therefore must be the same in both bodies. It is true that we may regard one body as attracting, another as attracted; but this distinction is more mathematical than natural. The attraction is really common of either to other, and therefore of the same kind in both.

And hence it is that the attractive force is found in both. The sun attracts Jupiter and the other planets; Jupiter attracts its satellites; and, for the same reason, the satellites act as well upon one another as upon Jupiter, and all the planets mutually one upon another. . . .

Perhaps it may be objected, that, according to this philosophy all bodies should mutually attract one another, contrary to the evidence of experiments in terrestrial bodies; but I answer, that the experiments in terrestrial bodies come to no account; for the attraction of homogeneous spheres near their surfaces are (by prop. 72) as their diameters. Whence a sphere of one foot in diameter, and of a like nature to the earth, would attract a small body placed near its surface with a force 20000000 times less than the earth would do if placed near its surface; but so small a force could produce no sensible effect. If two such spheres were distant but by ¼ of an inch, they would not, even in spaces void of resistance, come together by the force of their mutual attraction in less than a month's time; and less spheres will come together at a rate yet slower, viz. in the proportion of their diameters. Nay, whole mountains will not be sufficient to produce any sensible effect. A mountain of an hemispherical figure, three miles high, and six broad, will not, by its attraction, draw the pendulum two minutes out of the true perpendicular; and it is only in the great bodies of the planets that these forces are to be perceived. . . .

As the parts of the earth mutually attract one another, so do those of all the planets. If Jupiter and its satellites were brought together, and formed into one globe, without doubt they would continue mutually to attract one another as before. And, on the other hand, if the body of Jupiter was broke into more globes, to be sure, these would no less attract one another than they do the satellites now. From these attractions it is that the bodies of the earth and all the planets effect a spherical figure, and their parts cohere, and are not dispersed through the aether. But we have before proved that these forces arise from the universal nature of matter, and that, therefore, the force of any whole globe is made up of the several forces of all its parts. And from thence it follows (by cor. 3, prop. 74) that the force of every particle decreases in the duplicate proportion of the distance from that particle; and (by prop. 73 and 75) that the force of an entire globe, reckoning from the surface outwards, decreases in the duplicate, but, reckoning inwards, in the simple proportion of the distances from the centre, if the matter of the globe be uniform. And though the matter of the globe, reckoning from the centre towards the surface, is not uniform, yet the decrease in the duplicate proportion of the distance outwards would (by prop. 76) take place, provided that difformity is similar in places round about at equal distances from the centre. And two such globes will (by the same proposition) attract one the other with a force decreasing in the duplicate proportion of the distance between their centres.

Wherefore the absolute force of every globe is as the quantity of matter which the globe contains; but the motive force by which every globe is attracted towards another, and which, in terrestrial bodies, we commonly call their weight, is as the content under the quantities of matter in both globes applied to the square of the distance between their centres (by cor. 4, prop. 76), to which force the quantity of motion, by which each globe in a given time will be carried towards the other, is proportional. And the accelerative force, by which every globe according to its quantity of matter is attracted towards another, is as the quantity of matter in that other globe applied to the square of the distance between the centres of the two (by cor. 2, prop. 76); to which force, the velocity by which the attracted globe will, in a given time, be carried towards the other is proportional. And from these principles well understood, it will now be easy to determine the motions of the celestial bodies among themselves. . . .

Thus I have given an account of the system of the planets. As to the fixed stars, the smallness of their annual parallax proves them to be removed to immense distances from the system of the planets: that this parallax is less than one minute is most certain; and from thence it follows that the distance of the fixed stars is above 360 times greater than the distance of Saturn from the sun. Such as reckon the earth one of the planets, and the sun one of the fixed stars, may remove the fixed stars to yet greater distances by the following arguments: from the annual motion of the earth there would happen an apparent transposition of the fixed stars, one in respect of another, almost equal to their double parallax; but the greater and nearer stars, in respect of the more remote, which are only seen by the telescope, have not hitherto been observed to have the least motion. If we should suppose that motion to be but less than $20''$, the distance of the nearer fixed stars would exceed the mean distance of Saturn by above 2000 times. . . .

The fixed stars being, therefore, at such vast distances from one another, can neither attract each other sensibly, nor be attracted by our sun. But the comets must unavoidably be acted on by the circum-solar force; for as the comets were placed by astronomers above the moon, because they were found to have no diurnal parallax, so their annual parallax is a convincing proof of their descending into the regions of the planets. For all the comets which move in a direct course, according to the order of the signs, about the end of their appearance become more than ordinarily slow, or retrogade, if the earth is between them and the sun; and more than ordinarily swift if the earth is approaching to a heliocentric opposition with them. Whereas, on the other hand, those which move against the order of the signs, towards the end of their appearance, appear swifter than they ought to be if the earth is between them and the sun; and slower, and perhaps retrograde, if the earth is in the other side of its orbit. This is occasioned by the motion of the earth in different situations. If the earth go the same way with the comet, with a swifter motion, the comet becomes retrograde; if with a slower motion, the comet becomes slower however; and if the earth move the contrary way, it becomes swifter; and by collecting the differences between the slower and swifter motions, and the sums of the more swift and retrograde motions, and comparing them with the situation and motion of the earth from whence they arise, I found, by means of this parallax, that the distances of the comets at the time they cease to be visible to the naked eye are always less than the distance of Saturn, and generally even less than the distance of Jupiter.

THE CENTURY OF GENIUS

Alfred North Whitehead

The previous chapters were devoted to the antecedent conditions which prepared the soil for the scientific outburst of the seventeenth century. They traced the various elements of thought and instinctive belief, from their first efflorescence in the classical civilisation of the ancient world, through the transformations which they underwent in the Middle Ages, up to the historical revolt of the sixteenth century. Three main factors arrested attention—the rise of mathematics, the instinctive belief in a detailed order of nature, and the unbridled rationalism of the thought of the later Middle Ages. By this rationalism I mean the belief that the avenue to truth was predominantly through a metaphysical analysis of the nature of things, which would thereby determine how things acted and functioned. The historical revolt was the definite abandonment of this method in favour of the study of the empirical facts of antecedents and consequences. In religion, it meant the appeal to the origins of Christianity; and in science it meant the appeal to experiment and the inductive method of reasoning.

A brief, and sufficiently accurate, description of the intellectual life of the European races during the succeeding two centuries and a quarter up to our own times is that they have been living upon the accumulated capital of ideas provided for them by the genius of the seventeenth century. The men of this epoch inherited a ferment of ideas attendant upon the historical revolt of the sixteenth century, and they bequeathed formed systems of thought touching every aspect of human life. It is the one century which consistently and throughout the whole range of human activities, provided intellectual genius adequate for the greatness of its occasions. The crowded stage of this hundred years is indicated by the coincidences which mark its literary annals. At its dawn Bacon's *Advancement of Learning* and Cervantes' *Don Quixote* were published in the same year (1605), as though the epoch would introduce itself with a forward and a backward glance. The first quarto edition of *Hamlet* appeared in the preceding year, and a slightly variant edition in the same year. Finally Shakespeare and Cervantes died on the same day, April 23, 1616. In the spring of this same year Harvey is believed to have first expounded his theory of the circulation of the blood in a course of lectures before the College of Physicians in London. Newton was born in the year that Galileo died (1642), exactly one hundred years after the publication of Copernicus' *De Revolutionibus*. One year earlier Descartes published his *Meditationes* and two years later his *Principia Philosophiae*. There simply was not time for the century to space out nicely its notable events concerning men of genius.

461

I cannot now enter upon a chronicle of the various stages of intellectual advance included within this epoch. It is too large a topic for one lecture, and would obscure the ideas which it is my purpose to develop. A mere rough catalogue of some names will be sufficient, names of men who published to the world important work within these limits of time: Francis Bacon, Harvey, Kepler, Galileo, Descartes, Pascal, Huyghens, Boyle, Newton, Locke, Spinoza, Leibniz. I have limited the list to the sacred number of twelve, a number much too small to be properly representative. For example, there is only one Italian there, whereas Italy could have filled the list from its own ranks. Again Harvey is the only biologist, and also there are too many Englishmen. This latter defect is partly due to the fact that the lecturer is English, and that he is lecturing to an audience which, equally with him, owns this English century. If he had been Dutch, there would have been too many Dutchmen; if Italian, too many Italians; and if French, too many Frenchmen. The unhappy Thirty Years' War was devastating Germany; but every other country looks back to this century as an epoch which witnessed some culmination of its genius. Certainly this was a great period of English thought; as at a later time Voltaire impressed upon France.

The omission of physiologists, other than Harvey, also requires explanation. There were, of course, great advances in biology within the century, chiefly associated with Italy and the University of Padua. But my purpose is to trace ,the philosophic outlook, derived from science and presupposed by science, and to estimate some of its effects on the general climate of each age. Now the scientific philosophy of this age was dominated by physics; so as to be the most obvious rendering, in terms of general ideas, of the state of physical knowledge of that age and of the two succeeding centuries. As a matter of fact, these concepts are very unsuited to biology; and set for it an insoluble problem of matter and life and organism, with which biologists are now wrestling. But the science of living organisms is only now coming to a growth adequate to impress its conceptions upon philosophy. The last half century before the present time has witnessed unsuccessful attempts to impress biological notions upon the materialism of the seventeenth century. However this success be estimated, it is certain that the root ideas of the seventeenth century were derived from the school of thought which produced Galileo, Huyghens and Newton, and not from the physiologists of Padua. One unsolved problem of thought, so far as it derives from this period, is to be formulated thus: Given configurations of matter with locomotion in space as assigned by physical laws, to account for living organisms.

My discussion of the epoch will be best introduced by a quotation from Francis Bacon, which forms the opening of Section (or 'Century') IX of his *Natural History*, I mean his *Silva Silvarum*. We are told in the contemporary memoir by his chaplain, Dr. Rawley, that this work was composed in the last five years of his life, so it must be dated between 1620 and 1626. The quotation runs thus:

'It is certain that all bodies whatsoever, though they have no sense, yet they have perception; for when one body is applied to another, there is a kind of election to embrace that which is agreeable, and to exclude or expel that which is ingrate; and whether the body be alterant or altered, evermore a perception precedeth operation; for else all bodies would be like one to another. And sometimes this perception, in some kind of bodies, is far more subtile than sense; so that sense is but a dull thing in comparison of it: we see a weatherglass will find the least difference of the weather in heat or cold, when we find it not. And this perception is sometimes at a distance, as well as upon the touch; as when the loadstone draweth iron; or flame naphtha of Babylon, a great distance off. It is therefore a subject of a very noble enquiry, to enquire of the more subtile perceptions; for it is another key to open nature, as well as the sense; and sometimes better. And besides, it is a principal means of natural divination; for that which in these perceptions appeareth early, in the great effects cometh long after.'

There are a great many points of interest about this quotation, some of which will emerge into importance in suceeding lectures. In the first place, note the careful way in which Bacon discriminates between *perception*, or *taking account of*, on the one hand, and *sense*, or *cognitive experience*, on the other hand. In this respect Bacon is outside the physical line of thought which finally dominated the century. Later on, people thought of passive matter which was operated on externally by forces. I believe Bacon's line of thought to have expressed a more fundamental truth than do the materialistic concepts which were then being shaped as adequate for physics. We are now so used to the materialistic way of looking at things, which has been rooted in our literature by the genius of the seventeenth century, that it is with some difficulty that we understand the possibility of another mode of approach to the problems of nature.

In the particular instance of the quotation which I have just made, the whole passage and the context in which it is embedded, are permeated through and through by the experimental method, that is to say, by attention to 'irreducible and stubborn facts,' and by the inductive method of eliciting general laws. Another unsolved problem which has been bequeathed to us by the seventeenth century is the rational justification of this method of Induction. The explicit realisation of the antithesis between the deductive rationalism of the scholastics and the inductive observational methods of the moderns must chiefly be ascribed to Bacon; though, of course, it was implicit in the mind of Galileo and of all the men of science of those times. But Bacon was one of the earliest of the whole group, and also had the most direct apprehension of the full extent of the intellectual revolution which was in progress. Perhaps the man who most completely anticipated both Bacon and the whole modern point of view was the artist Leonardo Da Vinci, who lived almost exactly a century before Bacon. Leonardo also illustrated the theory which I was advancing in my last lecture, that the rise of naturalistic art was an important ingredient in the formation of our scientific mentality. Indeed, Leonardo was more completely a man of science than was Bacon. The practice of naturalistic art is more akin to the practice of physics, chemistry and biology than is the practice of law. We all remember the saying of Bacon's contemporary, Harvey, the discoverer of the circulation of the blood, that Bacon 'wrote of science like a Lord Chancellor.' But at the beginning of the modern period Da Vinci and Bacon stand together as illustrating the various strains which have combined to form the modern world, namely, legal mentality and the patient observational habits of the naturalistic artists.

In the passage which I have quoted from Bacon's writings there is no explicit mention of the method of inductive reasoning. It is unnecessary for me to prove to you by any quotations that the enforcement of the importance of this method, and of the importance, to the welfare of mankind, of the secrets of nature to be thus discovered, was one of the main themes to which Bacon devoted himself in his writings. Induction has proved to be a somewhat more complex process than Bacon anticipated. He had in his mind the belief that with a sufficient care in the collection of instances the general law would stand out of itself. We know now, and probably Harvey knew then, that this is a very inadequate account of the processes which issue in scientific generalisations. But when you have made all the requisite deductions, Bacon remains as one of the great builders who constructed the mind of the modern world.

The special difficulties raised by induction emerged in the eighteenth century, as the result of Hume's criticism. But Bacon was one of the prophets of the historical revolt, which deserted the method of unrelieved rationalism, and rushed into the other extreme of basing all fruitful knowledge upon inference from particular occasions in the past to particular occasions in the future. I do not wish to throw any doubt upon the validity of induction, when it has been properly guarded. My point is, that the very baffling task of applying reason to elicit the general characteristics of the immediate occasion, as set before us in direct cognition, is a necessary preliminary, if we are to justify induction; unless indeed we are content to base it upon our vague instinct that of course it is all right. Either there is something about the immediate occasion which affords knowledge of the past and the future, or we are reduced to utter scepticism as to memory and induction. It is impossible to over-emphasise the point that the key to the process of induction, as used either in science or in our ordinary life, is to be found in the right understanding of the immediate occasion of knowledge in its full concreteness. It is in respect to our grasp of the character of these occasions in their concreteness that the modern developments of physiology and of psychology are of critical importance. I shall illustrate this point in my subsequent lectures. We find ourselves amid insoluble difficulties when we substitute for this concrete occasion a mere abstract in which we only consider material objects in a flux of configurations in time and space. It is quite obvious that such objects can tell us only that they are where they are.

Accordingly, we must recur to the method of the school-divinity as explained by the Italian medievalists whom I quoted in the first lecture. We must observe the immediate occasion, and *use reason* to elicit a general description of its nature. Induction presupposes metaphysics. In other words, it rests upon an antecedent rationalism. You cannot have a rational justification for your appeal to history till your metaphysics has assured you that there *is* a history to appeal to; and likewise your conjectures as to the future presuppose some basis of knowledge that there *is* a future already subjected to some determinations. The difficulty is to make sense of either of these ideas. But unless you have done so, you have made nonsense of induction.

You will observe that I do not hold Induction to be in its essence the derivation of general laws. It is the divination of some characteristics of a particular future from the known characteristics of a particular past. The wider assumption of general laws holding for all cognisable occasions appears a very unsafe addendum to attach to this limited knowledge. All we can ask of the present occasion is that it shall determine a particular community of occasions, which are in some respects mutually qualified by reason of their inclusion within that same community. That community of occasions considered in physical science is the set of happenings which fit on to each other—as we say—in common space-time, so that we can trace the transitions from one to the other. Accordingly, we refer to *the* common space-time indicated in our immediate occasion of knowledge. Inductive reasoning proceeds from the particular occasion to the particular community of occasions, and from the particular community to relations between particular occasions within that community. Until we have taken into account other scientific concepts, it is impossible to carry the discussion of induction further than this preliminary conclusion.

The third point to notice about this quotation from Bacon is the purely qualitative character of the statements made in it. In this respect Bacon completely missed the tonality which lay behind the sources of seventeenth century science. Science was becoming, and has remained, primarily quantitative. Search for measurable elements among your phenomena, and then search for relations between these measures of physical quantities. Bacon ignores this rule of science. For example, in the quotation given he speaks of action at a distance; but he is thinking qualitatively and not quantitatively. We cannot ask that he should anticipate his younger contemporary Galileo, or his distant successor Newton. But he gives no hint that there should be a search for quantities. Perhaps he was misled by the current logical doctrines which had come down from Aristotle. For, in effect, these doctrines said to the physicist *classify* when they should have said *measure*.

By the end of the century physics had been founded on a satisfactory basis of measurement. The final and adequate exposition was given by Newton. The common measurable element of *mass* was discerned as characterising all bodies in different amounts. Bodies which are apparently identical in substance, shape, and size have very approximately the same mass: the closer the identity, the nearer the equality. The force acting on a body, whether by touch or by action at a distance, was [in effect] defined as being equal to the mass of the body multiplied by the rate of change of the body's velocity, so far as this rate of change is produced by that force. In this way the force is discerned by its effect on the motion of the body. The question now arises whether this conception of the magnitude of a force leads to the discovery of simple quantitative laws involving the alternative determination of forces by circumstances of the configuration of substances and of their physical characters. The Newtonian conception has been brilliantly successful in surviving this test throughout the whole modern period. Its first triumph was the law of gravitation. Its cumulative triumph has been the whole development of dynamical astronomy, of engineering, and of physics.

This subject of the formation of the three laws of motion and of the law of gravitation deserves critical attention. The whole development of thought occupied exactly two generations. It commenced with Galileo and ended with Newton's *Principia*; and Newton was born in the year that Galileo died. Also the lives of Descartes and Huyghens fall within the period occupied by these great terminal figures. The issue of the combined labours of these four men has some right to be considered as the greatest single intellectual success which mankind has achieved. In estimating its size, we must consider the completeness of its range. It constructs for us a vision of the material universe, and it enables us to calculate the minutest detail of a particular occurrence. Galileo took the first step in hitting on the right line of thought. He noted that the critical point to attend to was not the motion of bodies but the changes of their motions. Galileo's discovery is formularised by Newton in his first law of motion: 'Every body continues in its state of rest, or of uniform motion in a straight line, except so far as it may be compelled by force to change that state.'

This formula contains the repudiation of a belief which had blocked the progress of physics for two thousand years. It also deals with a fundamental concept which is essential to scientific theory; I mean, the concept of an ideally isolated system. This conception embodies a fundamental character of things, without which science, or indeed any knowledge on the part of finite intellects, would be impossible. The 'isolated' system is not a solipsist system, apart from which there would be nonentity. It is isolated as within the universe. This means that there are truths respecting this system which require reference only to the remainder of things by way of a uniform systematic scheme of relationships. Thus the conception of an isolated system is not the conception of substantial independence from the remainder of things, but of freedom from casual contingent dependence upon detailed items within the rest of the universe. Further, this freedom from casual dependence is required only in respect to certain abstract characteristics which attach to the isolated system, and not in respect to the system in its full concreteness.

The first law of motion asks what is to be said of a dynamically isolated system so far as concerns its motion as a whole, abstracting from its orientation and its internal arrangement of parts. Aristotle said that you must conceive such a system to be at rest. Galileo added that the state of rest is only a particular case, and that the general statement is 'either in a state of rest, or of uniform motion in a straight line.' Accordingly, an Aristotelian would conceive the forces arising from the reaction of alien bodies as being quantitatively measurable in terms of the velocity they sustain, and as directively determined by the direction of that velocity; while the Galilean would direct attention to the magnitude of the acceleration and to its direction. This difference is illustrated by contrasting Kepler and Newton. They both speculated as to the forces sustaining the planets in their orbits. Kepler looked for tangential forces pushing the planets along, whereas Newton looked for radial forces diverting the directions of the planets' motions.

Instead of dwelling upon the mistake which Aristotle made, it is more profitable to emphasise the justification which he had for it, if we consider the obvious facts of our experience. All the motions which enter into our normal everyday experience cease unless they are evidently sustained from the outside. Apparently, therefore, the sound empiricist must devote his attention to this question of the sustenance of motion. We here hit upon one of the dangers of unimaginative empiricism. The seventeenth century exhibits another example of this same danger; and, of all people in the world, Newton fell into it. Huyghens had produced the wave theory of light. But this theory failed to account for the most obvious facts about light as in our ordinary experience, namely, that shadows cast by obstructing objects are defined by rectilinear rays. Accordingly, Newton rejected this theory and adopted the corpuscular theory which completely explained shadows. Since then both theories have had their periods of triumph. At the present moment the scientific world is seeking for a combination of the two. These examples illustrate the danger of refusing to entertain an idea because of its failure to explain one of the most obvious facts in the subject matter in question. If you have had your attention directed to the novelties in thought in your own lifetime, you will have observed that almost all really new ideas have a certain aspect of foolishness when they are first produced.

Returning to the laws of motion, it is noticeable that no reason was produced in the seventeenth century for the Galilean as distinct from the Aristotelian position. It was an ultimate fact. When in the course of these lectures we come to the modern period, we shall see that the theory of relativity throws complete light on this question; but only by rearranging our whole ideas as to space and time.

It remained for Newton to direct attention to *mass* as a physical quantity inherent in the nature of a material body. Mass remained permanent during all changes of motion. But the proof of the permanence of mass amid chemical transformations had to wait for Lavoisier, a century later. Newton's next task was to find some estimate of the magnitude of the alien force in terms of the mass of the body and of its acceleration. He here had a stroke of luck. For, from the point of view of a mathematician, the simplest possible law, namely the product of the two, proved to be the successful one. Again the modern relativity theory modifies this extreme simplicity. But luckily for science the delicate experiments of the physicists of to-day were not then known, or even possible. Accordingly, the world was given the two centuries which it required in order to digest Newton's laws of motion.

Having regard to this triumph, can we wonder that scientists placed their ultimate principles upon a materialistic basis, and thereafter ceased to worry about philosophy? We shall grasp the course of thought, if we understand exactly what this basis is, and what difficulties it finally involves. When you are criticising the philosophy of an epoch, do not chiefly direct your attention to those intellectual positions which its exponents feel it necessary explicitly to defend. There will be some fundamental assumptions which adherents of all the variant systems within the epoch unconsciously presuppose. Such assumptions appear so obvious that people do not know what they are assuming because no other way of putting things has ever occurred to them. With these assumptions a certain limited number of types of philosophic systems are possible, and this group of systems constitutes the philosophy of the epoch.

One such assumption underlies the whole philosophy of nature during the modern period. It is embodied in the conception which is supposed to express the most concrete aspect of nature. The Ionian philosophers asked, What is nature made of? The answer is couched in terms of stuff, or matter, or material—the particular name chosen is indifferent—which has the property of simple location in space and time, or, if you adopt the more modern ideas, in space-time. What I mean by matter, or material, is anything which has this property of *simple location*. By simple location I mean one major characteristic which refers equally both to space and to time, and other minor characteristics which are diverse as between space and time.

The characteristic common both to space and time is that material can be said to be *here* in space and *here* in time, or *here* in space-time, in a perfectly definite sense which does not require for its explanation any reference to other regions of space-time. Curiously enough this character of simple location holds whether we look on a region of space-time as determined absolutely or relatively. For if a region is merely a way of indicating a certain set of relations to other entities, then this characteristic, which I call simple location, is that material can be said to have just these relations of position to the other entities without requiring for its explanation any reference to other regions constituted by analogous relations of position to the same entities. In fact, as soon as you have settled, however you, do settle, what you mean by a definite place in space-time, you can adequately state the relation of a particular material body to space-time by saying that it is just there, in that place; and, so far as simple location is concerned, there is nothing more to be said on the subject.

There are, however, some subordinate explanations to be made which bring in the minor characteristics which I have already mentioned. First, as regards time, if material has existed during any period, it has equally been in existence during any portion of that period. In other words, dividing the time does not divide the material. Secondly, in respect to space, dividing the volume does divide the material. Accordingly, if material exists throughout a volume, there will be less of that material distributed through any definite half of that volume. It is from this property that there arises our notion of density at a point of space. Anyone who talks about density is not assimilating time and space to the extent that some extremists of the modern school of relativists very rashly desire. For the division of time functions, in respect to material, quite differently from the division of space.

Furthermore, this fact that the material is indifferent to the division of time leads to the conclusion that the lapse of time is an accident, rather than of the essence, of the material. The material is fully itself in any sub-period however short. Thus the transition of time has nothing to do with the character of the material. The material is equally itself at an instant of time. Here an instant of time is conceived as in itself without transition, since the temporal transition is the succession of instants.

The answer, therefore, which the seventeenth century gave to the ancient question of the Ionian thinkers, 'What is the world made of?' was that the world is a succession of instantaneous configurations of matter—or of material, if you wish to include stuff more subtle than ordinary matter, the ether for example.

We cannot wonder that science rested content with this assumption as to the fundamental elements of nature. The great forces of nature, such as gravitation, were entirely determined by the configurations of masses. Thus the configurations determined their own changes, so that the circle of scientific thought was completely closed. This is the famous mechanistic theory of nature, which has reigned supreme ever since the seventeenth century. It is the orthodox creed of physical science. Furthermore, the creed justified itself by the pragmatic test. It worked. Physicists took no more interest in philosophy. They emphasised the anti-rationalism of the Historical Revolt. But the difficulties of this theory of materialistic mechanism very soon became apparent. The history of thought in the eighteenth and nineteenth centuries is governed by the fact that the world had got hold of a general idea which it could neither live with nor live without.

This simple location of instantaneous material configurations is what Bergson has protested against, so far as it concerns time and so far as it is taken to be the fundamental fact of concrete nature. He calls it a distortion of nature due to the intellectual 'spatialisation' of things. I agree with Bergson in his protest: but I do not agree that such distortion is a vice necessary to the intellectual apprehension of nature. I shall in subsequent lectures endeavour to show that this spatialisation is the expression of more concrete facts under the guise of very abstract logical constructions. There is an error; but it is merely the accidental error of mistaking the abstract for the concrete. It is an example of what I will call the 'Fallacy of Misplaced Concreteness.' This fallacy is the occasion of great confusion in philosophy. It is not necessary for the intellect to fall into the trap, though in this example there has been a very general tendency to do so.

It is at once evident that the concept of simple location is going to make great difficulties for induction. For, if in the location of configurations of matter throughout a stretch of time there is no inherent reference to any other times, past or future, it immediately follows that nature within any period does not refer to nature at any other period. Accordingly, induction is not based on anything which can be observed as inherent in nature. Thus we cannot look to nature for the justification of our belief in any law such as the law of gravitation. In other words, the order of nature cannot be justified by the mere observation of nature. For there is nothing in the present fact which inherently refers either to the past or to the future. It looks, therefore, as though memory, as well as induction, would fail to find any justification within nature itself.

I have been anticipating the course of future thought, and have been repeating Hume's argument. This train of thought follows so immediately from the consideration of simple location, that we cannot wait for the eighteenth century before considering it. The only wonder is that the world did in fact wait for Hume before noting the difficulty. Also it illustrates the anti-rationalism of the scientific public that, when Hume did appear, it was only the religious implications of his philosophy which attracted attention. This was because the clergy were in principle rationalists, whereas the men of science were content with a simple faith in the order of nature. Hume himself remarks, no doubt scoffingly, 'Our holy religion is founded on faith.' This attitude satisfied the Royal Society but not the Church. It also satisfied Hume and has satisfied subsequent empiricists.

There is another presupposition of thought which must be put beside the theory of simple location. I mean the two correlative categories of Substance and Quality. There is, however, this difference. There were different theories as to the adequate description of the status of space. But whatever its status, no one had any doubt but that the connection with space enjoyed by entities, which are said to be in space, is that of simple location. We may put this shortly by saying that it was tacitly assumed that space is the locus of simple locations. Whatever is in space is *simpliciter* in some definite portion of space. But in respect to substance and quality the leading minds of the seventeenth century were definitely perplexed; though, with their usual genius, they at once constructed a theory which was adequate for their immediate purposes.

Of course, substance and quality, as well as simple location, are the most natural ideas for the human mind. It is the way in which we think of things, and without these ways of thinking we could not get our ideas straight for daily use. There is no doubt about this. The only question is, How concretely are we thinking when we consider nature under these conceptions? My point will be, that we are presenting ourselves with simplified editions of immediate matters of fact. When we examine the primary elements of these simplified editions, we shall find that they are in truth only to be justified as being elaborate logical constructions of a high degree of abstraction. Of course, as a point of individual psychology, we get at the ideas by the rough and ready method of suppressing what appear to be irrelevant details. But when we attempt to justify this suppression of irrelevance, we find that, though there are entities left corresponding to the entities we talk about, yet these entities are of a high degree of abstraction.

Thus I hold that substance and quality afford another instance of the fallacy of misplaced concreteness. Let us consider how the notions of substance and quality arise. We observe an object as an entity with certain characteristics. Furthermore, each individual entity is apprehended through its characteristics. For example, we observe a body; there is something about it which we note. Perhaps, it is hard, and blue, and round, and noisy. We observe something which possesses these qualities: apart from these qualities we do not observe anything at all. Accordingly, the entity is the substratum, or substance, of which we predicate qualities. Some of the qualities are essential, so that apart from them the entity would not be itself; while other qualities are accidental and changeable. In respect to material bodies, the qualities of having a quantitative mass, and of simple location somewhere, were held by John Locke at the close of the seventeenth century to be essential qualities. Of course, the location was changeable, and the unchangeability of mass was merely an experimental fact except for some extremists.

So far, so good. But when we pass to blueness and noisiness a new situation has to be faced. In the first place, the body may not be always blue, or noisy. We have already allowed for this by our theory of accidental qualities, which for the moment we may accept as adequate. But in the second place, the seventeenth century exposed a real difficulty. The great physicists elaborated transmission theories of light and sound, based upon their materialistic views of nature. There were two hypotheses as to light: either it was transmitted by the vibratory waves of a materialistic ether, or—according to Newton—it was transmitted by the motion of incredibly small corpuscles of some subtle matter. We all know that the wave theory of Huyghens held the field during the nineteenth century, and at present physicists are endeavouring to explain some obscure circumstances attending radiation by a combination of both theories. But whatever theory you choose, there is no light or colour as a fact in external nature. There is merely motion of material. Again, when the light enters your eyes and falls on the retina, there is merely motion of material. Then your nerves are affected and your brain is affected, and again this is merely motion of material. The same line of argument holds for sound, substituting waves in the air for waves in the ether, and ears for eyes.

We then ask in what sense are blueness and noisiness qualities of the body. By analogous reasoning, we also ask in what sense is its scent a quality of the rose.

Galileo considered this question, and at once pointed out that, apart from eyes, ears, or noses, there would be no colours, sounds, or smells. Descartes and Locke elaborated a theory of primary and secondary qualities. For example, Descartes in his 'Sixth Meditation' says:[1] 'And indeed, as I perceive different sorts of colours, sounds, odours, tastes, heat, hardness, etc., I safely conclude that there are in the bodies from which the diverse perceptions of the senses proceed, certain varieties corresponding to them, although, perhaps, not in reality like them. . . .'

Also in his *Principles of Philosophy*, he says: 'That by our senses we know nothing of external objects beyond their figure [or station], magnitude, and motion.'

Locke, writing with a knowledge of Newtonian dynamics, places mass among the primary qualities of bodies. In short, he elaborates a theory of primary and secondary qualities in accordance with the state of physical science at the close of the seventeenth century. The primary qualities are the essential qualities of substances whose spatio-temporal relationships constitute nature. The orderliness of

[1] Translation by Professor John Veitch.

these relationships constitutes the order of nature. The occurrences of nature are in some way apprehended by minds, which are associated with living bodies. Primarily, the mental apprehension is aroused by the occurrences in certain parts of the correlated body, the occurrences in the brain, for instance. But the mind in apprehending also experiences sensations which, properly speaking, are qualities of the mind alone. These sensations are projected by the mind so as to clothe appropriate bodies in external nature. Thus the bodies are perceived as with qualities which in reality do not belong to them, qualities which in fact are purely the offspring of the mind. Thus nature gets credit which should in truth be reserved for ourselves; the rose for its scent: the nightingale for his song: and the sun for his radiance. The poets are entirely mistaken. They should address their lyrics to themselves, and should turn them into odes of self-congratulation on the excellency of the human mind. Nature is a dull affair, soundless, scentless, colourless; merely the hurrying of material, endlessly, meaninglessly.

However you disguise it, this is the practical outcome of the characteristic scientific philosophy which closed the seventeenth century.

In the first place, we must note its astounding efficiency as a system of concepts for the organisation of scientific research. In this respect, it is fully worthy of the genius of the century which produced it. It has held its own as the guiding principle of scientific studies ever since. It is still reigning. Every university in the world organises itself in accordance with it. No alternative system of organising the pursuit of scientific truth has been suggested. It is not only reigning, but it is without a rival.

And yet—it is quite unbelievable. This conception of the universe is surely framed in terms of high abstractions, and the paradox only arises because we have mistaken our abstraction for concrete realities.

No picture, however generalised, of the achievements of scientific thought in this century can omit the advance in mathematics. Here as elsewhere the genius of the epoch made itself evident. Three great Frenchmen, Descartes, Desargues, Pascal, initiated the modern period in geometry. Another Frenchman, Fermat, laid the foundations of modern analysis, and all but perfected the methods of the differential calculus. Newton and Leibniz, between them, actually did create the differential calculus as a practical method of mathematical reasoning. When the century ended, mathematics as an instrument for application to physical problems was well established in something of its modern proficiency. Modern pure mathematics, if we except geometry, was in its infancy, and had given no signs of the astonishing growth it was to make in the nineteenth century. But the mathematical physicist had appeared, bringing with him the type of mind which was to rule the scientific world in the next century. It was to be the age of 'Victorious Analysis.'

The seventeenth century had finally produced a scheme of scientific thought framed by mathematicians, for the use of mathematicians. The great characteristic of the mathematical mind is its capacity for dealing with abstractions; and for eliciting from them clear-cut demonstrative trains of reasoning, entirely satisfactory so long as it is those abstractions which you want to think about. The enormous success of the scientific abstractions, yielding on the one hand *matter* with its *simple location* in space and time, on the other hand *mind*, perceiving, suffering, reasoning, but not interfering, has foisted onto philosophy the task of accepting them as the most concrete rendering of fact.

Thereby, modern philosophy has been ruined. It has oscillated in a complex manner between three extremes. There are the dualists, who accept matter and mind as on an equal basis, and the two varieties of monists, those who put mind inside matter, and those who put matter inside mind. But this juggling with abstractions can never overcome the inherent confusion introduced by the ascription of *misplaced concreteness* to the scientific scheme of the seventeenth century.

SUMMATION OF ORIGIN OF SPECIES

Charles Darwin

Authors of the highest eminence seem to be fully satisfied with the view that each species has been independently created. To my mind it accords better with what we know of the laws impressed on matter by the Creator, that the production and extinction of the past and present inhabitants of the world should have been due to secondary causes, like those determining the birth and death of the individual. When I view all beings not as special creations, but as the lineal descendants of some few beings which lived long before the first bed of the Cambrian system was deposited, they seem to me to become ennobled. Judging from the past, we may safely infer that not one living species will transmit its unaltered likeness to a distant futurity. And of the species now living very few will transmit progeny of any kind to a far distant futurity; for the manner in which all organic beings are grouped, shows that the greater number of species in each genus, and all the species in many genera, have left no descendants, but have become utterly extinct. We can so far take a prophetic glance into futurity as to foretell that it will be the common and widely spread species, belonging to the larger and dominant groups within each class, which will ultimately prevail and procreate new and dominant species. As all the living forms of life are the lineal descendants of those which lived long before the Cambrian epoch, we may feel certain that the ordinary succession by generation has never once been broken, and that no cataclysm has desolated the whole world. Hence we may look with some confidence to a secure future of great length. And as natural selection works solely by and for the good of each being, all corporeal and mental endowments will tend to progress towards perfection.

It is interesting to contemplate a tangled bank, clothed with many plants of many kinds, with birds singing on the bushes, with various insects flitting about, and with worms crawling through the damp earth, and to reflect that these elaborately constructed forms, so different from each other, and dependent upon each other in so complex a manner, have all been produced by laws acting around us. These laws, taken in the largest sense, being Growth with Reproduction; Inheritance which is almost implied by reproduction; Variability from the indirect and direct action of the conditions of life, and from use and disuse: a Ratio of Increase so high as to lead to a Struggle for Life, and as a consequence to Natural Selection, entailing Divergence of Character and the Extinction of less-improved forms. Thus, from the war of nature, from famine and death, the most exalted object which we are capable of conceiving, namely, the production of the higher animals, directly follows. There is grandeur in this view of life, with its several powers, having been originally breathed by the Creator into a few forms or into one; and that, whilst this planet has gone cycling on according to the fixed law of gravity, from so simple a beginning endless forms most beautiful and most wonderful have been, and are being evolved.

THE FORBIDDEN EXPLORATION

Sigmund Freud

If in what follows, I bring any contribution to the history of the psychoanalytic movement, nobody must be surprised at the subjective nature of this paper, nor at the rôle which falls to me therein. For psychoanalysis is my creation; for ten years I was the only one occupied with it, and all the annoyance which this new subject caused among my contemporaries has been hurled upon my head in the form of criticism. Even today, when I am no longer the only psychoanalyst, I feel myself justified in assuming that nobody knows better than I what psychoanalysis is, wherein it differs from other methods of investigating the psychic life, what its name should cover, or what might better be designated as something else.

In the year 1909, when I was first privileged to speak publicly on psychoanalysis in an American university, fired by this momentous occasion for my endeavors, I declared that it was not I who brought psychoanalysis into existence. I said that it was Josef Breuer, who had merited this honor at a time when I was a student and busy working for my examinations (1880-1882).[1] Since then, well-intentioned friends have frequently repeated that I at that time expressed my gratitude to Breuer out of all due proportion. They maintained that, as on previous occasions, I should have dignified Breuer's "cathartic procedure" as a mere preliminary to psychoanalysis, and should have claimed that psychoanalysis itself only began with my rejection of the hypnotic technique and my introduction of free association. Now it is really a matter of indifference whether one considers that the history of psychoanalysis started with the cathartic method or only with my modification of the same. I enter into this uninteresting question only because some of my opponents of psychoanalysis are wont to recall, now and then, that the art of psychoanalysis did not originate with me at all, but with Breuer. Naturally, this only happens to be the case when their attitude permits them to find in psychoanalysis something that is noteworthy; on the other hand, when they set no limit to their repudiation of psychoanalysis, then psychoanalysis is always indisputably my creation. I have never yet heard the Breuer's great part in psychoanalysis had brought him an equal measure of insult and reproach. As I have recognized long since that it is the inevitable fate of psychoanalysis to arouse opposition and to embitter people, I have come to the conclusion that I must surely be the originator of all that characterizes psychoanalysis. I add, with satisfaction, that none of the attempts to belittle my share in this much disdained psychoanalysis has ever come from Breuer himself, or could boast of his support.

The content of Breuer's discovery has been so often presented that a detailed discussion of it here may be omitted.[2] Its fundamental fact is that the symptoms of hysterical patients depend upon impressive, but forgotten scenes of their lives (traumata). The therapy founded thereon was to cause the patients to recall and reproduce these experiences under hypnosis (catharsis), and the fragmentary theory

[1] "On Psychoanalysis." Five lectures given on the occasion of the twentieth anniversary of Clark University, Worcester, Mass., dedicated to Stanley Hall. Second edition, 1912. Published simultaneously in English in the American Journal of Psychology, March, 1910; translated into Dutch, Hungarian, Polish and Russian.

[2] Cf. Breuer and Freud: Studies in Hysteria, translated by A. A. Brill, Monograph Series of the Journal of Nervous and Mental Diseases.

deduced from it was that these symptoms corresponded to an abnormal use of undischarged sums of excitement (conversion). In his theoretical contribution to the "Studies in Hysteria," Breuer, wherever obliged to mention the term *conversion*, has always added my name in parenthesis, as though his first attempt at a theoretical formulation was my spiritual property. I think this allotment refers only to the nomenclature, whilst the conception itself occurred to us both at the same time.

It is also well known that Breuer, after his first experience with it, allowed the cathartic treatment to remain dormant for a number of years and only resumed it after I urged him to do so, on my return from Charcot. He was then an internist and taken up with a rather busy medical practice. I had become a physician quite reluctantly, but was, at that time, impelled by a strong motive to help nervous patients, or, at least, to learn to understand something of their conditions. I had placed reliance on physical therapy and found myself helpless in the face of the disappointments that I had with W. Erb's "Electrotherapy," so rich in advice and indications. If I did not, at that time, pilot myself independently to the opinion later announced by Moebius, that the successes of electrotherapy in nervous disorders are the results of suggestion, it was mainly due to the fact that these promised successes failed to materialize. The treatment by suggestion in deep hypnosis seemed to offer me at that time sufficient compensation for the loss of confidence in electrical therapy. I learned this treatment through the extremely impressive demonstrations of Liébault and Bernheim. But the investigation under hypnosis with which I became acquainted through Breuer, I found, owing to its automatic manner of working and the simultaneous gratification of one's eagerness for knowledge, much more attractive than the monotonous and violent suggestive command which was devoid of every possibility of inquiry.

As one of the latest achievements of psychoanalysis, we have lately been admonished to put the actual conflict and the cause of the illness into the foreground of analysis. This is exactly what Breuer and I did in the beginning of our work with the cathartic method. We guided the patient's attention directly to the traumatic scene in which the symptom had arisen, we endeavored to find therein the psychic conflict, and to free the repressed affect. We thus discovered the procedure characteristic of the psychic processes of the neuroses which I later named *regression*. The associations of the patients went back from the scene to be explained, to earlier experiences, and forced the analysis which was to correct the present, to occupy itself with the past. This regression led even further backwards. At first, it went quite regularly to the time of puberty. Later, however, such failures as gaps in the understanding tempted the analytic work further back into the years of childhood which had, hitherto, been inaccessible to every sort of investigation. This regressive direction

became an important characteristic of the analysis. It was proved that
psychoanalysis could not clear up anything actual, except by going
back to something in the past. It even proved that every pathological
experience presupposes an earlier one, which, though not in itself
pathological, lent a pathological quality to the later occurrence. But
the temptation to stop short at the known actual cause was so great,
that even in later analyses I yielded to it. In the case of the patient
called "Dora," carried out in 1899,[3] the scene which caused the
outbreak of the actual illness was known to me. I tried uncounted
times to analyze this experience, but all that I could receive to my
direct demands was the same scanty and broken description. Only
after a long detour, which led through the earliest childhood of the
patient, a dream appeared in the analysis of which the hitherto
forgotten details of the scene were remembered, and this made
possible the understanding and solution of the actual conflict.

From this one example, it may be seen how misleading is the
admonition just mentioned, and how much of a scientific regression
it is to follow the advice of neglecting the regression in the analytic
technique.

The first difference of opinion between Breuer and myself came to
light on a question of the more intimate psychic mechanism of
hysteria. He still favored a physiological theory, so to speak, and
wished to explain the psychic splitting of hysterics through the
non-communication of various psychic states (or states of consciousness, as we then called them). He thus created the theory of the
"hypnoid states," the effects of which were supposed to push the
unassimilated foreign bodies into the "waking consciousness." I
formulated this situation less scientifically. I perceived everywhere
tendencies and strivings analogous to those of everyday life, and
conceived the psychic splitting itself as a result of a repelling process,
which I at that time called "defense," and later "regression." I made
a short-lived attempt to reconcile the two mechanisms, but as experience showed me always the same and only thing, my defense theory
soon stood in opposition to his hypnoid theory.

I am quite certain, however, that this difference of opinion had
nothing to do with the parting of the ways which occurred between
us soon thereafter. The latter had a deeper reason, but it happened in
such a manner that at first, I did not understand it, and only later
did I learn from many good indications how to interpret it. It will be
recalled that Breuer had stated, concerning his first famous patient,
that "the sexual element in her make-up was astonishingly undeveloped" and had never contributed anything to her very marked
morbid picture.[4] I have always wondered why the critics of my
theory of the sexual etiology of the neuroses have not often opposed
it with this assertion of Breuer, and up to this day, I do not know

[3] Gesammelte Schriften Bd. VIII, Translation in Collected Papers, Vol.
III, Hogarth Press.
[4] Breuer and Freud, l.c. p. 14.

whether in this reticence I am to see a proof of their discretion, or of their lack of observation. Whoever will reread the history of Breuer's patient in the light of the experience we have gained since then, will have no difficulty in understanding the symbolism of the snakes and her rigidity, and the paralysis of the arm; and by taking into account also the situation at the sick-bed of the father, he will easily guess the actual meaning of that symptom-formation. His opinion as to the part sexuality played in the psychic life of that girl will then differ greatly from that of her physician. To cure the patient, Breuer utilized the most intensive suggestive *rapport*, which may serve as prototype of that which we call "transference." Now I have strong reasons for thinking that after the removal of the symptoms, Breuer must have discovered the sexual motivations of this transference by new signs, but that the general nature of this unexpected phenomenon excaped him, so that he stopped his investigation right there, as though hit by "an untoward event." He did not furnish me with any direct information about this, but at different times he gave me enough clues to justify this deduction. Later, when I emphasized more and more the significance of sexuality in the etiology of the neuroses, Breuer was the first to show me those reactions of resentful rejection, with which it was my lot to become so familiar later on, but which at that time I had not yet recognized as my inevitable destiny.

The fact that a gross sexual, tender or inimical, transference occurs in every treatment of a neurosis, although this is neither desired nor induced by either party, has always seemed to me the most unshakable proof that the forces of the neuroses originate in the sexual life. This argument has by no means received the serious consideration it deserved, for if it had, there would have been no arguments. For my own conviction, it has remained the decisive factor beside and above the special results of the analytic work.

I felt some solace for the poor reception of the sexual etiology of the neuroses even among the closer circle of my friends (an empty space soon formed itself about my person) in the thought that I had taken up the fight for a new and original idea. But, one day my memories grouped themselves in such a way as to disturb this satisfaction. However, in return I obtained an excellent insight into the origin of our activities and into the nature of our knowledge. The idea for which I was held responsible had not at all originated with me. It had come to me from three persons, for whose opinions I entertained the deepest respect: from *Breuer* himself, from *Charcot*, and from *Chrobak*, the gynecologist of our university, probably the most prominent of our Vienna physicians. All three men had imparted to me an insight which, strictly speaking, they had not themselves possessed. Two of them denied their communication to me when later I reminded them of it; the third (Charcot) would have also done so had it been granted me to see him again. But these identical communications, received without my grasping them, had lain dormant within me, until one day they awoke apparently as an original discovery.

One day, while I was a young hospital doctor, I was accompanying Breuer on a walk through the town when a man came up to him and urgently desired to speak to him. I fell back, and when Breuer was free again, he told me in his kindly-teacher-like manner, that this was the husband of a patient who had brought some news about her. The wife, he added, behaved in so conspicuous a manner when in company, that she had been turned over to him for treatment as a nervous case. He ended with the remark: "Those are always secrets of the alcove." Astonished, I asked him what he meant and he explained to me the word, alcove (conjugal-bed), for he did not realize how strange this matter appeared to me.

A few years later at one of Charcot's evening receptions, I found myself near the venerated teacher who was just relating to Brouardel a very interesting history from the day's practice. I did not hear the beginning clearly, but gradually the story obtained my attention. It was the case of a young married couple from the far East. The wife was a great sufferer and the husband was impotent, or exceeding awkward. I heard Charcot repeat: *"Tâchez donc, je vous assure vous y arriverez."* Brouardel, who spoke less distinctly, must have expressed his astonishment that such symptoms as those of the young wife should have appeared as a result of such circumstances, for Charcot said suddenly and with great vivacity: *"Mais, dans des cas pareils, c'est toujours la chose génital, toujours—toujours—toujours."* And while saying that, he crossed his hands in his lap and jumped up and down several times, with the vivacity peculiar to him. I know that for a moment I was almost paralyzed with astonishment, and I said to myself, "Yes, but if he knows this, why does he never say so?" But the impression was soon forgotten; brain anatomy and the experimental induction of hysterical paralyses absorbed all my interests.

A year later, when I had begun my medical activities in Vienna, as a *Privatdozent* of nervous diseases, I was as innocent and ignorant in all that concerned the etiology of the neuroses as could only be expected of a promising academician. One day I received a friendly call from Chrobak, who asked me to take a patient to whom he could not give sufficient time in his new capacity as lecturer at the university. I reached the patient before he did and learned that she suffered from senseless attacks of anxiety, which could only be alleviated by the most exact information as to the whereabouts of her physician at any time of day. When Chrobak appeared, he took me aside and disclosed to me that the patient's anxiety was due to the fact that although she had been married eighteen years, she was still a *virgo intacta*, that her husband was utterly impotent. In such cases there is nothing that the physician can do but cover up the domestic misfortune with his reputation, and he must bear it if people shrug their shoulders and say, "He is not a good doctor if in all these years he has not been able to cure her." He added, "The only prescription for such troubles is the one well-known to us, but which we cannot prescribe. It is:

> Penis normalis
> dosim
> Repetatur!"

I had never heard of such a prescription and would like to have shaken my head at my patron's cynicism.

I have certainly not uncovered the illustrious origins of this wicked idea in order to shove the responsibility for it on others. I know well that it is one thing to express an idea once or several times in the form of a rapid *aperçu*, and quite another to take it seriously and literally to lead it through all opposing details and conquer a place for it among accepted truths. It is the difference between a light flirtation and a righteous marriage with all its duties and difficulties. *Épouser les idées* (to be wedded to ideas) is, at least in French, a quite common figure of speech.

Of the other contributions that were added to the cathartic method through my efforts, which thus transformed it into psychoanalysis, I emphasize the following: the theories of repression and resistance, the installation of the infantile sexuality, and the method of dream interpretation for the understanding of the unconscious.

The theory of repression I certainly worked out independently. I knew of no influence that directed me in any way to it, and I long considered this idea to be original until O. Rank showed us the passage in Schopenhauer's "The World as Will and Idea," where the philosopher is struggling for an explanation for insanity.[5] What he states there concerning the striving against the acceptance of a painful piece of reality agrees so completely with the content of my theory of repression, that once again, I must be grateful to my not being well read, for the possibility of making a discovery. To be sure, others have read this passage and overlooked it without making this discovery and perhaps the same would have happened to me if, in former years, I had taken more pleasure in reading philosophical authors. In later years I denied myself the great pleasure of reading Nietzsche's works, with the conscious motive of not wishing to be hindered in the working out of my psychoanalytic impressions by any preconceived ideas. I have, therefore, to be prepared—and am so gladly—to renounce all claim to priority in those many cases in which the laborious psychoanalytic investigations can only confirm the insights intuitively won by the philosophers.

The theory of repression is the pillar upon which the edifice of psychoanalysis rests. It is really the most essential part of it, and yet,

[5] Zentralblatt für Psychoanalyse, 1911, Vol. I, p. 69.

it is nothing but the theoretical expression of an experience which can be repeatedly observed whenever one analyses a neurotic without the aid of hypnosis. One is then confronted with a resistance which opposes and blocks the analytic work by causing failures of memory. This resistance was always covered by the use of hypnosis; the history of psychoanalysis proper, therefore, starts with the technical innovation of the rejection of hypnosis. The theoretical value of the fact, that this resistance is connected with an amnesia, leads unavoidably to that concept of unconscious psychic activity which is peculiar to psychoanalysis, and distinguishes it markedly from the philosophical speculations about the unconscious. It may, therefore, be said that the psychoanalytic theory endeavors to explain two experiences, which result in a striking and unexpected manner during the attempt to trace back the morbid symptoms of a neurotic to their source in his life-history; viz., the facts of transference and of resistance. Every investigation which recognizes these two facts and makes them the starting-points of its work may call itself psychoanalysis, even if it leads to other results than my own. But whoever takes up other sides of the problem and deviates from these two assumptions will hardly escape the charge of interfering with the rights of ownership, if he insists upon calling himself a psychoanalyst.

I would very energetically oppose any attempt to count the principles of repression and resistance as mere assumptions instead of results of psychoanalysis. Such assumptions of a general psychological and biological nature exist, and it would be quite to the point to deal with them elsewhere, but the principle of repression is an acquisition of the psychoanalytic work, won by legitimate means, as a theoretical extract from very numerous experiences. Just such an acquisition, but of much later days, is the theory of the infantile sexuality, of which no account was taken during the first years of tentative analytic investigation. At first, it was merely noticed that the effect of actual impressions had to be traced back to the past. However, "the seeker often found more than he bargained for." One was lured further and further back into the past and one finally hoped to be permitted to tarry in the period of puberty, the epoch of the traditional awakening of the sexual impulses. In vain the tracks led still further backward into childhood and into its earliest years. On the way down there an obstacle had to be overcome, which was almost fatal for this young science. Under the influence of the theory of traumatic hysteria, following Charcot, one was easily inclined to regard as real and as of etiological importance the accounts of patients who traced back their symptoms to passive sexual occurrences in the first years of childhood—speaking frankly, to seductions. When this etiology broke down through its own unlikelihood, and through the contradiction of well-established circumstances, there followed a period of absolute helplessness. The analysis had led by the correct path to such infantile sexual traumas, and yet, these were not true. Thus, the basis of reality had been lost. At that time, I would gladly have dropped the whole thing, as did my esteemed predecessor, Breuer, when he made his unwelcome discovery. Perhaps I persevered only because I had no longer any choice of beginning something else. Finally, I reflected that after all no one has a right to despair if he has been disappointed in his expectations; one must merely revise them. If hysterics trace back their symptoms to imaginary traumas, then this new fact signifies that they create such scenes in phantasy, and hence psychic reality deserves to be given a place next to actual reality. This was soon followed by the conviction that these phantasies were intended to hide the autoerotic activities of the early years of childhood, to embellish and raise them to a higher level, and now the whole sexual life of the child came to light behind these phantasies.

In this sexual activity of the first years of childhood, the congenital constitution could finally also attain its rights. Disposition and experience here became associated into an inseparable etiological unity, insofar as the disposition raised certain impressions to inciting and fixed traumas, which otherwise would have remained altogether banal and ineffectual, whilst the experiences evoked factors from the disposition which, without them, would have remained dormant and, perhaps, undeveloped. The last word in the question of traumatic etiology was later on spoken by Abraham, when he drew attention to the fact that the very peculiar nature of the child's sexual constitution is prone to provoke sexual experiences of a peculiar kind—that is to say, traumas.[6]

My formulations concerning the sexuality of the child were founded at first almost exclusively on the results of the analyses of adults, which led back into the past. I lacked the opportunity of direct observations on the child. It was, therefore, an extraordinary triumph when, years later, my discoveries were successfully confirmed for the greater part by direct observation and analyses of very young children, a triumph that gradually became tarnished on reflecting that the discovery was of such a nature that one really ought to be ashamed of having made it. The deeper one penetrated into the observations on the children, the more self-evident this fact became, and the more strange, too, became the circumstances that such pains had been taken to overlook it.

To be sure, so certain a conviction of the existence and significance of the infantile sexuality can be obtained only if one follows the path of analysis, if one goes back from the symptoms and peculiarities of neurotics to their ultimate sources, the discovery of which then explains what is explicable in them, and permits modifying whatever can be changed. I understand that one can arrive at dif-

[6]Klinische Beiträge zur Psychoanalyse aus den Jahren 1907-1920, Intern. Psychoanalyt. Bibliothek. Vd. X, 1921.

ferent conclusions if, as was recently done by C. G. Jung, one first forms a theoretical conception of the nature of the sexual instinct and then tries to explain thereby the life of the child. Such a conception can only be selected arbitrarily or with regard to secondary considerations, and runs the danger of becoming inadequate to the sphere for which it was to be utilized. To be sure, the analytic way also leads to certain final difficulties and obscurities in regard to sexuality and its relation to the whole life of the individual; but these cannot be set aside by speculations; they must wait till solutions will be found by other observations or by observations in other spheres.

I shall briefly discuss the history of dream-interpretation. It came to me as the first-fruits of the technical innovation when, following a dim presentiment, I had decided to replace hypnosis with free associations. It was not the understanding of dreams towards which my curiosity was originally directed. I do not know of any influences which had guided my interest to this or inspired me with any helpful expectations. Before Breuer and I stopped collaborating, I had only just time to tell him in one sentence that I now knew how to translate dreams. During the development of these discoveries, the symbolism of the language of dreams was about the last thing which became known to me, since the associations of the dreamer offer but little help for the understanding of symbols. As I have held fast to the habit of first studying things themselves before looking them up in books, I was, therefore, able to establish for myself the symbolism of dreams before I was directed to it by the work of Sherner. It was only later that I came to value fully this mode of expression in dreams. This was partly due to the influence of the works of Steckel, who at first did very meritorious work, but later became most perfunctory. The close connection between the psychoanalytic interpretation of dreams and the once so highly esteemed art of dream interpretation of the ancients only became clear to me many years afterwards. The most characteristic and significant portion of my dream theory, namely, the reduction of the dream distortion to an inner conflict, to a sort of inner dishonesty, I found later in an author to whom medicine, but not philosophy was unknown. I refer to the engineer, J. Popper, who had published his work, "Phantasies of a Realist," under the name of Lynkeus.

The interpretation of dreams became a solace and support to me in those difficult first years of analysis, when I had to master at the same time the technique, the clinical material, and the therapy of the neuroses; when I was entirely isolated and in the confusion of problems and the accumulation of difficulties, I often feared lest I should lose my orientation and my confidence. It often took a long time before the test of my assumption, that a neurosis must become comprehensible through analysis, was seen by the perplexed patient, bu the dreams, which might be regarded as analogous to the symptoms, almost regularly confirmed this assumption.

Only because of these successes was I able to persevere. I have, therefore, acquired the habit of measuring the grasp of a psychological worker by his attitude to the problem of dream interpretation, and I have noticed with satisfaction that most of the opponents of psychoanalysis avoided this field altogether, or if they ventured into it, they behaved most awkwardly. The analysis of myself, the need of which soon became apparent to me, I carried out by the aid of a series of my own dreams, which led me through all the happenings of my childhood years. Even today, I am of the opinion that in the case of a prolific dreamer and a person not too abnormal this sort of analysis may be sufficient.

By unfurling this developmental history, I believe I have shown better than I could have done by a systematic presentation of the subject what psychoanalysis really is. The peculiar nature of my findings I did not at first recognize. I sacrificed unhesitatingly my budding popularity as a physician and a growing practice in nervous diseases because I searched directly for the sexual origin of their neuroses. In this way, I also gained a number of experiences which definitely confirmed my conviction of the practical importance of the sexual factor. I appeared once unsuspiciously as a speaker at the Vienna Neurological Society, then under the presidency of Krafft-Ebing, expecting to be compensated by the interest and recognition of my colleagues for my material losses, which I voluntarily incurred. I treated my discoveries as ordinary contributions to science and hoped that others would treat them in the same way. But the silence which followed my lectures, the void that formed about my person, and the insinuations directed at me, made me realize gradually that statements concerning the rôle of sexuality in the etiology of the neuroses cannot hope to be treated like other communications. I realized that henceforth I belonged to those who, according to Hebbel's expression, "have disturbed the world's sleep," and that I could not count upon being treated objectively and with toleration. But as my conviction of the general accuracy of my observations and the conclusions grew and grew, and as my faith in my own judgment and my moral courage were by no means small, there could be no doubt about the issue of this situation. I was imbued with the conviction that it fell to my lot to discover particularly important connections, and was prepared to accept the fate which sometimes accompanies such discoveries.

This fate I pictured to myself as follows: I should probably succeed in sustaining myself through the therapeutic successes of the new procedure, but science would take no notice of me during my lifetime. Some decades later, someone would surely stumble upon the same, now untimely things, compel their recognition and thus, bring me to honor as a forerunner, whose misfortune was inevitable. Meanwhile, I arrayed myself as comfortably as possible like Robinson Crusoe on my lonely island. When I look back to those lonely years, from the perplexities and pressure of the present, it seems to me like a beautiful and heroic era. The "splendid isolation" was not lacking in advantages and in charms, I did not have to read any of the medical literature or listen to any ill-informed opponents. I was subject to no influences, and no pressure was brought to bear on me. I learned to restrain speculative tendencies and, following the unforgotten advice of my master, Charcot, I looked at the same things again and again until they, themselves, began to talk to me. My publications, for which I found shelter despite some difficulty, could safely remain far behind my state of knowledge. They could be postponed as long as I pleased. *The Interpretation of Dreams*, for example, was completed in all essentials in the beginning of 1896, but was not written down until the summer of 1899. The analysis of "Dora" was finished at the end of 1899. The history of her illness was completed in the next two weeks, but was not published until 1905. In the meantime, my writings were not reviewed in the medical periodicals, or if an exception was made, they were always treated with scornful or pitying condescension. Now and then, a colleague would refer to me in one of his publications, in very short and unflattering terms, such as "unbalanced," "extreme," or "very odd." It happened once that an assistant at the clinic in Vienna asked me for permission to attend one of my courses. He listened very attentively and said nothing, but after the last lecture he offered to accompany me home. During this walk, he informed me that, with the knowledge of his chief, he had written a book against my views, but regretted very much that he had only become better acquainted with them through my lectures. Had he known these before, he would have written very differently. He had, indeed, inquired at the clinic whether he had not better first read *The Interpretation of Dreams*, but had been advised against it, as it was not worth the trouble. As he now understood it, he compared the solidity of the structure of my theory with that of the Catholic Church. In the interests of his soul's salvation, I will assume that this remark contained a bit of recognition. But he concluded by saying that it was too late to alter anything in his book, as it was already printed. This particular colleague did not consider it necessary later on to tell the world something of the change in his opinions of my psychoanalysis. On the contrary, as a permanent reviewer of a medical journal, he chose rather to follow its development with facetious comments.

Whatever personal sensitiveness I possessed was blunted in those years, to my advantage. I was saved, however, from becoming embittered by a circumstance that does not come to the assistance of all lonely discoverers. Such a person usually torments himself with a need to discover the cause of the lack of sympathy or of the rejection from his contemporaries, and perceives them as a painful contradiction against the certainty of his own conviction. That did not trouble me, for the psychoanalytic principles enabled me to

understand this attitude of my environment as a necessary consequence of fundamental analytic theories. If it was true that the
connections I had discovered were kept from the knowledge of the
patients by inner affective resistances, then these resistances would be
sure to manifest themselves also in normal persons as soon as the
repressed material is conveyed to them from the outside. It was not
strange that they should know how to motivate their affective rejections of my ideas on intellectual grounds. This happened just as often
in the patients, and the arguments advanced—arguments are as common as blackberries, as Falstaff's speech puts it—were just the same
and not exactly brilliant. The only difference was that with patients,
one had the means of bringing pressure to bear in order to induce
them to recognize and overcome their resistances, but in the case of
those seemingly normal, such help had to be omitted. How to force
these normal people to examine the subject in a cool and scientifically objective manner was an insoluble problem, the solution of
which was best left to time. In the history of science it has often
been possible to verify that the very assertion which, at first, called
forth only opposition, received recognition a little later without the
necessity of bringing forward any new proofs.

That I have not developed any particular respect for the opinion of
the world or any desire for intellectual compliance during those years
when I alone represented psychoanalysis, will surprise no one.

THE STABILITY OF ATOMS

Sir Ernest Rutherford

During the latter half of the nineteenth century it was generally
accepted that the atoms of the chemist and physicist were permanent
and indestructible, and were uninfluenced by the most drastic
physical and chemical agencies available. The existence of elements in
the earth that appeared to have suffered no change within periods of
time measured by the geological epochs gave a strong support to the
prevailing view of the inherent stability of the elements. The discovery at the beginning of the twentieth century that the radio-active
elements uranium and thorium were undergoing a veritable transformation, spontaneous and quite uncontrollable by the agencies at
our disposal, was the first serious shock to our belief in the per-
manency of the elements. The essential phenomena which accompanied the series of transformations soon became clear. The disintegration of an atom was accompanied either by the emission of a swift

atom of helium carrying a positive charge, or of a swift electron. With the exception possibly of potassium and rubidium, only the heavy radio-active elements showed this lack of stability. The great majority of the chemical elements appeared, as before, to be inherently stable and to be unaffected by the most intense forces at our disposal.

A number of attempts have been made from time to time to test whether the atoms of the elements can be broken up by artificial methods. Some thought they had obtained evidence of the production of hydrogen and helium in the electric discharge tube. It is, however, a matter of such great difficulty to prove the absence of these elements as a contamination in the materials used that the evidence of transformation has not carried conviction to the minds of the majority of scientific men.

In this lecture an account will be given of some preliminary experiments which indicate the possibility of artificial disintegration of some of the ordinary elements by a new method. Before discussing the results, it is desirable to say a few words on the modern conception of the structure of the atom. The results have been interpreted on the nuclear theory of atomic constitution. According to this view, the atom is to be regarded as consisting of a minute positively charged nucleus, in which most of the mass of the atom is concentrated, surrounded, at a distance by a distribution of negative electrons which make the atom electrically neutral. We know that one or more of these outer electrons can be easily removed from the atom. The atom thus undergoes a kind of transformation, but only a temporary one, for the missing electrons are readily recaptured from neighbouring atoms. It seems not unlikely that the whole of the exterior electrons might be removed from an atom without interfering sensibly with the stability of its nucleus. Under suitable conditions, the atom would promptly regain its lost electrons and be indistinguishable from the original atom. In order to produce a *permanent* transformation of the atom, it is necessary to disintegrate the nucleus. Such a disruption of the nucleus occurs spontaneously in the radio-active atoms, and the processes appear to be irreversible under ordinary conditions.

The nucleus, however, is very small, and its constituent parts are probably held together by strong forces; and only a few agencies are available for an attack on its structure. The most concentrated source of energy at our command is a swift α-particle, and it is to be expected that an α-particle would occasionally approach so close to the nucleus as to disintegrate its structure. It is, indeed, from a study of the deflexion of swift α-particles in passing through matter that we have obtained the strongest evidence in support of the theory of the nuclear constitution of atoms. In the region surrounding a heavy nucleus, the inverse square law holds for the forces of repulsion between the charged α-particle and positively charged nucleus. The particle describes a hyperbolic orbit round the nucleus, and the amount of its deflection depends on the closeness of its approach. It is from a study of this scattering of α-particles, combined with Moseley's interpretation of the X-ray spectra of the elements, that we know the magnitude of the resultant positive charge on the nucleus. This charge, in fundamental units, is equal to the atomic or ordinal number of the element, and varies between 1 for hydrogen and 92 for uranium. Recently Chadwick has shewn by direct measurements of the scattering of α-particles that the charge on the nucleus is in close accord with Moseley's deduction, and has thus verified the correctness of this fundamental conclusion.

Some information about the dimensions of the nucleus can be obtained by studying the amount of scattering of α-particles at large angles by different atoms. The general results indicate that the nucleus of a heavy atom, if assumed spherical, cannot have a radius greater than 6×10^{-12} cm. It is not unlikely that the dimensions may be smaller than this. No doubt the size of a nucleus decreases with its atomic mass, and it is to be expected that the nucleus of the light elements should be smaller than for the heavy atoms. It is thus clear that the volume occupied by the nucleus is exceedingly small compared with that occupied by the atom as a whole.

A direct collision of an α-particle with this minute nucleus is thus a rare occurrence. It can be estimated that even in the case of heavy elements only one α-particle in about 10,000 makes a close collision with the nucleus. On account of the powerful repulsive field of the latter, the α-particle may either be turned back before reaching the nucleus, or be so diminished in energy that it is unable to effect its disruption. The case of the lighter elements, however, is much more favourable; for the repulsive forces are so much weaker that we may expect the α-particle to enter the nucleus structure without much loss of energy, and thus to be an effective agent in promoting the disintegration of the atom.

One of the most interesting cases to consider is that in which an α-particle (helium nucleus) collides with the nucleus of a hydrogen atom. Marsden showed that in some cases the H-atom is set in such swift motion that it can be detected by the scintillation produced on a zinc sulphide screen. The maximum speed obtainable is 1·6 times that of the incident particle, and such a swift H-atom is able to travel four times as far as the α-particle before being stopped. For example, the maximum range of a H-atom set in motion by an α-particle from radium C—range 7 cm. in air—corresponds to 29 cm. of air.

A close examination of the production of swift H-atoms by this method showed that the number was about 30 times greater than that to be expected if the colliding nuclei behaved as point charges repelling each other according to the inverse square law. This, and other observations, show that the law of the inverse square ceases to hold in such intense collisions, where the closest distance of approach is of the order 3×10^{-13} cm. It is probable that this distance is comparable with the actual dimensions of the structure of the α-particle itself. Some recent experiments by Chadwick and Bieler indicate that there is an abrupt change in the law of force at distances of about 5×10^{-13} cm. So far, no definite evidence has been obtained as to the nature of these forces which arise in the close collisions between nuclei. Attention should be directed to the enormous intensity of the electrical forces that come into play in such close collisions—forces much greater than can be brought to bear on an atom by ordinary laboratory methods. Unless the nucleus is a very stable structure, it is to be anticipated that it should be greatly disturbed, if not disintegrated, under the influence of such intense forces.

We must now consider the experiments which indicate that some of the lighter elements can be disintegrated by the action of α-particles. When a stream of α-particles is passed through dry air or nitrogen, a number of scintillations are observed far beyond the range of the α-particle. These scintillations are due to swift charged particles which are bent in a magnetic field like H-atoms set in swift motion by α-particles, and which, indeed, are undoubtedly H-atoms. Since this effect is not observed in dry oxygen or carbon dioxide, it appears likely that some of the nuclei of nitrogen have been disintegrated by the action of the α-particles. Recently these experiments have been repeated by Mr. Chadwick and myself under much better optical conditions for counting these comparatively weak scintillations. It has been found that, using radium C as a source of α-rays, the maximum range of the H-atoms from nitrogen atoms corresponds to 40 cm. of air, while the maximum range of the H-atoms from hydrogen, or any combination of hydrogen, is only 29 cm. under similar conditions. This result negatives the possibility that the presence of these H-atoms can be ascribed to any hydrogen contamination in the ordinary chemical sense.

This observation opened up a simple method of examining other elements besides nitrogen. Experiments were made beyond the maximum range (29 cm.) of ordinary H-atoms, so as to be quite independent of the presence of free or combined hydrogen in the material under examination. In this way it has been found that similar particles are produced in boron, fluorine, sodium, aluminium, and phosphorus. No definite effect has so far been observed for other elements of the production of particles with ranges greater than 29 cm. of air. The question of the production of slower velocity H-atoms has not so far been examined. The range of penetration of the atoms from aluminium is specially marked, being more than 80 cm. While no definite proof has yet been obtained of the nature of these ejected particles, it seems probable that they are in all cases H-atoms liberated from the nuclei of the elements in question. It is of special interest to note that H-atoms are only liberated in elements whose mass is given by $4n + 2$ or $4n + 3$ where n is a whole number.

No *H*-atoms are observed from elements like carbon, oxygen, and sulphur, whose mass is given by $4n$. This is an indication that the α-particles are unable to liberate *H*-atoms from elements composed entirely of helium nuclei, but are able to do so from some elements composed of *H*-atoms as units as well as helium nuclei. It would appear as if the *H*-atoms were satellites of the main nuclear system and that one of them gained sufficient energy from a collision with an α-particle to escape from its orbit with a high speed. If the long-range particles from aluminium are *H*-atoms, it can be calculated that the maximum energy of motion is somewhat greater than that of the incident α-particle, indicating that the escaping fragment of the atom has gained energy from the system. It is of special interest to note that, in the case of aluminium, the direction of escape of the *H*-atom is to some extent independent of the direction of the α-particle. Nearly as many are shot in the backward as in the forward direction, but in the former case the average velocity is somewhat smaller. No element of mass greater than phosphorus (31) has been found to yield *H*-atoms. It would appear as if the constitution of the nucleus undergoes some marked change at this stage.

It should be remarked that the disintegration observed in these experiments is on a very minute scale. Only about one α-particle in a million is able to get close enough to a nucleus to effect its disintegration.

So far we have only been able to observe those fragments of atoms which escape with sufficient speed to travel further than the α-particles. Another very important method of examining the effects produced within the range of the α-particle has been recently examined by Mr. Shimizu. This depends on the discovery of Mr. C. T. R. Wilson that the tracks of ionising radiations can be made visible by sudden expansion of a moist gas, so that each ion becomes the centre of a visible globule of water. Wilson had previously observed an occasional bend in the track of an α-particle, with a short spur attached, indicating the collision of an α-particle with an oxygen or nitrogen nucleus. By taking a large number of photographs of tracks of α-particles, Mr. Shimizu found a number of cases in which the track of the α-particle near the end of its range showed two nearly equal forks. It can readily be shewn from the range and angle between the forks that these effects cannot be ascribed to a collision of the α-particle with a *H*-atom, or with a nucleus of hydrogen or nitrogen. It would appear not unlikely that these forks indicate an actual disruption of the atom in which a helium nucleus is released. While this conclusion is only tentative, it will be of great interest to follow up further this new method of attack of a fundamental problem. It is remarkable that while only one α-particle in a million is able to liberate a *H*-atom from nitrogen, about one α-particle in 300 appears to show a forked track, indicating that this type of disintegration occurs much more frequently than the liberation of a *H*-atom.

If this interpretation proves to be correct, it shows that the amount of energy required to liberate a helium nucleus from a complex nucleus of a light atom is not great. Such a result is not inconsistent with modern ideas of the relation between mass and energy, for the fact that the atomic masses of carbon and oxygen are very nearly integral multiples of the mass of the helium atom is an indication that the helium nuclei are bound loosely together. On the other hand, if we suppose the helium nucleus itself to be composed of four hydrogen nuclei and two electrons, the loss of mass in the structure indicates that the helium nucleus is so stable a structure that it should not be dissociated by even the swiftest α-particle. This conclusion is supported by experimental observations as far as they have gone.

ON LIVING IN A BIOLOGICAL REVOLUTION

Donald Fleming

Here are a dozen things that we have discovered in the last fifteen years.

1. We have discovered the structure of the genetic substance DNA—the double helix of Watson and Crick—the general nature of the process by which the chromosomal strands are replicated.

2. We have discovered in viruses how to achieve the perfect replication of DNA molecules that are biologically effective.

3. We have discovered the code by which DNA specifies the insertion of amino acids in proteins.

4. We have discovered how to produce hybrid cells between the most diverse vertebrate species, including hybrid between man and mouse; and some of these hybrids have gone on multiplying for several (cellular) generations.

5. We have discovered the power of viruses to invade bacterial and other cells and to insert the genes of the virus into the genome of the host; and we have good reason to conjecture, though not yet to affirm, that this phenomenon is involved in cancer.

6. We have discovered hormonal contraceptives and grasped in principle the strategy for devising a contraceptive pill for *both* sexes, by knocking out certain hormones of the hypothalamus, the master sexual gland of the body.

7. We have discovered on a large scale in the livestock industry that deep-frozen mammalian sperm, suitably mixed with glycerol, can be banked indefinitely and drawn upon as desired to produce viable offspring.

8. **We have discovered** in human females how to produce super-ovulation, the release of several eggs into the oviduct at the same time instead of the customary one, with the possibility on the horizon of withdrawing substantial numbers of human eggs for storage, culture in test tubes, or surgical manipulation, without destroying their viability.

9. **We have discovered** in rabbits how to regulate the sex of off-spring by removing fertilized ova from the female before they become implanted in the wall of the uterus, "sexing" the embryos by a technique entailing the deletion of some 200 to 300 cells, flushing embryos of the "wrong" sex down the drain, and then in a substantial minority of cases, successfully reinserting in the uterus embryos of the desired sex that proceed to develop normally.

10. **We have discovered** drugs, above all the hallucinogens, that simulate psychotic states of mind; and have thereby rendered it plausible that the latter are the product of "inborn errors of metabolism" and as such remediable by the administration of drugs.

11. **We have discovered** in principle, and to a certain extent in practice, how to repress the immunological "defenses" of the body.

12. **We have discovered** a combination of immunological and surgical techniques by which the kidney, liver, or heart can be transplanted with fair prospects of the recipient's survival for months or even years—the first constructive proposal for turning our death wish on the highways to some advantage.

Each of these is a major discovery or complex of discoveries in itself, but they add up to far more than the sum of their parts. They constitute a veritable Biological Revolution likely to be as decisive for the history of the next 150 years as the Industrial Revolution has been for the period since 1750.

Definitions of what constitutes a revolution are legion. An undoctrinaire formulation would be that every full-scale revolution has three main components: a distinctive attitude toward the world; a program for utterly transforming it; and an unshakable, not to say fanatical, confidence that this program can be enacted—a world view, a program, and a faith.

In this sense, Darwinism did not usher in a full-scale biological revolution. Darwinism was a profoundly innovating world view, but one that prescribed no steps to be taken, no victories over nature to be celebrated, no program of triumphs to be successively gained. Indeed, one of the most plausible constructions to be put upon it was that nothing much *could* be done except to submit patiently to the winnowing processes of nature.

This defect was not lost upon Darwin's own cousin Sir Francis Galton, who tried to construct an applied science of eugenics for deliberately selecting out the best human stock. But Galtonian eugenics was sadly lacking in any authentic biological foundation. Once the science of Mendelian genetics came to general notice about 1900, a more promising form of eugenics began to commend itself, the effort to induce artificial mutation of genes in desirable directions.

This was long the animating faith of one of the most extraordinary Americans of the twentieth century, the geneticist Herman J. Muller. He was the actual discoverer, in 1927, of artificial mutation through X rays. But this great achievement, for which he got the Nobel Prize, was a tremendous disappointment to Muller the revolutionary. There was no telling which genes would mutate in which direction, and he came to suspect that the vast majority of mutations were actually harmful in the present situation of the human race.

Muller at the end of his life—he died in 1967—was thrown back upon essentially Galtonian eugenics. He did bring this up to date by his proposal for sperm banks in which the sperm of exceptionally intelligent and socially useful men could be stored for decades and used for artificial insemination. He also envisioned, in the not too distant future, ova banks for storing superior human eggs. But none of these modern touches, these innovations in technique, could conceal the fact that this was still the old eugenics newly garbed, but equally subjective and imprecise.

BIOLOGICAL ENGINEERING

The Biological Revolution that Muller failed to bring off was already in progress when he died, but on very different terms from his own. There is a new eugenics in prospect, not the marriage agency kind, but a form of "biological engineering." When this actually comes to pass, chromosomes, segments of chromosomes, and even individual genes will be inserted at will into the genome. Alternatively, germ cells cultured in laboratories will be enucleated and entire tailor-made DNA molecules substituted. Alternatively still, superior genes will be brought into play by hybridization of cells.

The detailed variants upon these general strategies are almost innumerable. They all have in common the fact that they cannot be accomplished at present except in viruses and bacteria or in cell cultures. But it would be a bold man who would dogmatically affirm that none of these possibilities could be brought to bear upon human genetics by the year 2000.

That is a long way off for the firebrands of the Biological Revolution. The Nobel Prize winner Joshua Lederberg in particular has been pushing the claims of a speedier remedy, christened by him "euphenics," and defined as "the engineering of human development." The part of human development that fascinates Lederberg the most is embryology, seen by him as the process of initially translating the instructions coded in the DNA into "the living, breathing organism." Embryology, he says, is "very much in the situation of atomic physics in 1900; having had an honorable and successful tradition it is about to begin!" He thinks it will not take long to mature—"from 5 to no more than 20 years." He adds that most predictions of research progress in recent times have proved to be "far too conservative."

The progress that Lederberg has in mind is the application of new embryological techniques to human affairs. He is at once maddened and obsessed by the nine-months phase in which the human organism has been exempted from experimental and therapeutic intervention—such a waste of time before the scientists can get at us. But the embryo's turn is coming. It would be incredible, he says, "if we did not soon have the basis of developmental engineering technique to regulate, for example, the size of the human brain by prenatal or early postnatal intervention."

SEX CONTROL

Nothing as sensational as this has yet been attempted, but the new phase in embryology that Lederberg heralded is undoubtedly getting under way. The most conspicuous figure at present is Robert Edwards of the physiology laboratory at Cambridge University. In 1966 Edwards reported the culture of immature egg cells from the human ovary up to the point of ripeness for fertilization. He made tentative claims to have actually achieved fertilization in test tubes. The incipient hullabaloo in the newspapers about the specter of "test tube babies" led Edwards to clamp a tight lid of security over his researches in progress.

In the spring of this year, however, he and Richard Gardner announced their success in "sexing" fertilized rabbit eggs before implantation in the wall of the uterus and then inducing 20 percent of the reinserted eggs to produce normal full-term infants. The aspect of these findings that attracted general attention, the prospect of regulating the sex of mammalian offspring, is not likely to be of permanent interest. For this purpose, Edwards and Gardner's technique is obviously a clumsy expedient by comparison with predetermining the "sex" of spermatozoa—presently impossible but certainly not inconceivable within the next generation.

The real importance of Edwards and Gardner's work lies elsewhere. They have opened up the possibility of subjecting the early embryo to microsurgery, with the deletion and "inoculation" of cells at the will of the investigator, *and* the production of viable offspring from the results. The manufacture of "chimeras" in the modern biological sense—that is, with genetically distinct cells in the same organism—is clearly in prospect.

Work in this vein has just begun. The only branch of euphenics that has already become something more than a promising growth stock in science is the suppression of immunological reactions against foreign tissues and the accompanying, highly limited, successes in the transplantation of organs.

BIOLOGICAL REVOLUTIONARIES

The technical details and immediate prospects in eugenics and euphenics, however fascinating, are less important than the underlying revolutionary temper in biology. The most conspicuous representatives of this temper are Lederberg himself, the biochemical geneticist Edward L. Tatum, and Francis Crick of the model—all of them Nobel Prize winners, with the corresponding leverage upon public opinion. Robert Edwards, though slightly singed by the blast of publicity about test tube babies, is clearly in training for the revolutionary cadre.

One of the stigmata of revolutionaries in any field is their resolute determination to break with traditional culture. For a scientist, the most relevant definition of culture is his own field of research. All of these men would angrily resent being bracketed with biologists in general. Biology has always been a rather loose confederation of naturalists and experimentalists, overlapping in both categories with medical researchers. Today even the pretense that these men somehow constitute a community has been frayed to the breaking point.

At Harvard, for example, the revolutionaries have virtually seceded from the old Biology Department and formed a new department of their own, Biochemistry and Molecular Biology. The younger molecular biologists hardly bother to conceal their contempt for the naturalists, whom they see as old fogies obsequiously attentive to the world as it is rather than bent upon turning it upside down.

In one respect, the molecular biologists do overlap with the contemporary naturalists and indeed with most creative scientists in general—in their total detachment from religion. In a way, this is a point that could have been made at any time in the last seventy-five years, but with one significant difference. Herman Muller, for example, born in 1890, had no truck with religion. But he was self-consciously antireligious.

The biological revolutionaries of today are not antireligious but simply unreligious. They give the impression not of defending themselves against religion but of subsisting in a world where that has never been a felt pressure upon them. They would agree with many devout theologians that we are living in a post-Christian world, to such an extent that some of the most doctrinaire biological revolutionaries are able to recognize without embarrassment, and even with a certain gracious condescension, that Christianity did play a useful role in defining the values of the Western world.

The operative word here is in the past tense. Francis Crick says that the facts of science are producing and must produce values that owe nothing to Christianity. "Take," he says, "the suggestion of making a child whose head is twice as big as normal. There is going to be no agreement between Christians and any humanists who lack their particular prejudice about the sanctity of the individual, and who simply want to try it scientifically."

This sense of consciously taking up where religion left off is illuminating in another sense for the revolutionary character of contemporary biology. The parallel is very marked between the original Christian Revolution against the values of the classical world and the Biological Revolution against religious values.

All the great revolutionaries, whether early Christians or molecular biologists, are men of good hope. The future may or may not belong to those who believe in it, but cannot belong to those who don't. Yet at certain points in history, most conspicuously perhaps at intervals between the close of the Thirty Years' War in 1648 and the coming of the Great Depression in 1929, the horizons seem to be wide open, and the varieties of good hope contending for allegiance are numerous. But the tidings of good hope don't become revolutionary except when the horizons begin to close in and the plausible versions of good hope have dwindled almost to the vanishing point.

For the kind of good hope that has the maximum historical impact is the one that capitalizes upon a prevalent despair at the corruption of the existing world, and then carries conviction in pointing to itself as the only possible exit from despair. Above everything else, revolutionaries are the men who keep their spirits up when everybody else's are sagging. In this sense, the greatest revolutionaries of the Western world to date have been precisely the early Christians who dared to affirm in the darkest days of the classical world that something far better was in process and could be salvaged from the ruins.

Both of these points are exemplified in the Biological Revolution that has now begun—despair at our present condition, but infinite hope for the future if the biologists' prescription is taken. Anybody looking for jeremiads on our present state could not do better than to consult the new biologists. "The facts of human reproduction," says Joshua Lederberg, "are all gloomy—the stratification of fecundity by economic status, the new environmental insults to our genes, the sheltering by humanitarian medicine of once-lethal genes."

More generally, the biologists deplore the aggressive instincts of the human animal, now armed with nuclear weapons, his lamentably low average intelligence for coping with increasingly complicated problems, and his terrible prolificity, no longer mitigated by a high enough death rate. It is precisely an aspect of the closing down of horizons and depletion of comfortable hopes in the second half of the twentieth century that conventional medicine is now seen by the biological revolutionaries as one of the greatest threats to the human race.

Yet mere prophets of gloom can never make a revolution. In fact,

the new biologists are almost the only group among our contemporaries with a reasoned hopefulness about the long future—if the right
path is taken. There are of course many individuals of a naturally
cheerful or feckless temperament, today as always, but groups of men
with an articulated hope for the future of the entire race are much
rarer. The theologians no longer qualify, many Communists have lost
their hold upon the future even by their own lights, and the only
other serious contenders are the space scientists and astronauts. But
just to get off the earth is a rather vague prescription for our ills.
Few people even in the space program would make ambitious claims
on this score. In a long historical retrospect, they may turn out to
have been too modest.

This is not a charge that is likely ever to be leveled against the new
biologists. It is well known by now that J. D. Watson begins his
account of his double-helix double by saying that he had never seen
Francis Crick in a modest mood. But after all, modesty is not the
salient quality to be looked for in the new breed of biologists. If the
world will only listen, they *know* how to put us on the high road to
salvation.

CUSTOM-MADE PEOPLE

What exactly does their brand of salvation entail? Perhaps the most
illuminating way to put the matter is that their ideal is the manufacture of man. In a manufacturing process, the number of units to
be produced is a matter of rational calculation beforehand and of
tight control thereafter. Within certain tolerances, specifications are
laid down for a satisfactory product. Quality-control is maintained by
checking the output and replacing defective parts. After the product
has been put to use, spare parts can normally be supplied to replace
those that have worn out.

This is the program of the new biologists—control of numbers by
foolproof contraception; gene manipulation and substitution; surgical
and biochemical intervention in the embryonic and neonatal phases;
organ transplants or replacements at will.

Of these, only contraception is technically feasible at present.
Routine organ transplants will probably be achieved for a wide range
of suitable organs in less than five years. The grafting of mechanical
organs, prosthetic devices inserted in the body, will probably take
longer. Joshua Lederberg thinks that embryonic and neonatal intervention may be in flood tide by, say, 1984. As for gene manipulation
and substitution in human beings, that is the remotest prospect of
all—maybe by the year 2000. But we must not forget Lederberg's
well-founded conviction that most predictions in these matters are
likely to be too conservative. We are already five to ten years ahead
of what most informed people expected to be the schedule for organ
transplants in human beings.

The great question becomes, what is it going to be like to be living in a world where such things are coming true? How will the Biological Revolution affect our scheme of values? Nobody could possibly take in all the implications in advance, but some reasonable conjectures are in order.

It is virtually certain that the moral sanctions of birth control are going to be transformed. Down to the present time, the battle for birth control has been fought largely in terms of the individual couple's right to have the number of babies that they want at the desired intervals. But it is built into the quantity-controls envisioned by the Biological Revolution, the control of the biological inventory, that this is or ought to be a question of social policy rather than individual indulgence.

Many factors are converging upon many people to foster this general attitude, but the issue is particularly urgent from the point of view of the biological revolutionaries. In the measure that they succeed in making the human race healthier, first by transplants and later on by genetic tailoring, they will be inexorably swamped by their own successes unless world population is promptly brought under control. The irrepressible Malthus is springing from his lightly covered grave to threaten them with catastrophic victories.

LICENSED BABIES

The only hope is birth control. The biologists can contribute the techniques, but the will to employ them on the requisite scale is another matter. The most startling proposal to date for actually enforcing birth control does not come from a biologist but from the Nobel-Prize-winning physicist W. B. Shockley, one of the inventors of the transistor. Shockley's plan is to render all women of childbearing age reversibly sterile by implanting a contraceptive capsule beneath the skin, to be removed by a physician only on the presentation of a government license to have a child. The mind boggles at the prospect of bootleg babies. This particular proposal is not likely to be enacted in the near future, even in India.

What we may reasonably expect is a continually rising chorus by the biologists, moralists, and social philosophers of the next generation to the effect that nobody has a right to have children, and still less the right to determine on personal grounds how many. There are many reasons why a couple may not want to be prolific anyhow, so that there might be a happy coincidence between contraception seen by them as a right and by statesmen and biologists as a duty. But the suspicion is that even when people moderate their appetite in the matter of babies, they may still want to have larger families than the earth can comfortably support. The possibility of predetermining sex would undoubtedly be helpful in this respect, but might not be enough to make people forgo a third child. That is where the conflict would arise between traditional values, however moderately indulged, and the values appropriate to the Biological Revolution.

This issue is bound to be fiercely debated. But some of the most profound implications of the Biological Revolution may never present themselves for direct ratification. In all probability, the issues will go by default as we gratefully accept specific boons from the new biology.

Take, for example, the role of the patient in medicine. One of the principal strands in Western medicine from the time of the Greeks has been the endeavor to enlist the cooperation of the patient in his own cure. In certain respects, this venerable tradition has grown much stronger in the last century. Thus the rising incidence of degenerative diseases, like ulcers, heart trouble, and high blood pressure, have underscored the absolute necessity of inducing the patient to observe a healthful regimen, literally a way of life.

This has been the whole point of Freudian psychiatry as a mode of therapy, that cures can be wrought only by a painful exertion of the patient himself. We often forget, for good reasons, how traditional Freudianism is after the one big shock has been assimilated. In the present context, it actually epitomizes the Western tradition of bringing the patient's own personality to bear upon his medical problems.

Where do we go from here? The degenerative diseases are going to be dealt with increasingly by surgical repair of organs, by organ transplants, and later on by the installation of mechanical organs and eventually by the genetic deletion of weak organs before they occur. The incentive to curb your temper or watch your diet to keep your heart going will steadily decline.

As for mental illness, the near future almost certainly lies with psychopharmacology and the far future with genetic tailoring. Though the final pieces stubbornly decline to fall into place, the wise money is on the proposition that schizophrenia and other forms of psychosis are biochemical disorders susceptible of a pharmacological cure. If we are not presently curing any psychoses by drugs, we are tranquilizing and antidepressing many psychotics and emptying mental hospitals.

Neuroses, the theme of Freudian psychoanalysis, are another matter. It is not easy to envision a biochemical remedy for them. But even for neuroses, we already have forms of behavioral therapy that dispense with the Freudian tenet of implicating the patient in his own cure. For the *very* long future, it is certainly not inconceivable that genetic tailoring could delete neurotic propensities.

Everywhere we turn, the story is essentially the same. Cures are increasingly going to be wrought upon, done to, the patient as a passive object. The strength of his own personality, the force of his character, his capacity for reintegrating himself, are going to be increasingly irrelevant in medicine.

GENETIC TAILORING, BOON OR BANE?

This leads to what many people would regard as the biggest question of all. In what sense would we have a self to integrate under the new dispensation? The Princeton theologian Paul Ramsey has now been appointed professor of "genetic ethics" at the Georgetown University Medical School, presumably the first appointment of its kind. He thinks that genetic tailoring would be a "violation of man." To this it must be said that under the present scheme of things, many babies get born with catastrophic genes that are not exactly an enhancement of man. Our present genetic self is a brute datum, sometimes very brutal, and anyhow it is hard to see how we can lose our identity before we have any.

As for installing new organs in the body, there is no evident reason why the personality should be infringed upon by heart or kidney transplants per se. Brain transplants would be different, but surely they would be among the last to come. States of mind regulated by drugs we already possess, and obviously they do alter our identity in greater or lesser degree. But even here we must not forget that some identities are intolerable to their distracted possessors.

We must not conclude, however, that the importance of these developments has been exaggerated. The point is that the immediate practical consequences will probably not present themselves as threatening to the individuals involved—quite the contrary. Abstract theological speculations about genetic tailoring would be totally lost upon a woman who could be sure in advance that her baby would not be born mentally retarded or physically handicapped. The private anxieties of individuals are likely to diminish rather than increase any effective resistance to the broader consequences of the Biological Revolution.

One of these is already implicit in predicting a sense of growing passivity on the part of patients, of not participating as a subject in their own recovery. This might well be matched by a more general sense of the inevitability of letting oneself be manipulated by technicians—of becoming an article of manufacture.

The difficulty becomes to estimate what psychological difference this would make. In any Hegelian overview of history, we can only become articles of manufacture because "we" have set up as the manufacturers. But the first person plural is a slippery customer. We the manufactured would be everybody and we the manufacturers a minority of scientists and technicians. Most people's capacity to identify with the satisfactions of the creative minority is certainly no greater in science than in other fields, and may well be less.

The beneficiaries of the Biological Revolution are not likely to feel that they are in control of the historical process from which they are benefiting. But they will not be able to indulge any feelings of alienation from science without endangering the specific benefits that they are unwilling to give up.

The best forecast would be for general acquiescence, though occasionally sullen, in whatever the Biological Revolution has to offer and gradually adjusting our values to signify that we approve of what we will actually be getting. The will to cooperate in being made biologically perfect is likely to take the place in the hierarchy of values that used to be occupied by being humbly submissive to spiritual counselors chastising the sinner for his own salvation. The new form of spiritual sloth will be not to want to be bodily perfect and genetically improved. The new avarice will be to cherish our miserable hoard of genes and favor the children that resemble us.

AMERICA IN THE TECHNETRONIC AGE

Zbigniew Brzezinski

Ours is no longer the conventional revolutionary era; we are entering a novel metamorphic phase in human history. The world is on the eve of a transformation more dramatic in its historic and human consequences than that wrought either by the French or the Bolshevik revolutions. Viewed from a long perspective, these famous revolutions merely scratched the surface of the human condition. The changes they precipitated involved alterations in the distribution of power and property within society; they did not affect the essence of individual and social existence. Life—personal and organised—continued much as before, even though some of its external forms (primarily political) were substantially altered. Shocking though it may sound to their acolytes, by the year 2000 it will be accepted that Robespierre and Lenin were mild reformers.

Unlike the revolutions of the past, the developing metamorphosis will have no charismatic leaders with strident doctrines, but its impact will be far more profound. Most of the change that has so far taken place in human history has been gradual—with the great "revolutions" being mere punctuation marks to a slow, eludible process. In contrast, the approaching transformation will come more rapidly and will have deeper consequences for the way and even perhaps for the meaning of human life than anything experienced by the generations that preceded us.

America is already beginning to experience these changes and in the course of so doing it is becoming a "technetronic" society: a society that is shaped culturally, psychologically, socially and economically by the impact of technology and electronics, particularly computers and communications. The industrial process no longer is the principal determinant of social change, altering the mores, the social structure, and the values of society. This change is separating the United States from the rest of the world, prompting a further fragmentation among an increasingly differentiated mankind, and imposing upon Americans a special obligation to ease the pains of the resulting confrontation.

THE TECHNETRONIC SOCIETY

The far-reaching innovations we are about to experience will be the result primarily of the impact of science and technology on man and his society, especially in the developed world. Recent years have seen a proliferation of exciting and challenging literature on the future. Much of it is serious, and not mere science-fiction.[1] Moreover, both in the United States and, to a lesser degree, in Western Europe a number of systematic, scholarly efforts have been designed to project, predict, and possess what the future holds for us. Curiously, very little has been heard on this theme from the Communist World, even though Communist doctrinarians are the first to claim their 19th-century ideology holds a special pass-key to the 21st century.

The work in progress indicates that men living in the developed world will undergo during the next several decades a mutation potentially as basic as that experienced through the slow process of evolution from animal to human experience. The difference, however, is that the process will be telescoped in time—and hence the shock effect of the change may be quite profound. Human conduct will become less spontaneous and less mysterious—more predetermined and subject to deliberate "programming." Man will increasingly possess the capacity to determine the sex of his children, to affect through drugs the extent of their intelligence and to modify and control their personalities. The human brain will acquire expanded powers, with computers becoming as routine an extension of man's reasoning as automobiles have been of man's mobility. The human body will be improved and its durability extended: some estimate that during the next century the average life-span could reach approximately 120 years.

These developments will have major social impact. The prolongation of life will alter our values, our career patterns, and our social relationships. New forms of social control may be needed to limit the

[1] Perhaps the most useful single source is to be found in the Summer 1967 issue of *Daedalus*, devoted entirely to "*Toward the Year 2000: Work in Progress.*" The introduction by Professor Daniel Bell, chairman of the American Academy's Commission on the Year 2000 (of which the present writer is also a member) summarises some of the principal literature on the subject.

indiscriminate exercise by individuals of their new powers. The possibility of extensive chemical mind-control, the danger of loss of individuality inherent in extensive transplantation, and the feasibility of manipulation of the genetic structure will call for a social definition of common criteria of restraint as well as of utilisation. Scientists predict with some confidence that by the end of this century, computers will reason as well as man, and will be able to engage in "creative" thought; wedded to robots or to "laboratory beings," they could act like humans. The makings of a most complex—and perhaps bitter—philosophical and political dialogue about the nature of man are self-evident in these developments.

Other discoveries and refinements will further alter society as we now know it. The information revolution, including extensive information storage, instant retrieval, and eventually push-button visual and sound availability of needed data in almost any private home, will transform the character of institutionalised collective education. The same techniques could serve to impose well-nigh total political surveillance on every citizen, putting into much sharper relief than is the case today the question of privacy. Cybernetics and automation will revolutionise working habits, with leisure becoming the practice and active work the exception—and a privilege reserved for the most talented. The achievement-oriented society might give way to the amusement-focused society, with essentially spectator spectacles (mass sports, TV) providing an opiate for increasingly purposeless masses.

But while for the masses life will grow longer and time will seem to expand, for the activist élite time will become a rare commodity. Indeed, even the élite's sense of time will alter. Already now speed dictates the pace of our lives—instead of the other way around. As the speed of transportation increases, largely by its own technological momentum, man discovers that he has no choice but to avail himself of that acceleration, either to keep up with others or because he thinks he can thus accomplish more. This will be especially true of the élite, for whom an expansion in leisure time does not seem to be in the cards. Thus as speed expands, time contracts—and the pressures on the élite increase.

By the end of this century the citizens of the more developed countries will live predominantly in cities—hence almost surrounded by man-made environment. Confronting nature could be to them what facing the elements was to our forefathers: meeting the unknown and not necessarily liking it. Enjoying a personal standard of living that (in some countries) may reach almost $10,000 per head, eating artificial food, speedily commuting from one corner of the country to work in another, in continual visual contact with their employer, government, or family, consulting their annual calendars to establish on which day it will rain or shine, our descendants will be shaped almost entirely by what they themselves create and control.

But even short of these far-reaching changes, the transformation that is now taking place is already creating a society increasingly unlike its industrial predecessor.[2] In the industrial society, technical knowledge was applied primarily to one specific end: the acceleration and improvement of production techniques. Social consequences were a later by-product of this paramount concern. In the technetronic society, scientific and technological knowledge, in addition to enhancing productive capabilities, quickly spills over to affect directly almost all aspects of life.

This is particularly evident in the case of the impact of communications and computers. Communications create an extraordinarily interwoven society, in continuous visual, audial, and increasingly close contact among almost all its members—electronically interacting, sharing instantly most intense social experiences, prompting far greater personal involvement, with their consciousnesses shaped in a sporadic manner fundamentally different (as McLuhan has noted) from the literate (or pamphleteering) mode of transmitting information, characteristic of the industrial age. The growing capacity for calculating instantly most complex interactions and the increasing availability of bio-chemical means of human control increase the potential scope of self-conscious direction, and thereby also the pressures to direct, to choose, and to change.

The consequence is a society that differs from the industrial one in a variety of economic, political and social aspects. The following examples may be briefly cited to summarise some of the contrasts:

1. In an industrial society, the mode of production shifts from agriculture to industry, with the use of muscle and animals supplanted by machine-operation. In the technetronic society, industrial employment yields to services, with automation and cybernetics replacing individual operation of machines.

2. Problems of employment and unemployment—not to speak of the earlier stage of the urban socialisation of the post-rural labour force—dominate the relationship between employers, labour, and the market in the industrial society; assuring minimum welfare to the new industrial masses is a source of major concern. In the emerging new society, questions relating to skill-obsolescence, security, vacations, leisure, and profit-sharing dominate the relationship; the matter of psychic well-being of millions of relatively secure but potentially aimless lower-middle class blue collar workers becomes a growing problem.

3. Breaking down traditional barriers to education, thus creating the basic point of departure for social advancement, is a major goal of social reformers in the industrial society. Education, available for

<hr>

[2] See Daniel Bell's pioneering "Notes on the Post-Industrial Society," *The Public Interest*, Nos. 6 and 7, 1967.

limited and specific periods of time, is initially concerned with overcoming illiteracy, and subsequently with technical training, largely based on written, sequential reasoning. In the technetronic society, not only has education become universal but advanced training is available to almost all who have the basic talents. Quantity-training is reinforced by far greater emphasis on quality-selection. The basic problem is to discover the most effective techniques for the rational exploitation of social talent. Latest communication and calculating techniques are applied to that end. The educational process, relying much more on visual and audial devices, becomes extended in time, while the flow of new knowledge necessitates more and more frequent refresher studies.

4. In the industrial society social leadership shifts from the traditional rural-aristocratic to an urban "plutocratic" élite. Newly acquired wealth is its foundation, and intense competition the outlet—as well as the stimulus—for its energy. In the post-industrial technetronic society plutocratic pre-eminence comes under a sustained challenge from the political leadership which itself is increasingly permeated by individuals possessing special skills and intellectual talents. Knowledge becomes a tool of power, and the effective mobilisation of talent an important way for acquiring power.

5. The university in an industrial society—rather in contrast to the medieval times—is an aloof ivory-tower, the repository of irrelevant, even if respected wisdom, and, for only a brief time, the watering fountain for budding members of the established social élite. In the technetronic society, the university becomes an intensely involved *think-tank*, the source of much sustained political planning and social innovation.

6. The turmoil inherent in the shift from the rigidly traditional rural to urban existence engenders an inclination to seek total answers to social dilemmas, thus causing ideologies to thrive in the industrial society.[3] In the technetronic society, increasing ability to reduce social conflicts to quantifiable and measurable dimensions reinforces the trend towards a more pragmatic problem-solving approach to social issues.

7. The activisation of hitherto passive masses makes for intense political conflicts in the industrial society over such matters as disenfranchisement and the right to vote. The issue of political participation is a crucial one. In the technetronic age, the question increasingly is one of ensuring real participation in decisions that seem too complex and too far-removed from the average citizen. Political alienation becomes a problem. Similarly, the issue of politi-

[3] The American exception to this rule was due to the absence of the feudal tradition, a point well developed by Louis Hartz in his work *The Liberal Tradition in America* (1955).

cal equality of the sexes gives way to a struggle for the sexual equality of women. In the industrial society, woman—the operator of machines—ceases to be physically inferior to the male, a consideration of some importance in rural life, and she begins to demand her political rights. In the emerging society, automation discriminates equally against males and females; intellectual talent is computable; the pill encourages sexual equality.

8. The newly enfranchised masses are coordinated in the industrial society through trade unions and political parties, and integrated by relatively simple and somewhat ideological programmes. Moreover, political attitudes are influenced by appeals to nationalist sentiments, communicated through the massive growth of newspapers, relying, naturally, on native tongues. In the technetronic society, the trend would seem to be towards the aggregation of the individual support of millions of uncoordinated citizens, easily within the reach of magnetic and attractive personalities effectively exploiting the latest communication techniques to manipulate emotions and control reason. Reliance on TV—and hence the tendency to replace language with imagery, with the latter unlimited by national confines (and also including coverage for such matters as hunger in India or war scenes)—tends to create a somewhat more cosmopolitan, though highly impressionistic, involvement in global affairs.

9. Economic power in the industrial society tends to be personalised, either in the shape of great *entrepreneurs* like Henry Ford or bureaucratic industrialisers like Kaganovich in Russia, or Minc in Poland. The tendency towards de-personalisation of economic power is stimulated in the next stage by the appearance of a highly complex interdependence between governmental institutions (including the military), scientific establishments, and industrial organisations. As economic power becomes inseparably linked with political power, it becomes more invisible and the sense of individual futility increases.

10. Relaxation and escapism in the industrial society, in its more intense forms, is a carry-over from the rural drinking bout, in which intimate friends and family would join. Bars and saloons—or fraternities—strive to recreate the atmosphere of intimacy. In the technetronic society social life tends to be so atomised, even though communications (especially TV) make for unprecedented immediacy of social experience, that group intimacy cannot be recreated through the artificial stimulation of externally convivial group behaviour. The new interest in drugs seeks to create intimacy through introspection, allegedly by expanding consciousness.

Eventually, these changes and many others, including the ones that affect much more directly the personality and quality of the human being itself, will make the technetronic society as different from the industrial as the industrial became from the agrarian.

THE AMERICAN TRANSITION

America is today in the midst of a transition. U.S. society is leaving the phase of spontaneity and is entering a more self-conscious stage; ceasing to be an industrial society, it is becoming the first technetronic one. This is at least in part the cause for much of the current tensions and violence.

Spontaneity made for an almost automatic optimism about the future, about the "American miracle," about justice and happiness for all. This myth prompted social blinders to the various aspects of American life that did not fit the optimistic mould, particularly the treatment of the Negro and the persistence of pockets of deprivation. Spontaneity involved a faith in the inherent goodness of the American socio-economic dynamic: as America developed, grew, became richer, problems that persisted or appeared would be solved.

This phase is ending. Today, American society is troubled and some parts of it are even tormented. The social blinders are being ripped off—and a sense of inadequacy is becoming more widespread. The spread of literacy, and particularly the access to college and universities of about 40% of the youth, has created a new stratum—one which reinforces the formerly isolated urban intellectuals—a stratum not willing to tolerate either social blinders nor sharing the complacent belief in the spontaneous goodness of American social change.

Yet it is easier to know what is wrong than to indicate what ought to be done. The difficulty is not only revealed by the inability of the new social rebels to develop a concrete and meaningful programme. It is magnified by the novelty of America's problem. Turning to 19th-century ideologies is not the answer—and it is symptomatic that the "New Left" has found it most difficult to apply the available, particularly Marxist, doctrines to the new reality. Indeed, its emphasis on human rights, the evils of depersonalisation, the dangers inherent in big government—so responsive to the felt psychological needs—contain strong parallels to more conservative notions about the place and sanctity of the individual in society.

In some ways, there is an analogy here between the "New Left" and the searching attitude of various disaffected groups in early 19th-century Europe, reacting to the first strains of the industrial age. Not fully comprehending its meaning, not quite certain where it was heading—yet sensitive to the miseries and opportunities it was bringing—many Europeans strove desperately to adapt earlier, 18th-century doctrines to the new reality. It was finally Marx who achieved what appeared to many millions a meaningful synthesis, combining utopian idealism about the future of the industrial age with a scorching critique of its present.

The search for meaning is characteristic of the present American

scene. It could portend most divisive and bitter ideological conflicts—
especially as intellectual disaffection becomes linked with the increasing bitterness of the deprived Negro masses. If carried to its
extreme, this could bring to America a phase of violent, intolerant,
and destructive civil strife, combining ideological and racial intolerance.

However, it seems unlikely that a unifying ideology of political
action, capable of mobilising large-scale loyalty, can emerge in the
manner that Marxism arose in response to the industrial era. Unlike
even Western Europe or Japan—not to speak of Soviet Russia—where
the consequences and the impact of the industrial process are still
re-shaping political, social, and economic life, in America science and
technology (particularly as socially applied through communications
and increasing computarisation, both offsprings of the industrial age)
are already more important in influencing the social behaviour of a
society that has moved past its industrial phase. Science and technology are notoriously unsympathetic to simple, absolute formulas.
In the technetronic society there may be room for pragmatic, even
impatient, idealism, but hardly for doctrinal utopianism.

At the same time, it is already evident that a resolution of some of
the unfinished business of the industrial era will be rendered more
acute. For example, the Negro should have been integrated into U.S.
society *during* the American industrial revolution. Yet that revolution
came before America, even if not the Negro, was ready for full
integration. If the Negro had been only an economic legacy of the
pre-industrial age, perhaps he could have integrated more effectively.
Today, the more advanced urban-industrial regions of America, precisely because they are moving into a new and more complex phase,
requiring even more developed social skills, are finding it very difficult to integrate the Negro, both a racial minority and America's only
"feudal legacy." Paradoxically, it can be argued that the American
South today stands a better long-range chance of fully integrating the
Negro: American consciousness is changing, the Negro has stirred, and
the South is beginning to move into the industrial age. The odds are
that it may take the Negro along with it.

Whatever the outcome, American society is the one in which the
great questions of our time will be first tested through practice. Can
the individual and science co-exist, or will the dynamic momentum of
the latter fundamentally alter the former? Can man, living in the
scientific age, grow in intellectual depth and philosophical meaning,
and thus in his personal liberty too? Can the institutions of political
democracy be adapted to the new conditions sufficiently quickly to
meet the crises, yet without debasing their democratic character?

The challenge in its essence involves the twin-dangers of fragmentation and excessive control. A few examples. Symptoms of alienation
and depersonalisation are already easy to find in American society.

Many Americans feel "less free"; this feeling seems to be connected with their loss of "purpose"; freedom implies choice of action, and action requires an awareness of goals. If the present transition of America to the technetronic age achieves no personally satisfying fruits, the next phase may be one of sullen withdrawal from social and political involvement, a flight from social and political responsibility through "inner-emigration." Political frustration could increase the difficulty of absorbing and internalising rapid environmental changes, thereby prompting increasing psychic instability.

At the same time, the capacity to assert social and political control over the individual will vastly increase. As I have already noted, it will soon be possible to assert almost continuous surveillance over every citizen and to maintain up-to-date, complete files, containing even most personal information about the health or personal behaviour of the citizen, in addition to more customary data. These files will be subject to instantaneous retrieval by the authorities.

Moreover, the rapid pace of change will put a premium on anticipating events and planning for them. Power will gravitate into the hands of those who control the information, and can correlate it most rapidly. Our existing *post*-crisis management institutions will probably be increasingly supplanted by *pre*-crisis management institutions, the task of which will be to identify in advance likely social crises and to develop programmes to cope with them. This could encourage tendencies during the next several decades towards a technocratic dictatorship, leaving less and less room for political procedures as we now know them.

Finally, looking ahead to the end of this century, the possibility of bio-chemical mind-control and genetic tinkering with man, including eventually the creation of beings that will function like men—and reason like them as well—could give rise to the most difficult questions. According to what criteria can such controls be applied? What is the distribution of power between the individual and society with regard to means that can altogether alter man? What is the social and political status of artificial beings, if they begin to approach man in their performance and creative capacities? (One dares not ask, what if they begin to "outstrip man"—something not beyond the pale of possibility during the next century?)

Yet it would be highly misleading to construct a one-sided picture, a new Orwellian piece of science-fiction. Many of the changes transforming American society augur well for the future and allow at least some optimism about this society's capacity to adapt to the requirements of the metamorphic age.

Thus, in the political sphere, the increased flow of information and more efficient techniques of co-ordination need not necessarily prompt greater concentration of power within some ominous control agency located at the governmental apex. Paradoxically, these developments also make possible greater devolution of authority and responsibility to the lower levels of government and society. The division of power has traditionally posed the problems of inefficiency, co-ordination, and dispersal of authority; but today the new communications and computer techniques make possible both increased authority at the lower levels and almost instant national co-ordination. It is very likely that state and local government will be strengthened in the next ten years, and many functions currently the responsibility of the Federal government will be assumed by them.[4]

The devolution of financial responsibility to lower echelons may encourage both the flow of better talent and greater local participation in more important local decision-making. National co-ordination and local participation could thus be wedded by the new systems of co-ordination. This has already been tried successfully by some large businesses. This development would also have the desirable effect of undermining the appeal of any new integrating ideologies that may arise; for ideologies thrive only as long as there is an acute need for abstract responses to large and remote problems.

It is also a hopeful sign that improved governmental performance, and its increased sensitivity to social needs is being stimulated by the growing involvement in national affairs of what Kenneth Boulding has called the Educational and Scientific Establishment (EASE). The university at one time, during the Middle Ages, was a key social institution. Political leaders leaned heavily on it for literate confidants and privy counsellors, a rare commodity in those days. Later divorced from reality, academia in recent years has made a grand re-entry into the world of action.

Today, the university is the creative eye of the massive communications complex, the source of much strategic planning, domestic and international. Its engagement in the world is encouraging the appearance of a new breed of politicians-intellectuals, men who make it a point to mobilise and draw on the most expert, scientific and academic advice in the development of their political programmes. This, in turn, stimulates public awareness of the value of expertise—and, again in turn, greater political competition in exploiting it.

A profound change in the intellectual community itself is inherent in this development. The largely humanist-oriented, occasionally ideologically-minded intellectual-dissenter, who saw his role largely in terms of proffering social critiques, is rapidly being displaced either by experts and specialists, who become involved in special governmental undertakings, or by the generalists-integrators, who become in effect house-ideologues for those in power, providing overall intellec-

---

[4] It is noteworthy that the U.S. Army has so developed its control-systems that it is not uncommon for sergeants to call in and co-ordinate massive air-strikes and artillery fire—a responsibility of colonels during World War II.

tual integration for disparate actions. A community of organisation-oriented, application-minded intellectuals, relating itself more effectively to the political system than their predecessors, serves to introduce into the political system concerns broader than those likely to be generated by that system itself and perhaps more relevant than those articulated by outside critics.[5]

The expansion of knowledge, and the entry into socio-political life of the intellectual community, has the further effect of making education an almost continuous process. By 1980, not only will approximately two-thirds of U.S. urban dwellers be college-trained, but it is almost certain that systematic "élite-retraining" will be standard in the political system. It will be normal for every high official both to be engaged in almost continuous absorption of new techniques and knowledge, and to take periodic retraining. The adoption of compulsory elementary education was a revolution brought on by the industrial age. In the new technetronic society, it will be equally necessary to require everyone at a sufficiently responsible post to take, say, two years of retraining every ten years. (Perhaps there will even be a constitutional amendment, requiring a President-elect to spend at least a year getting himself educationally up-to-date.) Otherwise, it will not be possible either to keep up with, or absorb, the new knowledge.

Given diverse needs, it is likely that the educational system will undergo a fundamental change in structure. Television-computer consoles, capable of bringing most advanced education to the home, will permit extensive and continuous adult re-education. On the more advanced levels, it is likely that government agencies and corporations will develop—and some have already begun to do so—their own advanced educational systems, shaped to their special needs. As education becomes both a continuum, and even more application-oriented, its organisational framework will be re-designed to tie it directly to social and political action.

It is quite possible that a society increasingly geared to learning will be able to absorb more resiliently the expected changes in social and individual life. Mechanisation of labour and the introduction of robots will reduce the chores that keep millions busy doing things that they dislike doing. The increasing GNP (which could reach approximately $10,000 per capita per year), linked with educational

---

[5] However, there is a danger in all this that ought not to be neglected. Intense involvement in applied knowledge could gradually prompt a waning of the tradition of learning for the sake of learning. The intellectual community, including the university, could become another "industry," meeting social needs as the market dictates, with the intellectuals reaching for the highest material and political rewards. Concern with power, prestige, and the good life could mean an end to the aristocratic ideal of intellectual detachment and the disinterested search for truth.

advance, could prompt among those less involved in social management and less interested in scientific development a wave of interest in the cultural and humanistic aspects of life, in addition to purely hedonistic preoccupations. But even the latter would serve as a social valve, reducing tensions and political frustration. Greater control over external environment could make for easier, less uncertain existence.

But the key to successful adaptation to the new conditions is in the effective selection, distribution and utilisation of social talent. If the industrial society can be said to have developed through a struggle for survival of the fittest, the technetronic society—in order to prosper—requires the effective mobilisation of the ablest. Objective and systematic criteria for the selection of those with the greatest gifts will have to be developed, and the maximum opportunity for their training and advancement provided. The new society will require enormous talents—as well as a measure of philosophical wisdom—to manage and integrate effectively the expected changes. Otherwise, the dynamic of change could chaotically dictate the patterns of social change.

Fortunately, American society is becoming more conscious not only of the principle of equal opportunity for all but of special opportunity for the singularly talented few. Never truly an aristocratic state (except for some pockets such as the South and New England), never really subject to ideological or charismatic leadership, gradually ceasing to be a plutocratic-oligarchic society, the U.S.A. is becoming something which may be labelled the "meritocratic democracy." It combines continued respect for the popular will with an increasing role in the key decision-making institutions of individuals with special intellectual and scientific attainments. The educational and social systems are making it increasingly attractive and easy for those meritocratic few to develop to the fullest their special potential. The recruitment and advancement of social talent is yet to extend to the poorest and the most underprivileged, but that too is coming. No one can tell whether this will suffice to meet the unfolding challenge, but the increasingly cultivated and programmed American society, led by a meritocratic democracy, may stand a better chance.

THE TRAUMA OF CONFRONTATION

For the world at large, the appearance of the new technetronic society could have the paradoxical effect of creating more distinct worlds on a planet that is continuously shrinking because of the communications revolution. While the scientific-technological change will inevitably have some spill-over, not only will the gap between the developed and the underdeveloped worlds probably become wider—

especially in the more measurable terms of economic indices—but a *new one* may be developing *within* the industrialised and urban world.

The fact is that America, having left the industrial phase, is today entering a distinct historical era: and one different from that of Western Europe and Japan. This is prompting subtle and still indefinable changes in the American psyche, providing the psycho-cultural bases for the more evident political disagreements between the two sides of the Atlantic. To be sure, there are pockets of innovation or retardation on both sides. Sweden shares with America the problems of leisure, psychic well-being, purposelessness; while Mississippi is experiencing the confrontation with the industrial age in a way not unlike some parts of South-Western Europe. But I believe the broad generalisation still holds true: Europe and America are no longer in the same historical era.

What makes America unique in our time is that it is the first society to experience the future. The confrontation with the new—which will soon include much of what I have outlined—is part of the daily American experience. For better or for worse, the rest of the world learns what is in store for it by observing what happens in the U.S.A.: in the latest scientific discoveries in space, in medicine, or the electric toothbrush in the bathroom; in pop art or LSD, air conditioning or air pollution, old-age problems or juvenile delinquency. The evidence is more elusive in such matters as music, style, values, social mores; but there, too, the term "Americanisation" obviously defines the source. Today, America is *the* creative society; the others, consciously and unconsciously, are emulative.

American scientific leadership is particularly strong in the so-called "frontier" industries, involving the most advanced fields of science. It has been estimated that approximately 80% of all scientific and technical discoveries made during the last few decades originated in the United States. About 75% of the world's computers operate in the United States; the American lead in lasers is even more marked; examples of American scientific lead are abundant.

There is reason to assume that this leadership will continue. America has four times as many scientists and research workers as the countries of the European Economic Community combined; three-and-a-half times as many as the Soviet Union. The brain-drain is almost entirely one-way. The United States is also spending more on research: seven times as much as the E.E.C. countries, three-and-a-half times as much as the Soviet Union. Given the fact that scientific development is a dynamic process, it is likely that the gap will widen.[6]

[6] In the Soviet case, rigid compartmentalisation between secret military research and industrial research has had a particularly sterile effect of inhibiting spill-over from weapons research into industrial application.

On the social level, American innovation is most strikingly seen in the manner in which the new meritocratic élite is taking over American life, utilising the universities, exploiting the latest techniques of communications, harnessing as rapidly as possible the most recent technological devices. Technetronics dominate American life, but so far nobody else's. This is bound to have social and political—and therefore also psychological—consequences, stimulating a psycho-cultural gap in the developed world.

At the same time, the backward regions of the world are becoming more, rather than less, poor in relation to the developed world. It can be roughly estimated that the per capita income of the under-developed world is approximately ten times lower than of America and Europe (and twenty-five times of America itself). By the end of the century, the ratio may be about fifteen-to-one (or possibly thirty-to-one in the case of the U.S.), with the backward nations *at best* approaching the present standard of the very poor European nations but in many cases (*e.g.*, India) probably not even attaining that modest level.

The social élites of these regions, however, will quite naturally tend to assimilate and emulate, as much as their means and power permit, the life-styles of the most advanced world, with which they are, and increasingly will be, in close vicarious contact through global television, movies, travel, education, and international magazines The international gap will thus have a domestic reflection, with the masses, given the availability even in most backward regions of transistorised radios (and soon television), becoming more and more intensely aware of their deprivation.

It is difficult to conceive how in that context democratic institutions (derived largely from Western experience—but typical only of the more stable and wealthy Western nations) will endure in a country like India, or develop elsewhere. The foreseeable future is more likely to see a turn towards personal dictatorships and some unifying doctrines, in the hope that the combination of the two may preserve the minimum stability necessary for social-economic development. The problem, however, is that whereas in the past ideologies of change gravitated from the developed world to the less, in a way stimulating imitation of the developed world (as was the case with Communism), today the differences between the two worlds are so pronounced that it is difficult to conceive a new ideological wave originating from the developed world, where the tradition of utopian thinking is generally declining.

With the widening gap dooming any hope of imitation, the more likely development is an ideology of rejection of the developed world. Racial hatred could provide the necessary emotional force, exploited by xenophobic and romantic leaders. The writings of

Frantz Fanon—violent and racist—are a good example. Such ideologies of rejection, combining racialism with nationalism, would further reduce the chances of meaningful regional co-operation, so essential if technology and science are to be effectively applied. They would certainly widen the existing psychological and emotional gaps. Indeed, one might ask at that point: who is the truer repository of that indefinable quality we call human? The technologically dominant and conditioned technetron, increasingly trained to adjust to leisure, or the more "natural" and backward agrarian, more and more dominated by racial passions and continuously exhorted to work harder, even as his goal of the good life becomes more elusive?

The result could be a modern version on a global scale of the old rural-urban dichotomy. In the past, the strains produced by the shift from an essentially agricultural economy to a more urban one contributed much of the impetus for revolutionary violence.[7] Applied on a global scale, this division could give substance to Lin Piao's bold thesis that:

Taking the entire globe, if North America and Western Europe can be called "the cities of the world," then Asia, Africa and Latin America constitute "the rural areas of the world." ... In a sense, the contemporary world revolution also presents a picture of the encirclement of cities by the rural areas.

In any case, even without envisaging such a dichotomic confrontation, it is fair to say that the underdeveloped regions will be facing increasingly grave problems of political stability and social survival. Indeed (to use a capsule formula), in the developed world, the nature of man as man is threatened; in the underdeveloped, society is. The interaction of the two could produce chaos.

To be sure, the most advanced states will possess ever more deadly means of destruction, possibly even capable of nullifying the consequences of the nuclear proliferation that appears increasingly inevitable. Chemical and biological weapons, death rays, neutron bombs, nerve gases, and a host of other devices, possessed in all their sophisticated variety (as seems likely) only by the two super-states, may impose on the world a measure of stability. Nonetheless, it seems unlikely, given the rivalry between the two principal powers, that a full-proof system against international violence can be established. Some local wars between the weaker, nationalistically more aroused, poorer nations may occasionally erupt—resulting perhaps even in the total nuclear extinction of one or several small nations?— before greater international control is imposed in the wake of the universal moral shock thereby generated.

The underlying problem, however, will be to find a way of avoiding somehow the widening of the cultural and psycho-social gap inherent in the growing differentiation of the world. Even with gradual dif-

[7] See Barrington Moore's documentation of this in his pioneering study *Social Origins of Dictatorship and Democracy* (1967).

ferentiation throughout human history, it was not until the industrial revolution that sharp differences between societies began to appear. Today, some nations still live in conditions not unlike pre-Christian times; many no different than in the medieval age. Yet soon a few will live in ways so new that it is now difficult to imagine their social and individual ramifications. If the developed world takes a leap—as seems inescapably the case—into a reality that is even more different from ours today than ours is from an Indian village, the gap and its accompanying strains will not narrow.

On the contrary, the instantaneous electronic intermeshing of mankind will make for an intense confrontation, straining social and international peace. In the past, differences were "livable" because of time and distance that separated them. Today, these differences are actually widening while technetronics are eliminating the two insulants of time and distance. The resulting trauma could create almost entirely different perspectives on life, with insecurity, envy, and hostility becoming the dominant emotions for increasingly large numbers of people. A three-way split into rural-backward, urban-industrial, and technetronic ways of life can only further divide man, intensify the existing difficulties to global understanding, and give added vitality to latent or existing conflicts.

The pace of American development both widens the split within mankind and contains the seeds for a constructive response. However, neither military power nor material wealth, both of which America possesses in abundance, can be used directly in responding to the onrushing division in man's thinking, norms, and character. Power, at best, can assure only a relatively stable external environment: the tempering or containing of the potential global civil war; wealth can grease points of socio-economic friction, thereby facilitating development. But as man—especially in the most advanced societies—moves increasingly into the phase of controlling and even creating his environment, increasing attention will have to be given to giving man meaningful content—to improving the quality of life for man *as man*.

Man has never really tried to use science in the realm of his value systems. Ethical thinking is hard to change, but history demonstrates that it does change. . . . Man does, in limited ways, direct his very important and much more rapid psycho-social education. The evolution of such things as automobiles, airplanes, weapons, legal institutions, corporations, universities, and democratic governments are examples of progressive evolution in the course of time. We have, however, never really tried deliberately to create a better society for man *qua* man. . . .[8]

The urgent need to do just that may compel America to redefine its global posture. During the remainder of this century, given the perspective on the future I have outlined here, America is likely to become less concerned with "fighting communism" or creating "a

[8] Hudson Hoagland, "Biology, Brains, and Insight," *Columbia University Forum*, Summer 1967.

world safe for diversity" than with helping to develop a common response with the rest of mankind to the implications of a truly new era. This will mean making the massive diffusion of scientific-technological knowledge a principal focus of American involvement in world affairs.

To some extent, the U.S. performs that role already—simply by being what it is. The impact of its reality and its global involvement prompts emulation. The emergence of vast international corporations, mostly originating in the United States, makes for easier transfer of skills, management techniques, marketing procedures, and scientific-technological innovations. The appearance of these corporations in the European market has done much to stimulate Europeans to consider more urgently the need to integrate their resources and to accelerate the pace of their own research and development.

Similarly, returning graduates from American universities have prompted an organisational and intellectual revolution in the academic life of their countries. Changes in the academic life of Britain, Germany, Japan, more recently France, and (to even a greater extent) in the less developed countries, can be traced to the influence of U.S. educational institutions. Indeed, the leading technological institute in Turkey conducts its lectures in "American" and is deliberately imitating, not only in approach but in student-professor relationships, U.S. patterns. Given developments in modern communications, is it not only a matter of time before students at Columbia University and, say, the University of Teheran will be watching, *simultaneously*, the same lecturer?

The appearance of a universal intellectual élite, one that shares certain common values and aspirations, will somewhat compensate for the widening differentiation among men and societies. But it will not resolve the problem posed by that differentiation. In many backward nations tension between what is and what can be will be intensified. Moreover, as Kenneth Boulding observed:

The network of electronic communication is inevitably producing a world super-culture, and the relations between this super-culture and the more traditional national and regional cultures of the past remains the great question mark of the next fifty years.[9]

That "super-culture," strongly influenced by American life, with its own universal electronic-computer language, will find it difficult to relate itself to "the more traditional and regional cultures," especially if the basic gap continues to widen.

To cope with that gap, a gradual change in diplomatic style and

[9] Kenneth Boulding, "Expecting the Unexpected," *Prospective Changes in Society by 1980* (1960).

emphasis may have to follow the redefined emphasis of America's involvement in world affairs. Professional diplomacy will have to yield to intellectual leadership. With government negotiating directly—or quickly dispatching the negotiators—there will be less need for ambassadors who are resident diplomats and more for ambassadors who are capable of serving as creative interpreters of the new age, willing to engage in a meaningful dialogue with the host intellectual community and concerned with promoting the widest possible dissemination of available knowledge. Theirs will be the task to stimulate and to develop scientific-technological programmes of co-operation.

International co-operation will be necessary in almost every facet of life: to reform and to develop more modern educational systems, to promote new sources of food supply, to accelerate economic development, to stimulate technological growth, to control climate, to disseminate new medical knowledge. However, because the new élites have a vested interest in their new nation-states and because of the growing xenophobia among the masses in the third world, the nation-state will remain for a long time the primary focus of loyalty, especially for newly liberated and economically backward peoples. To predict loudly its death, and to act often as if it were dead, could prompt (as it did partially in Europe) an adverse reaction from those whom one would wish to influence. Hence, regionalism will have to be promoted with due deference to the symbolic meaning of national sovereignty—and preferably also by encouraging those concerned themselves to advocate regional approaches.

Even more important will be the stimulation, for the first time in history on a global scale, of the much needed dialogue on what it is about man's life that we wish to safeguard or to promote, and on the relevance of existing moral systems to an age that cannot be fitted into the narrow confines of fading doctrines. The search for new directions—going beyond the tangibles of economic development—could be an appropriate subject for a special world congress, devoted to the technetronic and philosophical problems of the coming age. To these issues no one society, however advanced, is in a position to provide an answer.

Counterrhetoric

THE GRAND ACADEMY OF LAGADO

Jonathan Swift

This Academy is not an entire single Building, but a Continuation of several Houses on both Sides of a Street; which growing waste, was purchased and applyed to that Use.

I was received very kindly by the Warden, and went for many Days to the Academy. Every Room hath in it one or more Projectors; and I believe I could not be in fewer than five Hundred Rooms.

The first Man I saw was of a meagre Aspect, with sooty Hands and Face, his Hair and Beard long, ragged and singed in several Places. His Clothes, Shirt, and Skin were all of the same Colour. He had been Eight Years upon a Project for extracting Sun-Beams out of Cucumbers, which were to be put into Vials hermetically sealed, and let out to warm the Air in raw inclement Summers.[1] He told me, he did not doubt in Eight Years more, that he should be able to supply Governors Gardens with Sun-shine at a reasonable Rate; but he complained that his Stock was low, and intreated me to give him something as an Encouragement to Ingenuity, especially since this had been a very dear Season for Cucumbers. I made him a small Present, for my Lord had furnished me with Money on purpose, because he knew their Practice of begging from all who go to see them.

I went into another Chamber, but was ready to hasten back, being almost overcome with a horrible Stink. My Conductor pressed me forward, conjuring me in a Whisper to give no Offence, which would be highly resented; and therefore I durst not so much as stop my Nose. The Projector of this Cell was the most ancient Student of the

---

[1]The experiments described in this chapter are based on actual experiments undertaken or proposed by Swift's contemporaries.

Academy. His Face and Beard were of a pale Yellow; his Hands and Clothes dawbed over with Filth. When I was presented to him, he gave me a very close Embrace, (a Compliment I could well have excused). His Employment from his first coming into the Academy, was an Operation to reduce human Excrement to its original Food, by separating the several Parts, removing the Tincture which it receives from the Gall, making the Odour exhale, and scumming off the Saliva. He had a weekly Allowance from the Society, of a Vessel filled with human Ordure, about the Bigness of a *Bristol* Barrel.

I saw another at work to calcine Ice into Gunpowder; who likewise shewed me a Treatise he had written concerning the Malleability of Fire, which he intended to publish.

There was a most ingenious Architect who had contrived a new Method for building Houses, by beginning at the Roof, and working downwards to the Foundation; which he justified to me by the like Practice of those two prudent Insects the Bee and the Spider.

There was a Man born blind, who had several Apprentices in his own Condition: Their Employment was to mix Colours for Painters, which their Master taught them to distinguish by feeling and smelling. It was indeed my Misfortune to find them at that Time not very perfect in their Lessons; and the Professor himself happened to be generally mistaken: This Artist is much encouraged and esteemed by the whole Fraternity.

In another Apartment I was highly pleased with a Projector, who had found a Device of plowing the Ground with Hogs, to save the Charges of Plows, Cattle, and Labour. The Method is this: In an Acre of Ground you bury at six Inches Distance, and eight deep, a Quantity of Acorns, Dates, Chestnuts, and other Maste or Vegetables whereof these Animals are fondest; then you drive six Hundred or more of them into the Field, where in a few Days they will root up the whole Ground in search of their Food, and make it fit for sowing, at the same time manuring it with their Dung. It is true, upon Experiment they found the Charge and Trouble very great, and they had little or no Crop. However, it is not doubted that this Invention may be capable of great Improvement.

I went into another Room, where the Walls and Ceiling were all hung round with Cobwebs, except a narrow Passage for the Artist to go in and out. At my Entrance he called aloud to me not to disturb his Webs. He lamented the fatal Mistake the World had been so long in of using Silk-Worms, while we had such plenty of domestick Insects, who infinitely excelled the former, because they understood how to weave as well as spin. And he proposed farther, that by employing Spiders, the Charge of dying Silks would be wholly saved; whereof I was fully convinced when he shewed me a vast Number of Flies most beautifully coloured, wherewith he fed his Spiders; assuring us, that the Webs would take a Tincture from them; and as he had them of all Hues, he hoped to fit every Body's Fancy, as soon as he could find proper Food for the Flies, of certain Gums, Oyls, and other glutinous Matter, to give a Strength and Consistence to the Threads.

There was an Astronomer who had undertaken to place a Sun-Dial upon the great Weather-Cock on the Town-House, by adjusting the annual and diurnal Motions of the Earth and Sun, so as to answer and coincide with all accidental Turnings of the Wind.

I was complaining of a small Fit of the Cholick; upon which my Conductor led me into a Room, where a great Physician resided, who was famous for curing that Disease by contrary Operations from the same Instrument. He had a large Pair of Bellows, with a long slender Muzzle of Ivory. This he conveyed eight Inches up the Anus, and drawing in the Wind, he affirmed he could make the Guts as lank as a dried Bladder. But when the Disease was more stubborn and violent, he let in the Muzzle while the Bellows was full of Wind, which he discharged into the Body of the Patient; then withdrew the Instrument to replenish it, clapping his Thumb strongly against the Orifice of the Fundament; and this being repeated three or four Times, the adventitious Wind would rush out, bringing the noxious along with it (like Water put into a Pump) and the Patient recovers. I saw him try both Experiments upon a Dog, but could not discern any Effect from the former. After the latter, the Animal was ready to burst, and made so violent a Discharge, as was very offensive to me and my Companions. The Dog died on the Spot, and we left the Doctor endeavouring to recover him by the same Operation.

I visited many other Apartments, but shall not trouble my Reader with all the Curiosities I observed, being studious of Brevity.

I had hitherto seen only one Side of the Academy, the other being appropriated to the Advancers of speculative Learning; of whom I shall say something when I have mentioned one illustrious Person more, who is called among them *the universal Artist*. He told us, he had been Thirty Years employing his Thoughts for the Improvement of human Life. He had two large Rooms full of wonderful Curiosities, and Fifty Men at work. Some were condensing Air into a dry tangible Substance, by extracting the Nitre, and letting the aqueous or fluid Particles percolate: Others softening Marble for Pillows and Pin-cushions; other petrifying the Hoofs of a living Horse to preserve them from foundring. The Artist himself was at that Time busy upon two great Designs: The first, to sow Land with Chaff, wherein he affirmed the true seminal Virtue to be contained, as he demonstrated by several Experiments which I was not skilful enough to comprehend. The other was, by a certain Composition of Gums, Minerals, and Vegetables outwardly applied, to prevent the Growth of Wool upon two young Lambs; and he hoped in a reasonable Time to propagate the Breed of naked Sheep all over the Kingdom.

We crossed a Walk to the other Part of the Academy, where, as I have already said, the Projectors in speculative Learning resided.

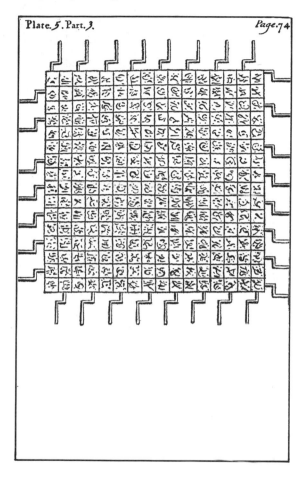

The first Professor I saw was in a very large Room, with Forty Pupils about him. After Salutation, observing me to look earnestly upon a Frame, which took up the greatest Part of both the Length and Breadth of the Room; he said, perhaps I might wonder to see him employed in a Project for improving speculative Knowledge by practical and mechanical Operations. But the World would soon be sensible of its Usefulness; and he flattered himself, that a more noble exalted Thought never sprang in any other Man's Head. Every one knew how laborious the usual Method is of attaining to Arts and Sciences; whereas by his Contrivance, the most ignorant Person at a reasonable Charge, and with a little bodily Labour, may write Books in Philosophy, Poetry, Politicks, Law, Mathematicks and Theology, without the least Assistance from Genius or Study. He then led me to the Frame, about the Sides whereof all his Pupils stood in Ranks. It was Twenty Foot square, placed in the Middle of the Room. The Superficies was composed of several Bits of Wood, about the Bigness of a Dye, but some larger than others. They were all linked together by slender Wires. These Bits of Wood were covered on every Square with Papers pasted on them; and on these Papers were written all the Words of their Language in their several Moods, Tenses, and Declensions, but without any Order. The Professor then desired me to observe, for he was going to set his Engine at work. The Pupils at his Command took each of them hold of an Iron Handle, whereof there were Forty fixed round the Edges of the Frame; and giving them a sudden Turn, the whole Disposition of the Words was entirely changed. He then commanded Six and Thirty of the Lads to read the several Lines softly as they appeared upon the Frame; and where they found three or four Words together that might make Part of a Sentence, they dictated to the four remaining Boys who were Scribes. This Work was repeated three or four Times, and at every Turn the Engine was so contrived, that the Words shifted into new Places, as the square Bits of Wood moved upside down.

Six Hours a-Day the young Students were employed in this Labour; and the Professor shewed me several Volumes in large Folio already collected, of broken Sentences, which he intended to piece together; and out of those rich Materials to give the World a compleat Body of all Arts and Sciences; which however might be still improved, and much expedited, if the Publick would raise a Fund for making and employing five Hundred such Frames in *Lagado*, and oblige the Managers to contribute in common their several Collections.

He assured me, that this Invention had employed all his Thoughts from his Youth; that he had emptied the whole Vocabulary into his Frame, and made the strictest Computation of the general Proportion there is in Books between the Numbers of Paricles, Nouns, and Verbs, and other Parts of Speech.

I made my humblest Acknowledgments to this illustrious Person for his great Communicativeness; and promised if ever I had the good Fortune to return to my native Country, that I would do him Justice, as the sole Inventor of this wonderful Machine; the Form and Contrivance of which I desired Leave to delineate upon Paper as in the Figure here annexed. I told him, although it were the Custom of our Learned in *Europe* to steal Inventions from each other, who had thereby at least this Advantage, that it became a Controversy which was the right Owner; yet I would take such Caution, that he should have the Honour entire without a Rival.

We next went to the School of Languages, where three Professors sat in Consultation upon improving that of their own Country.

The first Project was to shorten Discourse by cutting Polysyllables into one, and leaving out Verbs and Participles; because in Reality all things imaginable are but Nouns.

The other, was a Scheme for entirely abolishing all Words whatsoever: And this was urged as a great Advantage in Point of Health as well as Brevity. For, it is plain, that every Word we speak is in some Degree a Diminution of our Lungs by Corrosion; and consequently contributes to the shortening of our Lives. An Expedient was therefore offered, that since Words are only Names for *Things*, it would be more convenient for all Men to carry about them, such *Things* as were necessary to express the particular Business they are to discourse on. And this Invention would certainly have taken Place, to the great Ease as well as Health of the Subject, if the Women in Conjunction with the Vulgar and Illiterate had not threatned to raise a Rebellion, unless they might be allowed the Liberty to speak with their Tongues, after the Manner of their Forefathers: Such constant irreconcileable Enemies to Science are the common People. However, many of the most Learned and Wise adhere to the new Scheme of expressing themselves by *Things*; which hath only this Inconvenience attending it; that if a Man's Business be very great, and of various Kinds, he must be obliged in Proportion to carry a greater Bundle of *Things* upon his Back, unless he can afford one or two strong Servants to attend him. I have often beheld two of those Sages almost sinking under the Weight of their Packs, like Pedlars among us, who when they met in the Streets, would lay down their Loads, open their Sacks, and hold Conversation for an Hour together; then put up their Implements, help each other to resume their Burthens, and take their Leave.

But, for short Conversations a Man may carry Implements in his Pockets and under his Arms, enough to supply him, and in his House he cannot be at a Loss; therefore the Room where Company meet who practice this Art, is full of all *Things* ready at Hand, requisite to furnish Matter for this Kind of artificial Converse.

Another great Advantage proposed by this Invention, was, that it would serve as an universal Language to be understood in all civilized Nations, whose Goods and Utensils are generally of the same Kind, or nearly resembling, so that their Uses might easily be comprehended. And thus, Embassadors would be qualified to treat with foreign Princes or Ministers of State, to whose Tongues they were utter Strangers.

I was at the Mathematical School, where the Master taught his Pupils after a Method scarce imaginable to us in *Europe*. The Proposition and Demonstration were fairly written on a thin Wafer, with Ink composed of a Cephalick Tincture. This the Student was to swallow upon a fasting Stomach, and for three Days following eat nothing but Bread and Water. As the Wafer digested, the Tincture mounted to his Brain, bearing the Proposition along with it. But the Success hath not hitherto been answerable, partly by some Error in the *Quantum* or Composition, and partly by the Perverseness of Lads; to whom this Bolus is so nauseous, that they generally steal aside, and discharge it upwards before it can operate; neither have they been yet persuaded to use so long an Abstinence as the Prescription requires.

THE FERTILIZING ROOM

Aldous Huxley

The hands of all the four thousand electric clocks in all the Blooms-bury Centre's four thousand rooms marked twenty-seven minutes past two. "This hive of industry," as the Director was fond of calling it, was in the full buzz of work. Every one was busy, everything in ordered motion. Under the microscopes, their long tails furiously lashing, spermatozoa were burrowing head first into eggs; and, fertil-ized, the eggs were expanding, dividing, or if bokańovskified, budding and breaking up into whole populations of separate embryos. From the Social Predestination Room the escalators went rumbling down into the basement, and there, in the crimson darkness, stewingly warm on their cushion of peritoneum and gorged with blood-sur-rogate and hormones, the foetuses grew and grew or, poisoned, languished into a stunted Epsilonhood. With a faint hum and rattle the moving racks crawled imperceptibly through the weeks and the recapitulated aeons to where, in the Decanting Room, the newly-unbottled babes uttered their first yell of horror and amazement.

The dynamos purred in the sub-basement, the lifts rushed up and down. On all the eleven floors of Nurseries it was feeding time. From eighteen hundred bottles eighteen hundred carefully labelled infants were simultaneously sucking down their pint of pasteurized external secretion.

Above them, in ten successive layers of dormitory, the little boys and girls who were still young enough to need an afternoon sleep were as busy as every one else, though they did not know it, listening unconsciously to hypnopaedic lessons in hygiene and sociability, in class-consciousness and the toddler's love-life. Above these again were the playrooms where, the weather having turned to rain, nine hun-dred older children were amusing themselves with bricks and clay modelling, hunt-the-zipper, and erotic play.

Buzz, buzz! the hive was humming, busily, joyfully. Blithe was the singing of the young girls over their test-tubes, the Predestinators whistled as they worked, and in the Decanting Room what glorious jokes were cracked above the empty bottles! But the Director's face, as he entered the Fertilizing Room with Henry Foster, was grave, wooden with severity.

"A public example," he was saying. "In this room, because it contains more high-caste workers than any other in the Centre. I have told him to meet me here at half-past two."

"He does his work very well," put in Henry, with hypocritical generosity.

"I know. But that's all the more reason for severity. His intellectual eminence carries with it corresponding moral responsibilities. The greater a man's talents, the greater his power to lead astray. It is better that one should suffer than that many should be corrupted. Consider the matter dispassionately, Mr. Foster, and you will see that no offence is so heinous as unorthodoxy of behavior. Murder kills only the individual—and, after all, what is an individual?" With a sweeping gesture he indicated the rows of microscopes, the test-tubes, the incubators. "We can make a new one with the greatest ease—as many as we like. Unorthodoxy threatens more than the life of a mere individual; it strikes at Society itself. Yes, at Society itself," he repeated. "Ah, but here he comes."

Bernard had entered the room and was advancing between the rows of fertilizers towards them. A veneer of jaunty self-confidence thinly concealed his nervousness. The voice in which he said, "Good-morning, Director," was absurdly too loud; that in which, correcting his mistake, he said, "You asked me to come and speak to you here," ridiculously soft, a squeak.

"Yes, Mr. Marx," said the Director portentously. "I did ask you to come to me here. You returned from your holiday last night, I understand."

"Yes," Bernard answered.

"Yes-s," repeated the Director, lingering, a serpent, on the "s." Then, suddenly raising his voice, "Ladies and gentlemen," he trumpeted, "ladies and gentlemen."

The singing of the girls over their test-tubes, the preoccupied whistling of the Microscopists, suddenly ceased. There was a profound silence; every one looked round.

"Ladies and gentlemen," the Director repeated once more, "excuse me for thus interrupting your labours. A painful duty constrains me. The security and stability of Society are in danger. Yes, in danger, ladies and gentlemen. This man," he pointed accusingly at Bernard, "this man who stands before you here, this Alpha-Plus to whom so much has been given, and from whom, in consequence, so much must be expected, this colleague of yours—or should I anticipate and say this ex-colleague?—has grossly betrayed the trust imposed in him. By his heretical views on sport and *soma*, by the scandalous unorthodoxy of his sex-life, by his refusal to obey the teachings of Our Ford and behave out of office hours, 'even as a little infant,' " (here the

Director made the sign of the T), "he has proved himself an enemy of Society, a subverter, ladies and gentlemen, of all Order and Stability, a conspirator against Civilization itself. For this reason I propose to dismiss him, to dismiss him with ignominy from the post he has held in this Centre; I propose forthwith to apply for his transference to a Sub-Centre of the lowest order and, that his punishment may serve the best interest of Society, as far as possible removed from any important Centre of population. In Iceland he will have small opportunity to lead others astray by his unfordly example." The Director paused; then, folding his arms, he turned impressively to Bernard. "Marx," he said, "can you show any reason why I should not now execute the judgment passed upon you?"

"Yes, I can," Bernard answered in a very loud voice.

Somewhat taken aback, but still majestically, "Then show it," said the Director.

"Certainly. But it's in the passage. One moment." Bernard hurried to the door and threw it open. "Come in," he commanded, and the reason came in and showed itself.

There was a gasp, a murmur of astonishment and horror; a young girl screamed; standing on a chair to get a better view some one upset two test-tubes full of spermatozoa. Bloated, sagging, and among those firm youthful bodies, those undistorted faces, a strange and terrifying monster of middle-agedness, Linda advanced into the room, coquettishly smiling her broken and discoloured smile, and rolling as she walked, with what was meant to be a voluptuous undulation, her enormous haunches. Bernard walked beside her.

"There he is," he said, pointing at the Director.

"Did you think I didn't recognize him?" Linda asked indignantly; then, turning to the Director, "Of course I knew you; Tomakin, I should have known you anywhere, among a thousand. But perhaps you've forgotten me. Don't you remember? Don't you remember, Tomakin? Your Linda." She stood looking at him, her head on one side, still smiling, but with a smile that became progressively, in face of the Director's expression of petrified disgust, less and less self-confident, that wavered and finally went out. "Don't you remember, Tomakin?" she repeated in a voice that trembled. Her eyes were anxious, agonized. The blotched and sagging face twitched grotesquely into the grimace of extreme grief. "Tomakin!" She held out her arms. Some one began to titter.

"What's the meaning," began the Director, "of this monstrous . . ."

"Tomakin!" She ran forward, her blanket trailing behind her, threw her arms round his neck, hid her face on his chest.

A howl of laughter went up irrepressibly.

". . . this monstrous practical joke," the Director shouted.

Red in the face, he tried to disengage himself from her embrace. Desperately she clung. "But I'm Linda, I'm Linda." The laughter drowned her voice. "You made me have a baby," she screamed above the uproar. There was a sudden and appalling hush; eyes floated uncomfortably, not knowing where to look. The Director went suddenly pale, stopped struggling and stood, his hands on her wrists, staring down at her, horrified. "Yes, a baby—and I was its mother." She flung the obscenity like a challenge into the outraged silence; then, suddenly breaking away from him, ashamed, ashamed, covered her face with her hands, sobbing. "It wasn't my fault, Tomakin. Because I always did my drill, didn't I? Didn't I? Always . . . I don't know how . . . If you knew how awful, Tomakin . . . But he was a comfort to me, all the same." Turning towards the door, "John!" she called. "John!"

He came in at once, paused for a moment just inside the door, looked round, then soft on his moccasined feet strode quickly across the room, fell on his knees in front of the Director, and said in a clear voice: "My father!"

The word (for "father" was not so much obscene as—with its connotation of something at one remove from the loathsomeness and moral obliquity of child-bearing—merely gross, a scatological rather than a pornographic impropriety); the comically smutty word relieved what had become a quite intolerable tension. Laughter broke out, enormous, almost hysterical, peal after peal, as though it would never stop. My father—and it was the Director! My *father!* Oh, Ford, oh Ford! That was really too good. The whooping and the roaring renewed themselves, faces seemed on the point of disintegration, tears were streaming. Six more test-tubes of spermatozoa were upset. My *father!*

Pale, wild-eyed, the Director glared about him in an agony of bewildered humiliation.

My *father!* The laughter, which had shown signs of dying away, broke out again more loudly than ever. He put his hands over his ears and rushed out of the room.

MAN'S CONQUEST OF SPACE

Hannah Arendt

Has Man's conquest of space increased or diminished his stature? The question raised is addressed to the layman, not the scientist, and it is inspired by the humanist's concern with man, as distinguished from the physicist's concern with the reality of the physical world. To understand physical reality seems to demand not only the renunciation of an anthropocentric or geocentric world view, but also a radical elimination of all anthropomorphic elements and principles, as they arise either from the world given to the five human senses or from the categories inherent in the human mind. The question assumes that man is the highest being we know of, an assumption which we have inherited from the Romans, whose *humanitas* was so alien to the Greek frame of mind that they had not even a word for it. (The reason for the absence of the word *humanitas* from Greek language and thought was that the Greeks, in contrast to the Romans, never thought that man is the highest being there is. Aristotle calls this belief *atopos*, "absurd.") This view of man is even more alien to the scientist, to whom man is no more than a special case of organic life, and to whom man's habitat—the earth, together with earthbound laws—is no more than a special borderline case of absolute, universal laws, that is, laws that rule the immensity of the universe. Surely, the scientist cannot permit himself to ask: What consequences will the result of my investigations have for the stature (or, for that matter, for the future) of man? It has been the glory of modern science that it has been able to emancipate itself completely from all such truly humanistic concerns.

The question propounded here, insofar as it is addressed to the layman, must be answered in terms of common sense and in everyday language (if it can be answered at all). The answer is not likely to convince the scientist, because he has been forced, under the compulsion of facts and experiments, to renounce sense perception and hence common sense, by which we coordinate the perception of our five senses into the total awareness of reality. He has also been forced to renounce normal language, which even in its most sophisticated conceptual refinements remains inextricably bound to the world of the senses and to our common sense. For the scientist, man is no more than an observer of the universe in its manifold manifestations. The progress of modern science has demonstrated very forcefully to what an extent this observed universe, the infinitely small no less than the infinitely large, escapes not only the coarseness of human sense perception but even the enormously ingenious instruments that have been built for its refinement. The phenomena with which modern physical research is concerned turn up like "mysterious messenger[s] from the real world," according to Max Planck in *The Universe in the Light of Modern Physics*, and we know no more about them than they affect our measuring instruments in a certain way, suspecting all the while with Eddington that "the former have as much resemblance to the latter as a telephone number has to a subscriber."

The goal of modern science, which eventually and quite literally has led us to the moon, is no longer "to augment and order" human experiences (as Niels Bohr, still tied to a vocabulary that his own work has helped to make obsolete, described it); it is much rather to discover what lies *behind* natural phenomena as they reveal themselves to the senses and the mind of man. Had the scientist reflected upon the nature of the human sensory and mental apparatus, had he raised questions such as *What is the nature of man and what should be his stature? What is the goal of science and why does man pursue knowledge?* or even *What is life and what distinguishes human from animal life?*, he would never have arrived where modern science stands today. The answers to these questions would have acted as definitions and hence as limitations of his efforts. In the words of Niels Bohr, "Only by renouncing an explanation of life in the ordinary sense do we gain a possibility of taking into account its characteristics."

That the question proposed here makes no sense to the scientist *qua* scientist is no argument against it. The question challenges the layman and the humanist to sit in judgment over what the scientist is doing, and this debate must of course be joined by the scientists themselves insofar as they are fellow citizens. But all answers given in this debate, whether they come from laymen or philosophers or scientists, are nonscientific (although not antiscientific); they can never be demonstrably true or false. Their truth resembles rather the validity of agreements than the compelling validity of scientific statements. Even when the answers are given by philosophers whose way of life is solitude, they are arrived at by an exchange of opinions among many men, most of whom may no longer be among the living. Such truth can never command general agreement, but it frequently outlasts the compellingly and demonstrably true statements of the sciences which, especially in recent times, have the uncomfortable inclination never to stay put, although at any given moment they are, and must be, valid for all. In other words, notions such as life, or man, or science, or knowledge are prescientific by definition, and the question is whether or not the actual development of science which has led to the conquest of terrestrial space and to the invasion of the space of the universe has changed these notions to such an extent that they no longer make sense. For the point of the matter is, of course, that modern science—no matter what its origins and original goals—has changed and reconstructed the world we live in so radically that it could be argued that the layman and the humanist, still trusting their common sense and communicating in everyday language, are out of touch with reality, and that their questions and anxieties have become irrelevant. Who cares about the stature of man when he can go to the moon? This sort of bypassing the question would be very tempting indeed if it were true that we have come to live in a world that only the scientists "understand." They would then be in a position of the "few" whose superior knowledge entitles them to rule the "many," namely, the laymen and the humanists and the philosophers, or all those who raise prescientific questions because of ignorance.

This division between the scientist and the layman, however, is very far from the truth. The fact is not merely that the scientist spends more than half of his life in the same world of sense perception, of common sense, and of everyday language as his fellow citizens, but that he has come in his own privileged field of activity to a point where the naive questions and anxieties of the layman have made themselves felt very forcefully, albeit in a different manner. The scientist has not only left behind the layman with his limited understanding, he has left behind himself and his own power of understanding, which is still human understanding, when he goes to work in the laboratory and begins to communicate in mathematical language. Max Planck was right, and the miracle of modern science is indeed that this science could be purged "of all anthropomorphic elements," because the purging itself was done by men. The theoretical perplexities that have confronted the new nonanthropocentric and nongeocentric (or heliocentric) science because its data refuse to be ordered by any of the natural mental categories of the human brain are well enough known. In the words of Erwin Schrödinger, the new universe that we try to "conquer" is not only "practically inaccessible, but not even thinkable," for "however we think it, it is wrong; not perhaps quite as meaningless as a 'triangular circle,' but much more so than a 'winged lion.' "

Even these perplexities, since they are of a theoretical nature and perhaps concern only the few, are nothing compared to such paradoxes existing in our everyday world as electronic "brains," devised and constructed by men, which can not only do man's brain work incomparably better and more swiftly (this, after all, is the outstanding characteristic of all machines), but can do "what a human brain cannot *comprehend*," as George Gamow recently put it in a very interesting essay on the "Physical Sciences and Technology," in *The Great Ideas Today 1962*. The often mentioned "lag" of the social sciences with respect to the natural sciences or of man's political development with respect to his technical and scientific know-how is no more than a red herring drawn into this debate, and can only divert attention from the main problem, which is that man can *do*, and successfully do, what he cannot comprehend and cannot express in everyday human language.

It may be noteworthy that among the scientists it was primarily the older generation, men like Einstein and Planck, Niels Bohr and Schrödinger, who were most acutely worried about this state of affairs which their own work had chiefly brought about. They were still firmly rooted in a tradition that demanded that scientific theories fulfill certain definitely humanistic requirements such as simplicity, beauty and harmony. A theory was still supposed to be "satisfactory," namely, satisfactory to human reason in that it served to "save the phenomena," to explain all observed facts. Even today, we still hear that "modern physicists are inclined to believe in the validity of general relativity for aesthetic reasons, because it is mathematically so elegant and philosophically so satisfying" (Sergio de Benedetti). Einstein's extreme reluctance to sacrifice the principle of causality as Planck's Quantum Theory demanded is well known; his main objection was of course that with it all lawfulness was about to depart from the universe, that it was as though God ruled the world by "playing dice." And since his own discoveries, according to Niels Bohr, had come about through a "remolding and generalizing [of] the whole edifice of classical physics . . . lending to our world picture a unity surpassing all previous expectations," it seems only natural that Einstein tried to come to terms with the new theories of his colleagues and his successors through "the search for a more complete conception," through a new and surpassing generalization. Thus Max Planck could call the Theory of Relativity "the completion and culmination of the structure of classical physics," its very "crowning point." But Planck himself, although fully aware that the Quantum Theory, in contrast to the Theory of Relativity, signified a complete break with classical physical theory, held it to be "essential for the healthy development of physics that among the postulates of this science we reckon, not merely the existence of law in general, but also the strictly causal character of this law."

Niels Bohr, however, went one step further. For him, causality, determinism, and necessity of laws belonged to the categories of "our necessarily prejudiced conceptual frame," and he was no longer frightened when he met "in atomic phenomena regularities of quite a new kind, defying deterministic pictorial description." The trouble is that what defies description in terms of the "prejudices" of the human mind defies description in every conceivable way of human language; it can no longer be described at all, and it is being expressed, but not described, in mathematical processes. Bohr still hoped that, since "no experience is definable without a logical frame," these new experiences would in due time fall into place through "an appropriate widening of the conceptual framework" which would also remove all present paradoxes and "apparent disharmonies." But this hope, I am afraid, will be disappointed. The categories and ideas of human reason have their ultimate source in the human senses, and all conceptual or metaphysical language is actually and strictly metaphorical. Moreover, the human brain which supposedly does our thinking is as terrestrial, earthbound, as any other part of the human body. It was precisely by abstracting from these terrestrial conditions, by appealing to a power of imagination and abstraction that would, as it were, lift the human mind out of the gravitational field of the earth and look down upon it from some point in the universe, that modern science reached its most glorious and, at the same time, most baffling achievements.

In 1929 shortly before the arrival of the Atomic Revolution, marked by the splitting of the atom and the conquest of universal space, Planck demanded that the results obtained by mathematical processes "must be translated back into the language of the world of our senses if they are to be of any use to us." The three decades that have passed since these words were written have proved not only that such translation seems less and less possible, and that the loss of contact between the physical world view and the sense world has become even more conspicuous, but also—and in our context this is even more alarming—that this has by no means meant that results of this new science are of no practical use, or that the new world view, as Planck had predicted in case the translation back into ordinary language should fail, "would be no better than a bubble ready to burst at the first puff of wind." On the contrary, one is tempted to say that it is much more likely that the planet we inhabit will go up in smoke as a consequence of theories that are entirely unrelated to the world of the senses, and defy all description in human language, than that even a *hurricane* will cause the theories to burst like a bubble.

It is, I think, safe to say that nothing was more alien to the minds of the scientists, who brought about the most radical and the most rapid revolutionary process the world has ever seen, than any will to power. Nothing was more remote than any wish to "conquer space" and to go to the moon. Nor were they prompted by an unseemly curiosity in the sense of a *temptatio oculorum*. It was indeed their search for "true reality" that led them to lose confidence in appearances, in the phenomena as they reveal themselves of their own accord to human sense and reason. They were inspired by an extraordinary love of harmony and lawfulness which taught them that they would have to step outside any merely given sequence or series of occurrences if they wanted to discover the overall beauty and order of the whole, that is, the universe. (This may explain why they seem to have been less distressed by the fact that their discoveries served the invention of the most murderous gadgets than they have been disturbed by the shattering of all their most cherished ideals of necessity and lawfulness. These ideals were lost when the scientists discovered that there is nothing indivisible in matter, no *a-tomos*, that we live in an expanding, nonlimited universe, and that chance seems to rule supreme wherever this "true reality," the physical world, has receded entirely from the range of human senses and from the range of all instruments by which their coarseness was refined.)

The modern scientific enterprise began with thoughts never thought before (Copernicus, we are told by J. Bronowski in *Science and Human Values*, imagined he was "standing in the sun . . . overlooking the planets") and with things never seen before (Galileo's telescope pierced the distance between earth and sky and in his own words delivered the secrets of the stars to human cognition "with all the certainty of sense evidence"). It reached its classic expression with

Newton's law of gravitation, in which the same equation covers the movements of the heavenly bodies and the motion of terrestrial things on earth. Einstein indeed only generalized this science of the modern age when he introduced an "observer who is poised freely in space," and not just at one definite point like the sun, and he proved that not only Copernicus but also Newton still required "that the universe should have a kind of center" although this center of course was no longer the earth. It is in fact quite obvious that the scientists' strongest intellectual motivation was Einstein's "striving after generalization," and that if they appealed to power at all, it was the interconnected formidable power of abstraction and imagination. Even today, when billions of dollars are spent year in and year out for highly "useful" projects that are the immediate results of the development of pure, theoretical science, and when the actual power of countries and governments depends upon the performance of many thousands of researchers, the physicist is still likely to look down upon all these space scientists as mere "plumbers."

The sad truth of the matter, however, is that the lost contact between the world of the senses and appearances and the physical world view has been reestablished not by the pure scientist but by the "plumber." The technicians, who account today for the overwhelming majority of all "researchers," have brought the results of the scientists down to earth. And even though the scientist is still beset by paradoxes and the most bewildering perplexities, the very fact that a whole technology could develop out of his results demonstrates the "soundness" of his theories and hypotheses more convincingly than any merely scientific observation or experiment ever could. It is perfectly true that the scientist himself does not want to go to the moon; he knows that for his purposes unmanned spaceships carrying the best instruments human ingenuity can invent will do the job of exploring the moon's surface much better than dozens of astronauts. And yet, an actual change of the human world, the conquest of space or whatever we may wish to call it, is achieved only when manned space carriers are shot into the universe, so that man himself can go where up to now only human imagination and its power of abstraction, or human ingenuity and its power of fabrication, could reach. To be sure, all we plan to do now is to explore our own immediate surroundings in the universe, the infinitely small place that the human race could reach even if it were to travel with the velocity of light. In view of man's life span—the only absolute limitation left at the present moment—it is quite unlikely that he will ever go much farther. But even for this limited job, we have to leave the world of our senses and of our bodies, not only in imagination but in reality.

It is as though Einstein's imagined "observer poised in free space"—surely the creation of the human mind and its power of abstraction—is being followed by a bodily observer who must behave as though he were a mere child of abstraction and imagination. It is at this point that all the theoretical perplexities of the new physical world view intrude as realities upon man's everyday world and throw out of gear his "natural," that is, earthbound, common sense. He would, for instance, be confronted in reality with Einstein's famous "twin paradox," which hypothetically assumes that "a twin brother who takes off on a space journey in which he travels at a sizeable fraction of the speed of light would return to find his earthbound twin either older than he or little more than a dim recollection in the memory of his descendants." For although many physicists had found this paradox difficult to swallow, the "clock paradox," on which it is based, seems to have been verified experimentally, so that the only alternative to it would be the assumption that earthborn life under all circumstances remains bound to a time concept that demonstrably does not belong among "true realities," but among mere appearances. We have reached the stage where the Cartesian radical doubt of reality as such, the first philosophical answer to the discoveries of science in the modern age, may become subject to physical experiments that would make short shrift of Descartes's famous consolation, *I doubt therefore I am*, and of his conviction that, whatever the state of reality and of truth as they are given to the senses and to reason, you cannot "doubt of your doubt and remain uncertain whether you doubt or not."

The magnitude of the space enterprise seems to me beyond dispute, and all objections raised against it on the purely utilitarian level—that it is too expensive, that the money were better spent on education and the improvement of the citizens, on the fight against poverty and disease, or whatever other worthy purposes may come to mind— sound to me slightly absurd, out of tune with the things that are at stake and whose consequences today appear still quite unpredictable. There is, moreover, another reason why I think these arguments are beside the point. They are singularly inapplicable because the enterprise itself could come about only through an amazing development of man's scientific capabilities. The very integrity of science demands that not only utilitarian considerations but even the reflection upon the stature of man be left in abeyance. Has not each of the advances of science, since the time of Copernicus, almost automatically resulted in a decrease in his stature? Man, insofar as he is a scientist, does not care about his own stature in the universe or about his position on the evolutionary ladder of animal life; this "carelessness" is his pride and his glory. The simple fact that physicists split the atom without any hesitaticns the very moment they knew how to do it, although they realized full well the enormous destructive potentialities of their operation, demonstrates that the scientist *qua* scientist does not even care about the survival of the human race on earth or, for that matter, about the survival of the planet itself. All associations for "Atoms for Peace," all warnings not to use the new power unwisely, and even the pangs of conscience many scientists felt when the first bombs fell on Hiroshima and Nagasaki cannot obscure this simple, elementary fact. For in all these efforts the scientists acted not as scientists but as citizens, and if their voices have more authority than the voices of laymen, they do so only because the scientists are in possession of more precise information. Valid and plausible arguments against the "conquest of space" could be raised only if they were to show that the whole enterprise might be self-defeating in its own terms.

There are a few indications that such might indeed be the case. If we leave out of account the human life span, which under no circumstances (even if biology should succeed in extending it significantly and man were able to travel with the speed of light) will permit man to explore more than his immediate surroundings in the immensity of the universe, the most significant indication that it might be self-defeating consists in Heisenberg's discovery of the uncertainty principle. Heisenberg showed conclusively that there is a definite and final limit to the accuracy of all measurements obtainable by man-devised instruments. In his own words, "We decide, by our selection of the type of observation employed, which aspects of nature are to be determined and which are to be blurred." He holds that "the most important new result of nuclear physics was the recognition of the possibility of applying quite different types of natural laws, without contradiction, to one and the same physical event. This is due to the fact that within a system of laws which are based on certain fundamental ideas only certain quite definite ways of asking questions make sense, and thus, that such a system is separated from others which allow different questions to be put." From this he concluded that the modern search for "true reality" behind mere appearances, which has brought about the world we live in and resulted in the Atomic Revolution, has led into a situation in the sciences themselves in which man has lost the very objectivity of the natural world, so that man in his hunt for "objective reality" suddenly discovered that he always "confronts himself alone."

The truth of Heisenberg's observation seems to me to transcend by far the field of strictly scientific endeavor and to gain in poignancy if it is applied to the technology that has grown out of modern science. Every progress in science in the last decades, from the moment it was absorbed into technology and thus introduced into the factual world where we live our everyday lives, had brought with it a veritable avalanche of fabulous instruments and ever more ingenious machinery. All of this makes it more unlikely every day that man will encounter anything in the world around him that is not man-made and hence is not, in the last analysis, he himself in a different disguise. The astronaut, shot into outer space and imprisoned in his instrument-ridden capsule where each actual physical encounter with

his surroundings would spell immediate death, might well be taken as
the symbolic incarnation of Heisenberg's man—the man who will be
the less likely ever to meet anything but himself the more ardently
he wishes to eliminate all anthropocentric considerations from his
encounter with the nonhuman world around him.

It is at this point, it seems to me, that the humanist's concern with
man and the stature of man has caught up with the scientist. It is as
though the sciences had done what the humanities never could have
achieved, namely, to prove demonstrably the validity of this concern.
The situation, as it presents itself today, oddly resembles an elaborate
verification of a remark by Franz Kafka, written at the very beginning of this development: Man, he said, "found the Archimedean
point, but he used it against himself; it seems that he was permitted
to find it only under this condition." For the conquest of space, the
search for a point outside the earth from which it would be possible
to unhinge, as it were, the planet itself, is no accidental result of the
modern age's science. This was from its very beginnings not a
"natural" but a universal science, it was not a physics but an
astrophysics which looked upon the earth from a point in the
universe. In terms of this development, the attempt to conquer space
means that man hopes he will be able to journey to the Archimedean
point which he anticipated by sheer force of abstraction and imagination. However, in doing so, he will necessarily lose his advantage. All
he can find is the Archimedean point with respect to the earth, but
once arrived there and having acquired this absolute power over his
earthly habitat, he would need a new Archimedean point, and so *ad
infinitum*. In other words, man can only get lost in the immensity of
the universe, for the only true Archimedean point would be the
absolute void behind the universe.

Yet even if man recognizes that there might be absolute limits to
his search for knowledge and that it might be wise to suspect such
limitations whenever it turns out that the scientist can do more than
he is capable of comprehending, and even if he realizes that he
cannot "conquer space," but at best make a few discoveries in our
solar system, the journey into space and to the Archimedean point
with respect to the earth is far from being a harmless or unequivocal-
ly triumphant enterprise. It could add to the stature of man inasmuch as man, in distinction from other living things, desires to be at
home in a "territory" as large as possible. In that case, he would only
take possession of what is his own, although it took him a long time
to discover it. These new possessions, like all property, would have to
be limited, and once the limit is reached and the limitations established, the new world view that may conceivably grow out of it is
likely to be once more geocentric and anthropomorphic, although not
in the old sense of the earth being the center of the universe and of
man being the highest being there is. It would be geocentric in the

sense that the earth, and not the universe, is the center and the home of mortal men, and it would be anthropomorphic in the sense that man would count his own factual mortality among the elementary conditions under which his scientific efforts are possible at all.

At this moment, the prospects for such an entirely beneficial development and solution of the present predicaments of modern science and technology do not look particularly good. We have come to our present capacity to "conquer space" through our new ability to handle nature from a point in the universe outside the earth. For this is what we actually do when we release energy processes that ordinarily go on only in the sun, or attempt to initiate in a test tube the processes of cosmic evolution, or build machines for the production and control of energies unknown in the household of earthly nature. Without as yet actually occupying a point where Archimedes had wished to stand, we have found a way to act on the earth as though we disposed of terrestrial nature from outside, from the point of Einstein's "observer freely poised in space." If we look down from this point upon what is going on on earth and upon the various activities of men, that is, if we apply the Archimedean point to ourselves, then these activities will indeed appear to ourselves as no more than "overt behavior," which we can study with the same methods we use to study the behavior of rats. Seen from a sufficient distance, the cars in which we travel and which we know we built ourselves will look as though they were, as Heisenberg once put it, "as inexcapable a part of ourselves as the snail's shell is to its occupant." All our pride in what we can do will disappear into some kind of mutation of the human race; the whole of technology, seen from this point, in fact no longer appears "as the result of a conscious human effort to extend man's material powers, but rather as a large-scale biological process." Under these circumstances, speech and everyday language would indeed be no longer a meaningful utterance that transcends behavior even if it only expresses it, and it would much better be replaced by the extreme and in itself meaningless formalism of mathematical signs.

The conquest of space and the science that made it possible have come perilously close to this point. If they ever should reach it in earnest, the stature of man would not simply be lowered by all standards we know of, it would have been destroyed.

VII

A Postscript

"I say we had best look our times and lands searchingly in the face, like a physician diagnosing some deep disease."
Walt Whitman, *Democratic Vistas*

REVOLUTION IN AMERICA?

Barrington Moore, Jr.

Are there grounds for taking seriously the prospects of revolution in American society? One way to answer this question is to examine the variety of conditions that in the past have led to the creation of revolutionary situations and movements, and that have affected the subsequent fate of these movements. Then one can try to determine the extent to which such conditions may or may not apply, currently or in the future, to the situation in the United States.

It is hardly necessary for me to stress that the procedure cannot yield perfect answers. By the nature of the case, everyone interested in the problem, activist or observer, suffers in varying degrees from the same limitations. Revolutionaries themselves, like generals and scholars, march into the future facing resolutely backward. Puritan revolutionaries looked back to the Bible; the French to the Romans and the Greeks; the Russians to the French and to what Marx thought he saw of the future in looking at nineteenth-century capitalism, an imaginary world that was about as far from Russian conditions as could be imagined; latest of all comers, the Chinese Communists looked back to the Russians and again to Marx while they went ahead and did something that had very little to do with either of them.

To the extent that revolutionaries did succeed, they often did so in large measure by avoiding slavish adherence to past models and by displaying ingenuity in devising new social mechanisms and new policies for unprecedented situations. Granting the importance of these considerations I still think that historical reflection may help us to distinguish between rhetorical pipe dreams and real possibilities. Significant though the element of creative improvisation in politics may be, it never starts from scratch, and it always works within a set of limiting conditions.[1] Finally, the past and the present provide the

---

[1] For a brilliant discussion of the limiting conditions on revolutionary movements see Otto Kirchheimer, "Confining Conditions and Revolutionary Breakthroughs," *American Political Science Review*, Vol. LIX, No. 4 (December, 1965).

only possible evidence we can have in any effort to think rationally
about these issues.

In previous patterns of revolutionary change it is possible to discern
three sets of mutations that have occurred within the dominant
classes prior to the outbreak of serious revolutionary violence. One of
these Crane Brinton has named "the desertion of the intellectuals." It
is something much deeper than desertion: a challenge to the prevailing modes of thought and to the whole perception of the possible
causes of and remedies for human suffering. In the modern world
generally, we are at a point where both reigning orthodoxies, official
liberalism and official Marxism, are subject to vigorous challenge.
Neither one can any longer provide a convincing explanation of the
causes of human misery in the twentieth century. The justifications
for horrifying forms of cruelty and oppression that both liberalism
and Marxism have put forward, in the service of great powers, have
more and more discredited both ideologies. So far, on the other
hand, no intellectual current has emerged as a clear alternative,
certainly not in the sense that Enlightenment doctrines, for all their
variety, came to constitute an alternative to traditional views of the
social hierarchy.

A second mutation has been the appearance of very sharp conflicts
of interest within the dominant classes themselves. In all major
revolutions so far, the symptom has been apparently insoluble
financial problems. Behind the symptom have been acute disagreements—insoluble contradictions might for once do as a meaningful
empirical term here—over how to resolve stresses posed by the rise of
new social relationships and, more specifically, over which social
groups are to bear the costs of these new arrangements. This split in
the dominant classes has quite different causes in successive historical
epochs and in different countries. Hence there is little to be gained
by efforts to reduce it to a single pattern of events. Whether such a
split will occur in the United States depends upon how long and how
satisfactorily the predatory solution of token reform at home and
counterrevolutionary imperialism abroad continues to work. In my
judgment the system has considerable flexibility and room for
maneuver, including strategic retreat. There is even a slim chance of
peaceful change within the democratic framework, or rather of re-
creating this framework with and through a limited amount of disorder that falls short of real revolutionary upheaval. Indeed, it is
worth noticing that these two generalizations about the dominant
classes apply, with only slight modifications, to non-revolutionary
changes.

They cease to apply when we come to the third mutation among
the dominant classes—loss of unified control over the instruments of
violence: the army and the police. Where a section of the dominant
classes breaks off and takes with it part of the armed forces, his-

torians are accustomed to calling the result a Civil War. When the police and the armed forces refuse to obey, they are likely to call it a revolution. Actually, as in the Chinese Revolution, there can be a mixture of the two processes. In the United States now, there is no more than a hint that the decomposition of the military forces may be beginning. And without control or neutralization of the government's armed forces, revolutionary movements do not have the shimmer of a ghost of a chance.

If we consider the lower classes, we find in general more variety in the patterns that experience so far has revealed. Here it is important to distinguish between revolutions whose main base has been in the cities and those in the countryside.

An urban revolutionary mass provided the main destructive impetus in the French Revolution; in the continental revolutions of 1848, particularly in the most important upheavals in Paris; in the Paris Commune of 1871; in the revolutions of 1905 and 1917 (both February and October) in Russia; and in the abortive revolution of 1918 in Germany. One process is common to these events: the transformation of a more or less atomized and diffuse urban plebs or of a proletariat into a politically active revolutionary mass.[2] These were all revolts of desperation, certainly not of rising expectations as some liberal theorists of revolution might lead one to anticipate.[3] Contrary to what one might expect on the basis of Leninist theory too, there is almost no evidence that prior organizational work and propaganda played a significant role and a good deal of evidence to the contrary. (Bolshevik organization did play a part in the October revolution of 1917 in Russia, but not in the more important February revolution that overthrew the Tsar and inaugurated a period of disorder upon which the Bolsheviks were able to capitalize.) Though the influence of prior forms of social organization, pre-existing habits, and general outlook is a topic that requires further investigation, I have come to suspect that it too plays a much less important role than immediate circumstances in creating a revolutionary mass. However, organization does play a part in sustaining revolutionary élan

---

[2] The term plebs is convenient for the sans-culottes and similar movements made up mainly of small shopkeepers, artisans, journeymen; proletariat for factory workers. There has yet to be a successful revolution (in the sense of seizing and holding power) in a country where the proletariat constitutes a larger segment of the lower classes.

[3] There is, on the other hand, an element of hope produced by some break in the ranks of the dominant classes, some sign, such as the Supreme Court's decision on educational desegregation in 1954, that changes are possible after all. In situations where people feel utterly hopeless their response is more likely to be apathetic acceptance of "fate"; in extreme cases, found for example in concentration camps, people may give up and die in response to the general situation, not as a result of any single act of cruelty.

and making the mass politically effective, a state that apparently can be sustained for no more than a few years at most. (The Great Cultural Revolution in China, about which we know very little, might just possibly disprove this generalization.)

The main factors that create a revolutionary mass are a sudden increase in hardship coming on top of quite serious deprivations, together with the breakdown of the routines of daily life—getting food, going to work, etc.—that tie people to the prevailing order. The grievances of man as a consumer appear to be more important than those of man as a producer in providing fuel for such explosions. However, their proximate cause is the general breakdown of the flow of supplies into the city. If there are no goods upon which to work, artisans cannot go to their workshops nor factory workers to their factories. (Or if they do, as in Petrograd in 1917, it may be mainly to stir each other up.) The final spark that sets off the conflagration among floating groups of desperate men (and sometimes more desperate women, who face even more directly the problem of getting food and keeping the household going) is likely to be some punitive act or threat by those in authority. If the authorities are already quarreling severely among themselves, the result may be a revolutionary upheaval, especially if the police and the army have ceased to be dependable. Otherwise there may be no more than a brief period of bloody disorder.

Hence in an urban lower-class population the creation of revolutionary solidarity resembles what happens when a bolt of lightning fuses into a single mass some chunks of metal that happen to be lying close to one another. Dramatic threat overcomes the atomization that the proliferation of different occupations creates in the city. This type of rapidly created solidarity breaks up again rather easily as individual interests reassert themselves. Such a breakup is not a matter of individual versus collective interests, at least not in any metaphysical sense. When a person joins a revolutionary crowd or even goes to a dramatic political demonstration, as an individual this person gains certain psychological satisfactions by seeing that other people have similar passions and by merging his own with those of the crowd.

Under such circumstances there is a release of inhibitions, an opportunity to vent feelings of moral outrage, sentiments of moral superiority toward those in authority to whom respect is ordinarily due, in other words a whole set of pleasures whose indulgence is ordinarily unsafe and imprudent. But the revolutionary crowd does not and cannot provide an adequate social mechanism for meeting the individual's other needs for food and shelter on a regular and recurring basis. Therefore the solidarity of the urban mass sustains itself only so long as it promises results. When all the food stores have been pillaged,[4] to speak metaphorically, the revolutionary crowd may turn on its own leaders or desert them. That is a theoretical extreme point, rarely approximated in real life, where revolutionary solidarity dissolves of its own accord.

More often solidarity dissolves as more and more people return to the search for a private and more familiar everyday solution to their problems. There is a drift back to work. In the meantime a new authority armed with revolutionary legality may speed up the process with a judicious application of terror, accusing the leaders of the revolutionary crowd of anarchist and counterrevolutionary tendencies. Or, as happened in 1848, the forces of the old order may retain control of the army and be able to defeat the revolutionary crowd in bloody pitched battles at the barricades– real confrontations instead of symbolic ones. In either case, whether revolutionary solidarity evaporates of its own accord or suffers violent suppression–or some combination of the two–once destroyed it is impossible to recreate it for at least a generation.

So far, then, urban revolutionary movements have been very short-lived, even if very important, agents of social change. There has never been any such thing as a long-term revolutionary mass movement in an urban environment. That is, there has not been a movement with a mass basis that has sustained a revolutionary impetus for more than a generation. *A fortiori* there has never been a long-term urban revolutionary movement that has succeeded. Sooner or later, urban movements that start off with the aim of revolutionary change either turn into reformist movements or succumb in competition with reformism and pure trade unionism. That is what has happened in England, France, Germany, the United States, even to a great extent in Tsarist Russia.

Among the many reasons for the failure of revolutionary movements to take deep root in an urban setting, the following seem to be the most important: 1) the very great division of labor and consequent atomization that work produces in the urban setting; 2) at least in industrial societies, a rising productivity that makes it possible to grant substantial benefits to the working classes, easing their social, legal, and cultural incorporation into the larger society; 3) the overwhelming political and economic power of the dominant group that closes off the prospect of revolutionary changes so long as this group remains reasonably united. All these factors drive urban revolutionary movements in a reformist direction.

The situation is, or rather can be, different in a rural setting,

---

[4]Or all the land distributed, as Harold Hinton points out for an area he observed in China. There are *some* similarities between urban and rural revolutionary movements.

especially the kind conducive to successful peasant-revolution. Though our concern here is with America, it is worth pointing out where the differences lie because an important current in American radicalism tries to apply, in an urban setting, strategy and tactics taken from rural movements.

The essential feature in peasant revolutions is the establishment of what are often called liberated areas. The Chinese Communist movement is the only one that has so far used this strategy successfully. It is actually a modernized version of one that has deep roots in specifically Chinese history and institutions.[5] The Chinese Communists were able to make a liberated area into what some American radicals might call a genuine counter-community. It was a place that provided real protection and security for its members. Here the peasants were free from the demands of the more rapacious tax collectors and landlords. In this fashion the liberated area provided the same kind of protection that a trade union does in a capitalist society. But, unlike the capitalist trade union, a liberated area undermines the prevailing "legal" order instead of supporting it. The liberated area can do this because it is self-sufficient, territorially independent of the legal central government, and more attractive to the mass of the population. As a matter of daily routine its members do not depend on anything except one another for food and for work. They are not tied to the existing order by depending upon it for jobs and through jobs for practically everything else.

Because of their stake in better conditions within the liberated area, peasants are likely to be more willing to furnish recruits to revolutionary armies than to government forces. Chinese experience demonstrates once again the independently crucial importance of revolutionary control over military force. Liberated areas, especially in the early stages, are not strong enough to defend themselves on their own. Both Harold Hinton's and Jan Myrdal's accounts give convincing evidence about the peasants' fear and hesitation to commit themselves to the Communist cause because they were afraid Chiang's troops might return, and about the temporary demoralization that occurred when government troops did return. Without their isolation (the result of the Long March) and the fact that the Communists

[5] Unlike previous rebels Mao used peasant hostilities to create an entirely new social system based on new economic relationships. Another major innovation in the Chinese revolution is the effort to create artificially a revolutionary mass of the type described above *after* the seizure of power and use it to prevent the ossification of the regime. That has apparently been one of the purposes of the Great Cultural Revolution. Evidently the Chinese are trying to use Trotsky's permanent revolution as a mechanism for social adaptation and rejuvenation comparable to the way the democratic process is supposed to work in the West. It is unlikely that permanent revolution will do the job any better.

were able to detach a part of Chiang's army at the very beginning, the Communist liberated areas probably could not have survived at all.

It is easy enough to see that the essential conditions of a successful peasant revolution are almost impossible to reproduce in an urban setting. The long period of prior disruption upon which the Chinese Communists built is something no industrial society would be likely to tolerate. The creation of a liberated area that is really independent culturally, economically, and politically would be extraordinarily difficult, if not impossible. To sustain itself, any oppositional political movement needs to be able to obtain for its members day-to-day benefits and protect them against reprisals. In modern industrial societies this necessity has so far always led to compromise with the existing order, to working within it to achieve piecemeal benefits. That is very clear in the history of trade unions. The same process has eroded the militancy of communist parties in western countries, turning them into what amounts to social democratic parties.

It is also precisely this need for protection and continuing benefits that New Left semi-revolutionary movements cannot provide through such symbolic gestures as offering sanctuary to draft resisters or "liberating" a university through a student riot. Neither of these is a step toward setting up a real working community, a base from which influences can be expected to spread outward and transform the existing social order. Such a strategy could be successful only if processes in the larger society rapidly created a "surplus" population of utterly hostile irreconcilables immune to the blandishments of the affluent world. Such groups have barely begun to put in an appearance, mainly as a result of the war in Vietnam. It seems to me highly unlikely that they can create and sustain a revolutionary sub-culture on any significant scale.

Finally, it seems to me highly unlikely that a revolutionary sub-group can establish itself and get a solid start without some form of military shield to protect it in the beginning. Those in authority are not so stupid as to fail to be aware of what is at stake. And the mass of the underlying population, especially in an industrial society, has enough fear of the prospects of liberation (and suppressed desires for it) to make excellent recruits for "spontaneous" violence and pogroms, which would make the Spanish Inquisition look like a Boy Scout picnic.

There might be just a chance for the growth of liberated areas or communes, or something similar, in the American setting if the process proceeded slowly and quietly and managed to establish communities with considerable autonomy and more attractions than either the black ghetto or the rat race of so-called normal white society. Some such goal may well be worth working for in its own right. There remains, nevertheless, the question whether it is possible to change the larger society in this fashion.[6] The movement toward a distinct form of community might easily become and remain distinct, but only in trivial ways, such as dress, eating habits, tastes in art and music—perhaps even sexual practices where deviance now scarcely threatens the status quo. The result would be to leave the new forms of social life as tourist attractions that don't change anything. The surrounding society could proceed serenely in its normal path of growing investment in destruction. In modern industrial society the counter-community is likely to remain parasitic upon the larger society. Even if it grows at the expense of its host, it is unlikely to be able to strike at the instruments of domination or to undermine them in the ways that liberated areas succeeded in doing in a peasant revolution.

So far we have been discussing revolutionary and near-revolutionary forms of change in American society based on the creation of mass support for these changes prior to some kind of violent outbreak and the collapse of the existing order. We have seen that it is vastly more difficult to build this support within a modern industrial society than it is in at least some varieties of a peasant society, that the embryo of a new social order cannot easily form within the womb of the old one under modern conditions. We have also noticed the crucial part that the military forces and the police can play, that no violent transformation can possibly take place unless the insurgent elements can neutralize or gain control of the instruments of violence.

There remains at least one other possible contingency: a major breakdown or collapse of the political apparatus without prior mass support for serious social changes. Such a collapse might provide the opening for a revolutionary takeover in quasi-Leninist fashion by some tiny but resolute minority. Though by no means an immediate prospect, such an eventuality does seem to me a distinct possibility. In the light of obstacles to other forms of change, including those within the democratic framework, there is even some reason for suspecting that collapse without prior mass support could be the most likely possibility. It is also one that a segment of young American radicals apparently seeks, though perhaps not explicitly or consciously. In any case this kind of collapse constitutes the maximum goal of the tactic of radicalization through disruption.

There are some good historical and sociological reasons too for holding that such a collapse might both occur and permit a revolutionary takeover. As pointed out above, in an urban setting the creation of a revolutionary mass is a quite rapid transformation.

[6]We can leave aside further problems of getting started. In modern society it is almost impossible to find physical and social breathing space for any city dweller who is not quite rich. In our cities there is nothing like the catacombs to which the early Christians could retreat; their modern equivalents bring in a good rent.

Fundamentally it comes about through the breakdown of the supply of goods and services upon which a city is dependent. In recent years there have been numerous partial breakdowns from a variety of causes that have nothing to do with revolution as ordinarily conceived, such as strikes or near-strikes by key city employees: police, fire, sanitation workers, teachers. They have exposed the vulnerability of the city to disruption.

One of the most threatening and sociologically interesting possibilities is a repetition of the electrical power failure that affected much of the Northeast not so long ago. Beneath the good humor of the last blackout there was an undertone of anxiety, not necessarily eased by frequent broadcasts to assure the population that the Pentagon was functioning normally and that it felt sure there was no emergency. Electricity means even more to a modern city than the supply of wheat meant to eighteenth-century Paris. France in May, 1968, demonstrated the vulnerability of a whole modern industrial state to spontaneous and yet concerted disruption. But it also demonstrated some of the obstacles that stood in the way of carrying through to a revolutionary conclusion. Though a revolutionary mass can form in a modern industrial society and can paralyze the society briefly, it cannot take power on its own. For a revolution to take place there must exist some group, such as the Russian Bolsheviks in 1917, that knows what it wants to accomplish and is willing to seize power in the midst of chaos and exercise it ruthlessly to restore order.

It would be a curious historical irony if the anarcho-syndicalist dream of the general strike and revolution somehow came true, several generations after the theory behind it had passed into the museum of social history, and in a country such as the United States where it has flourished only very briefly. It is not out of the question that further attempts along these lines may be made and even that one attempt on a big scale might induce some form of temporary collapse. But it seems to me highly unlikely that the attempt could turn out the way its proponents wish. It is almost certain to have quite the opposite result.

In the first place, even if black and white radicals in America could work together long enough to get the process started, it seems highly unlikely that in this country they could persuade workers in essential services to join them. There is the even smaller likelihood that they could neutralize the police and the army. There is a less obvious and perhaps even more important consideration. Should disorder somehow proceed far enough to create a revolutionary mass, would its temper and objectives be at all similar to that of the sans-culottes in eighteenth-century Paris, or Russian workers and—for a brief moment—central European workers at the end of World War I? The urban masses in these situations had undergone considerable hardships for some time. When the bonds of the status quo snapped under sudden additional strains, there were many in the mass who were already angry at what was clearly to them an oppressive social order. They were emotionally ready to try something new, to support leaders who promised something new, though the evidence we have indicates fairly clearly that the masses had no more than very vague notions about what the new society should be.

It is conceivable that the black population, the real masses in many major American cities, might display a similar temper in the course of a general collapse. The white population, on the other hand, while it might get very angry, would be rather more likely to be angry at disorder and chaos, to throw its support to whatever person or group promised to get the electricity turned on, the gas pumps and television sets working, the stores open. By and large it seems safe to predict that the groups interested in disruption would be on opposite sides of the barricades: police and other city employees on the one side, blacks, student radicals, a few intellectuals on the other.

Hence any such major disruption would very likely result in martial law or worse. Unless events and trends that no one can now foresee intervene to generate both widespread support for a revolutionary break and a more passive willingness to go along with it, any temporary collapse within the next twenty or thirty years would probably have utterly tragic consequences. Even if it succeeds in taking power, a revolution that tries to remold society against the mores and folkways of the mass of the population must turn to terror and propaganda on a gigantic scale in order to stay in control. In America a black dictatorship of the proletariat or even a black and white version—something as far as I am aware no one takes very seriously— might claim to have poetic justice on its side, but practically nothing else. It would almost certainly be a failure.

What is it that we mean by the success or failure of a revolutionary movement? I have deliberately saved this question for the end. Actually there is no such thing as complete success or complete failure, only differences of degree. Yet these differences of degree have decisive importance. A revolution that is crushed by its enemies we can call a failure even if its legend survives as an inspiration (perhaps a thoroughly misleading one) for later generations. On the other hand, taking power and even staying in power for a couple of generations are not by themselves sufficient grounds for us to call a revolution successful. In the longer run it is necessary to define success as making some lasting contribution to human freedom.

So far, I think it is fair to assert that no radical revolutionary movements have made such contributions on their own, at least not yet. They have made them only as part of the "bourgeois" or "liberal" revolutionary movements—the great surges of the Puritan and French Revolutions and our own Civil War, which belong to an historical epoch that is now drawing to a close. The first revolution that took power mainly as the result of a radical movement, the Bolshevik Revolution, turned into a vicious form of oppression that has yet to be shaken off. In China the issue is still doubtful. I believe very firmly that unless future radical movements can somehow synthesize the achievements of liberalism with those of revolutionary radicalism, the results for humanity will be tragic.

Given a commitment to minimizing the social causes of human misery and allowing human beings to obtain happiness in a variety of ways, some form of democratic and humane socialism may well be the most desirable social arrangement. But the obstacles are enormous. Where socialism has come to power by revolutionary means it has done so in backward countries and under conditions that have largely destroyed what humane aspects there were in the original tradition. In its effort to achieve power by peaceful and legal means in advanced industrial countries, socialism has had to compromise so deeply with the crimes of law and order that it has lost its capacity for bringing about fundamental change. The collaboration between the German socialists and the General Staff during the First World War was only one of the more dramatic instances of this general trend. Communists too have become parties of law and order, most notably in France. In American society the prospects for any synthesis between the liberal and radical traditions are dim. The prospects for any transformation of American society by purely peaceful and democratic means are dimmer still.

These are the reasons behind a very somber sense of the world to come. A somber view is not, on the other hand, a passive and fatalist one. One task of human thought is to try to perceive what the range of possibilities may be in a future that always carries on its back the burden of the present and the past. Though that is not the only task of the intellectual, it is a very important and very difficult one. No one can do it with complete success. Only those with a religious conviction of the infallibility of their own beliefs can take seriously notions of inevitable catastrophe and inevitable utopia. To give up such consolations is to become really serious about a very deadly and very serious world.